The Bloomsbury Companion to
M. A. K. Halliday

The Bloomsbury Companion to M. A. K. Halliday

Edited by
Jonathan J. Webster

Bloomsbury Academic
An imprint of Bloomsbury Publishing Plc

B L O O M S B U R Y
LONDON • NEW DELHI • NEW YORK • SYDNEY

Bloomsbury Academic
An imprint of Bloomsbury Publishing Plc

50 Bedford Square	1385 Broadway
London	New York
WC1B 3DP	NY 10018
UK	USA

www.bloomsbury.com

BLOOMSBURY and the Diana logo are registered trademarks of Bloomsbury Publishing Plc

First published 2015

British Library Cataloguing-in-Publication Data
A catalogue record for this book is available from the British Library.

ISBN: HB: 978-1-4411-7275-4
    ePDF: 978-1-4411-9758-0
    ePub: 978-1-4411-0254-6

Library of Congress Cataloging-in-Publication Data
The Bloomsbury Companion to M.A.K. Halliday / Edited by Jonathan J. Webster.
pages cm. – (Bloomsbury Companions)
Includes bibliographical references and index.
ISBN 978-1-4411-7275-4 (hb : alk. paper) – ISBN 978-1-4411-0254-6 (epub) –
ISBN 978-1-4411-9758-0 (epdf)　1. Language and languages.　2. Functionalism
(Linguistics)　3. Linguistics.　4. Halliday, M. A. K. (Michael Alexander Kirkwood),
1925-　I. Webster, Jonathan, 1955- editor.　II. Halliday, M. A. K. (Michael Alexander
Kirkwood), 1925- honouree.
PE1106.B55 2015
410.92–dc23
2014024663

Series: Bloomsbury Companions

Typeset by Newgen Knowledge Works (P) Ltd., Chennai, India
Printed and bound in Great Britain

Contents

Contents

PART IV   Directions of Development from Halliday

Preface

This Bloomsbury Companion focuses on M. A. K. Halliday as the originator of Systemic Functional Linguistics, a powerful theory of language which accommodates new perspectives capable of adding to our understanding of how language works in the affairs of humanity.

This Companion volume begins with a brief biography introducing Halliday's life, followed by five chapters elaborating on the various influences which have impacted on Halliday's thinking about language. With this foundation, the reader will have a better understanding of Halliday's life and times, how he has responded to the changing challenges, and how he is positioned in the modern philosophical landscape, especially as a theoretician of language.

Readers are introduced to how Halliday's work selectively elaborates on ideas from great linguists of this century such as Saussure and Hjelmslev; as well as his valued teachers – J. R Firth (London University) and Wang Li (Peking University); and colleagues with whom he worked closely, such as Jeffrey Ellis, Dennis Berg, Jean Ure, Trevor Hill and Peter Wexler – co-thinkers on the relevance of Marxist themes to the study of language. In addition, his association with Basil Bernstein in London (1964–71) continued this integration of socially aware Marxist orientations in Halliday's approach to the study of language.

Both Professor M. A. K. Halliday and Professor Ruqaiya Hasan have contributed chapters which provide not only fresh academic insight into the theory but also very personal perspectives on how the theory developed out of the various encounters and events that have occurred over the course of his life. At my request, Professor Halliday wrote on the influence of Marxism on his thinking about language. Professor Hasan, in her chapter on Systemic Functional Linguistics: Halliday and the Evolution of a Social Semiotic, rightly points out that while chance most certainly had a role to play, nevertheless, 'at some point, chance had to give way to choice in order to maintain the commitment to understanding how language works'. Both Halliday's and Hasan's contributions to this volume make this a landmark publication not just in the discipline of linguistics, but also in related disciplines in the human sciences.

Subsequent chapters explain the major architecture of Halliday's theory, and also discuss various directions of development in the theory. Today's leading scholars in Systemic Functional Linguistics have come together to write about Halliday's ideas about language, in particular, those areas where Halliday's contribution is most notable – Halliday's conception of language as a probabilistic system, language development in early childhood, intonation, stylistics, text linguistics as well as Halliday the grammarian, and Halliday as an international educator. Future directions of development of the theory, building on the foundation provided by Halliday, include studies in multimodality, translation, language comparison and typology and computational linguistics.

This book is a celebration of a pioneering scholar who as Christian M. I. M. Matthiessen points out, has been often ahead of his time and has never been a scholar who adopted (or adapted to) the intellectual fashion of the day.' This being the case, Matthiessen predicts 'the second decade of the 21st century will certainly continue to be very conducive to Halliday's ideas about language.'

In which case, this volume should be required reading for those who recognize that the future of linguistics as a discipline which is dedicated to the study of language lies in the exploration of the functional origins of language as a social semiotic.

Acknowledgement

'"Social realistic linguistics": The Firthian tradition', from *International Journal of the Sociology of Language,* vol. 31, De Gruyter, 1981, pp. 65–90. Reprinted with permission from De Gruyter.

Notes on Contributors

Annabelle Lukin is Research Fellow of the Centre for Language in Social Life, Macquarie University. She is part of a research team investigating the interaction of intonation with other levels of the language system, grammar and semantics. She has contributed expertise in theories and analysis of semantics, in particular with the analysis of 'speech function' and 'semantic networks', as developed by Emeritus Professors M. A. K. Halliday and Ruqaiya Hasan. She has also been interested in child language development and language evolution, and in 2004 co-edited a volume of papers with Geoff Williams called *Language Development: Functional Perspectives on Species and Individuals* (Continuum: London).

Bradley A. Smith has focused his studies on spoken language, particularly the use of intonation systems, multimodal discourse, and register language (types of language use corresponding to particular contexts, such as interviews, medical discourses, casual conversation, academic discourse, commercial interactions, business discourses). He also has had a long-term interest in the performance, composition and study of music and sound-as-art in general. His current main research interests are in: spoken business discourse; the changing roles of spoken and written language in contemporary interactive digital culture; multimodal competencies in higher education and in business, in particular the use of speech, writing and visual design for composition and interaction in digital teaching-&-learning environments.

Braj B. Kachru (b. 1932) is Professor Emeritus of Linguistics, Education, English as an International Language, and Comparative Literature (sociolinguistics, World Englishes, multilingualism, and language and ideology), University of Illinois at Urbana-Champaign. He has pioneered, shaped and defined the scholarly field of world Englishes. He is the founder and co-editor of *World Englishes*, the associate editor of *the Oxford Companion to the English Language* and contributor to *the Cambridge History of the English Language*. His research on world Englishes, the Kashmiri language and literature, and theoretical and applied studies on language and society has resulted in more than 25 authored and edited volumes and more than 100 research papers, review articles, and reviews.

Christian M. I. M. Matthiessen is Chair Professor and Head in the Department of English at The Hong Kong Polytechnic University, Hong Kong. He has worked in areas as diverse as language typology, linguistics and computing, grammatical descriptions, grammar and discourse, functional grammar for English-language teachers etc. He is an author of *Rhetorical Structure Theory*, along with Bill Mann and Sandra Thompson. He also co-authored *An Introduction to Functional Grammar* (3rd edition) with M. A. K. Halliday.

David G. Butt is Associate Professor of Linguistics, Macquarie University, Sydney. His research covers a wide range of text-based questions: e.g. the stylistic analysis of latent patterns in verbal art; the semantic and grammatical structure of abstract tools in classroom talk; the semiotic analysis of contexts of critical care (viz. surgery; psychiatry); the modelling of context by networks; the history of linguistics and of rhetorical theory; and linguistics in relation to other sciences. Currently, he is working in collaborations on the analysis of language in Borderline Personality Disorder; on the complexity of meaning-based ('realizational') systems; and on the representation of latent rhetorical structures in extended discourse.

Erich Steiner has been Chair of English Linguistics and Translation Studies, later on English Translation Studies, Department of Applied Linguistics, Translating and Interpreting, University of Saarland, Saarbrücken; he has also served as Head of Department, Pro-Dean and Dean at the University. His major research interests include Functional Linguistics, Translation Theory, Comparative Linguistics and Computational Linguistics. He has attracted major research projects from the European Union (ESPRIT/FRAMEWORK, LEONARDO, MINERVA), the Deutsche Forschungs Gemeinschaft (DFG/ German Research Council) and the German Academic Exchange Service (DAAD).

Geoff Williams is Honorary Professor at the University of Sydney and an Emeritus Professor at the University of British Columbia, where he was previously Head of the Department of Language and Literacy Education. He has contributed to a range of international professional organizations, including the International Systemic Functional Linguistics Association, of which he was Chair for several years. He is particularly interested in social semiotic theory, semantic variation, and children's language and literacy development. His current research includes work on children's recontextualization of discourse, modelling semantic variation in children's language development, and literacy development in rural Ethiopia.

Jane Torr is Associate Professor at Faculty of Human Sciences, Macquarie University, Australia; she also works in the University's Institute of Early Childhood, and is committed to the provision of high-quality educational experiences for young children prior to school. For the last 25 years she has researched and taught in the areas of early childhood language development, children's literature and literacy. She is interested in all aspects of early childhood education, learning and development. She has a strong commitment to the provision of quality early childhood services in Australia. She is particularly interested in the role of language in shaping adults' and children's understandings of the world.

J. R. Martin is Professor of Linguistics at the University of Sydney. His research interests include systemic theory, functional grammar, discourse semantics, register, genre, multimodality and critical discourse analysis, focusing on English and Tagálog – with special reference to the transdisciplinary fields of educational linguistics, forensic linguistics and social semiotics. Recent publications include a book on genre (*Genre Relations*, Equinox, 2008), an introduction to the genre-based literacy pedagogy of the 'Sydney School' (*Learning to Write, Reading to Learn*, Equinox, 2012), and with Clare Painter and Len Unsworth, a book on children's picture books (*Reading Visual Narratives*, Equinox, 2012).

John Bateman has a distinguished research background in applied linguistics and has contributed to a wide range of research areas since the 1980s. He started working on natural language generation in 1982 and was awarded the degree of Ph.D. in artificial intelligence in 1986 at Edinburgh University. Since then, he has engaged in research projects on language generation, translation science, discourse structures, and descriptive linguistics at Kyoto University, the Information Sciences Institute of the University of Southern California, the University of the Saarland in Saarbrücken, the former GMD Institute of Integrated Publication and Information Systems in Darmstadt, and the University of Stirling. In 1999, he was appointed Professor of Applied Linguistics at the University of Bremen within the Department of English, where he has initiated several linguistic projects on ontology, language, and space.

Jonathan J. Webster is Professor at the Department of Chinese, Translation and Linguistics; and Director at The Halliday Centre for Intelligent Applications of Language Studies, City University of Hong Kong. He is also the Managing Editor of the International Linguistics Association's journal *WORD*, and the editor of the forthcoming *Journal of World Languages* (2014). He has edited numerous publications by world-renowned scholars including *The Collected Works of M.A.K. Halliday* (Bloomsbury), *The Collected Works of Ruqaiya Hasan* (Equinox), *Continuing Discourse on Language*, volumes 1 & 2 (Equinox) and many more.

Kay L. O'Halloran is Director of the Multimodal Analysis Lab, Deputy Director of the Interactive Digital Media Institute, and Associate Professor in the Department of English Language and Literature at the National University of Singapore. Her areas of research include multimodal analysis, social semiotics, mathematics discourse, and the development of interactive digital media technologies and mathematical and scientific visualization techniques for multimodal and sociocultural analytics.

Kazuhiro Teruya, obtained his Ph.D. in Linguistics from Macquarie University, Australia in 1999, is Assistant Professor, Department of Chinese and Bilingual Studies, The Hong Kong Polytechnic University. His work in linguistics embraces systemic functional linguistic theory and description, comparative linguistics, language typology, discourse analysis, profiling of registers, and advanced second/foreign language learning.

M. A. K. Halliday was born in Yorkshire in 1925 and educated at S.O.A.S., Peking University and Cambridge. He taught Chinese for a number of years before moving into the field of linguistics, where he specialized in grammatical theory and in language in education, the language of early childhood, computational and quantitative linguistics, the language of science, and the meaningful roles of intonation. He retired as Emeritus Professor of Linguistics from the University of Sydney at the end of 1987. His Collected Works, edited by Professor Jonathan J. Webster (City University of Hong Kong), have recently been published in ten volumes by Continuum (2002–7).

Marissa K. L. E is a Teaching Fellow at the Centre for English Language Communication at the National University of Singapore. Her research interests include systemic functional linguistics, multimodal discourse analysis and their applications in analyzing the constitution, perpetuation and evolution of ideologies and culture as manifested in traditional and emergent forms of media communication. She has worked on inter-disciplinary projects at the Multimodal Analysis Lab at the National University of Singapore involving the application of mathematical modeling techniques to the analysis of multimodal data and the development of interactive and collaborative software for multimodal analysis for research and educational purposes.

Michael O'Toole, also known as Lawrence M. O'Toole (1934–), Emeritus Professor of Communication Studies at Murdoch University, Western Australia, has a long and distinguished career in applied linguistics, including the development of pioneering approaches to language studies and multimodal semiotic analysis, culminating in his highly influential systemic functional (SF) approach to displayed art, which has provided a foundation for contemporary multimodal research.

Mick O'Donnell is currently a lecturer in English Studies at the Universidad Autónoma de Madrid, Spain, where his main research interest is the exploration of second language development in a University context using learner corpora and natural language processing. He has developed various corpus annotation tools including UAM CorpusTool, Systemic Coder and RSTTool. He has previously worked as a computational linguist in major research centres around the world, and as a team leader within a medical informatics company.

Peng Xuanwei is Professor at the School of Foreign Languages and Literatures, Beijing Normal University; he is also the Director of the Centre for the Study of Functional Linguistics. Under the paradigm of linguistic theory and application, Professor Peng now directs his research of language on philosophy, construction, language process and dimension model of discourse analysis, metaphor, evaluation theory, evaluation of stylistics, evaluation corpus, bilingual lexicography, language teaching etc.

Ruqaiya Hasan received her doctoral degree from the University of Edinburgh. Thereafter as a research officer, she worked on cohesion in English (with M. A. K. Halliday), and on the sociolinguistic analysis of children's stories (with Basil Bernstein). An international scholar, she has held visiting positions at many universities worldwide. Her areas of especial interest are semantics, context, register and text, sociolinguistics, and the theory of verbal art. She has published in all these areas. Her Collected Works edited by Jonathan J. Webster are being published in seven volumes by Equinox in English. She retired as Emeritus Professor in 1994 from Macquarie University (Australia).

Dr Sabine Tan is Research Fellow at the School of Education, Faculty of Humanities, Curtin University. Previously she was Research Associate at the Multimodal Analysis Lab, Interactive and Digital Media Institute, at the National University of Singapore. Her main research interests include critical multimodal discourse analysis, social semiotics, and visual communication. She has worked on interdisciplinary projects involving the development of interactive and collaborative software for the multimodal analysis of images and video texts for research and educational purposes.

William S. Greaves is Emeritus Associate Professor in the English Department at Glendon College, York University, Toronto, which he joined in 1967. He is co-author, with James D. Benson of *Functional Dimensions of Ape-Human Discourse* (Equinox, 2005); and with M. A. K. Halliday, of *Intonation in the Grammar of English* (Equinox, 2008).

Part I

Halliday's Life

1 Michael Alexander Kirkwood (M. A. K.) Halliday – A Brief Biography[1]

Jonathan J. Webster

Born Easter Monday 13 April 1925 in Leeds, Yorkshire, England, Michael Alexander Kirkwood MAKH grew up with two fascinations: one being to go to China – he recalls writing a story when he was about 4 years old about a little boy who went to China. His other fascination was language, nurtured by both his parents. His mother had been a teacher of French and as a child he heard French spoken, and listened to French rhymes and songs. His father, a dialectologist and dialect poet, was an English teacher with equal love for grammar and Elizabethan drama.

Although happy at school, he felt rather trapped in a system which was so overspecialized that from the age of about 14, he was spending most of his time studying the classics, either Latin or Greek, or else classical history. His only respite from the classics came by way of the few hours of classes in English literature. While he enjoyed studying literature, nevertheless he felt that what his teachers had to say about the language in literature was out of touch with what was actually there. Though not yet able to be explicit about what it was exactly that he was looking for, still he felt that there ought to be some way of talking about the language in literature beyond what he was hearing from his teachers. This curiosity about language led to his first encounter with 'linguistics' having discovered in the library 'a book about language by an American professor called Bloomfield'. But Bloomfield proved difficult to understand, and MAKH recalls not getting 'very far with it!'

In early 1942, MAKH volunteered for the national services' foreign language training course. The initiative for conducting this intensive course came from J. R. Firth, who pointed out at the beginning of the war that Britain was obviously going to be involved in the war in Asia and it was high time that they trained some service people in Asian languages. Those who applied for the training course were taken out of school and brought to London and given a wide-ranging aptitude test, which evidently had also been designed by Firth.

The test had two parts, the first being a general language aptitude test, which included, among other things, decoding made-up languages. The second part focused on the specific character of each of the four languages which had been selected to be offered in the first course: Chinese, Japanese, Turkish and Persian. One of the tasks in this part required applicants to repeat from memory an increasingly long list of monosyllables with different tones. Had MAKH been unable to hear a falling tone from a rising tone, he would have probably ended up studying Persian or some other language, but in fact he succeeded in being selected to study Chinese, his first choice, and, shortly after his seventeenth birthday, he had his first lesson in Chinese, from Dr Walter Simon.

After 18 months' training, MAKH joined up with the services, doing half a year's army training in Britain, followed by a year of serving overseas in India. During the year in India, he was with the Chinese Intelligence Unit in Calcutta, doing counterintelligence work. Besides interviewing those who came out of Japanese-occupied China about the situation there, finding out about the fighting at the front, who was fighting who, and how it was going, they would also read and censor the mail going in and out of China.

After that year and a half, he along with three others from the first batch who had learned Chinese – including John Chinnery, who went on to become head of the Chinese Department at Edinburgh, Cyril Birch who later taught at Berkeley, and Harry Simon who ended up at Melbourne as Head of the Department of Chinese – were pulled back to London from their respective postings, to teach Chinese to new recruits. It was 1945, and everyone figured there were still years of war ahead against the Japanese, so the number of those being trained in Chinese and Japanese for the three services was increased. This, of course, meant that they needed more teachers of Chinese. So MAKH spent most of his last two years in the army teaching Chinese. To this day, he remembers the first Chinese class he ever had to teach, on 13 May 1945, during which he gave dictation to a group of very high-powered air force officers.

The course which was offered in the Services Unit for Language Training was taking place at S.O.A.S (School of Oriental and African Studies); although because of the bombing, S.O.A.S. was not in fact located in a single place, but scattered around London. Realizing that these service instructors might be interested in studying language academically, Eve Edwards, who was the Professor and Head of the Chinese Department at S.O.A.S, and Walter Simon, who was then Reader, organized things in such a way that the service instructors taught their courses in the morning and studied Chinese in the afternoon. One could specialize in either modern or classical Chinese. Most, like MAKH, were interested in modern Chinese, so they mainly studied modern Chinese literature and did as much as they could by way of conversation.

As a learner, MAKH often had been puzzled by the grammar of Chinese, and wanted explanations to questions like 'how does one actually know what can (or cannot) be said?' This struggle to engage with the grammar of Chinese became all the more pressing when he began teaching Chinese, and was put in the position of having to explain things to his students. He began with very straightforward questions about the grammar, because he found that there were so many things about Chinese grammar which just simply hadn't been described at all, and fell outside the scope of both traditional and then current grammars of Chinese. This interest in exploring such pedagogical questions about Chinese became his first source of attraction to linguistics.

When MAKH came out of the army in 1947, he decided he wanted to go on studying Chinese. He did not yet have a degree, so he thought he would pursue his degree from the University of London externally in China. Walter Simon happened to know the president of Peking University, Hu Shih; so he wrote to him to ask if he would take MAKH on as a student and help him find some way of earning a living, perhaps by teaching English in a high school.

About this time the Ministry of Education was offering grants to ex-servicemen to complete their higher education if this had been interrupted by the war; normally this offer was taken up to pay fees at a university in the United Kingdom; MAKH applied to be given this grant for use to travel to China where he intended to complete his higher education. When he arrived in China, and turned up at Peking University, Hu Shih said, 'Good. You start teaching next week in our English Department'. So in 1947, at the beginning of classes, he enrolled as a student at Peking University in the Chinese Department, and began teaching English in the English Department. MAKH had never taught any English before; but they were desperate for speakers of English. English had been totally banned under the Japanese occupation and most of their students were beginners. Not knowing what he wanted to do afterwards, except that he needed to prepare himself for the examinations for the London degree, he took classes in the Chinese Department in modern Chinese literature, and also in the Chinese classics.

After one year at Peking University, in June 1948, MAKH flew down to Nanking, where the British Council had made the necessary arrangements for him to take the University of London examination, which was exactly the same examination as the internal exam. The examination was on Modern Chinese: nine papers on a combination of language and literature, including the history of Chinese literature from 500 BC to the present day – all in one paper! As MAKH recalls, there was one question that you knew you were going to get, which was 'Write about the author of your choice'. MAKH had in fact been to see his author, the playwright Cao Yu, who was living and working in Shanghai at the time, and had even spent a whole day with him; so he was, of course, ideally prepared for that question!

After completing his London degree, at that point in his life, he had no intention of going on to do postgraduate study, so he took a job in China working for the Chinese Industrial Cooperatives, whose founder was a New Zealander, Rewi Alley. Taking this job meant going up to a remote part of northwest China, where there were these village cooperatives that had been a kind of industrial base in the unoccupied areas during the Second World War. The cooperatives were about the only source of industrial production in wartime, because all the cities had been occupied by the Japanese. Most were pretty well defunct by this time, killed off by inflation and civil war, but about 350 of them were still going. MAKH travelled with a young Chinese who was an accountant, and helped to keep the books. MAKH, meanwhile, wrote publicity in English which would be used to help in appeals for money back in New Zealand, Australia, Britain and North America. MAKH worked for the cooperative for about four months; until, in some small village up in Shaanxi, a letter arrived which had been chasing him for about three months, saying he'd been given a scholarship from England for postgraduate study. He had not applied for it; but Professor Edwards had seen his results and said 'Let's apply for him.' So she had applied on his behalf for this government scholarship.

The letter read 'Proceed back to Peking immediately' (or words to that effect!). The conditions were that MAKH could spend two more years studying in China before returning to England to do a higher degree. 'Well do I do this, or not?' he thought, but in the end, he finally decided to accept, knowing that they probably wouldn't ask him again if he turned it down. That meant he would have to get back to Peking, which would not be easy, however, since he was miles away from any city, and much of the countryside around was in Communist hands, with fighting still going on. After travelling five days by bus he got to Lanzhou, where there was an airport, and there he was able to catch a plane going by some devious route to Peking. He arrived in Peking just a few days before the Communists occupied Peking airport. Any later and he would never have been able to get back in.

It was towards the end of November when MAKH re-enrolled at Peking University. Professor Luo Changpei, who MAKH had met during his first year at Peking University when he attended one of Luo's courses on the history of Chinese, took MAKH on and started training him in historical linguistics and Sino-Tibetan studies. Luo, who had worked on the reconstruction of early Chinese, was familiar with the comparative method as worked out in Indo-European linguistics; but his own specialization was in Sino-Tibetan studies.

After about six months or so, however, it became clear to Luo that MAKH really wanted to work on modern Chinese dialects, so Luo told him, 'Well then you need to go and do some work in synchronic studies; next year you should go and study with my friend Wang Li.' Wang Li was Dean of the Faculty of Arts at Lingnan University in Canton, about 1,500 miles to the south of Peking. Wang Li was both a grammarian, a phonologist and phonetician, and also a dialectologist. He, who had been trained in Europe, was very much influenced by

Jespersen. MAKH credits Wang Li with teaching him the tradition of Chinese linguistics, as well as the principles of Chinese grammar and phonology.

Around this time, other influences included the Marr school of linguistics, which grew out of his interest in Russian ideas dating back to 1946 when he studied Russian in London. MAKH once wrote a long essay for Wang Li about convergence versus divergence as a model of linguistic history, because the Marrist position was that the traditional view of the history of languages as divergence from a common ancestor was largely wrong. Marr argued that the process should be seen much more as one of convergence. During this time in Canton, MAKH also became aware of some of Firth's notions after reading his paper 'Personality and language in society'. MAKH felt very sympathetic with what Firth was saying about language; Firth's ideas made sense to MAKH both in terms of his own experience and his own interests. He looked forward to exploring these ideas further with Firth when he returned to England.

It was May, 1949, and getting to Canton was complicated by the very heavy fighting then going on in central China. Only a few months earlier, in February, the Communists had liberated Peking, and by May, the last big battles of the civil war were going on in central China. So MAKH travelled by boat from Tientsin to Korea, then down to Hong Kong; and from there back into China, arriving in late August in Canton, which at the time was still Nationalist, but would be liberated just a few weeks after his arrival there.

Wang Li was doing a survey of the widely differing varieties of Cantonese of the Pearl River Delta. But because there was too much chaos all around, Wang Li and his students could not do their survey work in the surrounding villages. Instead, they surveyed university students who were natives of these small towns and villages, and who spoke their own local dialects in addition to standard Cantonese. When it came to the analysis, MAKH did the tones – Wang Li said he was the best among his research students at hearing and identifying tones! MAKH also developed a grammar questionnaire which he used to get the students to give him the versions of the Cantonese sentences in their own local dialects. MAKH was fascinated by the differences between Mandarin and Cantonese grammar, and also by how these local dialects differed in their grammar from Cantonese.

The terms of his scholarship required MAKH to return to England to complete his PhD. MAKH anticipated that he not only would be working on the material from his dialect work with Wang Li but also would be working under Firth while teaching Chinese in the Chinese department at S.O.A.S. But, in fact, he was in for some bitter disappointment. Three years on from when he left in 1947, England in 1950, was at the height of McCarthyism. Known to be sympathetic to the Chinese communists, MAKH was asked when he went for the job at S.O.A.S. whether he was a member of the Communist Party (that was the only question, in fact). He answered, 'No', because he wasn't. But he also refused to undertake that he would not become a member of the Communist Party in the future. In the end, he didn't get the job. When MAKH later asked the person who had questioned him whether that was the reason for him not to get the job, the interviewer replied simply, 'Political considerations were not absent.'

Witch-hunted out of the more politically sensitive S.O.A.S, MAKH got shunted off to the Chinese department at Cambridge, where there was no Modern Chinese at all, only classical. Not only would he not be working with Firth, but also he could not pursue his Chinese dialect studies as part of his Ph.D. research. There was simply no one at Cambridge qualified to supervise him on modern Chinese dialects. Neither did he consider himself suited to working with classical Chinese. Being someone who learns exclusively by ear, he had always felt quite put off by the idea of 'engaging with dead languages'. As a compromise, his supervisor at Cambridge, Gustav Haloun, then Professor of Chinese, suggested that MAKH work instead on the C14 Chinese translation of the so-called *Secret History of the Mongols* [元朝祕史].

The Secret History, a traditional Mongolian biography of Genghis Khan, was the earliest known text in the Mandarin dialect. The reason it was in Mandarin was that it had been translated into Chinese to be used as a textbook for Chinese civil servants who had to learn the official language of the civil service, Mongolian. The fact that it was not supposed to be a work of literature, but rather intended to be more like a language manual, made it an interesting case study into an earlier stage of modern Mandarin.

MAKH negotiated with Professor Haloun to be allowed to go up to London to study with Firth, who had agreed to take him on for informal supervision. But then Haloun died, quite suddenly, at the end of that year; so MAKH went to ask if Firth would be willing to become his supervisor, officially, if it could be arranged. Firth agreed, and MAKH, although still a student at Cambridge, was allowed to transfer to the supervision of Professor Firth, travelling regularly to S.O.A.S. As well as giving MAKH time himself, Firth also arranged for Professor R. (Bobby) H. Robins to see him for tutorial sessions and assign him essays to write.

Being supervised by Firth was 'a wonderful experience', recalls MAKH. Though Firth could be 'very tough', intellectually, even occasionally 'bullying', still 'if you said to him, "Hang on, I don't think I agree with you", he would listen, and say "Oh yes, you might be right"'. Besides sharing 'speech fellowship bonds' – both MAKH and Firth came from Yorkshire – there were also family connections (which, as MAKH is careful to note, were never referred to): MAKH's mother had known Firth (then known as Rupert) as a child – they were at the same elementary school, in Bramley, a suburb of Leeds. The principal, Miss Firth, was Rupert Firth's aunt. Rupert was 5 years older than MAKH's mother; Miss Firth sometimes asked him to help with teaching the younger children; according to his mother, Firth was very nice to them. Later she often travelled on the same train with him when he was a student of history at Leeds; during the trip, Firth would quiz the high school girls on historical dates.

MAKH attended lectures by both Firth and Robins, and also courses in phonology given by Eugenie Henderson and Eileen Whitley. These lectures gave MAKH both a theoretical foundation to underpin everything he had learned from Wang Li and also a direction in which a methodology might be developed. He also attended lectures by visiting scholars whenever possible, including a series of three lectures given by Louis Hjelmslev, who spoke on the semiotics of traffic lights. On one occasion, MAKH was among a few privileged postgraduate students who were invited to afternoon tea in the Senior Common Room where he was introduced to Hjelmslev by Firth. MAKH recalls Firth saying, 'The trouble with you, Louis, is that you are too stratospheric.' 'No, John', Hjelmslev replied. 'You are stratospheric. I have no ceiling.'

Firth's general theoretical view of language, and his post-Saussurean system-structure descriptive model, provided the sort of insights MAKH felt were needed. The problem MAKH faced was how to build on Firth's system-structure theory so that it became a way of talking about the language of the *Secret History*. The text was closed, in the sense that you couldn't go out and get any more data; this was, after all, fourteenth-century Mandarin. Modern Mandarin could serve comparatively, as a point of departure, but not as a source of further textual data. So it had to be treated as it was. Taking the lexicogrammar as the core, MAKH used quantitative methods to test internal predictions based on proportionality.

Firth wanted his students to be broadly grounded in the branches and schools of linguistics. Given that Firth's orientation was primarily European, his students tended to be more familiar with Hjelmslev and the Danish school, Prague school linguists, Martinet and the French linguists. Though Firth was less keen on American structuralism, still his students read Bloomfield and Sapir and also Pike. MAKH does acknowledge having drawn on the Sapir-Whorf tradition, but less so the post-Bloomfield school. MAKH also notes the influence from having been taught Chinese phonological theory, his studies in historical linguistics in relation to Sino-Tibetan rather than Indo-European; and his dialectology work on Chinese dialects.

When he got back to Cambridge, MAKH became politically active, trying to combine the role of being a graduate student in linguistics with being active in the local Communist Party, setting up a branch of the Britain-China Friendship Association. He soon found the two roles clashed. There was just not enough time in the day, to do both, making it necessary for him to decide which he was better at. In the end, he decided there were others who could do the political spade-work, and it would be better for him to focus on his study of language. 'The trouble was', recalls MAKH, 'that I found it too much to be both politically active and a scholar. I couldn't do both, and I thought I will do better and will make more of a contribution as a linguist than as a politician'.

MAKH became increasingly committed to general linguistics, and especially to working with an inspirational group of colleagues in the Linguistics Group of the British Communist Party – in particular Jeffrey Ellis, Dennis Berg, Trevor Hill, Jean Ure and Peter Wexler. They wanted to unpack current views of language which they believed to be the outcome of having prioritized certain varieties of language over others: standard languages were privileged or prioritized over dialects; written language over spoken; classical languages over modern ones; formal language over colloquial; dominant languages over emergent ones; literary language over everyday language; majority languages over minority languages. To what extent, they asked, were mainstream views of language derived from an overemphasis on highly valued forms of languages at the expense of those which were traditionally under-valued and neglected. Reflecting critically on the way mainstream approaches represented grammar, the Linguistics Group sought, on the one hand, to discover the background which motivated development of mainstream theories, while, on the other hand, working out a theory which would address this neglect and give value to these socially induced low-visibility forms of language.

Around this time MAKH describes the beginning of a gradual shift in his thinking away from the classical Marxist view of language as 'a kind of second-order phenomenon, where essentially it was reflecting rather than construing' to seeing language as 'a product of the dialectic between material processes and semiotic processes, so the semiotic became constructive-constitutive'.

Firth once told MAKH: 'Of course, you'd label me a bourgeois linguist'. When MAKH replied: 'I think you're a Marxist', Firth laughed. Though at the other end of the political spectrum, Firth once said that he didn't see anything in his own work which he considered as being contrary to Marxist principles. In fact, there was considerable compatibility between MAKH's understanding of what constituted a Marxist linguistics and Firth's emphasis on the social nature of language, his central concern with meaning, his integration of the paradigmatic and syntagmatic modes of order, his sense of multiple patterning in language, his requirement of flexibility ('rigour' he parodied as rigor mortis), and his clear distinction between general (theoretical) and particular (descriptive) categories.

In 1952, MAKH applied for a job in Firth's department, but didn't get it. Had he gotten the job, he would have had closer contact with his colleagues, and been better able to monitor whether his work on grammar was developing along 'Firthian' lines. As it was, he felt left very much on his own, especially after being appointed (in 1954) as Assistant Lecturer in Chinese at Cambridge, with a teaching load of between 12 to 14 hours a week – twice the number of hours then stipulated by the university as a maximum, which left him little time for writing, let alone trips to London. So when he finally submitted his thesis – at four o'clock on the last day of the final extension, 31 December 1954 – the grammatical framework had diverged somewhat from what was clearly recognizable as Firth's teaching. Whereas Firth defined the system by its environment in largely syntagmatic terms, it seemed to MAKH that the environment is instead better thought of as paradigmatic. Nevertheless, Firth still acknowledged the thesis as having been produced under his guidance, and supported its publication; he also agreed to let MAKH dedicate it to him.

It would be another six years, however, before MAKH would complete what would be the first journal article in systemic functional linguistics – a lengthy article, called 'Categories of the theory of grammar'. Hoping to show it to Firth before submitting it, he took the article with him to a conference arranged by the British Council on English language teaching, where Firth was to be the opening speaker. The date was 14 December and everyone had taken their seats in the conference room, waiting for Firth to appear, when the convener came in and reported that Firth had died, suddenly, during the night. The article appeared in *WORD* in 1961.

While at Cambridge, MAKH also took part in the activities of the Cambridge Language Research Unit, which was founded by Margaret Masterman. The immediate goal was to model the processes involved in translating an Italian text into Chinese. Whereas computer specialists saw machine translation as essentially an engineering problem, the CLRU instead considered it to be primarily a linguistic problem, requiring powerful theoretical tools for analysing and synthesizing text. In the course of their discussions on the principles for representing linguistic structure, MAKH recalls putting forward his arguments for formalizing the paradigmatic relations. However, as he recalls, 'I did not know how to do it – and I totally failed to persuade anyone else of this!' MAKH also saw a political role for machine translation: 'There were lots of cultures around the world where people were beginning to be educated in a mother tongue, and if you could possibly have a machine to translate a lot of text books at least it would help the process.'

Around this same period, MAKH developed a growing sense of language as a variable system, or what came to be called 'register' variation – the term 'register' coming from T. B. W. Reid (1956), the professor of Romance Philology at Oxford. This insight was prompted, on the one hand, by Firth's notion of 'a restricted language', and, on the other hand, by the interest of the Marxist Linguistics Group in the development of technical registers for legal and administrative purposes in newly emerging national languages.

In 1956, one year after Professor MAKH completed his Ph.D. at Cambridge, but three years before the subsequent publication of his Ph.D. dissertation 'The Language of the Chinese "Secret History of the Mongols" ' (1959), his paper 'Grammatical categories in Chinese' was published in the *Transactions of the Philological Society*. In this paper, he put forward a scheme of grammatical categories for the description of 'Modern Pekingese formal colloquial', or as he described it, 'the type of Chinese which a foreigner learns' (Halliday, [1986] 2005a: 210). The textual basis for this description came from a small corpus of spoken material, which he recorded in Peking and elsewhere.

In 1958, MAKH moved to Edinburgh where he became a Lecturer in General Linguistics, a new position created in Angus McIntosh's department, the Department of English Language and General Linguistics. Whereas, for the past 13 years, he had taught mainly Chinese, now he had to learn how to teach undergraduate courses in introductory linguistics and stylistics. Besides also lecturing on English grammar for the applied linguistics programme, MAKH was also asked by David Abercrombie to teach intonation for his Summer School in English Phonetics.

What made Edinburgh such a memorable intellectual environment for MAKH was not only how everyone seemed to interact with openness and a sense of going somewhere, but also how phonetics, general linguistics and applied linguistics interpenetrated at every level. That each corresponded to a different department was irrelevant to the genuine intellectual well-being of the collective. The academic culture was one of inclusion.

Since most of his students would go on to become teachers in the Scottish school system, MAKH, along with Ian Catford, John Sinclair, and Peter Strevens, began interacting with teachers to find out what they found useful from their study of linguistics. They held regular Saturday morning sessions with groups of teachers in Edinburgh or Glasgow. MAKH came away from these encounters with teachers with the realization that linguists working at the tertiary level had both much to offer to and much to learn from their secondary and primary level colleagues.

It was also around this time that MAKH got to know Basil Bernstein, who was invited to Edinburgh to give a seminar on his research into the reasons for educational failure and possible links to social class. The push from the school teachers with whom MAKH was interacting, on the one hand, and Basil Bernstein's sociological research, on the other, prompted MAKH to look closely at the relevance of language variation to education.

Arriving in Edinburgh from Pakistan in 1960, Ruqaiya Hasan became one of MAKH's first doctoral students (and later his wife). With a background in teaching English literature in Pakistan, she wrote her thesis on the language of two modern novels. She later joined the Nuffield / Schools Council Project in Linguistics and English Teaching, which MAKH set up when he moved back to London in 1963 to become the Director of the Communication Research Centre that had been set up at University College by A. H. Smith and Randolph Quirk.

The materials developed through this collaborative effort of primary, secondary and tertiary-level teachers included *Breakthrough to Literacy*, *Language in Use* and, indirectly, *Language and Communication*. The insights from this project plus his involvement in the *Linguistics Properties of Scientific English* project also contributed to his systemic description of English grammar over a three-part series, entitled 'Notes on transitivity and theme in English', which was published over three successive issues of the *Journal of Linguistics* in 1967–8. MAKH saw this development of a grammar for educational purposes as addressing the need of social accountability – 'although it wasn't directly political, it was, as [MAKH] saw it, trying to make a contribution to society'.

MAKH continued to offer workshops for school teachers who were using the *Breakthrough to Literacy* and *Language in Use* materials. The fact that teachers often asked him about the language experience of children before they come into school sparked his own interest in how children develop language.

He continued to explore those theories which were becoming mainstream in the discipline. MAKH even tried to come to terms with the Chomskian paradigm, as demonstrated by his paper on 'Some notes on deep grammar' ([1966] 2002a). Still, it seemed that more interesting questions were being asked by those working outside linguistics, including Basil Bernstein, whose research into cultural transmissions – how the social order was reproduced and potentially transformed, through language – demanded a theory of semantics beyond the current power of existing linguistic theory.

In 1965, the Communications Research Centre was incorporated into a new Department of General Linguistics headed by MAKH, whose goal was to develop linguistics as an undergraduate subject, appropriate for a first degree. In one of his courses, MAKH used Malinowksi and Whorf 'as a way in to functional theories of meaning'. Influenced by Bernstein and others, MAKH came to see the semantic systems of different languages as construing different pictures of human experience.

MAKH left University College to take up an appointment at the University of British Columbia. However, after a long wait, the Canadian government in the end refused him entry into Canada. So the next year was spent at home in London, before leaving in the latter half of 1971 to take up various appointments in the United States. Taking advantage of that gap year, MAKH decided to begin an intensive study as a participant-observer of his new son's developing linguistic ability from 9 months to 2½ years of age. The methodology was simple – using notebook and pencil to record Nigel's utterances. The data proved rich, providing a wealth of insight into how a child learns how to mean.

After leaving London in 1971, MAKH took up visiting appointments, first at Brown University, and then the University of Nairobi, each for a semester, before taking up a fellowship at the Centre for Advanced Study in the Behavioural Sciences, located on the UC Stanford campus.

This was followed, first, by a year spent at the University of Illinois, Chicago Circle, and then a year at the University of Essex, before moving in 1976 to the University of Sydney as Foundation Professor of Linguistics, where he also served as head of the Department of Linguistics for its first ten years. While on study leave at U. C. Irvine in 1980, he assisted on Bill Mann's text generation 'Penman' project, working together with Christian Matthiessen – who was then working part-time on the project while completing his Ph.D. at UCLA – to implement and expand a clause system network which MAKH had developed for English.

In 1979 MAKH was elected a Fellow of the Australian Academy of the Humanities, and in 1989 he became a Corresponding Member of the British Academy. He is also a Foreign Member of the Academia Europaea. He received the David H. Russell Award for distinguished Research in the Teaching of English, National Council of Teachers of English (USA) in 1981. In 1986 he was the Lee Kuan Yew Distinguished Visitor at the National University of Singapore. He retired as Emeritus Professor from the University of Sydney at the end of 1987.

In the early 1990s, MAKH spent some time working with the COBUILD project at the University of Birmingham. It was there that he collaborated with Zoe James in a study whose findings are reported in *A Quantitative Study of Polarity and Primary Tense in the English Finite Clause* (1993). Their aim, as MAKH explains, was not simply to count things, but to test 'the hypothesis that grammatical systems fell largely into two types: those where the options were equally probable – there being no "unmarked term", in the quantitative sense; and those where the options were skew, one term being unmarked'. They carried out their investigation by looking at between 1 and 2 million instances of polarity and primary tense in the COBUILD corpus.

In 2002, MAKH became the inaugural recipient of the AILA gold medal award for exemplary scholarship in the field of applied linguistics. In 2007, he was the recipient of an honorary doctorate from the University of British Columbia in recognition of his contribution to linguistics, including especially educational linguistics. He was the recipient of an honorary doctorate (Doctor of Education *honoris causa*) from the Hong Kong Institute of Education in 2008.

Professor M. A. K. Halliday is currently advisor to *The Halliday Centre for Intelligent Applications of Language Studies* (City University of Hong Kong), which is honoured to bear his name.

Note

1. This brief biography is an expanded version of one which appeared earlier in Ruqaiya Hasan et.al.'s *Continuing Discourse on Language*, Volume 1, Equinox: London, 2005. As with the earlier version, the account here is told as far as possible in Halliday's own words as taken from interviews which have been conducted with him over the years and which were recently compiled by Jim Martin into the book, *M. A. K. Halliday: Language Turned Back on Himself* (London: Bloomsbury, 2013). See also Webster's (2013) entry on M.A.K. Halliday in *The Encyclopedia of Applied Linguistics* (Blackwell Publishing Ltd.).

PART II

Halliday: The Making of a Mind

2 The 'History of Ideas' and Halliday's Natural Science of Meaning

David G. Butt

Chapter Overview

There can be no semiotic act that leaves the world exactly as it was before.

M. A. K. Halliday ([1994] 2002: 254)

1 Introduction

Can there be a natural science of meaning? And if so, what would such a science be like – what would be its dimensions, its architecture and its conventions? What problems would it confront? And what matters might it resolve? Furthermore, how would such a theory stand comparison with other theories or proposals which may lay claim to all, or to parts, of the same theoretical space – how might it falsify, or at least measure the efficacy of, alternative proposals?

My primary aim here is to set out how Halliday's theoretical work – language as social semiotic – constitutes such a natural science for investigating the processes of meaning, those processes that both connect us and construct us as human beings. In fulfilling this aim, I first set out by considering the milieu in which the values – which recur like motifs throughout Halliday's work – appear to me to be grounded (1). In the following sections (2–7) I take up direct evidence of Halliday's scientific values by scanning his methodical 'dialogues' with the many aspects of language; I also draw on an influential neuroscientist who is opposed to the possibility of meaning as a legitimate 'object' of scientific enquiry: 'except in some trivial sense'. Included in my enquiry are those problems and ideas that have provided Halliday with most support in the development of his work: for example, the relation to the work of his supervisor J. R. Firth on the one hand, and the work of Darwin, on the other. A Marxist social perspective is contextualized by the whole idea of a material basis for understanding the social roots of higher-order thinking, an order based on meanings rather than on the usual appeal to inferred 'cognitive' structures (e.g. Halliday, [1995] 2003b; Halliday and Matthiessen, 1999). From these perspectives and a wide spectrum of other traditional sources, we can see Halliday integrate linguistics with social theory and natural sciences. This integration is illustrated through the toolpower of system networks – an elegant, 'parsimonious' means of representation which combines the foundational linguistic notion of paradigm with the metaphor of 'choice'. Through this indicative case of scientific description (see Section 8), I argue that the activities of functional linguists constitute an extension of sciences into activities that change, dramatically, our capacity for conceptualizing and managing the complexity of experience, from casual conversation and child language development to verbal art and scientific debate. Illustrated throughout is the critical consciousness which Halliday applies to theoretical distinctions: for instance, in the way his functional grammar has been developed, and through his attitudes to theories more generally (Section 9), that is theories across various sciences and language arts. Ultimately (in Section 10), I return to the questions 'thrown down' (hence the 'ob jecta' in Latin) of the opening paragraph, above.

2 A Milieu of Enquiry

Some personal aspects are important background in such an interpretation. This is not because they are criterial for the attribution of science; but they do assist in understanding the deep and continuing currents that link ideas to the flow of individual and community motivations and values. For instance, Halliday comes from a language-focused family of teachers: his mother a teacher of French and his father a teacher and still cited dialectologist and cartographer of British dialects (see Joseph and Janda, 2003: 63). The positive aspects and values of nineteenth-century England appear to have been formative for Halliday: they are instances in which human effort through organization could create improved ideas and social conditions – Fabian societies and social movements focused on rational reform; systems of public transport; postal communication; a new commitment to broaden education; the exempla of novels as an evolving genre of social analysis; the Romantic movement with its re-animation of natural forces, its emphasis on the complex interplay of personal elements, and its tropes of walking and wending along common ways . . . And, crucially, Darwin and Wallace – their extension of a 'materialist' account of nature, and of humans in nature, extended also for differences of consciousness in those novels (for example, of George Eliot or Elizabeth Gaskell: see Beer, 2000).

This tradition of rational enquiry and respect for nature was in evidence in the eighteenth-Century Romantic and Industrial ethos of Britain and Europe. Darwin's grandfather, Erasmus Darwin, England's leading physician, was a forceful evolutionist, an acclaimed poet, and part of the Lunar Society of ingenious industrialists, including figures like James Watt (Uglow, 2002: 426ff.). The poetry of Erasmus Darwin directly influenced his acquaintance, the poetic theorist of British Romanticism: Samuel Taylor Coleridge. Also a member was Josiah Wedgewood. Members of the wealthy Darwin family married into the Wedgewood family – by then themselves wealthy from their production of porcelain. In short, Charles Darwin had the access and resources to focus for years on the research which produced his 19 books and his personal exchanges with Britain's leading authorities on all natural sciences. This spirit of 'secularized enquiry', clearly a force in Europe from the 1760s, encompassed linguistic, cultural and psychological investigations. Key figures of influence were Alexander and Wilhelm von Humboldt (the latter still seen today as a foundational figure by linguists from contrastive theories). Darwin wrote of how he read and reread Alexander's works; and he expected others to do so with him (Ridley, 2000).

Halliday has inherited, and carefully assimilated, this legacy of reasoning about nature.

It is important to remember that the most crucial component of Darwin's work on evolution was actually sparked by social theory and metaphors like the 'economy of nature'. It was the work of Malthus which helped Darwin leap to 'natural selection' and 'descent with modification'. Furthermore, in order to persuade people to his final views in 'On the Origin . . . ', Darwin used the example of gradual variations and differing rates of variation in a reflection on the origins of languages (see the final section of 'On the Origin . . .' (Darwin,

[1859]1998: 562ff.). Dawkins also uses languages to illustrate Darwinism in his powerful young people's science book: *The Magic of Reality* (Dawkins and McKean, 2011: 61–4).

The point to emphasize is the way linguistics, and a broader 'science of language', have been at the leading edge of scientific reasoning and persuasion. Semiotics is a site at which issues of matter, life and meaning are inextricably implicated with the social order. I will later claim that, in the history of ideas, and in science more specifically, reflection on languages has been a leading edge to development, not a late arrival to human sciences (see also the continuing interest in the work of Jakob von Uexkull in biosemiotics: Favareau, 2010). Halliday's methods, I further stress, provide opportunities for a new understanding of transactions between matter, organization and meaning in an era in which what people actually do can be analysed empirically at a wide range of scales.

The emphasis in the title here on the binomial 'natural science' is motivated by Halliday's own emphasis on 'doing linguistics'. In this we are likely to come closest to a reliable sense of linguistics as one way of 'doing science' – its character as an activity (Halliday, [1992] 2003a). The point is that we are not likely to decide what counts as science through a philosophical dictum. Halliday is a reflective reader into the growth of science (for instance, through the works of G. E. R. Lloyd, 2002 and Stephen Toulmin, 1961, 1972). His work not only addresses how science may represent a defining human endeavour (its phylogenetic role in the development of hominids and their ongoing development through cultures), but also how its discourse is a revealing object of enquiry in relation to the evolution of culture and consciousness (see the discussions of grammatical metaphor: [1988] 2004, [1998] 2004, 2010; Halliday and Matthiessen, 1999). The general approach to science as a higher order of our semiotic system demonstrates the remarkable human construction of 'theory': what Halliday sees as an order of organization of meaning worked out by the reworking of linguistic expressions that already have had a non-technical role in common speech. The consequences of Halliday's approach to theory, in particular through his account of grammatical metaphor, will be central to my later argument for the *forensic* and *predictive* potential in Halliday's linguistic theory.

Overall, I argue for the contemporaneous character of Halliday's science, building as it does on the 'prescience' in the work of his teacher, J. R. Firth (1890–1960). Firth's gnomic formulations, emphasizing the purpose of linguistics as the production of 'statements of meaning', were baffling to neo-Bloomfieldians and later Generative linguists alike (Langendoen, 1968). Even more challenging were formulations concerning how 'meaning is made at all levels' (i.e. not just at the semantics). The techniques of linguistics were to be (according to Firth) relegated to 'scaffolding' that, like the linguistic system itself, should not be 'reified' or 'hypostatized' into beadlike structures ([1950] 1957). Language was not to be detached from concrete instantiation in the pattern of social process. Firth also dismissed dualisms as misleading idealizations. Whether through the materiality of social contexts, or in emphasizing the organic embodiment of speakers (or in his own 'prosodic' rendering of the materiality of sound in phonetics), Firth's views, with their emphasis on polysystemic heterogeneity and actual speech data, now appear to anticipate the values of our current era of 'complexity' theory and 'text mining'. Firth's insights are activated and worked through in Halliday's wide spectrum of investigations – for instance, from the phonology of Mandarin (Halliday, [1992] 2005b and Butt, 2008a) to the analysis of functional motivation in the clause patterns of English or Chinese, as well as in the adaptation of semantic varieties (i.e. registers) in the specific evolution in each culture.

The aim of my account is to explain links and motivations in Halliday's work that may be not so well understood, including Halliday's published and conversational views on the growth of science as a historical stream of institutions and discourses. These include Halliday's study of Chinese culture and civilization – for example, the findings and career of Joseph Needham; the consistent attention to developments in a range of information sciences, developments which throw light on the mathematical 'proportions' in coding systems. These assist in interpreting the 'meaning potential' of different channels and of shifting tendencies in a grammar. Examples of these considerations include information theory following Shannon's work in 1949 (see the elaboration of this work in Gleick, 2011: chapters 7 and 8); natural language processing with the Cambridge Group in the 1950s led by Margaret Masterman (Masterman, 2005); the project with Mann and Matthiessen (see Matthiessen, 1995) to complete a paradigmatic model of English Grammar for computational purposes; and continuing attention to a similar goal through the Cardiff Grammar (Fawcett, 2010). It is noteworthy, in this line of thinking, that Winograd's influential work in modelling SHRDLU was based on Halliday's networks and grammar (see the summary of systemic grammar in Winograd, 1983).

Crucial to the whole development of functional linguistics has been the study of language and the child – the links with Trevarthen's work on intersubjectivity; the early studies edited by Margaret Bullowa (1979); and the difference between evolved and designed systems, in particular, as such differences depend on 'metaredundancy' – the fact that realizational relationships are 'nested' and not sequential, and certainly not causal. This concept – metaredundancy – clarified in the collaboration with the physicist/semiotician Jay Lemke (1995), provides a way of construing the 'implicate order' of emergent protolanguage and of a functional, polyphonic grammar. In this interpretation of child language development, the focus is on how a child moves from a personalized two-level sign system up into the three or more levels of a natural language.

In step with this professional, linguistic focus on 'learning how to mean', Halliday has monitored developments in neuroscience – its 'neural Darwinism' and various approaches to the brain through populations of neurons and the increasing emphasis on affective or interpersonal states as a platform for ideation. Then there are the images of the brain with a polysystemic dynamism and emphatic 'wiring' to itself – its 're-entrant' connections (e.g. see Edelman, 1988, 1992, 2006). In the Darwinian empiricism of current neuroscience, there has been an opportunity for revisiting interpretations of higher-order thinking in a way that seems to have been lost during the cognitive revolution of the 1960s and 1970s. The contrast with the 'autonomous syntax' of Chomsky (e.g. 1975) and the promissory notes of psycholinguistics is dramatic: consider here the current position of Chomsky, behind a minimal redoubt of 'recursion' for grammar, and 'merge' for the componential nature of knowledge (Chomsky and McGilvray, 2012, e.g. 14–15 and 176 ff.; Berwick, 1997).

The abstract dimensions in Halliday's theory have emerged from the reconciliation of empirical investigations; this is to say, from asking questions of a spectrum of problems that both specialists and 'lay' persons experience. These can be thought of as including: How does language vary between speakers and situations? What is the difference between spoken and written forms of expression? How should a teacher talk about language to students of different ages? Why is a work of literature valued in the ways that it is? What is a useful translation between languages? Why are scientific texts difficult to read? Is language a social or mainly organic ability of humans? What is the relationship between our meanings and our thoughts? Can governments or institutions plan their language, or intervene in language practices? How does a child take on the meanings of those around, from the earliest stages of life? How is learning a second language like and unlike learning the first? How 'big' is a language? How can our choices in language be mapped out so that we can see or anticipate options for meaning, whether as users/consumers, or as teachers? How has language been recruited to ideologies in which power and control dominate over the interests of a community? Can (and should) linguistic theory assist in the semiotic analysis of non-linguistic forms – in art, architecture and film studies (O'Toole, 2011)?

Alongside these problems 'looking out' to the world, there are also the questions students ask – whether linguists or not – when looking 'into' language. These start to take on a more technical idiom: What is grammar? Is intonation part of the system or an 'add on' to the system (viz. 'emphasis'; supra-segmentals; proxemics)? How does the context determine or change the meaning? How does Chinese manage time without tenses? Should Traditional (Latin) Grammars be applied to other varieties of languages around the world? If not, how should we proceed in describing languages from distinct language families? Where does grammar end and lexicography begin? What is 'semantics'?

What is a thesaurus? How should it be organized? How might a computer become more proficient at answering human enquiries? What is dialogue, and when does it begin, say, between mother and child? What do languages have in common, even as these commonalities might appear in mixed forms (e.g. a mix of properties of transitivity and ergativity in the case systems)? What kind of properties do language systems exhibit as systems? And how might these properties be evident across other forms of human institutions (across eco-social systems in general)? Which species, other than humans, have elaborate communication systems? Are such systems languages? How do human brains communicate with themselves and their personal history of experiences?

3 The 'Implicate Order' of Linguistic Tradition

In this section, I try to indicate briefly a peculiarity about the working context of linguists in the latter half of the twentieth century. It is difficult for anyone outside linguistics to evaluate what currently counts as linguistic tradition, and what of the research activities of today constitute a tradition predating the rhetorical onslaught of generative linguistics since the 1960s (Allan, 2010, offers a valuable survey of the legacies of tradition and the diversity of contemporary theory). Much of the linguistic tradition has operated as an 'implicate order': a less visible structure making progress behind the overt appearance of psycholinguistics and its exclusive claims to U.G. and 'the science of language'. This subsection, then, is directed to the problem of rhetorical inversion – the situation of academics who have been trained to see the longer-term traditions of linguistics as aberrant and non-scientific (see Chomsky, 1993: 51). The foreground of empirical research became background to a hunt for a chimera of pre-semantic 'grammaticality' (again, explained at length in his disputes with Searle: Chomsky, 1975. For the case against this direction in linguistics, see e.g. Ellis, 1993 and Halliday, [1995] 2003a).

A broad range of ideas drawn from linguistic traditions has been characteristic of Halliday's publications. Yet, this is quite in contradiction of the way Halliday's work and the tradition of Firth has been positioned in America, namely, as if it involves neologisms of an eccentric character (Thomas, 2011 and personal communication). The fact is that the more than ten volumes of Halliday's *Collected Works* encompass a broad range of established problems and concepts from linguistics, a spectrum comparable to the virtuoso range of even Roman Jakobson. A case in point concerns the terms of his grammatical theory: they all have an historical depth, or 'pedigree', which demands some reorientation when brought to the description of non-classical languages and, in particular, when applied to languages outside the Indo-European family. Furthermore, the functional meanings of grammatical terms need to be integrated into a consistent general framework (a point discussed below). It is one of the remarkable aspects of contemporary discourse in linguistics how traditional notions have been made to seem weird, and then later reintroduced under supposedly novel or formalistic motivations. See, for example, the functional contrast discussed by Miyagawa et al. (2013) in a 'novel account' of the evolution of 'human language syntax': namely, as the 'adventitious' combination of an E-Language ('Expressive': as from birdsong, leading to mood; modality variations) and a L-Language ('Lexical': meanings that are supposedly constant in establishing a predication, as in the honeybee dance). The combination of these two finite systems are the basis, we are told, for the infinite and unique system of human language. This seems to be a combination of many 'non-M.I.T. elements', including another way of invoking the many to many relations that are traditionally seen as realization across linguistic strata and systems, as in SFL or the work of Hjelmslev (1953) and Lamb (1973).

Due to the controversies surrounding the allocation of the title 'science' in linguistics, the following scan of influences will highlight some direct connections between the Firthian approach and the history and methods of linguistics. There is also the leadership of ideas from the Prague School and from related concepts in the work of figures like Sapir. A connection here is through Sapir's 'That certain cut' in a language – its pattern of distinctive regularities and tendencies seen in a form of 'characterology', as the Prague school referred to such analyses (see Halliday's paper on Mandarin, ISFC 40, *Functional Linguistics*, Vol. 1, in Guangzhou: 2013).

Sapir's student and colleague, Benjamin Lee Whorf, has been a more often cited stimulus to Hallidayan thought: the ideas of phenotypic versus cryptotypic patterning in a grammar, as well as 'reactance' and 'covert category'. These concepts demonstrate how subtle and psychological Whorfian thinking on language was from its inception, when examined in the actual writings of Whorf – and free of textbook caricatures (see, for instance, the exceptional insights of Dan 'Moonhawk' Alford (2002) and other postings on his experience of studying linguistics). The conditions of enquiry into semiotic systems create a strong case for Whorfian effects across languages: certain meanings are going to be prioritized by the configuration of systems in any language, certain meanings will be 'facilitated' by the choices foregrounded in a grammatical system. This is not to claim that other thoughts are impossible, but that they may be realized implicitly, or by a heavier load of choice in 'circumlocutions' (see Hasan's close analysis of 'subject' and restricted exophoric reference across a comparison of upper-middle-class English and upper-middle-class Urdu, [1984] 1996).

In work that bears most directly on the empiricism and methodical conduct of sociolinguistic enquiry, Ruqaiya Hasan has turned Halliday's networks to an investigation of alignments between social class and semantic patterning. Her work reveals an astoundingly consistent relationship between the workplace autonomy of the family (in first place, through the history of the mother) and the prioritizing of particular meanings. The most relevant of these alignments are how the child is projected through talk as:

(1) an independent agent of thought, of opinion, and of responsible action; and

(2) how the child–parent relationship can be construed as a domain in which one expects explanations based on personal, localistic principles of authority OR where decontextualized, quasi-objective meanings are foregrounded.

This project elaborated one of the most profound implications of Halliday's way of understanding and describing language – namely, that semantic variation is an inevitable consequence of a sociological semantics . . . of any semantics that uses language as the primary evidence for what people do and know (see Halliday [1992] 2003a and 1973a). The research involved the development of a comprehensive network for semantics. This characterized more than 70 dimensions of a 'message', along with realization statements directly to the forms 'at risk' in the lexicogrammar. Hasan's empirical, archival study involved more than 20,000 messages from higher and lower autonomy families across Sydney (all naturally recorded by mothers themselves who could just push a recorder button in contexts of daily care).

As with the writings of Firth, other European traditions have created paths for Halliday's programme of enquiry. These traditions include not only the Prague School but also the work of Russian theorists and 'Formalists'. This may be easiest to cite from Halliday's work in stylistics, in which concepts like 'prominence', marked/unmarked, foregrounding, dominant, and 'de-automatization' are examined and illustrated (see Jakobson, 1987; Striedter, 1989). The views of Tynjanov and Jakobson (1978) and Tynjanov (1978) from the 1930s are congruent – they may have been the first to use the term 'systemo-functional' in characterizing texts (see Steiner, 1984: 137, 109, 112). The Hjelmslevian and relational theory of Sydney Lamb has also provided interesting parallels in that it has shown that complex cognitive and linguistic junctures could be represented practically and economically through Lamb's extended version of Halliday's network diagrams. This is to say that the network conventions (treated in detail in section below) can be adapted to represent 'relations of relations' across phenomena as divergent as phonological alternatives, at one level, and the differences between roles in a family, at another (e.g. Lamb, 1973: 60–83 and 1984).

Despite the universalist assumptions of the main period of Chomskyan influence, Halliday's orientation to meaning was maintained in the development of *An Introduction to Functional Grammar* (now in four editions), in Halliday's work in education, and also in child language studies. The focus on meaning was also comprehensively explored in a volume written with Christian Matthiessen (1999): *Construing Experience through Meaning*. This offers a profound exploration of the way sciences of the mind might work from a meaning or semiotic base, rather than from their usual assumption of a 'prior' level of inferred cognitive structures (see also the work of Michio Sugeno at the RIKEN Brain Science Institute, Tokyo, as reported in Kobayashi et al., 2006). The topics covered in *Construing Experience through Meaning* provide a bridge of signs – through realization and its implications – over to the way registerial expansion can develop, particularly through the diversification of grammatical strategies for textual purposes. By this latter description I am referring again to Halliday's concept of grammatical metaphor: the strategic deployment of lexical items to grammatical categories in which the goals of the register potential can be realized more directly: for example, rather than the report that 'The glass cracked' and that 'The crack got longer by 2cms each day', one can nominalize to 'The glass crack growth rate IS 2 cms per day'. Such formulations both reflect the anaphoric pressure on the text – the need to summarize its preceding topics – as well as the goals of quantification and abstraction to more general principles, that is, for activation across contexts. The implications of the 13 trans-categorizations set out in Halliday's work address the 'drift', the changing texture, of technical writing in science and related activities ([1998] 2004). The lexical density of certain registers creates, then, a contrast with the dialogic choreography of spoken discourse.

4 What We Expect in Speaking of Science

Various terms are invoked when the specialist or the lay person describes knowledge as 'science'. I now wish to reflect on such terms and how they stand up to review in relation to linguists and their activities. Whether or not science can be defined for practical purposes, there is clearly something very important at stake in defending the notions which motivate scientists and the activities of those who are committed to scientific methods and ethics. But we need to reflect on what the motivations, methods, and ethics have been in actual cases, rather than in some vague popular ideal, potentially the product of social propaganda. Given the kudos of science with funding bodies and in medical research, 'propaganda' is not an exaggerated term for the argumentation that has characterized debates over the twentieth century in relation to, for example: 'reality' and hidden variables in quantum theory (see Whitaker, 2006 on Einstein, Bohr, Heisenberg, Schrodinger, Bohm and the EPR experiments; Cassidy, 1992); genetics and the shifts from the Dogmas of Crick 1958 (see Shapiro, 2011); genes and I. Q. (Rose, Lewontin and Kamen, 1984 and Lewontin, 2000a: chapter 1); sociobiology (E. O. Wilson's work, including 'Genetic Social Evolution' in

Holldobler and Wilson, 2009); and Feyerabend (1975) or Brooks (2011) on the 'anarchism' of scientists.

Work in the history and philosophy of science, during the 1960s and 1970s, was particularly focused on the idea of criteria for what was and was not science (Chalmers, 2013, 4th extended edition). This work in part responded to an emphasis on the sociological formation of scientific groups, groups whose discourse delimited the paradigm of current knowledge (viz. Kuhn in Lakatos and Musgrave, 1970: 1–24, 231–78; Chalmers, 2013: chapter 8). More programmatic was the work, decades earlier, on a criterion for science proposed by Popper: namely, that a claim was scientific when it stated the conditions for its own falsification (e.g. Popper, 1979; and Chalmers, 2013: chapters 5, 6, 7). This criterion has been influential in practical ways (e.g. the work on the neuron by J. Eccles: see Popper and Eccles [1977] 1983), and it created a chain of debate and some 'testing' against historical cases, and against counter-proposals. Foremost in the commentaries were the responses of Lakatos (e.g. Lakatos and Musgrave, 1970: 91–196; Chalmers, 2013: chapter 9), who suggested that science takes place within more encompassing programmes of enquiry, with falsification not supplying an unequivocal guide to what counts as progress. More dramatic were the claims of Feyerabend (e.g. Lakatos and Musgrave, 1970: 197–230; Feyerabend, 1975; Chalmers, 2013: chapter 10), who stressed the 'anything goes' and the non-methodical 'advance' in what scientists later present as methodical and rational science. The recent study by Brooks (2011) offers extended exemplification of the skulduggery and intuition in the history of modern science. While there may be much that is deeply shocking in the ethics and behaviours of celebrated scientists, also, as argued by Chalmers and Medawar (1984), there is much to defend in the activity of experimentation and the reconciliation of relevant 'facts'.

The environment or milieu of enquiry is a key factor in the evaluation of scientific change and of the work of scientists. The monastic chain of 'research centres' that supported Mendel's work in the nineteenth century (see Lewontin, 2000b: chapter 3) provides an unnerving comparison with the context of funded support in America in the 1960s, as described and criticized by Chargaff (e.g. 1978: 134–5). The latter highlights the ruthless administration of resources to which even a Nobel Laureate was subjected: you exist only to the extent that you have a funded project – a social ethos, like politics, that only backed the most recent winners!

But 'scientific' principles warrant attention **and** defence. The fact that there is so much psuedo-science in public domains attests to the significance of rational enquiry in being human: why would agencies mimic scientific methods if such methods did not impart power? Contemporary medicine and industrial technologies have provided unequivocal evidence of reliability of methods and outcomes, of the 'efficacy' of knowledge, even though medicine and technology have been equivocal in particular cases. The 'progress' related to science has also been tightly bound up with measurement (Crosby, 1997). Scientists have a task, perhaps even shared with poets: they supply 'a response to the daily necessity of getting the world right' (the poet, Wallace Stevens, 1957: 201). When our reasoning about a broad spectrum of possibilities depends on experience, and must be 'taken back' to experience for the test of consistency, one is in a domain of rational enquiry. Any conduct that counts as a 'rational enterprise', after the formulation offered by Stephen Toulmin (1972), should be included in the spectrum of 'sciences'.

More specifically, I suggest that science is characterized simply by the reconciliation of diverse reports about experience. Humans have to conduct themselves, first, by giving weight to the individual reports available to them, whether personal or distal (i.e. on the basis of various forms of authority). They then need to act in the light of some co-ordination of what may seem like differing or even contradictory accounts of experience. The most reliable job of reconciliation we call 'science'. Its reliability will be the source of further reports, since we need to act on, or perform, our social roles in deep seriousness. Wellbeing and efficacy of action depend upon the reconciliation of such accounts, although such a dependency may be not be as direct as scientists might seek in problems of great complexity (for example, involving populations, not just isolated instances).

This means that we need to see science as context bound, yet reaching for 'sub specie aeternitatis', aspiring to the conditions of eternity (Grant, 1997). How any human or human society gives weight to a report from experience depends on the historical moment: ideas are plausible only when they are perceived as both relevant and credible. They have a cultural or historical timeliness – the Greek notion of 'kairos'. One can ask whether the atomism of Epicurus and of his Latin follower Lucretius (1992) was 'rational' or merely a prejudice of belief. If there is no technology to settle an issue, is reasoning enough to be science? In the case of these classical authors, many reasons were proposed to readers concerning, for instance, emptiness and matter, much as we might understand the emptiness of matter in the twenty-first century. Furthermore, Lucretius is credited with the first of the 'thought experiments' of physical science – on the infinite cosmos (Cohen, 2005: 52). This secularization of the universe challenged others to offer better reasons and was therefore part of a programme of rational extension in humans (Johnson, 2000). In fact, Greenblatt (2011) has described the rediscovery of Lucretius's poem 'De Rerum Natura' as a catalyst for the development of European humanism in the Renaissance, since the 7,000-line poem showed that a secularization of natural philosophy was possible and plausible.

Freud's theories also illustrate the importance of historical moment and particular location. I cannot fully develop the claim here, however. What I wish to point out is the changing respect for Freud's work as science, especially as

a 'watershed' in the sciences of mind. After a period in the mid-twentieth century when Freud's methods and theories were even lampooned, the greater
understanding of the dynamics of the brain, based on brain imaging and the
emphasis on systems of feelings (rather than on cognitive modules) has led to a
re-affirmation of the 'general' findings of Freud and of his status as a leader in
'science' (Kandel, 2012: 47 and 2005: 65ff.; and Gregory, 1981: 353–8 and chapter 14). Also relevant to the context of what counts as 'science', we can see that
Pierre Janet, Freud's equal in influence in the early twentieth century (and arguably a scientific superior), is relatively unknown today (Janet, 1924). The case
of the neurologist Hughlings Jackson (1835–1911) is also relevant – the first to
use the 'self' in a medical context, and one who made various sound predictions
about evolutionary aspects of human brains (Meares, 2005, 2012: 48–54). The
question one might ask then is: what justification can there be for discriminating between 'scientific' and 'pre-scientific'? (Note, I may need to recant on my
earlier use of 'prescience' with respect to J. R. Firth.)

Only with this context dependency in mind can we proceed to the cluster
of characteristics which are often cited as the hallmarks of science: *evidence;
objectivity; explanation of causes; prediction; universalism; proof; coherence; formality;
simplicity; parsimony; reliability and duplication; elegance; pragmatism* . . . No significant scientific theory accommodates all these characteristics. A 'favourable'
selection of such terms is typically combined and tossed around rhetorically by
those engaged in claiming the prestige, and funding, of sciences. Therefore, I
suggest, these are a secondary set of descriptions. Some combination of these
characteristics will need to be activated in debate for anyone to extend the 'family resemblance' of science to an activity, method or idea. **These characteristics
will be far more challenging and complex and difficult to secure in the most
important cases – those which involve deep innovation, those which must
involve a number of disciplines and those which cut across the seams of our
most deeply felt values.** But such cases are precisely those in which a culture
needs to support research.

The scientific process is the 'most rational' reconciliation of reports offered
by human transactions with experience. In the study of language, the relevant
reports are long standing, diverse and sensitive to changing technologies (as in
most issues of human significance). While there may be no simple technique
for resolving 'most rational', it is possible to take guidance from the degree
of openness to a diversity of sources (or perspectives), and in the degree of
relevance of a report (based on the proximity of the information to the 'nub' of
the experiential problem). Similarly, diversity of sources and relevance can be
refined through extrinsic considerations: for instance, by authorship. Questions
in this regard are straightforward: 'Is there a conflict of interest or a vested interest with respect to the source?' and 'Does the author of a report have authority
in the domain of enquiry or debate?' These questions have been prominent in

public forums, with Thucydides' account of the Mytilene debate of Athens (c. 428 BCE) illustrating the failure of rhetorical standards under a strategy by the violent demagogue Cleon (Leff, 1996: 88–94). It is truly astonishing today, in what purports to be an 'Information Era', that we still have so few demands on purveyors of information to declare their *ethos* in detail – simply even to declare all their sources of earnings. This has critical consequences for the public understanding of scientific debates, since there are certain requirements in specialist environments that are not extended to the wider forums of public legislation (i.e. demands for disclosure and restrictions on cronyism).

In this regard, it is germane to ask how current expressions about the limits of the study of meaning or consciousness or 'qualia' compare with the introduction of scientific ideas that today we 'take for granted'. In the case of 'The Calculus', for example, we should note that the notions introduced by Newton and Liebniz were ridiculed by powerful minds when they were proposed in the seventeenth century. The idea of 'infinitesimals' and 'limits' and 'fluxions' and other fundamental heuristic fictions (Vaihinger, 1924) were lampooned by Bishop Berkeley as so outlandish that nothing in the New Testament need be a problem of belief by comparison. The historian of mathematics Kline (1953: 267–8) wrote that a sound explanation of calculus did not eventuate till nearly 200 years after its proposal, despite the toolpower, or practical utility, that recommended the technique.

Calculus applied symbols to capture change. Linguistic and semiotic theory has to 'dimensionalize' the symbolic order; but this 'order' is an object of enquiry which is also the instrument of enquiry. Furthermore, both the object and the instrument are subject to change. Such problems of 'language turned back on itself' may not be unique. They could be analogous to beams of electrons interfering with electrons in the process of measuring electrons. The paradoxes in the theories of matter continue to run out ahead of the human ability to reconcile fully the relationships between rest-mass, mass-energy, energy-time, dark matter vs (our) baryonic matter, real vs virtual photons (undetectable except for their putative effect on real particles! See McMullin, 2010, especially pp. 14 31; and Davies and Gregersen, 2010: all articles. For an emphasis on realism in quantum phenomena, however, see recent work reported by Deutsch and Ekert, 2012).

In the life sciences, population behaviours, even among single cell life forms, involve 'decision points' and paradoxical exchanges of information: 'quorum sensing' and purpose-driven 'mutualisms'. These phenomena, and the evidence of self-engineering of DNA sequences in various life forms, present scientists with new epistemological problems concerning 'self-awareness' and goal directedness in living systems (Shapiro, 2011: 137). According to Shapiro, there is a need to reconstrue life forms in terms of systems of information with teleological properties – not theological, but rather molecular and cellular processes that are goal oriented. This reconstrual of goal-directed behaviour in living systems was inaugurated by Rosenblueth, Wiener, and Bigelow in 1943, if we set aside the four types of cause proposed by Aristotle. Jakobson wrote a brilliant response to the analogies and potential homologies between linguistic systems and biological systems (1972). But this ran counter to the 'uniqueness' of language urged by Chomsky, and has made a rather belated contribution to historical linguistics and notions of change (see Antilla's views 2003; and the systems ideas in Lass, 1997). Other authorities discuss the incompleteness of nature when addressed without consideration of teleodynamic systems (e.g. Deacon, 2012: 270ff.); and some even venture to allocate rudimentary consciousness to cells (viz. Margulis, 2006). All this suggests we might reconsider the 'pan-experientialism' of A. N. Whitehead, which now appears to be moving closer to an 'orthodoxy' (Birch, 1990; Cobb, 1993). These developments and controversies make the 'objects' of various sciences appear more like the linguists study of, say, the system of *mood* in grammar: our potential to enact various forms of striving in our exchanges with the world about – an 'ecosocial system', as these were described by Lemke (1995).

Despite the difficulty of paradoxes involved in the study of matter and life, I suspect (to caricature and dramatize) that the human role in the analysis of processes of meaning is even more challenging – akin to being 'one' of the interfering electrons probing electrons – one in a population which is itself 'shifted' by the enquiry and its purpose. Rather than opposing matter and information, or matter and meaning, Halliday is open to the implications of organization as a form of information. He notes that it may be conceivable that the weight of scientific formulations may move towards 'matter as a special case of meaning, rather than (as in our usual way of thinking) the other way round' (Halliday, [2005] 2013: 208).

We need to apply the test of William James also when evaluating the abstractions and dimensions of theory that may be needed to manage the complexity of enquiries concerning language: namely, we need to ask how the theory increases our potential for better outcomes in the problems and questions we take up. The problems taken up in Hallidayan linguistics are on display throughout this volume; they are clustered around the issue of variation and diversity, much like the problem facing Darwin, with the 'speciation' applying to language families, languages, dialects and registers – systems, users and uses. Again, it might be emphasized that the study of genealogy in languages was the first clear theory of 'descent with modification', a point noted by close readers of Darwin (see Jones, 2000: 12–13 for an analogy with variation in forms of HIV; and note the recent support for the genealogical approaches to word order regularities in Dunn et al., 2011).

In the rational integration of human reports that is at the centre of science as an activity, platonic oppositions like *induction* versus *deduction*, or *empiricist* versus *rationalist*, I suggest, are unrealistic and misleading (as if any enquiry can be conducted from one or other pole!). Such terms are rhetorical props in the theatre of academic politics: was Darwin empirical or rational? Was he working by induction or deduction? The *Origin of Species* appears to me to be the very acme of a reasoned reconciliation between evidence and competing accounts of nature. The volume, written in haste in response to the work of Alfred Wallace (and a third its original 'planned' size), invites the reader to share in its steps of observation and rational reflection. The reasoning was supported by 20 years of 'antagonistic' note taking – every possible counterargument to his theory that Darwin came across he wrote down and considered.

Consequently, it may be that no major theory has ever been explained with such deep anticipation of opposing arguments and with such candour over difficult cases: a natural application of Popper's criterion of falsification. Consider, in particular, chapter 6 (p. 189) of *On the Origin of Species* ([1859] 1998) 'Difficulties on Theory'. In this section, Darwin discusses 'organs of extreme perfection' as possible contradictions to his main thesis. Immediately following the quoted passage, Darwin wrote on this search for any counterexamples: 'But I can find out no such case.' As pointed out by Halliday ([1990] 2002) in his textual analysis of Darwin's expository style, the whole discourse of 'Origin of Species . . .' functions as a preparation for the imaginative leap of the last paragraph of the book – a reflection on the 'certain grandeur' of nature under this concept of natural selection. Such is the textual accumulation that introduces 'evolved': the verb only appears in the book's final sentence.

Furthermore, Darwin's argument had to deal with the problem of a crucial gap in 'theory': no mechanism was known at that time to carry the selected traits across to a following generation (assumptions of 'averaging' or 'pangenesis' proving inaccurate). This only changed with the re-evaluation in 1900 of experiments by Gregor Mendel (1821–84). In reviewing our criteria of science, we might ask therefore: could any concrete *prediction* be made about evolution as a result of Darwin's theory at the time of his publication of '*On the Origin* . . .'? What kind of *predictions* are made currently? Well, yes . . . the continuity of the principles at work in evolution can be reconfirmed in a myriad of ways. But no individual prediction could be drawn with regard to particular instances (of natural species or of individuals). Evolution as a process is dependent on contingencies of the momentary environment (hence Lewontin's notion of a 'triple helix', 2000a). These contingencies are so complex as to seem tantamount to 'chance'. On the other hand, the virtuoso physical, perceptual and mental powers of different species make it difficult to imagine how the vagaries of environment could provide a context for such high degrees of order or organization. In fact, Darwin had dealt with the incremental logic of instinct and complex behaviour as a challenge to natural selection in *On the Origin of Species* (chapter 8):

> The subject of instinct might have been worked into the previous chapters; but I have thought that it would be more convenient to treat the subject separately, especially as so wonderful an instinct as that of the hive-bee making its cells will probably have occurred to many readers, as a difficulty sufficient to overthrow my whole theory. I must premise, that I have nothing to do with the origin of the primary mental powers, any more than I have with that of life itself. **We are concerned only with the diversities of instinct and of the other mental qualities of animals within the same class** [chapter 8: emphasis added].

The 'dance of the honey bee', as later explained by von Fritsch (see Dawkins, 1995), is an important case of bio-semiotics. It involves the challenge of explaining a complicated routine of communicative behaviour which has an ideational purpose and precise indices of direction and distance (from the dancer to the sources of nectar).

As pointed out by Popper and various scholars, knowledge can take on a diachronic depth that supervenes the minds of individuals. Humans keep records and work out tables for future reference; what may be done under one motivation can become vital to those of quite different motivation; and cultural institutions can send groups in distinct directions, only to be brought together by historical circumstances of a different era. Geoffrey Lloyd has emphasized the strong, predictive record keeping of Chinese astronomical 'bureaucrats', by contrast with the demonstrations of Greek astronomical thinkers who sought to attract pupils through individualized renown (2002: 136–7). Science becomes a 'collective consciousness' which projects its cultural characteristics and which carries implicit knowledge beyond the range of any individual 'knower'. Popper emphasized this through his notion of World 3 (Popper, 1979), namely with respect to the tool power of knowledge storage and knowledge without a human knower (e.g. the power of the book of logarithms, which no one sets out to 'know').

This intricacy of population effects in nature's evolutionary change has clear analogies with respect to the scale, direction, and diversity of 'linguistic drift', for instance, as described by Sapir (in 1921: 155). From the collective work of many linguists, the millennial creep of grammars and cultures has been clarified in a methodical way for its principles of regularity. The William Jones era and its predecessors, hardly William Jones alone (see Campbell, 2003 and 2006), brought to the consciousness of academic researchers the prospect of seeing languages as consisting of families, genealogical relations from earlier 'common ancestry'. The comparative method, as it ultimately emerged from the work of many scholars, gave to the sciences an example of what Darwin was to describe a hundred years after as 'descent with modification'. In this way we can claim that a science of meaning had already exemplified how variation and speciation (in languages) could have been the result of evolution from common ancestors. This led to a method of 'natural science', and like the variationist arguments of Darwin in 1859, left less interpretive space for any theological approach to languages (despite the complex of motivations of William Jones, as argued by Campbell, 2006).

One needs to ask, why this case – a form of 'descent with modification', 100 years before Charles Darwin – would not be counted as leadership in the sciences? The dominance of influence of ancestry between languages – over Chomskyan innate parameters and over Greenberg's universals (see below Section 10) – has been supported by Bayesian analysis applied to the nuclear word order patterns across hundreds of languages in four language families (Dunn et al., 2011). This method for checking taxonomies was taken from the biological sciences. The findings reaffirm the importance of the 'pre-scientific' work of historical linguists, and should moderate the hubris of those who claim to have transcended the taxonomists they supplanted and sleighted (consider Chomsky's dismissal of other linguists as 'taxonomists' and 'butterfly collectors', echoing Sir Ernest Rutherford's dismissal of scientists outside physics as 'stamp collectors').

As suggested above, the essence of the 'activity' of science appears to be the reconciliation of a large number of significant, validated reports, reports at different frontiers of experience, by different styles of enquirer and rapporteur, at different scales of observation, with different criteria of completeness or plausibility . . . And with, perhaps, quite distinctive (even contrastive) desires as to how such interpretations should be put to use in human affairs. We can all conceive of better or worse reconciliations of the diversity of reports concerning complex phenomena. Little of any enquiry is self-evident when investigated from a number of perspectives. Consider here the perennial and renewed scientific debate as to whether humans act as free agents (a topic of *Scientific American Mind*, 8 December 2011 and *Scientific American*, 22 March 2011). Depending on the ideologies we project and the responsibilities we have, one may choose to give priority to one form of report over another. In a law court, business will set out from the assumption of 'free will', even if then qualified by circumstances which need to be established unequivocally. In such a forum, there is little role for the characteristically qualified conclusions of scientists. In psychiatry, on the other hand, the ideal of a 'free agent' or a 'less constricted' life can be a goal to which the treating experts aspire for their patients (Meares et al., 2012). There is no single way to define the experience of human value; and, ultimately, languages consist of paradigms of values, not just linear strings. Halliday has focused on meaning as a cultural artefact, a tool elaborated through 'choice' and the prioritization of one aspect of contextual meaning over another (see Halliday [2011] 2013b).

Different priorities provide us with motivation for evidence based sub-disciplines (investigators take up dimensions of a problem rather than all dimensions of a problem); hence, strong differences of approach can be exhibited by scholars who may seem sociologically similar in their academic demeanour. This paradox is explored in detail by Kusch in a comparison of the Schools of Psychology in Germany in the first two decades of the twentieth century: e.g. the followers of Wundt and of Buhler. Kusch emphasizes how the use of intuitive as against public forms of evidence divided the three main schools he researched.

It is a situation repeated in the schools of linguistics that characterized the second half of the twentieth century, and which became the contrastive careers of Halliday and Chomsky, among many others. Chomsky not only prioritized intuitions, he lambasted all other forms of linguistic evidence; he not only prioritized syntax as a 'level', he claimed it was **the** essential component of any science concerning 'homo loquens'; he not only prioritized the computational strand of linguistic production, he has now backed into defending recursion alone as the unique property of the FLN: Faculty of Language – narrow (Hauser, Chomsky and Fitch, 2002; see also comments from Thibault, 2005).

Even an apparent similarity in political commitments has tended to contrast academic careers. Halliday's career took shape under the experience of field work on tonal and grammatical variation among dialects of the Pearl River Delta, and his study with Wang Li over the period of the conflict between Kuomintang and Communists in China. On returning to England, he could not work at the School of Oriental and African Studies in London (since they required students to sign a contract that they would never join a communist party). Halliday was accepted at Cambridge and ultimately supervised by J. R. Firth, nonetheless. Chomsky, 3 years younger, studied with luminaries like the philosopher Nelson Goodman and the linguist Zellig Harris before attacking the narrowness of American behaviourism, and taking up his 6 decade assault on flagrant contradictions in US government policies. Chomsky's activism and influence have been maintained in one place (at M.I.T.), despite his uncompromising support of US government opponents like Daniel Ellsberg (whose release of the 'Pentagon Papers' on the Vietnam War saw him labelled as the 'most dangerous man in America'). Halliday's left-wing history and views have dislodged him on a number of occasions. He now spends much of his time between home in Australia and academic forums in Hong Kong and China.

It is with many issues in mind, then, that we interpret the linguistic projects of Halliday, since the late 1940s, and the ways in which these language-based activities are in accord with what we take to be characteristics of science and scientists. We should leave open the possibility here that some characteristic claims about science need to be re-examined, not only in the light of the demands of a specifically semantic science, but also under fresh evaluations of what history can confirm (or contradict) about enquiry in physics, mathematics, life sciences, chemistry, neuroscience, and those social sciences which are seen by many – in contradiction of historical fact – to be only recent contributors to 'human sciences'.

5 Arguments against a Science of Meaning

Of those who deny the possibility of a natural science of meaning, it is practical to set out from the reasoning offered by Edelman and Tononi (2000: 222), not just because of the stature of Edelman's legacy in neurosciences (and in immunology before that), but because Halliday has drawn attention to the importance of Edelman's concept of 'Neural Darwinism'. Furthermore, the observations made at the close of their book *A Universe of Consciousness* are representative of both learned discourses and popular assumptions about meaning and verbal creativity.

The central points raised by Edelman and Tononi are that, while language (in its unique forms, like 'everyday conversation' or 'poetry') is a product of the natural order, it can never genuinely become an 'object' of scientific enquiry. According to those authors, its very 'uniqueness' undermines the methods and requirements of scientific enquiry. They refer more vaguely to something like an adaptive freedom (freeplay) in the 'grammatical soup' of human interaction. And I will return to the potential of this suggestive metaphor in an attempt to show the linguistic correlates for adaptation and freedom in the Hallidayan model.

Let us first deal with the problem of 'uniqueness' and the 'impossible' objects of scientific enquiry. Evolution is itself unique. In its specific unfolding, in its instances or actual states. So too the 'big bang' (now viewed as 'cosmic inflation'). This hardly precludes the scientific investigation of evolution's regularities; of the source of its dynamics (natural selection); of the claims and 'dogmas' concerning genetic mutations and mechanism (viz. Crick, 1958 as criticized by Shapiro, 2011: 24–5); and the roles of systemic properties in 'correcting', 're-writing', and intervening in the ongoing reciprocation between maintenance and change (Shapiro, 2011: 56ff.). Edelman's own 'Neural Darwinism' demonstrates the reconciliation between underlying pattern and actual process, between the generality of human brains and the uniqueness of each brain as a function of the specific 'weight' of experiences that recruit 'populations' of neurons and that participate in the 're-entrant mapping' of each brain's 'conversation' with itself (if I can be permitted that metaphor). While science may be the rational pursuit of invariance in human experience, the framework of evolution means that principles of invariance have to be construed within the variation of a dynamic cosmic order in which, for all matters of critical significance for humans, specific histories have to be built into the search for 'universals', not shut out for the convenience of heuristic formalisms.

As Halliday's works in the analysis of dialogue and in stylistics have shown, these areas of human choice are more breathtaking as 'evolved' performance when seen against the regularities of the systems which they utilize as their 'ground' or symbolic resources. Analysis does not prejudice the 'grammatical soup' or freeplay of meaning in the mind, just as astrophysics cannot dull human interest in the cosmic 'soup': rather, both put the intricacies of natural organization on display. In fact, the work of Edelman, with 'Neural Darwinism' and the resonance of a brain in touch with itself ('re-entrant mapping'), has supplied, along with works by Damasio (2012) and Meares (2012), a means for construing the semiotic dimension of 'self' construction in evolution. The central problem is of how a value becomes salient in the lived experience of the child. With this we can return to Halliday ([1994] 2002: 'How do you mean?' See Section 7 below).

6 Co-Ordinates for Scientific Enquiry into Texts and their Contexts

To know where we are in space, we need co-ordinates from a system we impose on nature, on nature's changing reference points. Latitude and longitude are not natural, but use nature. In order to manage the complexity of languages, Halliday has proposed a system of dimensions. In these, he has taken the basic variables of traditional approaches to semiosis and brought them into a consistent relationship. These dimensions provide investigators with control of their enquiry: one can be clear about the 'semiotic address' of questions and actions currently on the 'work bench' of research. In Figure 2.1, the main concern of the linguist might be thought of as the dominating matrix of systems in a language – a co-ordinate system for knowing where we are in the 'polysystemic' heterogeneity that Firth emphasized. So, we have the conventional division of the linguists' task into codings of codings of codings . . . producing, in the case of SFL: the levels of context, semantics, form (lexicogrammar), phonology, expression substance (phonetics/graphology/sign gesture). Similarly, we can observe that terms from the traditional toolkit of linguists are allocated precise roles with respect to each other: for example, language *levels* (*strata*) are distinct from the constituency expressed by *rank*; and *depth* pertains to the degrees of dependency in taxis or combination. There is a role, then, for constituency and dependency in the work of analysis, along with the central concept of '*realization*': the relationship between *exponents* on different levels in the mode.

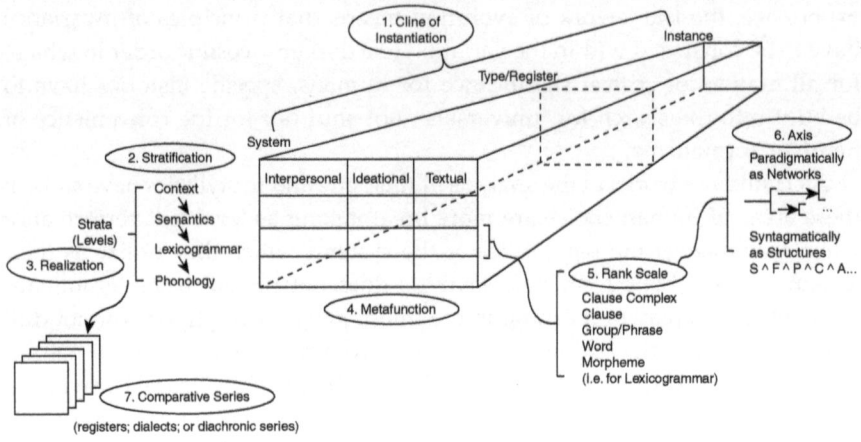

(After Halliday and Matthiessen, various.)

Figure 2.1 Dimensions of language

Realization characterizes the distinctive, semiotic demands of linguistic theory. We have the challenge with language of many things having to happen together on different levels, or 'nothing' takes place at all! The levels do not cause each other, even though language as a totality may be the most consequential system in human ecology. As Halliday reflects on the situation: 'There can be no semiotic act that leaves the world exactly as it was.' One has to ask how it could be that simultaneous alignments between units on a number of levels have the potential to create meaning-bearing behaviours by which persons in a collective (a population) can calibrate their actions and thoughts. Furthermore, one has the conundrum of how such a system of alignments (i.e. signs) gets started; how a human child gets started into it; and how the semogenic process continues in the history of a culture (that is, how the plasticity of semiotic 'materials' is continuously elaborated for the changing needs of an open future, and under pressures for adaptation, all within the 'natural selection' of a Darwinian framework).

The chief characteristic of a realizational system is not that it provides the linear recursion that has become the redoubt of Chomsky's Language Faculty ('narrow': Hauser et al., 2002), but that the 'system' overall is infinite in its potential to provide potential. The alignments are not simply of, say, sound with meaning; they are at many levels, and so involve a creativity that can evolve in many, many ensembles of contextual, semantic and grammatical values (Saussure's 'valeurs'). According to Halliday, the simultaneous strands of meaning integrated in grammatical structures constitute a vast 'polyphony'. These different kinds of meaning are drawn from his observations on interrelations in grammar: the fact that the 'wiring' between different systems of choice tended to indicate a pattern of three blocs: one with an *interpersonal* orientation; one with an *ideational* orientation; and a third that seemed to supply choices by which the other modes of meaning can be facilitated in their *textual* combination, as well as their linking within the context of the *instance* of speech itself. These more abstract functions in language Halliday refers to as *metafunctions*. They supply the other side of the 'strata : metafunction' matrix (i.e. Figure 2.1).

But the matrix only gives a way of moving around the language as *system*. Halliday compares this perspective to that of a specification of 'climate' – what history has shown us to expect in a broad, probabilistic way. We need the complementary perspective of conditions in a given *instance* – the text under consideration. This may be compared to the 'weather': the actual variables from which the climate undergoes continuous readjustments.

While network representation can be taken up and left off according to the task at hand, it is nevertheless the case that, in order to be a useful placeholder in a description, the network itself needs to be clearly situated in an overall theory. This is quite different from the full exploration of all the connections and dependencies, ad infinitum, that any component of description may imply. The network, so as to speak, requires an 'address' in the theory – its position as a task against the topography of metadescriptive tasks needs to be specified. This follows from the practical goal of integrating different descriptions in order to model, for example, linguistic behaviour in a machine. Part of the problem of integration is that, while the conventions of a linguistic network remain the same across different tasks, the many orders of pattern or organization in language result in the descriptions themselves having a varying status. This is to say contextual, semantic, lexicogrammatical and phonological networks all vary somewhat in their own status or meaning. They contribute differently to a global picture or model. The optimum demonstration of these points can be found by comparing Hasan's networks for lexicogrammar of depositive verbs (1987, 1996: 73ff.), for semantics (1996: 104–31) and more recent accounts of field in context (1999a). Consequently, one needs the address – at least, metaphorically, we ought to supply the area code. In the diagram (i.e. again Figure 2.1), taken or modified from Halliday (1998), the site of a network in the total theory can be clearly specified. With the seven concepts set out, one can settle on the co-ordinates for the 'map' of systemic functional theory. The concepts supply the text analyst with the necessary distinctions for narrowing down both the task of description and the status of what has been achieved. In this way they, the concepts, function like the multiple term expressions on a topographic map. Only here the space being systematically specified is abstract space – the potential to mean metalinguistically.

The first setting for text analysis is the most difficult to resolve in categorical terms. I will open the discussion of the cline of instantiation and return to it again in some final remarks about the context of a text and the context of the analyst. A text description must be situated either closer to demonstrating the patterns of the overall system, that is patterns that texts are likely to share (at least those that might be shared across a text type) or, towards the other end of the cline, closer to the foregrounding of the text's particular, even idiosyncratic relations. The analyst has to consider: will the description foreground the actual (the instance), the typical-actual (the registerial), the typical (the systemic), or the type of typical (the typological/ 'universal')? These distinctions on the cline of instantiation are usefully demonstrated by a larger-scale structure like narrative. A given instance can be characterized by the details of its actual unfolding, its textural tendencies, its subject matter and so on. Furthermore, it can be set at exemplifying its narrative type – mystery, nursery tale, romantic encounter, or any taxon in a schema of genres and sub-genres. More abstractly, the basis for the generic term itself – narrative – could be the main focus of descriptive effort and argument. Beyond this degree of abstraction, we can still move towards the putative universalism of narrative structures and their relation to broad functionalist claims (like a narrative ensues from any state of affairs which is disturbed by a complication). These last vaguer generalizations can have a place as part of an attempt to establish cross-cultural similarities and differences. But one would hope that narratologists did not focus all their resources at any single point alone along this cline.

Moving the exemplification over to the units of grammar, we might say that the description of a text can focus (i) on the plethora of particularities that constitute the actual instance; (ii) on the emerging patterns of typical, registerial choice like the probability of complex nominal groups in scientific exposition or the way tense options vary systematically with genre variation in French (see Caffarel, 2006a); (iii) on an account of all the interlocking structures down a rank scale of units in the grammar as system; or (iv) on the characteristic resource in a grammar for managing a meaning for instance, the way tense in English can be expressed by a serial, or 'choose-over-again', pattern, while other languages might utilize contrastive elements or particles (Halliday and Matthiessen, 2014: e.g. 406–10)).

The second dimension of the diagram – metafunction – is more straightforward in that it is more easily related to wider discussions in linguistics. Still there are at least two aspects of Halliday's use of function, or metafunction, that need to be carefully differentiated from the general ideas concerning linguistic function. Halliday sees the resources for meaning in a language as sets of options which fall out into three or four distinctive blocks of potential: (1) the interpersonal, comprising the choices which have a direct bearing on how speakers can maintain and further their goals in the social context, how the politics of interaction can be managed person to person, role to role, group to group, message by message, clause by clause, tone group by tone group; (2) the ideational resources for building a model which represents categories of experience: process, event, participant, and circumstance, along with how these might be spliced together according to different logical principles (this is the fourth metafunction) or architectures; and (3) the textual resources which offer choices to speakers as to how messages can be tied in with other messages (before and after) as well as with the semantically relevant dimensions of the context.

A distinction that needs to be made here is in the way Halliday motivated the idea of metafunctions. Initially, the proposal was a consequence of seeing the systems of grammatical choice actually fall out into more and less tightly dependent networks of options. The metafunctions, then, are an abstract characterization of degrees of proximity or involvement in the lexicogrammatical network.

The third co-ordinate of a linguistic address is stratal allocation. The abundant overlay of patterns in language are of necessity 'in parallel' – they have to be treated as simultaneous or overlapping to the linearity of processes of construction and interpretation (think of the major systems of the different metafunctions in relation to a clause, for example: mood, transitivity and theme-rheme choices). But some of the parallel events or patterns are also in a realizational relation – higher-order units, say of meaning, have to find realization in another order of reality, in the lexicogrammar and the expression (phonology or graphology). The lower strata are our (only) access to the higher. The patterns of units on these different levels or strata must be separated out for the regularity and variation of text to be visible.

The fourth aspect of address is a rank scale of constituent relations. On each stratum it can be proposed that certain units of a given rank can be combined to constitute a unit at the rank or ranks above. Halliday refers to this principle simply as composition because it does not only apply to the constituency of lexicogrammar or phonology. While linguists have debated whether their grammars should be organized around dependency or constituency, in a model based on networks of differences/choices, this debate ceases to have the consequences it might have for a theory which places so much responsibility on rules and syntagma. Both constituency and dependency are ways of seeing the organization of language, and so the issue becomes not a case of either/or but one of 'where?' (i.e. where to use the two kinds of relations in the overall model).

Other crucial details of Halliday's map for system networks, his co-ordinates for the address of a description, include the semantic units of *sequence, figure,* and *element*; and the characteristic realizations in a given metafunction: are they constituent 'particles'? or prosodic 'waves'? or a dispersed pattern, a 'field' of significant choices outside the syntagma of clause or tone unit?

Returning to the motivation for the cline of instantiation, we can say that the context we are making (the instance) becomes the culture we are experiencing (the background system), much as the weather we are experiencing day by day becomes, from a broader perspective, the basis for describing our climate. Instance and system are not two phenomena, but the same experience viewed from different depths of field. Once again, an old conundrum – namely, how does language reflect the culture? – ceases to be an issue in that we can see more practically how texts construct the culture, context by context, semiotic process by semiotic process. In the texture of text, in the structures of exchanges; in the parameters of context; the variables which are consequential for meaning are the realia upon which the larger-scale generalizations concerning ideology, class, gender, and culture can be set out with systemic evidence.

Such evidence can be described, I would claim, as an argument against randomness. Essentially, when a pattern of selection appears to have no logical explanation from the context, then there is a prima facie case that it is 'motivated'. One then has reason to ask what could have been the motivation for this semantic consistency, this possibly unnoticed pressure to make sense in just this way when other options appear to have offered just as 'natural' versions of experience. Halliday's ability to put this kind of argument to work has been breathtaking, and resolves the content vs form, or the context vs text impasses that have bedevilled studies by literary analysts and by those in pragmatics and the analysis of ideology.

At this point, with the weather-climate analogy, one can see further evidence of the congruence between the Hallidayan systemic networks and those developed by Lamb (1984). One can move from the conception of linguistic representation right through to cultural representation, the culture as a system of semiotic systems, each in itself not intractable as a descriptive task, just a network of distinctions that are observable and therefore interpretable against the background of other relations. Distinctions of sound can be interpreted because they realize distinctions of form, which realize distinctions of meaning. These construe and construct the situation such that it can take those directions of unfolding, of social process, which are the recognizable forms of life for the culture (see Hasan, 1996: 1).

7 Halliday on the 'Science of Linguistics'

Halliday has, under different headings and sub-disciplines, expressed views directly on the 'science' in Linguistics. As first raised in Section 1 above, Halliday takes up the distinction between 'doing science' and science as a category ([1992] 2003a). In fact, the discussion makes a number of relevant distinctions. It notes that special conditions may well apply to semiotic systems, and these may make people withhold the title of 'science', as least as far as the inner group of physics, chemistry, biology . . . are concerned. He goes on to distinguish between theories which purport to define science, and the day-to-day pattern of scientists at work. When doing linguistics, linguists engage in activities which look like the actions designated as science in other groups of experts. To this alliance with those conducting rational investigations into the natural world, he seems satisfied. I have begun to elaborate on this designation 'science' – in particular, on the importance of a core activity, namely: simply reconciling the diverse reports that exist about the phenomenon under investigation. In a summarizing section, I will return to this underrated characteristic of scientific activities – of rationally reconciling diverse reports.

In this subsection, I wish to consider some of the key clarifications necessary to understand the complexity of linguistic enquiry. The point is to set out how, as in all sciences, provision needs to be made to manage such complexity and produce the optimum 'line of vision' with respect to the object of enquiry. Such anticipation and management of complexity was inaugurated by Saussure in his *'Course.'* (1959). But Halliday brings the discussion back to the activities of linguists today in what Firth referred to as the necessary 'renewal of connection to the patterns and processes of living' (Firth, [1957] 1962). From my reading of Halliday, in particular from the 'Ineffability of Grammatical Categories' ([1988] 2002), something like Saussure's notion of 'valeur' has to be applied both to a language and to the terms of language for describing that language. One then has to add to this complexity of point of view the further refraction that results from the power we can exercise when we intervene (consciously or unconsciously) in our language, moment to moment (through the systems of the textual metafunction). Then there is the effect of the different purposes to which we can orient our metalinguistic descriptions (that is, towards phylogenetic, ontogenetic or logogenetic projects). Taken together, these issues show how challenging can be the complexity of the linguist's point of view. It is hard to hide from the perspectivism, the relativism, inherent in the epistemological conditions of semiotic enquiry.

But is this not, I would ask, the 'perspectivism' of problems in relativity and space-time, and in any cosmology that has to impose a co-ordinate system to secure a 'locus' from which to assign facts? Is there not also, for linguists, the relativism of dealing with population phenomena – analogous to the statistical problems raised by Boltzmann in thermodynamical systems (1895 discussed in Mainzer, 2004). Even more pressing may be the analogy with the complementarity of the Bohr-Heisenberg account of the electron and the limits of possible knowledge of single particles (Heisenberg, 1958). Heisenberg and Bohr make no equivocations: we are not reflecting on knowledge we do not yet have in 'complementarity'; the different views cannot be reduced because there is an impasse – the knowledge for which we strive in measuring some phenomena must be qualified by the position we adopt with respect to the phenomena (Bohr, 1961). Complementarities (see Halliday, [1987] 2003, 2008) tell us there are aspects of knowledge we can never have without sacrificing or diminishing the claims of another point of view.

This intersection of problems was raised for language by Saussure (e.g. Saussure's the 'point of view creates the object'); at least, the problems emerge as you work to apply his concepts while holding to the complexities he makes conditions of semiology. These conditions were then elaborated by Hjelmslev (1953) and, in striking contrast, by Firth. Hjelmslev's 'semiotic calculus' may have become a 'Copenhagen theory' of sign systems. J. R. Firth combined the concreteness of anthropology with the motifs of 'process and pattern' taken from A. N. Whitehead's 'process philosophy' (see Butt, 2001 and 2008a). Saussure was struck by the complexity of the 'object' of enquiry in linguistics and semiology. He appears to have thought (quite erroneously) that these complexities were not a condition of other sciences; he believed that sciences typically involved basic units that were unequivocal. In fact, contemporaneous with his own lectures (1906–11), the units of the natural sciences had been subject to interpretive pressures that reformed the investigative methods of every science.

Halliday's method is to keep different perspectives active in the treatment of linguistic complexity. This is in keeping with the way sciences now require of its investigators that they accept a relativity of procedure, the fuzzy nature of descriptive categories, and an incompleteness of any account (see Deacon, 2010 and 2012). In 'Language and the Order of Nature' ([1987] 2003), Halliday argues that complementarities are characteristic of grammars of natural languages. This is not just because evolved systems typically have fuzzy boundaries. Tendencies towards transitive and ergative patterns in a grammar, between tense and/or aspect in a system, for instance, indicate tensions between alternative construals of phenomena. The dominant ways of representing the outer to inner experiences, and the transactions between matter and meaning, are constantly open to the pressure of change through social variation. In speaking and writing, the innumerable small choices of the 'collective consciousness' can be sampled; but language is an arena of populations, not of individuals (Firth actually expunged the notion of individual from his linguistics by writing of persons as a bundle of roles or 'personae' ([1950] 1957)).

The discussion is significant for many reasons – in particular for the lucid account of the difference between theoretical and descriptive categories. The theoretical terms are those one invokes to create an account of semiotic processes: hence – system; metafunction; rank; stratum; instance; and, in particular, the general concept of realization. These are derived from confronting those various epistemological limits, those inherent relativities in the analysis of meanings. The semogenic character of evolution in a culture, of development between a mother and child, and in the way the scope of meaning expands in an unfolding text (all of which are elaborated in the article discussed below: 'How do you mean?' ([1992] 2002a).

By contrast, the descriptive categories are not dimensions of the paradoxical 'architecture' of theory (Halliday, 2003c). Terms like mood: indicative: interrogative; transitive: intransitive; active: passive; theme: rheme . . . are the application of categories passed on from previous linguistic studies. They constitute both the potential to represent choices that speakers may use, and the chance to be utterly misled. Halliday's exposition shows how one should not go imposing your expectation of descriptive categories on 'exotic' situations; rather, one needs to 'ask' how a certain function may or may not be taken up by speakers in a community: Is there a system for signalling the psychological pre-eminence of an element in a message? If so, how is this signalling manifested (what is its exponent?)? With what does this 'exponent' interact most in the grammar overall?

Ultimately, a linguist may apply the traditional descriptive term – as the optimum way of orienting others to the linguistic phenomenon under discussion. But the comparison is offered conditionally, in clear view of how the valeur of the descriptive category differs when the place of a system in the overall language is itself quite different. Firth had put this in his compressed style: noun and verb are not universal categories because they mean something different in each language.

One can see the implications. Searching for descriptive categories from the starting point of English, for example, produces the linguistic presuppositions of 'Pro-drop' – the weird assumption that languages ought to manifest Subject with the purpose and frequency of English (which is reasonably described as typologically odd in this specific 'expectation'). With the variability of semantic styles that result from sociolinguistic parameters (class, age, region, exposure to professional registers . . .), it becomes clear that, in concord with evidence from dialect and register studies, a whole vista of socio-stylistics opens up (Hasan: personal communication). In fact this conceptual breadth and social method in stylistics echoes the early direction of style studies in Britain in the 1960s, and also outlined in Firth's 'personality studies' and 'modes of meaning' (see the synopsis in Firth, [1957] 1962).

We have considered the inherent variability in the way meanings grow through the contingencies of living. Yet the potential for change and semantic variation across cultures is a function of the relativity of systems overall, combined with those contingencies of living conditions. As in evolution with natural selection, we find a 'triple helix' – as in the title of Lewontin's thesis on the interaction of genes and environmental 'niches' or opportunity (2000a).

The grammar of a language constitutes a legacy, a body of past information, a history of 'success' (Dunn et al., 2011, cited above, a Bayesian study of the dominance of 'family' relationships over other factors between languages). But legacy has to adapt to contingency, and history. One might expect then that the default position on typological work, or in any semiotic comparison, would be variationist, even Whorfian (see Evans and Levinson, 2009: 'The myth of

45

language universals'). To make claims of universals in the experience of meaning, one needs to find evidence to neutralize the factors that create variation AND/OR one must operate at a very abstract order of generalization for a cross system comparison viz. the way Halliday uses 'metafunction' as part of his 'semantic compass'. Such a compass creates opportunities for comparison and characterizations of languages – with consistencies and motifs (see Caffarel, Martin and Matthiessen, 2004, chapter 10: 537–658).

In his characteristically measured approach, Halliday points out that the descriptive categories need to be utilized in a way mindful of the differences. He also urges that a language should be described by categories drawn from its own linguistic forms (not from Latin, Greek and Sanskrit). This limits the 'baggage'. But we invoke terms like transitivity; mood; theme-rheme; word-mor-pheme; phoneme in the light of the way that language utilizes its own plasticity to a semantic purpose. So, for example, 'transitivity' is an important descriptive concept in English, and in typological work generally; but it can hardly be construed or confined to the way it was invoked in Latin (i.e. as a feature of verbs, at the rank of word, or group), given the synthetic character of Latin. In English, the transitive-intransitive distinction is expressed only at the rank of the whole clause, with the reactance that many verbs are entered in dictionaries as both 'trans. and intrans.'

We might also agree that every language has a minimal unit of sound. The term 'phoneme' might be applied; but, as Halliday demonstrates in his study of the syllable in Mandarin, it produces only absurd results to try to make that minimum unit anything 'smaller' than the syllable in Chinese. On the other hand, the phoneme in English may prove to be a useful provisional unit for the description of English, notwithstanding the arguments by Firth as to the prosodic reality of linguistic patterns (see Palmer's misunderstanding of Halliday's notion in relation to the phoneme and other terminological attitudes of Halliday in the Introduction to Firth, 1968: 8–9, a consequence of Palmer's apparent focus on 'Categories of a theory of grammar', 1961).

We can also consider the situation of the tense system in English – that there are disputes over the existence of a future tense, for example, with scholars arguing for a system of two tenses and a modal structure for future (e.g. Palmer, 1974: 36ff. and Huddleston, 1984: 133). Anglo-Saxon / Old English (c. 1000 CE) had only past versus non-past (Saussure commented on the mistake of reading three tenses into the two-term system of Proto-Germanic). But, in Anglo-Saxon, through periphrastic verbal groups (e.g. with *willan* and *sculan* as verbal operators translating futurity), one could see the evidence of an expanding system (Cummings, 2010: 42, 118–20). The modal verbs of later Middle English (c. 1380) were different in their force and in their relationship to moods (for instance, with the expectation of the selection of subjunctive mood). But today, in the English of speakers across the world, the evidence is of a consistent serial tense system (Halliday and Matthiessen, 2014: 406–10), albeit with some dramatic variants in the way the morphology is chosen to align the speaker, context by context, with the most relevant social membership (La Page, as discussed in Milroy, 1987: 115). The point is that the dynamic open system of a language has to be interpreted in terms of its current transactions with social contexts, not by applying an alien metalanguage, or by interpreting its current morphology on the basis of a history of its forms.

The interrelated problems of relativity and complementarity of perspectives have brought the natural sciences towards the predicaments of social science – an impasse not unlike the paradoxes of Saussure, in which the issues around point of view were urgent, but insoluble. Physics became subject to the problems of point of view in a way that shifted them more closely to the relativism of 'synchronic linguistics', and to the complexity of literature (e.g. Albright's *Quantum Poetics: Yeats, Pound, Eliot and the Science of Modernism*). Even politically 'reactionary' spirits like Yeats, Pound, and Lawrence tried to understand the shifts in science, especially the analogies between quanta and units of verbal art. Ultimately, the experiments by A. Aspect in 1982 gave support to the bizarre problem in physics of 'spooky action at distance'. Such utterly inexplicable influence between entangled, distant electrons (DeWitt, 2004: 296–8; Gilder, 2008) is in contradiction of the strategies of 'reductio ad absurdum' pursued by Einstein, Podolsky and Rosen (viz. the 'EPR experiments'). It is relevant to recall that the physicist Niels Bohr offered his idea of complementarity as a concept that might assist the work of those in more complex fields – where the comparative simplicity of physics can give a lead in epistemological conundrums with social and human layers (1961).

The intellectual impasse for conventional views of scientific certainties came in at least two forms: (1) in the rational reconciliation of experimental results like those of Aspect in quantum physics, and (2) in attempts to re-establish formal systems which could be consistent and self-sufficient (i.e. without referring outside themselves: contra Godel's proof). The epistemological limits that Heisenberg propounded were boundaries to human activities which humans had to accommodate as rational enquiry. Cultures confronted a new and infinite universe with no co-ordinate system for restoring the ideal of objective descriptions (Kline, 1980).

8 Transactions between Matter and Meaning: 'How Do You Mean?'

Halliday has been particularly methodical in pursuing the implications of the interface between matter and meaning, and how transactions across these planes of experience can then be enfolded into more complex planes of social and semiotic complexity.

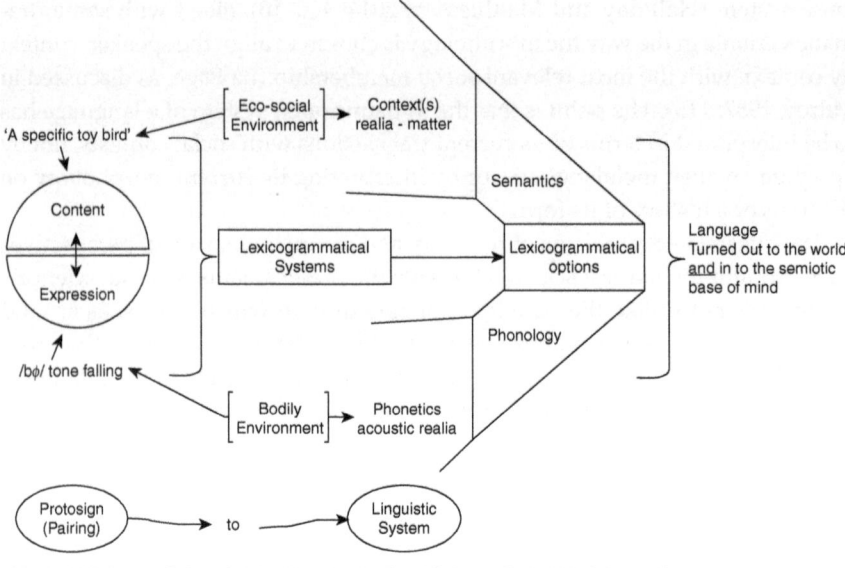

(After M. A. K. Halliday, Collected Works: Vol. 3 (2003: 13) and Collected Works: Vol 4 (2004: 36).)

Figure 2.2 Protosign to linguistic sign

The drama around such transactions begins within the sign, where the 'concept' of an ideational unit (within an order of such units) has to be merged with the concept of a unit of material manifestation (drawn from a spectrum of such divisions of potential units). A profound account of the origins of such a rapprochement between signification and value, and between semantics and physics, is in the succinct 'How do you mean?' ([1992] 2002a: 352–68). It sets out the way a two-dimensional semantic space can result from the projection of the material onto the conscious, and then how this can be further divided by, for example, interpersonal categorization (viz. *you and me* versus *others*). This two-level structure then has the potential to be 'doubly articulated': the content and expression of protolinguistic signs (both of which combine 'concepts' of matter and of consciousness) can be projected back out onto experience, but now freed of any direct dependence on the motivation of a moment – the sign system becomes dual in directing responses rather than just 'having' responses. This freedom of systemic development also multiplies the semiotic dimensions, or 'plasticity', as speakers combine choices that were mutually excluding into simultaneous options in expanding systems of choice. Grammar is thus a process, subject to the legacy of norms available through a collective consciousness, and open to the creativity devised from cultural 'opportunities' or contingencies.

In 'Learning how to mean' ([1975] 2003), Halliday had put this incremental, creative semiosis on display – from intersubjective signs to a fuller grammatical and social membership. The study is a 'map' of the growth of the meaning potential in his son (while the mother had believed the diarising was for phonological report, not for semantic argument). In this, Halliday also demonstrates that the child can build a semiotic and grammatical consciousness without theorists needing to invoke 'poverty of the stimulus' or a specific mental organ for syntax.

The priorities of homo loquens are not, then, with how an individual generates strings, but how one turns a blending of subjectivities into a material manifestation of shared understanding. Language directs, and can be directed by, its users because it has recruited the potential of matter into a material projection of shared minds ('collective consciousness'). There is a semiotic continuum between inner and outer phenomena as experienced by humans (Favereau, 2010), even though there is an organic break at the boundary of the body. This assists in understanding the origins, I believe, of the paradox of a 'collective consciousness'. The process is mapped by Halliday through the expansion of choices in system networks.

9 Networks of Choice – A Test Case for a Science of Meaning

How then does Halliday represent languages? The first step in understanding Halliday's approach is to share the perspective of language as choice: 'We do one thing and not another. We mean one thing and not another' (Plenary address, ISFC Beijing 2009, and [2011] 2013b). Crucial in this emphasis is the potential for mapping choices – how does a community member negotiate through a situation by meaning this rather than that, opting for that and not the other choices. This is a beguilingly direct representation of the human transacting between the material order of the social situation and the meaningful choices that a situation offers to the speaker. One task for the linguist is to produce such transactional 'maps' – contextual, semantic, lexicogrammatical, phonological and phonetic.

The notion of 'choice' is the optimum idea for conceptualizing the speaker's ability to act – there is little point in haggling over conscious choice, unconscious choice or sub-conscious choice. Language can be seen as a system of systems into which we are apprenticed before we can reflect deeply on the processes with which we are engaged. The path we follow across the points of possible divergence – the decision points in our behaviour – can be thought of as our semantic style. Such 'decision points' can be thought to extend down and back in time to the 'quorum sensing' and decision points evident in single cell archaea (e.g. Shapiro, 2011: 137 and Margulis, 1998: 107–9). A critical problem for the linguist, however, is to demarcate the 'linguistic' behaviours. This means we are seeking a tool for mapping what the human speaker can DO by way of symbolic behaviour.

49

Halliday's response to this problem of mapping is the system network. Out of five basic conventions, all possibilities of semiotic divergence ('choice') can be captured. It is a diagrammatic representation that is built up from iconic 'wiring' of five basic relationships between options. These basic terms are: OR; AND; WHEN X or Y then . . .; ONLY WHEN BOTH or ALL then . . .; and CHOOSE OVER AGAIN. As wordings they have the opacity of logical operators in general; but, as parts of a network diagram, they permit the linguist or semiotician to build up a 'polysystemic' picture that reconciles Saussure's emphasis on 'valeur' and 'relations of relations' with Firth's radical concreteness and contextualization (at all levels!).

Important to note here are the practical, instrumental motivations for the representation and its ability to be tailored to the specific goals of the analyst. The semantic character of the different choices in the sample expressions can be brought out in different ways and elaborated to different degrees of *delicacy*. The systems a, b and c are relevant to one (minimal) step in semantic clarification; but any dimension of meaning may be built in and pursued to the delicacy that a project demands in order to distinguish the speakers or social groups involved. For instance, recall here the different semantic styles of mothers. Hasan has elaborated just such networks of choice and the class variants in the patterns of mothers' control and typical rhetorical styles (Hasan, 1989; Hasan and Cloran, 1990). This form of network representation begins in extremely simple terms (or primitives) which do not themselves bring a high order of interference from the analytic apparatus. Essentially, the network begins from Figure 2.3 OR and Figure 2.4 AND

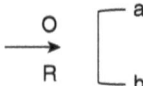

Figure 2.3 OR

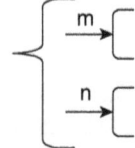

Figure 2.4 AND

From these terms an involved interconnection can be developed which accounts for the interdependencies of language, including the valeurs established by the choices within a given system and the valeurs that result from the allocation of semantic responsibilities across the polysystemic architecture. The basic terms can give greater tool power by being used left to right and right to left. Hence:

1. Select in systems **a** or **b**
2. Select in both systems **m** and **n**
3. When either system **a** or **b** is entered, then either **c** or **d** must be selected (Figure 2.5)
4. Only when (if?) systems **o** and **p** are both selected can you then select between **q** and **r** (Figure 2.6)

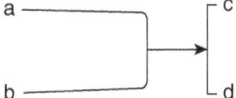

Figure 2.5 When a OR b are selected, then c OR d must be selected

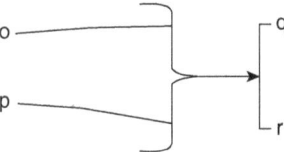

Figure 2.6 Only when o AND p are both selected then select either q OR r

The networks also manage the description of 'recursion' by the less platonic notion of **'choose over'**. This has the advantage of not implying that the chooser holds an idealized conception of an infinite output: merely, that the context may be indicative of the fact that the same options can be selected over again.

5. If option b is selected, return to a previous entry condition and make further selections (Figure 2.7).

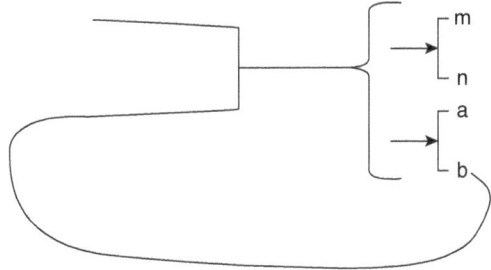

Figure 2.7 Recursion; select over

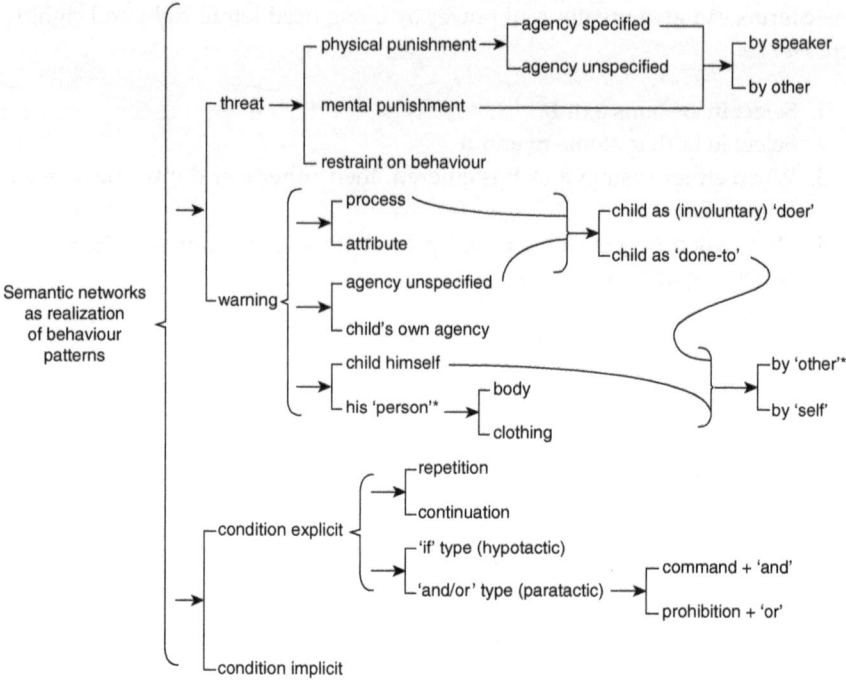

Figure 2.8 Revised network for threats and warnings

The 'delicacy' of the description can go as far as the analyst's power to discriminate a difference of meaning, or as far as is demanded by the issue which motivated the description. Halliday develops the picture of a mother's control to enhance the opposition between threat and warning (see Figure 2.8), as well as the delicacy of distinction concerning agency (child as 'doer').

The conventions discussed here as the basis of semantic networks are, then, the Hallidayan method for accounting for the meaning potential of speakers in specific contexts of situation. As mentioned above, unlike other linguistic models (except stratificational theory, which has an isomorphic network theory), systemic functional linguistics utilizes the same conventions for all strata. The statements of linguistic meaning are then congruent; at least, they are consistently organized around the principles of *choice/system* or *paradigm*. It must be conceded that these terms of meta-description necessarily take on a somewhat different value on each stratum: for example, 'choice' may not have precisely the same value in the meta-theory at the levels of context, say, and at the level of expression in the phonology. But, nevertheless, the patterns of different strata can still be accommodated by the polysystemic approach, namely, the number of alternatives in the specific environment, and the environment in its environment and so on in serial contextualization (Firth, [1935] 1957: 32–3).

The status of the network itself needs to be discussed, since the emphasis on argumentation in contemporary linguistics has been used as a distinguishing mark of the scientific approach and apparently as a reason for self-congratulation in formal models.

Networks are, in themselves, a form of argument. They are a consistent means of checking what is the better motivated proposal in linguistic description. The network either accounts for the linguistic options and their consequences, choice by choice, or it does not. It is straightforward to check and redraw, so it maintains adequacy through a transparent *accountability* and *modifiability*. One system of choices and its consequences in realization statements can be wired in with parallel systems so that the relevant patterns of a unit, like the clause in lexicogrammar, can be described in blocks of simultaneous and dependent options. The metafunctions reflect the interdependency of particular options and systems of options. Ideational, interpersonal and textual are, then, a response to order in the grammar, not ideas that have been introduced extrinsically, i.e. from outside semiotics.

System networks were first introduced by Halliday in 1964 (Personal communication from Sydney Lamb). Through the mapping of choice using only five primes or conventions of representation, Halliday can give an evidence-based (empirical) account of the variants active at any level or scale or linguistic enquiry. One can set out from any social setting, or from any 'persona' whose semantic variation (or 'style') is an object of enquiry. This latter task has been an urgent issue for functional linguists working on the sociology of class-based semantic variation (Bernstein's codes), on pedagogical styles and genre, and those in collaboration with psychiatrists and psychotherapists (Meares et al., 2012: chapter 8).

Networks diminish the need to appeal to mental organs. And by creating plausible models of accumulating structure, networks could offer ways of conceptualizing the emergence of organization without imputing to evolution the power to produce mental organs in a single evolutionary step, or at least, without seemingly adequate, preceding, incremental stages. (See early criticisms by Toulmin, 1972: 446–77 on biological and evolution-based objections to Chomsky's claims about innateness, objections which are now even more forceful in this era of greater neuroscientific 'mapping' and imaging. Also see Edelman on non-biological 'organs', 1992: 211–52. For Chomsky's recent views on 'recursion' and 'merge', follow the interviews of Chomsky in Chomsky and McGilvray, 2012 and work by Berwick, 1997 which uses the motif of 'syntax facit saltum'. A succinct summary of biological and other arguments against autonomous syntax, by a specialist in the formal modelling of human systems, can be found in Arbib, 2012: 43ff.).

Each network is a thesis about the structure under description; and the accountability of the thesis derives from the output of the path through the network. Either a network produces the relevant realization, or it does not. As a descriptive tool, then, networks tend to declare their qualities and weaknesses. They enforce explicitness by having practical consequences – in linguistic terms, a network can be accountable because it will not produce the required expressions and/or because it produces other expressions which it 'should' not. In a sense, it is truly generative; but rather than imply the existence of knowledge of abstract linguistic rules, a network implies only strata of organization based on differences and connections, as well as the primitive notion of the potential to 'choose over', or simply 'do the same again'.

Networks do not require separate and distinctive forms of representation for encoding and decoding. Linguistic, or semiotic, networks can be read from the perspectives of either (a) how can a particular structure be built up? or (b) how does this given structure fit into the relational matrices of the semiotic system more broadly? These questions correspond, respectively, to 'how is something said?' and 'how does one establish the value (valeur) of what is being said?'.

The network is not there to explain the semantic/linguistic consequences of, say, changing group membership. I am thinking here of the kind of radicalization of individual speech (accent) patterns which are discussed by Milroy with respect to individuals whose work takes them outside the dense, multiplex social connections which are so reconfirming of behaviour, so 'norm enforcing' (Milroy, 1987: 136–44).

Similarly, a network does not purport to be an explanation of pattern stability and its consequences.

The best cases here would again be Hasan's work (1989, 1986, 1991; Hasan and Cloran, 1990), which shows how the semantic orientation of mother-child dyads is predicted by class background (of the mother) and the gender (of the child). The representation does not make claims about gender and class and why certain mothers seem constrained to elaborate topics in particular contexts and why others do not. The representation does not explain why some patterns of behaviour change and others (the majority) are reproduced. Rather, network representations put both change and stability on display so that just such aetiological, teleological and process-based accounts can be offered. **Essentially, then, the network declares a state of relations along with the variability of states.**

If one can map out, in terms of the simple notion of a perceived difference, the contrasts that need to be accounted for in order to encompass the meaning potential of a speaker (at least when the speaker's speech fellowships and context can be stated), one can claim to have diminished the need for certain kinds of descriptions, claims, and explanations – first of all, those kinds that claimed the impossibility of ever achieving a useful description.

Halliday emphasizes that language is a semogenic process, not just a semiotic structure. This is to say it is staged biologically, culturally and socially (see, for instance, Luria's discussion of what he and Vygotsky called their anti-Cartesian experiments, 1979: chapter 3). There is less special pleading in an approach which sets out from the assumption of gradualism, levels of behavioural complexity and variability based on differing contexts of group membership. The utility of a network derives in part from the fact that it can bring out the complexity and the variability: a network can be drawn with any specific problem or domain of relations in mind. Similarly, the degree of delicacy in the description can be set – the description can start and stop without having to state all its wider responsibilities of connection. So, a system of potential choice in the grammar, say the *mood* or *transitivity* systems, can be mapped out in such a way that the relevant distinctions in grammatical meaning can be displayed and then that network itself be left as a placeholder in the wider map of the theory (see Halliday and Matthiessen, 1999: figures 1.1, 1.7, 1.8).

As already outlined above, networks permit the modification of the description in line with differences of use. One modification of growing significance is the potential for incorporating probabilities, including different rates at which a choice is taken up by a specific group. Such a modification is relevant in at least three ways:

(1) Halliday has pointed out how the systemic choices of a language appear to fall into two main tendencies – those that are roughly 50/50 in their take up in text; and those that fall out at about 80/20 or 90/10 (see Halliday, 2013 in Fontaine et al., chapter 1). Shifts around these proportions can assist in characterizing what is dominant in a register. Consider, for example, an increase in the selection of passive away from the 80/20 pattern: it would be one of the statistical indices of a specific variety of meaning-making.

(2) Hasan's investigations of semantic variation and code across mother-child dyads in Sydney is essentially a 'quantitative' treatment of semantic 'qualities'. This is to say, the 'typical actual' of each dyad is established by tracking c. 70 choices in the pathways through the available options of meaning against the tasks of daily life: eating; bathing; preparing for kindergarten. These interactions (c. 20,000 messages) around offering goods & services and (crucially) giving information were analysed for principal components, thereby providing a basis for graphing the like, the less like, and the unlike between the meanings made by the dyads. The consistency of alignments between semantic styles and vocational autonomy in the family was dramatic, with the only 'outlier' being a clear case of one whose 'circumstances' had changed significantly with motherhood (Hasan, 2009).

(3) Matthiessen remains the de facto chief 'cartographer' of systemic functional grammar (see Halliday and Matthiessen, 2014), and with this leadership he has also built up a spectrum of representations of texts and registers, and typographical comparisons (Matthiessen, 1995a; Caffarel et al., 2004). These tools are motivated by statistical analyses and/or have statistical implications (Matthiessen, 2006). In collaboration with his colleague Wu Canzhong, a statistical and database package of tools – SysAmanuensis – has been developed. The graphic representations capture the changes in systemic choices as a text develops (logogenesis), the systemic parameters that underpin the nomination of a register, the semantic profile of a persona or an institution, and many relationships displayed by system networks. This work demonstrates, I would argue, the importance of 'process' based modelling, even models of language which could, paradoxically, systematize chance. Such developments in SFL relate directly to phase space and phase portrait characterizations discussed by mathematicians: where there are many ways a 'potential' can be utilized, the particular choices actualized by an agent negotiating the space constitute a **phase portrait** for that agent (Cohen and Stewart, 1995: 198ff.). Linguistically there is also a distinction to be made between the portrait of different choices and the different order in which choices are taken up. This has special relevance, for example, to the analysis of teaching strategies: different purposes may have a similar semantic goal but require quite different sequencing in their pedagogical staging.

After the fact of its development, the networks of SFL seem beguiling straightforward (as many of the tools of one's culture appear to be on reflection). Yet in their simplicity, a number of previously disjointed dimensions of linguistic theory are brought together.

10 Comparing Descriptions of Meaning

In the multi-stratal cartography of Halliday's systemic theory, the realizations of meaningful behaviours are given detailed profiles. Every semiotic act is an ensemble. The patterning of sign systems requires an account that combines the complexities of matter, of meaning, and of transactions between collective values established in the world (in the social milieu to which a child is born) and values established in a nervous system (including in the 'personalized' brain). Anything less than this potential in a metalinguistic framework is likely to be misleading by being simplistic.

At this point, it is useful to ask ourselves why it is that non-linguists are so often the arbiters of statements about meaning – both as theorists, and as critics of what can be known or studied in relation to language. It is not linguists who direct debate. While linguists are left to the somewhat lampooned role as wardens of the labyrinths of phonology, morphology, and grammar (and lexicography), it seems that persons without such specializations feel fully licensed to dictate the terms of debates over meaning in language, speech acts or pragmatics. Perhaps, this is as it should be – language is critical to life and to maintaining the conditions for living. We all have a stake in meaning, so perhaps we all need to be part of the debate. But I remain surprised that, out of all the luxuriant complexity of languages and their grammars, we should still see books on 'semantics' dominated by the ex cathedra simplicities of Searle's speech acts and Gricean maxims. Neither theory is data driven; neither theory appears to explore falsification from actual cases (see by contrast, for instance, Stephens, 1995, and Jones, 1998: 28–9 on Mekeo in Western Papua and Ochs and Keenan, 1979 on the 'conditions of the use of speech' in Malagasy).

Saussure argued that language is, in essence, a collective behaviour for attending to differences which, in themselves, make a difference to those living out the distinctions actively used in that collective consciousness. The distinctions are not built up as an accumulating 'lexicon' (through reference, or anything akin to Russell's logical atomism or Wittgenstein's early ideas of 'primes'). As Saussure argued, and as Halliday described empirically and in detail (in 'Learning How to Mean'), we come into a world already organized around semiotic transactions, already construed according to linguistic categorizations. The neonate works at the intersubjective creation of a 'system', in fact an expanding system of systems, first with mother and then in the cross-contextual roles offered to her or him by the specific social conditions bequeathed by the structure of families, neighbourhoods, schooling, available work, and ideological spaces – those behaviours that a society legitimates through laws, rewards, censures, and by semantic occlusions, by excluding and obscuring the contradictions and 'gaps' in making sense.

Saussure's system of oppositions, when taken into Hallidayan contexts and with his emphasis on the notion of 'choice', takes on a revolutionary tool power – namely through the practical representation of 'value'. Semiotic behaviour takes on value according to the significance of what is chosen and the specific value of what was NOT. From the numinous and paradoxical (but necessary) oppositions of Saussure's *Course in General Linguistics*, the paradigmatic emphasis of Halliday provides a methodical consistency for describing language variation according to 'use' as well as 'user'. This is achieved by the parsimony and elegance of system networks.

By contrast to Saussure's 'synchronic linguistics', Halliday's science of meaning builds history and change into the investigation of the regularities in language. This enquiry into what Firth called 'pattern and process' has to deal with profound difficulties which may be peculiar to semiotic behaviour: the relational nature of signs (and the derivative, secondary nature of reference in meaning making); and the 'ineffable' character of the concepts by which we sort out the complexity of relations in language (Halliday, [1984] 2002). Problem (1) is inherited from Saussure's insights, though Halliday's response is, like that of his teacher Firth, to move closer to the social actualities of linguistic transactions rather than to the idealism of Saussure's 'langue'. In essence, where the paradoxes of the sign are confronted, Halliday's method is to maintain the principles of choice and 'meaning potential', but to apply them, like Firth, to the 'typical-actual', not just to the 'ideal-potential'. With problem (2), the 'ineffable' nature of linguistic categories, the practical problems of categorization confirm the heuristic character of all linguistic 'scaffolding', and yet demonstrate the practical value of centuries of linguistic thinking (viz. the science of language families).

11 Return to a Natural Science of Meaning

The questions from which we set out can be rounded upon now, in the cultural context offered here. It is NOT that there may be a science of meaning – that 'science' has been developing in various branches for as long as we have had records of human experience. This development is comparable to the disciplinary histories of astronomy and medicine, although the long history of rhetoric (Roochnik, 1996) may have been more consistently efficacious than these two superstition-plagued activities (e.g. Lloyd, 1970: chapter 5 on the Hippocratic Writers). Critical concepts like objectivity, replication, causation, prediction, coherence, evidence and measurement have all been erratic factors across different phases of scientific efforts by communities and individuals. Quantum Theory is often lauded for its outstanding success at prediction, yet its coherence with respect to the human macro scale of Newtonian physics has been under challenge (first from Einstein, and from Bohm, 1980. For a balanced view of the history of this challenge, see Whitaker, 2006 and, on the boundary between Newtonian and Quantum theories, see Leggett, 2008). Evolutionary theory may be the greatest re-construal of the world in scientific terms (i.e. rather than by animistic beliefs). Yet Darwinism does not predict specific outcomes: it does predict the principles and processes that make sense of outcomes (somewhat retrospectively). Genetics gives evolutionary theory its missing mechanism for 'descent with modification'; but it brings with it new challenges from the realms of protists and bacteria, from the virosphere and from 'natural genetic engineering' which should 'temper theorizing in psychology and linguistics based on 20th Century genetic determinism' (Shapiro, 2012: 146 and 142–7. Note: 145: 'Today the major focus in scientific enquiry is to understand how systems change over time, whether they are atoms, molecules, organisms, ecosystems, climates, galaxies, black holes, or universes'). The legacy of Freud went through a period of dismissal as unscientific, despite the observations of his life's work. More recently, neuroscientists have attested to the strengths of his general outline of mind, brain and personality (see Kandel, 2012, especially p. 49; Solms, 2006, though there are still, in fact, strong claims even against Freud's integrity as a scientist). It is reasonable to conclude, therefore, that the conventional views of science do not accommodate its actual history: the strengths of sciences and of scientists do not apply to all stages of the development of consequential ideas, and in similar degree across different branches of science (Brooks on 'The secret anarchy of science', 2011; and see Chargaff, 1978: 100–03 on the biological 'bona fides' of Crick and Watson in 1952, the year before their publication on the double helix!).

With these historical reflections in mind, I will conclude with a focus on prediction – the most contentious of the issues in a human culture (the battleground of sciences, politics, and some religions: Toulmin, 1961). Prediction seems the extreme test of explanation. But how does one predict with 'evolved' systems, systems with unique histories: for example, at the scales of evolution and the expansion of the universe? A consequential case to consider comes from Halliday's study of the emergence of scientific English ([1988] 2004). Following the development of lexical density in English scientific writing, Halliday analyses Chaucer's discussion of the astrolobe (fourteenth century), writing of Newton (seventeenth century) and the work of Clerk-Maxwell at the inauguration of twentieth-century physics. He demonstrates how the grammatical texture of English has undergone an extreme shift. This shift is a syndrome of cross-categorizations, especially those in which the semantics of verbs and logical relators have 'drifted' into the noun groups of increasingly dominant verbal equations. Verbs are functioning, through nominalization, as abstract processes and entities. Such equations answer to the semantic pressures associated with sciences, especially reconstruing one thing as another thing or as a value. Such Token and Value structures in the grammar of English are directly related to transformations of phenomena (i.e. change) and that crucial platform to sciences: measurement (Crosby, 1997). The textual virtuosity of equational structures in English presents a 'chreod' or 'canal' of favoured choices for the social task to hand, for the 'pragma' of meaning (see Waddington, 1977 on 'chreod' and other representations of system dynamics). This power of verbal equations is particularly true when seen against the narrower potential of attributive copula clauses. The equational structures in English maximize one's textual options, the options which most mark off human languages from other communications between natural species. We can intervene in arranging our equations by reversing the wording, which reverses both theme-rheme and subject-complement roles, but retains the token to value in transitivity (giving a latent passive form to the equative). In attributive clauses, such reversal affects only theme and rheme (see the full account in Halliday and Matthiessen, 2014: chapter 5). In the attributive, one ends up with only a marked theme, while in the equation the theme is unmarked, as if a covert passive has been bestowed on the verb 'be'. The result is a naturalization of changes in a semantics of switching symbolic forms: a flexibility for intervening in our forms of symbolic address.

This goes to the core of a grammatical tide which characterizes the intensification of semantics around the living and the discourse habits of modernity. These trends towards abstraction and heuristic thinking have been dimensions of thinking under industrialization. Their pervasiveness is attested by corpus studies of noun phrases and nominalization (see Mair and Leech, 2004, who remark on the deep mathematical significance of the shift in British English; Biber, 2006; Biber et al., 1998). The changes are not, however, merely a perversity of nominal style, of 'bureaucratese': the pressure to measure and equate dominates every register now from sciences to marketing, sport, and 'theories' of intimate relations.

It is here that we find the basis of the troubling changes in the most measured characteristic of human minds, in the inflation of I.Q. scores known as the Flynn effect (Flynn, 2007). Flynn has offered a number of explanations of this need to re-normalize I.Q. tests around the c. 20 points of inflation over the records since 1947, and before. He has generally described the phenomenon as a function of industrialization and modernity and he has offered a number of key words as indices of changes in public discourse since 1800 (in *Scientific American Mind*, December 2007). As I have argued previously (Butt, 2008b), the tide of linguistic change explained by Halliday through grammatical metaphor constitutes an extraordinary confirmation of the role of linguistics within the human sciences. The linguistic changes adumbrated and then explained by Halliday's analyses offer an account of semantic change that the wider world eventually confronted through the careful, iconoclastic analysis of the most measured feature of human mental behaviour. The findings of Flynn's critical acumen have been attributed, anachronistically, by references to television and computer screen cultures since 1947. Clearly such cultures are what Flynn might refer to as environmental 'multipliers'; but their effects were much later than the first evidence of dramatic change. The change in the thinking came from the new ways of discussing the world in measures and hypothetical values (see, for example, the work on heuristic fictions by Hans Vaihinger, 1924, but from writings from the 1890s).

Grammatical metaphor has been a conduit for this kind of change, a mechanism for the 'speciation of registers' in our new habits of modernity.

Halliday's theory can be viewed as an integration of the strands of scientific endeavour around meaning and its variation. The tools and cartography of systemic functional linguistics extend the practical activities of linguists. The central problems of language cluster around variation. The interrelation of system, strata, metafunction, composition, and cline of instantiation, assist in analysis and help to bring the reports of overt differences between speakers and different registers into a principled framework. This means that the variation we see from language types, from dialects, from registers, and from different modes (spoken, written, sign, . . .) constantly inform on one another in Halliday's work. In this variation theory and social research, we can map the selections of communities against sub-groups. We can track priorities in our patterns of living – our socially 'logical' options in meaning.

3 Halliday in China: Legacies and Advances from LUO, WANG and Beyond[1]

Peng Xuanwei

1 Introduction

Halliday often acknowledges those whose insights have influenced his own thinking about language and linguistics. Elaborating on what he learned from the 'traditional and modern linguistics as developed in China' (Halliday, [1994] 2003: 433), Halliday refers, in particular, to two of his former teachers from his early years in China: 'Luo Changpei gave me a diachronic perspective and an insight into a language family other than Indo-European; and Wang Li taught me many things, including research methods in dialectology, the semantic basis of grammar, and the history of linguistics in China' (Halliday, [1985] 2003: 188). In his paper 'Wang Li and Halliday', Hu Zhuanglin, one of Halliday's former students at the University of Sydney, identifies certain key points where Halliday's approach aligns closely with that of Wang Li, including views on language (that it is a social phenomenon, that it is more or less contextually appropriate rather than grammatical or ungrammatical; that description is particular to each language; and that grammar is based on meaning); on methodology (textual data as the main source of evidence); and on the nature of some fundamental grammatical categories (such as mood and modality, transitivity and voice) (Hu, 1991). Taking Hu's discussion a step further, here we argue that the holistic epistemology of SFL is deeply rooted in the holisticality of traditional Chinese thinking.

2 Holisticality Epistemology of SFL

Holisticality – one of the key principles in traditional Chinese learning (Fung, 1948, passim) – is most apparent in the panchronic, dialectic and interactional nature of SFL.

2.1 Panchronic Angle of SFL Model Design

When Saussure proposed the synchronic-diachronic distinction in linguistics, he considered the former as 'static', the 'evidence' for which came from 'the language users' while the latter he considered to be 'dynamic' in both 'prospective' ('the course of time') and 'retrospective' (looking back) ([1916] 1983: 89). It is practically impossible, he argued, to have a 'panchronic point of view' (p. 94). Since Saussure, there have been constant modifications of and even refutations to this sharp distinction (e.g. Bloomfield, [1933] 2002: 18–19; Jakobson, [1942] 1990, [1977] 1985: 143; Jakobson and Waugh, [1979] 1987; Ullmann, 1957: 261; Gao, 1960: 29–34; Birch, 1988; Štekauer et al., 2001; Kiełtyka, 2010; cf. Čermák, 1997). The key development point lies in a more or less panchronic perspective in terms of which synchrony is dynamic and diachrony is constantly inevitable in synchronic data analysis.

SFL is no except to this; further, it makes an extraordinary contribution of theorizing the panchronic methodology by advocating the priority status of SYSTEM from the simultaneity of langue (system) and parole (speech or instance) as well as paradigmatic and syntagmatic discrimination. On the one hand, a systemic perspective may at first appear to be diachronic in its approach to the study of language since it addresses the phylogenetic development of language. On the other hand, it is synchronic in so far as it observes language in use at a given point in time and space. However, compared with the typical Saussurian diachronic-synchronic division ([1916] 1983: 79–98), SFL is better thought of as **panchronic** since the phylogenetic and ontogenetic processes of evolution and accumulation in context of culture (diachronic) provide the basis for the system of language to be instantiated in context of situation (synchronic). Therefore, the distinction between diachrony and synchrony is then effectively neutralized, and, in particular, '[w]hat we think of as "modern

English" is actually an assortment of many divergent components – a complex product of semantic creolization, in which conflicting models from different stages in our history (pre-settlement, agro-pastoral, iron age, scientific-technological) compete with and complement each other' (Halliday, [1993] 2003: 217). '[A] written text can be contextualized at any moment from the time of its being written down, so that its context could be presented **"diachronically"** in a series of **"synchronic"** statements' (Halliday, [1959] 2006: 12; emphases mine).

He further specifies the point into 'four strands or dimensions of history that are forerunners of every sentence, by virtue of which it becomes an act of meaning': the intertextual, the developmental, the systemic and the intratextual (Halliday, [1992] 2003: 360–1). The intertextual is associated with phylogenetic evolution of language, which relates to the individual's own ontogenetic linguistic growth and maturation. These two dimensions of history – the phylogenetic and ontogenetic – are represented in the networks of one's language system, which are in turn activated in the logogenetic process of the text unfolding as discourse (Halliday, [1998] 2004: 88–9). The meanings of a sentence (in the here-&-now sense) are the product of these four dimensions of history which are presently available to the speaker.

Comprehensive studies from phylogenetic, ontogenetic and logogenetic perspectives have been implemented under such headings as grammatical metaphor in scientific texts, child language development into adulthood, and text creating process through time and space (e.g. Halliday, [1975] 2003, 2004, 2008; Martin, 1992). 'Meanings are made by people who have meant before; they relate to prior acts of meaning; and their source is a meaning potential that has been transmitted, as a metastable system (one that persists by constantly changing, in interaction with its environment), over a very long time. The impact of a text is dependent on its location in this complex semo-history, at the intersection of the various dimensions of that history **where we ourselves are located when we enact it or hold it up for investigation**' (Halliday, [1992] 2003: 373; emphasis mine). In one word, all studies are studies of the past; and all relevant past should be presently present for the ongoing concern. Or even more generally, history does not lie behind, as people generally think of it, but rather is an organic part of the present: past and present are one.

The systemic paradigm in this panchronic sense has certain epistemological implications: it represents a distinct theoretical ideology embracing a general functional view of language from a descriptive-ethnographic perspective (anthropological, cultural, communicative, activity-natured, semantic-oriented, anomalistic, resourceful, rhetorical, selective); more in keeping with the Protagoras-Plato tradition, than with the philosophical-logical stance originating with Aristotle (for further discussion of this point see Halliday, [1977]

2003). It is a 'form of argumentation' or even a way of thinking and behaving: always being aware of a linguist's duty to stand at the systemic crossroad to look (i) both backward from the phylogenetic and ontogenetic perspectives and (ii) along the text logogenetically.

Halliday's two Chinese teachers, Luo Changpei and Wang Li, contributed much to the development of traditional Chinese phonology, adopting a pan-chronic perspective on the phonological system of Chinese by starting from the initials and finals of character pronunciation across longitudinal time and geographical space. This unique approach requires one to learn dozens of basic characters (varying from 36, 40, 47 to 51 to different criteria) that represent the initial system of consonants of all characters in Chinese and 206 basic characters that stand for the final system of rhymes (including medial, vowel, ending and one of level, rising, going or entering tone; see, e.g. Wang, 1936; Luo, 1949). Long and repetitive reciting and configuring of such systems for recovering the proper mid-ancient and ancient pronunciations, most probably along with the Greek and Latin morphological paradigms that have long been built into the memory, may inspire Halliday with a predominant view to look at language, and hence to sort out its paradigmatic items 'into their contrasting sets: to identify the system, and its terms, and to locate it at an explicit point of origin – the environment in which the selection is made, irrespective of where and how it is expressed' (Halliday, 2005b: xxvi–xxvii).

2.2 Dialectic and Interactional Natures of SFL

Lao Tzu (or Lao Zi) makes the following observation in chapter 42 of *Dao De Jing* (*Tao Te Ching*): 'Tao gave birth to the One; The One gave birth successively to two things, Three things, up to ten thousand. These ten thousand creatures cannot turn their backs to the shade Without having the sun on their bellies, And it is on this blending of the breaths that their harmony depends' (Lao, 1934). We would not claim this bit of Taoist wisdom responsible for the numerous tripartite classifications in SFL; nevertheless, there is no denying such a conceptualization of language phenomena would more or less make for a linguistic theory with Chinese nature. The 'trinocular vision' that characterizes a systemic functional approach to the study of language can be most representatively evidenced, for example, with the summarization made by Halliday (see also Halliday, [1970] 2005):

> The 'trinocular' principle in the grammatics can be simply stated. In categorizing the grammar, the grammarian works 'from above', 'from roundabout' and 'from below'; and these three perspectives are defined in terms of strata. Since the stratum under attention is the lexicogrammar, 'from

roundabout' means 'from the standpoint of the lexicogrammar itself'. 'From above' means 'from the standpoint of the semantics: how the given category relates to the meaning (what it "realizes")'. 'From below' means 'from the standpoint of morphology and phonology, how the given category relates to the expression (what it "is realized by")'. What are being taken into account are the regularities (proportionalities) at each of the three strata. (Halliday, [1996] 2002:408)

Also pervasive in SFL is the dialectic idea: anti-language and language, anti-society and society – 'an antilanguage stands to an antisociety in much the same relation as does a language to a society' (Halliday, 1978: 164), and diatypic (use) versus dialectal (user) for language varieties (Halliday, 1978: 35, 225).

Once when asked if his point of view is 'too behaviouristic', Halliday replied 'no', arguing that 'behaviourist models will not account for linguistic interaction or for language development' (Halliday, 1978: 54). In fact, the seemingly contradictory relationship between language as behaviour and language as knowledge is not something incompatible at all, but should be better characterized as 'complementary' and 'inseparable': 'Therefore, it is possible, and is in fact quite usual in what is nowadays called 'sociolinguistics', to look at language behaviour as a type of knowledge; so that although one's attention is focused on the social aspects of language – on language as communication between organisms – one is still asking what is essentially an intra-organism kind of question: how does the individual know how to behave in this way? We might refer to this as psychosociolinguistics: it is the external behaviour of the organism looked at from the point of view of the internal mechanisms which control it' (Halliday, 1978: 13).

Dialectics in traditional Chinese philosophy dates back at least to the sixth century BC and has had a radical impact on Chinese thinking, not just among scholars but also in daily life (Fung, 1948: 1–6). Of course, Hegel obviously demonstrates that dialectics should not be unique to Chinese thinking. Incidentally, Halliday has also been influenced by Marxist thinking.

3 Key Concepts in SFG

This section discusses the formulation of some of the key concepts in systemic functional grammar. Jespersen and Bloomfield are also mentioned because they are constantly referred to while Wang is elaborating his comparative views of Chinese and the Indo-European languages. This of course does not mean that these works were not accessible to Halliday before he came to study in China; rather, they may have reinforced their awareness to him.

3.1 Ranks

Taking the 'sentence' as the point of departure for linguistic analysis (Wang, 1947: 9), Wang proceeded to differentiate between 'phrase' and 'word group' (pp. 47–8). For example, while explaining Bloomfield's notions of endocentric and exocentric construction, Wang noted that *John* and *poor John* are both 'proper-noun expression' and their function is the same. Halliday further elaborates the observation by stating it as 'a combination of words built up on the basis of a particular logical relation' (i.e. 'group of words'); and it is also 'the reason why in the western grammatical tradition it was not recognized as a distinct structural unit: instead, simple sentences, (that is, clauses, in our terms) were analyzed directly into words' (Halliday, 1994: 180).

The hierarchy from morpheme to word to phrase to sentence is discussed by Bloomfield ([1933] 2002); but Halliday ([1961] 2002) characterizes it in terms of Rank Theory. Typical ranks are word, group (phrase), clause, and each of these is a unit of grammar, i.e. a stretch that carries grammatical patterns (Halliday, 2002a: 43, 78) and functions as the source of 'grammatical potential' (Halliday, 1994: 29, elsewhere, e.g. 1973a: 101). Halliday also singles out the hierarchy of meaning units: element – figure – sequence (Halliday, [1998] 2004), which is structured in terms of ranks.

Wang applied the notion of 'part of speech' to Chinese words on 'ideational' grounds, since there is no morphological marker as a basis for discrimination. As for English, Wang admits: 'Honestly, as for the general way of classifying parts of speech of words in modern English, it seems better to put them in sentences to observe their functions' (1947: 22).

Similarly, Halliday preferred Minimal (Ranked Constituent) Bracketing to Maximal Bracketing (or Immediate Constituent Analysis) because the latter 'says nothing about the function that any of the pieces have in any construction; in fact it does not imply that they have any function at all' (Halliday, 1994: 24). Accordingly, the structures of lower ranks are defined by those at higher ranks; for example, 'word classes' are 'defined by group structure' and 'clause-classes' by the structure of clause complex (Halliday, [1963] 2002: 95).

3.2 Process Types

Wang identified several sentence types, including narrative, descriptive and determinative on the one hand, and optative, causative, dispositive, passive, pivotal, compressive forms on the other. Wang (1947: 61) noted that, in the European languages, like English, French, German, a sentence must have a verb, 'since almost every sentence in such languages may be said to be an actor-action construction. In fact, each daily sentence must narrate an action;

so a sentence – whether it needs to describe an action or not – should have a verb'.

SFG's notion of relational process resembles Wang's distinction between Descriptive and Determinative. Descriptive describes the lasting or constant 'attribute' of a thing, the nature or property, represented by adjective or nominal, as *brave* and *(much) courage* in *he is brave* and *he has much courage*. Determinative accounts for a thing by using a title or the like, with something like a nominal group, as *four legs* in *a horse has four legs* (Wang, 1947: 95).

This preliminary division is systematically extended in SFG to cover a wider range of clause phenomena. Halliday distinguishes between Attributive and Identifying modes, so, for example, *he is brave* and *a horse has four legs* are assigned to the Attributive mode as the attributes *brave*, *(much) courage* and *four legs* are qualities ascribed or attributed to the respective Carriers *he*, *he* and *a horse*. In addition, Halliday describes *Tom is the leader* and *the leader is Tom*; *tomorrow is the 10th* and *the 10th is tomorrow*; and *the piano is Peter's* and *Peter's is the piano* as identifying since the function of such clauses is to identify the roles of the two entities.

Wang's (1947: 96) narrative sentence – *he is at home* – and the determinative – *stars are in the sky* belong to what Halliday classifies as circumstantial-identifying. While Wang identified the main types of relational processes, nevertheless the matrix of process types configured in SFG is more systematic in coverage (see Halliday, 1994: 119–38).

Wang introduced the concepts of 'causative form' and 'passive form' from Jespersen (Wang, 1947: 153–64, 175–87). He stated that, generally, scholars in China overlooked the structural characteristic of the causative form. The Chinese causative is realized by means of a connection between two clauses (Wang, 1947: 155–60). As for the passive form, Wang, following Jespersen (1924: 165), distinguished between notional passive (e.g. *the book sells well*) and syntactic passive (e.g. *Jill is loved by Jack*) (Wang, 1947: 177, 184–5).

Halliday integrates both the causative and passive forms into his ergative model. On the one hand, the clause as representation is divided into two general categories: middle and effective. As for the middle voice, the process appears as active, as in the *glass broke*. The effective is further divided into active and passive. The active contains an agent as subject and the process is active, as in *the cat broke the glass*; the passive has medium as subject and an agent as adjunct (with *by*), and the process is passive, as in *the glass was broken by the cat*. The passive is further classified into a series, such as location-passive, as in *the bed hadn't been slept in*, and manner-passive, as in *this pen's never been written with*: 'Normally these are also medio-passives, i.e. they are middle not effective clauses' (Halliday, 1994: 169). Such a construction, whether active, middle or passive, is better analysed as ergative because there is a causation meaning implied in the structure, where medium is the centre and agent optional.

Other categories such as Beneficiary, Range and Circumstance can find their origins in Jespersen (e.g. 1949: 229–52); Wang (1947: 164–97, 220–1); Lv (1947, [1959] 1984), Chao (1968 passim) and others, even though most were discussed in traditional terms and lacked adequate attention to their semantics, a drawback SFG has overcome.

3.3 Clause Complex

Above the clause is the clause complex, where Halliday has been essentially influenced by Wang, and in turn Wang's observation is mainly rooted in Jespersen and Bloomfield, in particular Jespersen.

Wang classifies the 'Composite Sentence' (1947: 111–27), including coordinate and subordinate clauses (*cf.* Gao, 1948: 213–65; Jespersen, 1949; Bloomfield, [1933] 2002), as follows: coordinate clauses include: (i) cumulative, as suggested by the use of *and* in *Both Father and elder brother have come back* and *Mr. Zhang reads and writes*; (ii) disjunctive, as indicated by *or* in *We just start to perform or wait for a while?*; (iii) adversative, with *but* as in *He's got rich, **but** is still unhappy*; (iv) deductive, as signalled by *so* in *That man is unfaithful to friends, **so** you should have less contact with him*; and (v) explicative, as marked by *for* in *He was serving here **for** there did not lack enough ones to attend the guests in the front*.

The subordinates include: (i) time – ***When** you want to eat something, just tell me*; (ii) condition – ***If** you want to eat something, just tell me*; (iii) concession – ***Although** he's got rich, he's still unhappy*; (iv) reason – ***Since** that man is unfaithful to friends, you should have less contact with him*; (v) cause – *(**Because**) He saw there did not lack enough ones to attend the guests in the front, so he was serving here*; (vi) purpose – *I will secretly send clothes to you in the evening **so that** you should wear them earlier or later*; (vii) result – *He was **so** poor **that** he quitted schooling*; and (viii) compressive – *I hated him for **having not helped me***.

Wang further explicated the constructions identified by Jespersen under the headings of Parallelism and Comparison. The former may be exemplified with *The older you grow, the more careless you have become*. The latter is merely a type of determinative sentence, as in *She was married to such a husband, just like a piece of lovely flower stuck in a dunghill*.

Wang (1947: 126–7) also pointed out that there are some sentence constructions in English that do not have equivalents in Chinese, such as the relative clause, e.g. *He slew all the prisoners, **which** was a very barbarous act; He is clear at planting young trees; **for which** purpose every one is glad to employ him; I shall be back before midnight, **when** we shall send for the police; The formulation is possible **only because** the change occurred regularly*. (For further and more detailed studies in this area, see also Lv, 1947, vol. 3.)

Halliday acknowledges the two sub-type relations in Wang's paratactic sentences, namely, coordinate and subordinate; and, following Jespersen (1949), recategorizes the coordinate with paratactic and the subordinate with hypotactic (both from Jespersen, 1949). While treating these two as an exclusive pair, he further introduces what he calls 'logico-semantic' relations: expansion and projection. These two pairs constitute what is known as the matrix of 'basic types of clause complex' (Halliday, 1994: 220).

3.4 Mood and Modality

Wang describes mood phenomenon in Chinese in the following way: 'mood elements do not represent the mood of narrative sentence (like the moods expressed by verbs in the western languages). Rather, they represent the mood of the whole sentence; so the natural place for a mood element is at the end of sentence. Mood elements have their respective grammatical meanings, such as determination, question, retorting (tag) and exaggeration, but they bring more or less with them some emotion. Therefore, if they are translated into English, moods may be called emotional moods and mood elements emotional particles' (Wang, 1947: 301; see also Gao, 1948: 435–58; Lv, 1947, vol. 2: 271–307).

Similarities between SFG and Wang's formulation include (i) mood and modality are associated (see Halliday, [1970] 2005, 1994: 68–99; Wang, 1947: 140–53); (ii) the clausal conception of mood; and (iii) mood is meaningful. The second point agrees well with Halliday's theorization in terms of the interpersonal metafunction. Unlike models associated with pragmatics, Halliday starts from the grammatical angle and generalizes two categories for social exchanges (giving and demanding) and two for what are exchanged (goods-&-services and information) (Halliday, [1975] 2003: 79–81). The two dimensions, when put together, produce four interactive/negotiation categories or speech functions: offer, command, statement and question. In grammatical terms, Subject and Finite as Mood elements of the English clause realizes the following mood alternatives: declarative (subject-finite order), interrogative (subject-finite order reversed) and imperative (mood element omitted), which play the roles of the various speech functions.

Halliday's four speech functions can be seen as further refinement of Wang's 12 semantic meanings of grammatical mood based on Jespersen (1924: 313–21): (i) Determinative, with emotional sigh, regret, delight, admiration, yearning, threat, *etc.*, as in, e.g., *when I think about benevolence, benevolence comes!* (ii) Explanative, as in *Just now it's I who was naughty and did not allow to open the door for you!* (iii) Emphatic; (iv) Interrogative; (v) Rhetorical Question; (vi) Hypothesis; (vii) Conjecture; (viii) Command; (xi) Urgency; (x) Resignation;

(xi) Indignation; and (xii) Persuasion. Many of the categories are concerned with modality and served as a basis for subsequent SFG conceptions of modalization and modulation (Halliday, [1970] 2005, 1994: 88–9). Halliday synthesizes Wang's and Jespersen's (e.g. 1924: 313–21) account of mood elements, producing a highly generalized account of speech functions which distinguish social meanings on grammatical grounds.

4 Concluding Remarks

Halliday has maintained a life-long interest in Chinese (see Halliday, 2006), in particular, Chinese phonology. Building on Luo and Wang's diachronic methodology, he has contributed new ideas by reclassifying the syllabic initial and final systems (Halliday, [1981] 2006). His systemic description of the Peking syllables (Halliday, [1992] 2006) has encouraged Chinese scholars working in this area too.

Apart from that, Halliday has continued his study of modern Chinese grammar and discourse in comparison with English (e.g. Halliday, [1984, 1993, 2001] 2006). He has a commanding view of the Chinese language from both typological and general linguistic perspectives (see Halliday, 2008 passim).

To sum up, Halliday started his linguistics career in China, which has led to outstanding achievements both in general linguistics and in specific descriptions and other applications.

Note

1. The author is most grateful to Professor Halliday and Professor Hasan who are so kind to read through the manuscript of this chapter and hence guide it to the present shape.

4 'Socially Realistic Linguistics': The Firthian Tradition

Braj B. Kachru

1 Introduction[1]

The 1960s and 1970s saw a period of search for 'socially realistic' paradigms applicable to linguistic research and methodology (Labov, 1970, 1972: xiii).[2] This activity was much more intense in North America than elsewhere, and there was an understandable reason for it. In the United States the 1950s and 1960s were essentially the decades of one dominant paradigm. With the publication of Chomsky's influential *Syntactic Structures* in 1957, the structural linguistic tradition of Bloomfield and his followers came under attack, and the transformational-generative paradigm became predominant. This domination continued up to the end of the last decade. However, the scene seems to have changed again, and it is with that changed linguistic scene that I am concerned here.

The 1970s saw serious discussion about theoretical validity, and applications of various linguistic models, not excluding those which rejected the main thrust of what is known as Chomskyan linguistics (see, e.g. Smith and Wilson, 1979). In a number of contemporary approaches, prominence was given to terms such as *social*, *socio-* and *sociological*. There was renewed concern for a *social person*, interacting as a *social being* within the network of *social roles* determined by the social and cultural context in which the person functions. The emphasis rightly was on looking at language in terms of function in context (see, e.g. Halliday, 1973, 1975, 1978; Helmer, 1969; Hymes, 1969 and later).

This concern was manifest in recent work in generative semantics (see, e.g. Cicourel, 1969),[3] pragmatics (see, e.g. Cole, 1978; Mitchell, 1978; Morgan, 1977)[4] and the seminal research done on discourse analysis (see, e.g. Schenkein, 1978). It is, however, true that the underlying assumptions and the formal analytical apparatus used in each theory were not identical. But the change in refocusing research areas was very clear, and serious concern was expressed for the neglect of the functional aspects of language in earlier linguistic theories (see, e.g. Givón, 1979). Some socially oriented or functionally oriented models were presented and enumerated, for example, in the work of Bernstein (e.g. 1958, 1959, 1971), Fishman (e.g. 1965, 1971), Gumperz (e.g. 1964, 1967), Halliday (1973 and later), Hymes (e.g. 1962, 1964, 1969, 1971a, 1971b, 1974) and Labov (e.g. 1963, 1966, 1970, 1972). It is clear that not all these models drew upon linguistic theories per se, but their concern with language and its function in society was clearly evident. George Lakoff and John Ross, among others, attempted to redirect linguistics towards what they call 'human linguistics'. These were some of the reactions against the one-sided direction which linguistics took since the 1950s. It was this *human* aspect of linguistics which concerned Firth from as early as 1930. Mitchell (1975: 1) succinctly summarized this aspect of Firth: '. . . he [Firth] was also deeply concerned with the full humanness of language, not with the question of our mental "specification" for language but rather with the uses and concomitant forms to which we adapt this "gift of tongues".'[5] Robin Lakoff (1975: 329), an American linguist, expressed a typical Firthian position in the following words: '. . . a theory was needed which did not separate levels of analysis, did not assume the autonomy of any part of language, that did not, further, assume that language use was necessarily independent of other means used to achieve communication, that allowed for the incorporation of non-linguistic information into our grammar.' Hymes (1969: 113) rightly felt that 'linguists today usually describe language in terms of just one broad type of function, which I term "referential meaning" whereas language is organized in terms of a second broad type of function, which I term "social meaning"' (1969: 112). Therefore, he was concerned that the current practice of linguistics 'perpetuates a fragmented, incomplete understanding of man'.

The subsequent direction in linguistics and the search for 'socially realistic' paradigms therefore provided an ideal context to re-evaluate an earlier and rather neglected tradition of linguistics. This tradition has vaguely been termed the 'British tradition', particularly with reference to the work of J. R. Firth (see, e.g. Langendoen, 1968; Mitchell, 1975; Monaghan, 1979).

This chapter is primarily a postscript to current discussion on the study of language in social context and focuses on the views of Firth on this aspect of language study and research. This attempt at taking another look at Firth's approach to language is not merely for antiquarian interest, but it is appropriate and relevant to the ongoing debate on redefining the goals of linguistic study. In Firth's approach we also detect valuable insights for the type of research which is well established in the United States as a sub-discipline of linguistics under the term 'sociolinguistics'.[6] In Britain, however, traditionally the dichotomy between 'sociolinguistics' and 'general linguistics' was not used. What is 'sociolinguistics' in America has been considered as a vital part of 'general linguistics' in the British approach to language.

The discussion of Firth's approach is appropriate for other reasons, too. Firthian linguistics, especially Firth's concept of contextualization, never seems to have received serious consideration in America. During Firth's linguistically productive years mainly two paradigms overshadowed the American linguistic scene. First came the behaviourist school following the Bloomfieldian tradition. It was, as Palmer (1968: 9) rightly says, 'against this that Firth directed most of his attack'. And later Firth was clearly impatient with the mentalism (and formalism) of the transformational group which followed Bloomfieldian structuralism and completely neglected the role of language in social context.[7]

Earlier some attention had been paid to one component of Firthian linguistics, namely, prosodic analysis (see, e.g. Davis, 1973; Haugen, 1958; Hill, 1961; Langendoen, 1968; Lyons, 1962; Oyelaran, 1967; Palmer, 1970; Stockwell, 1959; Vachek, 1959). But the other component, termed 'contextualization' or 'context of situation' (see, e.g. Langendoeri, 1968; Lyons, 1966), which is the theme of this chapter, was either ignored or rather hastily rejected. Again, the reason for it was that the linguistic scene of the 1950s and 1960s in America was not conducive to such an approach. But this is not the whole story, and part of the blame must go to Firth, too, for his 'obscure' style, for his lack of explanations and paucity of illustrations. There is no well-enumerated and clear explanation of contextualization in the work of Firth. Often even the adherents of Firth have mentioned Firth's obscure writing as one of the reasons for the vagueness of his concepts and consequent misunderstanding by readers. It is therefore not surprising that impatience has been shown towards his 'philosophy of language'. Among his own adherents consider, for example, the opinion of the following. Palmer (1968: 2) feels that 'Firth was himself largely to blame for the fact that he was both during his lifetime and afterwards so misunderstood'. And Firth's close associate Mitchell (1975: 2) recognizes that there was 'some stylistic obscu-rity, considerable inconsistency, and an unfortunate lack of exemplification in his [Firth's] writings'. Kress (1976: xv) notes two 'shortcomings' of Firth. First, Firth 'never attempted to provide a fully worked out and systematic exposition of his theory'. Second, he 'did not provide a set of terms or categories which could systematically relate all the descriptive statements on all levels to each other'. Dixon (1965: 91) – not necessarily a Firthian or a neo-Firthian – feels that Firth's 'theoretical remarks were vague, and often mutually inconsistent, so that it is difficult to see how they could be used for a comprehensive description'.

The neglect of Firthian linguistics, however, was not complete. There are sev-eral examples of the Firthian model being embedded into American linguistic models (e.g. Pike in [1959] 1967). Pike's model, however, never became a domi-nant paradigm in America, though his tagmemic model has been applied to a large body of Western and non-Western languages. In spite of these limitations, we find that around the 1960s, Firth was being recognized in a wider circle as one who had provided what Bell (1976, see especially 75–82) terms 'the func-tional models' of language.

It was not until the 1960s in America that there was renewed interest among linguists towards incorporating social context in language study as a relevant component. Labov's work is a clear example of such awareness, with convinc-ing examples to show the inadequacies of the type of research which neglects social context. Labov presented his position very aggressively, with a wealth of empirical data and refined analytical techniques. In the introduction to his collection of papers written mainly during the 1960s, Labov (1972: xiii) sums up the main argument of such an approach in the following words: 'There is a growing realization that the basis of intersubjective knowledge in linguistics must be found in speech – language as it is used in everyday life by members of the social order, that vehicle of communication in which they argue with their wives, joke with their friends, and deceive their enemies.' These words remind one of what Firth said in 1935 (see Firth, 1957a: 29): 'The multiplicity of social roles we have to play as members of a race, nation, class, family, school, club, as sons, brothers, lovers, fathers, workers, churchgoers, golfers, newspaper read-ers, public speakers, involves also a certain degree of linguistic specialization.' Again ([1935] 1957a: 29): 'The grown man has to play many parts, functioning in many characters, and unless he knows his lines as well as his role he is no use in the play. If you do not know your part and your lines, there are no cues for the other fellow, and therefore no place or excuse for his lines either.'

Labov was not attacking only the goals of the linguistics of the post-1957 period (and earlier structuralism) but also the methodology of such approaches (see, e.g. Labov 1978: 339–42). There were other dissidents against the domi-nant paradigm, e.g., Pike, but as compared to Labov, their impact on theoreti-cal discussions of the period remained marginal. But earlier in the 1960s there seemed to be only a remote possibility that 'socially realistic linguistics' would be acceptable to the practitioners in the profession in the 1970s. The dominant paradigm continued to be Transformational Grammar or the variations of this paradigm.

It is within this context of American linguistics that one has to consider the earlier reactions to Firthian linguistics (e.g. that of Langendoen, 1968), and later, in the changed context, the renewed interest in Firth's 'philosophy of language'.

2 British Linguistics: A Vague Tradition

The term 'British linguistics' is as misleading as the term 'American linguistics', except that there is more vagueness attached to it. The British tradition of linguistics embodies primarily the linguistic insights of Henry Sweet (1845–1912), Daniel Jones (1881–1967) and J. R. Firth (1890–1960). The first two provided primarily the phonetic tradition, and Firth developed it into what he fondly called a tradition of 'general linguistics'. In later literature, both in Britain and elsewhere, terms such as 'London school' (e.g. Langendoen, 1968), 'prosodic analysis' (Hill, 1961; Palmer, 1970; Robins, 1957), 'Firthian linguistics' (Mitchell, 1975; Palmer, 1968: 1), and 'Levels analysis' (BursillHall, 1961), as well as the term 'London group' (Firth, 1957a: 170), have been used. The beginning of the British phonetic tradition, however, is much earlier than the work of Sweet, Jones and Firth (for details see Abercrombie, 1948; Firth, 1956). And Firth was fond of reminding us of the words of Abercrombie, 'that our antecedents are older and better than we think' (1957a: 168), especially in phonetics.

While building a tradition in London, Firth also attempted to demonstrate that his view of language and linguistic analysis was different from the Saussurian view and the structural formalism of Bloomfield.[8] In his two popular books *Speech* (1930) and *The Tongues of Men* (1937), we find Firth's first ideas about what later became known as the Firthian approach to language. *The Tongues of Men* was published four years after Bloomfield's *Language*. 'One fact that becomes obvious with the publication of these works is that British linguistics is not a variant of Bloomfieldian linguistics' (Strevens, 1964: ix). However, these two books, as Strevens correctly notes, are 'almost entirely unknown to linguists trained in the American tradition' (1964: vii).

It is in 'The techniques of semantics' (1935) that Firth presented his 'philosophy of language',[9] claiming that he has ceased 'to respect the duality of mind and body, thought and word' (1957a: 19). This disagreement with the behaviourists and formalists was partially responsible for separating him – and for some time isolating him – from the linguists of the 1930s and 1940s.

What are then the basic characteristics of the British tradition, if any? It is claimed (e.g. by Mitchell) that in the British tradition, as manifested and developed in Firth's work, the emphasis is on (a) the study of the function of language in social context, (b) the primacy of speech and 'the potential meaningfulness of phonetic minutiae', (c) the inductive approach to language analysis, and (d) 'the priority of syntagm and the resulting importance of finding the syntagmatic limits beyond which linguistic choice is unpredictable' (see Mitchell, 1975: 2–13). This view of language was, as Firth says (1956 [Palmer, 1968]: 90), 'first stated in 1930', and 'maintained and developed since'. In Firth's view then 'the whole of our linguistic behavior is best understood if it is seen as a network of relations between people, things and events, showing structures and systems, just as we notice in all our experience . . . Such an approach requires no dichotomy of mind and body, thought and its expression, form and content'. This approach, as Firth says, 'implies rather a different general philosophical attitude towards speech from that which has set our scale of linguistic values hitherto' ([1935] 1957a: 32).

3 Language as Function

In Firth's view, language is primarily viewed as *function*. The emphasis is on 'a hierarchy of techniques' by which a linguistic event is seen as a spectrum of statements at various levels, e.g., phonetic, phonological, morphological, lexical, syntactic, contextual.

Firth does not use the term 'meaning' in its general sense, since for him any linguistic statement at any level is a statement of 'meaning'. At first sight, therefore, one might consider his use of the term 'mischievous' and 'perverse' (Lyons, 1966). Firth's use of the term does not refer to lexicographical or conceptual meaning of an 'item'. Rather it is the linguistic function of an item, and the term 'linguistic' is applied to those disciplines and techniques which are concerned with institutionalized languages. For Firth (1957a), therefore, 'a statement of the meaning of an isolate of any of these cannot be achieved at one fell swoop by one analysis at one level'. The 'meaning' at each level 'disperses' like a spectrum till at the *contextual level* a restricted language is related to the social process of which it forms a part, since 'speech at all levels is regarded as a social and bodily process' (1957a: 170). There is, thus, a relationship between linguistic form and its function (or 'meaning') in context. In this sense, then, a *restricted* language is a functionally determined 'language' within the total language. In Firth's view, a total language could be seen as comprising a 'multiplicity of languages'. There are clearly definable situations which determine (and influence) language. Let me try to explain the concept of 'function in context' with the following illustrations from the Indian English novel *Untouchable* by Mulk Raj Anand:

(1) 'Why did you sit down on my footstep? You have defiled my religion . . . now, I will have to sprinkle holy water all over the house.'

(2) 'He caught the jelebis [pretzel-shaped Indian sweets] which the confectioner threw at him like a cricket ball, placed four nickel coins on the shoe-board for the confectioner's assistant who stood ready to splash some water on them.'

(3) 'Do you know you have touched me and defiled me?'

These illustrations are examples of formally and functionally Indianized texts of English as used in fiction. The Indianization is functionally determined by 'creating' what might be called a 'restricted' language of caste in Indian English. The appropriateness of this 'restricted' language has to be seen in the 'contextual unit' of the caste system which provides a 'defining context' for it, and the meaning of the text is not clear unless a *relationship* is established with the Indian context of situation. It is much more difficult in this context, since a second language (English) has been used to recreate a context which originally exists in Hindi or Punjabi. Anand, therefore, makes a meaningful use of formal devices such as extended collocations and 'semantic equivalence' of English lexical items with the lexical items from his native language, e.g., *footstep, shoe-board, defile, holy water, touch* and *defile*. The cohesion of the text, thus, creates a *casteness*, appropriate to the situation. Contextually, then, the above examples can be understood only within the Indian context of situation with reference to contextual parameters such as the following. The transaction involves a traditional confectioner (*halvai*) who is a Brahmin, and a buyer who is an 'untouchable'. It is within this context that items such as *shoe-board, threw, sprinkle, holy water, touch, defile*, etc., acquire specific contextual meanings. In this case the extended meanings have been given to these items from Indian lexical items. The written text does not specify the phonetic/phonological characteristics of the speech act, but if such information were available it would be further illuminating. We have to keep in mind, as Mitchell ([1957] 1975: 186) points out, that:

A text is a kind of snowball, and every lexical item and every collocation in it is part of its own context, in the wider sense of this term; moreover, the snowball rolls now this way, now that. To make progress in statement at all possible it is necessary for the linguist to select from his material and to focus attention on some elements to the exclusion of others. Not every part of a text lends itself to collocational statement, nor will it always be necessary to make statements about *every* (habitual) collocation in a text.

Another example, again from Indian English, is from the matrimonial advertisements published in national newspapers in India. These provide some examples of semantic nativization of English lexical items and use of code-mixing for contextualizing the advertisements in the Indian situation.

(a) Wanted well-settled bridegroom for a Kerala fair, graduate, Baradwaja otram, Astasastram girl . . . subsect no bar. Send horoscope and details (*The Hindu* 1.7.79).

(b) on-Koundanya well qualified prospective bridegroom below 30 for graduate Iyengar girl, daughter of engineer. Mirugaserusham. No dosham. Average complexion. Reply with horoscope (*The Hindu* 1.7.79).

(c) Suitable match for Kanyakubja post-graduate girl 24, educated throughout in convents (*The Pioneer* 31.12.78).

The Firthian approach to language seeks the appropriateness of the behaviour of participants in a language event, and the whole background of their coming together which determines their use of language in a certain way in a particular context. The crucial backdrop for such a relationship is the CONTEXT OF SITUATION (see, for references, Kachru, 1966; Robins, 1971).[10]

4 Context of Situation

As is well documented, Firth borrowed the term 'context of situation' from British anthropologist Bronislaw Malinowski (1884–1942), who used it for a semantic analysis of ethnographic data. In turn, it is believed that Malinowski owed his earlier use of the term to Wegener's (1885) concept of *Situationstheorie*.[11] In Malinowski's view language is separated from mental processes and is described as a mode of *action* rather than a *counter-sign of thought*. This, as Firth (1957b: 94) says, was in line with British empiricism, 'and of the philosophic radicals and utilitarians, whose influence was far-reaching and is obvious in the works of the Vienna Circle'. Malinowski was interested in an analytical and functional study of culture; for him, therefore, linguistics was subordinate to anthropological research. And he considers language to be the 'ethnographer's most important apparatus, that is, his linguistic apparatus' (see Firth, 1957b: 94).

The main features of Malinowski's context of situation are: the meaning of an utterance is determined by taking the context of a whole utterance in a context of situation. The general condition in which an utterance is spoken should be considered relevant. A word without the *linguistic context* is a mere fragment and stands for nothing by itself. Gestures and motions are essential factors for understanding speech. Meaning should be defined in terms of experience and situation. One might say that for Malinowski the context of situation is 'the physical environment' in which a linguistic activity is performed. Robins (1971: 36) attempts to put Malinowski's concept of the context of situation in a historical perspective. In his view

> Malinowski's challenge to the semantic priority of the word ran counter to the theory of the West from Aristotle to our own day. But in ancient India (though to my knowledge Malinowski was not interested in this field) the question of priority was keenly debated: does word meaning arise from sentence meaning or are sentence meanings built up from word meanings? Bhartrhari (c. seventh century AD) argued that a sentence conveyed its meanings undivided at first, like a picture, and that analysis into individual word meanings is a subsequent critical, metalinguistic operation. He instances the sentence 'Fetch a cuckoo from the woods' (in Sanskrit, of course); unless and until the meaning of the 'cuckoo' is known as well, the meaning of 'fetch' remains vague and undefined, since fetching a log and fetching a bird are a very different operation.

It is only in their broad underlying assumptions that there is a similarity between Malinowski and Firth. In Firth's hands, context of situation is an important part of his general philosophy of language. Contextualization applies to *restricted* [12] forms of speech and writing as these are actually *used* by persons in varied social roles.

In 1930, when Firth first used this concept, he specifically mentioned that 'the linguist, however, must keep the language text in the focus of attention, and his main work is the linguistic analysis of the language data collected in the corpus inscriptionum' (1957b: 96). For Malinowski, context of situation is 'a bit of social process which can be considered apart and in which a speech event is central and makes all the difference, such as a drill sergeant's welcome utterence on the square, "*Stand at-ease!*" The context of situation for Malinowski is an ordered series of events considered as *in rebus*' (Firth, [1950] 1957a: 182). For Firth it was a suitable schematic construct to apply to language events. The abstracted categories consist of verbal and non-verbal constituents and are 'observable' and 'justifiable' in the text.

In Firth's view, language is better considered as having a creative function, 'effect' or 'meaning' in the context of situation. Firth would claim that if you want to know what an utterance means, you must see what happens after it is said (cf. also Wittgenstein).[13] Firth is concerned with *mutually expectant* interrelations of elements of structure and terms of systems, and constituents of context of situation.[14] It is through contextualization that the text, or portions of the text, can be said to exemplify special functions. This *relationship* is not restricted to phonology or grammar but can be extended to lexis in terms of the structure of collocations, and extended collocations [15] generally in a restricted language (see also Halliday, 1966; Kachru, 1965, 1966). The Firthian use of context of situation is an abstraction from situation, and as Mitchell says (1978: 227), it is 'as abstract as the grammatical, lexical, phonological, and other categories that are relevant to the interpretation of transactional linguistic behavior; it is not on a par with, say, phonic "realizations" of phonological categories'. It is the situation which provides the *context of experience* and *context of culture* to the language used by the *speech fellowship, speech community* or a *language community*. The situation is *extra-linguistic*, and it is through *form* that a linguist is able to show its relevance (appropriateness) to linguistic behaviour.[16] Therefore, contextualization for Firth involves abstraction of the same nature as the structures and systems of phonology and grammar. Thus *contextualization* implies a unitary approach in which linguistic *form* and *meaning* are not separated. Language is seen as meaningfully organized – both formally and functionally – in maintaining patterns of *living*. The interrelationship of 'levels' may tentatively be shown in the following way:[17]

Subject concerned	*Phonetics*			*Linguistics*	
Level (general)	SUBSTANCE (phonic or graphic)	relation of form and substance	FORM	CONTEXT (relation of form and situation)	situation (non-linguistic phenomena)
Level (specific)	PHONETICS	PHONOLOGY	GRAMMAR & LEXIS (vocabulary)	SEMANTICS	
	SCRIPT	'GRAPHOLOGY' (writing system)			

Note: See Halliday et al., 1964: 18.

One might ask: Does the context of situation *determine* the linguistic behaviour? Mitchell (1978: 239) believes that Firth did not think so 'and was completely misunderstood on the score by Chomsky and his followers, who saw no prospect of the context of situation ever contributing to theoretical knowledge'. The context of situation 'was simply thought of as infusing every linguistic element with relevance, or, as Firth put it, with some "mode of meaning"' (Haas, 1966: 118).

5 Constituents of Context of Situation

Firth does not provide a methodology for structuring context of situation. Perhaps one reason for this vagueness is Firth's belief that there is no one *procedure* for such analysis. He rejected proceduralism, this being one reason for his disagreement with American structuralism. Firth did, however, suggest some broad (and general) categories for establishing the *relevant* features of context of situation.

(a) The relevant features of participants: Persons, personalities
   (i) Verbal actions of participants
   (ii) Non-verbal actions of participants
(b) The relevance of objects
(c) The effect of the verbal action

The other features to be considered are

(a) Economic, religious, social structures to which participants belong
(b) Types of discourse – monologue, narrative
(c) Personal interchanges – age, sex of participants
(d) Types of speech – social flattery, cursing

In using such a schema one has to take note of *creative effect* or *effective result* as a link with context of situation. The structure and system of a text are to be related with the 'structure' and 'system' *outside*.

The above schema provides what may be termed CONTEXTUAL PARAMETERS. These are formal and contextual variables which determine the effective operation of a *text* in a CONTEXTUAL UNIT. A delimited text may be said to be the exponent of a contextual unit on the basis of those formal features which mark it off from other delimited texts and, more importantly, which make it 'effective' in a specific context. A contextual unit may be viewed as a 'substitution frame' and the *relevant* parameters as the distinctive markers of the frame. A contextual unit is by and large culturally determined and has 'meaning' with reference to a specific culture. It is worth remembering that 'we are born into a vast potential cultural heritage, but we can only hope to succeed to a very small part of the total heritage and then only in stages . . . for each stage of childhood and youth, of each type of child, there are relevant forms of language' (Firth, [1935] 1957a: 29). A linguistic activity then has two dimensions, i.e., syntagmatic and paradigmatic. Syntagmatically one might think of the 'time dimension', that is, the beginning and the end of a ROLE. Paradigmatically it comprises a 'bundle of features' in terms of the participants, age, sex, etc., within a context of situation. (For illustrations see Kachru, 1965, 1966; Mitchell, 1957.) Mitchell ([1957] 1975: 169–70) rightly warns us that:

> In order to make a satisfactory statement, the linguist constantly has to select some features and suppress others of both the text and its environment. When

doing so, however, he should not lose sight of the text as a whole. Arabic 'Subáah ilxáyr' (Good morning), taken *in vacuo*, may be said to belong to the language of greetings, and differs in many respects from, say, 'yaftuħálla', which is only used as the refusal of a bid in buying and selling. But, as a rule, greetings form part of a complex pattern of activity which is peculiar to buying and selling; therefore, 'Subáah ilxáyr' – as far as it contributes to the pattern – may be considered, like 'yaftuħálla', as belonging to buying and selling, provided that texts of adequate extent are given in support.

Extending this proceduralism a little further, one might say that in order to determine the 'appropriateness' of contextual units two types of substitution are involved, namely, *contextual substitution* and *textual substitution*. It is through such substitution that one can provide a *correlation* between the contextual parameters and their formal exponents. One must accept the warning of Mitchell (1978: 237) here and not think of correlation as 'neatly compartmentalizing the several dimensions of speech events', since, as we know, 'the forms of language are too often mixed and fuzzy with shifts of style occurring to and fro within utterances and their parts'.

6 Firthian View of the Sociology of Language, Sociological Linguistics and Linguistic Theory

In Firth's writings at least 15 linguistic 'levels' have been mentioned, out of which *social* and *sociological* are crucial for linguistic description. In his view 'the linguist studies the speaking person in the social process' ([1951] 1957a: 190), and he emphasizes this point in various ways. Firth disagrees with the earlier formalistic and comparative schools and believes that 'such linguistics cannot throw even the dimmest indirect glimmer on personality and language in society, which I submit is a major concern of science' ([1950] 1957a: 178–9).

In his approach there is a relationship between 'linguistic patterns' and 'activity'. In establishing this relationship a 'sociological approach' and 'synthesis' are vital for a linguistic description. Firth ([1948] 1957a: 143) presents his position unambiguously in the following words:

We must expect therefore that linguistic science will also find it necessary to postulate the maintenance of linguistic patterns and systems (including adaptation and change) within which there is order, structure, and function. Such systems are maintained by activity, and in activity they are to be studied . . . in emphasizing the personal as well as the systemic and typic character of descriptive linguistics, there is no implied neglect of the sociological approach and synthesis.

At the same time, Firth ([1935] 1957a: 28) reminds us that 'we are not aiming at linguistic sociology, but building on the foundations of linguistics'. This obviously is an important distinction.[18]

Perhaps Firth was one of the first linguists to use the term 'the sociology of language'[19] and claim that this area is one of the 'autonomous group of related disciplines' under 'descriptive linguistics' ([1950] 1957a: 144). In 1935 Firth had prophesied (see 1957a: 27) that 'sociological linguistics is the great field for future research'.

But in spite of this relationship the two fields are 'autonomous', and their goals and methods are not identical. The aim of a linguist is to study '. . . the speaking person in the social process. . . . The linguist deals with persons habitually maintaining specific forms of speech or writing which can be referred to dialects or languages operating in close or open social groups' ([1951] 1957a: 190). The approach of linguistics, in Firth's view, contrasts with that of sociologists. Compare the above, for example, with the following (Firth, [1951] 1957a: 191): 'The study of linguistic institutions is thus more specific and positive and on the whole less speculative than the sociological study of societies. Sociologists and social anthropologists are much bolder than linguists in what they find it possible to state in general human terms. To what lengths sociological abstractions can be extended is well exemplified in Pareto's theory of residues and derivations.'

In later research on language the difference between the approaches of a linguist and a sociologist was clearly demonstrated in Labov (e.g. 1966, 1970) as a linguist, as opposed to, for example, Fishman (e.g. 1965, 1971), a sociologist.

In his often-quoted *Papers in Linguistics*, Firth emphasizes that the goal of his 'linguistic theory' is not to 'attempt to establish universals for general linguistic description'. He expects his theory to be 'useful in renewal of connection with experience' (1957a: xii).

The 'experience' manifests itself in ROLES which are to be understood (interpreted) in the framework of the context of situation. 'In that context are the human participant or participants, what they say, and what is going on' ([1935] 1957a: 27). For a linguist the SOCIAL ROLES are to be determined by the formal exponents which are related to each role (see Firth, [1935] 1957a: 28). The social roles of an individual are in turn determined by the social organization, 'and the chief condition and means of that condition is learning to say what the other fellow expects us to say under the given circumstances' ([1935] 1957a: 28). Hence, social *activity* and *expectations* are conditioned by the context of situation. Therefore, Firth says: 'Once someone speaks to you, you are in a relatively determined context and you are not free just to say what you please' ([1935] 1957a: 28).

According to this approach, therefore, monolithic description does not bring out the socially (or contextually) determined characteristics of language.

Firth adopts a rather unconventional position and claims that 'unity of language is the most fugitive of all unities whether it be historical, geographical, national, or personal. There is no such thing as *une langue une* and there has never been' ([1935] 1957a: 29). For adopting such a view Firth has been criticized by, among others, Langendoen (1968) who, as Robins (1971: 44) says, 'chides Firth and those following up his ideas with making context of situation "a convenient dumping ground for people's knowledge about the world, their own culture, etc." (1968: 50) and assigns Mitchell's study of the language of buying and selling "to the realm of ethnography and not of semantics" (1968: 65). But this is verbal play. It is just such areas of experience and knowledge, call them what you will, that are somehow involved in the individual's acquisition and retention of his knowledge of his vocabulary. The linguist must somehow try to experience this'. It seems to me that the non-monolithic view of Firth does make sense in terms of *functions* of language, since in his view 'multiplicity of social roles' ([1935] 1957a: 29) is under the focus of attention. These multiple roles include the roles which we have to play 'as members of a race, nation, class, family, school, club, as sons, brothers, lovers, fathers, workers, churchgoers, golfers, newspaper readers, public speakers' ([1935] 1957a: 29).

These roles provide a contextual network within a context of situation and entail 'a certain degree of linguistic specialization' ([1935] 1957a: 29). The problem with having such a wide network is that it is easier to talk about it than to describe and analyse it in *linguistic* terms. Firth is aware of that fact and rightly says that it is 'easier to suggest types of linguistic function than to classify situations' ([1935] 1957a: 31).

Various labels have been used for such contextualization (or classification of 'situations') (see, e.g. Gumperz, 1964; Halliday, 1978; Hymes, 1964, 1969; Kachru, 1966, forthcoming). Firth has provided some illustrative labels which are useful for defining those 'language-types' in which there is a relationship between form and function (see, e.g. [1935] 1957a: 31). One might, for example, classify the language of personal relationships in terms of *agreement, condemnation, endorsement* and *disagreement*. And language is constantly used to reflect *attitudes*. These attitudes become meaningful again within the context of culture by choosing culturally determined language types. Consider, for example, typical contexts in which language is used *to appeal, to annoy, to bless, to blame, to boast, to belittle, to curse, to challenge, to cold-shoulder, to flatter, to hurt, to make love* and *to praise*.

The use of language has, of course, other functions, too. One might use words, as Firth says, 'to inhibit hostile action, or to delay or modify it, or to conceal one's intention' ([1935] 1957a: 31). Then there is the use of words for *advertising* and *propaganda* which is difficult to appreciate and analyse without proper contextualization, as illustrated in an earlier section.

85

7 Text and Context

In Firth's approach to 'meaning', a well-defined (and demarcated) text is crucial for 'renewal of connection' with its function in a context of situation. By the term 'text' is meant a 'piece' of language relevant to a specific context (again in a context of situation). Firth rightly warns us that 'without scrupulously identified forms and well-established text, Semantics is apt to be just gossip' ([1935] 1957a: 75). The analysis begins with the utterance, and the aim is 'establishing valid texts' ([1948] 1957a: 145). In 1951, Firth attempts to explain this concept with the use of a metaphor ([1951] 1957a: 192): 'Having made the first abstraction by suitably isolating a piece of "text" or part of the social process of speaking for a listener or of writing for a reader, the suggested procedure for dealing with meaning is its dispersion into modes, rather like the dispersion of light of mixed wave-lengths into a spectrum.' All language 'text' is thus 'attributed to participants in some context of situation' ([1951] 1957a: 226). The approach then focuses on 'the whole man in his patterns of living' ([1951] 1957a: 225). One therefore understands why Firth alternately termed his linguistic framework the 'monistic approach'.

Firth is well aware that for linguists this is too big a bite to chew. Therefore, he rightly says that 'the linguist has to reject most of these patterns, confining himself to the processes and patterns of life in which language "text" is the central feature and operative force' ([1951] 1957a: 225).

The generalizations which Firth makes are based on 'language events' without accepting a dichotomy in which 'minds', 'thoughts' and 'ideas' are excluded. Their presence is not denied, 'but the recognition of them in linguistics is indirect, and *if any reference to them is made it is in terms of linguistics*' ([1951] 1957a: 225; emphasis added). The 'meaning' is not in the text as Mitchell (1975: 7) rightly says but it is 'part of the linguistic organization of the speaker-hearer, who, as far as the practice of linguistics is concerned, is usually also the observer-analyst'.

In a later work Firth (1956 [Palmer, 1968]: 97) makes this point clearer when he says: 'My main concern is to make statements of *meaning* in purely linguistic terms, that is to say, such statements are made in terms of *structures* and *systems* at a number of *levels of analysis*: for example, in phonology, grammar, stylistics, situation, attested and established texts. I do not attempt statements about a speaker's or a writer's thoughts and intentions, ideas and concepts – these are for other disciplines.'

8 The Firthians in the 1970s

The main concentration of the Firthians has traditionally been at the School of Oriental and African Studies of London University. The peak period of their activity was 1948–65. Outside of his immediate group, as Palmer says (1968: 1–2), Firth was 'misunderstood and largely ignored', and 'alas, he was misunderstood' even by some of those who were in the 'immediate group'.

A large number of the members of this group primarily concentrated on prosodic phonology. Those who discussed other aspects of his 'philosophy of language' include, among others, Mitchell and Halliday. Palmer (1968: 9), however, takes the position that Halliday (and other neo-Firthians) 'have little in common with Firth's approach'. In Palmer's view, Halliday's 'essentially monosysternic categorization' seems to have little in common with Firth's 'essentially polysysternic' approach; and secondly, 'Halliday's theory retains the phoneme' which 'typifies the kind of segmentation and classification that Firth rejected' (1968: 9). In fact, Palmer goes a step further and warns us against equating Halliday's theory with that of Firth on the basis of the shared terminology: 'Of course the terminology [of Halliday] is largely Firth's, but Firth was particularly aware of the danger of equating terms in what were essentially different theories.' Halliday does not agree with this evaluation of Palmer (see Halliday, 1971: 664–7).

Is there then a neo-Firthian school, and in what sense is Halliday a chief representative of such a school? Kress (1976: xv) claims that 'Halliday's theory depends more strongly on Malinowski and Whorf, the label neo-Firthian which has been applied to him obscures the main thrust of Halliday's thinking about language'.

What then is Firth's importance for and influence on Halliday? Kress (1976: xiv) believes that Firth's importance lies 'in the attempt which Firth made to provide the linguistic component to go with the sociolinguistic insights of Malinowski'. He specifically mentions two categories (Kress, 1976: xiv):

(1) *Context of situation*, that is, a view of language as closely dependent on stateable general types of situation which influence language. From here Firth developed his theory of the multiplicity of 'languages' within the total language. This is an important insight which Halliday took over and developed in his work on *register*.

(2) *System*, which in redefined form has become the major formal category in Halliday's theory.

These are not the only influences: for instance, Halliday uses Firth's category of collocation in his work on lexis . . . but they are the significant ones.

In spite of the debate on who really is the *śiṣya* of Firth, and what is the validity of the term 'neo-Firthian', there is no doubt that it is in the work of Halliday that several 'socially realistic' aspects of Firth's theory have been expanded, elaborated and illustrated (see, e.g. Halliday, 1971, 1973, 1975, 1978). Consider, for example, what Robins (1971: 38), another vocal adherent of Firthian linguistics, has to say about the contribution of the neo-Firthians: '"neo-Firthian" linguistics associated with Professor M. A. K. Halliday at University College, London and his colleagues and pupils, derives more directly than other theories from the teachings of Firth, and incorporates a good many of the fundamental tenets of Firthian theory. Halliday regards context of situation as a central and essential part of his theory of languages, making it the bridge between grammar and lexis and actual phonation and audition . . .' It is, however, true that 'Halliday made no use of Firth's work in prosodic analysis, which many followers of Firth regard as Firth's major achievement' (Kress, 1976: xv).

9 Conclusion

The position of the Firthian approach to language has been like that of a lost linguistic paradigm. Whenever it has been mentioned in the literature, elaborate warnings are given about its being 'obscure' and vague. The result of such warnings has been that very few linguists have ventured to study the Firthian tradition carefully and evaluate its relevance to the present linguistic debate. One might, however, quote here Halliday's (1971: 666) response to this often-repeated criticism:

> Firth is often said to be obscure; my own experience as a teacher suggests not so much that he is obscure as that his writing provokes hostility in some readers – essentially I think because they find his relativism distasteful, although the reaction often manifests itself as a dislike of Firth's 'style' (can the two really be separated?) – who find it difficult then to read with the sympathy and care that all scholarly work demands.

There is, however, certainly some truth in the fact that reading Firth's writing is not the same as was listening to his lectures in class or having a personal interaction with him on a linguistic topic. In class one was under the spell of his personality and distinct charm mixed with idiosyncracies. It seems to me that in a sense Firth had acquired some characteristics of a traditional Indian *guru*, transmitting his knowledge essentially through the spoken word, repeating himself in various ways. After all, his eight-year stay (1920–8) in India had not left him without its impact on both his personality and scholarship. At the same time, he was a proud Englishman, respecting and eager to contribute to what he termed 'the British tradition' of linguistics.

As a teacher, Firth preferred to have long study sessions with his students. These sessions were replete with digressions about his opinions of his colleagues and former and present students. These he gave in generous doses with a characteristic Firthian flavour. These sessions were full of political and cultural asides, and above all forthright linguistic judgements about other scholars and 'schools'. It was therefore not possible to be indifferent to Firth. One was either under his spell or one avoided him – in either case one *noticed* him. This was also true of the attitude of his students towards him. It was essentially in the role of a student of Firth, as Halliday (1971: 667) rightly emphasizes, that one saw the 'whole man' which is missing in his writings and without which it is difficult to relate the man to his writings.

The next generation of British linguists generally ignored Firth, and the 'London School' in its original sense has almost disintegrated. There are a number of linguistic, historical and other reasons for it, one perhaps being that 'it is not our custom, in Britain, to boast much of our achievements, we are ill-educated and have bad memories. We are taught only the smallest fraction of what we have done, and even that we cannot remember' (Eric Linklater; quoted in Firth, [1946] 1957a: 92).[20]

The main reason for this neglect of Firth is not the relative value of the Firthian paradigm, but that his paradigm was almost lost among the conflicting paradigms of his time.

In the 1960s Lyons (1966) took a rather dim view of Firth's 'contextual theory of meaning' in a paper which, ironically, appeared in *In Memory of J. R. Firth*. But even that critical (and certainly perceptive) paper conceded that there are several points of value in Firth's theory. These, according to Lyons, are 'situations in which language functions and the degree to which what we say at any time is determined by the situation we are in and the particular social role we are playing at the time; and his refusal to describe languages as monolithic, unified systems, writing off as paralinguistic and outside the range of linguistic description everything that distinguishes particular "styles" and "registers"' (1966: 300).

Two decades later, Lyons (1978: xi) noted 'parallels between Labov's approach to linguistics and that of the so-called "British" school, which draws its inspiration from J. R. Firth'. He specifically stated that (1978: xvi):

For Firth, as for Labov, the most important fact about language is its social function: the fact that it serves to establish and maintain socially prescribed patterns of behavior. The whole of Firth's theory of meaning, and his rejection of what he took to be a facile and misguided dichotomy between the twin 'bogies' of mechanism and mentalism, is based upon his commitment to the primacy of the social function of language. He would refuse, on principle, to consider any sentence as being fully meaningful unless it either had been uttered in some actual situation of language-use or could be 'referred to typical participants in some generalized context of situation'. (Firth, 1957: 226)

What is crucial is to evaluate the underlying similarities of 'socially real-istic' approaches to language and not to see these as isolated and unrelated developments.[21]

Notes

1. This attempt to interpret Firth is clearly indicative of my going into an area where angels fear to tread. But the urge to make an attempt has been so irresistible that, in spite of my fears, I decided to attempt it. If I have been able to clarify any points, or show Firth's relevance to the contemporary linguistic context, the credit goes to several readers of an earlier version, who discussed it with care and interest, gave many comments and suggestions and expressed disagreements. The comments of the following have been particularly of value, C. Thomas Mason, Peter Trudgill and Ladislav Zgusta. Mason has also made several specific suggestions which I have incorporated at the relevant places and duly acknowledged. If this chapter achieves any clarity, and makes readers interested in reading the Firthian literature, the credit goes to these and other patient readers of an earlier version. All the shortcomings, of course, reflect my limitations. The term 'socially realistic linguistics' was originally used in Labov (1972: xiii). I am using it here in the sense in which Labov uses it.
2. This does not mean that in earlier linguistic traditions, say before the 1950s, there was no concern within linguistics for the type of research which has been termed 'sociolinguistics'. A summary of such earlier 'sociolinguistic concerns . . . within lin-guists' is presented in Hymes, 1969 (esp. 115 ff.).
3. In this paper Cicourel proposes 'some invariant presuppositions basic to the pro-duction of everyday social activities, and argue[s] that these presuppositions consti-tute sociological cognitive elements of what I [Cicourel] shall be calling a generative semantics central for an understanding of all human communication. Further, the explication of these presuppositions is fundamental to the development of socio-linguistics and an understanding of social interaction as contingent possibilities of specific settings' (1969: 174). The paper also discusses the main works of generative semantics.
4. Mitchell (1978) is an insightful and critical review of the traditions of research on pragmatics. This paper provides a Firthian view of pragmatics and takes the position that 'J. R. Firth in London was talking about pragmatics from a linguistic standpoint long before Morris' (1978: 225).
5. See also Palmer (1968: 9–10) who takes an identical position about Firth: 'Firth never forgot that the task of linguists was to talk about language and languages; he rejected utterly "linguistics without language". At the same time he wished to avoid "dehu-manizing" language. For him, undoubtedly, part of the meaning of his texts was that they were uttered (or written) by human beings.'
6. Note, however, that the sub-field of 'sociolinguistics' is not accepted by all American linguists. Consider. for example, the following observation of Chomsky: 'But the existence of a discipline called "sociolinguistics" remains for me an obscure matter' (1979: 56).
7. It is true that in his writing Firth has not directly alluded to Transformational Grammar. But then, by 1960, the impact of Transformational Grammar – as devel-oped by Chomsky – had not been felt. In his class lectures in Edinburgh, Firth certainly expressed his impatience with the linguistic models of Zellig Harris as pro-posed in Harris' *Methods in Structural Linguistics* and Chomsky's *Syntactic Structures*.

Firth clearly expressed his dissatisfaction when Yamuna Kachru started her dissertation on Hindi, following the transformational model, under C. E. Bazell at the School
of Oriental and African Studies. Note also what Palmer (1968: 5) has to say on this
point: 'he [Firth] regarded his own approach as a combination of the theoretical
and the empirical approaches . . . and reacted most strongly against the essentially
procedural approach of Z.S. Harris' *Methods in Structural Linguistics.*'

8. For Firth's comments on de Saussure see [1950] 1957a: 179–81; on Bloomfield see
[1935] 1957a : 1516, [1949] 1957a: 167–88. Note, however, Mitchell's observation that
'Firth himself did not seem to realize that the Saussurean *signe,* the intangible link
between an essentially unitary *signifiant* and *signifié,* also escaped any deterministic
implication, and he consequently did de Saussure less than justice' (note 45: 251).

9. This term has been used by Mitchell (1975) and seems to be more appropriate than a
theory or the more fashionable term *model.*

10. The following observation of Straumann (1935: 58–61) provides a historical perspective for understanding 'context and situation':

> It must be emphasized that, to a certain degree, the importance of situation and
> context has long been recognized in some way or other, but, oddly enough, only
> few philologists have actually tried to draw the consequences for their research
> work. Among the first who saw an essential factor in the situational elements
> were Ph. Wegener, and H. Paul. From the point of view of logic, the observations
> of Ed. Husserl were a decisive step forward, and of late J. Jørgensen has dealt with
> the subject. Meanwhile, Ch. Bally, M. Bréal, and F. Brunot had made their obser-
> vations in French, whilst in Germany J. Reis, K. Vossler, K. Bühler, L. Morsbach.
> Th. Kalepki, and above all H. Ammann had touched on the subject in greater or
> less detail. Among these Kalepki and Ammann especially dwelt at some length
> on the importance of situation, the former by stating that words are not used for
> such things as may be expressed by the situation, and the latter by emphasiz-
> ing that any sentence if brought into a context (Zusammenhang) where it has
> no sense would automatically become nonsense. Among the Scandinavian and
> Dutch scholars it was O. Jespersen, K. Sundén, and J. van Ginneken who noticed
> the problem.
>
> In England and America the question has likewise been touched upon by A. D.
> Sheffield, E. B. Titchener, G. A. de Laguna, J. Hubert Jagger, C. K. Ogden and I. A.
> Richards, Mildred Lambert, I. Fry, W. L. Graff, and of late especially by J. R. Firth,
> and A. H. Gardiner most of whom are sufficiently known to English philologists.
>
> For full bibliographical reference for the above see Straumann (1935: notes 58–60).
> Note also that Straumann (1935) *Newspaper Headlines: A Study in Linguistic Method*
> shows the influence of Firth and the author expresses his 'deepest obligation to
> Mr. J. R. Firth of University College (London) for having made a number of most
> valuable suggestions in matter of terminology as well as in the arrangement of the
> Systematic Survey'. (1935: 9)

11. There is some doubt about this claim. In a private communication, C. Thomas Mason
(3 April 1980) makes the following observation concerning this point:

> While I realize that this statement comes from Firth himself ([1957] 1968a: 139). it's
> not clear that Malinowski derived anything so significant as his notion of Situation
> from Wegener. I think that Firth here is simply wrong, unless he is remembering –
> thirty years later – something Malinowski told him in conversation. In any case, as
> far as I can ascertain, Malinowski's writings contain only one reference to Wegener,
> whom he mentions in a meaningless laundry-list of linguists: 'It is enough to men-
> tion the names of W. von Humboldt, Lazarus and Steinthal, Whitney, Max Müller,
> Misteli, Sweet, Wundt, Paul, Finck, Rozwadowski, Wegener, Oertel, Marty,

Jespersen and others, to show that the Science of Language is neither new nor unimportant' (1923: 297). There is no implication that he had read all of these, let alone derived important concepts of theory from them ... Malinowski would most likely have gotten an acquaintance he had of Wegener through Sir Alan Gardiner, with whom he has corresponded during his fieldwork days on linguistic questions (cf. Gardiner, in *Man* 19 1919]: 2–6). However, Gardiner, although he dedicated his 1932 *The Theory of Speech and Language* to Wegener's memory, does not mention Wegener in his early articles with regard to the notion of Situation, but rather to the questions of sentences and predication (cf. Gardiner, 'The definition of the word and the sentence', *British J. Of Psychology*, 12 (1922): 35–361). I personally think that it is very unlikely that Malinowski took his notion of Situation from either Wegener or Gardiner; I think it is much more probable that he simply invented the concept out of the exigencies of his fieldwork. After all, to arrive at a notion of 'context of situation', it only takes an examination of real live language and a bit of common sense.

What was the influence of Wegener on Firth? It seems that Firth had not seen Wegener's book until after the publication of Speech (1930). According to C. Thomas Mason (private communication 3 April 1980), it was not 'until late 1934, when Heinrich Straumann (Zurich), author of *Newspaper Headlines*) sent him a copy'. Mason has obtained a copy of the letter which Firth wrote to Straumann (5 November 1934) after receipt of the book. The letter says:

> Thank you very much indeed for the Wegener which I received on Saturday. I spent Sunday going through it for the first time! It seems incredible! The bit about Der Lowe is the most striking coincidence – though there are lots of differences ... 'Great minds', I suppose. His book, I feel certain, has influenced many subsequent writers who thought him fair game and passed on and perhaps improved on him without acknowledgement. I have recognized bits of Amman and stranger still Scripture the phonetician, to say nothing of whole chunks of Gardiner – especially in Congruence. I am very glad I have it and he will receive his need of tardy recognition as one of the moderns in my book. His Situationen are curiously different. The only one that really corresponds is *Kultursituation*. He also has *Situation der Anschauung*
>
> > *der Erinnerung*
> > des ewusstseins
> > des nweisens

I don't think I need these . . . On the whole he deserves a place in the history of Bedeutungslehre – the coming thing.

12. See Palmer (1968: 7).
13. One might then say that there was some overlap between the Firthian approach and the approach of the behaviourists.
14. See Firth's (1957c) description of these terms. See Kress (1976: vii–xxi) for the use of these terms by Firth and Halliday, and specifically for Firth's use, see Palmer (1968: 5–7).
15. See Halliday (1966) and Kachru (1965, 1966).
16. Note also that in the Hallidayan model 'the two important categories' are *context of situation* and *system*. Context of situation is explained as 'a view of language as closely dependent on stateable general types of situation which influence language. From here Firth developed his theory of the multiplicity of "languages" within the total language. This is an important insight which Halliday took over and developed in his work *on register*' (Kress: xiv). Furthermore, 'Halliday is convinced that it is possible to show a systemic relationship between the text, the linguistic system,

and the situation, provided that the situation is interpreted not as the material environment (in however abstract terms) but as a semiotic structure whose elements are social meanings, and into which "things" enter as the bearers of social values' (Kress, 1976: xxi).

17. This diagram was originally suggested by Halliday (1961). In the opinion of several Firthians, it does not represent the typical Firthian position.

18. My attention was drawn to this quote by C. Thomas Mason (private communication, 3 April 1980).

19. Firth was also perhaps one of the first linguists to hold the position of 'Assistant in the Sociology of Language in the London School of Economics and Political Science' (Robins, 1961: 544).

20. One might not necessarily agree with this quote since 'boasting' is a relative term.

21. An earlier version of this article appeared in *Studies in the Linguistic Sciences* 10 (1), 85–111.

5 The Influence of Marxism

M. A. K. Halliday

The editor asked me to write this chapter myself – because, sadly, all those who would have been able to write it from their own personal knowledge are no longer alive. So I agreed. I ought to try and avoid making it read like a chapter of autobiography. Yet that, from my point of view, is what it is: an account of the origin and development of one dimension in my own thinking which was critically, though not exclusively, involved in my thinking about language.

In the middle of the Second World War, I volunteered for a language course, and began an intensive study of Chinese just after my seventeenth birthday. The course was given at the School of Oriental and African Studies, University of London; both the design of the course and its implementation in teaching were consistently of a high standard. Among the students on the course, the one I came to know best was John Derry Chinnery, who later in life became Professor of Chinese at the University of Edinburgh. Unlike myself at the time, Derry was already politically aware, and had strong left-wing leanings. He never forced his views; but over those years when we knew each other well, first as students and then, after we had been serving in different military units, as instructors in the later Chinese language courses, I came to share his communist outlook and his interest in marxist thought.

Released from military service, I went to study in China for the better part of three years, from 1947 to 1950, during which time the communist forces decisively won the civil war and established their own national government. I was one among the crowd watching them as they paraded through the streets of Peiping (as it was called then) in February 1949. The general attitude that I encountered was, well, we don't know much about them, but they can't be worse than the last lot. As it turned out, they were a great deal better: they stabilized the currency, which had descended into runaway inflation; they put an end to corruption; and, in my view most important of all, they carried through a land reform which provided the foundation for all China's subsequent prosperity, despite the disasters that came along in between.

When I returned to England, in the middle of 1950, the world – or much of it – was embroiled in a meaningless 'cold war', with the United States leading a 'crusade' against the threat of world-wide communism. I was not convinced that communism was the best solution for my own country; but I wanted to find out, and in particular I wanted to tell people from first hand about what was happening in China. So I joined the British Communist Party, and was fairly active politically for some seven or eight years. I was lucky to be in the same university as Joseph Needham, who knew everything about the history of science and technology in China and was active, like myself, in the Britain–China Friendship Association;[1] and in the same party branch as Eric Hobsbawm, who was our authority on anything at all to do with Marx and with marxism.[2]

When studying in China I had specialized in language studies, and I had been introduced into linguistics by two distinguished scholars, Luo Changpei and Wang Li;[3] so back in England I contrived to work for my Ph.D. degree under the supervision of J. R. Firth. Meanwhile I had started to explore the recent Soviet Russian work in linguistics, particularly that of Meščaninov, who claimed to be developing a marxist theory of language that was distinctively soviet in character. Derry Chinnery was interested in Chinese literature rather than in the study of language; but he passed on my name to one of a small group of linguists who were in the Communist Party and were investigating the question of marxism in linguistics. The core members of this Communist Party Linguistics Group were Jeffrey Ellis, Jean Ure, Dennis Berg, Trevor Hill and Peter Wexler; and I enthusiastically joined them. Our regular discussions over a number of years provided a powerful impetus to thinking hard about the nature and functions of language.

What did the notion of 'marxist linguistics' mean, to all of us and, perhaps, specifically to me? It did not mean discarding or combating all previous wisdom about language; that would obviously be absurd. It did mean examining previous scholarship objectively, and trying to recognize and correct distortions that might arise from 'bourgeois' habits of thought; for example, from the assumption that written language is somehow superior to spoken language and represents a more advanced stage of development in grammar or in semantics. But many covert prejudices of this kind had already been penetrated and largely overcome, at least by linguists; and it seemed to me that in this respect Firth's linguistic theory was entirely compatible with general marxist principles. On one occasion, in fact, Firth said the same thing to me himself.[4]

More important, in our view, was the task of using linguistics to tackle current problems of social and political life. The 1950s was a period of rapid decolonization, when newly independent countries were having to work out their language policies and find resources for developing a new national language, (or more than one) and making it acceptable, and accessible, to the population in general; while at the same time maintaining an international language, usually that of the former colonial power (in practice mainly English or French), as the channel of communication and of ongoing interaction with all the rest of the world. This imposed a huge strain on their limited available resources; and this could easily be made worse by wrongheaded decisions, such as setting up planning agencies to design changes in the national language (inventing new vocabulary for administration and for science and technology) without first trying to understand how new registers evolve in general, and how the particular language of their own creates new meanings when simply left to itself.[5]

In more general terms, we felt that a marxist linguistics should give value to languages, and varieties of language, that were usually regarded as of little value, and often ignored altogether: minority languages, unwritten languages, languages of hybrid origin (creoles), non-standard, or non-literary, varieties, spoken languages (especially casual speech), trade languages, underworld languages and so on. Language planning meant working out policies and priorities, particularly educational policy, to determine how limited funding and energy should be distributed among competing agencies and institutions.

These were practical considerations, and we tried to identify what were the relevant factors; not harbouring any illusions about whether anything we said would make any impact, but thinking that it was important to put our ideas on record. But we were also concerned with the more theoretical issue of the underlying relationship between language and society – the interaction between linguistic and social processes and systems. Not long before I joined the group, there had been a heated controversy about linguistics in the Soviet Union, with articles by linguists on both sides of the argument appearing in supplements to the national newspaper Pravda over a period of about ten weeks. On one side were Meščaninov and his colleagues, the 'Marrists', who validated themselves as successors to the late N. Ya. Marr; Marr had rejected some of the accepted tenets of comparative historical linguistics, such as that sound change inevitably leads to more and more divergence among daughter languages, and argued for a complementary principle of convergence, introducing some rather questionable 'sound laws' of his own. Meščaninov put forward the theory that language was part of the superstructure that evolved on top of the economic base of society, and so changed as the social structure changed, along with changes in the mode of production.[6] On the other side were the mainstream of comparative historical linguists, who rejected the Marrists' rewriting of linguistic history and their claim to be the sole purveyors of a truly marxist theory of language.[7]

One of the leading spokesmen for the second, traditional viewpoint was the Georgian linguist Chikobava, and it was said that he was the one who persuaded Stalin to intervene, and perhaps contributed largely to the text of his intervention. At all events Stalin did join in, with a sarcastic denunciation of the Marrists, and that put an end to the controversy.[8] The dispute did not seem to have brought us any nearer to a specifically marxist account of language. But a large amount of serious descriptive linguistic work was going on in the Soviet Union at this time, without any reference to the controversy; and that was increasing the total store of knowledge about language, even if – or perhaps because – it was not designed to promote a specially privileged variety of linguistic science.

A year or two after this, Sidney Allen, a specialist in Indian languages at the School of Oriental and African Studies, published an article entitled 'Relationship in comparative linguistics', in which he argued against a belief in the reality of reconstructed ancestral languages and challenged some of the basic assumptions that underpinned comparative philology.[9] We discussed this at some length in relation to the theoretical position being expounded by J. R. Firth. I felt that Allen was making some valid points, although perhaps in a rather polemical fashion, about the nature and use of linguistic evidence, whereas Jeff Ellis considered that his argument was directly opposed to a marxist way of thinking; this led to some very interesting discussions which among other things forced me to make explicit the reasons why the Firthian model, as I had been trying to adapt it in my Ph.D. thesis, seemed to me essentially marxist in its orientation.

So how far did the motif of marxism persist, and has it had any continuing relevance to my professional work? To the extent that this is simply a matter of labelling, then if the significance of calling something 'marxist' has been largely forgotten, it has no relevance at all. But if there is still any interest in what a marxist approach implies, then it is perhaps worth saying that I think that this motif has continued to inform my linguistic work, both in general and in certain specific aspects. At a very general level, I have always thought of linguistic theory as something to be applied, to real problems either in research or in some domain of practice; eventually I came up with the term 'appliable' linguistics to encapsulate this preoccupation with a theory as a mode of action that is based on understanding. It is of course not specifically marxist, except perhaps in the notion that there are cycles of mutual reinforcement between practice and theory: theory improves the effectiveness of practice, and practice contributes to the ongoing refinement of theory.

I am a slow worker, and a slow thinker; so whatever I am engaged in is likely to take me rather a long time. After six or seven years of fairly active involvement in the work of the party, during the first half of which I was writing my thesis and during the second half designing and teaching a course in modern Chinese (up to then Chinese at Cambridge had been limited to classical Chinese studies), I decided that I couldn't do both. Either I could be a teacher and researcher, or I could be a political worker; it had to be one or the other. I enjoyed teaching, and thought that I was reasonably good at it (after all, both my parents had been teachers), whereas I knew my abilities as a party activist were extremely limited; so the decision was made for me almost before I had faced up to it. But the actual transition was more gradual, because I hadn't changed my mind on the underlying issues. We all had to recognize that the first attempt at designing a socialist society was failing – somewhat later, after following the progress of 'applied linguistics' in foreign language teaching, I was able to formulate a historical principle, the law of the failed first try, or FFT; this law states that whenever a human agency intervenes by design in a process which has hitherto taken place naturally, the first attempt always fails. But this is not a sufficient reason for giving up on the whole enterprise. Half a century later, I still feel the same, though perhaps with rather a greater sense of urgency.

I hoped that what I was trying to achieve as a linguist might make some contribution to improving the human condition, however minuscule and oblique. This is what I meant by calling the theory 'appliable'.[10] The term is less specific than 'applicable', which denotes applicable to some specific task, and therefore less immediate, and more indirect; its relevance is less obvious, but more long term. But other than this feature of being appliable, what other aspect of the theory might be considered as marxist? I think the answer lies in the underlying notion of functionality, which has been present in my thinking in three distinct manifestations: functional variation, functional grammar and metafunction.[11] Functional variation is what our group, following Jean Ure's suggestion, called 'register'[12]: the way that a language varies, on the content plane, and sometimes also on the plane of expression, according to the situational context – who is doing what, with whom, when, where and why. This notion was made explicit in Firth's category of 'restricted languages'; we had in fact considered using this term, but we thought it too much emphasized the restriction: some registers are in effect closed, so that you cannot extend their meaning potential beyond a specified inventory, but most registers are open-ended. A typical register is characterized by its pattern of relative frequencies, its statistical profile, rather than by absolute limitations on what is possible. But the general point being made here is that a language is regarded as being a functionally variable system.

A functional grammar is one in which functional labelling, with elements such as Subject, Actor, Process, Beneficiary, Theme and so on, takes precedence over labelling in terms of classes, like verb, noun, adverb or noun phrase. This locates grammatical structure in its place within the realizational cycle, by relating structure to system (e.g. in English, a declarative clause realized by Subject preceding Finite); it enables us to show that one occurrence of a class may have multiple functions (e.g. a nominal group as simultaneously Subject, Actor and Theme), and that the same function may be realized by different classes (e.g. Beneficiary either by prepositional phrase or by nominal group); and its meaning is defined by the configurations in which it occurs (e.g. Medium by its occurrence in the configuration Process • Medium • Agent). But the crux of this functionality lies in what it is that is taken as explanation. In a functional grammar, explaining something means explaining it in functional terms;

for example, the fact that in English, unlike most other languages, indicative clauses typically require a Subject is related to the fact that the sequence of Subject • Finite is discursively significant: it distinguishes a yes / no question from a statement ('That was John.' / 'Was that John?'), and you can't put two things in sequence if one of them happens to be missing. Of course, other features are also implicated; such explanations are too ramified to expound within one move. They are not just isolated pairings of cause-&-effect, but rather fragments of a more general pattern in which a number of grammatical features are involved.

Most far-reaching of all aspects of functionality is the phenomenon that I called 'metafunction', with apologies offered for the Graeco-Latin hybrid. This encapsulates the principle that language evolved, along with the human species, at a particular moment in space-time and in a particular set of historical conditions, and its organization reflects the eco-social context of its evolution. On the one hand, language functioned to construe the human experience, to constitute the 'reality' with which human beings were confronted and of which they themselves formed a part. I referred to this as the 'ideational' metafunction (borrowing the term from Freud). On the other hand, language functioned to enact human relationships, those of an inherently social species, and in this way to establish and maintain a coherent social order. I referred to this as the 'interpersonal' metafunction, meaning the combination of interactional and personal. But both these, in turn, depend on achieving modes of discourse which cohere in themselves and with the context; and this made further demands on the way language functioned as the essential meaning-making resource. I called this the 'textual' metafunction. These three functional origins are clearly recognizable in the way a language works, when its lexicogrammar and semantics are represented in systemic functional terms.

It seems to me that this overall conceptualization of language, which had been developing slowly in my own thinking across several decades, is essentially – though not aggressively – marxist in its orientation. If I never proclaimed this out loud, this was because it would be too much open to misunderstanding: there are too many different ideas about what 'marxist' means, and most people nowadays wouldn't think it was worth discussing. One attribute of my ideas that is at least compatible with a marxist ideology is the way they have always developed in conversation with other people, often as a by-product of my activities as a teacher; I have tried to acknowledge those who have been part of this enterprise, though I am conscious of having done so only very inadequately. It is impossible to track the provenance of scientific ideas, and with our modernist ways of thinking we attach too much importance to the individual anyway. It was my privilege to encounter so many congenial and thoughtful colleagues.

Notes

1. W. S. Allen (1953), 'Relationship in comparative linguistics', *Transactions of the Philological Society*.
2. J. Ellis and R. Davies (1951), 'The Soviet linguistics controversy', *Soviet Studies*, University of Glasgow.
3. J. Ellis and J. Ure (1974), 'Register in descriptive linguistics and linguistic sociology', *International Journal of Sociolinguistics*.
4. J. R. Firth (1957a), *Papers in Linguistics 1934–1951*. Oxford: Blackwell.
5. M. A. K. Halliday ([1990] 2003), 'New ways of meaning: a challenge to applied linguistics', *Greek Journal of Applied Linguistics*, 6. Reprinted in Jonathan J. Webster (ed.) *The Collected Works of M.A.K. Halliday*, vol. 3, *On Language and Linguistics*. London and New York: Bloomsbury Academics, pp. 139–74.
6. Halliday.
7. M. A. K. Halliday (2008a), 'Working with meaning: towards an appliable linguistics', Webster (ed.) *Meaning in Context*. London and New York: Continuum.
8. E. Hobsbawm (2011), *How to Change the World: Tales of Marx and Marxism.* Yale University Press.
9. G. Meščaninov Glagol [The verb] or Myšlenie i Yazik [Thought and Language].
10. J. Needham (1985), *The Shorter 'Science and Civilisation in China'*, Cambridge: Cambridge University Press.
11. E. Pollock (2006), *Stalin and the Soviet Science Wars*. Princeton University Press.
12. L. Wang ([1947] 1971), *Zhongguo Yufa Lilun* [Theory of Chinese Grammar]. Shanghai: Commercial Press.

6 Systemic Functional Linguistics: Halliday and the Evolution of a Social Semiotic*

Ruqaiya Hasan

Chapter Overview

---

1 Introduction: From the School to the War

Perhaps the first unplanned, invisible step towards systemic functional linguistics (SFL) was taken in 1942 when Michael Halliday left Rugby for London to attend the Joint Services Course in Oriental Languages at the School of Oriental and African Studies (SOAS).[1] This would be his first encounter with the Chinese language – specifically Mandarin – as he was going to be trained there to become proficient in that language to serve in the war effort. The intensive course he attended was inspired by the work of J. R. Firth at SOAS and was perhaps prepared under his guidance: Firth held the first and only Chair of General Linguistics in the whole of England then, and his popular book *The*

Tongues of Men had been published a few years back: its first paragraph opens as follows:

> Men are strange creatures. And they know it. They recognize the gulf which separates them from what they call the dumb animals, and on the strength of speech have exalted themselves towards Heaven. This speaking business has gone to their heads, and they have held all manner of beliefs about themselves and their words. They have believed themselves to have been created in the image of God and to have been given a voice in the world by God himself, the voice, the Word, Vak, being the source of wisdom, power, creation. (Firth, 1937: 1)

Hidden behind the seeming simplicity of these sentences are ideas which have the power to explain much that has been said and done in the name of linguistics even within our living memory. With hindsight, knowing the un-designed design of Halliday's academic trajectory, we might say today: what a coincidence! But can we really be sure that this was Halliday's first step towards linguistics? After all, the other young men who joined the same course with him had had exactly the same two unique experiences: there was no Chinese in the English schools then, so they too were encountering Chinese for the first time; and of course the one who had inspired the course design was reportedly the same socially aware linguist, namely, Firth..

That sobering thought might return one to Halliday's home background: one should perhaps take into account the fact that, between them, his parents had provided him with a model for interest in the social and the intellectual. His mother, a lively extrovert and deeply interested in how people lived their lives, a feminist before the feminist movement, and a believer in the equality of the human race, had been quite active in politics as a university student. Equally active out of the university, she loved her job as the teacher of French. Forced by regulations to quit that job when she got married, she found part-time work in education, and played an active part in politics, standing as a Liberal candidate at the Leeds City Council elections. His father, a thoughtful and quiet man, the Senior Master and later Head of a Grammar School in his home town in Yorkshire, had taken a deep interest in dialect studies: after retirement he became involved in the English Dialect Survey as the editor of the volumes on the Northern Counties; the survey was located at Leeds University under the directorship of Professor Harold Orton. Wilfrid Halliday's interest in dialect was not a post-retirement 'hobby': after his return from the First World War, he became an active member of The Yorkshire Dialect Society, and remained so throughout his life, holding office in various capacities in the Society and contributing to its Transactions. These experiences were not very common: they could have oriented the young Michael Halliday towards linguistics, towards social awareness about language, from an early age. But who can say for certain?

The point I am making is that reading cause-and-effect in individual and/or communal lives after they have become biography and history is one thing, and knowing that *that* history is actually happening and tending in *that* particular direction, is quite another. This explains the choice of the word 'evolution' in my title. In this, the last chapter of Part II of this volume, I hope to present my view of 'the evolution of a social semiotic', which is known as systemic functional linguistics and has been associated with Halliday as its primary energizer. What I am able to tell is not 'the truth and nothing but the truth': rather, it is a reading of something that has come into being by the repeated timely conjunctions of a number of 'naturally occurring' events. The effort will be to draw attention to continuities – how a chance happening turned later into a deliberate choice, how the effects of that choice penetrated moves in the evolution of a social semiotic theory, hardly any of the moves arriving as the last word, perfect in its formation. I will begin this journey with the apparently fanciful opening claim about the momentous nature of Halliday's journey from Rugby, where he was being brought up on Virgil and Homer, on conjugations and declensions, to a course designed by expert scholars for teaching modern spoken Chinese. In the perspective, adopterd here, the most important thing that happened – important to tracing why SFL is as it is – was implicit neither in the nature of 'modern', 'spoken' or 'Chinese' nor in the new ways of teaching and learning a foreign language: I doubt if Halliday paid more attention to these facts than an ordinary intelligent observer. Of at least equal importance was the friendship that developed between Michael Halliday and one of his fellow students, John Chinnery, a highly intelligent and thoughtful person who was already well aware of social and political issues. Though perhaps not easily recognizable in the earliest documents (Halliday, [1959] 2005, [1961] 2002) which lead up to SFL, the trace of their many conversations soon begins to appear clearly in the motif of 'language as social semiotic', which became prominent in the second half of the 1960s, and has developed in strength along with the theory. But of course many other things were also happening.

In interweaving those other events, happenings and opportunities that finally brought Halliday to linguistics I will need to move back and forth in real time, while hinting at the continuities between his experience of living in two different continents 'in interesting times', and drawing attention to occasions leading to the emergence of ideas about language which would finally lead him into linguistics. These ideas could not have been anywhere on the horizon for Halliday as he devoted himself to learning Chinese, while enjoying the company of his fellow students and discovering a London which still retained its charm though under attack and somewhat frayed by the long struggle to win a war that just could not be lost.

2 Enter Action with Words: From Language towards Linguistics

Halliday was being taught Chinese for a purpose. At the completion of the course, mid-1943 saw him in British India (as it then was) assigned to a post in an Intelligence Unit in Calcutta. This would involve collecting information coming from and going to China, particularly résumés of news items and other important documents for use by people who did not know Chinese. Some effort must have been made to cultivate the ability to focus on the central issues relevant to the task in hand, even though the last decision and assessment of the information worth forwarding to the United Kingdom rested with his superiors. This was an opportunity to add to what the course had taught him about China. Sometime in 1945, Halliday was called back to London with three other classmates including John Chinnery to teach Chinese on the same Joint Services Unit for Language Training which had prepared them for action just about 18 months earlier: he would be affiliated with SOAS for this service. Landing in the United Kingdom on VE day in 1945, he found that his task in London was to teach Chinese to services personnel, some of them were much higher in rank than he was himself.[2] This experience could have hardly left him untouched; he must have wondered – even if not systematically, not with a sustained effort at analysis, but at least in a general way – about the nature of Chinese language, its meanings, its grammar, its sounds and its writing, perhaps comparing them with English, which was the mother tongue of the learners. As he put it in an interview *With Ruqaiya Hasan, Gunther Kress and J.R. Martin* 'The first two years I was teaching Chinese. So the problems first arose in that and again I doubt whether I could have formulated them terribly clearly except for the need simply to understand the grammar and the structures of the language that I was teaching' (Martin, 2013a: 97). So while it did focus his attention towards the Chinese language, this was still just a prelude to linguistics. Talking of that course to the same interviewers, Halliday himself had said '. . . I was becoming aware that something like linguistics existed and that there was a rather good department of linguistics just down the street' (Martin, 2013a: 97); he had heard Firth's name but not met him.

Two years later, at the end of his wartime service, instead of looking to join a degree course at one of the prestigious Universities in United Kingdom, Halliday was heading over to China. He had been offered a junior post at Peking University where he would himself be enrolled in some undergraduate courses, preparing himself as an external candidate towards a Bachelor of Arts degree from London university, while teaching English to Chinese learners at the University. This teaching of a second language was different from the one he had done at SOAS: the learners were young, and their teacher was the native but naïve speaker of the language that he was teaching. But never having taught that language, this experience must have been remarkable: did he feel 'the need simply to understand the grammar and the structures of the language' that he was teaching, as he had done at SOAS in teaching Chinese to mature learners?

At the end of the academic year 1948, having sat the exams for the degree from London, he took off to have some authentic experience of life in China. A job as a journalist became available with the Chinese Industrial Cooperatives, courtesy of an acquaintance, Peter Townsend. Since the end of Manchu dynasty in 1911, there had been decades of instability in China, culminating in the Japanese invasion of 1933–45. The Japanese were now defeated, but Chiang Kai-Shek, the leader of the Nationalist Party and president of the country, seemed more interested in winning the war against the Chinese Communist Party led by Mao Zedong than in improving the conditions of living for the ordinary man. The last stage of this civil war was being fought between them as in 1948 Halliday travelled in a China ravaged by the long and hostile Japanese occupation and by the ensuing neglect and unrest in the country: the situation, to put it mildly, was unstable. The fabric of trade and commerce had been torn apart, the ordinary citizen was grappling with inflation, that lapped up the value of currency even as it changed hands in ordinary buying and selling; all around was evidence of hardship and poverty for the ordinary persons. These memories were still with Halliday when in the later 1980s we attended a conference in Suzhou: 'this is so different from when I was here last', he remarked, 'in 1948, you couldn't have walked in the streets without plunging your shoes into garbage.' The Co-ops he was working for in 1948 had been set up in western China in areas that had not been occupied by the Japanese. A friendly initiative by an international group, led by a New Zealander, and assisted by some Australian and British businessmen, had financed the venture; but with all the unrest around, the number of enterprises at this time had shrunk to around 400 from a healthy 4,000 some time back. Halliday's work was to travel from one branch to another, interviewing people working in the cooperatives with a view to preparing reports on their activities, to inform its benefactors, and encourage them to continue the funding.

It was at one of these locations that a letter from London University caught up with him. He had done well at his BA (Hons) exam and a scholarship awaited him to allow the pursuit of post-graduate studies; he must return immediately to Peking. Up to this point Halliday had not thought about a career; the job with the cooperative was much too interesting. He describes his reactions to the letter as follows:

The conditions were that I could spend two years in China studying and then have to go back to England to do a higher degree. And I thought 'well do I do this?' I thought that they probably won't ask me again if I turn it down, so I took it. And that meant getting back to Peking. This was difficult because I was way up in a little village miles outside any city in northwest China. I finally found a bus and it took me about five days to get to Lanzhou. Then I found an aeroplane and it got me back to Peking just before the communists occupied the airport; otherwise I would never have got back in. (Martin, 2013a: 100)

Halliday was enrolling for a postgraduate degree at Peking University, but even up to this moment without a well thought out plan about what he wished to do. When it came to the actual enrolment, a decision had to be made. To do postgraduate in Chinese studies he had to be more specific – what will he choose to specialize in: language or literature? This was where the experience of the last five years spoke the words to him: Halliday chose to do language studies, not literature.

The relevant trajectory of Halliday's life since the 1942 journey to London had so far been something like the above play of chance and choice: he himself described the underlying design of the process of natural learning by referring to another such feat of natural learning as *Three aspects of children's language development: learning language, learning through language, learning about language* ([1980] 2004). And of course as he would also alert us in one of his papers written around the late 1970s (Halliday, [1978] 2007), learning a second language is not exactly like learning a first language: there were some differences. For the last five years, Chinese had been a focal interest in his life: first, learning a second language, then learning through that language about the country of that language – first on the Services course, and then in Calcutta and then even more by living in China – and finally 'opting freely' to learn about the language – to find out about its grammar and structures. The events after this are well chronicled: Halliday spent the first year of his postgraduate studies working largely with the historical linguist Luo Changpei in Peking. Recognizing Halliday's interest in modern spoken Chinese, the professor advised him to go and work with Professor Wang Li, who turned out to be miles away in Guangzhou at Sun Yat-Sen University. The first year had been spent looking into the historical aspects of Sino-Tibetan languages; 1949–50 would bring him to the modern linguistics under Wang Li's supervision; with abilities to work as a good listener, Halliday worked on the current dialect survey under the supervision of Wang Li, beginning at last to learn also about 'the grammar and structures' of the language.

The second year of his Chinese studies completed at Sun Yat-Sen University, Halliday needed to return to England in 1950. The valuable influence of these years of education in China is described in scholarly detail elsewhere (Peng, Chapter 3, this volume). One might be tempted to claim with hindsight that everything in Halliday's life had led up to this moment, but it is perhaps now as he returns to London, having had a favourable experience of linguistics and hoping to continue his work on the Chinese dialect survey as the focus of his doctoral research, that we can be certain about the direction his career was moving in. At his point, one might ask: coming out of Marxist China, was Halliday a Marxist now? To this, I would say both 'yes' and 'no': if being a Marxist means registering with the Communist Party or joining in events designed specifically by a Marxist institution, then the answer is 'no, in that sense Halliday was not a Marxist as he left Communist China'. If, however, one asks about his considered ideas about the role of Marxism in society particularly in relation to the life of ordinary citizens, then the answer would be 'yes! he was a Marxist'. In view of what he had witnessed as ordinary life in China, what the Communist Party was attempting to achieve must have seemed miles better than anything done by anyone before for the man in the street. But then neither individual nor communal histories are fully inscribed at the time when the first steps are taken.

3 Apprenticeship in Linguistics: Halliday in London/Cambridge

Halliday was under the impression that he was returning to a job combined with the pursuit of a doctoral research: this was indicated by the terms of his scholarship, and there was no reason to imagine that all this would be done anywhere else than at SOAS; after all it was *the* institution for oriental studies in London, and Halliday had been associated with it during the war years, as also afterwards (see above, and also Martin, 2013a: 95ff.). SOAS was his *alma mater*, so on arrival he reported there, and began to settle down. For the first time in his life he would actually meet J. R. Firth, the linguist to have the deepest influence on his future career as a linguist. All seemed set, and he had begun attending seminars at SOAS, looking forward to starting his research on some Chinese dialect, for which he had brought the data from China. But there would be another twist: the Korean war had just begun, and it was the McCarthy era in the United States whose tolerance of communism has never been anything but low. Here was Halliday freshly returned from a communist country, neighbour to Korea, settling down in SOAS, where, as already evident, high ranking officers in the Services could be sent for training; inevitably they would encounter the likes of Halliday. The government in the United Kingdom was under obligation to the United States for helping them in the war against Hitler. Clearly, contamination by communism in high places could not be tolerated. Halliday was interviewed; on being questioned, he stated that he was not a member of the Communist Party, but refused to promise he would never join it, which meant he had to leave SOAS. With typical quiet efficiency, everything was smoothly and quickly organized: Halliday was to go to Cambridge – which had already refused to witch-hunt its students or staff on grounds of their religious or political beliefs.

The move from SOAS to Cambridge was a serious blow to Halliday: he had set his heart on researching modern Chinese dialects for his postgraduate degree, but Cambridge only recognized classical Chinese and did not have anyone on the staff who could supervise doctoral research on modern spoken Chinese! There was no choice for Halliday but to leave SOAS, where he could have worked in the department of Chinese studies while being supervised by Firth. This was not to be; so Halliday went to Cambridge. But perhaps the first thing he did on arrival was to become a member of the University branch of the Communist Party. This I suspect was less because he wanted to be recognized as a Marxist, but more to be viewed as an independent agent not cowed by draconian rules motivated by paranoia. His supervisor in Cambridge, Gustav Haloun, professor of classical Chinese, was a well-known scholar. The dialect studies had to be abandoned; Professor Haloun helped Halliday choose an appropriate text, The Chinese 'Secret History of the Mongols', which would become a significant name for anyone choosing to become familiar with Halliday's systemic functional linguistics. But there would be another unforeseen change: at the end of that year, before the research had got very far, Professor Haloun died. So on Halliday's request, Firth accepted to act externally as his supervisor, and Halliday had Firth's permission to attend his lectures/seminars.

Some time soon after this, a British linguist Jeff Ellis sought Halliday out: he was working on a comparative analysis of temporal categories in some languages of the world, including Chinese. Ellis did not know Chinese, but the data he had brought with him proved extremely interesting. Working on this became the basis of a close friendship between them which lasted until Jeff Ellis died in the late 1980s. Halliday and Ellis, working together on the Chinese data, came to the conclusion that this analysis by itself would provide enough material for a scholarly article. They completed that work in 1951, but for 'various reasons' it did not get published until much later (Halliday and Ellis, [1951] 2005: 177–208). The first introduction to Chinese language in the early 1940s had created a lasting friendship that had led Michael into conversations about sociopolitical issues; this new friendship with Ellis was to bring his linguistics closer to Marxist thoughts particularly in relation to language and human action: for Marx, 'human' had meant social. Jeff Ellis and Jean Ure were also active members of the Communist Party. With some other like-minded friends, Jeff had initiated what came to be known as the Linguistics Group of the Communist Party: the group met regularly, sometimes to discuss linguistics, on other occasions to listen to invited scholars who had specialized in various languages, or in areas related to language and to Marxist studies. How these events influenced Michael Halliday's own ideas about language and linguistics will be found elsewhere in this volume in Halliday's own words (Halliday, Chapter 5, this volume).

It is interesting to recall that two somewhat distinct currents were running side by side in this early period: there was this issue of exploring 'Marxist linguistics', and along with this preoccupation ran Firth's supervision of

Halliday's doctoral thesis. Although Firth's linguistics is not incompatible with Marxist ideas, it cannot be said that Firth (1957a, 1968) was sympathetic to Marx; but he was a good linguist: thus not bound by the conventional ideas about language. Long before 'embodiment' became a fashionable term, Firth already thought of language as embodied in its speakers; and a case could be made that he would be happy with Vygotsky's idea of internalization and voluntary recall of sociogenetically mediated knowledge.[3] I do not recall clearly if Firth ever talked about the system and process of language in quite the way that Hjelmslev did, but for him the 'process' of language was nothing less than language playing integral part in the living of life (Firth, 1957a, 1968).[4] In an age when the study of meaning still lingered in its quasi 'philological' stage (Bréal, [1897] 1900), Firth, like that other great linguist, Whorf (1956) would elevate meaning as 'the essence of linguistics', and like Whorf, he too would refuse to draw strong boundaries between culture and language. Although radically modified and renewed, a great deal of Firthian linguistics has found a place in the architecture of Halliday's systemic functional linguistics (Butt, 2001; Hasan, Matthiessen and Webster, 2005, 2007): Halliday's views on language, lexicogrammar, phonology and on his 'science of meaning' are presented in other chapters of this volume (e.g. Butt, Chapter 2; Matthiessen, Chapters 7 and 8; Martin, Chapter 10; and Smith and Greaves, Chapter 11, all in this volume). From among the many themes of Firthian linguistics that in one form or another constitute part of the architecture of SFL, I pull out a couple here because they resonated particularly well with Halliday's ideas around this time about (1) giving value to the different varieties of language irrespective of their standing in bourgeois societies, and in bourgeois scholarship; and (2) doing linguistics as a form of social action that might bring a better conceptualization of the relations of individuals to their culture.

The first of these Firthian themes was his forceful denial of 'unity' as a feature of human language:

> Unity is the last concept that should be applied to language. Unity of language is the most fugitive of all unities, whether it be historical, geographical, national, or personal. There is no such thing as *une langue une* and there never has been. (*The technique of semantics*, Firth, 1957a: 29)

Published first in the *Transactions of the Philological Society 1935*, this remark came exactly two decades *after* Saussure's *Cours de Linguistique Générale* (1959) and three decades *before* Chomsky's *Aspects of the Theory of Syntax* (1965): for quite different reasons, both these scholars wanted to make invariant/ homogeneous language the focus of linguistics proper. Time has proved both wrong. Halliday would take Firth's view and in a characteristic manner, he would interpret Firth's remark at a higher level of abstraction – as the theoretical concept of 'inherent variation in language' (more in Section 6 below).

The second Firthian theme, that Halliday transformed similarly, was that of context. A couple of years before Halliday was born, Malinowski (1923) had introduced his much to be misinterpreted concept of 'context of situation' (for some discussion of these misinterpretations, see Hasan, 1985b). Malinowski was primarily an anthropologist; the main problem that concerned him was that of translation between remarkably distinct languages that belonged to two remarkably distinct cultures, namely European and Kiriwinian. Closely related to this problem of how culturally alien meanings could be made intelligible across this cultural gulf was another equally fundamental question, highly relevant to any linguistics that sees itself as 'a quest for meaning' as did Firth's: taking on board Saussure's ideas about language as a semiological system, Malinowski asked how the Saussurean theory would explain the entry of a new learner, such as the neonate, into this hermetically sealed system of meaning which is produced by the 'relations of relations of sign . . .'? (Hasan, 1985b) Malinowski answered his own questions by postulating 'context of situation' as the mediator of meaning in all kinds of linguistic interaction: language in use occurs in time and space, and the properties of that space and time bear a systematic relation to what is said and meant (Halliday and Hasan, 1985b). Seen thus, the context of situation is a resource which, given certain conditions, will enable the infant to enter the meaning system of any first language: three essential ingredients are required in this context of situation, (i) what is going on in the situation, which includes (ii) the speakers' bodily actions and the interactants' mutual relations, and (iii) at least one adult interactant belonging to the child's culture and speaking the child's mother tongue. Firth immediately grasped the value of Malinowski's context of situation as relevant to the study of language as a whole: in fact, he presented the concept as capable of explaining the entire makeup of language; every scholar wishing to study language from the phonetician to the lexicographer could get all the information they needed by focusing on 'context' at every stratum (1957a: 27). Years later Halliday would develop the Firthian concept of context so as to make it far more amenable to the study of what Firth called 'language event', akin to Halliday's 'language in action'(Section 6); he would go on to build a powerful theory which claimed that learning a language is learning how to mean (for some details, see Torr, Chapter 9, this volume); and later still in one simple move of theorization Halliday ([1991] 2007) would resolve the Saussurean langue-parole paradox, by postulating a realizational relation between language and culture as well as between context and text; their mutual relations were further strengthened with context as instantiating culture just as text instantiated language (Hasan, 2009).

With Firth supervising Halliday's research, he enjoyed nearly all the benefits of actually being at SOAS. Interaction with many brilliant scholars such as

W. S. Allen, Eugenie Henderson, R. H. Robins, Eileen Whitley and others made up for the absence of discourse on linguistics in Cambridge, which at that time did not have a department of linguistics. The nearest he would come to the study of language in Cambridge was his involvement with the machine translation project that developed into the Cambridge Language Research Unit under the directorship of Margaret Masterman: he would be drawn here to think about the problems of translation perhaps for the first time from a linguistic perspective, as well as coming in contact with computational linguistics. After submitting his thesis in 1954, Halliday took up the teaching of Chinese: this would be the first Modern Spoken Chinese course ever introduced or taught at Cambridge; that meant he would be the one to prepare the course design and the teaching materials. The course was intended for students specializing in Chinese; but Halliday also prepared and taught a special course for the interested researchers or staff members. Auditing this course was one remarkable scholar and polymath, A. F. Parker-Rhodes, who would some decades later author a book, with the title *Inferential Semantics* (1978), 'that presents a new theory on the structure of meaning, based on logical and mathematical analysis of what is accomplished in a successful speech act'. In this study Parker-Rhodes had used some of Halliday's later work on grammar and intonation. In presenting the Parker-Rhodes Memorial lecture, Yorick Wilks described Parker-Rhodes as a great scholar and 'an original thinker in information retrieval, quantum mechanics and computational linguistics'. There were other attractions as well at Cambridge: as the secretary of the local Britain China Friendship Association, Halliday had the experience of working closely with the great Sinologist Joseph Needham, who was then the president of that association. Through the Communist Party he also met Eric Hobsbawm, a remarkable historian. He met other like-minded scholars, many actively and consciously attempting to build in a perspective in their work that was clearly inspired by Marxism.

In 1958 Halliday was offered a position at the University of Edinburgh as a lecturer in Linguistics. Over this period, as a member of the Communist Party Linguistics Group, he had become seriously committed to the project of creating a Marxist linguistics, which was substantially different from what had been put forward as Soviet Linguistics in the recent controversy in Pravda (Ellis and Davies, 1951). But at the same time he found himself being increasingly drawn to understanding how language works as an 'agency' in the social processes. Gone was that insouciant attitude with which he had chosen to do 'Language studies' rather than 'Literature studies' at Peking University in 1948. Wang Li and Firth had between them succeeded in showing him how central language was to human social existence. He found that actively participating in both politics and linguistics would be impossible, at least for him, and this is where the concept of doing linguistics from the perspective of socially aware action seemed the best choice: there is an interesting discussion on this topic in Martin

(2013a: 117 ff.). Scholars have long suggested that serious change in societies is actually equal to bringing change in the community's ways of thinking, saying and doing: the change that is produced in individuals via semiotic mediation has a greater degree of permanence than that imposed by official 'revolutionary activity'. But by the same token, change via semiotic mediation demands a comparatively much longer period of continuous and complex social action. So the choice facing Halliday at that point was 'do something "revolutionary" here and now and in all likelihood see a quick result that would most probably not last long' or 'contribute towards an understanding of doing something via a battery of complex social semiotic activities and wait for its effect to "sink into the communal mind" perhaps some generations later but most probably lasting a good deal longer'.[5] Before leaving Cambridge to join Edinburgh in 1958 was the obvious moment for Halliday to make this choice: he decided he would not actively enlist himself in a branch of the Party in Edinburgh; and the Cambridge membership would obviously lapse. This final choice determined the focus of intellectual activities that would preoccupy Halliday for a long time to come. But when we ask if there had been a definite move yet towards the social semiotic turn in Halliday's linguistics, the answer would depend on how one interprets 'towards' in 'towards language as a social semiotic'. It is one thing to recognize that language is active in the community's life; it is quite another to demonstrate that language is inherently a social semiotic.

4 Edinburgh 1958–63: Learning Linguistics, Teaching Linguistics

Halliday's first teaching experience (1945–7) had been to teach selected adult learners a foreign language, which had been foreign to him as well, but just 'mastered' a couple of years back (1942–3). However, he had started the teaching with a given well-organized course – the very one he had himself experienced as a learner. His next assignment at Peking University (1947) had also been to teach adult learners a foreign language; but this time the language was his own mother tongue and the learners were native speakers of Chinese, quite new to English. There would of course be a University outline for the course content and assessment; and these would have to be observed. In Cambridge, where he again had to teach a foreign language, modern spoken Chinese, to adult learners at the University, he had to design the course from a clean slate. So far he had had varied experience of teaching a foreign language, mostly Chinese; but he had not taught 'about language' in a formal sense ever before.

Now, specialized in linguistics with regular experience of interaction with top-ranking linguists at SOAS and with mathematical and computational thinkers at the Cambridge Language Research Unit, quite apart from his experience of discourse on the social aspects of language in the Communist Linguistics

Group, the challenges he faced would be quite different in Edinburgh. Here, his job would be to teach 'about language' in a formal set-up, for the first time since linguistics courses were being formally introduced at the University. This naturally involved designing linguistics courses for undergraduate and graduate levels to be taught at the Department of English Language (which would later become Department of English language and General Linguistics). In addition, he would also teach a postgraduate Diploma course on English grammar to mainly foreign students in the School of Applied Linguistics. He would also be expected to supervise research undertaken by the Diploma, MA (Hons), and Doctoral candidates. This was an exciting challenge; and around him were exciting colleagues. Angus McIntosh, professor and head of the department, was a specialist in medieval English dialectology; James Thorne had just joined the department and Robert Dixon would do so a couple of years later, followed by Jeff Ellis. Nearby was Ian Catford, Director of the School of Applied Linguistics and a formidable expert in phonetics and phonology. Next door to Applied Linguistic was Trevor Hill, then working with the Survey of Scottish dialects – the originator of 'institutional linguistics'. David Abercrombie, Professor and Head of the Department of Phonetics, himself an erudite scholar and a fabulous lecturer, had collected in his department a number of experts including Peter Strevens, Peter Ladefoged, Betsy Uldall, Bill Jones and others. The doctoral candidates ready to start work with Halliday were Hannah Ulatowska, who would become a Professor at Austin (Texas), Braj Kachru, who would be Professor and Chair of Linguistics at Illinois (Urbana), internationally known for his work on World Englishes, Ayo Bambose, working on the Grammar of Yoruba, who would be Professor and Head of the Department of Linguistics at the University of Lagos, and John McH. Sinclair, to become a Professor and Head of the Department of English (Birmingham) and an international trail blazer in Corpus Linguistics. The year before, in 1957–8, Firth had been a visiting scholar at the School of Applied Linguistics: the place was a-buzz with context, system, prosody and meaningful linguistics. To put it mildly, Halliday would not have much time to miss Cambridge. But I suspect he missed London all the same: for one thing, weather-wise Edinburgh was too cold for him, though the scene at the work place must have been hot with activity; those were the days for friendly competition in knowledge production and diffusion, not for making more money for the universities starved for funds by the official policies and systems.

Judging by its publication date, December 1961, in the journal called *WORD*, Halliday's *Categories of the Theory of Grammar* must have been written while he was designing and elaborating its contents in the courses he was teaching in the early Edinburgh years. *The Linguistic Sciences and Language Teaching* co-authored with Angus McIntosh and Peter Strevens, known to close colleagues as *SHAM*, must have been a work freshly started after Halliday's arrival in Edinburgh, but it must have been close to ready for submission to publishers near the end of 1961, because that is when I was given access to Chapter 4 of Part I: 'The users and uses of language'. I had arrived in mid-1960 to qualify for the Diploma in Applied Linguistics, with the intention of exploring the possibility of doing further research, and at the completion of that course had joined as a doctoral candidate to be supervised by Halliday and McIntosh. Both these documents were a clear declaration of independence from the rising empire of Chomsky's TG: Lyons (1969) was yet to have his *Structural Semantics* published before Chomsky's theories of linguistics would really take over.

Unaware of any of these intellectual currents in contemporary United Kingdom, I had arrived mid-1960 in Edinburgh with two problems more or less clearly formulated in my mind but with hardly any knowledge of what I needed to do to work towards a solution (Hasan, 2006: 29–43, 2011b). When I first discovered that knowing English was not sufficient for teaching it as it should be taught, I had made a serious attempt to read Bloomfield's *Language* in the British Council Library in Lahore. But without any background in language study as such, Bloomfield had not seemed easy to relate to either of my problems. As a postgraduate of English literature, I had read on the sublime, on the texture of prose, the threads of melody in poetry, and the craft of drama where the staging of the plot rose in a crescendo towards the dénouement: something about that teaching had made me love English literature and to guess at its potential for shaping human minds. But in the classroom where the undergrads were struggling between 'my father are . . .' and 'my father is . . .' or between 'he can be go . . .', and 'he is went . . .' and other such puzzles, it was clear I needed help and that help was not coming from learning about the language of literature. As for the problem in teaching literature (in whatever tongue), all I knew then was that society, text and evaluation go hand in hand; but how you stopped people from simply mouthing others' opinions remained a mystery.

Advised and enabled by the British Council to try a Diploma in Applied Linguistics at Edinburgh, I had arrived there but without even a suspicion of how linguistics and grammar were to help with either of my problems. The grammar books I had tried to use in teaching English to my students had certainly not inspired trust. With hindsight I now know what I was searching for: a quick and efficient way of telling my students about words and structures in terms of their 'default meaning', as well as those principles which would explain when and why the same words and structures could convey a different meaning, i.e., 'a conditioned meaning' (Hasan, 2011a: 336–79). But given this degree of naivety about language, the first couple of months at the new course in Edinburgh had been a little disappointing: what I could grasp was the history and psychology of language learning; what I did not understand at all was how the phonetic drills, ear training and the course on grammar taught by Halliday were going to be any help in teaching my students what they really needed.[6] In this frame of mind, reading Firth's Tongues of Men had seemed like a breath of fresh air, meaningful and comforting. Here there was at least some linguistics that could actually be understood; it could relate to things I knew a little about, like myths, like stories of how language began; and interspersed with this kind of discourse were things like how to make sense out of non-sense, and 'the elements of utterance' giving an intuitive understanding that a sound in language had an identity of its own when seen in comparison with another. The chapters on 'context of situation' and 'revue: 1937 and after' raised the hope that I could do something with this kind of learning. As part of the Diploma course assessment, I was required to do a 'pilot project' (today's equivalent of 'independent research'). I decided to do a partial linguistic analysis of Necessity's Child, a short story by Angus Wilson. With Catford's permission, I requested Michael Halliday, who was well known to have worked closely with Firth, to act as my supervisor. That research gave me hope (Hasan, 1967): first, I could see that grammar 'applied' in a particular way would help with how social life is re-construed by language and what that does in the structuring of the literary text; secondly, it was gratifying to find that my teachers approved of the finished piece; I did not realize then how kind they were being, but it certainly encouraged me to enrol for a doctoral research in the area of linguistic stylistics. It had, mercifully, not been clear to me then that to tackle the problem of teaching literature (to which, regretfully, I have never really returned), I would ideally have to interweave a deep understanding of the nature of four distinct domains of knowledge: society, language, art and the nature of aesthetic evaluation changeful across time and place. For the time being, it seemed that with what I was learning I would be able to say something worth saying about society and literary texts, using notions of cultural context, register, grammar and lexis (see Halliday, McIntosh and Strevens, 1964: 18; 'levels for linguistic description in tabular form'). This is how 'Chapter 4: *Users and uses of language*' became essential reading for me then, and even today it pays to go back to it to appreciate the length of the theoretical distance between Firthian monistic, polysystemic, contextual linguistics and Halliday's systemic functional linguistics. It seems to me that in a very true sense, the coming together of systems and functions is where Halliday's linguistics definitely took off in the direction of a social semiotic (dare I add, 'proper'?), which I believe is not contra Firth in spirit but which had definitely not been articulated *methodically* and *theoretically* in Firth's writings. Which is just a way of saying that Halliday et al. (1964) is, in spirit and in theory, still largely Firthian, even though in enumerating there the three dimensions of discourse, it takes the very first step that offers a qualitatively different opening. And this first step towards social semiotic was taken very much in the same way as was the step towards linguistics in choosing 'Chinese Language studies' as opposed to 'Chinese literature studies': neither was pre-planned but both were a manifestation of the 'orientation' towards language – ways of meaning, thinking, and saying are aspects of the struggle to externalize some experience; and it is this externalization that is needed to make the claim that the experience of living is what 'personalizes the brain', shaping it into the human 'mind' (Greenfield, 1977), at once unique and the same as others in our immediate community. Halliday would take the next steps towards a social semiotic approach over a long period of time, but not in Edinburgh: the majority of these steps would be taken at UCL – University College London – to which Halliday moved in 1963 as the Director of the Communication Centre in the Department of English. That things were moving in Halliday's linguistics is quite evident from his paper 'Class in relation to the axes of chain and choice in language' ([1963] 2002). This paper was written, presented and printed at least one year later than the completion of SHAM, which in manuscript form must have definitely left Halliday's table earlier than any initiation of the [1963] 2002 paper.

Throughout this chronicle, I have been deliberately avoiding ascribing 'cause-effect' to any singled out event, but in the case of . . . *the axes of chain and choice*, it seems to me Halliday began to take a much closer look into some issue which had hitherto been accepted perhaps too readily. Taking this piece of writing as a harbinger we will find many indications from now on of how, by exploring the resources of systemic description, Halliday would build-in 'context' as the test for the efficacy of language as a meaning potential. Although I suspect the choice of the word 'motivated' is somewhat unfortunate, here I would readily agree that going about the description of grammar systemically, i.e., paradigmatically, was a variety of 'motivated selection' in the evolution of Halliday's 'science of social semiotic' (Butt, Chapter 2; Matthiessen, Chapter 7, both this volume) – one whose 'motivations' we can appreciate actually only after the event. This path would lead him soon to recognize the roll of 'metafunctions' as an argument which would *suggest strongly* that language is suffused inherently with functionality; and it will become clear a little later that, in the last analysis, the secret of context-metafunction resonance lies in the inherently social nature of linguistic actions (Hasan, in press). But I am running way ahead of historical time and place: it will take Michael Halliday over a decade – most of it while attached to UCL – to arrive at this point; and it would take longer still to absorb its significance fully into the theory. I hope to describe some of these details in the sections below.

5 London 1963–71: From Systems and Functions to a Social Semiotic

Halliday arrived in London – not at once but 'gradually' – in the first half of 1963: he commuted for a few months as he still had some commitments to

Edinburgh but needed also to guide the moves in his new job in London. The Bloomsbury area was, as usual, throbbing with activity, and the intellectual scene in and around UCL was a source of excitement with many research projects in the social sciences. Within the college, less than 5 minutes away from Halliday's Communication Research Centre, was Randolph Quirk's Survey of English Usage, one of those 'data-based' research projects which, in defiance to the predominant 'data scorning' Transformational Generative theory, would pioneer the discipline of 'Corpus Studies'. Quirk's project attracted a number of scholars, some working with him such as Geoffrey Leech and Jan Svartvik, and others visiting such as Nelson Francis (Brown University) and Arthur Delbridge (Macquarie University). Not so close but still within reach were scholars such as Mary Douglas, the anthropologist at UCL, whose brilliant analysis of 'other religions, other cultures' (1966, 1975) would resonate with both Halliday's and Bernstein's thinking. Bernstein's Sociological Research Unit was just two Squares away from Halliday's Centre: and here some research projects would attract Halliday most, perhaps initially because they concerned language, such as those by Turner and Turner & Mohan. As scholars Bernstein and Halliday meet at the junction of two major social science boundaries – *Sociology, the science of society, and Linguistics, the science of language as the semiotic social;*[7] these two sciences, between them, have the power to unravel the underlying nature of the disciplines of *Politics and Economics;* together they could analyse the entire social universe. Both Basil Bernstein and Michael Halliday were committed to Marxism in a true sense and therefore deeply interested in each other's area of specialization, with a clear sense of its importance for their own work. A life-long friendship developed between them, and for nearly a decade with Halliday at UCL the two Research Centres would work very closely in harmony.

Having arrived at the Centre, which was metamorphosing into the Department of General Linguistics at UCL, Halliday himself had immediately set about exploring resources for setting up research projects under the aegis of the Communication Research Centre; and it is interesting to note what he chose as his foci (Halliday, 2014). In a deeper sense, the general name of anything one tries to *do* by way of making a difference to the social has to be 'pedagogy': Halliday went for varieties of both of what Bernstein would much later refer to as *official* and *private* pedagogic agencies (1973a, 1990). One of Halliday's research projects, funded by The Nuffield Foundation, was The Nuffield Programme in Linguistics and English Teaching, and its domain of action was official pedagogy, i.e., educational activities implemented through officially recognized and controlled institutions such as the schools, colleges and universities. Specifically this project aimed to explore the principled bases for teaching English as the mother tongue from KG right through to the Upper Secondary levels. The other project, funded by the Office of Scientific Technical Information

(OSTI), concerned a wider social spectrum from the official to 'private' in terms of Bernstein (2000): this project was a linguistic study of three scientific register varieties addressed to three distinct groups of addressees. The corpus of texts for this project was organized under the three Hallidayan parameters (i) field (ii) mode and (iii) tenor. The mode choice is constant as 'written' throughout the entire collected data, while the field and the tenor each had three variables; the field under study was either (1) physics, or (2) chemistry or (3) biology, while tenor could be either (1) popular, or (2) educational, or (3) specialized. This as Eirian Davies (2014) reminds, was the first research project to *formally* study registerial variation, and is perhaps the first instance of large-scale discourse analysis in the framework proposed by Halliday (Huddleston, Hudson, Winter and Henrici, 1968: mimeo). Both these projects needed descriptive categories in terms of which the research data could be interpreted/analysed: what does it mean to differentiate particular educational levels in terms of language already learned, and/or language yet to be taught? How would one teach and how test the efficacy of that teaching? What did the Kindergarten children know as they first toddled into their classroom? How do infants learn their mother tongue? Can classroom learning be seen as just a natural continuation of learning at home? Halliday's variety of Marxist linguistics was to be severely tested, as was also Bernstein's, since he was researching 'primary socialization' – to be known as 'local pedagogy' later – and seeking its genesis in human interaction among socially positioned speakers.

Between the research projects conducted at that moment under the directorship of Halliday and Bernstein was an impressive spectrum focused on language and learning in society; Halliday would much later capture its scope in his account of language development as consisting of 'learning language, learning through language, learning about language' ([1980] 2004). His Nuffield research was focused on both 'learning language and learning about language' but with an interesting perspective: this learning was not restricted to pupils only; the teachers across the entire range of the relevant educational levels were also to learn about language, and when it came to learning about language by the pupils, this learning-teaching discourse had to be modulated according to who the addressee was. What David Mackay (and his team) would use, and how, as the resource for 'learning language and learning about language' for his Primary (years 1–3) (Breakthrough to Literacy 1970) was different from what Ian Forsythe and Catherine Wood (Language and Communication 1977) or Peter Doughty (and his team) would use (Language in Use 1971). The project's aim was to ensure that all teachers learned about language before they were required to intervene in the learners' learning about language. The research project concerned with the activity mentioned as the middle one in Halliday's 1980 title, namely, 'learning through language' was the one that formed the heart of Bernstein's research projects. It is this learning – hidden and unselfconscious for both the learner and the teacher, and not foregrounded in any way by institutional 'paraphernalia' – that in the end was the most relevant to Bernstein's theory of codes.

Today, with hindsight, Bernstein's concept of code can be seen properly as part of the architecture of a sociological/cultural theory whose concern it is to provide an explanatory model of society. And within the architecture of this theory, the concept 'code' would be positioned at the most abstract level descriptive of human social existence. Seen dispassionately, this 'code theory' would have the task of accounting for cultural/social variation.[8] So, clearly, 'code theory' would go beyond the realm of language, embracing all forms of cultural existence and action – i.e., ways of being, thinking, doing and evaluating. To put it very simply, the theory's claim is that cultural systems are not invariant and that variation in their forms correlates with variation in the social subjects' material and social existence. In specifying the code-sensitive social/cultural variables, Bernstein foregrounded 'social class' as exerting the most powerful effect on a wide range of human behaviour; and although our own dominant cultural system, namely the capitalist one, could not possibly survive without the imbalance of social classes, the well-known fact about the genteel section of our society is its refusal to recognize 'hierarchy by class' as an undeniable fact. The attitude is based on the belief that a characteristic of our advanced progressive society/ culture is our respect for and observance of equality; that, being democratic, the culture in fact offers equal opportunity and equal freedom of choice to every member of the community. In my reading, Bernstein believed he had viable reasons for rejecting these suppositions, and as clearly evident from his work, he struggled to demonstrate that the maintenance of cultural variation based on class inequalities is in the last resort coercive: maintaining any privilege in this environment is logically equal to exercising irrational control. The title of four out of the five volumes of his writing include the words 'class', 'codes' and 'control'. Among the modalities of cultural transmission, the one that Bernstein had singled out, as the most significant and powerful, even before code theory had surfaced, was the modality of language (if for the simple reason that it was the most pervasive means of transmission): as early as 1958, he was already struggling with a classification of variant forms of language use (Bernstein, 1971a: chapters 1–3), *public language*, and '*formal language*' as a means of identifying the variety that enabled one to master the kind of discourse which would be known much later as 'disembedded language' (Donaldson, 1978). But it is clear that so far as actual language description was concerned, up to the mid-1960s, he was at sea: his observation of variation was certainly viable, but his efforts at viable recognition criteria were far from acceptable. As a Marxist, Halliday was sympathetic to Bernstein's general position, but of course the true nature of what Bernstein's project needed was not clarified even into the late 1960s. So right up to this stage Bernstein's sociological hypotheses offered linguistic criteria that would in actual fact be off the mark: Bernstein's theory of variation could not be handled easily by grammatical and/or lexical criteria: they needed to be connected to semantics. And usable semantics was yet to emerge in many linguistic models, including that of Halliday's.

I arrived from Leeds where I had been working on a Nuffield project which was closely collaborating with the French project CRÉDIF: I was in charge of the Child Language Survey, collecting naturally occurring spoken interaction among children in small groups of three friends. A large number of cohorts of pupils of 7–11 years old from a range of selected schools were to be audio-recorded and a framework was to be set up for the linguistic analysis of the data. This analysis was to be used as a resource for producing classroom text books for teaching English to French children of the same age ranges, and as a guide for those teaching French to English children. When I arrived in London, in early 1965, the Department at UCL had been up and running for some time; and the two research projects were hard at work. Eirian Davies, my closest colleague, and I were to produce linguistic descriptions of certain areas of English grammar: as I recall I was in charge of the work on cohesion.[9] One of our duties was to keep up regular interaction with the team of teachers on the Nuffield project: we discussed issues of language description which they raised as arising from their work. It was an effective way of interacting with teachers: my teacher colleagues made me understand the pressures under which teachers typically work. Getting to know them as dedicated thinkers caught up in a web whose strings they are far from controlling has deeply influenced my own thinking about the educational process.

This scene setting is a poor substitute for the actual excitement of the research, the seminars, the informal discussion sessions, though, with hindsight, all were proceeding in the same direction towards the evolution of a social semiotic theory as the new identity for the early Hallidayan linguistics framework. As the *Categories* (Halliday, [1961] 2002) became known and used, the theory was christened (probably in 1965, as I recall) by Margaret Berry as a 'scale and category grammar' at a seminar at UCL. The last two years of Halliday in Edinburgh had been much preoccupied with the description of English grammar: being Firthian, one could ignore neither the axis of chain nor that of choice; what was needed was clarity about their relations; syntagm and paradigm were calling for closer attention. It is interesting to note that two thirds of some 30 papers that Halliday published between 1963 and 1970 concerning grammatical and/or phonological description, raised issues such as the definition of class, elements of structure, syntax, stratification, realization, relations of units within strata, and relations of the strata within the overall theoretical framework; the theory was under constant and intensive scrutiny. At this point, another, a transatlantic, friendship needs to be foregrounded: I am referring now to Sydney

Lamb whom Michael Halliday first met in 1964 at a Georgetown Round Table Meeting. Lamb, who had developed 'Stratificational linguistics' (Lamb, 1962, 1964) and who was an impressively clear interpreter of Hjelmslev (Lamb, 1966), and Halliday, a Firthian linguist who deeply respected Hjelmslev, found much in their work that was closely related: both were concerned with the relations between the strata, and those within the networks on each stratum: the discourse was mutually stimulating.

6 Halliday's Social Semiotic: Functionality and Sociality

Back in London, Halliday discussed the formalism of system networks with Alex Henrici, a mathematician attached to the OSTI project and familiar with the growing trends of computational linguistics. These interactions together with the many descriptions and discussions built up a momentum. As the description of some fragments of English grammar grew in extent, Halliday noted that the overall disposition of their representation began to reveal lines of demarcation: the choices in the system networks seemed to create 'chunks', with denser systemic relations among the choices within each chunk but weaker, i.e., sparser relations across the chunks. And this remarkable demarcation of descriptive areas could be explained by exploring the characteristic nature of each chunk: each chunk was specializing for a particular kind of description. Thus transitivity seemed to form one chunk: its choices did not become the entry condition for choices in mood; and neither seemed to affect the description of the thematic organization of the clause. But why? What were these chunks representing? The answer could be stated in terms of meanings on the premise that grammar has evolved in human language – and only in human language – as a resource for construing meanings: human beings use signs as signals, that is to say for meaning something thereby. So to say that each demarcated chunk of grammatical description was indicative of a certain type of meaning is to simply state what meanings the grammar was signalling, without any necessary implication that the organization was an *exclusive* characteristic of the stratum of semantics alone: this solidary relation between meaning and grammar had been recognized by Saussure, Hjelmslev and Firth. The chunking was not such as to suggest that each demarcated area was an island unto itself, but the interconnections between them were fewer: in terms of the density of the interrelated choices within the chunk, they could be viewed as exceptions capable of being explicitly described in terms of the conjunction of certain systemic facts (Halliday, 1970, [1979] 2002; Hasan, 2013, 2014, in press [a]). Halliday first presented his interpretation of these, so to speak, 'naturally' occurring phenomena of the systemicity of language in terms of an inherent functional organization as revealed by the form of language (Halliday, 1970: 141):

> Why is language as it is? The nature of language is closely related to the nature of the demands we make on it, the functions it has to serve. In the most concrete terms, these functions are specific to a culture . . . But underlying such specific instances of language use, are more general functions . . .

> A purely extrinsic account of linguistic functions, one which is not based on an analysis of linguistic structure, will not answer the question; . . . At the same time an account of linguistic structure that pays no attention to the demands that we make of language is lacking in perspicacity, since it offers no principles for explaining why the structure of language is organized in one way rather than in another.

He went on to describe four 'more general functions' used universally by human beings for organizing life (one can almost 'hear' Firth saying language is 'for the living of life'): the functions Halliday recognized there are now familiar as (i) the experiential, realised as transitivity and reference and construing our experience of the world around and within us; (ii) the logical, realized as iterative and modifying structures which construe the amplification of meaning (which Halliday would put together with the experiential, referring to the combination as 'ideational'); (iii) the interpersonal, realized as choices in the system of mood, aspects of modality/ modulation and of polarity, which enact human relations by creating, maintaining or changing these relations; and (iv) the textual, realized as the lexicogrammatical devices for construing textual continuities, that forms the basis of relevance in human interaction.

This more abstract concept of function, which Halliday later referred to as 'metafunction', energized the theory. It needs to be stressed that the social had never been entirely ignored in the study of language, but the two had been presented as two distinct, at times almost irreconcilable aspects: if language was viewed as functional/social, then it could not be formal. And as often pointed out by Halliday, they seemed to be like the two ends of a see-saw: when one end was up the other had to be down. It so happened that at that particular moment in the history of linguistics, according to the dominant TG model 'doing linguistics proper' was to pay attention exclusively to the 'syntactic' without any regard for the social: language was a 'mental organ' though I do not recall the model explaining why this organ was unlike others which had developed adaptively in serving some function in human life. And even when/ if the discourse of linguistics accepted the social as an aspect of language, what was foregrounded was the contribution of the social: thus language was seen as representing some *social* processes, or *social* speakers, or the *social* relations of the interactants, the individual's intentions and actions; in all these cases, what the semiotic system of language was doing was just to represent even when being 'expressive' or 'conative'.[10] All such represented entities existed independent of language: the job of language as a social instrument was to represent them. The Firthian-Hallidayan linguistics had respected these relations. But now with the new metafunctional perspective presented by Halliday, this attitude would change though it would take some time for the change to become obvious: whatever the evolutionary impetus for the genesis of functionality in language, the metafunctions as described by Halliday (1973a, 1975, 1978a, [1979] 2002 etc.) suggested that there was, in the semiotic mechanism of language, an affordance, a power, which was essentially independent of the physical, physiological and the material.[11] The view of language as a surrogate simply running parallel to physical/material reality had already been rejected implicitly or explicitly by verbal artists and visionary thinkers on language, e.g., Whorf (1956), Vygotsky (1978), Wittgenstein (1953): but with metafunctions as conceptualized by Halliday, one could begin to suspect how, in a very real sense, language actually creates that universe which the speakers contend with in the living of life. The semiotic resources that power language in representing the world are the same that allow it also not only to create parallel universes, but also to go beyond the parallel to entirely virtual realities. It is this powerful signing system that also shapes the human mind, interpreting everything surrounding the sensing, thinking, acting human beings. It would be decades before neuroscience would begin to recognize human 'mind' as a 'personalized brain', thus implicitly confirming, with Bernstein (1971a, especially chapters 8 and 9) 'the role of language in the formation of consciousness'.

But my account is again running ahead, this time both ahead of time and ahead of the arguments that would support the above assertions. So let me return to that moment when in introducing Halliday's 1970 paper, Lyons (1970: 140) on the one hand pointed to its similarity to Anderson (1968) and Fillmore (1968), and on the other implied that Halliday's critique of 'competence' and 'performance' was perhaps misguided. At that point in the history of linguistics, the idea of language as having functions was, after all, not new: functions of language had much engaged European scholars, such as Buhler, Mathesius and Jacobson in the Vienna and Prague Circles. So one is entitled to ask, what was distinctive about the functions introduced by Halliday to support the view of language as a powerful semiotic system capable of not only *representing* reality but also *creating, changing* and *maintaining* it? I would name three interrelated characteristics specific to the metafunctions in SFL: the SFL metafunctions are (1) *intrinsic* to language as both system and process; (2) *each equally essential* in the formation of the semantic and grammatical units; and (3) each is *nonhierarchical*. Before attempting to explain the significance of these three attributes, it is useful to present one particular presupposition voiced most clearly and emphatically by Saussure (1959, 2008): to put it simply and somewhat cryptically, linguistic meanings are 'formed meanings'; the talk of meaning *and* form as two separate entities or aspects of language is an analytic convenience – linguistic meaning (semantics) cannot in reality be separated from linguistic form since it is the formal relations that produce those meanings, and it is the pressure of those meanings that lies behind the speakers' use of the formal devices. It follows that to identify four distinct metafunctions in terms of meaning is to also identify four distinct families of formal relations each 'forming' a distinct kind of meanings in parallel.[12]

Turning to the *first* characteristic of the metafunctions, namely that meanings are 'intrinsic': this follows directly from the presupposition discussed above. Though the example Wittgenstein uses is too simple to even hint on the complex details of how the relations of linguistic form produce linguistic meanings, his challenge to the reader to 'say "It's cold here" and mean "It's warm here." Can you do it?' is all the same relevant to this discussion (Wittgenstein, 1953: 140). Clearly, in the absence of some evidence of linguistic process, there will be no linguistic meaning, even though we often ascribe some 'content' to silence. The same philosopher also tells us: 'To understand the meaning of a sentence means to understand a language' (1953: 81). I do not deny that people have intentions; but equally true is the fact that a wording means what it means quite independent of the intentions of the sayer. There are both theoretical and practical reasons for maintaining with Halliday that metafunctions are 'intrinsic' to language: the identity of the metafunctions is unknowable except by the characteristic ways of making a certain order of meaning-wording patterns whose specificity is also the mark of that specific metafunction.

The *second* attribute, the fact that each metafunction is essential and indispensable means that none of the metafunctions can be excluded from the system or the process of language. If a kind of meaning-form relation could be excluded from the system or the process of language, this would simply mean that that particular kind of meaning-form relation could not be one of those 'more general functions', general in the sense of being present in every case of language. In the European discussions of functions, the 'expressive' and /or 'conative' functions of language were treated as dispensable: in fact the only indispensable function for most scholars in Vienna or Prague was the 'referential'/ 'representational'. This is like saying that it is possible to speak so that the speech informs about something in the world but does not indicate any relation between speaker and addressee. A little reflection will show that the position is untenable. In SFL the metafunction concerned with the interactants' relation to each other, just cannot be excluded: either the saying will *maintain* the existing relation, or *change* it; in other words the message will always indicate some interpersonal relation. From this view point, there is no speech event that leaves the world unaltered. The issue is never the presence or absence of a metafunction; it is simply a question of the identity of the relation being brought into being as formed meaning.

The *third* and final characteristic denies any hierarchic relation across the metafunctions: in this, SFL again differs from the view favoured by both Buhler and Mathesius. The SFL view specifically rejects the long-standing and widely held assumption that the 'representational'/'referential' function of language is the *sine qua non* of human language. In fact if we examine the nature of the structure that is specific to transitivity (Halliday, [1979] 2002), it becomes obvious that 'giving information' in this sense without enacting a role-relation, or indicating points of relevance or logical relation is impossible.

These three characteristics are shared by all four metafunctions recognized in Halliday's SFL, which, between them, exhaust *the kinds* of meaning-wording found in language: every language has these generalized orders of meaning-wording, with each particular language varying from all the others in respect to the more specific meanings. As I commented earlier, the concept of metafunctions energized SFL. A battery of concepts – system and structure, delicacy, strata, realization, rank, and units – i.e., concepts that are essential to language as a semiotic system – were all on the table to be viewed and reviewed in relation to each other from the perspective of the metafunctional hypothesis. But the changes in the theory were not instantaneous or cataclysmic; there was no sudden disjunction between the last version of the theory and the next one: the theoretical developments occurred as problems arose. An account of these developments has been described stage by stage by various colleagues (for example, Butt, 2001; Matthiessen, 2007b: 505–61) and again here in this volume (see Part III, especially Matthiessen, Chapters 7 and 8 in this volume). My own concern in this chapter is with those developments that have led to the creation of a reciprocal relation between the social and the semiotic as partners engaged in a single enterprise. These will be briefly discussed here under three headings in the order shown below:

(i)   metafunctions and the repositioning of linguistic meaning in SFL;
(ii) metafunctionality and the theorization of the process of language;
(iii) metafunctionality and the positioning of linguistics as a discipline – reconciling nature and culture.

To begin with meaning, the position of semantics had remained somewhat ambiguous: in the Firthian model, it seemed there was nothing particular one needed to do about semantics per se; instead, semantics was something that got described and accounted for if one attended appropriately to context, grammar and phonology (and of course, phonetics). It has taken a good deal of time for this view to admit change; and the first impetus towards that change came with the metafunctional hypothesis. This led to the valuable concept of language as meaning potential, and semantics began to be repositioned vis a vis other strata: the ambiguity of the 'tabular formulation' that voiced the Firthian position began to weaken. In that position somehow 'relations of form' jumped up to context, creating semantics. Today, semantics is thought of as a stratum of language, itself standing in a realizational relation to the strata of context of situation and lexicogrammar. The basis for my comments is a numbers of statements such as the following that elaborates the relations of action, meaning and meaning potential:

> . . . 'can do' by itself is not a linguistic notion; it encompasses types of behaviour other than language behaviour. If we are to relate the notion of 'can do' to the sentences and words and phrases that the speaker is able to construct in his language – to what he can say, in other words – then we need an intermediate step, where the behaviour potential is as it were converted into linguistic potential. This is the concept of what the speaker 'can mean'.

> The potential of language is a meaning potential. This meaning potential is the linguistic realisation of the behaviour potential; 'can mean' is 'can do' when translated into language. The meaning potential is in turn realised in the language system as lexicogrammatical, which is what the speaker can say. (Halliday, 1973a: 51)

Arguably the options in acts of meaning are what semantics is about: if there is 'behaviour' that reveals itself as an act of linguistic meaning, then the study of that is what constitutes semantics. Once meanings can be viewed as having some identity by their three-way relations to context that activates them, to lexicogrammar that construes them and to the paradigmatic relations of other meaning options indicative of the scope of signification, then it (semantics) can begin to be viewed in its own right. It would then be possible to ask the question: what is the character of this meaning potential that is language? What does this potential do for its speakers, and how? How do speakers learn to use language? and what accounts for linguistic variation? Halliday had already been asking such questions – or to be more precise, his research projects together with those of Bernstein's, which he became familiar with, were foregrounding issues of this kind since Halliday first arrived in London. The papers in the slim volume *Explorations in the Functions of Language* (Halliday, 1973a) indicate Halliday's take on the question of what it is to learn the mother tongue, and how code variation may be studied as choice in context. I was already working with Bernstein and had presented a paper at London School of Economics, where I attempted to examine the relationship of code, register and social dialect (Hasan, 1973). It was in examining the semantic options in the contexts of socialization that Halliday's linguistic analysis came closest to Bernstein's work.

At this time Halliday was working on many fronts at once, and I shall give up the effort to say what happened in what order. Preoccupied as most of us were with these intense intellectual activities, we were not entirely unaware of the first postwar crisis of capitalism which was just unfolding in the shape of cuts to university funds. Halliday, in particular, had been spending time and energy on sources of funding so as to maintain the level of research activity in the department: this constant struggle had, not unreasonably, appeared to eat up time which was urgently needed for work on language. At that point in time, there arrived an attractive offer from the University of British Columbia at Vancouver. Nigel had been born late 1969, and if we were going to move out of England altogether then this seemed a good moment to do so, and that part of Canada seemed fine to us. So we both resigned in 1971 in anticipation of a visa from Canada, which never arrived.[13] This was, to say the least, a nuisance. The saddest part was that the momentum of discourse among those who were part of the development of ideas had been fractured, and as I turn to the second issue, namely, how metafunctions impacted on the 'theorization of the process of language', it occurs to me that in fact the hypothesis introduced in Halliday 1973a was not picked up in any real sense until we settled in Sydney in 1976, Michael as the Professor and the founding Head of Linguistics at Sydney University, and I at Macquarie University in a large and lively department of linguistics. This was after a good few years of constant – though exciting – moves in Africa, England and the United States. Cohesion in English (Halliday and Hasan, 1976) arrived just as we were settling down in the new surroundings and discourse analysis was becoming *the* topic.

As I remember, we did not return to context and register in a big way until after Halliday (1977) and Hasan (1978). It was in the latter paper that I first published my thoughts on Generalized Structure Potential (GSP), on which I had been working since my last year with Bernstein (Hasan, in press). With publication of those papers and courses, the issues of register and context opened up again. According to Martin (1985) the approach in my paper was 'synoptic'; he advocated a dynamic approach, which would be able to account for all kind of 'twists and turns' in discourse as it happened rather than describing the text after the event. It was in this connection that the question of context/register was foregrounded. Now, turning to what Halliday had to say about register from the perspective of metafunctions, it seems to me that the comments he presented (Halliday, 1973a) are even to this day highly relevant, for both a principled analysis of register as linguistic variation, and for bringing to attention a feature about the context of discourse which as it were contributes to the genesis of the metafunctions themselves (Hasan, 1995, in press). In the debates at that time the 1973a hypothesis was (wrongly) referred to as 'context metafunction hook up hypothesis'. But what was the burden of this hypothesis?

The three now very familiar dimensions of field, tenor and mode had been introduced in 1964 as the three dimensions of the text's context that would correlate with the linguistic features realizing registerial variation: register variation correlated with variation in the dimension of field, and/or of tenor, and/or of mode. But the 1964 accounts of what would count as field, tenor or mode, or what specific linguistic patterns of the text would correlate with which of those dimensions of variation had not proved extremely helpful (for some discussion see Hasan, in press): after all, the 1960s were early days for Halliday's linguistics. Halliday (1973a: 100) had suggested that the linguistic features could be better examined functionally:

> ... With only minor exceptions, whatever the speaker is doing with language he will draw on all these [functionally identified, RH] components of the grammar. He will need to make some reference to the categories of his own experience – in other words, the language will be *about* something. He will need to take up some position in the speech situation; at the very least he will specify his own communication role and (will) set up expectations for that of the hearer – in terms of statements, questions, response and the like. And what he says will be structured as 'text' — that is to say, it will be operational in the given context.... (Halliday, 1973a: 100)

This hypothesis, which, borrowing Halliday's expression, I will from now on refer to as Context-Metafunction Resonance (CMR) hypothesis, is important to Halliday's SFL for at least two reasons. First, it offers a much more viable way for identifying meaning-wording that would be realizationally related to each contextual dimension; all that was needed now was to recognize how the formally identified metafunctions are actualized in language use (for some discussion of paradigmatic and syntagmatic relations see Matthiessen, Chapter 7, this volume). The information about the structural actualization of the systemic potential was first detailed in Halliday ([1966–8] 2005, [1969] 2005, [1979] 2002) and later exemplified in many SFL documents (including much later, Halliday, 1985a, 1994; Halliday and Matthiessen, 2004, 2013; see also Martin, this volume).[14] To my mind, the CMR hypothesis cannot be rejected without rejecting the current profile of the metafunctions as well as their current use in the model to underpin the lexicogrammar. The second important issue again brought to our attention in 1973 was Halliday's claim that 'The nature of language is closely related to the nature of the demands we make on it, the functions it has to serve. In the most concrete terms, these functions are specific to a culture . . .' (Halliday, 1970: 141). But there was now a difference: the claim was made sharper by reference to evidence from register analysis. In relating the genesis of metafunctions to what people do with their language, Halliday provided the basis for bringing the social and the semiotic together: at the same time by demonstrating that functionality is intrinsic, i.e., supported by the semiotic mechanism of language – its form – he also confirmed the creative power of language. One outcome of the inherent nature of the metafunctions has been to suggest that language *use* is not an unmanageable chaos, subject just to the local whims of an individual speaker: in theory at least it is as amenable to a 'scientific' (?synoptic) study as the language system itself. In this perspective, there is no viable ground for 'langue' (i.e. system) to be the exclusive concern of linguistics; a linguistics that banishes parole would be handicapped, and this is not simply because linguistics without parole can neither have evidence of linguistic variation nor offer an explanation for it (Weinreich, Labov and Herzog, 1968). Perhaps more important is the fact that a linguistics, with no place for parole, would have neither any evidence for the 'morphology of meaning', which Saussure considered to be 'the heart of the linguistics of langue', nor any idea about the complex relations underlying it (Hasan, 2013, 2014, in press). Saussure had placed the genesis/evolution of language with community: he implied that the history of language and community moved in step, and that langue is the property of the community. The theorization of both the system and the process of language, enabled by Halliday's metafunctional hypothesis has, in the end, produced a linguistics that comes closest to realizing the Saussurean dream to produce a linguistics of langue (Hasan, 2013, 2014). That dream has not come true because SFL was following Saussure, but because it was pursuing the aim it had set itself (Halliday, [1961] 2002, 1964) which is to explain how language works in society and why – this could only be achieved if the theory attended to both the system and the process.

Turning now to the third theme – how the metafunctions position linguistics as a discipline, Halliday (1974a, and elsewhere) has pointed out that the recognition of functions of language was not a new movement: both the function and the form have been recognized in some way or other from early studies of language. However, the tendency, perhaps more noticeable in the human/ social sciences, has been to polarize issues; so nature and culture have gone up and down as the two ends of the 'intellectual' see-saw. Form was up when Halliday put forward his concept of metafunctions and function was down. For Chomsky, language was a mental organ; every child was born with a Language Acquisition Device (LAD) intact in the brain; and the rules of syntax were innate – all the new born had to do was to match that internal grammar with the grammar of the community he was born in.[15] Now, no one, not even Skinner, was insisting on going back to babies with brains clean as the slate: Saussure had always maintained that human beings must have a mental affordance for language learning. This claim is qualitatively different from one that gives language the status of a mental organ. With hindsight, in terms of SFL now, it was not clear at what level of generalization Chomsky's hypotheses were operating. Starkly different from those views was the understanding provided by

Malinowski (1923) about children's learning of their mother tongue: the role of context and of functions was uppermost in explaining the efficacy of that process. Today, Halliday's accounts of the continuity in neonate learning from moving to meaning (Halliday, [1998] 2003: 9) does not seem that far out, but when in early 1970s he began to study Nigel's semiotic development he was out almost all by himself, explaining in functional terms what the child's (to ordinary ears) inchoate noises were doing by way of communicating, and even before that was the 'pre-symbolic stage' where small points of difference in body movements were presented as bodily movements specializing for distinct meanings. It is not necessary here to repeat the whole story: there is an account of 'language development in early childhood: learning how to mean' in this volume (Torr, Chapter 9). What I would emphasize again is the continuity in the process: the small child's language learning was always hitched to 'doing something'; this doing was purposive and the agenda was set by the baby; the modality of communication was not 'formed linguistic meanings'; rather it was the baby's body – protolinguistic 'vocal gestures' together with other kinds of bodily activity; and the addressee was someone from the child's 'meaning group', someone the child recognized and trusted. There was in that early stage no semantics, but there was semiotics and social context.

Years later in summarizing this state of affairs, I came to analyse the contextual frame for the child's communicative activities (Hasan, [2001] in press) as consisting of Action, Relation and Contact (ARC): with reference to these ARC dimensions one could describe what the child was getting at by addressing whom and how. I mention this here in order to draw attention to two relevant issues, one relating to the nature/culture debate and the other to the metafunctional hypothesis. To the extent that children's language learning was being presented by the dominant model as evidence for the innateness of grammar (or language *tout cours*), the functional account of language learning was a good rebuttal of that 'evidence': it provided richer details about the learning that was going on, and while not limited to syntax, it accounted for what the child could do, and how forms of interaction develop in children. That language learning is a social act, performed in cooperation with others in the society, and that one thing that engagement in interaction teaches is how to participate in discourse with others – these facts seem to favour the Saussurean view, namely that language belongs to the community and that it is not a biological inheritance but a social convention to be learned in society. The second point to note is that the neonates are awesome learning machines, but they are not 'biddable' – or rather are impervious to what we think of as 'instruction' in the very early stages: in terms of Bernstein, official pedagogy is nothing to the baby: it is the baby's bio-genetic foundations (Vygotsky, 1978) that is at work. So what the contextual frame of ARC indicates is something 'innate' – not the words, not the syntax, but the urge to be, to do, to change the world to suit the needs of his little body. In achieving this end, naturally and instinctively, the small body of the baby acts, – the urge to do is there, but also the recognition of members of the meaning group and the bodily 'modes of discourse' – these things no one can teach the baby; they are 'natural'. If the baby's acts of communication are to be taken as interactive acts of a kind, it is remarkable that, they presents the three dimensions which are a more generalized form of the contextual parameters identified by Halliday's SFL. I have suggested (Hasan, in press) that this is the 'template' for carrying out any social practice including that of the social practice of discourse. The latter may have different aims and purposes, they may be real or counterfeit, and they may or may not be attained; but one thing is certain that every adult discursive act calls for a specialized version of Action (field), Relation (tenor), and Contact (mode) (; it is the 'of discourse' that makes the contextual parameters a more delicate version of ARC. Related as these parameters are to the metafunctions by the CMR hypothesis, their genesis can be traced back to the 'natural' ARC frame used by the baby.

7 Concluding Remarks: The Relations of Language and Culture

So as I see it, the route Halliday took to his brand of social semiotic was anything but planned or direct. We cannot even say that there is any evidence of early orientation towards doing linguistics, leave aside one that was to become a social semiotic, though the experience which came purely by chance in the shape of friendly discourse on sociopolitical issues with John Chinnery must, with hindsight, count for something. Thereafter as events unfolded, there was always in the background an awareness of the social world, though up to the last minute chance did intervene. What if McCarthy had come ten years later? What if Firth had not been so positive about 'sociological linguistics'? Indeed, what if an undertaking to stay away from Marxism had not been an implied condition of being able to stay on at SOAS to work with Firth? Would he still have joined the Linguistics Group of the Communist Party? But at some point, chance had to give way to choice in order to maintain the commitment to understanding how language works. For those who share his view of the social it seems that once Halliday had begun to ask how and why language works in society, he would inevitably wish to foreground the social aspects, if only because understanding about language cannot be complete without it. But some readers may be inclined to ask if I have actually talked about the evolution of the social semiotic. On the face of it, in as much as I have talked about Halliday's linguistics, it has been about functionalism. There was, one might say, hardly anything about 'social semiotic'. And there is some truth in this though I did this deliberately. I believe what I have done is to foreground in this discourse the moment when the theory was given a momentum that could only lead to the evolution of the kind of social semiotic that SFL represents. There may be one interpretation of 'social semiotic' which requires language to satisfy social demands: this calls on language to represent communal beliefs, to reveal a person's individuality, to be indicative of social variation, be it class, gender, age or social status. And of course whether a linguistic theory recognizes this or not, every language performs these services. But this is not all that a social semiotic should be doing. By insisting on the intrinsicality of metafunctions, by arguing for their non-hierarchic status, by showing that our utterances over-whelmingly display all metafunctional strands of meaning-wording, Halliday leads to a new way of thinking about language: language goes beyond refer-ence or 'correspondence to reality'; it creates the meanings that need to be cre-ated. It is, in the last analysis, this quality of language that actually lies behind the value we attach to 'semiotic mediation' (Vygotsky, 1978) which is largely performed 'by means of the modality of language'. To say that mind is 'per-sonalized brain' is in fact also to claim that language is the most frequent, the most pervasive means of 'experiencing' if for no other reason than that there is simply no other modality as far reaching, as pervasive, as good at externalizing human experience as language. This is what a social semiotic linguistics such as Halliday's SFL is all about.

Notes

* I am grateful to Michael Halliday for helping me with chronological details and for his comments on this paper. I alone am responsible for the interpretation of events and of the theory as presented here.

1. What is SFL now did not begin under that name; the most recent partial history of its evolution is presented in Hasan, Matthiessen and Webster (2005, 2007) and partly in Halliday and Webster (2009); in the nature of things its changing names were not always in step with its own rate of change.
2. This training was thought necessary since the Japanese forces were still active.
3. See for example his *The Semantics of Linguistic Science* (1948/1957). In fact both anthol-ogies of Firth's writings (Firth 1957a, 1968) espouse ideas that would make the super-ficial interpretation of his writing e.g., by Langendoen, 1968, or even Lyons, 1966 difficult to sustain. I do not see eye to eye with Firth on the issue of how meaning is to be described, but his approach unlike that of a large number of very famous schol-ars is not limited to single words. And he had the courage to disagree with others without making impertinent comments. See also Kachru (this volume).
4. And again I would go so far as to say that Firth typically did not refer to examples such as 'board, boardroom, boardschool' as 'text'; unlike Hjelmslev, he would refer to such 'things' as 'item(s)' or 'form(s)' rather than 'text'.
5. The major problem is that the scope of 'semiotics' is wide, and the nature of those areas is far from clearly described; in any event it would be difficult to attend to all its processes simultaneously such as those described by Bernstein as 'official' and 'local' pedagogy, which requires the involvement of a vast area in order to educate the mind at home, in school, in neighbourhood, as well as attending to ways of being

saying and doing in not only real life but also in the virtual lives created by the media. We are only just beginning to see how complex a web of permanencies is woven invisibly around the social world, while overtly singing songs of praise for change and progress.

6. I have always thought that the linguistics of the 1960s was something like the 'nouveau riche'; it made claims about language teaching and about the nature of literature on the basis of the very little it knew about language. But even today, linguistics is only just beginning to see the ripples on the surface of language.

7. The inversion of 'social semiotic' to 'semiotic social' is intentional here: the 'social' certainly has its basis also in the material, but no part of our universe is 'thinkable' and certainly the sense of neither can be externalized as anything else but language. Sensing is real, but sense-making is what allows sociality.

8. In later years Bernstein himself preferred to characterize the code theory as a 'theory of cultural transmission'. I do not think there is any conflict here between these two views, since transmission is by definition at a lower level than cultural variation. Code theory is able to transmit all aspects of culture, but each aspect displays variability from local pedagogy to cuisine or concepts of cleanliness. Codes teach, but they are regulative, and the variants have to be learned by all according to who they are, even if to be defied later.

9. I was with the project at UCL just for 18 months. An attractive series of invitations just fell in place from Summer School at Urbana (the only opportunity for me to teach Urdu), to a visiting appointment teaching about Verbal Art in the Department of Rhetoric at Berkeley, followed by the possibility of visiting Yale where Lamb would employ me as a researcher to work on a stratificational project for describing English. When I left mid-1966, I had the work on reference ready for publication, and the first draft of work on substitution and ellipsis had been submitted to Michael Halliday for approval. It was in fact in 1975 that I learned that Eugene Winter had also done some work on cohesion for use at the OSTI project.

10. The tendency to believe that whatever language 'represents' must in some way be present in the world is based on 'collapsing' human history. Human 'evolution' is viewed as if speaking had made no difference in the human exosomatic evolution. So cultural objects are noted as important but language is not seen as playing any part in what Vygotsky 1978 drew attention to as sociogenetic in his writings. Popper's interpretation (1972) of Vygotsky's term elides the social and highlights the material.

11. Yes, the sign must 'be' material but no, the meaning-making function of the linguistic sign has had, despite my admiration for Firth, very little to do with linguistic meaning (especially if the prosodic organization is excluded from the material).

12. This debate is huge and goes far back in time; it cannot be pursued here but a very brief summary is presented. Assuming the SFL position to be as stated here, see Halliday and Matthiessen, 1999 and Hasan, 2009 for some discussion. The alternative position would be to think of meaning as extrinsic to language, and two fairly well-known approaches have been advanced. First, there is the truth functional (aka correspondence) theory where meaning is seen as representing material reality; this assigns language the function of a surrogate; there is then a problem in explaining the source of the creative power of language. Secondly extrinsic meaning may be viewed as psychological/mental in origin. In such theories the question of evidence often leads to circularity and so appears intractable, especially when viewed in relation to semantic variation across distinct cultural frames.

13. I was then in charge of the research on the study of variation in stories produced ex tempore by children from different social classes. In the to-ing and fro-ing with a little baby, the report on that research, though half written by 1973, was never

published: I was insisting on two volumes so as to include the details about the categories of analysis; the publishers did not want two volumes; 'mobile negotiations' were not successful.

14. The representation of lexicogrammar in SFL is presented in two parts: the potential is represented systemically, and its actualization as a set of simultaneous structure resolved as one syntagmatic display. This is in keeping with the conception of each metafunction as intrinsic, non-excludable and the non-hierarchic. For critiques of this 'syntax' see Fawcett, 2000, etc. It seems to me that this debate needs to be reviewed not from the perspective of what computers find easy to do today, but rather from the perspective of how this concept of grammar fares in renewal of connection with data. For the aim of linguistics is to explain how language works, not how the lack in an existing computational technology can be complemented.

15. I am aware that Chomsky's linguistics has undergone a cycle of revolutions; what I am describing here is what was being said in the late 1960s–early 1970s.

PART III

Halliday: Ideas about Language

7 Halliday on Language

Christian M. I. M. Matthiessen

1 Halliday on Language: Introduction

In this third part of the Continuum Companion to M. A. K. Halliday, we are concerned with his **ideas about language** – which echoes Halliday ([1977] 2003), where he identifies two ideas about language that have been part of the engagement with language in Europe since Ancient Greece: language as **resource** and language as **rule**. His own engagement with language has been based on the conception of language as resource. However, before I proceed any further, let me provide a way into 'Halliday on language' drawing on my own personal experience since I think this can be a helpful way of shedding light on the fundamental nature of his contribution to our understanding of language.

While I was studying in high school (1972–5), I started reading linguistics books because I was quite interested in language but also because very dissatisfied with the school grammars we were provided with for the various languages we studied: to me, they seemed unsystematic and fragmentary. Step by step I got hold of other books – for example, Jespersen's *Essentials of English Grammar*, which I found fascinating; but the two books that made the deepest impression on me were Bertil Malmberg's (1970) *Nya vägar inom språkveten-skapen* (literally, 'new paths in linguistics'; published in English as *New Trends in Linguistics*) and Alvar Ellegård's (1971) *Transformationell svensk-engelsk satslära* ('Transformational Swedish English syntax').

Malmberg's (1970) book, first published in 1959, provided a fascinating survey of different branches of linguistics before around 1960 (although later editions included an account of Chomsky's transformational grammar); but the part that intrigued me the most was his presentation of European structuralism – a theoretical development he was mainly responsible for introducing into Sweden, starting in the 1930s. The distinction between the **paradigmatic** axis and the **syntagmatic** one seemed like such a fundamental part of a theory of language.

Ellegård's (1971) book was also fascinating, and full of insight into syntactic structure: his introduction was in fact to a large extent based on generative semantics (as it had been developed in the second half of the 1960s by G. Lakoff, McCawley, Ross, Postal and others), so syntactic structures that had previously seemed purely syntactic could now be shown to be imbued with meaning – for example, the analysis of negation as a higher predicate (Ellegård, 1971: 51, 55–8).

However, these two fundamental insights – the structuralist insight into the axial organization of language and the generativist insight into the semantic foundation of syntax – did not seem possible to reconcile. Malmberg's examples of axis were taken mostly from phonology (and he also discussed lexical fields), so there was no clue in his book; and Ellegård did not refer to the European structuralist tradition in his presentation. So I had found these two regions of fascinating insights into language, but they were completely disconnected: there was no bridge or tunnel to link them (at the time, the Danish and Swedish governments were still debating whether to connect to two countries by means of a bridge or a tunnel).

I had a gap year between high school and university – the year of military service all men in Sweden had to endure in those days; it was the worst year of my life so far, but luckily I had been able to sign up for a correspondence course in English at university level, and this kept me going during my dreadful year of military culture (later, I came to know men who'd gone through this kind of experience in e.g. Israel, Turkey and Singapore; I gradually realized that my experience had been like a school picnic!). One of the textbooks was John Lyons' (1968) *Theoretical Linguistics*. It wasn't exactly easy reading for someone who'd just left high school, but it was certainly very rewarding (anticipating certain later developments, like the interest in categorial grammar). However, his book didn't contain anything at all to address the troubling mystery I had been left with after reading Malmberg and Ellegård.

I can imagine that today I might have found answers to my questions very quickly by searching the World Wide Web; the breakthrough to easy access to information has been absolutely dramatic. But in those days, it took me quite a long time to find the answers. Once I had been liberated from my military service, I went on to study linguistics, English, Arabic and philosophy at Lund University. In our linguistics undergraduate programme, we were trained in the then current version of transformational grammar (the textbook was Akmajian & Henry, *An Introduction to the Principles of Transformational Syntax*) – Extended Standard Theory, which, being purely focussed on syntactic form, was very disappointing to me after the insights into the semantics of syntax provided by Ellegård (1971); but we were encouraged to read widely and a number of our teachers were Ph.D. students, so we were infected with their excitement about being involved in research and discovery.[1] In the Department of English, I was introduced to work on cohesion, based on Halliday & Hasan's (1976) pioneering account of the textual resources for creating cohesive links. (And in the Department of Oriental Languages, I was told that Halliday's, 1956, work on Chinese was very hard to understand, but definitely worthwhile!)

However, it was not until I came across Halliday's (1973a) book with examples of system networks and realization statements that the puzzle that had mystified me since high school was solved – and as a bonus it also provided me with a sense of a comprehensive map of the lexicogrammatical resources of English in the form of a **function-rank matrix** (Halliday, 1973a: 141).

On the one hand, Halliday gave depth to the paradigmatic axis in the form of **system networks** – a totally new idea to me; and he showed how paradigmatic organization could in this way be extended far beyond the confines of phonological paradigms. On the other hand, terms in systems could have **realization statements** associated with them, and these realization statements turned out to be the bridge between the paradigmatic and syntagmatic axes that I had been looking for. I found the representation of linguistic resources by means of system networks very insightful; it revealed a form of organization that had remained hidden (later, I was able to understand this form of organization in terms of Bohm's, e.g. 1980, notion of **implicate order**), and this was reinforced when I got access to Halliday (1976) and to Halliday (1978).

In addition, of course, Halliday's work showed in a quite stunning way how grammatical structure was semantically natural (using terms that became more general by the mid-1980s): grammatical structure turned out to be **multilayered function** structure (also shown very clearly by Halliday, [1970] 2002). This was reinforced by the work by Prague School linguists, much admired in the Linguistics Department of Lund University; one of the Ph.D. students, Milan Bílý, gave us first-hand insight into Functional Sentence Perspective.

Halliday's (1973a) book thus contained the solution to a key problem that had been bothering me since high school; and more generally, this solution is one of the most fundamental contributions to our understanding of language in the last century or so – it was certainly a solution that Saussure had not been able to provide in his posthumous *Cours de Linguistique*.

Halliday's (1973a) book also contained the key to another major theoretical issue in 20th-century linguistics – the relationship between the equivalents of Saussure's *langue* and *parole* (and in another guise, between Chomsky's 'competence' and 'performance'). I don't think I had quite grasped that issue during my studies in the 1970s – although my struggle to understand the theories of Louis Hjelmslev and (very importantly) Gustave Guillaume had prepared the ground for me; but later it became very clear to me (cf. Matthiessen, 1993).

The key, which he has spelt out in more detail since the early 1970s (e.g. Halliday, [1991] 2007, [2002] 2005a), was to theorize *langue* and *parole* not as different phenomena but rather as the outer poles of a cline – the **cline of instantiation**. These outer poles were conceptualized as **potential** and **instance**: language was seen as both system (meaning potential) and text (instances of meaning, i.e. acts of meaning), with texts **instantiating** the system. Intermediate between these outer poles, he located patterns of functional variation, **register variation**, and then also **codal variation**, further up the cline towards the potential pole (see Hasan, 1973; Halliday, [1994] 2007: 236–7; cf. Matthiessen, 2007b, section 4.1.4). The significance of his cline of instantiation gradually became clear to me after I had become involved in a project concerned with the computational modelling of the generation of text; to model text generation, it is necessary to spell out how linguistic systems are instantiated in text (e.g. Matthiessen, 1983a). However, Halliday's cline of instantiation is also very significant in another way: it is the missing link in linguistics between the domain of theory – the linguistic system – and the domain of data – texts instantiating the system; and sorting this out has become increasingly important with the development of vast sources of data in the form of corpora and methods of automated analysis in the form of corpus tools.

Up through 1979, my experience had been with Halliday on paper; but around February 1980, I had the good fortune to meet him and Ruqaiya Hasan at Stanford University, purely by chance; and later in the first half of 1980, I attended a ten-week seminar he gave at UC Irvine, at the invitation of Benjamin Colby, in anthropology. By the time I had the chance to listen to his weekly lectures, I had had the opportunity to listen to talks and lectures by a number of great linguists (Los Angeles was, of course full of them, at UCLA and USC; and in December 1979, the annual LSA meeting was held in LA), ranging from say André Martinet to Jim McCawley. What struck me so profoundly about Michael Halliday's lectures was that I was given, for the first time, a holistic deep insight into what kind of resource language is (cf. Hasan, 1984). By then, I'd learned the scholarly games of doing linguistics; he cut through all that and gave me a sense of the overall organization of language – what I'd been looking for since high school.

Having sketched some aspects of my own personal experience of discovering Halliday's ideas about language, let me now take a step back and discuss 'Halliday on language' more systematically.

2 Language as Resource

When scholars develop theories of language, the nature of each theory depends on their *conception of the nature of language* upon which it is based. For example, if language is conceived of as an inventory of 'words', the theory is likely to be based on lexis in the first instance, and the primary source of data is likely to be corpora explored by means of standard lexis-oriented corpus tools such as concordancing programmes (cf. Halliday, [2002] 2005b). More generally, if we take a step back in order to be able to survey ideas about language and to discern the major motifs in the development of such ideas in the Western tradition, we can identify two very different conceptions of language. They have been discussed by Halliday ([1977] 2003) and Seuren (1998) under different headings. Halliday's earlier account is reinforced by Seuren's much longer overview of the development of Western Linguistics. I will start with Halliday's account.

Halliday ([1977] 2003) shows that when children begin to learn language, their conception of language is as a **resource** – a resource for making meaning. Learning language for them is thus 'learning how to mean' (e.g. Halliday, 1975) – building up the resources for making meaning. However, when children enter school, they are likely to meet a different image of language, language as **rule**; in school, 'language will be not a set of resources but a set of rules' (Halliday, [1977] 2003: 94). Halliday ([1977] 2003: 94) calls this the 'folk linguistics of the classroom', characterized by 'its categories and classes, its rules and regulations, its do's and, above all, it's don'ts'. He goes on to show that these two ideas about language have been present in Western Linguistics since Ancient Greek, with early versions of the resource view being developed by the sophists and of the rule view by Aristotle (Halliday, [1977] 2003: 99–100):

> We can follow these two strands throughout the subsequent history of ideas about language in the west. The one stems from Aristotle; it is 'analogist' in character, based on the conception of language as rule, and it embeds the study of language in philosophy and logic. The other has, for us today, less clearly defined origins, but it can probably be traced to Protagoras and the sophists, via Plato; it is 'anomalist' in character, and has a marked element of Stoic thought in it. It is not philosophical (the Stoics were the earliest scholars explicitly to separate linguistics from philosophy, and grammar from logic) but rather descriptive, or to use another term, ethnographic; and the organizing concept is not that of **rule** but of **resource**. [. . .]

> We can identify, broadly, two images of language: a philosophical logical view, and a descriptive- – ethnographic view. In the former, linguistics is part of philosophy, and grammar is part of logic; in the latter, linguistics is

part of anthropology, and grammar is part of culture. The former stresses analogy; is prescriptive, or normative, in orientation; and concerned with meaning in relation to truth. The latter stresses anomaly; is descriptive in orientation; and concerned with meaning in relation to rhetorical function. The former sees language as thought, the latter sees language as action. The former represents language as rules; it stresses the formal analysis of sentences, and uses for purposes of idealization (for deciding what falls within or outside its scope) the criterion of grammaticality (what is, or is not, according to the rule). The latter represents language as choices, or as a resource; it stresses the semantic interpretation of discourse, and uses for idealization purposes the criterion of acceptability or usage (what occurs or could be envisaged to occur).

Building on Halliday's characterization of the two images of language that have run as strands through Western Linguistics, language as resource and language as rule, let me summarize and elaborate his account in tabular form: see Table 7.1. When language is conceived of as resource, theories based on this image are **functional** ones; but when language is conceived of as rule, theories are **formal** ones.

Halliday's ([1977] 2003) contrast between 'language as resource' and 'language as rule', investigated in functional and formal theories, respectively, is reinforced by Seuren's (1998: 25–7) very similar or even identical contrast between approaches to language that he characterizes as '**ecologism**' and '**formalism**', though without a reference to Halliday's discussion. After introducing early engagements with language in Ancient Greece, Seuren (1998: 23) takes a step back to identify these two traditions in the history of Western Linguistics:

> We thus see the outlines of two different traditions emerging in Antiquity. On the one hand, there is the tradition that developed along Heraclitean, Platonic and Stoic lines. On the other hand, there is the tradition of Aristotle and the Alexandrine philologists.

Later he emphasizes the difference between these two approaches in terms of their *methods* (Seuren, 1998: 25):

> The point is one of method. It concerns the way in which linguistic theorists deal with the facts of language. Two main approaches can be distinguished in this respect, which we shall dub **ecologism** and **formalism**. [. . .] For the formalists, language is a formal system describable in terms of rule [. . .] In the ecological approach, on the other hand, language is primarily seen as a product of nature, and hence an object for empirical research.

Table 7.1 Language as resource and language as rule, theorized in functional and formal theories, respectively

	functional theories	*formal theories*
(i) conception of language	*resource* (Halliday, 1977a; Hasan, 1984)	*rule*
(ii) relationship of grammar to semantics	*natural* (Halliday, 1994; Halliday & Matthiessen, 1999; cf. Haiman, 1985)	*arbitrary and autonomous* ['standard theory', but increasingly challenged today]
(iii) principle of grammatical 'modularity'	*metafunction* — ideational [logical & experiential], interpersonal, textual], with no componential boundary between syntax & morphology (grammar = 'morpho- *syntax*') *(Halliday, 1967/8; 1978; 1994)*	*constituency* — yielding at least two components: syntax & morphology
(iv) principle of linguistic organization	*paradigmatic: system is the fundamental mode of organization (Halliday, 1966a; 1969; Hasan, 1996: Ch. 5; Martin, 1992; Matthiessen, 1995a)*	*syntagmatic: structure is the fundamental mode of organization*
(v) relationship between grammar and lexis	*continuous: grammar and lexis are not different phenomena, but rather different perspectives on the same phenomenon (Halliday, 1961; Hasan, 1996: Ch. 4; Martin, 1992: 277–86)*	*modular: syntax, morphology and the lexicon are different modules, but challenged more recently in construction-based approaches*
(vi) relationship between 'system' and 'text'	*one phenomenon — continuum: system and text are conceptualized as different 'phases' of the same phenomenon, related by the cline of instantiation as potential to instance (Halliday, 1991a; 2002a); the focus is on both system and text (seen as poles on a cline), with high value on naturally occurring text instances (hence corpus methods)*	*distinct phenomena — dichotomy: system and text are conceptualized as distinct phenomena, in terms of competence and performance, respectively (different from but recalling Saussure's dichotomy of langue and parole); the focus is on the system, typically with evidence from constructed examples, but now increasingly also with corpus evidence*
(vii) fundamental questions for theory	*large number derived from a wide range of contexts — linguistic, computational, educational, clinical, stylistic, etc., so highly powerful, flexible theory (Halliday, 1980)*	*small number derived from the context of Western philosophy concerning the nature and source of knowledge (the issue of innateness in the context of empiricism vs rationalism), so highly dedicated, constrained theory*
(viii) relationship between theory and application	*no clear distinction, with theory and application in ongoing dialogue; both are part of appliable linguistics (Halliday, 1985, 2002b)*	*sharp distinction, with formal theory within theoretical linguistics clearly separated from applied linguistics*

Table 7.1 Continued

	functional theories	*formal theories*
(ix) disciplinary orientation	*social semiotics and general systems theory as transdisciplinary formations; sociology, ethnography, education, stylistics (Halliday, 1978)*	*cognitive science as macro-disciplinary formation and within that cognitive psychology, natural language philosophy, philosophy of mind*
(x) mode of development	*evolution, building on immediate predecessors including earlier versions of itself*	*revolution, discarding immediate predecessors or even earlier versions of itself*
(xi) coverage of language in descriptions	*high priority on comprehensiveness in coverage (hence value on large corpora)*	*tendency towards fragments selected to probe theoretical issues (as in Montague grammar)*
Examples	*Halliday's (1950s —) systemic functional theory;*	*Chomsky's (1950s —) generative theories: phrase structure grammar, transformational grammar, standard theory, extended standard theory, government and binding, principles and parameters, minimalist programme*
	Other functional approaches: Prague School functionalism; Dik's functional grammar; West-Coast functionalism; Okuda's functional approach in Japan	*Formalist alternatives to Chomsky: generative semantics, Montague grammar, lexical functional grammar (LFG), generalized phrase structure grammar (GPSG), head-driven phrase structure grammar (HPSG)*

Ecologism corresponds to functional theories in Table 7.1, and formalism to formal theories. I have summarized his characterizations of these two approaches in see Table 7.2.

With respect to the role of description in Chomsky's influential version of formal theory, Seuren (1998: 252) notes:

> The paucity of Chomsky's actual grammatical analyses and descriptions is surprising for someone who has written so much on linguistics. Ironically, the only two thorough pieces of analysis produced by Chomsky to date are in morphophonemics (his 1951 MA dissertation on the Morphophonemics of Modern Hebrew) and, together with Halle, in phonology (Chomsky & Halle, 1968). In syntax there is not a single instance of anything approaching a thorough treatment of a construction or set of constructions in English or any other language. Hosts of general principles and constraints have seen the light in endless succession, but no actual analysis or description. All work of that nature produced within the confines of Chomsky inspired

Table 7.2 Seuren's (1998) characterization of ecological and formalist approaches to language

	ecologism [i.e. functional theories]	*formalism [i.e. formal theories]*
early manifestation	ancient anomalists ['lovers of exceptions']	ancient analogists ['lovers of regularity']
general	'. . . language is primarily seen as a product of nature, and hence as an object for empirical research. The expectation is that language, like nature, will manifest itself in all kinds of unexpected variations on and deviations from an as yet largely unknown rule or norm system'. [p. 25]	'language is a formal system describable in terms of rules for the acoustic or visual expression of meanings, and whatever appears to go against the system tends to be regarded as a nuisance, attributable to deplorable interference from outside sources. . . . They prefer to approach the task of analysing language with a formal system that has been developed elsewhere, usually in logic or mathematics, and then to impose their a priori, preconceived system on what they perceive as the facts of language.' [p. 25]
merits	'The ecologists . . . have the experience, the familiarity with the data, and the general knowledge of the terrain required for a judicious selection of a hypothesis that may have a reasonable chance of success'. [p. 26]	'Formalism gives the linguist a better awareness of the properties, mathematical and other, of the descriptive and analytical system he is using'. [p. 26]
drawbacks	'The ecologist runs the risk of ecologism [i.e. functional theories] becoming an antitheorist, rejecting anything formal and concentrating entirely on data collecting, without any theoretical perspective. Some ecologists have been seen to reject the very notion of an underlying system, on the pretext that the use of language is "free" and "creative", in some ill-defined sense.' [p. 26]	'The formalist risks becoming formalism [i.e. formal theories] blinkered by the mathematics of his system, losing sight of the reality the system should be about.' [p. 26]

grammar came from others, who then invariably found that the principles and constraints could not be maintained. Cp. Postal in Huck & Goldsmith (1995: 142):

> The significant point is then that there is an extraordinary contrast between the paucity of genuine results in Chomskyan linguistics and the forests of paper which have been, and continue to be, devoted to the linguistic ideas involved.

In the same way, in his article on the 'failure of generative grammar', Gross (1979), who had written about mathematical linguistics and worked with natural language processing (e.g. Gross, 1972) and came to use corpora in linguistic research, makes a very similar point about the lack of descriptive coverage in generative grammar, suggesting that Stockwell, Schacter & Partee's (1973) (in my view) valiant and valuable effort to integrate transformational grammar descriptions[2] did not in fact constitute an integrated account comparable to traditional reference grammars. Seuren's (1998) assessment may be compared with Halliday's (1985a / 1994: xxxiv) comment on 20th-century linguistics:

> Twentieth century linguistics has produced an abundance of new theories, but it has tended to wrap old descriptions up inside them; what are needed now are new descriptions.

And Halliday ([1992] 2005a: 76) reinforces this point, based on his personal research experience:

> It has always seemed to me, ever since I first tried to become a grammarian, that grammar was a subject with too much theory and too little data. [. . .] Back in 1949, when under the guidance of my teacher Wang Li I first put together a corpus of Cantonese sentences in order to study the grammar of the dialects of the Pearl River Delta (Wang Li was then conducting a survey of their phonology), I was struck by how little was known about how people actually talked.

In this context, McEnery & Hardie's (2011: Section 1.5) comments on Chomsky (1965) are also worth noting:

> In Chomsky (1965), twenty-four invented sentences are analysed; in the parsed version of LOB, a million words are annotated with parse trees.

Clearly, a great deal has happened in formal linguistics since the 1970s; and one aspect of these developments is a far greater commitment within certain frameworks with roots in the formal tradition to comprehensive descriptions – as in work based on HPSG (particularly at the CSLI Linguistic Grammars Online Lab at Stanford University; see e.g. Copestake & Flickinger, 2000). One reason for this was the increasing need for comprehensive descriptions in Natural Language Processing, starting in the late 1980s.[3]

Seuren's (1998) account of 'ecologism' and 'formalism' is balanced; he identifies 'merits' and 'drawbacks' with both approaches. Halliday's systemic functional linguistics is certainly a contribution within the ecological tradition; but it is interesting to explore where Halliday's development of SFL based on his 'ideas about language' is located in relation to these merits and drawbacks. This is actually quite revealing:

- In terms of the 'merits' of the formalist approach, it is important to note that Halliday has always been concerned with the properties of language in general, distinguishing very clearly between the theory of language as a general human semiotic system and descriptions of particular languages (e.g. Halliday, [1992] 2003a: 201–3, [1996] 2002); and this concern has, of course, been brought out in particular in the research context of computational modelling (see e.g. Matthiessen & Bateman, 1991) but also in language description, comparison and typology (see e.g. Caffarel, Martin & Matthiessen, 2004).
- In terms of the 'drawbacks' of the ecologist approach, it is equally important to note that Halliday has always been concerned with theory – he has never been 'antitheorist', as is very clear from his comments throughout the last half century or so (e.g. Halliday, [1961] 2002, [1992] 2005a, [1996] 2002, [2002] 2005b; and cf. Matthiessen & Nesbitt, 1996).

As far as the ecologist's 'risk of becoming antitheorist' is concerned, the antitheoretical stance has been a motif in certain areas of 'corpus linguistics', often associated with 'corpus-driven' as opposed to 'corpus-based methodology' – a motif that is explored and criticized by McEnery & Hardie (2011: Section 1.3 and chapter 6), who reject the distinction between 'corpus-based' and 'corpus-driven' linguistics.

Functional theories and formal ones have tended to be developed as mutually exclusive alternatives – as a thesis-&-antithesis pair; but they are, in principle, complementary rather than contradictory forms of theory, foregrounding different aspects of the vastly complex system of language. Halliday ([1992] 2003a: 203) articulates the distinction between formal vs functional grammars in terms of his principle of **trinocularity** (e.g. Halliday, 1978, [1996] 2002; Halliday & Matthiessen, 2004; Matthiessen, 1995a) whereby grammatical categories are identified and characterized (i) 'from above', from the level of semantics, (ii) 'from roundabout', from the level of lexicogrammar in terms of patterns of agnation, and (iii) 'from below', from lower ranks within lexicogrammar and the level of phonology (as illustrated by Figure 7.1):

In a formal grammar, perspective (iii) has priority; (i) is derived from (iii) and may not be stated at all (e.g. in some formal grammars the category corresponding to Subject in English would have no interpretation from above). In a functional grammar, such as systemic grammar, (i) has priority, and (iii) will typically be derived from it.

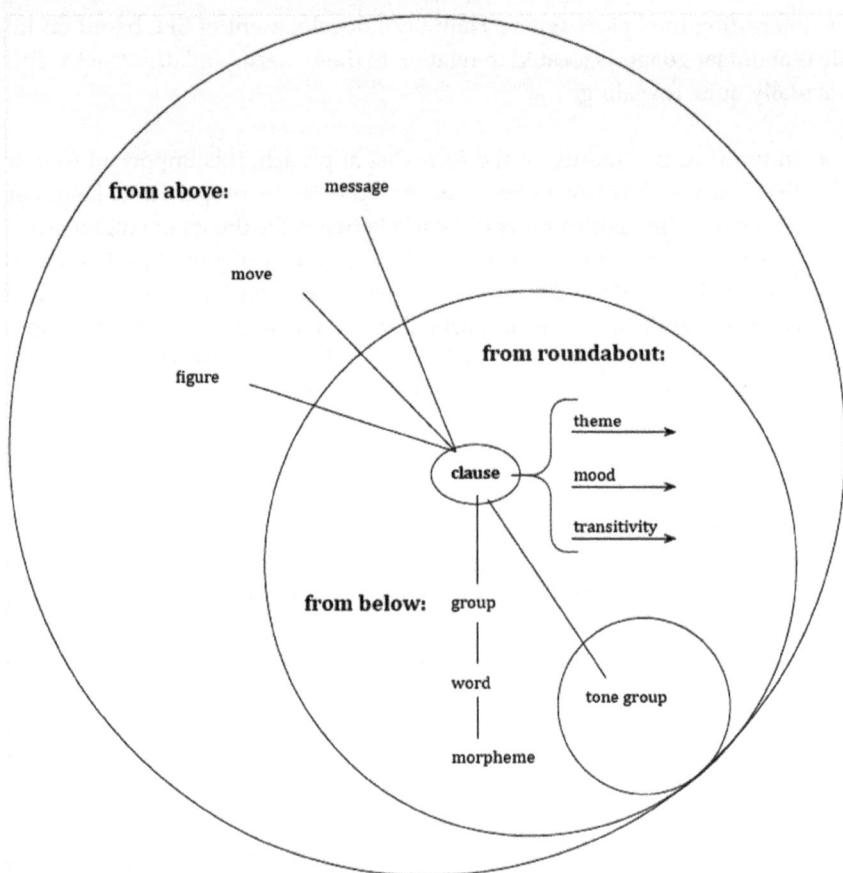

Figure 7.1 The clause viewed trinocularly – (i) 'from above' (semantics),
(ii) 'from roundabout' (lexicogrammatical agnation patterns), and
(iii) 'from below' (lower-ranking grammar, and phonology)

Since functional and formal theories are, in principle, complementary, it should be possible to develop a synthesis embodying both functional and formal insights into language. What would such a synthesis look like, and where is Halliday's systemic functional theory of language located within the overall landscape of theories of language?

Halliday's theory has certainly emerged out of the tradition of functional theories developed by 'ecologists' rather than 'formalists'. He has drawn on functional theories in linguistics (including centrally Firth's system-structure theory [see Butt, 2001; Kachru, this volume] and Prague School functionalism [see Halliday, 1974b; Davidse, 1986]) and in anthropological linguistics (the Sapir-Whorf tradition), and also on functional theories in anthropology

(Malinowski's functional anthropology with its emphasis on text in context; cf. Hasan, 1985b). Here Hjelmslev's (e.g. 1943) relational conception of language was important, with Lamb's (1966, 1999) work, inspired by Hjelmslev, on (what was originally called) stratificational linguistics as a key reference point.

At the same time, unlike many functional linguists, Halliday has developed representations of key aspects of his theory – system networks (representing the theory of the paradigmatic organization of language), realization statements (representing the theory of the relationship between paradigmatic organization and syntagmatic organization) and structural box diagrams (representing the theory of function structure as syntagmatic organization – e.g. Halliday ([1966] 2002a, 1976, 1978, 1985a, [2002] 2005a), and used them in computational linguistic research that he has been involved in. Computational applications have in fact been an important area of systemic functional research involving a number of researchers from backgrounds in both linguistics and computer science (see e.g. Winograd, 1983: Chapter 6; Matthiessen & Bateman, 1991; Teich, 1999a; O'Donnell & Bateman, 2005; Teich, 2009); and in the context of computational applications, researchers have explored system networks in more formal terms (e.g. Patten & Ritchie, 1987; Mellish, 1988; Bateman, Emele & Momma, 1992).

Thus we can see that while systemic functional theory is a full-fledged *functional* theory of language, it also has characteristics normally associated with *formal* theories rather than functional ones[4]; and one could argue that this would mean that it would be treated as 'taboo' based on Mary Douglas' (e.g. 1966) experiential account of taboo as a way of dealing with taxonomic conflicts in folk taxonomies, with anomalies in classifications: the taxonomic clash inherent in a category can be resolved interpersonally by making it taboo; systemic functional theory would thus join the company of shellfish and pigs.[5]

In fact, in the area of grammar, if we view the theory 'from below', from the vantage point of types of representation that are used to formalize aspects of the theory, we can recognize a **family of grammars** with similar properties that includes systemic functional grammar (SFG), Kay's (e.g. 1979) Functional Unification Grammar (FUG), Bresnan and Kaplan's Lexical Functional Grammar (LFG), Pollard and Sag's Head-driven Phrase Structure Grammar (HPSG), Sag's Sign-Based Construction Grammar (SBCG), Categorial Grammar (CG), and also Joshi's Tree Adjoining Grammar (TAG). These have been called **unification grammars** (e.g. Sag et al., 1986; Shieber, 1986) or **feature and function grammars** (Winograd, 1983: Chapter 6). Sag et al. (1986: 238) characterize the family of unification grammars as follows:

In such theories the linguistic objects under study are associated with linguistic information about the objects, which information is modeled by mathematical objects called **feature structures**. Linguistic phenomena are modeled by constraints of equality over the feature structures; the fundamental operation upon the feature structures, allowing solution of such systems of equation, is a simple merging of their information content called **unification**.

The work by Kasper (e.g. 1988a) provides a bridge between formalisms used in unification grammars and SFG (for example, one manifestation of unification in SFG is 'conflation').

It would take too long to explore the location of SFG in the family of unification grammars, but let me instead locate it diagrammatically in relation to other members of this family and in relation to a selection of formal and functional theories of grammar: Figure 7.2. Halliday's theory of grammar and his description of the grammar of English influenced Martin Kay in his development of what he came to call Functional Unification Grammar (see e.g. his descriptive examples in Kay, 1979), but, working with Ron Kaplan at Xerox PARC, Kay also drew on the notion of registers from Augmented Transition Networks (for part of the history, see Kay, 1994). In turn, Kaplan worked with Joan Bresnan to develop what came to be known as Lexical Functional Grammar, and in this way LFG was also influenced by Halliday's SFG.[6]

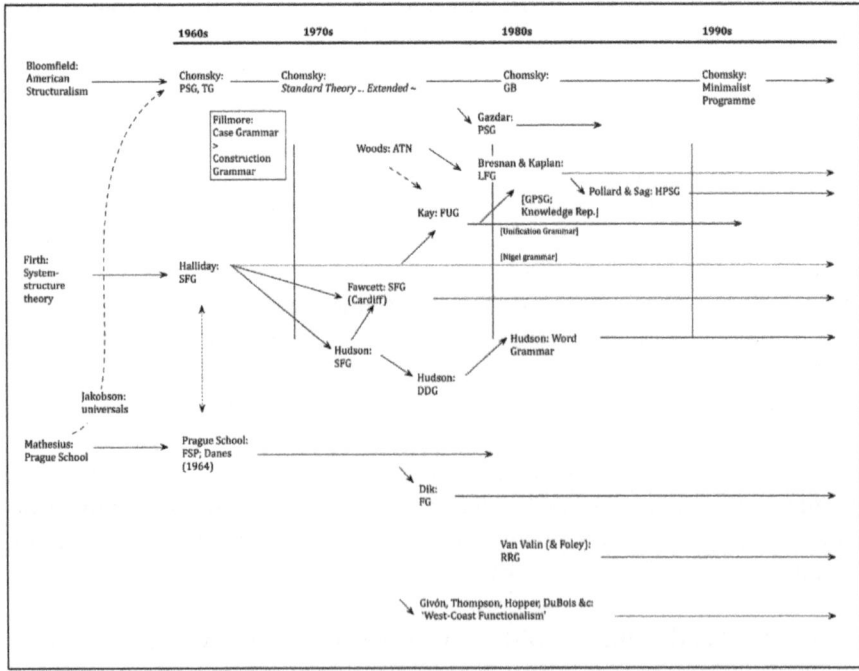

Figure 7.2 Systemic Functional Grammar in relation to the development of functional and formal theories of grammar

One difference between SFG and other members of the family is the primacy given in SFG to the paradigmatic axis, represented by means of system networks (e.g. Halliday [1966] 2002a). This form of organization has been explored in other unification frameworks, as in Elhadad's (e.g. 1990) use of typed features. The primacy given to the paradigmatic axis in systemic functional theory is not restricted to the theory of grammar; it applies to the theory of all the subsystems of language: semantics, phonology and phonetics also have a paradigmatic 'base'. This orientation towards the paradigmatic axis differentiates systemic functional theory not only from other members of the unification grammar family but also from other functional theories. (Formal theories tend to be very strongly oriented towards the syntagmatic axis, as part of their conception of language as rule.) So let me now turn to this central feature of Halliday's theory of language.

3 The Axial Rethink

The orientation towards the paradigmatic axis that Halliday developed in the first half of the 1960s can be characterized as an **axial rethink**. In the European tradition of structuralist theories, the paradigmatic and syntagmatic axes tended to be given equal weight, balanced as the axis of choice and the axis of chain; and this was certainly the case in Firth's (e.g. 1957a) **system-structure theory**: systems were located within places in the structures of units (see e.g. Fischer-Jørgensen, 1975; Dineen, 1967; Catford, 1969; de Beaugrande, 1991: Chapter 8; Butt, 2001); as Catford (1969: 225) puts it:

> Firth made explicit for both grammar and phonology a useful distinction not always observed by European 'structuralists' – namely, the distinction between *structure* and *system*.
>
> Structure is a syntagmatic ordering of elements; systems are the paradigmatic sets of units which can replace each other at any place, or element, in a structure. In simpler terms, structures may be thought of as a 'horizontal' ordering of elements; systems, as a 'vertical' set of terms or units which can occur at any given place in structure. Thus, in phonology, C_1VC_2 (initial consonant – vowel – final consonant) is a *structure*, exemplified in English by such words as *pit, bit, pin, pen*; whereas the sets of specific consonantal or vocalic units which may occur at C_1, V, or C_2 are systems (thus in English we have a system of initial consonants: p, b, t, d, k, g, . . .; a system of vowels: i, e, ae, . . .).

What Halliday (e.g. [1966] 2002a, [1969] 2005, 1976, in press [b]) did was in essence to free systems from particular places in the structure of units and give them whole units as their domains of operation.[7] As a result, systems could be organized into **system networks** – networks of simultaneous systems (like MOOD TYPE: indicative / imperative and PROCESS TYPE: material / behavioural / mental / verbal / relational / existential) and of systems ordered in delicacy (like MOOD TYPE: indicative / imperative and INDICATIVE TYPE: declarative / interrogative, with indicative as its entry condition). In addition, **terms** in systems could have associated realization **statements** (like declarative ↘ Subject ^ Finite – the systemic term 'declarative' is realized syntagmatically by the [specification of] the sequence of Subject followed by Finite); in other words, syntagmatic patterns were specified in paradigmatic contexts as realizations of systemic terms, as shown in Figure 7.3. Here is a key passage from Halliday ([1966] 2002a: 111–12):

> Systemic description may be thought of as complementary to structural description, the one concerned with paradigmatic and the other with syntagmatic relations. On the other hand it might be useful to consider some possible consequences of regarding systemic description as the underlying form of representation, if it turned out that the structural description could be shown to be derivable from it. In that case structure would be fully predictable, and the form of a structural representation could be considered in the light of this. [. . .] What is being considered . . . is that the part of the grammar which is as it were 'closest to' the semantics may be represented in terms of systemic features.

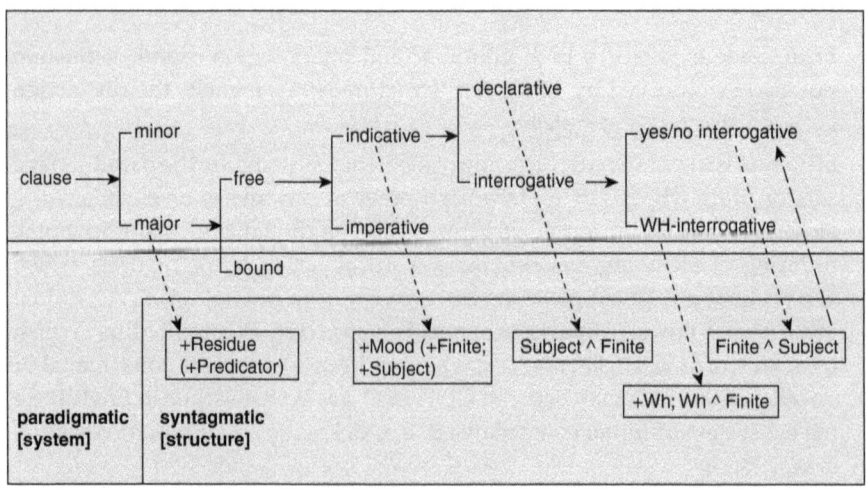

Figure 7.3 Simplified system network of MOOD (paradigmatic) with realization statements (syntagmatic)

His suggestion 'on the other hand it might be useful to consider some possible consequences of regarding systemic description as the underlying form of representation' represents a fundamental reconceptualization of the relation between the paradigmatic axis and the syntagmatic one. This axial rethink is a natural consequence of the conception of language as resource: to bring out the nature of language as resource, we can model it as choice – as paradigmatic options, treating syntagmatic patterns as realizations of one or more paradigmatic options.

System networks thus represent the overall, **global** organization of a given linguistic domain such as a unit of phonology or lexicogrammar, or a unit complex. This aspect of the axial rethink is brought out by Halliday ([1997] 2003: 249):

> I have always felt it important to try to view a language as a whole, to get a sense of its total potential as a meaning-making resource. This is not to imply that a language is some kind of a mechanical construct all of whose parts come together in a perfect fit, any more than if you try to see a human body as a whole you are conceiving of it as an idealized machine. Indeed it is precisely because the human body is not a mechanical assemblage of parts that it is important to view it paradigmatically as well as syntagmatically (to view it panaxially, if you like); and the same consideration applies to language.

In the system network, systems have intrinsic ordering: they are either dependent on one another in delicacy (as illustrated by the system network of mood shown in Figure 7.3), or else simultaneous in delicacy (as illustrated by the system network of the tone group in Figure 7.8); there is no extrinsic ordering of systems: simultaneous systems would in principle be processed in parallel in a model of the traversal of system networks in generation or analysis (see e.g. Matthiessen & Bateman, 1991: Chapter 10).

Realization statements are distributed across the system network, but each individual realization statement is local to a term in a particular system; its environment is thus paradigmatic, not syntagmatic. By virtue of the fact that systems are ordered in delicacy, the systemic environments of realization statements are ordered in delicacy: a given realization statement will specify exactly what is appropriate at a given point in delicacy, no more, no less. For example, the *presence* of Subject and Finite in the interpersonal structure of the clause is specified in the environment of 'indicative' – +Finite, +Subject. At that point, the *ordering* of these two elements is not specified because it could in fact be either Subject ^ Finite or Finite ^ Subject; these relative sequences are specified in systems of greater delicacy: declarative ↘ Subject ^ Finite (in INDICATIVE TYPE) and yes/no ↘ Finite ^ Subject (in INTERROGATIVE TYPE). Consequently, the problem of over-specification never arises; it was a characteristic problem in generative accounts based on syntagmatic rules in the 1960s (before many generative linguists moved to more declarative forms of representation, one source of influence being Halliday's systemic functional grammar: cf. the introduction to Section 4, and Section 2, Note 5).

The same applies to phonological system networks with realization statements. Phonological units serving in the structure of a higher-ranking unit, for example phonemes serving in the structure of syllables are never overspecified; they are only specified up to the appropriate degree of delicacy. This is of course possible because all phonological units (say, tone groups – feet – syllables – phonemes) are systemicized, i.e. represented systemically by system networks. Thus a phoneme is simply the syntagmatic realization of a combination of terms in phonemic systems, and a preselection from the unit above on the phonological rank scale, the syllable, can refer to any of these terms in phonemic systems. For example, if a syllable in Akan selects for 'nasal closure' : 'velar closure' : 'vocalic', the Peak of that syllable is preselected to be a phoneme with the features 'high' and 'back', but other features are left unspecified (e.g. 'advanced' [tongue root] / 'neutral'). (For the systemic description of the phonology of Akan, see Matthiessen, 1987a.)

If we compare the hierarchy of axis to the hierarchy of stratification, then it seems clear that the paradigmatic axis is analogous to a higher stratum and the syntagmatic axis to a lower one.[8] Like a higher stratum in relation to a lower one, it provides the environment in which the lower patterns operate. In this sense, the paradigmatic axis of a lower stratum mediates between that stratum and the stratum next above, as is illustrated within the content plane for semantics and lexicogrammar in Figure 7.4. Lexicogrammar is of course related

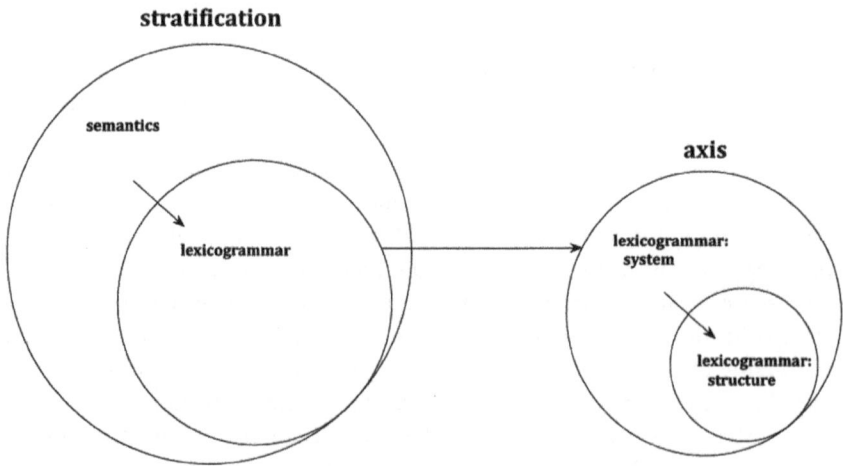

Figure 7.4 The hierarchies of stratification (global) and of axis (local)

to semantics in terms of both system and structure – as becomes very clear when we model the relationship explicitly for the purpose of computational modelling (e.g. Matthiessen & Bateman, 1991; Halliday & Matthiessen, 1999). However, it is the paradigmatic axis – the systemic organization of a given stratum – that organizes the relationship to the stratum next above.

Descriptions are thus organized or shaped systemically rather than structurally: structural descriptions are, as we have seen, contextualized by systemic ones. This does not mean that structural descriptions in lexicogrammar are not related to semantic ones – they are, and they must be (as is clear from Matthiessen & Bateman, 1991; Halliday & Matthiessen, 1999); but it is the paradigmatic axis that *organizes* the interface between semantics and lexicogrammar (whether we approach this interface 'from above' or 'from below'; cf. Matthiessen, 1990), also in as far as the syntagmatic axis is concerned. By the same token, lexico-grammatical structure interfaces with phonology; for example, the information structure of the information unit is realized by the structure of the tone group (see Halliday & Greaves, 2008).

The paradigmatic axis and the syntagmatic axis are both forms of order in language – implicate order and explicate order, respectively, to draw on the distinction proposed and elaborated for physical systems by Bohm (1980) (see also Butt, 1988: 75–6; Matthiessen, 1994). The implicate order of the paradigmatic axis engenders the explicate order of the syntagmatic axis; systemic terms are realized by specifications of fragments of structures, as illustrated above.

4 Consequences of the Axial Rethink

The axial rethink opened up a number of important new theoretical possibilities – possibilities that weren't readily available in syntagmatically based theories, whether they were functional or formal in orientation. I will consider the following developments (see also Halliday, 1996: Section 12):

- Halliday's discovery of the inherent functional organization of language in the **clustering** of systems in system networks, explained by him in the form of his theory of **metafunction** (e.g. Halliday, [1969] 2005, in press [b]).

- Halliday's comprehensive overview of the resources of a language based on major systems, in the form of **function-rank matrix** (e.g. Halliday, 1973a: 141, 1978; Halliday & Matthiessen, 2004).

- Halliday's integration of **intonation** in the description of phonology (as part of prosodic phonology) and (as a realizational resource) in the description of interpersonal and textual grammatical systems (e.g. Halliday, [1963] 2005a, [1963] 2005b, 1967; Halliday & Greaves, 2008).

- Halliday's **probabilistic** interpretation of the system of language (anticipated in Halliday, 1959), where probabilities are associated with terms in systems (e.g. Halliday, [1992] 2005a; Halliday & James, [1993] 2005).
- Halliday's modelling of the relationship between grammar and lexis as a continuum called **lexicogrammar** in terms of systems ordered in delicacy instead of as separate modules (anticipated in Halliday, [1961] 2002; Hasan, 1987; Halliday & Matthiessen, 1999).
- Halliday's modelling of all stratal subsystems of language in terms of the same type of axial organization by means of system networks with realization statements (e.g. Halliday, 1967, [1969] 2005, 1973, [1984] 2003, [1992] 2005b), thereby giving the axial organization the status of a **fractal principle** manifested in different environments throughout language.
- Halliday's account of **semogenesis** as systemic changes in the meaning potential, characterized in ontogenesis as an expansion and reorganization of this meaning potential (e.g. Halliday 1975, [1984] 2003, in press [b]).

These consequences of giving the theory of language a paradigmatic base, as an expression of the conception of language as resource, are represented diagrammatically in Figure 7.5. The diagram is designed to show how Halliday's 'stratal rethink' opened up news paths in linguistic theory and description.

Let me now discuss the consequences in Halliday's ideas about language of adopting the paradigmatic axis as the base of linguistics organization.

4.1 Systemic Clustering: Inherent Functional Organization

Halliday began developing a systemic description of English in the late 1950s (intonation, in particular) and the first half of the 1960s. This (evolving) description was the basis for a series of theoretical and descriptive papers in the next decade or so, including his comprehensive account of intonation and rhythm in relation to grammar (Halliday, [1963] 2005a, [1963] 2005b, 1967), his brief overview of the major systems of the clause (Halliday, [1969] 2005), his description of THEME and TRANSITIVITY (Halliday, 1967/8), his description of MODALITY (Halliday, [1970] 2005) and (with a delay in publication) his description of MOOD (Halliday, [1984] 2003). The 1964 version of his description, the 'Bloomington grammar', was published in Halliday (1976) and again in Volume 1 of his *Collected Works*, Halliday (2002a: 127–51).[9] As he developed the systemic description, he noticed that certain systems clustered together – that is, certain systems were more interdependent and other systems less so. This was the empirical basis of his theory of metafunction – a theory of the intrinsic

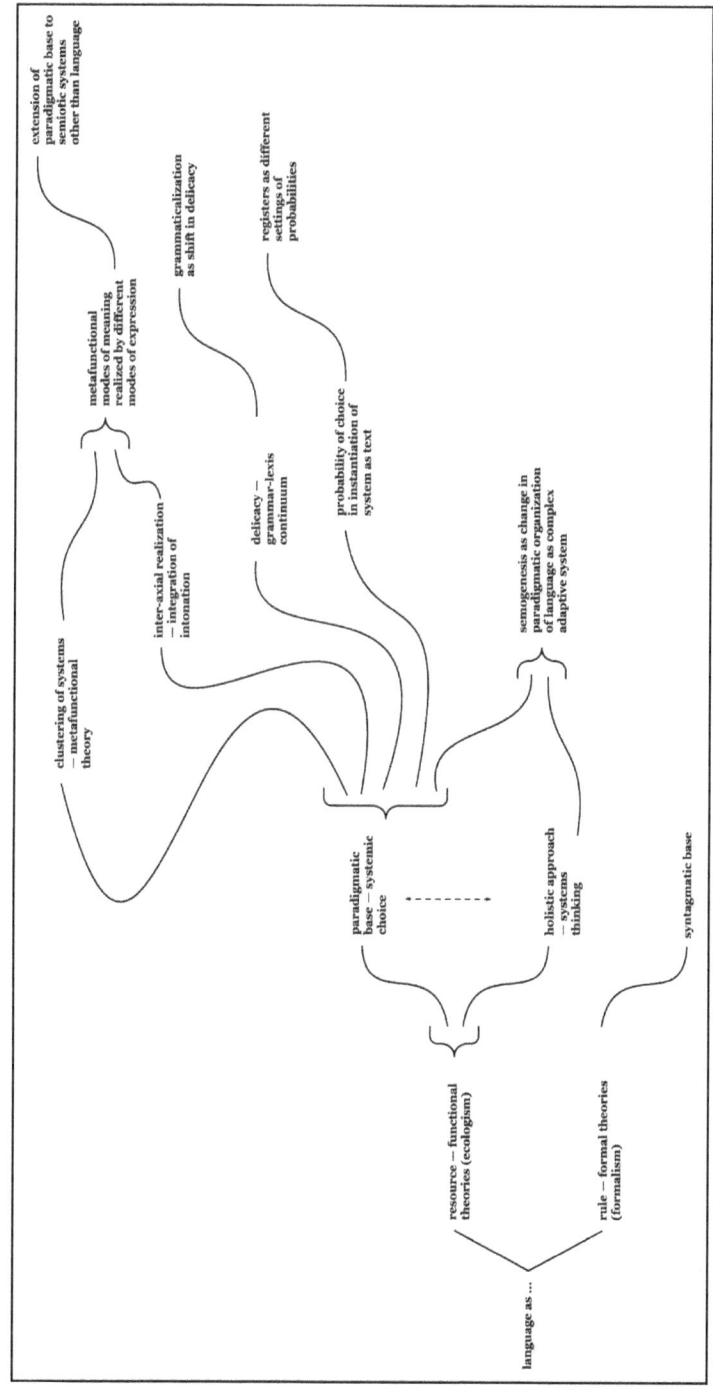

Figure 7.5 Consequences of image of language as resource

functional organization of language (cf. Martin, 1991). By the end of the 1960s, Halliday ([1969] 2005: 158) wrote:

> The assignment of clause options to the three components of transitivity, mood and theme reflects their interdependence: there is a relatively high degree of interdependence within each component and a relatively low degree (though not none) between the components.

(Compare also Halliday, in press [b]: Section 6.) In the Penman project at the Information Sciences Institute in Los Angeles, as we began to develop a computational version of Halliday's description of the clause grammar of English in 1980,[10] we were working with 'algebraic' representations of the systems in LISP, but it proved hard to manage the expanding and increasingly complex specification of the grammar in this format, so the project leader, Bill Mann (see Matthiessen, 2005), asked one of our team members, Yasutomo Fukumochi, to develop a programme that would enable us to plot the entire grammar with a Tektronix plotter on a multi-panel display that, once assembled, covered a large wall, making it possible for us to walk along the wall to examine different parts of the overall system network. This display made it possible to discern the differing degrees of interdependency that Halliday had already detected in the 1960s. Unfortunately, I can't reproduce this display here; instead, let me provide an index to the clause systems we represented in the form of system networks in Halliday & Matthiessen (2004), see Figure 7.6.

In Figure 7.6, the rectangular boxes represent individual systems in the three sets of systems of THEME, MOOD and TRANSITIVITY. The diagram shows connections between systems, but not the details; the entry conditions and terms of systems are 'invisible'. For example, the system of MOOD TYPE (free: indicative / imperative) is related to FREEDOM (major: free / bound) because the term 'free' in this system is its entry condition, and it is related to INDICATIVE TYPE (indicative: declarative / interrogative) because the term 'indicative' in MOOD TYPE is the entry condition to INDICATIVE TYPE (cf. Figure 7.3). Thus the diagram is not a system network but rather an index into a system network. However, it does capture the ordering of systems in delicacy (from left to right in the display) and interdependencies of the kind just illustrated, where a term in one system serves as an entry condition in one or more other systems.

As can be seen in Figure 7.6, systems tend to cluster; and these clusters can be interpreted metafunctionally – one cluster of textual systems (THEME, and also CONJUNCTION), one cluster of interpersonal systems (MOOD, including MODAL ASSESSMENT) and one cluster of experiential systems (TRANSITIVITY); a simplified version of these clusters is shown in the clausal system network provided by Halliday (1973a: 32). There are certainly interdependencies across these three sets of systems; for example, textual systems of VOICE operate in the

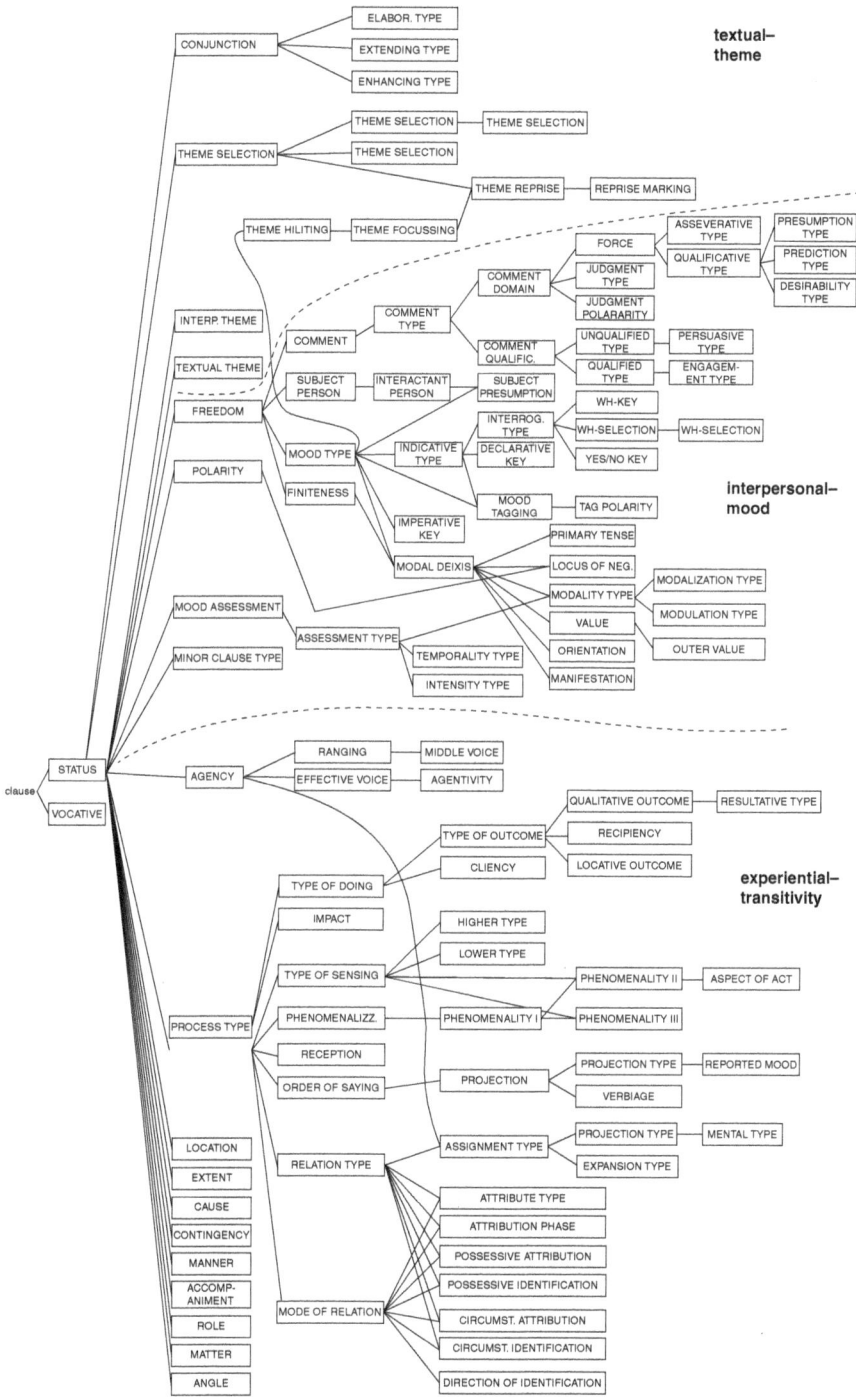

Figure 7.6 Index of clause systems in Halliday & Matthiessen (2004), with indication of metafunctional clustering

systemic environment of experiential systems of AGENCY, RANGE and BENEFAC-TION (cf. Matthiessen, 1995a), and THEME HIGHLIGHTING systems are only available in 'indicative' clauses, not in 'imperative' ones.

And then there are what appear to be more peripheral systems that are not part of a systemic cluster. In particular, the systems of CIRCUMSTANTIAL TRANSI-TIVITY like location, extent, manner and cause are represented simply as simultaneous systems with 'major' (clause) as their entry conditions. However, the current description of them as simultaneous with the more nuclear transitivity systems of AGENCY and PROCESS TYPE may in fact reflect a need for further descriptive work. When we consider relative frequency in text, we find significant quantitative associations between circumstantial systems and the systems of AGENCY and PROCESS TYPE even though they are not currently shown in the qualitative description of the system network. For example, circumstances of 'matter' are much more likely to be selected in 'verbal' or 'mental' clauses than in 'material' ones: see Matthiessen (1999, 2006). In addition, it seems very clear that additional interdependences between circumstantial and nuclear systems of TRANSITIVITY will begin to emerge when we extend the account in delicacy (cf. Hasan, 1987). Such more delicate interdependencies are likely to include patterns of agnation that have been discussed extensively in the tradition of case grammar, e.g. *provide somebody with something: provide something to somebody*, and in descriptions of 'constructions' in different versions of construction grammar (cf. further Section 4.5 below).

The situation is likely to be similar in the interpersonal domain with the core system of MOOD and types of MODAL ASSESSMENT. While they appear to be simply simultaneous in the system network index in Figure 7.6, interdependencies begin to emerge when we extend the description in delicacy. For example, assessments of the Subject's modal responsibility such as *rightly, wrongly, wisely, foolishly*, as in *he foolishly attempted to besiege the well-protected fortress of St. Malo*, can only be selected in 'indicative' clauses, not in 'imperative' ones (cf. Matthiessen, 1995a: 494).

4.2 Systemic Cartography

The diagram in Figure 7.6 provides us with an overview of the resources of the clause in English – an index to the clause systems presented in Halliday and Matthiessen (2004). The systems in Figure 7.6 can be located in terms of (i) metafunction and (ii) rank: textual – THEME, interpersonal – MOOD, and experiential – TRANSITIVITY, at the rank of clause, see Figure 7.7.

Figure 7.7 shows the location of a simple version of the system of MOOD (cf. Figure 7.3 above) in terms of a matrix where metafunction and rank are intersected. Such a matrix is called a **function-rank matrix**, and was introduced by

Halliday as a way of displaying an overview of the total system of a language at a particular stratum, in this case the stratum of lexicogrammar: see e.g. Halliday ([1970] 2005: 169, 1973a: 141, 1978) on English, Halliday & McDonald (2004) on Chinese, and Teruya (2007) on Japanese. In other words, when a language is described systemically, it becomes possible to map out its resources in the way illustrated by Figure 7.7. We can call the process of creating a map of language in this way **linguistic cartography** (cf. Matthiessen, 1995a, on lexicogrammatical cartography). As in the creation of maps of the extension of material systems in space, we use the maps to identify regions, using dimensions such as the

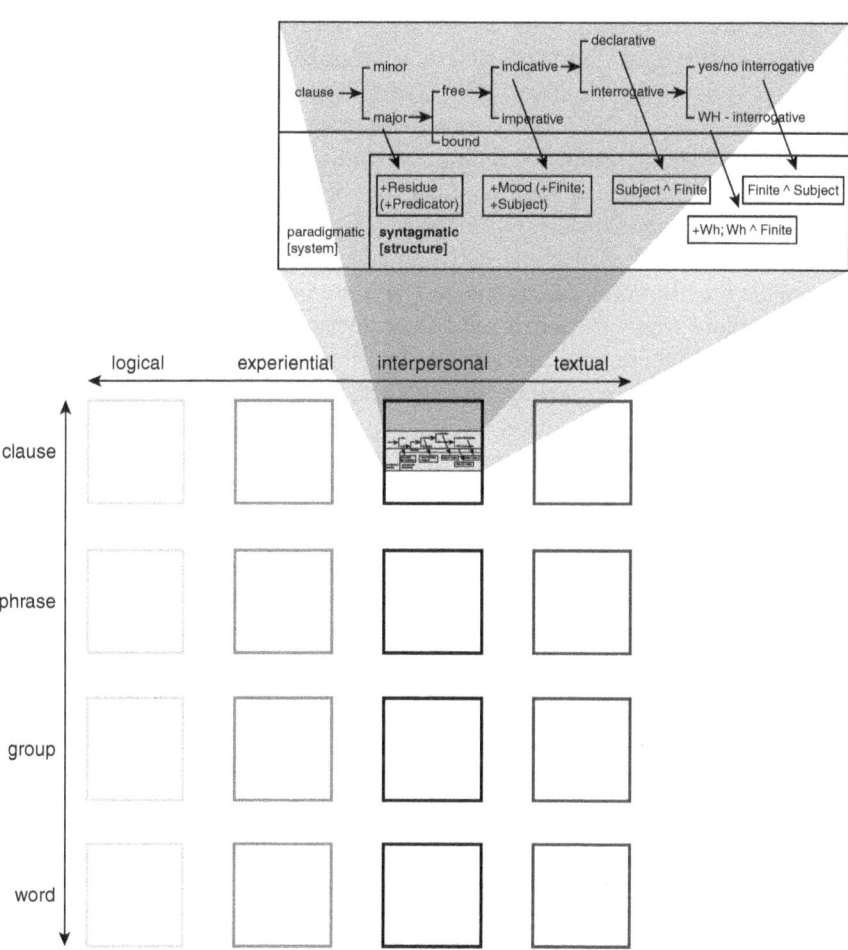

Figure 7.7 Schematic function rank matrix (lexicogrammatical stratum), showing the location ('semiotic address') of the system of mood in terms of metafunction (interpersonal) and rank (clause)

spectrum of metafunction and the hierarchy of rank as the analogues of longitude and latitude. By mapping out a language systemically, we can reason about
language as a system of systems. For example, we can explore recurrent systemic patterns manifested in different 'regions' of the language – what we have
called **fractal systems** (e.g. Matthiessen, 1995a; Halliday & Matthiessen, 1999).
In this way, the paradigmatic base used in the modelling of language makes it
possible to explore language as a complex adaptive system (cf. Matthiessen,
2009a; and also Beckner et al., 2009, for the interpretation of language as a **complex adaptive system** along the lines of research at the Santa Fé Institute).

Function-rank matrices are maps of the lexicogrammatical resources of
language; and comparing them across descriptions of different languages is
very illuminating, making it possible to undertake comparison and typology
based on systems (cf. Halliday, [1957] 2002). For example, the matrices providing overviews of the lexicogrammatical systems of Chinese (Halliday &
McDonald, 2004) and English (Halliday & Matthiessen, 2004: Chapter 2) make
it possible to identify and then contrast the different systems for construing
'process time' grammatically, ASPECT and TENSE, respectively (cf. Halliday &
Matthiessen, 1999). It is also instructive to add the semiotic dimension of delicacy to the function-rank matrix for lexicogrammar: by adding this dimension,
we can explore where meanings tend to be lexicogrammaticalized in different
languages, and where 'constructions' (in the sense of 'construction grammars')
are located somewhere midway between grammar and lexis (cf. Matthiessen,
2007b: Figure 7.13).

Similar maps can be drawn for the other strata of a language, although when
we survey the phonological system of a language, one of the dimensions will be
different: while we can retain rank, metafunction is only reflected indirectly at
the highest rank (that of the tone group) and it needs to be replaced with more
phonologically motivated considerations (cf. Matthiessen, 1987a).

A function-rank matrix is, of course, simply an intersection of two semiotic
dimensions – the hierarchy of rank and the spectrum of metafunction. In the
same way, other semiotic dimensions can be intersected – in particular, global
semiotic dimensions, giving us maps of the overall resources of language in
context:

- **stratification-instantiation matrix**: see Halliday ([2002] 2005a: 254–5)
- **metafunction-stratification matrix**: see Matthiessen (forthcoming b), and
  cf. the cover of Halliday & Matthiessen (2004).

It is, of course, even possible to work with three-dimensional matrices, like
the schematic **metafunction-stratification-instantiation matrix** on the cover
of Halliday & Matthiessen (2004). These global matrices provide the locations
of sets of systems like the meaning potential, the wording potential and the

sounding potential of a language. The general point is that Halliday's axial rethink enables us to explore the systemic organization of a language, viewing it holistically; in other words, the axial rethink enables us to investigate language in terms of systems thinking.

4.3 Systemic Integration: Intonation

Paradigmatic relations represented by system networks are 'freed' from the constraints of syntagmatic patterning. In theories based on structure, there will always be certain very significant non-segmental aspects of language that are very hard to accommodate theoretically and descriptively because they cannot be located within some variant of constituency structure (or dependency structure) since they are not manifested segmentally. This has certainly been true of accounts of intonation[11]; and similar considerations would apply to 'paralinguistic' features such as tamber, tempo and loudness (cf. Wan, 2011). However, once the paradigmatic axis is given priority, it becomes possible to describe systemic contrasts realized intonationally without being constrained by a particular form of syntagmatic expression. Intonation contours no longer have to be accommodated as sequences of some kind of segmental 'tonemes' but can instead be treated as prosodic realizations of terms in systems (cf. Halliday, [1979] 2002).

From a systemic point of view, what is important is simply that contrasts among terms in systems are maintained through syntagmatic realizations; it does not matter what the nature of the mode of expression is (cf. again Halliday, [1979] 2002), as long as the systemic terms are realizationally distinct. This principle is really the basis of Halliday's pioneering account of intonation (e.g. Halliday, [1963] 2005a, [1963] 2005b, 1967; Elmenoufy, 1969; Halliday & Greaves, 2008). He described the resources of intonation at their own level – the level of phonology, representing them by means of a network of options in the formation of 'melodies'; and then he also described them 'from above', showing how intonation was deployed as an expressive resource in the realization of delicate terms in the system of MOOD, see Figure 7.8 (a simplified representation based on the detailed descriptions in Halliday, 1967; Halliday & Greaves, 2008).

As Figure 7.8 shows, terms in the grammatical system of MOOD are realized in different ways in English. Fairly indelicate terms are realized by specifications of the modal structure of the clause (e.g. declarative ↘ Subject ^ Finite; yes/no interrogative ↘ Finite ^ Subject), but more delicate terms are realized by tonal distinctions – that is, by preselections of terms in systems forming part of the system network of intonation at the level of phonology. For example, 'neutral' yes/no interrogative key is realized by the preselection of the term 'tone 2' within the tone group realizing the clause at the stratum below, the stratum of

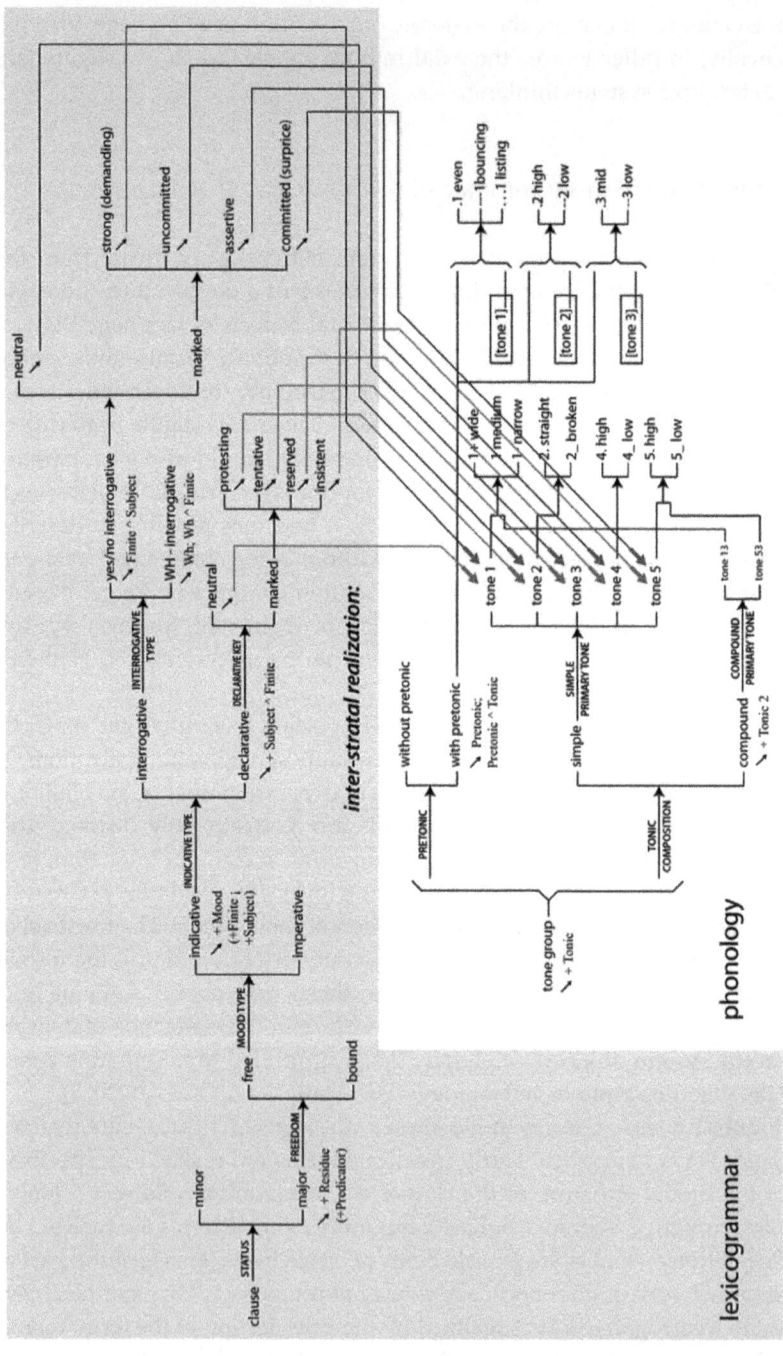

Figure 7.8 Systemic integration of intonation in the description of lexicogrammar and phonology in English

phonology; similarly, within MARKED DECLARATIVE KEY: 'protesting' ⬊ 'tone 2', 'insistent' ⬊ 'tone 5'. In languages other than English, we may find similar systemic distinctions within the system of MOOD but different syntagmatic realizations (see Teruya et al., 2007; and cf. Matthiessen, 2004a). For example, distinctions in MOOD in Cantonese, ranging from more general to more delicate ones, tend to be realized by modal particles rather than by contrasts in tone in the first instance (for Cantonese, see Tam, 2004; for Mandarin, see Halliday & McDonald, 2004).

By separating the statements of paradigmatic relations and syntagmatic ones and by representing them by means of system networks and realization statements, respectively, we can thus deal with modes of syntagmatic expression other than constituency, integrating them as expressive resources within the total account of the system of a language. In fact, the same principle can be extended to other semiotic systems. For example, terms in pictorial systems may be realized by specifications of different aspects of images, as in Kress & van Leeuwen's (1996) informal, discursively stated, realization statements. We need to find ways of making such statements explicit in terms of some form of syntagmatic representation of images; such realization statements could be called **rendering statements** (cf. Matthiessen, Kobayashi & Zeng, 1995).

4.4 Systemic Probability

Terms in the systems of a system network contrast with one another; in the course of instantiation (whether this is in generation or analysis), one term in a given system will be selected and the other terms won't be. This invites the question of how frequently the different terms in a given system are selected (e.g. Halliday, [1991] 2005a, [1991] 2005b, [1992] 2005a). As Halliday ([1991] 2005a: 45) puts it:

> Obviously, to interpret language in probabilistic terms, the grammar (that is, the theory of grammar, the *grammatics*) has to be paradigmatic: it has to be able to represent language as **choice**, since probability is the probability of 'choosing' (not in any conscious sense, of course) one thing rather than another. Firth's concept of 'system', in the 'system/structure' framework, already modelled language as choice. Once you say 'choose for polarity: positive or negative?', or 'choose for tense: past or present or future?', then each of these options could have a probability value attached.

This was in fact a question that Halliday had explored already in the 1950s, in his text-based research on Chinese.[12] In Halliday ([1956] 2005a), which he based on 'a small corpus of spoken material recorded by myself in Peking and elsewhere', he assigned probabilities to descriptive statements, using four degrees of probability: 'even, likely, almost certain and certain'. In Halliday ([1959] 2005), he gives counts of the occurrences of principal categories and items in his corpus, *The Secret History of the Mongols*. For example, in his text, there are 1009 instances of 'perfective' aspect in free clauses and 271 instances of 'imperfective' ones (Halliday, [1959] 2005: 207), which suggests that aspect is a skew system in terms of the probability of the selection of the two terms – perfective 0.8 / imperfective 0.2. What Halliday ([1959] 2005) had done was count occurrences, or instances, in his corpus of categories such as 'ergative', 'passive', 'perfective', 'imperfective', 'interrogative' and 'imperative' and items such as *yiu, duei, bei, zai, zuo* and other 'prepositive verbs'. Such counts can be reported as raw counts or relative frequencies. In either case, they are observations about quantitative patterns in texts, i.e. at the instance pole of the cline of instantiation. Just as qualitative patterns in texts instantiate qualitative patterns in the system – e.g. instances of 'passive' instantiate the term 'passive' in the system of voice, so quantitative patterns in texts instantiate quantitative patterns in the system: what this means is that frequencies in texts instantiate probabilities in the system, as shown in Figure 7.9.

Looked at from the potential pole of the cline of instantiation, systemic probabilities are inherent in systemic terms, or options; and the meaning of a systemic probability is 'probability of instantiation'. For example, in the system of polarity, the terms (with attached probabilities) are 'positive' 0.9 / 'negative' 0.1; that is, the probability that 'positive' will be instantiated (selected) is 0.9 and the probability that 'negative' will be instantiated is 0.1 (cf. Halliday & James, [1993] 2005). Viewed from the instance pole of the cline, texts unfold through repeated selections (instantiations) of different systemic terms (cf. Halliday, [1977] 2002; Matthiessen, 2002a). These selections form qualitative and quantitative patterns extending over the text – patterns which can be represented as **text scores** and visualized by means of graphs (see e.g. Matthiessen, 1995a: 47, 824–5, 2002a, 2009a: 209–12). Such scores show the frequency of selections of different systemic terms as the text unfolds. These frequencies constitute and reconstitute systemic probabilities higher up the cline of instantiation. As new

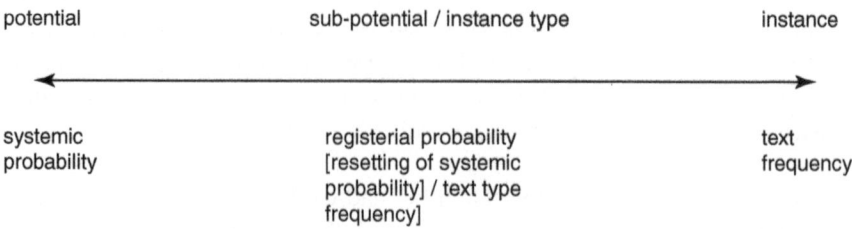

Figure 7.9 The location of probability and frequency along the cline of instantiation

text types emerge and become established (for a detailed study of the evolution of one new text type, see Nanri, 1993), they will have distinctive frequency profiles, constituted in the texts that contribute to the formation of text types. Halliday ([2010] 2013: Section 5) comments:

> Every act of meaning perturbs, however minutely, the probabilities of the language system, and so contributes to its ongoing evolution. The meaning potential is statistically modulated; this is how it is transmitted from one generation to the next.

As noted above, Halliday's conception of language as a probabilistic system can be traced back to the 1950s (and originates in his experience as a language learner and teacher); but it only became possible to investigate it on a more extensive scale once corpora and corpus tools had come of age (but cf. Halliday, [1992] 2005a: 81, on counts in the mid-1960s). In Halliday (2005), he summarizes a number of quantitative corpus-based studies within SFL, including the seminal work by Nesbitt & Plum (1988), and he explores a number of central theoretical issues – including different kinds of systemic probability such as transitional and conditional probabilities (cf. also Halliday, [1992] 2003b); but since this book contains a chapter devoted to Halliday on language as a probabilistic system, I won't go into further detail here.

4.5 Systemic Elaboration: Lexicogrammar

In rule-based, modular models of language, grammar (or syntax and morphology – 'morphosyntax', to use a term that has become common) and lexicon tended to be theorized as separate modules, the grammar book and the dictionary in commonsense ideas about language. This was reinforced in Bloomfield's ([1933] 2002: 269, 274) characterization of the 'grammar' and the 'lexicon', with the lexicon as a kind of repository of items and irregularities:

> A complete description of language will list every form whose function is not determined by structure or by a marker; it will include, accordingly, a *lexicon*, or list of morphemes, which indicates the form – class of each morpheme, as well as lists all complex forms whose function is in any way irregular. (p. 269)

> The lexicon is really an appendix of the grammar, a list of basic irregularities. This is all the more evident if meanings are taken into consideration, since the meaning of each morpheme belongs to it by an arbitrary tradition. (p. 274)

This conception of the relationship between grammar and lexis, arguably grounded in the commonsense understanding, was taken over by Chomsky[13] and other generative linguists (along with other ideas from American structuralist linguistics); and it was not until the transition from the 1960s to the 1970s that relationship began to be problematized and explored, including the distinction between syntactic and lexical rules (e.g. Chomsky, 1970; Wasow, 1977; Hoekstra, van der Hulst & Moortgat, 1980). So it was in the context of Bloomfield's conception of the relationship between grammar and lexis that Halliday ([1961] 2002: 54) introduced the idea of 'the grammarian's dream':

> The theoretical place of the move from grammar to lexis is therefore not a feature of rank but one of delicacy. It is defined theoretically as a place where increase in delicacy yields no further systems; this means that the description is constantly shifting as delicacy increases. The grammarian's dream is (and must be, such is the nature of grammar) of constant territorial expansion. He would like to turn the whole of linguistic form into grammar, hoping to show that lexis can be defined as 'most delicate grammar'.

At the time, this way of theorizing lexis as a basis for description was very different from what was rapidly becoming the dominant rule-based theory of language (cf. Note 9); and lexical items (lexemes, or 'formatives') were part of the structure- based conception of language, being inserted from the lexicon into structures. In systemic functional linguistics, the relation between grammar and lexis was theorized in terms of delicacy rather than in terms of composition (i.e. rank, in systemic functional terms), and the compositional approach was taken further in the lexical semantic models that began to be developed within certain linguistic and computational linguistic frameworks in the 1980s (for comparison of structural composition of lexical elements and systemic paradigms of lexical dimensions, see Halliday & Matthiessen, 1999); but the grammarian's dream had to wait to be presented in publications: it took a quarter of a century for a substantial example of the grammarian's dream to be presented (during this quarter of a century systemic functional linguists were working very hard on theories and descriptions of grammar, semantics and context) – Hasan's (1987) description of the extension of a field within 'material' processes in delicacy (cf. also Cross, 1992; Matthiessen, 1991). However, the principle was very clear: it was the paradigmatic base of the theory of language that made it possible for the grammarian to dream about expanding into lexis. In a way, this may seem like 'componential analysis' in anthropological linguistic accounts, notably Lounsbury (1956) and Frake (1961) (cf. also Leech, 1970, 1974). However, on the one hand, systemic features or terms are not syntagmatic components of (the senses of) lexical items; they are paradigmatic values defining the dimensions of the lexicogrammatical space within which lexical items can be located.[14] On the other hand, the grammarian's dream means extending the description in delicacy at the stratum of lexicogrammar, leaving space for complementary accounts one level up at the stratum of semantics.

It is difficult to illustrate the description of lexis through the extension of grammatical systems in delicacy precisely because quite a number of steps in delicacy must be taken before the description reaches the point where it is possible to distinguish even sets of lexical items by means of intersections of terms from simultaneous systems.[15] So let me use a simplified example, taken from Halliday & Matthiessen (2004: 44): see Figure 7.10. In this systemic description, there are only four steps in delicacy (i.e. systems ordered in delicacy) from the least delicate, most grammatical system, PROCESS TYPE, to the most delicate, most lexical systems, FORCE, AUTHORITY and LOADING. These three systems (and their more delicate subsystems, operating in the paradigmatic environment of the non-neutral options of the three systems) define the lexical space within which lexical verbs such as tell, order and ask can be located as the realizations of (the Event function in the verbal group realizing) the Process of the clause. That is, combinations of systemic terms from these systems are realized by lexical verbs; for example, the combination of 'neutral' (authority), 'neutral' (force) and 'neutral' (loading) is realized by tell.

This description is, of course, merely illustrative; taking account of a more extensive region of lexical resources would take many more steps (cf. Hasan, 1987; Matthiessen, 1995a, 2012; Neale, 2002; Tucker, 1998 – for an overview, see Warner, 1997: Chapter 5).[16] Thus the number of verbs that may realize (the Event function in the verbal group realizing) the Process of 'verbal' clauses is around 350, based on my classification and adaptation of Levin's (1993) verb classes, and these fall into 14 verb classes (see Matthiessen, 2014), and there are surely many more: systemicizing even this 'minor' process type is a huge task. It is also important to note that within the lexical zone there is quite a range from more general lexical terms to more specific ones, recognized in studies of folk taxonomies (see Halliday & Matthiessen, 1999, and references therein) and in general treatments of vocabulary (see e.g. Carter, 1987); and lexical items realizing combinations of terms along this range differ in frequency, from fairly high-frequency ones (shading into the region between grammar and lexis) e.g. with verbs such as *say, think, do* and *make* to very low frequency ones.

It is the paradigmatic base that has made it possible to explore the idea that lexis can be theorized and described as most delicate grammar – that is, not as a separate module but as part of a continuum within the stratum of lexicogrammar, illuminated by Halliday (2008: Chapter 2) as complementary perspectives on the resources of wording. He writes (p. 48):

So the lexicogrammar adopts two contrasting perspectives for construing all this complexity. The one is specific and openended; hence flexible, but low

169

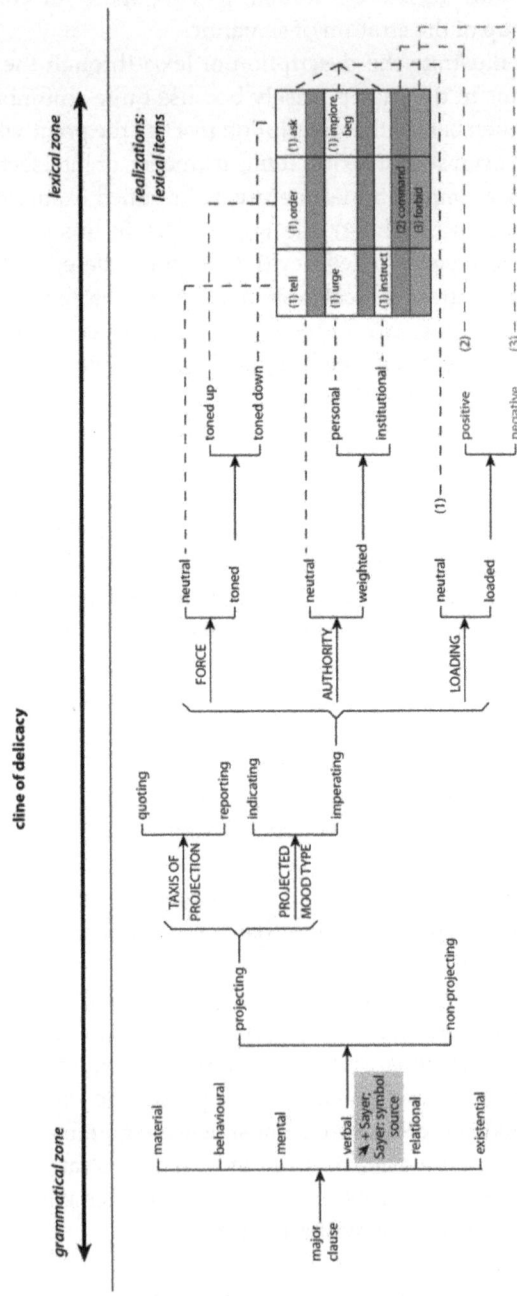

Figure 7.10 Simplified illustration of lexis as most delicate grammar

in information: this is the lexical perspective, good for seeing phenomena as particular. The other is general and systemic: hence high in information, but creating closure: this is the grammatical perspective, good for seeing phenomena as generality. The two are complementary; any phenomenon can be looked at in terms of either, but they will present two different images of the whole.

When we explore the relationship between grammar and lexis along these lines, in terms of the cline of delicacy, certain generalizations about paradigmatic and syntagmatic relations emerge: see Table 7.3 (cf. Halliday & Matthiessen 2004: 38–46).

Paradigmatically, the extension in delicacy from grammar to lexis is a gradual move from closed systems to open sets: lexis is more permeable than grammar; lexical items drift in an out of a language, whereas grammatical items tend to be more fixed by closed systems. In this respect, lexis provides a source of new resources for lexicogrammar; lexical items may be sucked into the vortex of grammar as expressive resources – a process that has been studied extensively in different languages in the last quarter century or so under the heading of **grammaticalization**. Based on the systemic way of modelling lexis and grammar, certain properties of grammaticalization in principle fall out automatically: terms in grammatical systems are selected much more frequently than are terms in lexical ones – so grammatical items are much more frequent than lexical ones and, as a Zipfian reflex on the expression plane, both phonologically shorter and more likely to be reduced (e.g. grammatical *the* vs lexical *supercalafragalisticexpealadocious*).

Syntagmatically, grammatical and lexical items thus differ significantly in terms of the nature of items; and whereas grammar engenders **structures** such as Theme + Rheme, Subject + Finite + Predicator + Complement, and Actor + Process + Goal, lexis engenders **collocations** (cf. Halliday, [1966] 2002b; Halliday

Table 7.3 The lexicogrammatical cline of delicacy in relation to the paradigmatic and syntagmatic axes

	low delicacy	*intermediate delicacy*	*high delicacy*
paradigmatic axis	systems (closed)	systems (semi-closed)	sets (open)
syntagmatic axis	structures	'constructions'	collocations
	grammatical items ('function words')	grammatico-lexical items (e.g. comment adverbs, cohesive conjuntions, attitudinal adjectives, general nouns, phasal	lexical items ('content words'
	low delicacy	intermediate delicacy verbs)	high delicacy

& Hasan, 1976) such as *strong + tea, powerful + argument, heavy + traffic, lay + table* and *make + bed*. But if grammar and lexis shade into one another along the cline of instantiation, how do structure and collocation relate to one another? I think many collocations actually involve lexical items serving in particular configurations of grammatical functions (cf. Matthiessen, 1995a); such configurations include Process + Medium (e.g. *shine + sun; twinkle + star; bark + dog; neigh + horse*); Process + Range (e.g. Process + Scope: *make + mistake; do + sum*; Process + Attribute: *turn pale; grow + old; run + dry; go + crazy*), Process + Manner: degree (e.g. *understand + completely; love + deeply; want + badly*), Epithet: degree + Thing (e.g. *powerful + argument, strong + tea, heavy + traffic*). Quite a few of these involve 'lexical functions', as they have been described by Mel'chuk (e.g. 1982) and his colleagues in the Meaning Text Model (cf. Matthiessen, 1995a). They seem to generalize beyond combinations of individual lexical items, which suggests that we can locate collocational patterns at different points along the cline of instantiation (see e.g. Matthiessen, 2009b, on Process: emotive + Manner: degree collocations). In other words, collocations can also be located at different points along the cline of delicacy.

Intermediate between the outer poles of the cline of delicacy – between grammar and lexis, we find patterns that have come into focus more recently under the heading of 'constructions' in different varieties of Construction Grammar [CxG] such as Berkeley Construction Grammar, Sign-Based Construction Grammar and Fluid Construction Grammar (e.g. Fillmore, Kay & O'Connor, 1988; Kay & Fillmore, 1999; Goldberg, 1995; Ruppenhofer et al., 2006; Sag, 2010; van Trijp et al., 2012; Steels, 2012) – but also under the heading of 'pattern grammar' in the work by Hunston & Francis (2000) in the Birmingham corpus linguistic tradition. The framework that Sag (2010) introduces is of particular interest in this context from a systemic functional point of view. It is called **Sign-Based Construction Grammar** (SBCG), and represents a merger of two distinct but related important traditions of research into lexicogrammar. Sag (2010: 29) characterizes SBCG as follows (footnotes omitted):

> a framework blending ideas developed over a quarter century of research in Head-Driven Phrase Structure Grammar (HPSG) with those presented within the tradition of Berkeley Construction Grammar (BCG) over roughly the same period. The goal is to expand the empirical coverage of HPSG, while at the same time putting BCG on a firmer theoretical footing.

The tradition of Berkeley Construction Grammar includes the work on FrameNet (e.g. Ruppenhofer et al., 2006), with a significant commitment to descriptive coverage of constructions; and FrameNet has been explored in systemic functional terms by Chow & Webster (2008). As noted earlier, descriptive coverage is also a priority in the HPSG tradition. Based on these two strands,

SBCG also includes the notion of typing; Sag (2010: 46) observes: 'In SBCG, the more general notion of "type hierarchy" takes over the inheritance functions that **constructional inheritance** performed in some earlier traditions of CxG.' This may thus be the emergence of a paradigmatic orientation, or at least the inclusion of paradigmatic considerations, in a tradition that began with a more syntagmatic focus – cf. also above the reference to Elhadad's (e.g. 1990) use of typed features (cf. also the use of 'ontologies', as in Huang et al.'s, 2010, work on the lexicon referred to above).

What are constructions? They are lexicogrammatical patterns located somewhere midway between grammar and lexis along the cline of delicacy (see Table 7.3). This suggests that we can approach them either from the lexical pole of the cline or from the grammatical pole. In work outside SFL, there has been a tendency to approach them from the lexical end, and then to look for generalizations. Perhaps we could call this the 'lexicologist's dream'. This approach is certainly facilitated by the way that corpora have tended to be represented and by the lexical orientation of corpus tools (cf. Halliday, [2002] 2005b; Manning, 2003, and also McEnery & Hardie, 2011). But we can also approach constructions from the grammatical end of the cline of delicacy, pursuing the 'grammarian's dream'. These two angles of approach are clearly complementary, not contradictory; but they are likely to foreground different considerations, at least in the early stages, before we arrive at a more well-rounded picture. Pursuing the grammarian's dream, we will be able to explore how the grammar engenders more delicate constructions based on more general grammatical configurations (cf. Matthiessen, 2012).

The systemic functional descriptions of lexis as most delicate grammar have tended to be focussed on experiential systems; but delicacy is of course a general dimension of organization that applies to all metafunctional domains. It is not surprising if the greatest extensions of lexicogrammar are found within the experiential metafunction: one key aspect of construing experience is, of course, precisely the construal of taxonomies of different fields of experience – with varying degrees of taxonomic depth depending on the degree of expertise, ranging from folk via expert to scientific (see e.g. Halliday & Matthiessen, 1999; Wignell, Martin & Eggins, 1993).

The logical metafunction – or rather the logical mode of construal within the ideational metafunction – is concerned instead with highly generalized logico-semantic relations, thus yielding taxonomies of grammatical items (e.g. structural conjunctions, and tenses in English) rather than of lexical items; and the textual metafunction provides a cohesive variant of these, extended further in delicacy (i.e. further from grammar towards lexis) but still not with great taxonomic depth.[17]

But what about the interpersonal metafunction? There are items that are purely interpersonal in nature; in English, these include grammatical items such as modal operators (*may, might, can, could, will, would, should, must* &c) and mood adverbs (e.g. *probably, surely; still, soon, already; sometimes, often; just, only; hardly, scarcely* &c), grammatico-lexical items (i.e. items realizing terms in more open systems located somewhere between grammar and lexis) such as comment adverbs (e.g. *sadly, honestly, wisely*) and attitudinal adjectives (e.g. *sweet, lovely, heavenly; vile, horrible, nasty*). There are also items that realize both experiential distinctions and interpersonal ones – traditionally discussed in terms of denotation and connotation, respectively; and these include general nouns with interpersonal loading (see Halliday & Hasan, 1976: Section 6.1[18]), located closer to the grammatical pole of the cline between grammar and lexis. To describe interpersonal distinctions that are realized lexically, whether on their own or in combination with experiential distinctions, we probably do not need to take as many steps in delicacy as we do in descriptions of experiential lexis (cf. the networking of classes of modal assessment in Halliday & Matthiessen, 2004). Halliday (2008: 49) comments:

> . . . in the interpersonal domain, the organization of meaning into the two regions, the lexical and the grammatical, is less polarized; there is not such a clear demarcation between the general and the particular in the management of human relationships. The two contrasting perspectives are still distinct; but it becomes more apparent that the difference between them is one of depth of focus, not one of discontinuity in the phenomena themselves.

The interpersonal deployment of lexical resources has, of course, been given a major descriptive boost in systemic functional linguistics through the work on APPRAISAL by J. R. Martin (e.g. 2000) and his colleagues; there is now an extensive literature – the major overview being Martin & White (2005). The description of appraisal covers both lexical items that are purely interpersonal (like the ones characterized above as grammatico-lexical items) and lexical items that realize both experiential and interpersonal features – as noted above, traditionally, denotation and connotation, respectively.

Martin & White (2005: Section 1.3) locate the system of appraisal within the interpersonal metafunction but at the semantic stratum rather than the lexico-grammatical one (cf. their Table 1.4):

> On the basis of the complementarities introduced above we can locate appraisal as an interpersonal system at the level of discourse semantics. At this level it co-articulates interpersonal meaning with two other systems – negotiation and involvement. Negotiation complements appraisal by focusing on the interactive aspects of discourse, speech function and exchange structure (as presented in Martin, 1992). Eggins & Slade 1997 present a detailed SFL framework for analysing interactive moves in casual conversation.

Involvement complements appraisal by focussing on non-gradable resources for negotiating tenor relations, especially solidarity.

This raises the interesting and important question of 'stratal address' of these systems within the content plane of language. Martin & White (2005) provide a number of informal system networks describing the potential for evaluation in English, but these networks lack 'root' features that would locate them within the overall description of either of the two content strata, semantics and lexicogrammar (e.g. Martin & White, 2005: Figure 1.8). Their account of evaluation includes both examples where the evaluation is made explicit ('inscribed') and examples where it has to be inferred ('evoked'); and these may of course differ in stratal location – inference clearly being a semantic rather than a lexicogrammatical process.

If evaluation – or assessment – is taken account of exhaustively within both of the content strata of language, semantics and lexicogrammar, I think the picture would have to be adjusted (cf. Matthiessen, 2007a). The semantic account would be more 'strategic' in nature – showing the strategies for assessing a range of phenomena, strategies drawing on both lexis and grammar (cf. Slade, 1996; and also Matthiessen, 2007a: Section 6); and the lexicogrammatical account would be 'lexis as most delicate grammar' in the interpersonal domain. If we pursue the description of interpersonal lexis systematically, treating it as extensions in delicacy of grammatical systems, I think we are likely to find that there are certain systemic prosodies: interpersonal systems that are manifested in multiple grammatical domains (cf. Matthiessen, 1988).

4.6 Fractality

One important finding in the development of accounts of intonation was that system networks can operate in domains with very different modes of expression. Thus even by the second half of the 1960s, Halliday's work had shown that two linguistic strata – lexicogrammar and phonology – could be represented by means of system networks accompanied by realization statements (e.g. Halliday, [1966] 2002a, [1969] 2005, 1967). In other words, the two formal strata of language, content form (lexicogrammar) and expression form (phonology), were organized along very similar lines.

At the time, this was very different from accounts in formal theories, as represented by Chomsky (1965) on syntax and Chomsky & Halle (1968) on phonology; and these two formal systems tended to be theorized in fairly different ways in generative linguistics, by means of different rule systems starting with different 'bases'. Later the generative theories of phonology tended to move in a more Firthian direction – from Chomsky and Halle's very abstract phonology via 'natural phonology' (as in the work by Theo Vennemann and Joan Hooper) to more prosodic conceptualizations of phonology, autosegmental and metrical phonology (as in Goldsmith, 1990; on these developments in relation to Firthian prosodic analysis, cf. also Henderson, 1987). The work on content form took off in another direction.

In contrast, in systemic functional work, both content form and expression form were conceived of as resources (with the term 'form' in Hjelmslev's, 1943: sense) – resources of wording and of sounding, respectively. Lexicogrammar was modelled as a **wording potential**, represented by means of lexicogrammatical system networks; and phonology was modelled as a **sounding potential**, represented by means of phonological system networks (as in Halliday, 1967; Tench, 1992; cf. also Matthiessen, 1987a). In this way, both lexicogrammar and phonology were 'generative'; they were represented as what speaker 'can say' and 'can sound', respectively. Thus a phonological system network with realization statements can specify all possible sound patterns in a language, not just those that are actually in use at a given point in time and listed as entries in a lexicon.

Thus the form strata, lexicogrammar and phonology, were theorized with a paradigmatic base and represented by means of system networks with realization statements. But what about substance – **content substance (semantics)** and **expression substance (phonetics)**?[19] Is it possible to formulate semantic and phonetic system networks, with semantic and phonetic realization statements? In principle, it should be, since these strata also provide resources as part of the overall meaning-making resources of language; as Halliday (2008: 65) observes:

> The network is a theory of what the speaker can do: what he can mean, at the semantic stratum; what he can say, or 'word', at the stratum of lexicogrammar; what he can say, or 'sound' at the strata of phonology and phonetics (cf. Matthiessen, 1995a; Butt, 2000).

However, the two substance strata are different in certain respects from the two form strata, one key difference being that they are **interface strata** (cf. Halliday, 1973a: on semantics as an 'interlevel').

Since the late 1960s, researchers have proposed a number of semantic system network, many of which are surveyed by Hasan et al. (2007); but there is no tradition of phonetic system networks – yet. While there is no comprehensive systemic description of the semantic system of any language (so far, nobody has produced the 'reference semantic' of a language comparable to the 'reference grammar' of a language), there have been a number of contributions illuminating various aspects of what the semantic system of language has evolved to deal with – including, semantics as the strategy for transforming what is not language into language in the form of meaning, in different situation types (e.g. Halliday, [1972] 2003, on the strategic semantics of maternal control; Turner, 1987) and across situation types, as a general meaning potential, with particular focus on interpersonal resources (e.g. Halliday, [1984] 2003, and the work by Hasan and her research group, summarized in Hasan et al., 2007). These accounts all involve semantic system networks with fully specified realization statements referring to lexicogrammatical features (cf. Fawcett, 1988). In a partly parallel long-term research programme, J. R. Martin and his research group developed system networks for semantics, what he calls 'discourse semantics' (e.g. Martin, 1992). These range across the metafunctions (although Eggins & Slade's, 1997, classic account of casual conversation focuses on interpersonal resources), but tend not to include explicit realization statements (cf. also the lack of explicit realization statement in the work on appraisal system presented in Martin & White, 2005).

Alongside these accounts – contributions that tended to be geared towards the task of manual semantic text analysis, there are also accounts of semantic networks developed in the research context of computational modelling. Drawing on Halliday ([1972] 2003), Patten (1988) shows how the notion of register-specific strategic semantic system networks resonates with ideas about planning in AI: such system networks serve as solutions that have been 'compiled' from the general semantic resources to deal with recurrent problems (cf. Matthiessen, 1990).

At the same time, there has been considerable work on general semantic systems in the context of computational linguistics, both in the 'Penman' tradition, with an ideational focus (e.g. Matthiessen & Bateman, 1991; Halliday & Matthiessen, 1999; Bateman et al., 1990) and in the 'Cardiff Grammar' tradition, with work across metafunctions, where system networks within the content plane are interpreted as semantic networks (since at least Fawcett, 1980): there is only one level of system networks, not two.

In the research context of computational modelling, various questions about semantic networks arise that have not tended to be addressed by those researchers who focus on applications involving manual text analysis. These questions relate both to the semantic networks themselves and to realization statements specifying fragments of semantic structure; for example:

- If reasoning and inference are theorized as semantic processes (rather than as cognitive ones[20]), how can they be supported by means of the representation of semantic resources – both systemically and instantially?
- Since semantics is the 'interface' within the content plane between language and other systems, how can semantic system networks be used to relate linguistic meaning to meaning construed or enacted in bio-semiotic systems such as perception (cf. Halliday & Matthiessen, 1999; Bateman et al., 2010[21])?

The concern with reasoning and inference has been one motivation in computational systems for using a form of representation of semantics other than system networks – some type of frame-based inheritance network, originally proposed in the late 1970s (for foundational proposals, see Brachman, 1978, [1979] 1985, in part a response to Woods' [1975] 1985, challenge to researchers working on semantic networks to develop theoretically and formally more explicit networks). Over the next couple of decades, researchers developed a family of frame-based inheritance networks such as KL-ONE, NIKL and LOOM (for some discussion from a systemic functional point of view and references to the original work, see Halliday & Matthiessen, 1999). These had well-understood mathematical properties, and included both paradigmatic inheritance and syntagmatic frames, the latter also represented in terms of instantial propositions supported by at least first-order predicate logic. Therefore, they support reasoning and inference both at the potential pole of the cline of instantiation and at the instance pole (cf. Halliday & Matthiessen, 1999). The developments in knowledge representation involving frame-based inheritance networks also influenced new initiatives in grammatical theory in the 1980s, in particular HPSG; so this form of representation takes us back to the role of paradigmatic order in the modelling of lexicogrammar discussed above (cf. also work on 'ontology' in relation to lexis: Huang et al., 2010) – highly relevant to explicit representations also of systemic functional grammars; see e.g. Bateman, Emele & Momma (1992).

It turns out that adopting what we might think of as an industrial-strength representational system for semantics also opens up new possibilities for interfacing with other non-linguistic models. One key example here is the research by John Bateman and his group to link a semantic model of space (related to the 'ideation base' part of the 'meaning base' of a language presented in Halliday & Matthiessen, 1999) to the kinds of models that robots need in order to engage with space as they perceive it and navigate around it: see Bateman et al. (2010). This is one of the crucial properties of semantics as an *interlevel* – to function as a resource for relating to other human systems (see Halliday, [1972] 2003), in this case systems designed for robots that are analogous to what we called bio-semiotic systems in Halliday & Matthiessen (1999).

It is probably not surprising that when we turn to semantics – to the interface level within the content plane (cf. again Halliday, 1973a), we find 'two cultures' (to echo C. P. Snow – but cf. also the principle embodied in Halliday's, 1964, notion of 'syntax and the consumer') within systemic functional linguistics: on the one hand, the culture of researchers who are focused on manual discourse analysis and the critically important problems in human communities that can be addressed by undertaking this form of analysis; and on the other hand, the culture of researchers who engage with computational modelling to solve other classes of problems of critical importance in human communities. The dialogue between members of these two communities of researchers has tended to be conducted with a somewhat narrow channel and to be a bit one-directional: members of the second community of researchers have typically engaged with the work by the first community, but the reverse has not usually been the case.

But what does this mean for the role of system networks in the description of semantic systems of languages? In a sense, this is an open empirical question; it will be illuminated by more extensive descriptions of the semantic systems of a variety of languages, descriptions with a clear focus on semantics as the inter-level of the content plane – the level embodying the strategies for transforming what is not language into language, into meaning. At the same time, we can address it by exploring the stratal organization of systemic theory itself as a metalanguage, see Section 6 below.

What about expression substance – phonetics, in spoken language?[22] As far as I know, while researchers have developed a fair range of phonological system networks (including realization statements), there are as yet no phonetic ones. Building on Abercrombie's (e.g. 1967) phonetic research, Catford (1977) was probably the linguist whose work on phonetics gives the clearest indication of what the ingredients of systemic phonetics would be (for a particular example, see Catford, 1985). His Fundamental Problems in Phonetics provides a very system-oriented – and I think systemic – view of phonetics; he says that the 'subject matter of general phonetics' is what he calls **the total sound-producing potential of man** (and in his book he includes the other phases of phonation as well), reminding us that Jan Baudouin de Courtenay had used the term 'anthropophonics'.[23]

In his review of Catford's contribution, Ladefoged (1979: 904) character-ized it as 'containing more original thought on phonetics than any book since Pike (1943)'. Ladefoged himself, who had also been at Edinburgh University and learned from Abercrombie there, like Catford & Halliday, worked over the years to produce a general inventory of phonetic features – more system-atic and phonetically motivated than Jakobson, Fant & Halle's (1952) pio-neering contribution; and Ladefoged's feature inventory can be interpreted as a **pre-systemic** account of the human phonetic potential as it is deployed in different ways in the languages around the world (a kind of 'etic' pool, in the sense of Tagmemic linguistics). The pressure on any form of representa-tion of the phonetic system of a language would, in principle, be the same as that exerted on the representation of the semantic system: the representa-tion would have to be such as to make it possible to capture the interface nature of phonetics, relating it to the articulatory and auditory systems of an organism.

4.7 Semogenesis

By giving priority to paradigmatic organization, Halliday has been able to shed new light on **semogenesis** – the processes by which meanings are created, recreated, extended and changed **logogenetically, ontogenetically** and **phylogenetically** (see e.g. Halliday & Matthiessen, 1999; Halliday, [1997] 2003: 250, [1992] 2005a, [1992] 2002a, [2002] 2005a). In other words, by viewing the creation and maintenance of meaning paradigmatically rather than only syntagmatically, Halliday and other systemic functional linguists have been able to bring out changes in the system over time. Change is thus interpreted as change pertaining to *choice* in the first instance, within the three time-frames of the unfolding of meaning in the text (logogenesis), the growth of meaning in persons as they develop (ontogenesis) and the evolution of meaning in the system over generations of speech fellowships (phylogenesis).

In each of the three time-frames, particular aspects of change pertaining to choice are easier to observe; some aspects stand out – are easier to observe – logogenetically, other aspects ontogenetically and yet other aspects phylogenetically.

(i) In the **logogenetic time-frame**, we see change in choice as a flow of systemic terms, selected with different frequencies as a text unfolds (e.g. Matthiessen, 2002a; cf. also Matthiessen & Bateman, 1991; see also Matthiessen, this volume: Figure 7.9).

(ii) In the **ontogenetic time-frame**, we see change in choice as the gradual expansion of a learner's meaning potential (e.g. Halliday, 1975; Painter, 1999; Painter, Derewianka & Torr, 2007; Christie & Derewianka, 2008; Matthiessen, 2009a); learners add new terms in existing systems, they add new systems, and they dissociate systemic variables from one another.

(iii) In the **phylogenetic time-frame**, we see change in choice as the gradual evolution of the collective meaning potential of a speech fellowship. This *may* involve an expansion of the meaning potential, e.g. when a language evolves new registers of science (e.g. Halliday, 1988), administration and commerce, adding them to the registerial make-up of the language, as part of becoming a standard language; but it always involves adaptation to the changing cultural environment, centrally through changes in the registerial make-up of the meaning potential. Underpinning these different manifestations of change in choice are the same systemic principles – the difference being where we observe them along the cline of instantiation.

(i) **Logogenetically**, meanings are created as texts unfold over time (cf. Halliday, [1992] 2003c, on the act of meaning). This can be modelled as changing states of the system in the course of the process of instantiation (cf. Matthiessen & Bateman, 1991): see Figure 7.11. The figure shows how the system of the clause is traversed in the course of instantiation. As systemic terms are chosen in the different systems that are entered (starting with 'clause', the root of all the clause systems), new systems become enterable (i.e. available for choice), and one term is chosen in each system that is currently enterable. The terms that are chosen as a unit of language emerges in the course of instantiation can be recorded as a **selection expression**, a record of the terms that have been instantiated. Some terms are chosen frequently, while other terms are chosen less frequently or not at all; the relative frequency of the selection of systemic terms in the course of logogenesis is an important aspect of the creation of instantial meaning (cf. discussions of foregrounding and de-automatization in verbal art, e.g. Halliday, [1971] 2002, [1982] 2002).

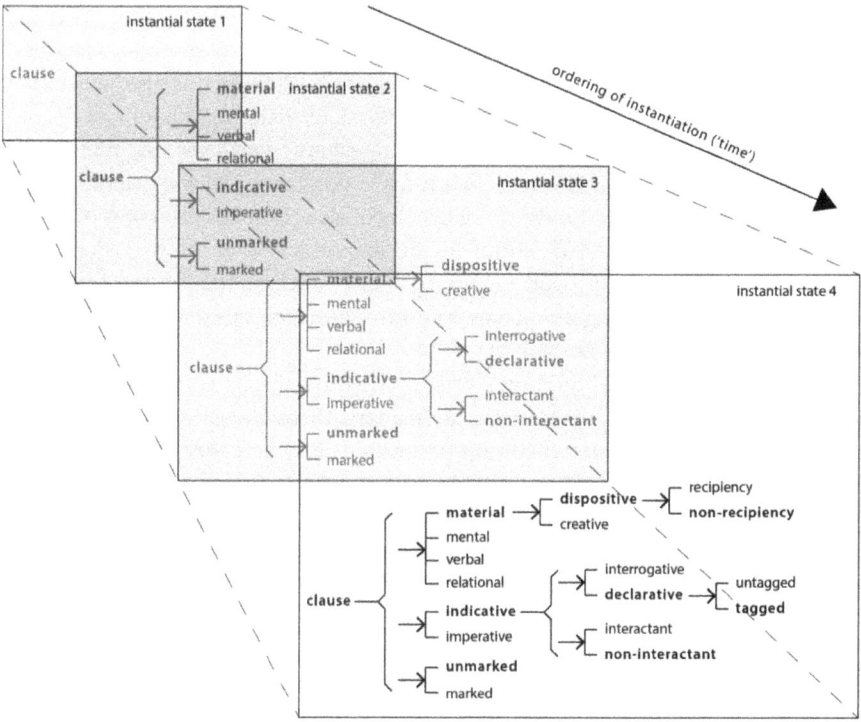

Figure 7.11 Successive instantial states of the systems of the clause

(ii) **Ontogenetically,** learners construct their meaning potentials out of innumerable processes of logogenesis: they engage with the instantial patterns of meaning in text, as they produce or analyse them; and out of these instantial patterns, they **distil** systemic generalizations, moving up along the cline of instantiation from the instance pole towards the potential pole (cf. Matthiessen, 2009a). These systemic generalizations include systemic probabilities inferred from relative frequencies in text (as e.g. Bod, Hay & Jannedy, 2003b: 6–7, emphasize, 'unlike categorical grammars, probabilistic grammars are learnable from positive evidence alone'; 'if the language faculty is probabilistic, the learning task is considerably more achievable'[24]). As learners develop, their meaning potentials **grow** – or, more specifically, follow the growth pattern characteristic of life: rapid growth through childhood (e.g. Halliday, 1975) and adolescence (e.g. Christie & Derewianka, 2008), steady growth through most of adult life, with the possibility of decline in late adulthood and ultimate death. It is difficult to illustrate the growth of the meaning potential, but let me give an indication of it by representing a sequence of the meaning potential for interaction (i.e. the meaning potential operating in interactional contexts) in Halliday's (1975) case study of Nigel, see Figure 7.12. The interactional meaning potential grows steadily; Nigel has more options in meaning at each interval described by Halliday. In the final version shown in Figure 7.12, there has been a qualitative change beyond the addition of new options of meaning: Nigel has deconstructed the personalized greeting into two systemic variables, the naming of the person being greeted ('Anna' / 'Mummy' / 'Daddy') and the orientation of the greeting ('seeking' / 'finding'). This deconstruction on the content plane was helped by his deconstruction on the expression plane into articulatory sequence (naming) and prosody (orientation). For Nigel, this served as a gateway into grammar, being able to mean more than one thing at the same time (e.g. Halliday, [1992] 2002a: 363–4).

(iii) **Phylogenetically,** members of speech fellowships evolve the *collective* meaning potential over generations of meaners, through both logogenesis and ontogenesis. This collective meaning potential is an *aggregate* of different dialectal, diatypic (registerial) and codal varieties of a language. In particular, as new registers gradually emerge and old ones disappear when they're no longer functional, the registerial make-up of a language changes over time, as has been shown by Halliday's (e.g. 1988) account of the evolution of scientific English over the last half millennium or so. The evolution of the registers of scientific English has involved an expansion of the meaning potential of the language, a key factor being the expansion of the metaphorical mode of meaning within the ideational resources of the language.

The evolution of the meaning potential is both qualitative and quantitative in character. Quantitative changes are probabilistic in nature – observable as changes in relative frequencies in texts over extended periods of time. One

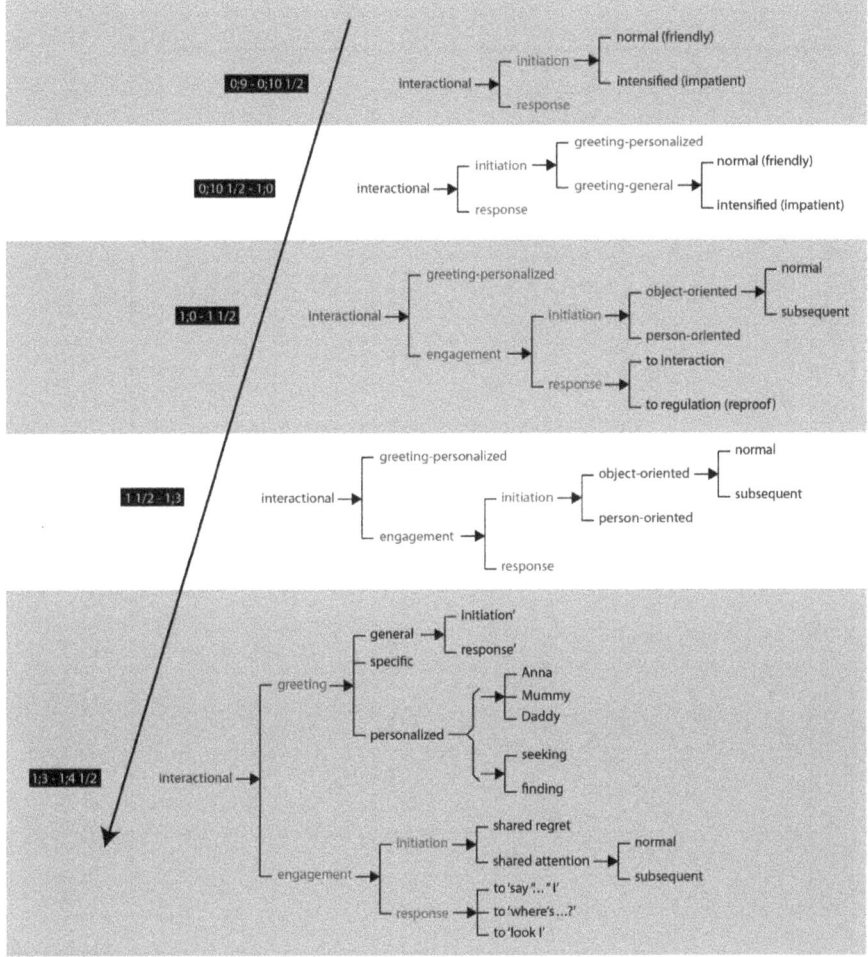

Figure 7.12 The gradual expansion of the interactional meaning potential during Nigel's protolinguistic phase, based on Halliday (1975)

classic (non-systemic) study shows this very clearly. This is Ellegård's (1953) text-based study of the gradual change in the systemic environments in which the auxiliary ('supportive' or 'periphrastic') do appears during a period of around 250 years, from Middle English in the 15th century to Modern English around 1700.[25]

The environment of *do* is determined by two systemic variables, MOOD ('imperative'/'declarative'/'interrogative') and POLARITY ('positive'/'negative'), and the frequency of do as a realization of Finite grew in so-called non-assertive clauses, i.e. clauses that are 'interrogative' and/ or 'negative', as shown schematically in

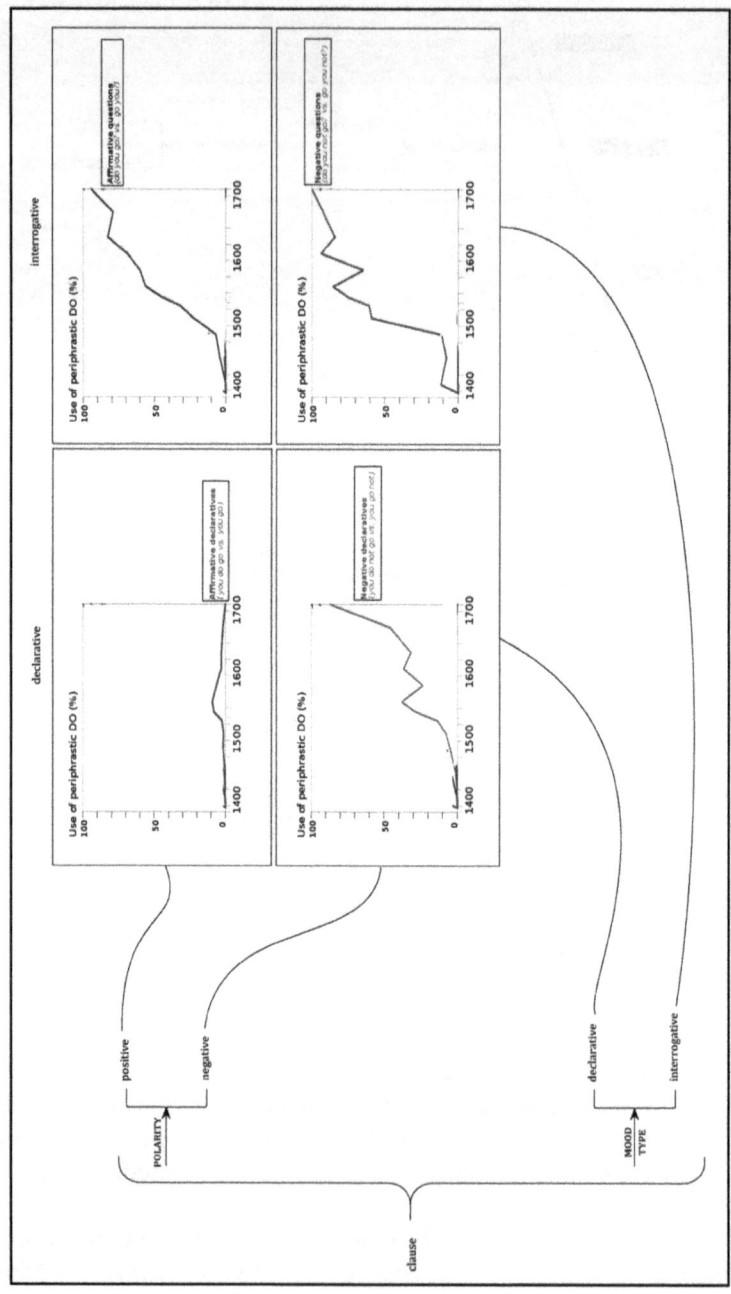

Figure 7.13 The gradual emergence of 'periphrastic *do*' since Middle English as a realization of Finite in interpersonal clause environments defined by the intersection of POLARITY and MOOD TYPE (simplified here as the contrast between 'declarative' and 'interrogative')

Figure 7.13.[26] (For the sake of simplicity, I have left out negative imperatives; but the frequency of *do* also increased steadily in such clauses during this period, reaching 100% by the early 18th century.) According to Ellegård's study, negative interrogatives led the way in terms of increase in frequency, followed by positive interrogatives and then by negative declaratives. The increases in frequency were gradual; for example, by around 1500, around 50 % of all negative interrogatives had *do* and by around 1700, close to 100 %. At the same time, while the frequency of *do* in (non-emphatic) positive declaratives increased for a while during the mid-16th century, it then decreased again and eventually became 0 %. Studies of this kind show very clearly that categorical change is simply the limiting case, either 0 % or 100 % in terms of relative frequency in text.

The kind of gradual change brought out by Ellegård's (1953) study illustrates a general principle in semogenesis: as just noted, states of the system that appear to be categorical are simply the *limiting cases of probability distributions*, either 0 or 1. Thus in Middle English, the probability of do as Finite in negative interrogatives was 0; but by the early 18th century, it was 1. To understand this change, we must interpret it as a gradual change in the probability of choice, as shown in Figure 7.13.

This general principle has been discussed by Halliday in various publications. In Halliday ([1992] 2002a: 360–3), he sets out a 'model of semogenesis' where associated variables are gradually dissociated from one another, providing a number of 'postulated examples of semogenic evolution in relation to some systems of Modern English' (Halliday, [1992] 2002a: Figure 4). The gradual dissociation is based on changing probabilities; as two features as 'prised apart', they begin by being very likely to be chosen together, and then gradually become more independently variable. This can be illustrated by reference to one of Halliday's 'postulated examples', the system of projection of speech and thought. Using Halliday's model of semogenesis, we can postulate three stages: see Figure 7.14.

In Stage I, there is just one system, which we can represent as 'locution = quote' / 'idea = report' – i.e. in traditional terms, 'direct speech' / 'indirect thought'. In Stage II, this one system begins to be split into two ('locution' / 'idea' and 'quote' / 'report'), with 'locution' and 'quote' and 'idea' and 'report' only partially (but strongly) associated with one another: 'locution' and 'quote' are very likely to be selected together, and 'idea' and 'report' are similarly very likely to be selected together; in other words, there are strong conditioning probabilities. In Stage III, these associations have weakened, and there are now two simultaneous systems, 'locution' / 'idea' and 'quote' / 'report'. These two systems could, in principle, have reached a state of being completely independently variable. However, text-based investigations have shown that certain combinations are favoured, other ones disfavoured. Drawing on a corpus of ethnographic interviews, Nesbitt & Plum (1988) found that 'locution' favours

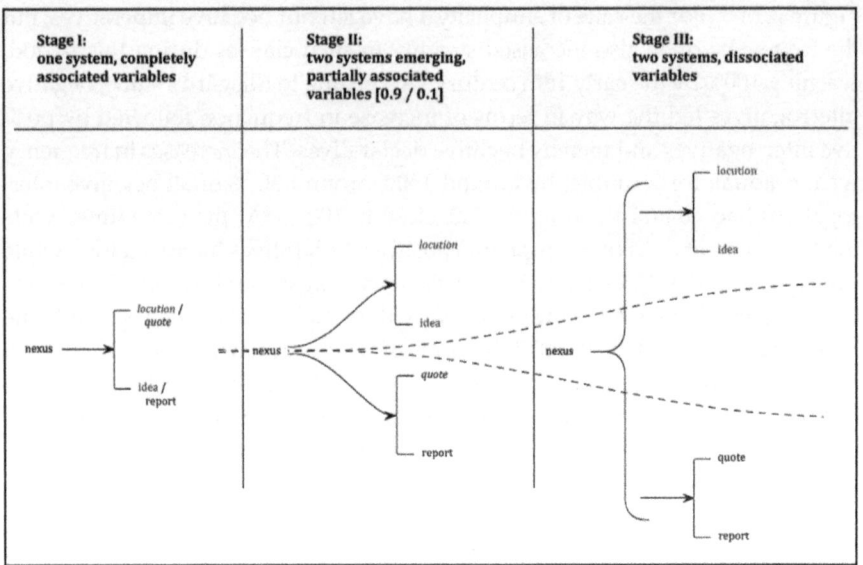

Figure 7.14 Halliday's model of semogenesis involving the gradual dissociation of associated variables (adapted from Halliday, [1992] 2002a: figures 3 and 4)

'quote', whereas 'idea' favours 'report' (for discussion, see also Halliday, 2005a). Drawing on a opportunistic sample from a range of spoken and written registers, I arrived at a different generalization (e.g. Matthiessen, 2002b): while 'idea' strongly favours 'report', 'locution' occurs approximately equally often with 'quote' as it does with 'report', see Figure 7.15.

Exploratory studies of semogenesis within the different time-frames – logogenetic, ontogenetic and phylogenetic – show very clearly that semogenesis is a systemic process in the first instance rather than a structural one. Semogenesis certainly involves changes in structure, as the now extensive literature on grammaticalization shows, but *the pressures behind such structural changes are systemic*. Studies outside systemic functional linguistics concerned with semogenesis – in particular, either with ontogenesis or phylogenesis – have been oriented largely towards the syntagmatic axis; but there are important exceptions: in their account of 'parametric linguistics', Heller & Macris (1967) give many examples of the role of what we might call 'paradigmatic pressure' in the evolution of languages. The work on grammaticalization, particularly in the last couple of decades, is another powerful example. While grammaticalization is usually investigated in syntagmatic terms, one key issue is really how grammatical systems gradually 'import' lexical items to serve as realizations of terms in these grammatical systems: lexical items move along the cline of delicacy from the lexical zone into the grammatical zone because of 'paradigmatic pressure' – the need to realize contrasts among terms in grammatical systems.

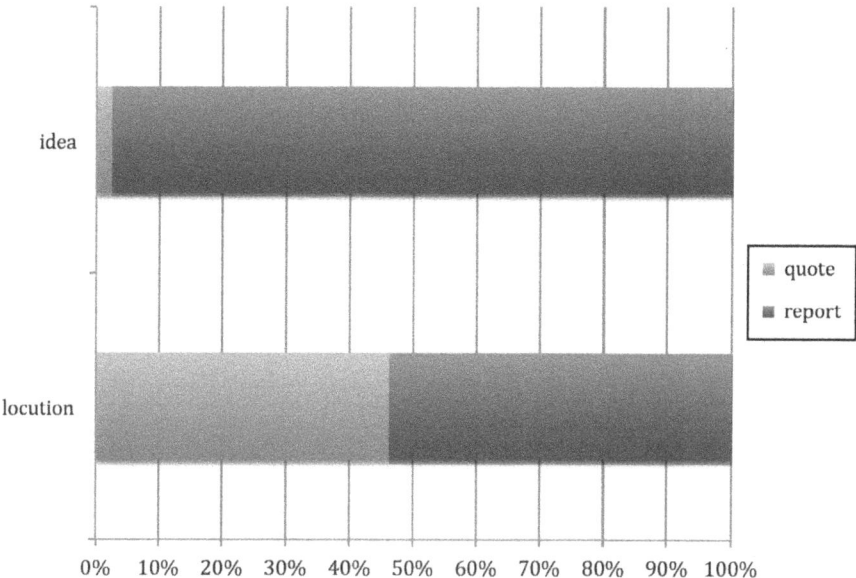

Figure 7.15 Intersection of 'locution' / 'idea' and 'quote' / 'report' in a registerially varied sample of texts (N = 1393 clause nexuses)

5 Language as a Higher-order Semiotic System

Central to Halliday's engagement with language is his conception of language as a resource for making meaning. This involves, as I have noted above (see Section 4.2), viewing language *holistically* as a complex adaptive system, adopting the approach of **systems-thinking** rather than that of **Cartesian Analysis**, the approach that came to dominate Western science (cf. Capra, 1996) in general and US American Structuralist and Generative Linguistics in particular. The holistic view of language in SFL has led to the expansion of the theory from language to semiotic systems in general. By applying systems-thinking, researchers have been able to locate language in relation to other semiotic systems – including centrally, protolanguage, making explicit how semiotic systems may differ in 'dimensionality'. For example, semiotic systems may differ in terms of the degree of stratification, in particular the bifurcation of the content plane and the expression plane into two sets of strata each (content – semantics and lexicogrammar; expression [for spoken language] – phonology and phonetics); and (related to this organizational difference) they may differ in terms of functional organization – one model being that of language development (e.g. Halliday, 1975, 2003b; Painter, Derewianka & Torr, 2007): micro-functional organization, macro-functional organization and metafunctional organization.

By another step, Halliday (e.g. [1996] 2002, [2005] 2013) has suggested that semiotic systems can be located in an ordered typology of systems operating within different phenomenal realms (see also e.g. Halliday & Matthiessen, 1999): 1st-order: **physical** systems – 2nd-order: **biological** systems [= physical + life] – 3rd-order: **social** systems [= biological + value] – 4th-order: **semiotic** systems [= social + meaning]. Each new order is characterized by the emergence of new forms of organization *superimposed* on the organization of lower-order systems. Thus higher-order systems *inherit* the organizational properties of lower-order ones (cf. Matthiessen, 2007b), see Figure 7.16. For example, by interpreting language as a social semiotic system (see Halliday, 1978), we assign it the properties of social systems in general – including the relationship between the individual

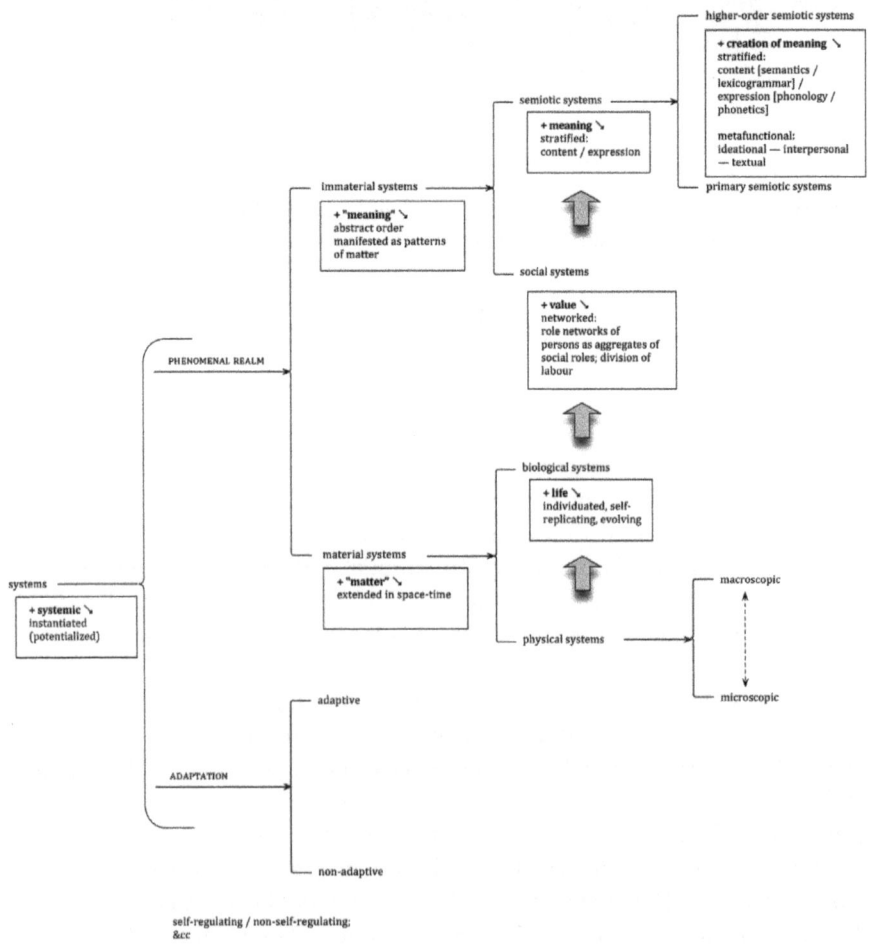

Figure 7.16 Ordered typology of systems operating in different phenomenal realms

and the collective modelled as roles in role networks (cf. Firth, [1950] 1957; Butt, 1991). In other words, the social properties of language – and of other social-semiotic systems – follow automatically from locating language in the ordered typology of systems; they do not have to be theorized and stated separately.

Halliday interprets language not just as a semiotic system but as a **higher-order semiotic system**, which means among other things that, in contrast with **primary semiotic systems**, it is stratified within both the content plane and the expression plane and that it is metafunctional, embodying the potential for the creation of simultaneous strands of meaning. Halliday (e.g. 1975, 2003b) has shown how language develops out of a primary semiotic system, protolanguage; and it seems plausible that his account of gradual increase in complexity is also a model of the evolution of language (see e.g. Matthiessen, 2004b).

Language thus *inherits* the properties not only from protolanguage, but also from the social, biological and physical systems through which it is manifested. This means that as linguists we must theorize and explain language as a particular kind of 4th-order system, noting carefully the properties it has because it is also at the same time a social, biological and physical system. In the last 30 years or so, linguists have written a great deal about the social nature of language in an attempt to reassert, in the context of the increasing dominance of cognitive science, what is of course an old insight into the nature of language. Such contributions are certainly important and valuable, but once we recognize the place of semiotic systems in the ordered typology of systems, it follows that they inherit the properties of social systems, including the enactment of individuals as persons through their participation in different social roles in different role networks (cf. Halliday, 1975, 1978; Butt, 1991 – both with references to Firth, [1950] 1957). Naturally, once language had emerged as a higher-order semiotic, it evolved together with the social order of modern humans, gradually paving the way for increasing social complexity (e.g. Halliday, [2010] 2013; Matthiessen, 2004b). By placing language in the ordered typology of systems, Halliday has made it possible to explore it in terms of a **general theory of systems**: we can ask what properties are shared by systems of all kinds, what properties emerge in systems as they increase in complexity. For example, compositional scales are found in systems of all kinds (cf. Koestler's notion of holarchy, discussed in Sheldrake, 1988); but individuation emerges only with biological systems – biological organisms, and is manifested with increasing complexity in social systems – persons (aggregates for personae, or social roles) and meaners (aggregates of meaning roles).

Let me round off the discussion of the ordered typology of systems by quoting from Halliday ([2011] 2013a):

I have referred elsewhere to the point made by the physicist George Williams, that as human beings we inhabit two incommensurable realms: the realm of **matter**, measurable in mass, heat, length and so on, and the realm of **information**, measured in bytes (Williams, 1995a; cf. Halliday, [2005] 2013). The realm of matter is investigated in the physical and biological sciences, and to some extent also in the social sciences; these got separated because our material world is made up of systems of different kinds. We can arrange these systems in a linear progression: first come physical systems; add **life**, then you have biological systems; add **value**, then you have social systems. At each step you are adding a new form of order: introducing more information by which the matter is becoming organized.

When we come to language, this is a system of a fourth order of complexity known as a **semiotic** system. Here what has been added is another component, that of **meaning**. In a semiotic system, information has replaced matter and taken over as the primary realm. It has been objected that all social systems are also semiotic; it is true that they have a lot of information in them, but there is still a significant distinction to be made. A hive of bees is not itself a semiotic system, although its members have evolved a system that is semiotic, the honey dance. What distinguishes the four different kinds of system is the different mix, the particular balance of matter and information that determines the properties of each.

6 Ideas about Linguistics

Halliday's ideas about language are of course related to his ideas about the *study* of language, linguistics: he has developed a kind of linguistics that will enable researchers to engage with language holistically as a resource, in both theory and application. He has written about the nature of the kind of linguistic theory that he and other systemic functional linguists have been developing since the 1960s – drawing attention to various features, e.g. its orientation to 'consumers' (e.g. Halliday, [1964] 2003), its multifunctional nature (e.g. Halliday, 1985a), its extravagance (e.g. Halliday, 1980), its differentiation as a theory of language as a general human system from descriptions of particular languages (e.g. Halliday, [1992] 2003a), its appliability (e.g. Halliday, [2002d] 2005), its variability (its nature as a flexi-theory; e.g. Halliday, 1980, [1997] 2003) and its social accountability (e.g. Halliday, 1984).

In Halliday ([1997] 2003), he explores linguistics as metaphor, suggesting five 'critical features' that linguistics shares with language: **comprehensiveness**, **extravagance**, **indeterminacy**, **non-autonomy** and **variability**. These five features are tabulated in Table 7.4 together with brief characterizations of their application to language and to linguistics.

Table 7.4 Halliday's (1997) five 'critical features' of language and linguistics

	phenomenon: language	*theory: linguistics*
comprehensiveness	language construes 'all of our experience, it enacts all of our interpersonal processes'	(i) comprehensive in coverage of the different orders of manifestation of language (semiotic, social, biological and physical); (ii) 'viewing the grammar of a language (or any other stratum) in its entirety' – 'language as resource'
extravagance	complementarities (see further Halliday, 2008), redundancy, metaphor	complementary ways of modelling the same phenomenon, e.g. lexicogrammar modelled either as grammar or as lexis
indeterminacy	blends, borderline cases, overlaps (cf. Halliday & Matthiessen, 1999: 547–52)	(i) the theory 'celebrates the indeterminacy in language itself', operating with 'descriptive categories that are themselves fluid and unstable'; (ii) 'the general theoretical framework offers ways of modelling indeterminacy', with probability as a central feature
non-autonomy	language is part of the human condition, and human history; it operates in context alongside other human systems	exploration of language as part of a general theory of meaning (semiotics); 'new understanding of the nature and typology of systems, and of processes of change'; applications in a growing range of institutional environments, e.g. 'in education, in medicine and in the law'
variability	language is inherently variable: dialectal variation, diatypic (functional, register) variation, codal variation	variation within the 'general model' that may be dialectal, registerial or codal in nature and which involves playing off different theoretical dimensions against one another (e.g. stratification and instantiation, stratification and axis)[27]

Like language and other semiotic systems, systemic functional theory is thus a **resource** – a resource for making meaning about semiotic systems. Systemic functional theory is itself a kind of semiotic system – like all theories, whether they are commonsense theories (folk theories) or uncommon sense ones (scientific theories and educational versions of them). In this respect, systemic functional theory is like all other theories: all theories are constructed out of the resources of semiotic systems – language, in the first instance, but also various semiotic systems designed for the purpose of representing theory, like various branches of mathematics like trigonometric functions used to represent various kinds of wave and differential calculus used to represent rates of change as in theories of motion. However, theories of social, biological and physical systems are of a different systemic order from the systems being theorized, whereas linguistic theories are of the same systemic order as the systems that they are theories of.

Linguists have explored this relationship using different terms; J. R. Firth ([1948] 1957: 190) talked about linguistics as language turned back on itself, Halliday ([1957] 2002: 30) emphasized the importance of the distinction between 'l.u.d.', language under description, and 'l.o.d.', language of description, a 'metalanguage', and Hjelmslev (1943: 105–6) had characterized linguistics as *metasprog*, metalanguage, which Weinreich (1980: 7) later characterized 'a specialized language for communication about another language (the "object language")'; see further Matthiessen & Nesbitt (1996: Section 3.2). One of the special challenges that arises in linguistics that Halliday ([1984] 2002) has identified and characterized is the 'ineffability of grammatical categories'.

Drawing on the insight that systemic functional linguistics is language turned back on itself, systemic functional linguists have explored the semiotic organization of this theory. Inspired by work by Brachman (e.g. 1978, [1979] 1985), by Hans Utzkoreit and by Hasan's (1985a) work on symbolic articulation and theme in verbal art (cf. Halliday's, [2011] 2013b: Section 3.2, exploration of theory and verbal science as higher-order values), we have explored the stratification of systemic functional linguistics into four strata – **theory, theoretical representation, computational representation** and **computational implementation** (e.g. Matthiessen, 1988; Matthiessen & Nesbitt, 1996; Halliday & Matthiessen, 1999; Teich, 1999a). This stratification of the metalanguage is illustrated in Figure 7.17 for the theory of paradigmatic organization.

Once we recognize that systemic functional linguistics can be modelled as a stratified metalanguage along the lines mentioned above, it becomes possible to be more precise about the unification-based family of grammars mentioned above in Section 2 and represented (in part) diagrammatically in Figure 7.2. Let me just make two observations here.

(i) Some of the grammatical frameworks are **functional in a high-level theoretical sense**, relating grammar to the kind of semantics that is concerned with text in context and drawing on large volumes of natural text examples. These include the European functional traditions of the Prague School and the Firthian and Hallidayan tradition, and the US American functional tradition of anthropological linguistics (including Sapir, Whorf and Pike). Later developments in the US include what has been referred to as 'West-Coast Functionalism', where a central concern since the 1970s has been to explain features of grammar by reference to discourse.

(ii) Some of the grammatical frameworks are **functional in a more representational sense**, involving structural functions (also referred to as roles, relations or deep cases) as well as classes in the representation of syntagmatic organization. One early prominent example is LFG, where a distinction was made

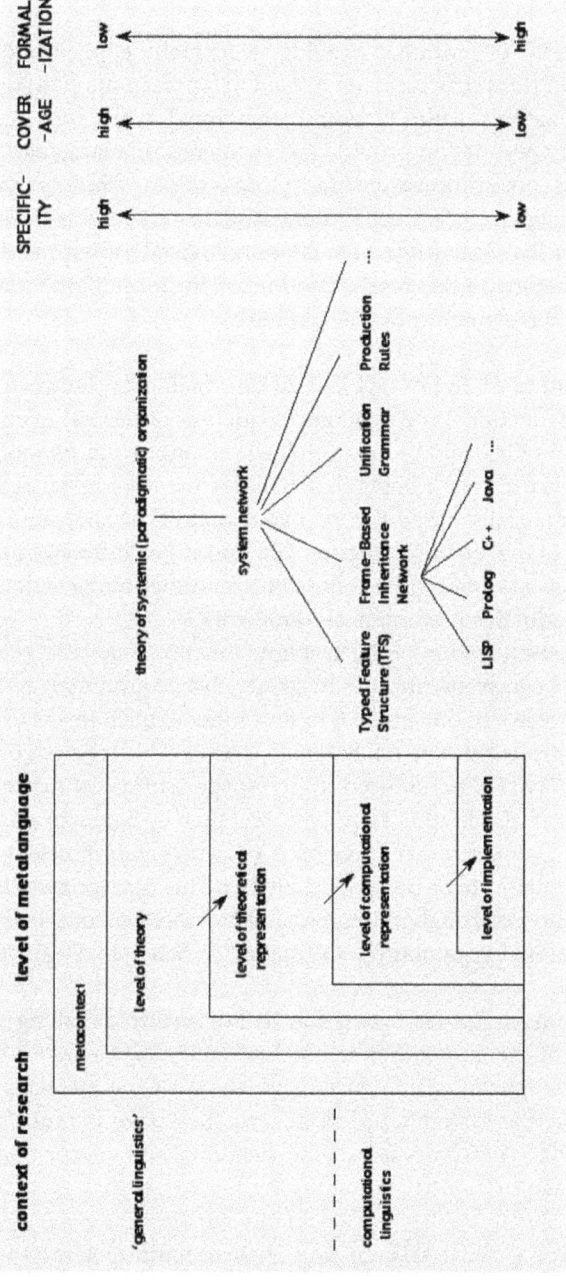

Figure 7.17 Stratification of the systemic functional metalanguage in context exemplified by reference to paradigmatic theory and system networks

between f-structure, function structure, and c-structure, constituent structure; for example, Bresnan (1982: 4) writes:

> The lexical theory of grammar provides a formally explicit and coherent theory of how surface structures are related to representations of meaningful grammatical relations. Rules of grammar defined in the formal system of grammatical representation provide each sentence of a language with dual representations consisting of a *constituent structure (c-structure)* and a *functional structure (f-structure)*. . . . The constituent structure represents the superficial constituency of the sentence (which is phonologically interpreted), and the functional structure is the representation of its meaningful grammatical relations (which is semantically interpreted).

This is reminiscent of Halliday's ([1966] 2002a) distinction between **structure** (configurations of functions) and **syntagm** (sequences of classes), even reflecting the stratal location of lexicogrammar between semantics and phonology – one significant difference of course being that Halliday incorporated this distinction within a paradigmatically based theory. I've used LFG as an example because its roots go back to the 1970s (cf. Figure 7.2), and it has influenced other later developments such as HPSG while at the same time continuing to develop in its own right as a productive grammatical framework.

Modelling the stratification of the systemic functional metalanguage makes it easier to identify complementarities in approaches to grammar, and opportunities to draw on research outside SFL to find more explicit forms of computationally oriented representation (cf. Bateman, 2008a). This research programme was initiated by Kay (1979), followed up by Kasper (1988a) at the Information Sciences Institute (cf. also Matthiessen, 1988) and then by Bateman and his group of researchers in German research contexts (e.g. Bateman, Emele & Momma, 1992); but it still remains to be developed further. This development is essential if there is to be a breakthrough in large-scale automated corpus analysis based on systemic functional grammar (cf. O'Donnell & Bateman, 2005; Teich, 2009; Wu, 2009).

The concerns I have just discussed can be interpreted as falling within the ideational realm of the systemic functional metalanguage – issues relating to the construal of language within successive strata of the metalanguage. But just like language, the systemic functional metalanguage is **multifunctional**; Halliday ([1985] 2003: 197) emphasized the ideational and interpersonal aspects of the metalanguage:

> I have often emphasized that language, both in its nature and in its ontogenetic development, clearly reveals a dual function; it is at once, and inseparably, a means of action and a means of reflection. Linguistics, as metalanguage, has

to serve the same twofold purpose. Systemic theory is explicitly constructed both for thinking with and for acting with.

Thus since the 1960s, systemic functional theory has been used as a means of action in many contexts – a concern that goes back to the efforts in the 1950s to develop a Marxist kind of linguistics (see Halliday, [1997] 2003: 223–4; this volume). Central to these efforts was the notion of **social account- ability** (e.g. Halliday, 1984),[28] which has been manifested in a wide range of applications, including critically the work in institutions of education by J. R. Martin, Joan Rothery, Fran Christie and their group (e.g. Martin & Rose, 2012; Christie, 2012), Geoff Williams, Bernard Mohan, Jay Lemke and many others. Social accountability includes being critical, what Halliday ([1997] 2003: 256) calls the 'prevailing stance'[29]; but it includes so much more – in general, it is concerned with strategies for addressing problems in the community, for improving the human condition (cf. Matthiessen, 2012). Describing a 'minor' language that is essential to its community but which is under threat (even if it is not yet classified as 'endangered' in the technical sense of the term) – a language such as Western Desert (Rose, 2001a), Òkó (Akerejola, 2005) or Bajjika (Kumar, 2009), or a 'major' language whose community of speak- ers play a key role in world affairs – a language such as Japanese (Teruya, 2007) or Arabic (Bardi, 2008) – may be much more important for communities around the world than critiquing some sample of discourses of power, and it is certainly a much harder task!

7 Conclusion

In this chapter, I have been concerned with Halliday's ideas about language – and by extension, with his ideas about linguistics. I have tried to show how his ideas about language flow from his conception of language as a **resource** – as a meaning potential giving the speakers of a language the power to mean (cf. Figure 7.5), the power to construe all of their experience as meaning, to enact all their roles and relations as meaning, and to transform these meanings into a flow of discourse that can be exchanged between speaker and addressee. My account has been partly chronological, but perhaps more logical (without chro- nos) in the sense that I have tried to bring out the theoretical force of what I called Halliday's **axial rethink** – the theoretical move whereby he developed a **paradigmatic base** for the modelling of language in order to bring out its orga- nization as a meaning-making resource.

Like many pioneering scholars, Halliday was often ahead of his time and he has never been a scholar who adopted (or adapted to) the intellectual fashion of the day,[30] so when he presented new proposals, they were often met with indifference or even hostility (as when he presented ideas about language as a probabilistic system in the 1960s). I remember being very impressed back in Sweden in the 1970s when I came across his article 'Syntax and the consumer' (Halliday, [1964] 2003) – it was so different from the prevailing ideology at the time, and sometime after I had met him in 1980, I asked him how his contribution to the Georgetown Roundtable was received. He smiled and said (as I recall) 'I was laughed out of court! There could only be one true theory of grammar.'

Many of his other ideas about language, and about linguistics, were, as I have just noted, met with indifference or even hostility when he first presented them.[31] I've suggested that Halliday was ahead of his time; if so, what is the situation at present? Views in linguistics in general have changed quite dramatically since the 1960s. Many of Halliday's key ideas have now been accepted, either by a wide group of linguists or by powerful sectors of the community of linguists – although too often without any reference to Halliday's work. Since it would take up too much space here to document this shift in the discipline of linguistics, I can only tabulate a few key areas here where the shift has been very significant: see Table 7.5. In this table, I have set out a number of Halliday's key contributions to the development of SFL, and compared them with views in non-systemic functional linguistics in the 1960s (when he introduced many of these key ideas) and at present.[32]

Thus ideas about language in linguistics in general have, not surprisingly, changed very considerably in the last 50 years or so; and as the table indicates, in a number of critical areas, non-systemic functional ideas ('mainstream ideas') are now much closer to Halliday's ideas about language – ideas that he began articulating in the 1950s and 1960s – than they were in the 1960s. The reasons are, naturally, many and complex; but let me mention a few of them.

(i) During the last 50 years, linguists have for the first time in the history of work on language gained access to large volumes of authentic **data** thanks to the technological advances that have made corpus-studies possible as a research methodology. Consequently, linguists have now revised earlier ideas about the relationship between grammar and lexis and about the role of probability in accounts of language, arriving at views resonating with those Halliday proposed over half a century ago.

(ii) During the same time, linguists have explored and tested theories and forms of representation that were very formal and segmental in orientation, and found them unworkable: transformations have (largely) disappeared, syntax is no longer treated as autonomous from semantics but is tightly aligned with it, sound structure is no longer represented only segmentally but also prosodically – and just as the stratal line between syntax and semantics is now treated as natural rather than arbitrary, so is the stratal line between phonology and phonetics.

Table 7.5 Some of Halliday's key ideas about language in non–systemic functional work, from the 1960s onwards and in current linguistics

	Halliday's SFL	*non-systemic functional linguistics*	
		1960s —	*current*
theory in relation to context of application	Halliday (1964): syntax and the consumer	no — only one 'true' theory	yes — generally accepted
relation between grammar and lexis	Halliday (1961): continuum [lexis as most delicate grammar]	no — separate modules	yes — accepted in various framework including those involving variants of 'construction grammar' and work based on corpus investigation
probabilistic nature of language	Halliday (1959 onwards): system inherently probabilistic	no — not seen as valuable or interesting	yes — 'probabilistic linguistics' (e.g. Bod, Jay & Jannedy, 2003a)
paradigmatic base	Halliday (e.g. 1966): systemic organization as primary, structure as derived	no — structure primary; system networks misunderstood as 'taxonomic' approach	no — structure still primary, but with interesting developments in the direction of type hierarchies
phonology: prosodic	Halliday (e.g. 1963b, 1967; 1992c)	no — approach to phonology segmental, with phonemes being composed of features [going back to Jakobson, 194932]	yes — in the development of autosegmental and metrical phonology [e.g. Goldsmith, 1990; cf. Henderson, 1987]
emergent complexity	Halliday (1975)	no — not yet on the agenda	yes — e.g. Steels (e.g. 1998), Larsen-Freeman, Ellis (e.g. Beckner et al., 2009)
language development	Halliday (1975): learning how to mean	language acquisition	maybe — powerfully by Larsen-Freeman (2011)

(iii) Since the 1950s, the intellectual climate outside linguistics has become more conducive to Halliday's ideas. In the 1950s, scholars from a number of fields took steps that led to the development of classical cognitive science, a kind of macro- discipline that included (the then nascent) cognitive psychology, artificial intelligence, segments of linguistics and philosophy, and also neuroscience. This version of cognitive science was conceived of as 'the science of mind', as Stillings et al. (1987: 1) put it, characterizing it further as follows (using common lexical and grammatical metaphors that I have discussed as part of my analysis of the discourse of cognitive science, e.g. Matthiessen, 1998):

> Cognitive scientists view the human mind as a complex system that receives, stores, retrieves, transforms, and transmits information.

This version of cognitive science did not produce an intellectual environment that resonated with Halliday's conception of human beings as persons and as meaners interacting with each other (see e.g. Halliday, 1978) – a point that becomes particularly clear in accounts of language development (e.g. Halliday, 1975). Even by the late 1980s, Stillings et al. (1987: Chapter 9) provide a very restricted, traditional account of 'language acquisition', suggesting that the early 'milestones in acquisition' begin with pre-linguistic 'babbling' while 'the first truly linguistic stage of language acquisition seems to be the one-word stage', which 'emerges within a few months of the child's first birthday' (Stillings et al., 1987: 366). This view of language development is of course fundamentally different from Halliday's (1975, 2003b) account of how young children learn how to mean in interaction with their immediate caregivers, starting with protolanguage somewhere around the middle of their first year of life.

However, the views of mainstream cognitive science have now been challenged in various fundamental ways. One important challenge was the introduction of Vygotsky's work in the West,[33] and his work is much more compatible with systemic functional ideas (cf. Wells, 1994; Byrnes, 2006), as has been shown by Hasan (e.g. 1994 [2007], 2002) in her research dealing with semiotic mediation. And, very importantly, the developments in neuroscience have been quite dramatic, aided by new brain scanning techniques; they have made it possible to explore and theorize the relationship between language and the brain – both now with a solid base in empirical research – without having to postulate an intermediate 'level' of cognition without a solid empirical foundation in either neuroscience or linguistics: see e.g. Deacon (1992, 1997) and Edelman (1992) and cf. Halliday ([1995b] 2003, [1997] 2003).[34]

Thus the second decade of the 21st century will certainly continue to be very conducive to Halliday's 'ideas about language'.

Notes

1. Later, the professor of linguistics who succeeded Bertil Malmberg, Bengt Sigurd, encourages me to specialize in 'Hallidayan linguistics', I remember him telling me that he thought this would also be very good for linguists in Denmark since they were still, as he put it, suffering from a 'post-Hijelmslevian hangover'.
2. In their preface, the authors write (p. iii): 'This work was originally undertaken under the title "Integration of Transformational Theories on English Syntax" in the

naïve expectation that most of the information about the transformational analysis of the grammar of English available up through the summer of 1968 could be brought together and integrated in a single format.'

3. The situation was different a decade earlier; when W. C. Mann and David Webber conducted a survey in the late 1970s of potential candidates to be used in a new text generation system, they chose Halliday's systemic functional grammar for various reasons (including Davey's, 1978, use of it in the Proteus text generation system); but a key reason was the commitment to comprehensive descriptions.

4. Other cross-overs can also be noted, including computational linguistics work within the Prague School tradition by Peter Sgall, Eva Hajičová, and others, and within Simon Dik's Functional Grammar, although the latter was arguably less functional in origin, not originally being centrally concerned with text in context (unlike Discourse Functional Grammar).

5. Douglas (1979) observes: 'A system of taboos covers up this weakness of the classification system. It points in advance to defects and insists that no one shall give recognition to the inconvenient facts or behave in such a way as to undermine the acceptability and clarity of the system as a whole. It stops awkward questions and prevents awkward developments.'

6. I haven't been able to find a succinct reference to this in the literature; but in response to a question about the influence of SFG on LFG after her talk at AILA at Waseda University in Tokyo, 1–6 August 1999 (Bresnan, 2000), Joan Bresnan drew attention to the flow of influence from Halliday via Kaplan on LFG. For a comparison of 'semantic relations' in SFG and LFG, see Steiner (1988).

7. The important principle that had been developed in Firthian system-structure phonology (prosodic analysis) that different systems operate at different places in a structure is captured by preselection: one general system is posited but different preselections are specified for different places in a structure.

8. In terms of ontogenesis, stratification and axis arguably develop out the hierarchic ordering of content and expression (cf. Matthiessen, 2007b: Section 2.4).

9. This version of his description 'was written between May and August 1964 and formed the substance of a course on the description of English at the University of Indiana' (Halliday, 2002a: 127).

10. See Halliday (2005a: 268–84) for his original set of systems we started with; Matthiessen & Bateman (1991) for discussion of the computational system; and Matthiessen (1995a) for a descriptive report based on an extended version of these systems.

11. As far as the description of English is concerned, there is a difference here between US American and British approaches to intonation (cf. Teich, Watson & Pereira, 2000; and also Ladd, 1996). In US American accounts, intonation contours tend to be described in terms of sequences of 'pitch levels' – ranging from Pike (1945, 1948: 15–16) to the current TOBI framework for intonation analysis (e.g. Beckman, Hirschberg & Shattuck-Hufnagel, 2005), where contours are essentially analysed as sequences of high (H) and low (L) tones (either pitch accents or boundary tones); in contrast, in British accounts (see e.g. Crystal, 1969), intonation contours tend to be analysed as prosodies, not broken down into sequences of segments: see Halliday (1967) and references therein. For an overview of phonetic research into intonation, see e.g. Nooteboom (1997).

12. His interest in grammatical frequencies had been stimulated as a language learner and as a language teacher (e.g. Halliday, [1993] 2005b: 131–2).

13. See e.g. Neef & Vater (2006: 35), who note that in his early work, Chomsky 'adopted Bloomfield's view of the lexicon as a list of morphemes (which he later cautiously termed "formatives")'. Chomsky (1965: 84) characterized the 'lexicon' as 'an

unordered list of all lexical formatives', 'a set of lexical entries, each lexical entry being a pair (D, C), where D is a phonological distinctive feature matrix "spelling" a certain lexical formative and C is a collection of specified syntactic features'; and later (p. 87) he reinforces the Bloomfieldian notion of irregularities belonging to the lexicon: 'In general, all properties of a formative that are essentially idiosyncratic will be specified in the lexicon.'

14. Just as articulatory dimensions define the vowel space as a topology: see Halliday & Matthiessen (1999) and cf. Matthiessen (1995b).

15. Roget's (1852) Thesaurus is, of course, a model in the sense that it provides a description of lexis as a resource (cf. Halliday, 1976; Matthiessen, 1991: 259–60, 275); but it is not grounded in grammar. In computational linguistic research, there is now also an extensive body of research on the taxonomic organization of lexis, explored under the heading of ontology: see Huang et al. (2010). This kind of taxonomic organization is implicit in traditional dictionaries in glosses, but it can be retrieved, as shown many years ago by Amsler's (1981) pioneering computational analysis of entries in *Webster's Dictionary*.

16. It is also important to note that the point in delicacy where lexical items realize combinations of lexicogrammatical features is not necessarily the endpoint in delicacy: see Halliday ([1996] 2002: 23).

17. In addition, the textual metafunction provides strategies for deploying orderings in delicacy in lexis within the other metafunction to achieve lexical cohesion (see Halliday & Hasan, 1976; and cf. Matthiessen, 1991, 1995a).

18. They write (p. 276): 'The expression of interpersonal meaning, of a particular attitude on the part of the speaker, is an important function of general nouns. Essentially the attitude conveyed is one of familiarity, as opposed to distance, in which the speaker assumes the right to represent the thing he is referring to as it impinges on him personally; hence the attitude may be either contemptuous or sympathetic, the two being closely related as forms of personal involvement (cf. the meaning of diminutives in many languages).'

19. And the comparable pairs of form and substance for written and signed languages.

20. The cognitive and the semiotic interpretations being complementary: see Halliday & Matthiessen (1999]).

21. The work by Bateman et al. (2010) is of enormous importance for the development of models of semantics because they 'interface' a semantic model of space with a model needed by robots to perceive space and navigate through it. See further below.

22. It is equally important to ask about the expression substance in written and signed languages; but I will focus on spoken languages here.

23. Or 'anthropophonetics'; in 'Linguistics in the Nineteenth Century', Baudouin de Courtenay characterizes it as 'a separate branch of science which deals with the investigation of the conditions of pronunciation and of the phonational-auditory production of language' (Baudouin de Courtenay, 1972: 246).

24. Compare Halliday's ([1984] 2002: 306) emphasis of the point that 'a child's semiotic experience is extraordinarily rich'; he notes that, by the age of 5, a child may have heard 'anything up to a quarter of a million Subjects' and observes that children 'model the language as a probabilistic system'. Halliday ([1993] 2005b: 136) again suggests that 'children seem to learn language as a probabilistic system', noting that 'they are surrounded by large quantities of data, probably at least a hundred thousand clauses a year, and they are sensitive to relative frequency as a resource for ordering what they learn'.

25. Since Ellegård's classic study, researchers have explored the history of 'periphrastic do' further, raising various issues such as differences during the period across registers ('genres'), as in Rissanen (1991) and Warner (2005). Registerial variation is to be

expected; the evolution of the overall meaning potential of a language is simply the composite of the evolution of and within the different registers that it is composed of – often with casual spoken language leading the development (cf. Halliday, [2002] 2005b). Compare also Halliday's (1988) account of the evolution of grammatical metaphor of the ideational kind as part of the evolution of scientific English in the last half millennium.

26. The source of the graph based on Ellegård (1953: 162) is in the common domain: http://en.wikipedia.org/wiki/File:Ellegard_Periphrastic_Do.svg.

27. Cf. Halliday ([1985] 2003: 192): 'Systemic theory is more like language itself – a system whose stability lies in its variation. A language is a "metastable" system; it persists because it is constantly in flux.'

28. Linguists and researchers in related fields have, not surprisingly, taken different positions. For example, as I recall the discussion in the early 1980s with respect to the use of military funding to conduct research in the US, Chomsky's position was that it was alright to accept military funding since what really mattered was how academics used their 'discretionary time'. In contrast, Terry Winograd's position was that one should not accept military funding because doing so strengthened the channels of funding through the military. Another view was that taken by my project leader, Bill Mann. He said that as long as the research was unclassified and thus publically accessible, military funding was acceptable since the military were too badly organized to make use of the results so that it was certain that the results would be in the public domain before the military got their act together. Chomsky and Halliday have, of course, taken very different positions on linguistics in relation to social accountability. Chomsky has separated his linguistics from his political activism – related to his point that what matters is what you do with your discretionary time. His two activities seem very far apart. However, I think there is actually a deep connection, viz. the individualism of his cognitive stance in linguistics and of his anarcho-syndicalism in his political activism – and since individualism resonates nicely with mainstream US America, he is tolerated by the ruling elite; he does not actually represent the kind of threat that a Marxist scholar and activist would. In contrast, Halliday has created a kind of linguistics that relates to social accountability – that can be used in various kinds of interventions (appliable linguistics: Halliday, [2002] 2007); systemic functional theory was never 'neutral' (cf. Halliday, 2003: 223).

29. Halliday ([1997] 2003: 256) writes: 'It is important, I think, in an age when the prevailing stance (on language, but also on other things besides) is the "critical" – and this often means only destructively critical – to place the enabling power of language clearly in the centre of the stage; otherwise, in our own praxis, whether educational, clinical, forensic or whatever else, we will come up only with problems, and never any solutions.'

30. There are many examples of this in his work; it is instructive to read his comments over the years on cognitive science, post-structuralism, postmodernism.

31. For example, Halliday ([1985] 2003) notes that Postal (1964) completely 'misread' Halliday ([1961] 2002) 'as a theory of constituent structure'; this was during Postal's Chomskyan period, before he helped develop generative semantics and became a critic of both Chomsky's linguistics and his politics.

32. In the Prague School phonology developed by Nikolai Trubetzkoy, phonological features had been interpreted as values along paradigmatic dimensions, just as terms in phonological systems in systemic phonology are. Jakobson ([1949] 1962: 420) instead interpreted 'distinctive features' as components of phonemes, thereby changing their status from paradigmatic to syntagmatic: 'Meanwhile the science of language continued to treat phonemes as the most minute (further indivisible) linguistic unit.

However, as the phonemes of a given language form a system of sequences, so the system of phonemes, in turn, is formed by their constituents, i.e. by distinctive features. And the breaking up of the phonemes into distinctive features follows precisely the same tested devices as the division of morphemes into phonemes.' As Fischer-Jørgensen (1975: 146) points out, this echoes Bloomfield's ([1933] 2002) statement that 'the distinctive features occur in lumps and bundles each one of which we call a phoneme'. For the drawback of Jakobson's reinterpretation, see also Halliday & Matthiessen (1999).

33. Vygotsky's *Thought and language* appeared in an English translation in 1962 with an introduction by Jerome Bruner; but it took a long time before his ideas were picked up more generally. (There is no reference to Vygotsky in Stillings et al., 1987; and Bruner is only mentioned in connection with his discussion of Piaget.)

34. Available from: http://www.cl.cam.ac.uk/~aac10/papers/lrec2000.pdf; also available at: http://framenet.icsi.berkeley.edu/index.php?option=com_wrapper&-Itemid=126.

8 Halliday's Conception of Language as a Probabilistic System

Christian M. I. M. Matthiessen

Chapter Overview

---

1 Introduction

This chapter is concerned with Halliday's ideas about language in terms of probability, viz. his conception of **language as a probabilistic system**. It elaborates on Section 4.4 in Matthiessen (this volume). I will not try to introduce the theory of probability as a branch of mathematics (developed originally with gambling as an application); nor will I discuss different interpretations of probability – objective vs subjective (Bayesian): the focus is on the probability of choice in language, not on the observer's subjective view. While it would be relevant to relate the probabilistic conception of language to indeterminacy in language more generally, I will simply focus on probability: indeterminacy in general is discussed in Part III of Halliday (2005a) and also in Halliday and

Matthiessen (1999), and certain aspects of indeterminacy are explored in Martin and Matthiessen ([1991] 2010) – system networks in relation to topological representations, and in Matthiessen (1995b) – system networks in relation to fuzzy theory.

Since his early descriptions of Chinese, Halliday (e.g. [1956] 2005a, [1959] 2005) has kept both qualitative and quantitative aspects of language in view; Halliday ([1991] 2005a: 45) comments on his early work:

> A linguistic system is inherently probabilistic in nature. I tried to express this in my early work on Chinese grammar, using observed frequencies in the corpus and estimating probabilities for terms in grammatical systems ([1956] 2005a, [1959] 2005).

Halliday conceived of terms (features, options) in systems as having probabilities attached, and this is also apparent in his early text-based descriptions of English (e.g. Halliday, [1963] 2005a, [1963] 2005b) with systemic contrasts where one term is 'neutral' or 'unmarked' and the other term or terms non-neutral or 'marked'. When he presented aspects of early systemic functional work on grammar at the Fifteenth Annual (First International) Round Table Meeting on Linguistics and Language Studies at Georgetown University, in a US American academic context, he characterized the work by him and other researchers in Britain as follows (Halliday, [1964] 2003: 40; my emphasis, CMIMM):

> If I were asked to characterize the work in which I have been engaged together with some of my colleagues, I would say that our aim is to show the *patterns inherent in the linguistic performance* of the native speaker: this is what we mean by 'how the language works'. This presupposes a general description of those patterns which the linguist considers to be primary in the language, a description which is then variably extended, on the 'scale of delicacy', in depth of detail. It involves a characterization of the special features, *including statistical properties*, of varieties of the language used for different purposes ('registers'), and the comparison of individual texts, spoken and written, including literary texts. This in turn is seen as a linguistic contribution towards certain further aims, such as literary scholarship, native and foreign language teaching, educational research, sociological and anthropological studies and medical applications. The interest is focused not on what the native speaker knows of his language but rather on what he does with it; one might perhaps say that *the orientation is primarily textual* and, in the widest sense, sociological.

> The *study of written and spoken texts* for such purposes requires an analysis of at least sentence, clause and group structures and systems, with extension where possible above the rank of sentence. The analysis needs to be simple in

use and in notation, variable in delicacy and *easily processed for statistical studies*; it needs to provide a basis for semantic statements, and to handle with the minimum complexity grammatical contrasts such as those in English expounded by intonation and rhythm; and it should idealize as little as possible, in the sense of excluding the minimum as 'deviant'.

In referring to 'the linguistic performance of the native speaker', Halliday was of course taking into account the audience's familiarity with the distinction between 'competence' and 'performance' that Chomsky had made, so he translated text as 'performance'. It was not a distinction that was in any way part of systemic functional theory as it was being developed, but the status of text in the overall engagement with language was, of course, critical to the exploration of 'statistical properties': see further below, Section 2. About a decade later, Halliday (1973a: 25, 51–3) characterized language as a **meaning potential** so that text could now be characterized as 'actualized potential', what a speaker **means** in some context of situation in reference to what he or she **can mean** within the context of culture.

The research conducted during the initial phases of systemic functional linguistics was largely text- and corpus-based, and thus provided material for quantitative information. This was true not only of Halliday's own work on phonology and lexicogrammar,[1] but also of the work by colleagues and research students, e.g. the work on scientific English by Huddleston et al. (1968), with many counts of different categories, Elmenoufy's (1969; cf. also 1988) account of the role of intonation in grammar (based on 4 hours of casual conversation, amounting to 7,012 tone groups), and of course the text-based research that led to the description of the system of COHESION (e.g. Hasan, 1968), presented comprehensively by Halliday & Hasan (1976). But, unfortunately, it was hard to get corpus-based linguistic research published in the 1960s, and the studies from this period remain unpublished.

However, during the 1960s, systemic functional linguistics was developed in a direction that made it easier to accommodate quantitative information. Halliday's development of a system-based theory with system networks as the representation of paradigmatic relations (see Matthiessen, this volume: Section 3) enabled him to reason about quantitative information in relation to both systems ordered in delicacy and systems simultaneous in delicacy. For example, Halliday ([1961] 2002: 48–9, 54) draws attention to the value of 'frequency counts' as the description is extended in delicacy:

As the description increases in delicacy the network of grammatical relations becomes more complex. The interaction of criteria makes the relation between categories, and between category and exponent, increasingly one of 'more / less' rather than 'either / or'. It becomes necessary to weight criteria and to make statements in terms of probabilities. With more delicate secondary structures, different combinations of elements, and their relation to groupings of the unit next below, have to be stated as more and less probable. [. . .] the 'more / less' relation itself, far from being an unexpected complication in grammar, is in fact a basic feature of language and is treated as such by the theory. It is not simply that all grammar can be stated in probability terms, based on frequency counts in texts: this is due to the nature of a text as a sample. (pp. 48–9)

The theoretical place of the move from grammar to lexis is therefore not a feature of rank but one of delicacy. It is defined theoretically as the place where increase in delicacy yields no further systems [. . .] No description has yet been made so delicate that we can test whether there really comes a place where increased delicacy yields no further systems: relations at this degree of delicacy can only be stated statistically, and serious statistical work in grammar has hardly begun. (p. 54)

And Halliday ([1964] 2003: 48–9) notes the possibility of accounting for 'partial dependence' between terms in simultaneous systems in probabilistic terms:

Partial dependence may also be manifested statistically, where the selection in one system affects the relative probabilities of selection in another system.

Halliday's conception of language as a probabilistic system is directly related to his image of language as **resource** (Matthiessen, this volume: Figure 4). But what aspects of systemic functional theory enabled him to model language probabilistically – and how was probability viewed during the 1960s at the time when Halliday developed systemic functional theory out of scale-and-category theory?

2 Locating Probability; Theory and Data

Leading up to the 1960s, there had been important contributions to the quantitative study of language that *could* have led to a general acceptance that language is a probabilistic system. These contributions included the work by George Zipf (e.g. 1935) and the seminal work on the quantification of information by Claude Shannon (1948) that led to the development of **Information Theory**. Shannon was concerned with information in a technical, engineering sense:

The fundamental problem of communication is that of reproducing at one point either exactly or approximately a message selected at another point.

> Frequently the messages have *meaning*; that is they refer to or are correlated according to some system with certain physical or conceptual entities. These semantic aspects of communication are irrelevant to the engineering problem. The significant aspect is that the actual message is one *selected from a set* of possible messages.

And in referring to information in this sense and certain key properties such as redundancy, Halliday has been careful to distinguish information, which is measurable, from meaning, which is not; information is in a sense meaning that can be measured, meaning being the more general category (e.g. Halliday, [1991] 2005a: 45). Information in this technical sense is inherent in systems of any stratum of language. In the early days, Information Theory was received with interest by some linguists (cf. the reviews by Van de Walle, 2009; Goldsmith, 2001; Manning, 2003), including Hockett (1955), Jakobson ([1961] 1971) and Gleason (1961: Chapter 19); but as Chomsky's generative linguistics came to dominate in the 1960s, Chomsky's dismissal of probabilistic considerations and of the kind of evidence that can be derived from corpora steered linguistics away from such concerns. As Manning (2003: 289) puts it:

> In the 1950s there were prospects for probabilistic methods taking hold in linguistics, in part owing to the influence of the new field of Information Theory (Shannon, 1948). Chomsky's influential remarks had the effect of killing off interest in probabilistic methods for syntax . . .

Similarly, Jurafsky (2003: 39) observes:

> Much research in linguistics and psycholinguistics in the 1950s was statistical and probabilistic. But this research disappeared throughout the '60s, '70s, and '80s.

The negative attitude towards the probabilistic nature of language in 'theoretical' linguistics was part of the same ideology according to which corpus studies had no theoretical value. After quoting Svartvik's (1966: vii) view that 'corpus-studies will help to promote descriptively more adequate grammars', Halliday ([1991] 2005b: 63) comments:

> This modest claim ran against the ideology prevailing at the time, according to which corpus studies had nothing to contribute towards an understanding of language. Chomsky's theory of competence and performance had driven a massive wedge between the system and the instance, making it impossible by definition that analysis of actual texts could play any part in explaining the grammar of a language – let alone in formulating a general linguistic theory.

Explicitly rejected was the relevance of any kind of quantitative data. Chomsky's sarcastic observation that '*I live in New York* is more frequent than *I live in Dayton Ohio*' was designed to demolish the conception that relative frequency in text might have any theoretical significance. [Footnote: Made in the course of a denunciation of corpus studies in a lecture at the Linguistic Society of America Summer Institute, Bloomington, July 1964.]

The separation of the system and the instance was one of two theoretical obstacles getting in the way of investigations of language as a probabilistic system, in the context of Chomsky's form of generative linguistics. I will discuss it in Section 3 below under the heading of the 'cline of instantiation'. The other theoretical obstacle was the focus on the syntagmatic axis to the exclusion of the paradigmatic one. I will discuss this obstacle in Section 4 under the heading of the 'hierarchy of axis'. Both theoretical obstacles meant that it was difficult to find a place for probability in the theory.

3 The Cline of Instantiation: Frequency (Instantial) and Probability (Potential)

If language is conceived of dichotomously as *langue* and *parole* along Saussurean lines or as 'competence' and 'performance' along Chomskyan (e.g. 1965) lines[2] (later 'I-language' and 'E-language', e.g. Chomsky, 2000), then linguists face the challenge of locating the probabilistic conception of language in relation to these two domains. What happened was that competence was conceptualized and theorized in **categorical** terms, and represented by rule systems that were equally categorical in nature (see e.g. the critical discussion by Ellis, 1993, and Halliday's, [1995] 2003a, comments based on the different views in systemic functional theory). This was the domain of 'theoretical linguistics'. At the same time, performance was studied, with attention given to quantitative features such as frequency, latency and duration; but such research was carried out mainly in psycholinguistics – see e.g. Jurafsky (2003), and there was no link to theoretical work on competence. In their introduction to *Probabilistic linguistics*, Bod, Hay and Jannedy (2003b: 1) characterize the view as follows[3]:

> One of the foundations of modern linguistics is the maxim of categoricity: language is categorical. Numbers play no role, or, where they do, they are artifacts of nonlinguistic performance factors. Thus, while it is widely recognized that real language can be highly variable, gradient, and rich in continua, many linguists would argue that the competence that underlies such 'performance factors' consists of well-defined discrete categories and

categorical grammaticality criteria. Performance may be full of fuzziness, gradience, and continua, but linguistic competence is not.

There was thus a fundamental disconnect between the domain of data (natural, elicited or experimental), 'performance', and the domain of theory, 'competence': theory and data couldn't be linked. This was the 'massive wedge between the system and the instance' identified by Halliday ([1991] 2005b: 63) in the passage quoted at the end of the last section. As long as the domain of theory and the domain of data are kept insulated from one another, it is difficult to see how observed frequencies in texts ('performance') can be theorized, i.e. incorporated within a theory of language.[4]

Halliday has developed a radically different alternative view – one that makes it possible to theorize observed **frequencies** in text as **probabilities** inherent in the system. The key point is that system and text are not two different phenomena but simply one phenomenon, language, seen from different observer perspectives: see Figure 8.1, where Halliday's theory (the top half of

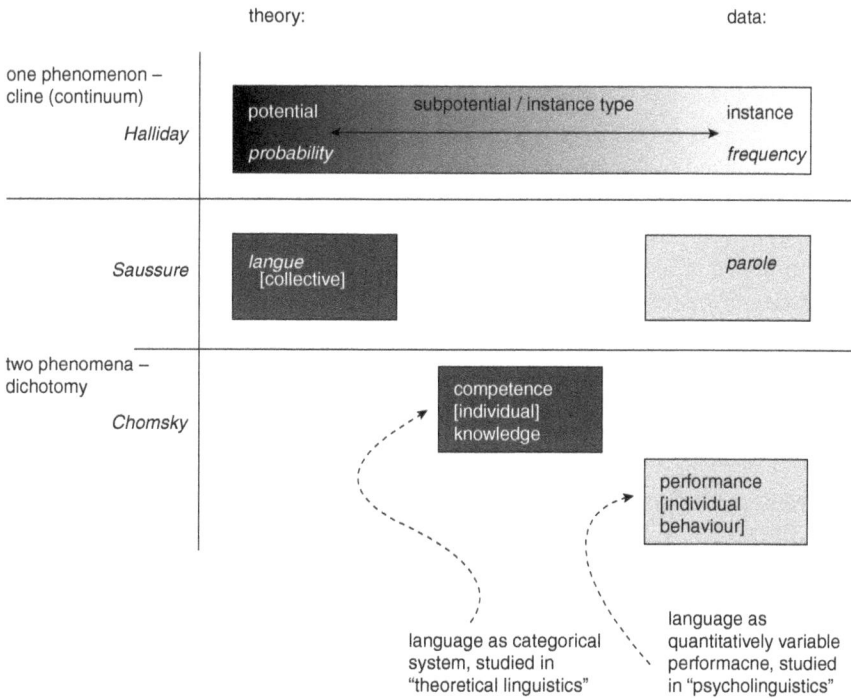

Figure 8.1 System and text – conceptualized as one continuous phenomenon extended along the cline of instantiation, or as two distinct phenomena forming a dichotomy

the figure) is contrasted with those of Saussure and Chomsky (the lower half of the figure). Let me introduce this in two steps.

(1) First, system and text are related to one another simply as **potential to actual**, or instantial, thus being *of the same phenomenal order*; this understanding was articulated by Halliday (1973a: 49–51) [already referred to above]:

> Language . . . is a range of possibilities, an open-ended set of options in behaviour that are available to the individual in his existence as social man. The context of culture is the environment for the total set of these options, while the context of situation is the environment of any particular selection that is made from within them.

> Malinowski's two types of context thus embody the distinction between the potential and the actual. The context of culture defines the potential, the range of possibilities that are open. The actual choice among these possibilities takes place within a given context of situation. [. . .]

> If we regard language as social behaviour . . ., this means that we are treating it as a form of behaviour **potential**. It is what speakers can do. But 'can do' by itself is not a linguistic notion; it encompasses types of behaviour other than language behaviour. [. . .] we need an intermediate step, where the behaviour potential is as it were converted into linguistic potential. This is the concept of what the speaker 'can mean'.

> The potential of language is a meaning potential. [. . .] The meaning potential is . . . realized in the language system as lexicogrammatical potential, which is what the speaker 'can say'.

System and text are thus one and the same phenomenon, simply viewed as either meaning potential or as meaning instances – acts of meaning (cf. Halliday, [1992] 2003c). In contrast, Chomsky theorized system and text as being of *different phenomenal orders*, knowing (competence) and behaving (performance); Halliday (1973a: 52–3) highlighted this problem, and criticized the distinction on these grounds:

> Meaning potential is defined not in terms of the mind [Chomsky's competence, CMIMM] but in terms of the culture; not as what the speaker knows, but as what he can do – in the special sense of what he can do linguistically (what he 'can mean', as we have expressed it). This distinction is important because 'can do' is of the same order of abstraction as 'does'; the two are related simply as potential to actualized potential, and can be used to illuminate each other. But 'knows' is distinct and clearly insulated from 'does'; the relation between the two is complex and oblique, and leads to the quest of a 'theory of performance' to explain the 'does'.

In addition, Chomsky's 'competence' is a feature of the *individual* speaker ('ideal speaker-listener'), whereas Halliday's 'meaning potential' is a feature of the *collective*, of the **speech fellowship** operating in a particular context of culture. The meaning potential is thus a collective resource, and individual meaners are trustees in this resource. In this respect, Saussure's *langue* is significantly different from Chomsky's 'competence'; like the meaning potential, *langue* is a feature of the collective. However, it is still insulated from *parole*.

(2) Second, potential and actual, or potential and instance, are theorized as part of an extended *continuum*, the outer poles of the **cline of instantiation**; Halliday ([1991] 2007) introduces a figure where he intersects 'instantiation' with 'realization', reproduced here as Figure 8.2. In this figure, he shows that instantiation is extended between 'system' and 'instance'; it is represented as a cline with intermediate regions, cultural domain / register and situation type / text type. These intermediate regions are specified further in Halliday ([2002] 2005a), as shown in Figure 8.3. (Note that at the stratum of context, 'cultural domain' in Figure 8.2 and 'institution' in Figure 8.3 both refer to sub-systems within the overall system of culture.)

Let me quote Halliday ([1992] 2002a: 359) at some length as he introduces the cline of instantiation:

Consider the notion of climate. A climate is a reasonably stable system; there are kinds of climate, such as tropical or polar, and these persist, and they differ in systematic ways. Yet we are all concerned about changes in the climate, and the consequences of global warming. What does it mean to say the climate is changing? Climate is instantiated in the form of weather:

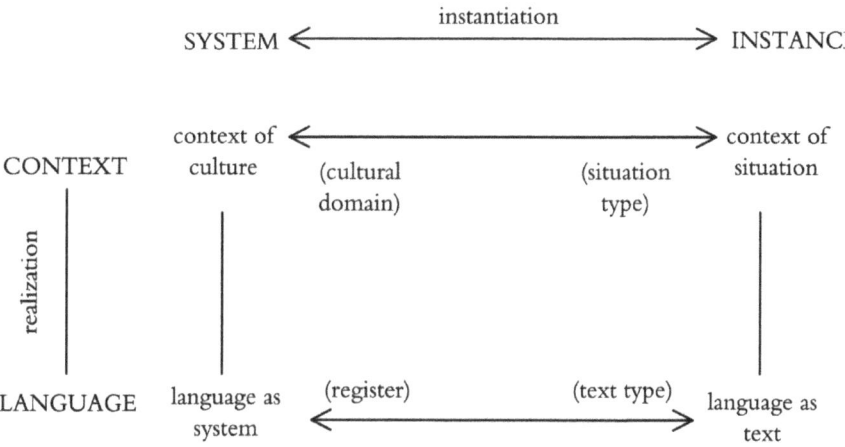

Figure 8.2 Halliday's ([1991] 2007) representation of the cline instantiation

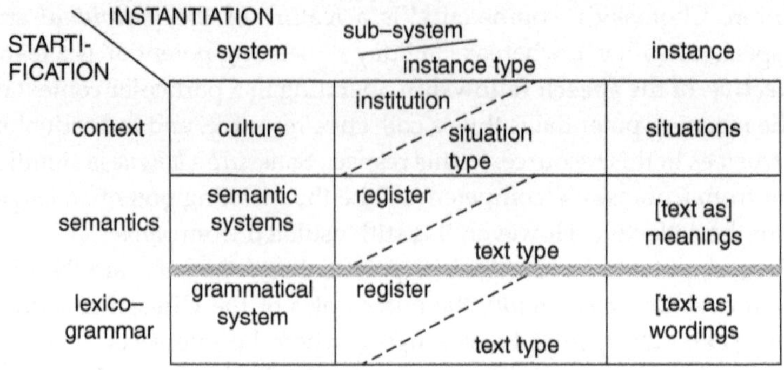

Figure 8.3 Halliday's ([2002] 2005a) representation of the cline of instantiation

today's temperature, humidity, direction and speed of wind, etc., in central Scotland are **instances** of climatic phenomena. As such they may be more, or less, **typical**: today's maximum is so many degrees higher, or lower, than **average** – meaning the average at this place, at this time of year, and at this time of day. The average is a statement of the **probabilities**: there is a 70 per cent chance, let us say, that the temperature will fall within such a range. The probability is a feature of the system (the climate); but it is no more, and no less, than the pattern set up by instances (the weather), and each instance, no matter how minutely, perturbs these probabilities and so changes the system (or else keeps it as it is, which is just the limiting case of changing it).

The climate and the weather are not two different phenomena. They are the same phenomenon seen by two different observers, standing at different distances – different time depths. To the climate observer, the weather looks like random unpredictable ripples; to the weather observer, the climate is a vague and unreal outline. So it is also with language; language as system, and language as instance. They are not two different phenomena; they are the same phenomenon seen by different observers. The system is the pattern formed by the instances; and each instance represents an exchange with the environment – an incursion into the system in which every language is involved. The **system** is permeable because each **instance** redounds with the context of situation, and so perturbs the system **in interaction with the environment**. Thus both realization and instantiation are involved in the evolution of language as a dynamic open system.

Now the relation of system to instance is in fact a cline, a continuous zoom; and wherever we focus the zoom we can take a look into history. But to know what kind of history, we have to keep a record of which end we started from. To the system observer, history takes the form of evolution; the system changes by evolving, with selection (in the sense of 'natural selection') by the material conditions of the environment. This is seen most clearly, perhaps, in the evolution of particular subsystems, or registers, where features that are functionally well adapted are positively selected for; but it appears also in the history of the system as a whole once we look beyond the superficial clutter of random fluctuations into the grammar's cryptotypic core. To the instance observer, on the other hand, history is individuation: each text has its own history, and its unique meaning unfolds progressively from the beginning. (Note that the probability of any instance is conditioned both systemically (a register is a resetting of the overall probabilities of the system) and instantially, by the transitional probabilities of the text as a Markoff chain.)

Halliday's theory of cline of instantiation is a fundamental contribution of the theoretical understanding of language. It provides the bridge between (a) quantitative information as frequency and quantitative information as probability, and (b) between the domains of data and of theory.

(a) At the instance pole of the cline of instantiation, we can observe the **relative frequency** of the instantiation (occurrence) of terms in systems; and at the potential pole of the cline, we can interpret these relative frequencies as **systemic probabilities**. (b) At the instance pole, we are analysing texts – the **data** constituting the basis for any generalizations we make, moving up the cline of instantiation towards the potential pole. At the potential pole, we **theorize** the system that we posit as the principles behind the instantial patterns that we can observe.

At the same time, we also recognize patterns that are intermediate between the outer poles of the cline of instantiation. We can interpret these intermediate patterns by approaching them from either pole. Looked at from the potential pole of the cline, they can be interpreted as **sub-potentials** – quantitatively, as resettings of the systemic probabilities of the potential pole (e.g. Halliday, [1991] 2005b: 65–6, 70, [1992] 2005a: 84–6, in press [b]). Looked at from the instance pole of the line, they can be interpreted as **instance types** – quantitatively, as averages of relative frequencies observed in instances.

4 The Hierarchy of Axis: Probabilities in Systems

Quantitative information is thus extended along the cline of instantiation, from systemic probabilities to relative frequencies in texts. But probabilities of what, frequencies of what? In a sense, any category in language can be counted; researchers in many disciplines have been counting words for a wide range of purposes. However, the categories that we count are *ultimately derived from contrasting options* in the systems that make up a system network[5] – from choice. This is thus central to the probabilistic interpretation of language, as Halliday ([1991] 2005a: 45) has emphasized:

> Obviously, to interpret language in probabilistic terms, the grammar (that is, the theory of grammar, the *grammatics*) has to be paradigmatic: it has to be able to represent language as **choice**, since probability is the probability of 'choosing' (not in any conscious sense, of course) one thing rather than another. Firth's concept of 'system', in the 'system / structure' framework, already modelled language as choice. Once you say 'choose for polarity: positive or negative?', or 'choose for tense: past or present or future?', then each of these options could have a probability value attached.

(The same remarks apply to any stratal subsystem of language in context; e.g. to interpret the sound system of a language in probabilistic terms, the theory of phonology has to be paradigmatic.) For example, we may count active and passive forms of the verb, or rather of the verbal group; but behind this is the systemic contrast in voice between 'active' and 'passive' verbal groups (cf. Halliday, [1991] 2005b; Halliday & James, [1993] 2005). Thus when Halliday ([1966] 2002a) developed the theory of language on a paradigmatic base – foregrounding system over structure, he made it possible to locate probabilities within the overall account of language: in the description of the system of language, *probabilities are attached to terms in systems*, e.g. 'active 0.9' / 'passive 0.1', and the system is thus the locus of probability (the distribution of probabilities, the probability profile of a system), of information and of redundancy (in the sense of Information Theory; see further below); and in the analysis of texts, we count the occurrences of terms in systems.

Thus in the system of PROCESS TYPE, we count each occurrence (selection) of one of its terms, 'material' / 'behavioural' / 'mental' / 'verbal' / 'relational' / 'existential' so that we can establish a **frequency profile** for this system: see Figure 8.4. The process types range in frequency from 'material' to 'existential': 'material [39.2%]' / 'relational [36.1%]'/ 'mental [10.8%]' / 'verbal [8.3%]' / 'behavioural [3.4%]' / 'existential [2.3%]'. Interpreted systemically, 'material' is the term that is the most likely to be selected and 'existential' the one least likely to be selected.

The system of PROCESS TYPE is a low-delicacy system within the experiential clause grammar; its entry condition is 'major clause'. Consequently, a reasonably high number of clauses have been analysed to establish the frequency profile in Figure 8.4 – around 8,700, although this is still very much in the exploratory pilot study range (cf. Matthiessen, 1999, 2006), However, as we explore systems ordered in delicacy, moving from less delicate (more general) systems to more delicate ones, the numbers will inevitably decrease. The

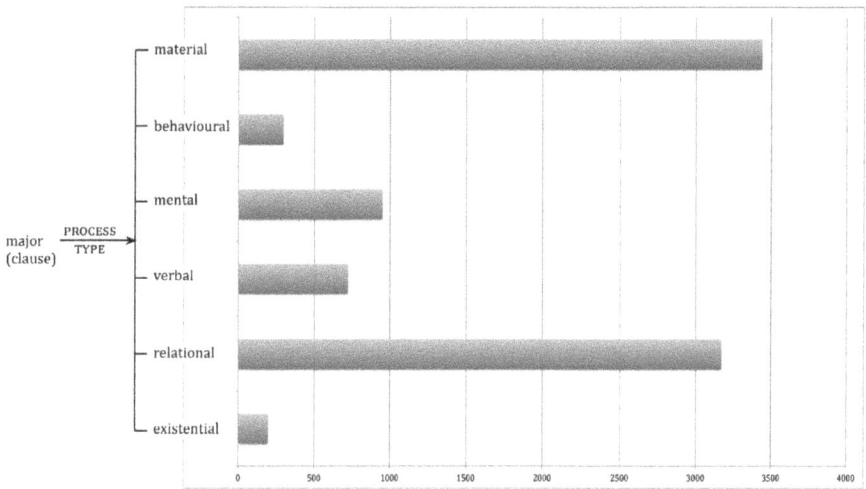

Figure 8.4 Relative frequencies of systemic terms in texts from
a registerially varied sample

analysis of relative frequencies in a set of systems ordered in delicacy can be
illustrated by reference to the interpersonal grammar of the clause in English:
see Figure 8.5.

There are four systems ordered in delicacy: STATUS (also called FREEDOM),
MOOD TYPE, INDICATIVE TYPE and INTERROGATIVE TYPE. The number of clauses
analysed for each step in delicacy is as follows:

- STATUS: 8,786 (out of 9,388 'major' clauses) – 'free' 6,821 / 'bound' 1,965
- MOOD TYPE: 6,330 (out of 6,821 'free' clauses) – 'indicative' 6,128 / 'imperative' 202
- INDICATIVE TYPE: 6,120 (out of 6,128 'indicative' clauses) – 'declarative'
5,679 / 'interrogative' 441
- INTERROGATIVE TYPE: 442 (out of 442 'interrogative' clauses) – 'wh-' 210 /
'yes/no' 232

While this is still very much work in progress, the general picture is clear: the
population of units (clauses, in this case) decreases, as delicacy increases (this
being the general inverse relation between extension and intension); and for
systems that have low-frequency terms as their entry condition, the effect is of
course magnified. Thus INTERROGATIVE TYPE has 'interrogative' as its entry condition, and 'interrogative' is much less frequent than 'declarative' in the system
of INDICATIVE TYPE. Consequently, as we increase the delicacy of the systemic

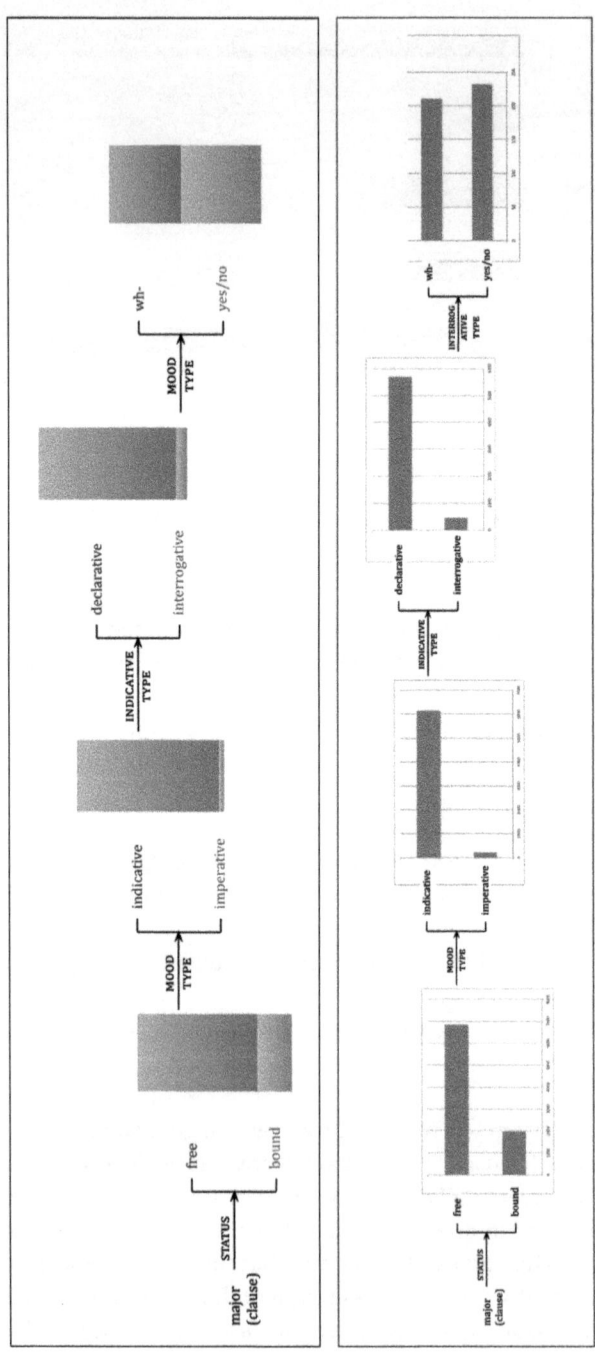

Figure 8.5 Relative frequencies of systemic terms in mood-type systems ordered in delicacy in texts from a registerially varied sample

analysis, we have to increase the size of the sample of texts that we analyse if we want our counts to be reasonably representative and reliable – which raises the question of the extent to which the analysis can be automated (see further below, Section 6; cf. also Halliday & James, [1993] 2005; Halliday, [1991] 2005b: 67, and endnote 7, p. 74).

There is another consideration that is also important: while the systems of increasing delicacy shown in Figure 8.5 all have simple entry conditions (thus in a sense forming a strict taxonomy of modal options in the clause), more delicate systems often have complex entry conditions – for example, I could have included mood tagging, which has a disjunctive entry condition of 'declarative' and 'imperative'.

Discussing the corpus-based study of systemic probabilities by Halliday and James ([1993] 2005) and their selection of systems to investigate, Halliday ([1993] 2005b: 145) draws attention to these methodological considerations relating to the study of systems of increasing delicacy:

> The systems to be counted had to be very general ones, not those of a more 'delicate' kind; they should be systems that apply to a large number of instances. This is partly to ensure that each term occurs with sufficient frequency; but there is a more significant factor, which is this – that any general hypothesis about probabilities ceases to apply when one moves to more specific sets of options, because these tend to have complex entry conditions. A system network is not a strict taxonomy.

When he carried out exploratory counts in the mid-1960s, Halliday adopted a 2000/200 instance criterion (Halliday, [1993] 2005b: 134; cf. also Halliday, [1992] 2005a: 81):

> I collected a small sample of four different registers of English, just big enough to yield a total of 2,000 occurrences of whatever category provided the entry condition to the systems I wanted to study. For example, in order to count instances of indicative / imperative mood, I had to have 2,000 independent clauses, because it is here that the choice is made: each independent clause selects one or the other. But to compare declarative with interrogative I had to count 2,000 indicative clauses, because it is the indicative clause that is either declarative or interrogative. The reason for settling on a figure of 2,000 occurrences was the following: first, I estimated it needed about 200 occurrences of the less frequent term to ensure a reasonable degree of accuracy; and second, that the less frequent term in a binary system seemed to occur about 10 per cent of the time. So if I restricted the counting to binary systems, 2,000 instances tended to yield around 200 occurrences of the less frequent term in the system.

This gives a very clear sense of methodological considerations involved in analysing texts in terms of systems of varying degrees of delicacy. In my pilot investigation interpersonal clause systems (Figure 8.5), equally exploratory as Halliday's work in the mid-1960s, the lowest number occurrences is of 'imperative' – 202 instances (which of course partly reflects the registerial composition of my opportunistic sample of texts; cf. Matthiessen, 2006).

5 Types of Probability and Probability Profiles

5.1 Types of Probability

In Halliday's characterization of probabilities in language, all probabilities are systemic: 'probability is the probability of "choosing" . . . one thing rather than another' (Halliday, [1991] 2005a: 45). As illustrated in Figure 8.4 and Figure 8.5, we can count the number of times terms in a given system are selected in a sample of texts, and interpret these relative frequencies as systemic probabilities. For example, in the system INDICATIVE TYPE (Figure 8.5), the relative frequencies are 92.8 % 'declarative' choices and 7.2 % 'interrogative' ones; so we can interpret this as approximating a probability ratio of 'declarative 0.9' vs 'interrogative 0.1'. In contrast, in the system interrogative type (Figure 8.5), the relative frequencies are 47 % 'wh-' choices and 52.5 % 'yes / no' ones; so we can interpret this as approximating a probability ratio of 'wh- 0.5' vs 'yes / no 0.5'. These two systems would thus have significantly different probability profiles: see further below, Section 5.2. Of course, we need to analyse vastly larger samples of text from a wide range of dialogic registers to get more reliable results.

The probabilities associated with terms in a system are subject to 'conditioning effects' deriving from the environment in which the system operates: see Table 8.1. Conditioning effects may be either (i) intrastratal, from roundabout the system whose probabilities are being conditioned, or (ii) interstratal, from above the system being conditioned. These are illustrated schematically for the system of MODALITY in Figure 8.6.

(i) **Intrastratal conditioning effect**. Intrastratal conditioning effects are systemic terms (with associated probabilities) located within the same stratum as the conditioned system.[6] They are either (1) simultaneous, **conditional** probabilities, or (2) sequential (linear), **transitional** probabilities. The former have been investigated by systemic functional researchers; the latter remain less explored.

(1) **Conditional probabilities**. Simultaneous systems are systems that are not ordered in delicacy in relation to one another but are of the same order of

Table 8.1 Types of systemic probabilities

type of probability		characterization	reference
probability		probability of choosing one term rather than another in a system	Halliday (1991b/2005: 45)
probability due to conditioning effect: intrastratal – 'from roundabout'	transitional probability	repeated successive selections in the same system as a text unfolds	Halliday (1992b/2005: 85)
	conditional probability	parallel selections in simultaneous systems within the same unit	Halliday (1992b/2005: 87)
probability due to conditioning effect: interstratal – 'from above'	(conditioned probability)	conditioning of probabilities 'from above', due to code or register	Halliday (1991b/2005: 48–52; 1991c/2005: 66)

delicacy, having the same entry conditions like MODALITY TYPE and MODALITY VALUE in Figure 8.6. Halliday ([1992] 2005: 88) characterizes conditional probabilities as follows:

> With conditional probabilities . . . the two choices are being made simultaneously, and so either can be treated as the environment for the other; . . . we could equally well ask, what is the effect on the probability of declarative / interrogative of choosing either active or passive in the same clause? The two effects may be reciprocal, but they may not: . . .

Thus in the example in Figure 8.6, each term in the two systems will have its own systemic probability; but, in addition, there may be **favoured** combinations and **disfavoured** ones. This was brought out for simultaneous systems in another grammatical domain, viz. that of the clause nexus, in a pioneering study by Nesbitt & Plum (1988). They analysed spoken texts – interviews with dog fanciers – in terms of the simultaneous systems of TAXIS and LOGICO-SEMANTIC TYPE. They found certain favoured combinations; for example, the combination 'hypotaxis' and 'enhancing' is favoured over 'parataxis' and 'enhancing' whereas 'parataxis' and 'extending' is favoured over 'hypotaxis' and 'extending'. The significance of their study is highlighted by Halliday in a number of his papers on probability and grammar from the early 1990s, collected in Halliday (2005a). He raises the issue of the 'direction' of conditioning. In Matthiessen (2002b), I examine the same set of simultaneous systems based on the analysis of a registerially varied sample of text. However, let me introduce another interesting example, one that will also be relevant to the discussion in Section 5.2 below of probabilistic profiles of systems.

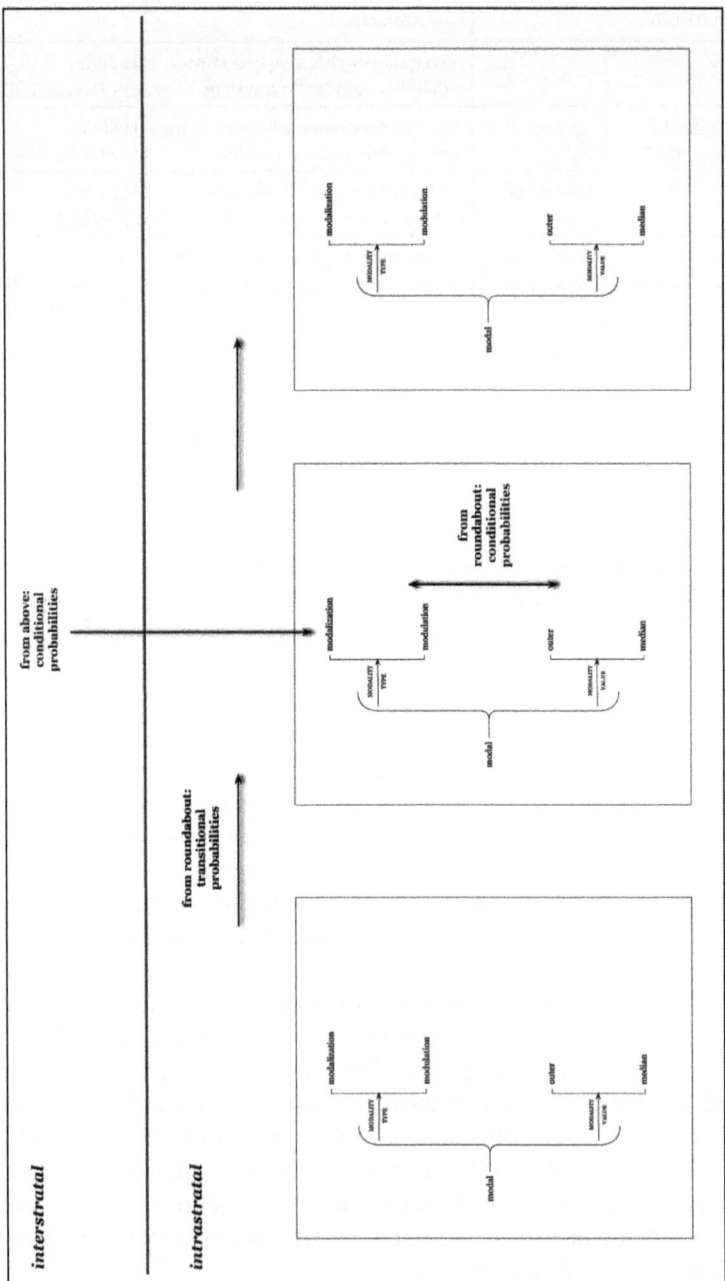

Figure 8.6 Schematic representation of conditioning effects on systemic probabilities

In the experiential grammar of the clause in English, the systems of PRO-CESS TYPE and of AGENCY are simultaneous; both have 'major clause' as their entry condition, and are thus very general, low delicacy systems. The system of PROCESS TYPE was represented in Figure 8.4. The system of AGENCY is the choice between 'middle' and 'effective', with the following relative frequencies: 'middle' 74.7 % / 'effective' 25.3 %. The intersection of these two simultaneous systems is shown in Figure 8.7. The picture is quite striking. If we look at the intersection in terms of AGENCY, we can see that the distribution of 'middle' and 'effective' across the process types is quite uneven: most 'effective' clauses are 'material', with just a fairly small proportion of 'relational' clauses. In fact, in 'material' clauses, the ratio of 'middle' to 'effective' is roughly 50 % / 50 %, but in all the other process types, it is 90 % or more / 10 % or less. (For these different probability profiles, see the next subsection.)

In other words, if we view the interaction between terms in the systems of AGENCY and PROCESS TYPE from the point of view of AGENCY, we can compare the predicted ratio of 'middle' to 'effective' for each process type based on the overall ratio of 'middle' 74.7 % / 'effective' 25.3 % with the actual ratio; this comparison is graphed in Figure 8.8. For 'material' clauses the predicted number of 'middle' clauses is higher than the actual number whereas the predicted number of 'effective' clauses is lower than the actual number; but for all other process types, it is the reverse: they all have a higher proportion of 'middle' selections over 'effective' ones based on the systemic frequencies in the system of AGENCY ('middle' 74.7% / 'effective' 25.3%).

(2) Transitional probabilities. As already noted, while conditional probabilities have been explored by systemic functional linguists, there has been less work (as far as I know) on transitional probabilities (probabilistic parsing would be one area where transitional probabilities are of interest). Like conditional probabilities, transitional probabilities are intrastratal rather than interstratal: they operate within the same stratum as the system whose probabilities are being conditioned, but unlike conditional probabilities, they are not located within the same cycle of instantiation of the system, but rather within an earlier cycle. In other words, transitional probabilities are linear in nature, being concerned with successive traversals of the same system. Halliday ([1992] 2003b: 370) characterizes transitional probabilities in terms of **intratextual history**:

The other is that of transitional probabilities: if the grammar of a language is represented as a probabilistic system, as I would consider it to be, then the intratextual history of any sentence is the perturbation of its inherent probabilities by the selections made earlier in the text. . . .

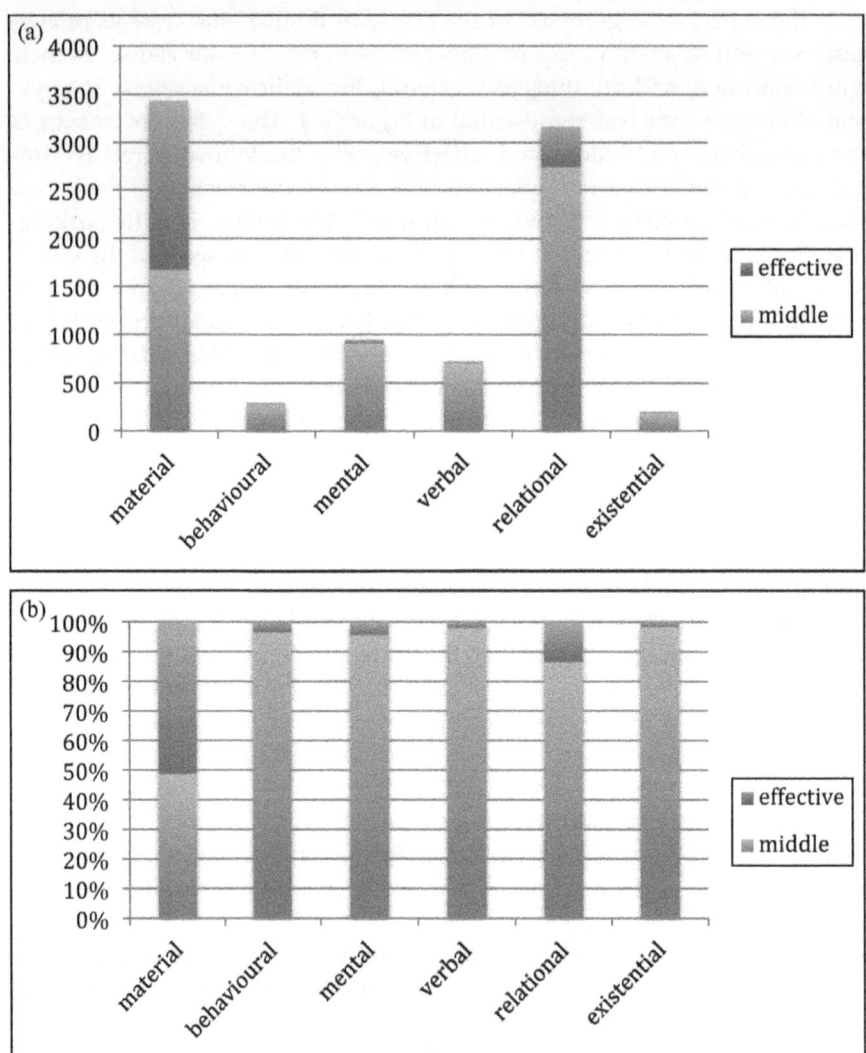

Figure 8.7 The intersection of the simultaneous systems AGENCY ('middle' / 'effective') and PROCESS TYPE ('material' / 'behavioural' / 'mental' / 'verbal' / 'relational' / 'existential') in terms of (a) absolute numbers and (b) percentages (N = 8,769 clauses)

and Halliday ([1992] 2005a: 85) relates transitional probabilities to the 'conception of a text as a Markoff process':

> Thirdly there is the question of whether, and if so how far, the probability of selecting one term in a given system is affected by previous selections made within the same system. [. . .] But the general conception of a text as a Markoff

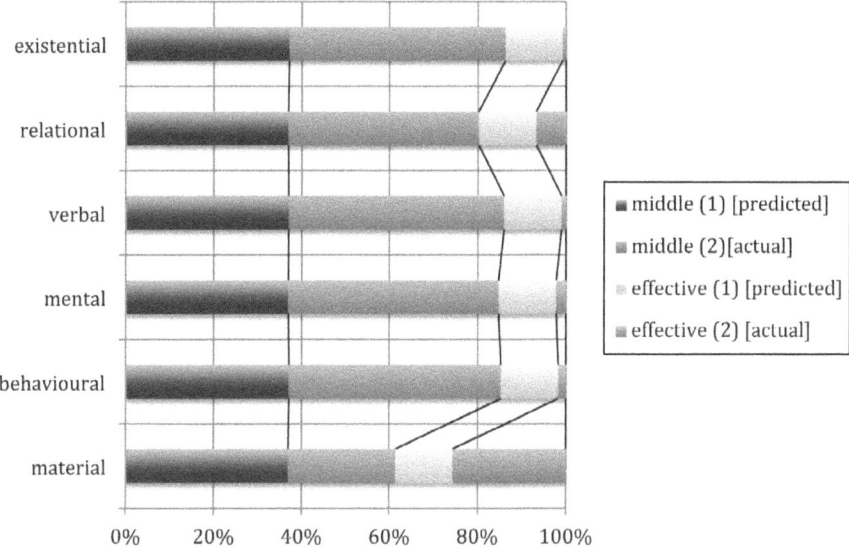

Figure 8.8 Conditioning between AGENCY and PROCESS TYPE represented as predicted and actual ratios between 'middle' and 'effective' AGENCY across the terms in PROCESS TYPE (N = 8,752 clauses)

process seems highly plausible; our expectances do play a significant part in our understanding of what we read and hear (for example in overcoming noise, as is demonstrated to every first-year student of phonetics.)

One way of exploring transitional effects is to examine texts as they unfold, tracking selections in different systems. This can be visualized as a **text score** (e.g. Matthiessen, 1995a, 2002a, using a term I have taken from Weinreich, 1972 ['Textpartitur']). A text score thus shows successive selections in one or more systems, unit by unit (e.g. clause by clause), as a text unfolds, as is illustrated for major interpersonal clause systems (cf. Figure 8.5) in a passage of a telephonic service encounter in Figure 8.9. Looking at the text score from left to right, we can see how local frequency patterns emerge clause by clause: in the system of MOOD TYPE, 'indicative' is consistently chosen over 'imperative'; and in the system of INDICATIVE TYPE, 'declarative' emerges over 'interrogative' as the (locally) unmarked selection. It is thus possible to see how relative frequencies gradually emerge as texts unfold. The text score does not, of course, show any transitional effects from one selection to another; but it may be possible to identify passages where such effects appear to be in operation.

Selections in certain systems are likely to appear periodically in the course of the unfolding of a text. Thus while most theme selections in a (traditional) narrative are likely to be 'unmarked', 'marked' selections are likely to appear

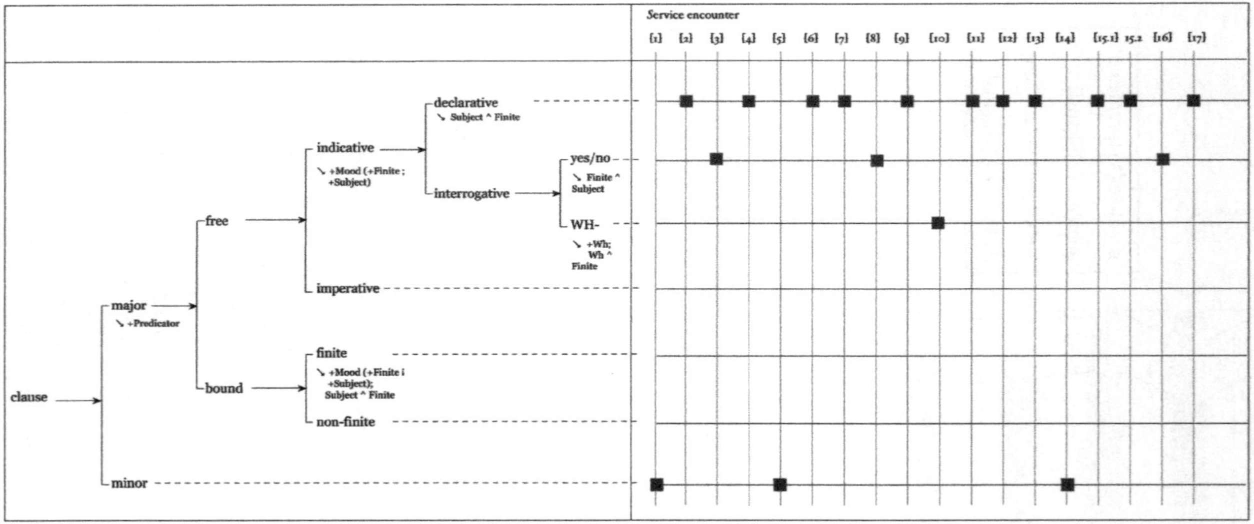

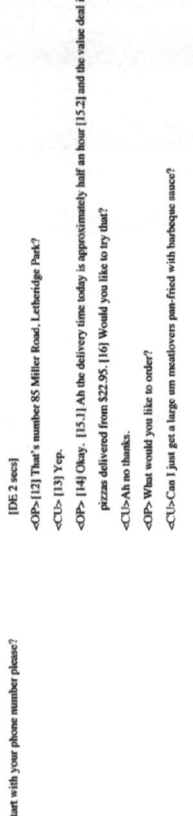

Figure 8.9 Text score showing selections (each selection being represented by a square) in interpersonal clause systems for a sequence of 17 clauses (each clause being represented by a numbered vertical line) in a passage from a telephonic service encounter

<OP> [1] Welcome to Pizza Hut. [2] My name's Sarah. [3] Can I start with your phone number please?

<CU> [4 <] 9628

<OP> [5] Uh-uh.

<CU> [>4] 9865.

<OP> [6] 96289865.

<CU> [7] Yeah.

<OP> [8] Would you like delivery or take away?

<CU> [9] Ah delivery thanks.

<OP> [10] Your surname and suburb there.

<CU> [11] Harding, Letheridge Park.

[DE 2 secs]

<OP> [12] That's number 85 Miller Road, Letheridge Park?

<CU> [13] Yep.

<OP> [14] Okay. [15.1] Ah the delivery time today is approximately half an hour [15.2] and the value deal is three large pizzas delivered from $22.95. [16] Would you like to try that?

<CU> Ah no thanks.

<OP> What would you like to order?

<CU> Can I just get a large um meatlovers pan-fried with barbeque sauce?

Figure 8.10 Successive selections of 'marked theme' (represented by diamonds) and 'unmarked theme' (represented by squares) in the course of the unfolding of a traditional narrative (a retelling for children of 'Noah's Ark')

periodically, as shown in Figure 8.10. In terms of transitional conditioning, we can note that 'marked' selections are very likely to be followed by 'unmarked' ones – usually a whole sequence of 'unmarked' Themes; there is only one exception in this text where 'marked' is chosen twice in a sequence. (This time the dove flew back to Noah with a green olive branch in its beak. Somewhere there was a bit of dry land.) We can explore successive selections of this kind in terms of intrastratal transitional probabilities; but it is of course also possible that larger-scale semantic patterns (and mediated by semantics, also contextual patterns) condition the probability of selecting 'marked' interstratally 'from above': in narratives, 'marked theme' selections tend to occur as part of the Placement, and then to signal the start of new episodes (cf. Hoey, 2006). There is of course no conflict between these two perspectives on the conditioning of the choice between 'marked' and 'unmarked' Theme.

Perhaps the limiting case of operation of transitional probabilities is the recursive kind of system characteristic of the logical mode of the ideational metafunction: see e.g. Halliday ([1992] 2005a: 90–1).

(ii) Interstratal conditioning effect. Systemic probabilities may be conditioned interstratally, 'from above'. In the case of phonology, this means lexicogrammatical conditioning in the first instance; and in the case of lexicogrammar, this means semantic conditioning in the first instance. The semantic conditioning will, of course, mediate conditioning from context. The two key areas here are (1) coding orientation and (2) register.

(1) Halliday ([1991] 2005a: 48–52) discusses two studies that bring out differences in coding orientation in probabilistic terms, Plum and Cowling (1987) and Hasan's large-scale research project concerned with interaction between mothers and children (e.g. Hasan, 1989, 2009; Hasan & Cloran, 1990; see further Chapter 6, this volume). For example, Plum and Cowling's (1987) study, based on interviews conducted for the Sydney Social Dialect Survey, shows that the relative frequencies of the selections in the system of PRIMARY TENSE of 'past' vs 'present' vary according to social class: see Figure 8.11. In particular, selections by lower-working-class speakers are skewed towards the 'present', whereas selections by middle-class speakers are skewed towards the 'past'. Commenting on this result, Halliday ([1991] 2005a: 50) observes:

This is a classic manifestation of Bernstein's principle of code, or (to give it the more accurate term) 'coding orientation'. If the linguistic system was not

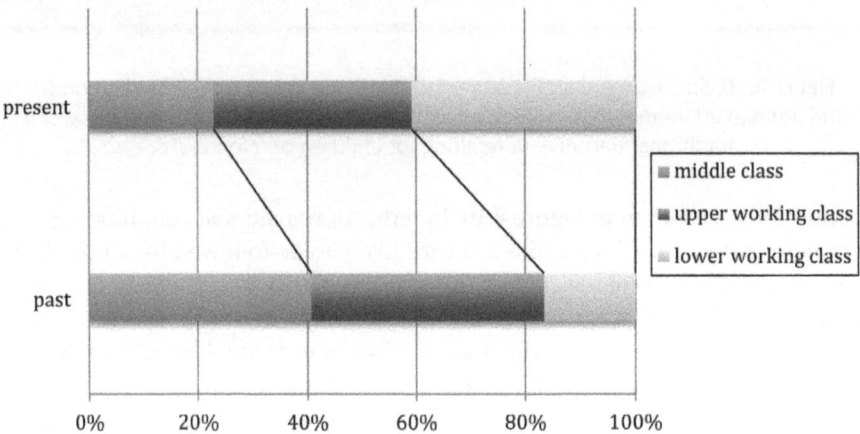

Figure 8.11 Variation in relative frequency in primary tense selections according to social class – graph of data from Plum and Cowling (1987)

inherently of a probabilistic kind it could not display these sociolinguistic effects. As it is, this kind of quantitative study can reveal important features relevant to the deeper social order.

(2) As already noted above, Halliday (e.g. [1991] 2005b: 65–6, 70, [1992] 2005a: 84–6, in press [b]) has characterized registers as resettings of systemic probabilities. Here the variation in systemic probabilities can be fairly dramatic, reflecting the fact that registers are different ways of using language, i.e. functional varieties of language. Let me use the system of PROCESS TYPE as an example: see Figure 8.12; average across a registerially mixed sample were shown in Figure 8.4. While we need much larger samples, there are some interesting patterns shown in Figure 8.12 that are likely to reflect general tendencies. For example, 'material' clauses are most dominant in narratives (traditional ones, like nursery tales, where they construe the event line of the narrative), 'mental' clauses are more prominent in casual conversation than in any of the other registers, and 'verbal' clauses are more common in news reports than in any of the other registers whereas they are absent in procedures.

Figure 8.12 shows how the relative frequency of each process type varies from one register to another. We can also look at this variation from the point of view of the conditioning register; Figure 8.13 shows how registers grouped according to the field of activity (socio-semiotic process) tend to attract different process types. For example, narratives (of the traditional kind) attract 'material' processes, scientific reports 'relational' processes, casual conversation 'mental' processes, and news reports 'verbal' processes. While 'material' and 'relational' clauses are the types most frequently selected across the different fields of activity, each field of activity (as represented here by one particular register each)

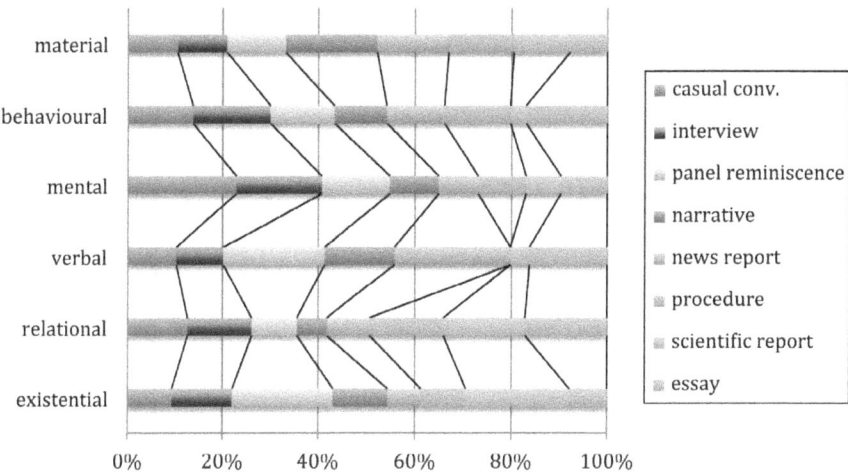

Figure 8.12 The relative frequency of terms in the system of PROCESS TYPE in eight different registers

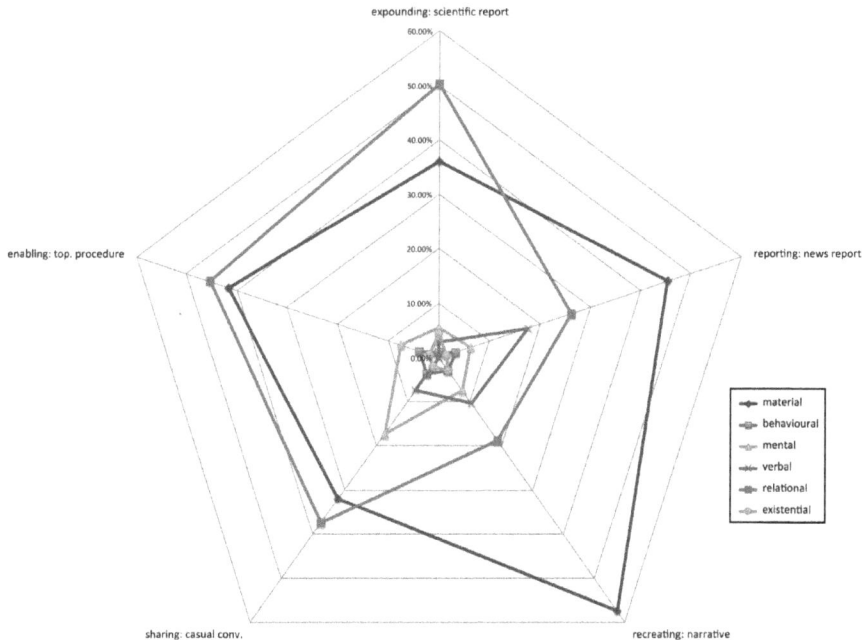

Figure 8.13 Registers grouped according to the field of activity (expounding, reporting, recreating, sharing, enabling) attracting different process types

constitutes a different angle on experience and thus needs to exploit the options provided by PROCESS TYPES in a distinct way.

5.2 Probability Profiles

Once a system is theorized as contrasting terms with probabilities attached, the question arises what **probability profiles** systems turn out to have – that is, what the possible probability distributions across the terms of the system are. For example, in systems with two terms ('binary systems'), should we expect to find profiles ranging across all values from 0.5 : 0.5 to 0.99 : 0.01 – that is m from equiprobable to the limiting case, bordering on categorical? In the example of interpersonal clause systems in Figure 8.6, there would appear to be two types of profile, roughly equiprobable (the system of INTERROGATIVE TYPE) and significantly skew (the other systems: STATUS, MOOD TYPE and INDICATIVE TYPE). This is not an accident. Halliday has shown both empirically and theoretically that these two probability profiles, **equi** and **skew**, are likely to be characteristic, at least of fairly general, indelicate systems. Discussing non-recursive systems, Halliday ([1991] 2005a: 47–8) writes:

> In principle these should be able to range over all probability distribution from 0.5/0.5 to approximately 0/1. But this kind of spread seemed to me to be highly unlikely. It would be unlikely for all systems to be equiprobable, since this would not leave enough redundancy. [. . .] But it would be equally unlikely for systems to take up all possible distribution of probabilities along the whole continuum from equiprobable to maximally skew.

> On the basis of what little counting I had done [in the 1960s, CMMIM], I suggested a bimodal distribution. The hypothesis was that systems tended towards one or other of two types, (i) equiprobable and (ii) skew, with the skew tending toward a ratio of one order of magnitude (which I represented for obvious reasons as nine to one, i.e. 0.9/0.1). This corresponds to one interpretation of the concept of marking: type (i), the equiprobable, have no unmarked term, while type (ii), the skew, have one of their terms unmarked.

Working with a member of John Sinclair's research group at Birmingham University, Zoe James, in the early 1990s, Halliday tested the hypothesis based on two systems, POLARITY ('positive' / 'negative') and PRIMARY TENSE ('past' / 'present'[7]). Halliday & James ([1993] 2005) examined these two systems in 18 million words of the Birmingham Corpus (before it expanded into the hundreds of millions of words of the 'Bank of English'). The findings were very clear (see also Halliday, [1993] 2005b: Part II): the probability profile of POLARITY was skew, while that of PRIMARY TENSE was equi.

The study by Halliday & James ([1993] 2005) was an important empirical investigation and, as Halliday (in press [b]) notes, it needs to be followed up for other systems on a similar scale (or increased by another order of magnitude). As far as I know, it hasn't yet been followed up – we only have additional exploratory small-scale investigations such as Matthiessen (2006). One reason is, of course, practical: the amount of work involved is very considerable – well beyond lots of small-scale manual investigations (cf. Section 6 below).

At the same time, Halliday has also backed up his hypothesis about the probability profiles of systems based on **Information Theory** (Shannon, 1948; Shannon & Weaver, 1949). This theory is rather technical and mathematical, involving entropy, information and redundancy (for a synopsis of Information Theory for linguists, see Goldsmith, 2001). But the key issue that Halliday identifies is the trade-off between **information** and **redundancy**: see Table 8.2 (based on numbers in Halliday's [1991] 2005b: 74, table in Endnote 9).

Roughly, in equi systems, information (H) is above 0.9 and redundancy (R) below 0.1; and in skew systems, information is below 0.7 and redundancy above 0.3. As I have indicated in the table (by means of the column and row headed '. . .'), there is thus a significant *gap* between equi systems and skew ones in terms of the relationship between information and redundancy. And this is the basis for Halliday's theoretical reasoning about the distinction between equi systems and skew ones. He has explained this in various places; for example, Halliday ([1991] 2005b: 69) writes:

> It is interesting to note that this skew profile of 0.9 : 0.1 is just at the point where, in Shannon and Weaver's theory of information, the redundancy measure works out at 50 per cent. (To be exact, H = R = 0.5 where the probabilities are 0.89 : 0.11.)

Table 8.2 The trade-off between information (H) and redundancy (R) for equiprobable (bold, dark shading) and skew (bold italics, light shading) system probability profiles (binary systems). The prototypical equi and skew profiles are shown in cells with heavy borders

	H = 1	H = 0.97	H = 0.91	. . .	H = 0.72	H = 0.47	H = 0.08
R = 0	0.5 : 0.5						
R = 0.03		0.6 : 0.4					
R = 0.09			0.67 : 0.33				
. . .							
R = 0.28					0.8 : 0.2		
R = 0.53						0.9 : 0.1	
R = 0.92							0.99 : 0.01

A little later, he develops this point further (Halliday, [1991] 2005b: 69–70):

> . . . it would be a matter of some significance if it turns out that grammatical systems tend towards a bimodal probability distribution where one mode is that of almost no redundancy and the other is that where redundancy is around 50 per cent. The actual values showing up in my own informal frequency counts would be defined by the following limits:
>
> (i) equiprobable
>
> p 0.5 : 0.5 ~ 0.65 : 0.35
>
> H 1 ~ 0.93
>
> (ii) skew
>
> p 0.8 : 0.2 ~ 0.89 : 0.11 ~ 0.95 : 0.05
>
> H 0.72 ~ 0.5 ~ 0.28

In other words, the redundancy was either (i) less than 10 per cent or (ii) somewhere in the region of 30–70 per cent, and often towards the middle of that range, close to 50 per cent. If this is in fact a general pattern, it would suggest that the grammar of a natural language is organized around the interaction between two modes of quantizing information: one where each act of choice – each instance – is maximally informative (it might equally well have been the opposite), and one where it is largely uninformative (since you could pretty well have guessed it already). Furthermore, it might be the case that these two kinds of system occur in roughly equal proportion.

As already noted, the two systems investigated by Halliday & James ([1993] 2005), viz. PRIMARY TENSE and POLARITY, fall into the probability profiles of equi and skew, respectively; primary tense is very close to the 'ideal' equi system in Table 8.2 (probability profile 0.5 : 0.5; information = 1, redundancy = 0), whereas polarity is very close to the 'ideal' skew system (probability profile 0.9 : 0.1; information = (approximately) 0.5, redundancy = (approximately) 0.5.

But what about other systems? We will have to wait until researchers take on the (perhaps daunting!) task of replicating Halliday and James's ([1993] 2005) study for systems other than PRIMARY TENSE and POLARITY. While we are waiting, let me just report on my own small-scale exploratory investigation (an ongoing effort, based on manual analysis; see Matthiessen, 2006, for an interim report).

Out of the wide range of systems that I have used in manual analysis of texts, I have chosen 38 clause nexus and clause systems as a basis for exploring Halliday's bimodal probability profile of equi vs skew systems. These 38 systems are all binary ones (thus non-binary systems like PROCESS TYPE are excluded): see Figure 8.14.

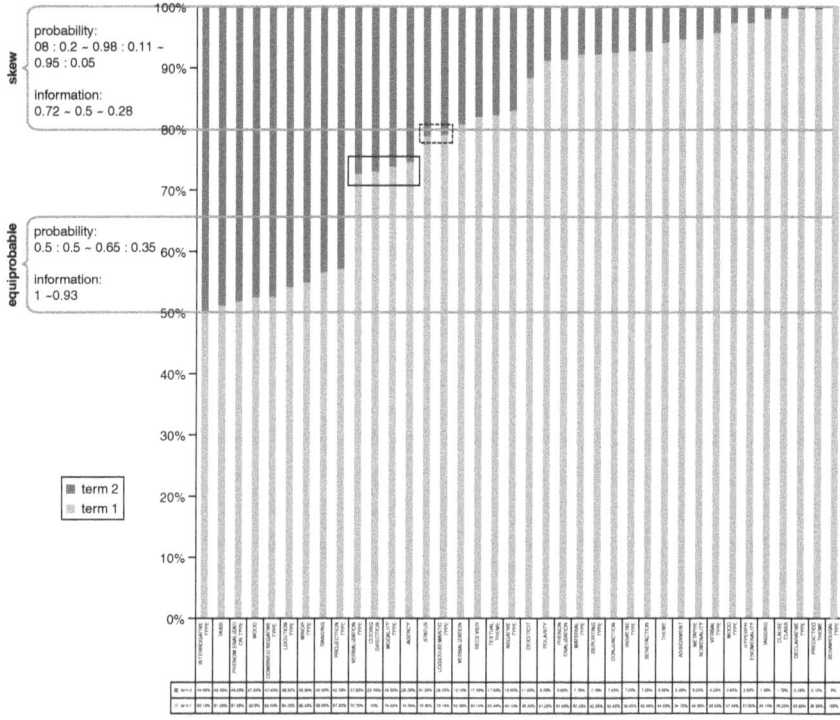

Figure 8.14 Systemic probability profiles in relation to Halliday's distinction between skew and equiprobable systems

Out of these 38 systems, 34 can be fairly clearly be interpreted as *either* equi *or* skew systems.[8] Four systems have profiles that fall in-between the probability ranges of 'skew' and 'equiprobable'; they all have a profile of approximately 0.25 : 0.75:

- VERBALIZATION TYPE: 'named' (+verbiage) 27.3% : 'locuted' (+projection) 72.7%
- CODING DIRECTION: 'encoding' 27% : 'decoding' 73%
- MODALITY TYPE: 'modalization' 26% : 'modulation' 74%
- AGENCY: 'effective' 25.3% / 'middle' 74.7%

Of these, the results for the system of AGENCY are the most robust: it is the least delicate system (simultaneous with PROCESS TYPE) of the four, and the absolute number of clauses analysed in terms of this system is fairly high (around 9,000). The other systems are all more delicate, so the absolute numbers are much lower, and we should set them aside for the time being until we have reached much higher numbers in our counting.

The system of AGENCY would thus seem to be an exception to the bimodal probability distribution hypothesized by Halliday (for low-delicacy systems). However, it is interesting to note that when we intersect AGENCY with the simultaneous system of PROCESS TYPE, as shown in Figure 8.8, it splits into two domains: in the environment of 'material' clauses, its probability profile is that of an equi system, but for the other process types, it is that of a skew system. This may be a general pattern with 0.25 : 0.75 system; but to assess the situation, we will have to wait for the results of extensive corpus-based studies.

5.3 Quantitative and Qualitative Correlations

As we have seen, in Halliday's account of the probabilistic nature of language, quantitative and qualitative aspects of choice are complementary ('probability is the probability of "choosing" . . . one thing rather than another'). But how is this complementarity manifested? This is of course in itself a major research question – and we could go back to Zipf (1935) to review findings in this area. Within the stratum of lexicogrammar, one manifestation of the complementarity is the cline between grammar and lexis. As is well known, if we count the frequency of occurrence of lexicogrammatical items, it turns out that the more frequent they are, the more likely they are to be grammatical rather than lexical – the highest-frequency items always being grammatical ('function words') rather than lexical ('content words'). As the frequency decreases, the proportion of lexical items increases: see Figure 8.15; and as we move towards grammatical items, the increase in frequency is exponential. And there is also, of course, a reflection of the frequency of wordings on the expression plane: the more frequent a lexicogrammatical item is, the 'shorter' and more reduced its expression tends to be.

In addition to the general correlation between the distinction between grammatical and lexical items, and frequency in text illustrated in Figure 8.15, there may be more specific pattern. One area that I have explored is the frequency of the different process types (see Figure 8.4) and their qualitative elaboration in the lexicogrammar measured crudely in terms of the number of verbs (or really verb senses) belonging to each process type (see Matthiessen, 1999, 2006, 2014). In general, it turns out that relative frequency and systemic elaboration correlate. There is one exception, viz. 'relational' clauses. Although they are almost as frequent as 'material' ones, there are many fewer verbs devoted to them. However, this is not surprising, given the nature of 'relational' clauses: the systemic elaboration is in the participants rather than in the process.

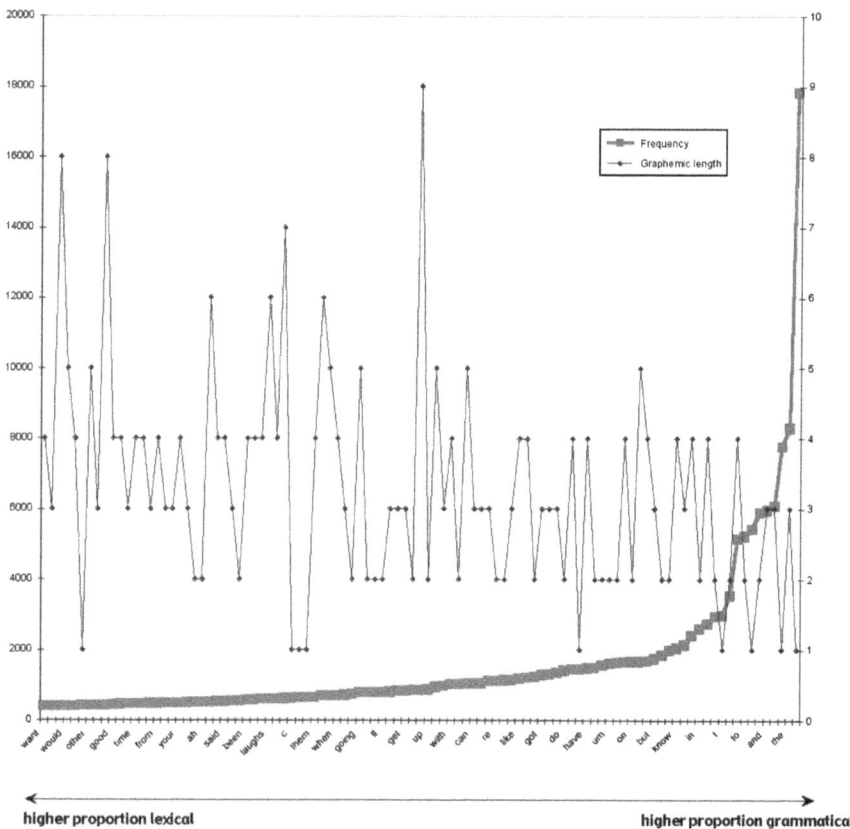

◀───▶

higher proportion lexical   **higher proportion grammatical**

Figure 8.15 Frequency of lexicogrammatical items and the cline
between lexis and grammar

6 Investigating the Corpus

Any investigation of quantitative patterns in language depends on the existence
of corpora and on tools for analysing them. In a sense, we are tantalizingly close
to a real breakthrough based in terms of the analysis of massive volumes of text;
but there are still severe constraints on what we can access as far as the grammar is concerned. Our access to the corpus is still fairly 'superficial'; the way
corpora are represented and the suite of corpus analysis tools are much more
supportive of lexical analysis than of grammatical analysis. Manning (2003:
294) characterizes the situation as follows:

> It's easy to search corpora for something like *as least as* constructions; it is
> far harder to search corpora for something like participial relative clauses or

locative inversion constructions. Such technological limitations have meant that corpus linguistic research has been largely limited to phenomena that can be accessed via searches on particular words. The average corpus linguist's main research tool remains the word-concordancing program, which shows a searched-for keyword in context (perhaps with morphological stemming, sorting options, etc.). However, a (theoretical) syntactician is usually interested in more abstract structural properties that cannot be investigated easily in this way.

This is very similar to the assessment Halliday has expressed over the years; for example, Halliday ([2000c] 2005: 171) notes:

> In principle, as I think is generally accepted, the corpus is just as useful, and just as essential, for the study of grammar as it is for the study of lexis. Only, the grammar is very much harder to get at. In a language like English, where words may operate all the way along the continuum, there are grammatical items like *the* and *and* and *to* just as there are lexical items like *sun* and *moon* and *stars*, as well as those like *behind* and *already* and *therefore* which fall somewhere in the middle; occurrences of any of these are easily retrieved, counted, and contextualized. But whereas *sun* and *moon* and *stars* carry most of their meaning on their sleeves, as it were, *the* and *and* and *to* tell us very little about what it going on underneath; and what they do tell us, if we just observe them directly, tends to be comparatively trivial. It is an exasperating feature of patterns at the grammatical end of the continuum, that the easier they are to recognize the less they matter.

In corpus studies in linguistics, there have tended to be two approaches to the processing of corpora. (i) One approach has been to represent corpora in standard orthography, and to analyse them directly using analysis tools – usually some kind of concordancing programme. In the UK, this approach was taken by John Sinclair and his team at the University of Birmingham. (ii) Another approach has been to develop software such as word class ('part of speech', 'POS') taggers and more full-fledged parsers to annotate corpora with additional information (a POS-tagged corpus, or a parsed corpus, a 'treebank' or 'treebanked' corpus), and then to analyse these annotated corpora using additional analysis tools to search annotated corpora. In the UK, this approach was taken by Geoffrey Leech and his team at the University of Lancaster.

Linguists adopting the first approach have argued that annotation introduces a theoretical or descriptive bias in the analysis of the corpus; but McEnery & Hardie (2011) address and (I think it is fair to say) demolish their argument. Even if a corpus has been annotated, it is of course perfectly possible to bypass the annotation; and whatever form of analysis we subject an unannotated corpus to will of course also embody a linguistic bias. By representing a corpus by

means of standard orthography, we have of course already made various theoretically significant decisions, and introduced a bias.

For any given research task, researchers will have to consider what kind of
corpus to use and what kinds of computational tools to use, including both
annotation tools and search tools. When Halliday & James ([1993] 2005) carried
out their corpus analysis of POLARITY and PRIMARY TENSE, they had access to the
unannotated Birmingham corpus of around 20 million words. They decided
that annotation would, at that time, not have been of great help; instead, they
searched the 'raw' corpus. Their account of how to go about looking for grammatical features based on orthographic words is methodologically very helpful, and still relevant today, at least if one hasn't got access to an annotated
corpus.

Even with an annotated corpus with good search tools such as COCA, the
Corpus of Contemporary American English (http://corpus.byu.edu/coca/), it
can be hard to carry out investigations into grammar. Assume that we want
to explore the probabilistic nature of the system of MODALITY in English (cf.
Figure 8.6). This will include searching for orthographic words that potentially realize modal operators such as *can, may, will, must* and modal adverbs
such as *perhaps, maybe, probably, certainly*. One problem is of course that one
and the same orthographic word can often realize different grammatical and
lexical words. For example, the orthographic word *will* can be a temporal or
modal operator (grammatical word) serving as Finite in the clause, a lexical
verb serving as Event in the verbal group or a lexical noun serving as Thing in
the nominal group (unless it is used as a Classifier in the nominal group). These
possibilities are represented schematically in Figure 8.16.

If we only have access to a 'raw' corpus, we will have to search for instances
of the orthographic word *will*; but all the instances that turn up will have to be
examined manually in some way – for example drawing on the methods used
by Halliday & James ([1993] 2005). However, what would the situation be if we
can search for *will* with tags representing different word classes? It will depend
on what tags are available and on how reliable they are. As an illustration, I
have tabulated tags in COCA that can be used in an attempt to pick out the right
kind of *will*: see Table 8.3.

Searches for forms of the lexical verb *will* and for the lexical noun *will* turn up
many instances of the operator *will*. However, the good news is that when one
searches for the 'modal auxiliary' *will* (i.e. will. [vm*]), the result seems reliable;
I examined the first 100 occurrences, and they are all instances of the operator
will. But that is as far as we can get at present: there are no tags to differentiate
between modal and temporal *will*, nor between the different modal senses of *will*.
This is not a criticism of COCA; it would indeed be quite hard to distinguish
these types automatically. Therefore, to continue the analysis, we would have
to examine 860,679 occurrences of the operator *will*, and analyse them manually
(and we could, of course, reasonably ask how much we have actually gained

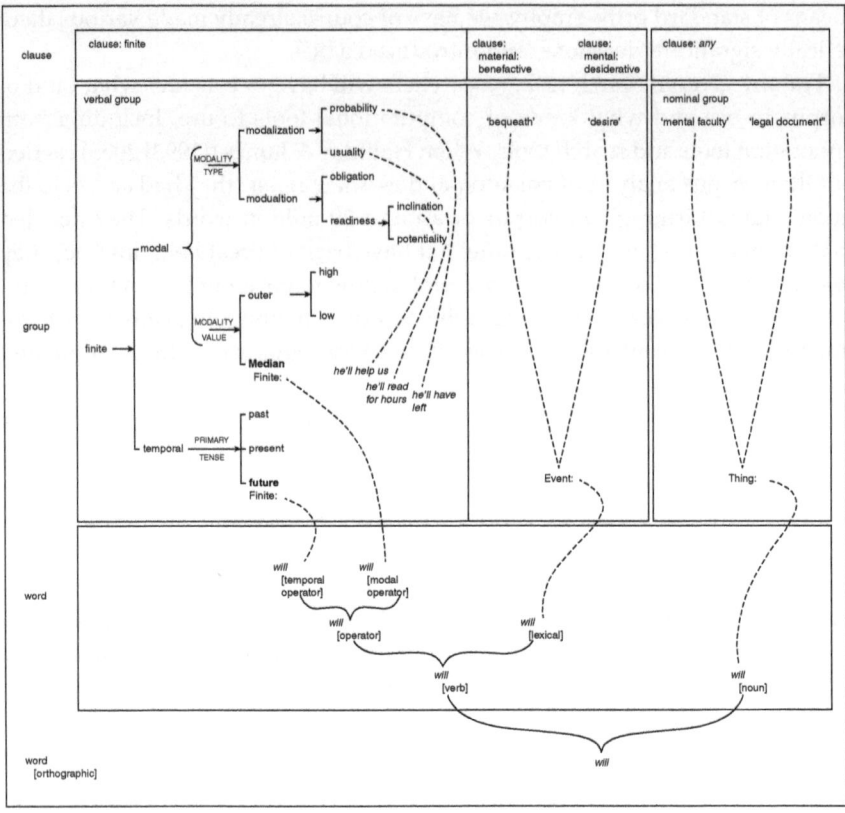

Figure 8.16 Lexicogrammatical differentiation of orthographic word will, first at word rank and then at group rank

from the tagging in this particular case – compare Halliday & James', [1993] 2005, decision not to try to produce a tagged version of the corpus they had access to).

Corpus studies as they developed in linguistics, 'corpus linguistics', have now been supplemented by extensive work within natural language processing (NLP), more specifically within **statistical NLP** (Manning & Schütze, 1999). This is an important development because, as McEnery & Hardie (2011: Section 2.5.3) observe, not much progress has been made in the further development of corpus tools in corpus linguistics since the 1990s because these tools tend to be developed by single researchers rather than by teams. A decade ago, Manning's (2003: 294) assessment of the potential for future research into the probabilistic properties of grammar was optimistic:

> Fortunately for such research, recent intensive work in statistical natural language processing (statistical NLP; Manning & Schütze, 1999) has led

Table 8.3 Examples of tags in COCA that can be applied in searches for instances of will in order to try to refine these searches

Class	COCA label	tag	occurrences	comment
operator [temporal / modal]	modal auxiliary	will.[vm*]	860,679	this seems reliable; the first 100 instances are all operators
lexical verb	base form of lexical verb	will.[wO*]	1891	most of the hits are operator *will*
	infinitive	will.[vʔi*]	128	
	3rd person singular	will.[vʔz*]	0	
	past (v-ed)	will.[vʔd*]	0	
	past participle (v-en)	will.[vʔn*]	0	
	present participle (v-ing)	will.[vʔg*]	0	
	lexical verb	will.fvv*]	2019	most of the hits are operator *will*
noun	noun	will.fn*]	50,060	this includes both common noun *will* and proper noun *Will*; operator *will* is also picked up, e.g. *Will thoroughbred racing have its historic moment?*

to the availability of both many more richly annotated text corpora that can support deeper investigations, and many more tools capable of being used with good accuracy over unannotated text in order to recover deep syntactic relationships. The prospects for applying these corpora and tools to probabilistic analysis are bright, but it remains fair to say that these tools have not yet made the transition to the Ordinary Working Linguist without considerable computer skills.

The Ordinary Working Linguist may be in a better position now than ten years ago; but many such linguists are still constrained in terms of how much of the power of statistical NLP they can tap into (cf. also McEnery & Hardie, 2011: Section 9.3, on the relative lack of interaction between 'corpus linguistics' and 'computational linguistics'). For discussions dealing specifically with corpus studies within SFL, see Wu (2009), Teich (2009) and cf. also Bateman (this volume).

The development of more powerful tools for corpus analysis will make it possible to extend the research into language as a probabilistic system based on Halliday's theoretical foundation. At the same time, his systemic functional linguistics has a great deal to offer in the further expansion of corpus studies. For example, in their review of criticisms of Biber's (1986, 1988, onwards) 'multidimensional' ('MD') approach in corpus studies, McEnery & Hardie (2011: Section 5.4.3) note that one problem is that his choice of features is not motivated, in addition to the fact that the features chosen are limited to only those that can be retrieved in the analysis of tagged corpora:

> So we might argue that the MD methodology could be more solidly founded if based on a selection of features which is both principled and exhaustive – a standard which Biber's feature-lists approach but do not reach. How might such a motivated list of lexicogrammatical features be derived? At this point we move into the realm of hypothesis. However, one possible approach is to consider the functions of a language as a feature tree. This could start at the very high level of nominal components versus verbal components (since the noun-verb distinction is one of the most universal features of language structure), and then diversify from there, with attention to contrasting linguistic options and category alternatives at each branch in the tree.

They provide an example of part of such a tree. An alternative to what they propose would be not to reinvent the linguistic wheel, but instead to draw on the extensive systemic functional literature and to use systemic descriptions in the form of system networks to derive principled selections of features from comprehensive (exhaustive) descriptions. Their 'tree' is simply a partial reflection of what would be covered by a comparable system network. Here corpus studies can benefit from Halliday's move to give the theory of language a paradigmatic base (see Martin& Matthiessen, this volume) and to theorize the corpus in terms of the cline of instantiation, thereby relating the domain of data (the instance pole of the cline) to the domain of theory (the system pole), as shown in Figure 8.1.

7 Conclusion

When Halliday began exploring the probabilistic nature of language, first in his text-based work on Chinese in the 1950s and then, moving from the late 1950s into the 1960s, also in his text-based work on English, it was conceivable that more linguists would have joined him in taking an interest in the probabilistic nature of language, stimulated by the development of Information Theory. However, the history of linguistics took a different turn – a turn towards the categoricity of competence, and the insulation of competence from performance, so that it was left to those taking an interest in performance, initially mainly psycholinguists, to deal with quantitative issues. In spite of this turn towards the categoricity of competence, Halliday and other systemic functional linguists continued to explore the probabilistic nature of language, taking advantage of the development of the technology of the corpus (starting in particular in the second half of the 1980s).

However, the academic climate was changing rather dramatically. One reason was of course precisely the development of corpus studies in linguistics. Another was the development in computational linguistics of what came to be known as statistical NLP (and also, importantly, in work on speech recognition[9]). This was related to the construction of grammatical frameworks such as LFG and HPSG designed to be used in computational systems; in this way, formal grammarians came to appreciate the value of the corpus and of a probabilistic understanding of language (probabilistic parsers were part of the convincing evidence[10]). It is also important to note that probabilistic insights have been taken into consideration in models of cognition (see e.g. Charter, Tenenbaum & Yuille, 2006).

A number of these developments are brought together by Bod, Hay and Jannedy (2003a) under the heading of **probabilistic linguistics**. Their own introduction and the various contributions to the book, including work on phonology, grammar (syntax and morphology) and semantics, make a very powerful case for a theoretical understanding of language as a probabilistic system. Thus there is now an interesting opportunity to relate the kind of work reported on by the contributors to 'probabilistic linguistics' to Halliday's conception of language as a probabilistic system. In Bod, Hay & Jannedy (2003a), there is only one reference to Halliday, viz. to the second edition of his *Introduction to Functional Grammar*, but not to any of his empirical and theoretical work on language as a probabilistic system since the 1950s. The reference is provided by Manning (2003) in his chapter on 'probabilistic syntax'.

Discussing the goals of joint research with other scholars, Manning (2003: 340) writes 'We want to be able to predict the overall rate of the different systemic choices (Halliday, 1994) that can be made for certain input.' This suggests that it would be possible to construct a bridge between these two communities of scholars concerned with the probabilistic properties of language. A number of the cases Manning discussed could certainly be interpreted and illuminated in systemic functional terms; some of his key examples (e.g. in reference to Optimality Theory) involve what I would interpret as competing motivations across metafunctions in the organization of the clause involving probabilistic considerations within the metafunctional systems that are in competition. In systemic functional research, one pioneering study that could serve as a model for future investigations informed by computational work is Munro (2004), who used the techniques of machine learning to 'infer an accurate description of functional categories' of the nominal group in English.

Halliday's conception of language as a probabilistic system is, of course, an integral and natural part of his conception of language as a (complex) dynamic open system (with reference to the work by Jay Lemke, e.g. Lemke, 1984). In this connection, it is interesting to consider Ball's (2004) comments on complexity; after a brief discussion of 'catastrophe theory' and 'chaos theory', he writes (pp. 4–5):

> The current vogue is for the third of these three C's: complexity. The buzzwords are now 'emergence' and 'self-organization', as complexity theory seeks to understand how order and stability arise from the interaction of many agents according to a few simple rules.

> The physics I shall discuss in this book is not unrelated to the idea of complexity – indeed, the two often overlap. But very often what passes today for 'complexity science' is really something much older, dressed up in fashionable apparel. The main themes in complexity theory have been studied by physicists for over a hundred years, and these scientists have evolved a toolkit of concepts and techniques to which complexity studies have added barely a handful of new items. At the root of this sort of physics is a phenomenon which immediately explains why the discipline may have something to say about society: it is a science of collective behaviour. At face value it is not obvious how the bulk properties of insensate particles of matter should bear any relation to how humans behave en masse. Yet physicists have discovered that systems whose component parts have a capacity to act collectively often show recurrent features, even though they might seem to have nothing in at all in common with one another.

The title of Ball's book is *Critical Mass: How One Thing Leads to Another*, and he has added an elaboration 'being an enquiry into the interplay of chance and necessity in the way that human culture, customs, institutions, cooperation and conflict arise'. Adding language to this mix would seem highly appropriate – language conceived of in probabilistic terms. When we conceive of language in probabilistic terms, we can examine the effect of 'collective behaviour'; the system that embodies systemic probabilities is located at the potential pole of the cline of instantiation embedded in the context of culture of a speech fellowship, as shown in Figure 8.1. Systemic probabilities are always being shaped by collective behaviour. Let me end my chapter by linking this understanding to a point made by Halliday (in press [b]) under the section heading of 'probability and prediction'):

> The concept of meaning as choice, or as choosing, whether or not it is being represented as a system network, may suggest a bias towards the individual meaner: the notion of an act of meaning, in particular, carries with it a suggestion of this kind. But choosing may be an activity of a whole population, as it is when they vote in an election or a referendum. Meaning as choice can likewise be thought of in the context of a population – in the statistical sense:

it may be concerned with very large quantities of acts of meaning, within which large-scale patterns and tendencies may be observed.

The network makes no prediction about what a particular person is going to mean on some particular occasion. It makes predictions about the behaviour of a population. It defines the range of options that is available to them as meaners, their meaning potential as producers and receivers in the social semiotic universe of language.

Notes

1. On Halliday's early compilation and use of corpora, first of Chinese (Cantonese, in 1949; Mandarin, in the 1950s) and then of English (beginning, in the late 1950s, with 1 hour of 'natural conversation'), see Halliday ([1992] 2005a: 76–8).
2. For example, Chomsky (1965: 4): 'We thus make a fundamental distinction between competence (the speaker-hearer's knowledge of his language) and performance (the actual use of language in concrete situations). [. . .] linguistic theory is mentalistic, since it is concerned with discovering a mental reality underlying actual behavior.'
3. Their characterizations of 'modern linguistics' is of course of a particular brand of modern linguistics – the kind of modern linguistics associated with Chomsky. It is important to emphasize that while his kind of linguistics dominated the scene for quite a while, there were other significant kinds of 'modern linguistics' around the world, including (but not restricted to) Pike's Tagmemic Linguistics (in the tradition of US anthropological linguistics), Lamb's Stratificational Linguistics (incorporating the European structuralist tradition as it had been developed by Hjelmslev), and the continuation of the Prague School – and of course the Firthian-Hallidayan tradition.
4. Lyons (1977: 29) suggested a distinction between 'system sentence' – 'the sentence as an abstract, theoretical model of the language-system' – and 'text-sentence' – 'the sentence as something that can be uttered (i.e. as the product of a bit of) language-behaviour'; but this distinction merely seems to emphasize the effect of the wedge Halliday ([1991] 2005b: 63) refers to, and it was never taken up by linguists in general.
5. This 'derivation' may involve one or more steps in a chain realization; but these steps are – or can be made – fully explicit, as is clear from computational models and implementations of systemic functional linguistics.
6. And also within the same ranked unit: in principle, there may be conditioning effects across units of different ranks. Qualitatively, such conditioning is represented by inter-rank preselection, but it seems very likely that there are also analogous quantitative effects.
7. This is of course really 'past' / 'present' / 'future'; but he excluded 'future' since it is much less common than 'past' and 'present'.
8. There are two systems that are on the borderline of skew systems (STATUS [or FREEDOM] and LOGICO-SEMANTIC TYPE); but they are very close to skew: 0.79 rather than 0.8.
9. See Goldsmith (2001), who makes a strong case for the value of Information Theory to phonological theory, noting the early interest by Roman Jakobson and other researchers concerned with phonology and phonetics.
10. In systemic functional linguistics, probabilistic parsing was explored by Robin Fawcett and his research team (e.g. Fawcett & Weerasinghe, 1993; Weerasinghe, 1994); cf. also Souter & Atwell (1992).

9 Language Development in Early Childhood: Learning How to Mean

Jane Torr

---

1 Introduction

Halliday's work on language development in early childhood, much of which is now available in a single volume (Halliday, 2003b), spans over a third of a century, and continues to hold great relevance for linguists, researchers and early childhood educators today. Halliday's thesis, which he explored from a variety of perspectives, is that infants are active participants in their own language learning, and that their developing language is at the same time a resource for learning more generally about the social, cultural and semiotic milieu in which they live. This powerful theory has enormous implications for early childhood education, pedagogy and practice, as it acknowledges the central role of language in the lives of young children, and explains why the social and cultural context in which language development occurs should be fully acknowledged and taken into account in the provision of educational environments for very young children.

The fundamental question posed by Halliday is 'How does a child learn language' (Halliday, 1975: 3). He endeavoured to answer this question through a detailed analysis of the manner in which a single child, his son Nigel, actively created for himself a unique communicative system for expressing his wants, needs and feelings with close family members. Halliday documented the changes which occurred in Nigel's language as he gradually made the transition from his 'child tongue' into the adult linguistic system in which he was immersed.

Halliday's model places meaning at the centre of language development: 'A child who is learning his first language is learning how to mean; in this perspective, the linguistic system is to be seen as semantic potential. It is a range of possible meanings; together with the means whereby these meanings are realized, or expressed' (Halliday, 1975: 8). By tracing Nigel's developmental trajectory from his prelinguistic communication through to his adoption of the basic features of the adult language system at the age of 2 years, Halliday was able to demonstrate the underlying continuities between the early manifestations of language in the first year of life, and the highly complex and abstract functional organization of the adult language.

The manner in which children make the transition from prelinguistic communication to language continues to be of major interest to both theoretical and applied linguists. From a theoretical perspective, an increased understanding of this developmental phase can assist us to learn more about the nature of language itself, while from an applied perspective, such knowledge can support early childhood educators and other specialists to provide targeted support and early intervention for society's youngest learners.

Contemporary sociocultural approaches to early childhood education and care have emphasized a view of the infant as an active participant in her or his own learning (Australian Government Department of Education Employment and Workplace Relations, 2009; Curtis & Carter, 2008; New Zealand Ministry of Education, 1996). While this image of the infant as an agentive, capable learner is frequently asserted in recent early childhood literature, however, it is not often explained in detail, nor is it often supported by empirical evidence. Halliday's insights into child language development provide an analysis of the infant as one who actively creates a system of meanings to achieve a range of purposes in interaction with others.

In this chapter, I shall provide an overview of the key features of Halliday's research into child language development and its implications for early childhood education and care. In doing so, I shall also refer to work by other researchers from a range of disciplinary backgrounds, whose findings provide supportive evidence for Halliday's model.

2 Prevailing Views of Language Development When Learning How to Mean Was Published

In order to understand the excitement which was generated by the 1975 publication of Halliday's volume *Learning How to Mean*, it is useful to consider the dominant view of language structure which had prevailed during the 1960s and 1970s when Halliday was undertaking his groundbreaking research. The publication of Chomsky's work on Transformational Grammar (Chomsky, 1957, 1965) was highly influential in the field of linguistics generally and child language research in particular. Transformational grammarians drew a sharp distinction between speakers' knowledge of language structure (*competence*), and speakers' actual use of language in everyday situations (*performance*), the latter being characterized as deficient as it was marked by 'grammatically irrelevant conditions . . . memory limitations, distractions, shifts of attention and interest and errors' (Chomsky, 1965: 3).

This dichotomy between competence and performance was problematic for child language researchers working within the theory of Transformational Grammar, as it posed a difficult question: how could infants possibly learn the underlying syntactic rules of the language on the basis of their exposure to such poor linguistic input? To address this conundrum, it was proposed that all human beings are born with an inbuilt mental construct referred to as a Language Acquisition Device. In order for this Language Acquisition Device to be activated, thus enabling the child to understand and produce syntactically correct linguistic forms, a child simply needed to have some exposure to his or her language in the early years of life. As language is seen by transformational grammarians primarily in terms of the acquisition of syntax, then the process of learning language was considered complete once a child had acquired all the basic syntactic structures of the adult language at around the age of 4 to 5 years. In other words, according to this theory, language acquisition is seen as the unfolding of an innate cognitive ability, which is relatively unaffected by social and environmental processes. Halliday (1975) characterized this perspective in the following way: 'The implication has been that the learning of structure is really the heart of the language learning process. And it is perhaps not too far-fetched to recognize in the use of the term acquisition, a further implication that structure, and therefore language itself, is a commodity of some kind that the child has to gain possession of in the course of maturation' (Halliday, 1975: 1).

3 Theories of Language and their Implications for Early Childhood Education

The view of language promoted by transformational grammarians and subsequent researchers working within this general paradigm has far-reaching implications for the quality of early childhood education and care services. If language development is the unfolding of an innate ability, and young children simply need exposure to language in order to learn language, then early childhood staff play a peripheral role in children's development. An implication of this perspective on language development is that aspects of the childcare environment such as the qualifications, experience and expertise of staff working with young children are irrelevant in terms of children's learning.

Yet this is demonstrably untrue. A large body of research from a range of disciplines has demonstrated that the quality and quantity of language addressed to young children has long-term consequences for their later academic achievement and opportunities throughout their lives (Hart & Risley, 2003; Hasan, 2009; Hoff, 2003; Mashburn et al., 2008; McCartney, 2002; Shonkoff & Phillips, 2000). Early childhood staff can potentially play a vital role in achieving positive educational outcomes for children under 5 years, especially infants and toddlers from disadvantaged backgrounds. While Halliday's systemic functional linguistic theory has been influential in shaping pedagogy and curricula at the primary and secondary school levels (Christie, 2002; Christie & Unsworth, 2005; Derewianka, 1998; Rose, Gray & Cowey, 1999; Rothery, 1984; Unsworth, 2002), it has had relatively little influence on curricula and pedagogy for children in the prior to school years, especially children under 3 years of age attending non-parental group care settings. Yet as will be argued in this chapter, a greater understanding of Halliday's model of language development has enormous potential for supporting early childhood staff to enhance the quality of the linguistic environment experienced by infants, toddlers and preschoolers in group care settings.

4 Halliday's Functional Model of Language

Other chapters in this volume provide a detailed exegesis of Halliday's systemic functional linguistic theory. I shall therefore only provide a brief overview here, in order to explain how the child's early communicative system relates to the adult language which will eventually replace it. According to systemic functional linguistic theory (Halliday, 1994) the functions which language serves in a speaker's life are thought to contribute directly to its formal organization. Each complete (major) clause encodes three types of meaning simultaneously: interpersonal, ideational and textual meaning. These meanings can be thought

245

of as abstract functions which language serves in the lives of speakers. They constitute what Halliday refers to as the semantic stratum of the language. Each function is expressed, or 'realized', in the words and structures of the language (referred to by Halliday as the *lexicogrammar*).

The **interpersonal function** of language is the function it serves as a means of interacting with others in an exchange. Halliday explains that

> in the act of speaking, the speaker adopts for himself a particular speech role, and in so doing assigns to the listener a complementary role which he wishes him to adopt in his turn. For example, in asking a question, a speaker is taking on the role of seeker of information and requiring the listener to take on the role of supplier of the information demanded. (Halliday, 1994: 68)

The interpersonal meanings are realized in the lexicogrammar through the Mood system, involving aspects such as the sequential ordering of the Subject and Finite verb, systems of Modality and Polarity.

The **ideational function** of language is the function it serves as a means of representing experience. Halliday explains that 'language enables human beings to build a mental picture of reality, to make sense of what goes on around them and inside them. Here again the clause plays a central role, because it embodies a general principle for modelling experience – namely, the principle that reality is made up of processes' (Halliday, 1994: 107). The ideational meanings in language, which specify the relationship between participants (nominals), processes (verbals) and circumstantial elements are realized in the lexicogrammar through the system of Transitivity.

The **textual** function of language is the function it serves in the production of coherent and cohesive stretches of text, in respect of which the other functions have meaning. Halliday notes that 'in all languages the clause has the character of a message: it has some form of organization giving it the status of a communicative event' (Halliday, 1994: 37). The textual metafunction realizes meanings such as Given and New, Theme and Rheme, and Cohesion across passages of text.

These three semantic functions are referred to by Halliday in his child language work as **metafunctions**, to distinguish them from the earlier functions or uses of language created by infants during the early years of life.

How does a child come to master this abstract linguistic system in the first 2 years of life? Halliday's model suggests that language development consists of a gradual reinterpretation of what language may be used for. The key notion is that of function. If meaning in the adult language is construed in terms of the metafunctional meanings referred to above, then we can look for the origins of this functional organization in the earliest utterances of the preverbal child. Such an approach suggests a deep continuity between preverbal communication and

the adult language, while the actual mechanisms of course require development across all domains, including intellectual, perceptual, motor, social and
emotional domains.

Halliday's model elucidates the underlying continuity of prelinguistic and
linguistic systems, because it is based on a theory of the adult language which
is functional: 'a language, then, is a system for making meanings: a semantic
system, with other systems for encoding the meanings it produces. The term
semantics does not simply refer to the meanings of words; it is the entire system
of meanings of a language, expressed by the grammar as well as by vocabulary'
(Halliday, 1994: xvii).

Halliday's functional model has many advantages for researchers and educators who are interested in language and learning in the early years of life.
First, it emphasizes the importance of the social context for early language
learning (which will be discussed in more detail later in this chapter). Secondly,
it integrates both pragmatic (speech function) and referential (content) aspects
of language within a single account of early development, thus obviating the
need to see a discontinuity between developments prior to 18 months (before
words and structures appear in the child's system) and development after this
period. This integration was possible because Halliday began with a functional theory of the adult language. This enabled him to inquire how the adult
language might have developed from the very early social and communicative behaviours of the infant. His longitudinal study showed how one child
reached adult grammar through a process of functional reorganization, from
very simple concrete early prelinguistic functions, to the highly abstract functions of the adult language. 'The transition from this phase [prelinguistic] into
the adult system can also be explained in functional terms, although it becomes
necessary to modify the concept of function very considerably in passing from
the development origins of the system, where "function" equals "use", to the
highly abstract sense in which we can talk of the functional organisation of the
adult language' (Halliday, 1975: 6).

Writing some 20 years after the publication of *Learning How to Mean*, Locke
(1996) claimed that few studies have attempted to explain why the prelingual
infant goes to the effort of inventing an elaborate system of idiosyncratic protowords, which he or she uses to communicate with others for some 9 months,
only to abandon this system around 18 months to 2 years of age, and adopt the
words and structures of the mother tongue. According to Locke (1996), despite
all the research on how infants learn to talk, language researchers have not
yet adequately considered the question of **why** infants begin to talk and 'what
causes the infant to emit particular behaviours at particular times' (Locke, 1996:
254). Echoing some of Halliday's (1975) insights, Locke (1996) says that it is
tautological to claim that prelinguistic behaviours occur in order that the infant
will know how to use language at a later stage in development. A prelinguistic

infant cannot know anything about the language system which he or she will eventually come to use. Halliday's model of language development provides an explanation of the relationship between communicative behaviours in the first year of life and the subsequent adoption of the words and structures of the adult system which will eventually replace them.

5 Data Collection

Halliday recorded his son Nigel's language over a 15-month period, commencing when he was 9 months of age and concluding on his second birthday. Powerful technologies for recording natural speech such as portable videocameras and digital recorders were not yet available to child language researchers in the 1970s. Halliday recorded Nigel's utterances by hand, using the symbols of the International Phonetic Alphabet until such time as the utterances began to resemble adult-like lexical items, after which he used standard English orthography.

Halliday obtained data in a range of contexts. At times he played the role of participant observer, interacting with Nigel while simultaneously recording his utterances. At other times, Halliday recorded Nigel's language while he, Nigel, was playing by himself or interacting with other close family members. Halliday's aim was always to record spontaneous natural language. He made particular note of meaningful expressions when Nigel used them for the first time, in addition to noting expressions which had been in Nigel's system for some time. In order to avoid interpreting chance one-off expressions incorrectly, Halliday decided that a meaningful utterance had to occur at least three times to be included in his data set.

The collection of diary-type records gathered over a period of time by a parent-observer has a long history in developmental research (Lytton, 1971). The diary method has many advantages: parents are intimately acquainted with and sensitive to the meanings expressed by their children and are therefore able to interpret them in the context of the child's life. Given the idiosyncratic nature of young children's productions, this is a real advantage for researchers, as it enables them to avoid underestimating the child's meaning potential at a particular time. As diary records are typically collected by parents in the natural setting in which language develops, the home and family, this method also avoids the presence of an unfamiliar adult, who may unintentionally inhibit the natural ebb and flow of family interaction. As Halliday notes 'of all forms of human activity, language is perhaps the one that is most perturbed by being performed under attention' (Halliday, 2003b: 328). There are limitations to the diary study as a methodology, however, as the data collected by parent observers are usually unstructured, the data cannot be subjected to the usual reliability and validation procedures, and the diary method requires a large investment of time.

Discussing the field of child language research, Snow, Pan, Imbens-Bailey and Herman (1996: 57–8) point out that 'few longitudinal analyses have been carried out from which the nature of earlier vs. later emerging communicative capacities could be inferred'. Infancy research does not usually extend to this transition period, and linguistic research has focused more on development after the age of 18 months than on the period from birth to 18 months. This makes Halliday's data particularly valuable, and a complete transcript of Nigel's conversations is now available (Halliday, 2003b).

6 Method of Analysis

A serious consideration for any researcher attempting to trace a child's development longitudinally lies in determining how best to analyse the data so as to capture both the changes in the system as well as the underlying continuities. Halliday decided to describe his son's system at six-weekly intervals, setting out Nigel's utterances diagrammatically using a series of 'system networks'. Halliday (1975: 7) explains that 'A system is defined as a set of options with conditions of entry: that is, it is a range of alternatives which may be behavioural, semantic, grammatical etc, together with a specification of the environment in which selection must be made among these alternatives.' Please see Table 9.1 for a fragment of a system network describing Nigel's system at the age of 9 months.

The six-weekly interval was found to be optimal in terms of noting broad trends in the data, while not becoming distracted by small shifts which had little significance in the overall developing system. The system networks represent the child's language as a series of frozen frames which enable the researcher to see development both in terms of an increase in the range of meanings expressed by the child, and in terms of increasingly delicate distinctions of meanings within existing networks. In the following sections, I set out the key features of Halliday's model. Since the publication of *Learning How to Mean*, other longitudinal studies of young children using systemic functional

Table 9.1 Fragment of a system network of Nigel's language at 9 months of age (reproduced from Halliday, 1975: 248)

Function	Content Systems	EXPRESSION: Articulation	Tone	GLOSS
Instrumental	demand, general	nã	mid	give me that
	demand, specific (toy bird)	bø	mid	give me my bird

theory as the informing framework have also been undertaken (Painter, 1984; Qiu, 1985; Torr, 1997). These studies all support the basic tenets of Halliday's developmental model, while also pointing to some individual differences in the children's path to linguistic maturity.

7 Developmental Overview

7.1 Phase 1: The Protolanguage

When Nigel was about 9 months of age, Halliday noted that Nigel began to communicate with others using distinctive vocalizations (or gestures), which consisted of a meaning of some kind (for example, 'give me that' or 'that's nice') and an expression (for example /nã/ or /a/ respectively). Halliday referred to these content-expression pairs as **signs**, and noted that most of Nigel's signs during the period from about 9 to 18 months were not imitations of words from the adult language, but were rather his own spontaneous creations. Another important feature of Nigel's signs was that the content did not correspond on a one-to-one basis with the meanings of words in the adult language. The content of the signs was best described as a generalized cluster of meanings such as 'nice to see you and shall we look at this together' or 'give me my bird'. Halliday referred to this developmental phase as the **protolanguage**, because while it is indeed a form of language in the sense that it involves the systematic and symbolic use of sound to express meanings in interaction with others, it does not yet have structure.

Halliday interpreted Nigel's signs in terms of the functions they served in his life, emphasizing that the signs of the protolanguage develop quite naturally out of the types of interaction already engaged in by parents and infants from birth. Halliday identified the following functions in Nigel's protolanguage over the nine-month period:

The Instrumental function is the child's use of signs to demand objects or services from the addressee, for example *give me that*, *give me my bird* and *yes I want that thing which you just offered me*.

The Regulatory function is the child's use of signs to control the behaviour of the addressee, for example *do that again*, and *let me play with the cat*.

The Interactional function refers to the child's use of signs to express, establish and maintain closeness with the addressee, for example *hello* and *let's look at this together*.

The Personal function refers to the child's use of signs to express his feelings about his experiences, for example *that's funny*, *I like this food*, *there's a cat* and *I'm sleepy*.

The Imaginative function refers to the child's use of signs to create imaginary situations or to engage in pretend play, either on his own or with an addressee. Examples include fragments of songs, rhymes and animal noises.

The Heuristic function refers to the child's use of signs to inquire about the world, in particular to request a name. It was the last of the protolanguage signs to appear in Nigel's system, at 15 months.

Halliday referred to the protolinguistic functions as *microfunctions* to distinguish them from the abstract metafunctions of the adult language. Nigel's system of signs enabled him to use sound symbolically to gain some control over his environment; to obtain food and objects, to make people behave in certain ways, to establish close bonds and intimacy with others, and to express personal feelings and reactions to the world. These very early uses or functions are, however, expressing goals which exist independently of language, and therefore do not necessarily require language for their achievement. For example, right from birth infants can in some ways communicate their feelings, demand food or attention, express affection with others and playfully produce a range of sounds.

The meanings Nigel expressed during the protolanguage were inextricably tied to the context in which they occurred. For example, the utterance /na/ was interpreted by his mother in the immediate situation in which it was uttered as 'give me that'. It was the use of this sign, in this particular context, which contributed to its meaning.

Gradually over the course of a 9-month period, the number of signs which could be interpreted within each microfunctional context expanded considerably. When Halliday first began to interpret Nigel's utterances at the age of 9 months, he had a system of 12 signs across 4 functions; instrumental, regulatory, interactional and personal. By the time he was 18 months of age, he had 145 signs in his system. By this stage, he had also introduced two additional functions to his range, the heuristic and imaginative functions. These signs constituted Nigel's 'meaning potential' during this period of his life.

Since Halliday documented the features of Nigel's protolanguage in 1975, other researchers have also undertaken studies of the communicative utterances of infants prior to the onset of adult words and structures. Within systemic functional linguistics, the studies of Painter (1984), Qiu (1985) and Torr (1997) documented the protolanguage systems of individual children who differed in terms of either home language, gender and/or birth order.

Studies by researchers working within other disciplinary frameworks have also been undertaken, many of which resonate with Halliday's findings. Children's early utterances have been referred to variously in the literature as 'phonetically consistent forms', 'vocables', 'protowords', 'quasiwords' or 'signs'. Bates (1979) noted that these forms appear in extremely constrained contexts and they have meaning only in relation to the whole of the context in which they are uttered (Bates, 1979; Bloom, 1993). Wetherby, Reichle and Pierce (1998) noted that the meanings expressed by the protowords are very generalized in nature and are usually tied to one speech function only, for example, they may be used *either* to make a demand *or* to direct attention to objects. Stoel-Gammon (1998: 95) noted that 'infant communication is linked to intention from around age 9 months; both gesture and vocal output can be linked to particular functions, such as requesting, showing, protesting, and commenting'.

Many quantitative studies have used spectrographic and acoustic analyses to investigate early protowords. For example, Blake & de Boysson-Bardies (1992) studied babbling in English and French infants aged from 9 to 14 months, and found that babbling was indeed tied to particular contexts. D'Ordrico & Franco (1991: 476) studied the suprasegmental characteristics in vocalization of 5 Italian infants aged between 4 and 12 months, and found a match between word-like utterances and context after 12 months, the so-called selective production hypothesis. They found that rising tone was used by the infants when the adult had a toy, and the child was looking from toy to adult, and falling tone was consistently used when the child was playing with the toy.

Interestingly, several phonological studies have also produced results which, while not necessarily undertaken within a functional theory of language, nevertheless support Halliday's claim of a systematic association of tone with context in infants. Stark, Bernstein & Demorest (1993) used Halliday's functions in their study of 51 infants, and found that all infants used protowords in instrumental / regulatory and personal / interactional contexts, at approximately the age that Halliday suggested from his case study of a single child.

Such studies provide support and validation for Halliday's characterization of the key features of the protolanguage phase of development.

7.2 Phase 2: The Transition from Protolanguage to Adult Language

At some stage, all typically developing children gradually give up their protolinguistic system of invented signs and begin to make the transition from the protolanguage into the metafunctional system of the adult language. How does this transition occur? Halliday has proposed a transitional phase (termed Phase II, the transition), during which the child's language continues to have some of the characteristics of the protolanguage, but also begins to adopt some of the characteristics of the adult language. This developmental phase typically extends from about 18 months to 2 years of age. According to Halliday (1975: 67), this period in children's language development 'corresponds to what is more usually regarded as the beginnings of language, because it is the point at which vocabulary (in the true sense, as distinct from imitations of word sounds) and structure start to appear; but from the present standpoint it is already transitional'.

Halliday identified a number of changes in Nigel's system. The child began to use adult-like words, which were sometimes used to refer to past and future, thus suggesting a gradually freeing of the utterance from the immediate context of its use. In Nigel's case, these words sometimes appeared as small recounts of experience in the form of strings of words which were related semantically but not grammatically, for example Nigel said *cars, buses, dogs, weathercocks, sticks, holes* after going for a walk and seeing these objects (Halliday, 1975: 28). On other occasions Nigel used his language to anticipate future experiences, for example the words *buses, weathercock, stones, sticks, star* were said by Nigel following his mother's promise that he would go for a walk the next morning (Halliday, 2003b: 403).

The child's 'words' are not yet functionally unrestricted, however, as is the case with the adult language. Rather, some of Nigel's early words and structures could only occur in the context of making a demand of some kind, while other expressions could only occur in the context of making a comment. In other words, the child's language had undergone a fundamental reorganization, such that it could now best be interpreted in terms of two more general functions, which Halliday called **macrofunctions** to distinguish them from the microfunctions of the protolanguage. The basic semantic distinction between these two more general functions hinged on their status as speech acts.

The **Pragmatic** function referred to the use of language to act upon the environment. This involved a demand for a response of some kind from the addressee, either goods and services or information. Examples from Nigel include: *get stick ball* ('I want the stick to get the ball with'), *Anna help greenpea* ('Anna, help me to eat the green peas'), *butter on knife* ('I want the butter on the knife') and *Dada put altogether egg* ('Daddy, put the eggs all together'). These pragmatic uses of language evolved out of the Instrumental and Regulatory microfunctions of the protolanguage.

The **Mathetic function** referred to the use of language to reflect on the environment, to learn about and classify objects and to comment on experience. When Nigel used his language within this functional context, he did not require a response from his addressee, although of course a response may have been provided. Examples from Nigel include: *Mummy book* ('it's mummy's book'), *that broke* ('that's broken'), *baby duck* (indicating a picture of a duck in his book) and *red jumber* ('there's the red jumper'). These mathetic uses of language evolved from the interactional and personal microfunctions of the prototanguage.

There are two pieces of evidence to suggest that Nigel himself was making a functional distinction between language used for acting on the environment (pragmatic) and language used for reflecting on the environment (mathetic), rather than the observer imposing this interpretation on the data. The first is the fact that, as stated above, the child kept the two sets of utterances functionally separate, with some vocabulary items only appearing in pragmatic contexts, and some only appearing in mathetic contexts. The second piece of evidence is that the child made the functional distinction explicit through the differential use of tone. All Nigel's pragmatic utterances were spoken on a rising tone, and all his mathetic utterances were said on a falling tone. Painter's son Hal (Painter, 1984) also used tone to differentiate the two functions of language, while Torr's daughter Anna (Torr, 1997) used voice quality, with all utterances which required a response spoken with a tense voice quality (pragmatic), and all utterances which did not demand a response spoken with a lax or breathy voice quality (mathetic).

We can thus see in the child's distinction between pragmatic and mathetic functions the origins of the adult Mood and Transitivity systems. However, where adult clauses encode both speech function and referential meaning simultaneously, the child at first was unable to do this; an utterance could have either a demanding function, or a commenting function. Before long, however, Nigel's pragmatic utterances began to take on more and more referential content, and his mathetic utterances began to occur with a range of speech functions. Once the child begins to encode a choice of both speech function and a choice of referential meaning within a single utterance, the basic organization of the adult grammar has been understood.

One of the major developments of the transition period is, according to Halliday (1975), the development of the **informative function** of language. The realization that language can be used to convey new information to an addressee who does not currently share that information occurs relatively late in the child's development of language. According to Halliday (1975: 31) 'The use of language to inform is a very late stage in the linguistic development of the child, because it is a function which depends on the recognition that there are functions of language which are solely defined by language itself.' Nigel made the semantic distinction between shared and unshared knowledge explicit through his own distinctive use of declarative and interrogative forms. Shared knowledge was expressed using a declarative form (for example *the tower fell down* would be uttered when playing with a companion who shared the experience). If the addressee had not shared the tower experience with Nigel, however, he would use the interrogative form, for example *did the tower fall down?* Neither Hal (Painter, 1984) nor Anna (1997) made explicit the distinction between imparting shared versus unshared information to an addressee. For Hal, information exchange emerged when Hal recounted some incident (*bump*) in order to obtain sympathy from his mother. Anna began to convey unknown information to her addressee when recounting what another family member had said about some incident or event in which she had participated. Veneziano & Sinclair (1995) have shown that children's justifications for their behaviour, especially in dramatic play situations, were contexts for the very early informative function of language in the French-speaking children they studied. One child, Camille, was putting a shoe on her doll, saying 'froid', that is, the baby is cold. Sometimes the informative function would be evident in justifications for a request, for example when one child said 'can't' to her mother, in order to get her mother to do the task (Veneziano & Sinclair, 1995).

The ability to use language to communicate unshared information to an addressee is crucial for the child's developing ability to engage in **dialogue** with other people, such that each step in a conversation becomes the point of departure for a new exchange. In order to do this, it is necessary for the child to take the listener's needs into account at least to some extent. Textual meanings also evolved in the course of the child's engagement in dialogue. These two developmental miletones, the informative function and dialogue, heralded Nigel's move into the adult language (Phase III), where ideational, interpersonal and textual meanings are simultaneously realized in all major clauses.

7.3 Phase 3: Into the Adult Language

Towards the end of Nigel's second year of life, it had become clear that his language could no longer be described in terms of macrofunctions. Utterances which had previously been classified as pragmatic could now not only act on the environment but could also be used to represent experience in terms of participants, processes and some circumstantial elements. Similarly, Nigel could now use words and structures which had previously been confined to reflective, mathetic contexts, to seek information about the environment using the Mood system of the adult language. Textual meanings were beginning to be realized lexiocogrammatically in narratives and recounts of experience.

Children gradually come to reinterpret the notion of function in language, from the very basic understanding that function is equivalent to use (as is evident in the microfunctions of the protolanguage) to the understanding that language can be used *either* to make demands *or* to comment on experience (as is evident in the macrofunctions of the transition), to the abstract understanding of the metafunctions embedded in the adult grammar.

8 Towards a Language-based Theory of Learning

For educators, one of the most valuable features of Halliday's systemic functional theory of language development is that it views language as a social phenomenon which shapes, and is shaped by, the, social context in which it occurs. As Halliday explains

> The essential condition of learning is the systematic link between semantic categories and the semiotic properties of the situation. The child can learn to mean because the linguistic features in some sense relate to features of the

environment. But the environment is a social construction. It does not consist of things, or even of processes and relations; it consists of human interaction, from which the things derive their meanings. (Halliday, 2003b: 302)

There are three elements within any context of situation which have implications for the language features that may be realized in that particular context. The social activity or subject matter of any situation will be expressed as particular choices from the ideational systems of the language. Halliday refers to this aspect as the **field**. The relationship between the participants, for example their degree of formality or intimacy, will lead to certain choices from the interpersonal systems of the language. Halliday refers to this aspect of the context as the **tenor**. Finally, the role played by language in the situation (whether it refers to aspects in the here-and-now context, or to topics which are more abstract and non-present) will be realized in choices from the textual systems of the language. Halliday refers to this aspect of the context as the **mode**. After a child's language system has become metafunctionally organized, the child will continue to learn his or her language; however, the learning process involves learning how to use language appropriately and effectively in a range of contexts of situation.

Halliday's model provides linguists and educators with a rich, nuanced understanding of how language develops in early childhood. It emphasizes the centrality of language and social interaction and places the child at the centre of her or his learning processes. There is still much to know about how children learn language. Our understanding of language development is based on a relatively small number of middle-class children, recorded while interacting with close family members in the home. As increasing numbers of infants attend formal childcare from as young as 6 weeks of age, it is important to understand more about how this distinctive learning environment influences the language learning process. Childcare staff have less time for one-to-one interactions with infants, and are less familiar with the everyday experiences of infants, compared with parents. Improving the quality of early childhood education and care has become an international priority (Organisation for Economic Co-operation & Development, 2006), and Halliday's model provides an ideal framework for detailed analysis of the potential of childcare to support and nurture children's development. One of the key principles of quality in early childhood care is to minimize the discontinuity between home and childcare; therefore, greater understanding of this critical phase of early language development in diverse communities would provide valuable information to inform early childhood practice. It is hoped that this chapter may encourage others to develop further current knowledge and understanding of how young children learn to mean.

10 Halliday the Grammarian: Axial Foundations

J. R. Martin

1 System and Structure

In this chapter[1] I will attempt to introduce Halliday's distinctive perspective on grammar, approaching this topic from a pedagogical perspective – inspired by a course on systemic functional grammar (hereafter SFG) I have delivered around the world over the past few years and for which I have recently published a textbook (Martin, 2013a). My aim in this course has been to introduce research students to the model of functional grammar which developed in London out of scale-and-category grammar (Halliday, [1961] 2002) from the early 1960s, as documented in the papers by Halliday, Henrici, Huddleston & Hudson collected in Halliday & Martin (eds) (1981; see also Martin & Doran 2015). This model privileged paradigmatic relations over syntagmatic ones in a way that had not been previously formalized in linguistic theory, and laid the foundations for rich accounts of grammar as a meaning-making resource across many language families around the world (e.g. Caffarel et al., 2004). By way of introducing this model I'll focus on examples from English, since Halliday's functional grammar of English is so well-known (e.g. Halliday & Matthiessen, 2014), and also from Tagalog, in order to clearly distinguish the reasoning inherent in Halliday's approach from the descriptions of particular languages to which it is applied (based on Martin, 2004b). I will not attempt here to review the work by Saussure, Hjelmslev, Whorf and Firth which in various ways influenced Halliday's perspective; for relevant discussion see the compilation of interviews recently compiled in Martin (2013b). Note in addition that I am not attempting to recapitulate the dialogue in London that led to this innovative SFG perspective on grammar; rather, the discussion is organized to move readers gradually from a syntagmatic perspective (which for most readers I predict is more familiar and easier to bring to consciousness) to the paradigmatic orientation foregrounded in Halliday's work.

2 Parsing

A glance at writing systems around the world tells us that one basic principle of organization in language has to do with parts and wholes – technically speaking constituency. Minimally, whole texts consist of symbols representing the sounds or words of a language; and systems that have evolved along the lines of the one I am using to write English here offer intermediate units of various kinds (minimally, sentences made up of words made up of letters). When I was in Hong Kong in 2001, shortly after the remarkable events of 9/11, I picked up a copy of a weekly life-style magazine and read its editorial, which included the following anecdote:

> Meanwhile (and we're not making this up), two Indian nationals on a flight from Singapore to Hong Kong were detained at Changi Airport after an American passenger said he heard one of the men calling himself a 'Bosnian terrorist.' (The man in fact said he was a 'bass guitarist.')

Here we find words, separated by spaces. And one of these 'words' itself has parts, separated by an apostrophe (*we're*); a grammarian would tell us that it's really two words (*we* and *are*) collapsed into one (an abbreviation, with writing reflecting the way two words are spoken as if one). Beyond this, the words are grouped into larger units, some into quoted phrases (in 'scare quotes') – *'Bosnian terrorist'* and *'bass guitarist'*, some into parenthetical comments – *(and we're not making this up),* and some into sentences beginning with an upper case letter and ending with a full stop.

These evolving graphological arrangements naturally invite grammarians to divide sentences up into parts and wholes. In the American structuralist tradition referred to as immediate constituent analysis (IC for short), grammar analysis was essentially a bracketing exercise (cf. Wells, [1947] 1957). In this style of analysis we take a clause such as the following:

two Indian nationals were detained at Changi Airport

... and group things together, either starting with the smallest things and working up in steps:

two Indian nationals were detained at Changi Airport

two (Indian nationals) (were detained) at (Changi Airport)

(two (Indian nationals)) (were detained) (at (Changi Airport))

(two (Indian nationals)) ((were detained) (at (Changi Airport)))

((two (Indian nationals)) ((were detained) (at (Changi Airport))))

... or starting with the biggest bit and working down:

two Indian nationals were detained at Changi Airport

two Indian nationals / were detained at Changi Airport

two Indian nationals / were detained // at Changi Airport

two /// Indian nationals / were detained // at /// Changi Airport

two /// Indian //// nationals / were //// detained // at /// Changi //// Airport

This tradition had a strong binary bias, usually insisting on grouping parts in pairs rather than in triplets or more. So the whole clause we're working on would typically be divided in half, as above (instead of having three parts – *two Indian nationals* + *were detained* + *at Changi airport*); and the first cut for *two Indian nationals* would involve two pieces (as above), not three (*two* + *Indian* + *nationals*). This preference for two rather than more parts has remained a strong one in grammars deriving from this tradition, such as the formal grammars associated with the school of linguists inspired by Chomsky in the second half of the twentieth century (now generally known as generative linguistics and naturalized as an analysis of 'syntax').

3 Class and Syntagm: Function and Structure

IC analysis tells us something about the compositional structure of clauses, but if we want to actually refer to the bits and pieces themselves we need some labels. The simplest kind of labelling tells us what kind of thing the bits and pieces are – terms like noun, verb, adjective, adverb,[2] noun phrase, prepositional phrase, clause and so on. Labels of this kind are class labels and tell us something about the potential of the labelled item to appear in different kinds of structure. In the structural and formal linguistics just introduced, letters are often used instead of words as class labels ('N' instead of noun, 'V' instead of verb, 'A' instead of adjective and so on). This reflects the concern of groups like the Bloomfieldian structuralists to rigorously define classes in linguistic terms and distinguish themselves from traditional grammarians with their notionally defined[3] parts of speech (Chomsky's teacher Harris was an important influence in this regard; see Harris, [1946] 1957; Bloch, [1946] 1957; Pittman, [1948] 1957). Using these abbreviations, the combinations of classes which a language uses can be stated as a kind of algebra. For *two Indian nationals* we can write A not N; for *at Changi Airport* we can write P N N and so on. As long as classes are carefully defined, it doesn't really matter whether we use words (like noun) or letters (like 'N') to represent them. Classes are generally referred to in formal linguistics as categories.

Inspired by Chomsky's work on generative grammar linguists often make use of labelled diagrams to display structure (Chomsky, 1957). These diagrams represent the part/whole structure of grammatical units, with larger units at the top and smaller units at the bottom, and labels for classes of different sizes. The diagrams give us an invaluable synoptic overview of the structure of a grammatical unit (often a sentence) as a whole, something that is much harder to get a sense of from a linear algebraic formula – such as S (NP (A A N)[4] VP (MV (Aux V) PP (P NP (N N))) for the example in Figure 10.1.

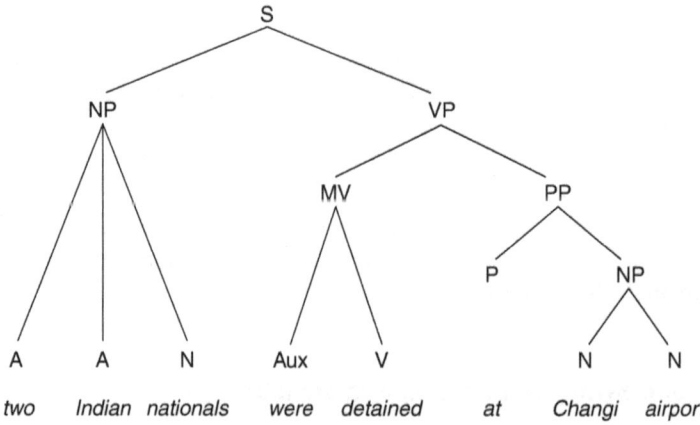

Figure 10.1 A tree diagram showing part/whole structure and class labels

In Figure 10.1,[5] I've drawn this kind of diagram for the IC analysis we did above of *two Indian nationals were arrested at Changi airport*, adding the kind of letter labels used in early Chomsky inspired diagramming of this kind. This kind of representation is often referred to as a tree diagram, or more technically as a phrase marker; if it looks more like the roots of a tree than its branches to you, then imagine if you can the shape of the conifers (e.g. pine, fir and spruce trees) outside linguists' windows in North America as they worked on images of this kind (or an up-side-down tree if you prefer).

The other kind of labelling used by grammarians tells us what something is doing in a particular structure, not just what class it is. These labels are called function labels, and include terms like Subject, Predicator, Complement and Adjunct. These labels can make it easier to talk about grammatical relations between parts of a structure. For example, in English we sometimes have to take the number of the Subject (singular or plural) into account to make sure the right form of the verb follows – as with *was* vs *were* below:

> **an Indian national was** detained (singular)
>
> **two Indian nationals were** detained (plural)

In English this same function, Subject, switches sequence with the same kind of verb to show MOOD – the difference between declarative (giving information) and interrogative (asking for information) for example:

> **two Indian nationals were** detained (declarative)
>
> **were two Indian nationals** detained (interrogative)

The Subject function is also important for analysing VOICE, since in the active voice it is the doer – but in the passive it is acted upon:

> **the authorities** detained two Indian nationals (active)
>
> **two Indian nationals** were detained by the authorities (passive)

If we draw our trees carefully enough, we can get by without actually having a label for the Subject, since we can infer it from the shape of the tree (Hudson, 1967). In Figure 10.2, for example the Subject is the NP attached directly to S (and so is an immediate constituent of S); and the Complement is the NP which is attached directly to VP (and so an immediate constituent of VP). As long as there is only one NP immediately dominated by S, and only one immediately dominated by VP, this works out fine – although when talking about number agreement, MOOD or VOICE, we either have to cheat a little by referring informally

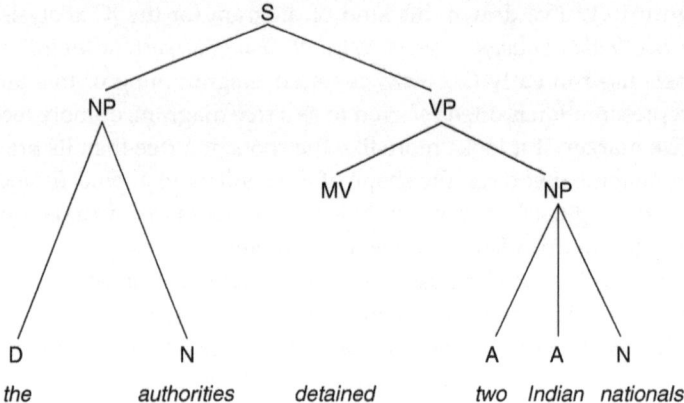

Figure 10.2 A tree structure with class labels and structure from which grammatical functions like Subject and Complement can be inferred

to categories like 'Subject' we don't really have explicitly available, or we have to be long-winded and avoid the term Subject by talking about the 'NP immediately dominated by S' all the time.

Alternatively we can introduce function labels into our description alongside class labels, and include them in our trees. This means that in some respects our trees can be simpler since we don't have to insist on binary branching to make sure we can infer function categories from the shape of trees; we can simply include this information explicitly in a flatter (in the sense of broader) tree structure such as that in Figure 10.3. Note that in formal grammars grammatical functions are generally referred to as grammatical relations.

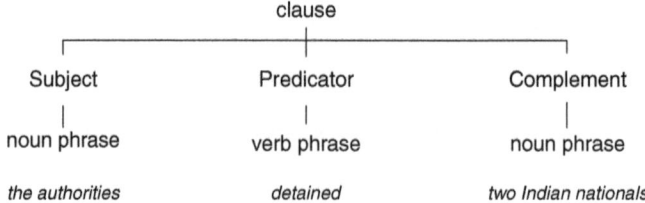

Figure 10.3 A flatter tree structure including both function and class labels

It's still important to have class labels alongside function labels of course since the relationship between function and class is not one-to-one (not bi-unique). Most grammatical functions can be realized by more than one class, just as a given grammatical class can usually perform more than one function. Nominal groups[6] for example serve two different functions in Figure 10.3 – Subject and

Complement. Conversely, the Subject function can be realized by either a nominal group or a clause:

The authorities upset the Indian nationals. [nominal group Subject & Complement]

Getting arrested like that upset the Indian nationals. [clause Subject, nominal group Complement]

The same kind of complex relationship between class and function is found in nominal groups. Adjectives for example typically describe the head noun (and so can be intensified and compared):

a **nervous** passenger   (a very nervous passenger)

a **brilliant** guitarist   (an even more brilliant guitarist)

And nouns typically subclassify the head noun (and as Classifiers don't accept intensification or comparison); note that we are following the convention here of using the symbol '*' before an example to mark it as ungrammatical (as something that can't be said in the language being described).

a **bass** guitarist (*a very bass guitarist)

an **train** passenger (*an even more train passenger)

But adjectives can be used to classify, for describing kinds of dog, disease or sugar for example:

red setter
yellow fever
brown sugar

And verbs can be used to describe, in place of adjectives:

an **agitated** passenger   (an extremely agitated passenger)

an **amazing** guitarist   (an even more amazing guitarist)

And in other contexts verbs are used to classify (and are thus not gradable):

running shoes
industrialized nations

If following Halliday we label the describing function Epithet (from the ancient Greek term for 'attributed') and the classifying function Classifier, then we can allow for the fact that Epithets can be realized by adjectives or verbs, that Classifiers can be realized by nouns or verbs, and that adjectives and verbs can function as Epithets or Classifiers as illustrated above.

Once again this means that we have more labelling in our tree diagrams (both function and class) but that the structure of our diagrams can be simpler (less branching). Double labelling for class and function in noun phrases is illustrated in Figure 10.4.

Figure 10.4 Class and function labelling in nominal groups

It is very important to keep in mind that if we label for both function and class then we have to have distinct criteria for each label, and more generally speaking for each set of labels. For the examples we're considering here we've insisted that Epithets can be intensified and compared whereas Classifiers can't. Turning to classes, count nouns are words which have singular or plural endings (*passenger/passengers*) and adjectives are words which have comparative morphology (*happy/happier, crazy/crazier, nervous/more nervous*). Of course words classes can't manifest this potential everywhere. As we've seen we can't intensify or compare adjectives when they function as Classifier (**yellower fever*), anymore than we can pluralize a noun when it has the same function (**basses guitarist*). Classes in other words get defined with respect to their potential; functions on the other hand are defined in terms of the work they do in a specific structural configuration. From this point in the discussion we'll consistently follow that SFG convention of writing class labels in lower case and beginning function labels with an upper case letter.

4 Tiers of Structure

The issue of motivating labels brings us to some important crossroads in the development of grammatical analysis. One has to do with whether we use just class labels with more complicated trees or use class and function labels with simpler ones. This is one important difference between the main formal theories (associated with Chomsky) and the main functional ones (associated with Halliday, Dik, van Valin[7] & others). Another crossroads has to do with what kind of function labels we use.

Linguists interested in English and related Indo-European languages (such as French, German, Danish, Italian, Spanish and so on), have tended to foreground functions such as Subject and Complement (or Object as it is often called). This makes it easier to talk about NUMBER, MOOD and VOICE as noted above, since in these languages (more so in some than others) the Subject tends to agree with the verb in NUMBER (and sometimes GENDER), and in English inverts with the verb to change MOOD (or to signal a dependent clause, as in German) and swaps 'doer' and 'done to' roles with the Complement as VOICE changes from active to passive. Subject and Complement can also be used to explain reflexive pronouns, which are used in the Complement when it refers the same entity as the Subject (but not when their identity is different):

the Indian nationals incriminated **themselves** (by saying they were terrorists)

the American passenger incriminated **them** (by saying they were terrorists)

For other languages linguists have been drawn to different kinds of function label – in part because these properties of Subjects and Complements don't seem to apply, and in part because different kinds of relation are foregrounded. Halliday's early grammatical work was on Chinese ([1959] 2005, [1956] 2005a) and attended for example to questions of 'given' and 'new' in relation to grammatical structure (cf. Halliday, [1959] 2005: 66). Accordingly, let's expand the discussion of labelling at this point, by turning our attention to another non-Indo-European language, Tagalog – a language spoken in the Philippines and the basis for the national language there, in which guise it is referred to as Filipino.

For Tagalog, Schachter and Otanes (1972) propose not a Subject but a Topic function, realized in the examples below by the *ang* phrase (and labelled 'T' in the morpheme by morpheme translation; examples based on Ramos, 1974). In Tagalog this phrase is informationally prominent[8] as far as unfolding discourse is concerned, and is related to the verb with respect to the role it plays as 'doer', 'done to', 'source' etc. in the clause. Essentially the verb morphology changes to display the role of the Topic, signalled by *ang* (in the examples below *ang*, *ng* and *sa* are pre-positions, with *ng* marking non-Topic Participants and *sa* marking Circumstances; verb affixation for the stem *hiram* is italicized).

'doer' / Topic:

h-*um*-iram   ang tao   ng pera   sa bangko
borrowed   T   man   money   bank
'The man borrowed some money from the bank.'

'done to' / Topic:

h-*in*-iram	ng tao	ang pera	sa bangko
borrowed	man	T money	bank

'The man borrowed the money from the bank.'[9]

'source' / Topic:

h-*in*-iram-*an*	ng tao	ng pera	ang bangko
borrowed	man	money	T bank

'The man borrowed some money from the bank.'

Essentially what we are looking at here is the way in which the Process and Participant or Circumstance preceded by *ang* interact with the verb. The verb stem realizing the Process in these examples is *hiram*, meaning 'borrow'; it comes out in different forms depending on the specific role of the *ang* phrase. In the first example, the *ang* phrase is doer, so the process has the form *humiram*, with the infix -*um*-; the clause tells us that the *ang* phrase is both information-ally prominent and the 'doer' or Actor. In the second example the *ang* phrase is affected by the Process (its 'done to' or Goal), and so we have a different form of the verb (*hiniram*, with the infix -*in*-). In the final example, to focus on the source of the money, we used *hiniraman*, with an infix -*in*- showing aspect (completed action) and a suffix -*an* showing that the *ang* phrase is the source.

Schachter (1976, 1977) argues in some detail why this Topic function realized by the *ang* phrase is so different in kind from an English Subject that it needs a different name. His basic argument is that properties typically associated with Subject in many other languages are more or less evenly split between the 'doer' ('role related' properties having to do with the Actor) and the Topic ('reference related' properties having to do with what in SFG would be called Theme) in Tagalog and Philippine languages in general. Li & Thompson (1976) generalize this kind argumentation for a range of languages, suggesting that languages can be more or less Subject or Topic prominent, typologically speaking, when we are comparing one of them with another. In general, functional linguists try and select function labels that reflect to some degree the grammatical proper-ties a function label has been used to describe; formal linguists are more con-servative, preferring to deal with traditional functions such as Subject (if any function labels are in fact used at all).

The idea that different kinds of function labels may be appropriate for differ-ent languages depending on the work they are doing raises a further question as to whether or not different kinds of function labels could be used for the same language, depending on how we are looking at the clause. In order to describe the *ang* phrase and verb morphology in Tagalog for example we had to refer to the role the Topic was playing – as 'doer', 'done to' or 'source' (the kind of Participant or Circumstance role they are playing in other words). And these are obviously critical grammatical categories in Tagalog since verbal affixes (the infixes *-um-* and *-in-*, and suffix *-an*) vary according to these roles. So alongside Topic, designated by the *ang* phrase, we might in addition recognize Actor, Goal and Location functions. If so, we could say that when the Topic combines with Actor, the action verb takes the infix *-um-*; when Topic combines with Goal it takes *-in-* and so on. In effect what we'd end up with is two kinds of labelling, one motivated by informational prominence (Topic) and others based on the Participant and Circumstance roles played by groups and phrases involved in a process (Martin, 2004b).

Double function labelling of this kind is more common in some functional theories than others. Linguists of the Prague School (e.g. Danes, 1974) are well known for their concern, beginning in the first half of the twentieth century, to introduce function labels such as Theme (comparable to Topic above), oriented to informational prominence. In their work on what they called 'functional sentence perspective' they tried to move beyond reasoning based purely on morphology, agreement, inversion and the like to include corpus evidence as part of the motivation for function labels. Partly inspired by their work, this and related reasoning was further extended by Halliday (e.g. Halliday & Matthiessen, 2014, 2009) and his colleagues in the second half of the century (Halliday and his colleagues began their work in Britain in the 1950s, as noted above, and continued developing their ideas in Sydney, Australia from 1975). This has resulted in a richer labelling system, involving three 'tiers' of function labelling, reflecting the different functions of constituents when probed from different points of view.

Let's explore now the nature of the reasoning behind tiers of function labels, beginning with the 'doer', 'done to', 'source' kind of labelling and considering how to grammatically motivate it for functions in the English clause.

Unlike Tagalog, English verbs don't provide us with very much overt morphology which we can use for distinguishing one role from another. Voice (active or passive) does tell us whether the Subject is a 'doer' or 'done to':

Authorities **detained** two Indian nationals at Changi airport.

Two Indian nationals **were detained** by authorities at Changi airport.

But English verbs don't distinguish between different kinds of 'done to' – for example the *two Indian nationals* vs *a new ticket* below:

The authorities issued two Indian nationals a new ticket.

Two Indian nationals were issued a new ticket by authorities.

A new ticket was issued by authorities.

Nor do English verbs distinguish morphologically between physical and mental activity.

> Authorities detained two Indian nationals at Changi airport.
>
> Authorities saw two Indian nationals at Changi airport.

Because of this implicitness, linguists working on role functions in English (e.g. Fillmore, 1968; Halliday & Matthiessen, 2014) have developed a complementary kind of reasoning introduced by Whorf (1937, [1945] 1956), an American linguist in the first half of the twentieth century who was much more interested in the relation between language and culture than his structuralist peers and so needed a richer conception of grammar. This involves looking at what happens to various functions in closely related sentences to see what kind of evidence pops up. If we put *a new ticket* instead of *two Indian nationals* next to *issued* for example, we need to add the preposition *to*:

> The authorities issued two Indian nationals a new ticket at Changi airport.
>
> The authorities issued a new ticket **to two Indian nationals** at Changi airport.

So what look like two affected participants turn out to be different kinds of 'done to' – something Halliday calls a Goal, a sub-type of participant in action clauses (*a new ticket*) and something he calls a Recipient, another kind of participant (*two Indian nationals*).

Similarly if we change the tense, and imagine a reporter giving a live commentary on goings on at Changi airport, then we'll discover that standard[10] English uses different kinds of present tense for physical and mental activity:

> At this very moment authorities **are detaining** two Indian nationals right now at Changi airport.
>
> Right now I **see** two Indian nationals (being detained).

For ongoing action English uses present continuous tense (*are detaining*), whereas simple present is deployed for mental activity concurrent with the moment of speaking (*see*).

As usual in linguistics, more criteria are better than one, so we might look for additional 'indirect' evidence that physical processes in English are different from mental ones. A further difference is that mental processes can report ideas, whereas physical processes don't:

> I see **that authorities are detaining two Indian nationals**.
>
> *Authorities are detaining that I see two Indian nationals.

Yet another difference is that the 'doer' in mental processes must be conscious, whereas in physical processes it need not be:

The security guard / the traffic is detaining two Indian nationals.

He / *the traffic sees that authorities are detaining two Indian nationals.

This kind of emergent criteria as we look from one related clause to another was referred to by Whorf as 'reactances'[11] ([1945] 1956: 89). Reactances enable us to move beyond explicit morphology (affixes), sequence and structural interdependencies (e.g. number agreement, reflexives) among the parts of a particular clause and consider the clause in relation to immediately related agnate[12] clauses varying the meaning in specific systematic ways (e.g. the shifts in information flow, process type and phenomenality just illustrated). On the basis of the reactances reviewed here (and additional criteria not discussed) Halliday (e.g. Halliday & Matthiessen, 2014) makes a distinction between material and mental processes, and uses distinctive function labels for each process type – Actor Process Goal Recipient for material processes, and Senser Process Phenomenon for mental ones. Actor, Goal and Recipient are all types of participant in physical processes (called material processes by Halliday), while Senser and Phenomenon are sub-types in mental ones.

Actor	Process	Recipient	Goal
authorities	*gave*	*two Indian nationals*	*a new ticket*

Senser	Process	Phenomenon
authorities	*saw*	*two Indian nationals*

In the examples just reviewed, the Actor, Recipient, Goal, Senser and Phenomenon functions are all realized by nominal groups, and the two Processes by verbal groups.

This kind of analysis, which explores the role of different participants in relation to different kinds of process, is referred to by Halliday as TRANSITIVITY[13] (concerned with what Fillmore (1968) referred to as case relations). It constitutes a tier of functional analysis concerned with the way in which a clause constructs experience. Alongside material and mental processes Halliday's functional grammar covers relational ones which deal with description, classification and identification. The anecdote we began with above was concerned with mistaken identity, and uses two clauses of this kind:

he was a 'bass guitarist'

one of the men calling himself a 'Bosnian terrorist'[14]

The story also reports on what an American passenger told authorities, a verbal process (which resembles mental processes in that it can report):

an American passenger said he heard one of the men . . .

Verbal processes allow an additional participant, the Receiver, who hears what was said; and their 'doer' need not be human – print and electronic media work just as well.

an American passenger said to authorities he heard one of the men . . .

the timetable said the plane was leaving at two o'clock.

Formal grammarians generally treat transitivity relations of this kind as semantics not grammar, arguably because they tend to be realized through reactances rather than explicit morphology in English and familiar Indo-European languages. As we've seen however, the picture is radically different in a language like Tagalog where there is a good deal of overt morphology and structural interdependency focusing on transitivity functions in relation to the verb. Looking across language families, functional linguists like Halliday have generally determined that typological interests are better served by broadening the criteria for motivating grammatical functions than by exporting the study of participant roles to a more abstract level of semantic analysis in some languages (like English) and having to include them as part of grammar in others (like Tagalog).

Alongside the tier of role-oriented function labels just introduced, Halliday also makes use of a set of function labels which look more like traditional ones – Subject, Finite, Predicator, Complement and Adjunct. The additional tier of labels must of course motivated by complementary criteria. In English, Halliday's Subject is the function that changes sequence with Finite to change MOOD (from declarative to interrogative as introduced above); these two functions are replayed in English tags, which can thus be used as a reliable diagnostic for Subject and Finite functions.

Subject	Finite	Predicator	Finite (tag)	Subject (tag)
two Indians	were	detained	weren't	they

Once the Subject and Finite are established, a Complement can be defined as a potential Subject (via a change in VOICE, as introduced above); and if a complete labelling is required, then the Predicator is the rest of the verbal group minus the Finite, and everything else is an Adjunct.

Rather than seeing these simply as formal categories, Halliday argues that they are meaningful ones – since they position a clause in interaction as giving information (declarative), asking for information (interrogative) or demanding goods and services (imperative):

Two Indian nationals were detained at Changi airport.
[declarative]

Were two Indian nationals detained at Changi airport?
[interrogative]

Detain two Indian nationals at Changi airport.
[imperative]

Beyond this, the Subject and Finite establish the arguability of the clause. The Subject is the nub of the argument (who or what we're arguing about) and the Finite realizes its terms (as temporal, through tense; or modal, in terms of probability, usuality, inclination, obligation or ability). Saying that *two Indian nationals were* sets the stage for a different argument . . .

Two Indian nationals were detained at Changi airport.

– Were they?

– Yes, they were.

– They weren't really, were they?

– Indeed they were.

. . .

. . . than one negotiating *the authorities shouldn't*:

The authorities shouldn't detain them.

– Yes, they should.

– No, they shouldn't, should they?

. . .

This kind of analysis exploring the role of clause functions to establish different kinds of interaction is referred to by Halliday as MOOD; for discussion of its discourse semantic function see Martin, 1992: chapter 6.

Halliday's third tier of grammatical functions is oriented to information flow, and takes us back to the kind of labelling we introduced earlier when discussing Topic in Tagalog and Theme for the Prague School. This time round Halliday is worried about variations like those illustrated below, where the way in which information is distributed changes from one clause to another. As far as TRANSITIVITY is concerned, we are saying the same thing (the 'content' stays the same); and as far as MOOD is concerned, the clauses interact in the same way as well (as declaratives giving information). But they all begin in different ways, with a pulse of informational prominence for which Halliday uses the Prague School term Theme.

Two Indian nationals were detained at Changi airport.

At Changi airport two Indian nationals were detained.

It was at Changi airport that two Indian nationals were detained.

What happened at Changi airport was two Indian nationals were detained.

This analysis sheds further light on why an English speaker chooses active or passive. Alongside proposing the nub of the argument, VOICE also makes one TRANSITIVITY role more informationally prominent than another; in what as called 'agentless passive' the Actor role might in fact be elided altogether. The anecdote were drawing on here did just this, leading off with a passive clause foregrounding the victims and not mentioning authorities – an appropriate choice in this case since the American passenger, not the authorities, was to blame for the wrongful arrest. The joke after all is at the American's expense, not that of the Singapore authorities.

Theme	Rheme
two Indian nationals	*were detained at Changi airport*

Theme	Rheme
two Indian nationals	*were detained by authorities at Changi airport*

Theme	Rheme
the authorities	*detained two Indian nationals at Changi airport*

A grammatics chapter of this kind is not the place to go into Halliday's functional tiers in more detail.[15] The main point we are making here is that once function labelling is deployed, then it has to be motivated. And there are different ways of motivating function labelling depending on how we look at the clause – the way we argue for function labels in other words depends on the kind of meaning we are looking at. Different kinds of meaning give rise to different kinds of criteria, which ultimately lead to tiers of structure (Participant and Process vs Subject and Finite vs Theme and Rheme). Halliday's general position is that clauses are concerned with three general types of meaning which he refers to as experiential, interpersonal and textual – and that looking at the clause from one or another of these points of view tells a different story about how to divide up the clause and label its parts. A crude outline of these different perspectives and the complementary ways in which they divide up[16] an English clause is presented as Figure 10.5.

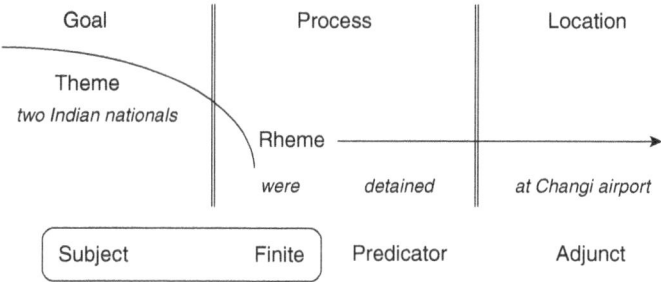

Figure 10.5 Complementary functional perspectives on a clause

It's possible of course to privilege one of these perspectives, and prescribe that it alone is grammar and the others are something else (or restrict ourselves to class labels for that matter, rejecting functions completely, adjusting the complexity of our tress accordingly and exporting some of the relations considered above to other levels of analysis). Bleached of interpersonal meaning and thus treated as purely formal categories, functions comparable to Halliday's MOOD functions (Subject, Finite etc.) are often treated as part of formal grammar in this way, with TRANSITIVITY roles (participant functions) exported to semantics and questions of Theme relegated to an even more abstract level of interpretation called pragmatics. But if our goal is to construct a theory that deals with how grammar makes meaning, then it's best not to privilege one kind of meaning over another – especially since from a typological point of view all three types of meaning are built more and less explicitly into the morphology and structural interdependencies of one language or another and we don't want to have to change our theoretical approach from one language to another just because of the way a particular language maps these different strands of meaning on to each other and manifests them more or less overtly as phenotypes[17] or cryptotypes in grammar.

5 System and Structure

As Figure 10.5 illustrates, looking at a clause from different points of view may lead us to recognize different kinds of structure depending on the kind of meaning we are focusing on. And for each type of meaning the question arises as to how structures are related to one another. What can we learn about language by comparing and contrasting structures? The strategy proposed by early generative grammarians involved deriving one structure from another by explicit rules called transformations. This was the dominant perspective in linguistics when Halliday and his colleagues addressed this issue in the 1960s. Their response was a different one, most clearly articulated in Halliday ([1964] 2003, [1966] 2002a, [1969] 2005) and also developed by Huddleston and Henrici in papers written in the same period but not published until 1981 (Henrici, [1965] 1981; Huddleston, 1981). Their suggestion was that rather than show relationships syntagmatically by deriving one structure from another (surface structure from deep structure in the parlance of the times), it would be more revealing to show relationships paradigmatically, as a network of choices reconfiguring grammar as meaning potential. To formalize a description of this kind, they designed[18] diagrams known as system networks to display what linguists call paradigmatic relations (choice relations), as a complement to tree diagrams which as we have seen display syntagmatic ones (chain relations). This gave Halliday and his colleagues a synoptic snapshot of the organization of grammar as a whole, by way of complementing formal grammarians' synoptic snapshots of the structure of single units of grammar such as the clause.

The idea of paradigmatic and syntagmatic relations of course goes back to Saussure ([1916] 1974), the Swiss linguist generally acknowledged as the father of modern linguistics; following him, paradigmatic analysis focuses on choice (what you say in relation to what you could have said), whereas syntagmatic analysis focuses on chain (the relations among the different parts of what you say). Hjelmslev developed this work, introducing the term paradigmatic in place of Saussure's 'associative'; and for Halliday's teacher Firth, the first principle of linguistics was to distinguish system and structure. The decisive move taken by Halliday and his colleagues with respect to this tradition was to privilege system over structure, thereby formulating 'deep grammar' in paradigmatic terms (Halliday, [1964] 2003, [1966] 2002a, [1969] 2005). This means that instead of focusing on the motivations for function labels, argumentation needed to be developed motivating systems. We have already introduced crytogrammatical argumentation in relation to TRANSITIVITY analysis above. Let's explore argumentation further now, from a 'paradigmatic privileged over syntagmatic' perspective – which is the distinguishing feature of Halliday's contribution to grammatical theory.

Take MOOD. When drawing systems networks the basic idea is to take a set of examples of different moods and look carefully at how each mood is realized (taking any morphology, structural interdependencies and relevant reactances into account). For English we can note that the imperative clause below is different from the other two moods in that it has neither a Subject nor a Finite; the declarative and interrogative have both, but in a complementary sequence (as we have seen above).

> Two Indian nationals were detained at Changi airport.
> [declarative]
>
> Were two Indian nationals detained at Changi airport?
> [interrogative]
>
> Detain two Indian nationals at Changi airport.
> [imperative]

On the basis of these similarities and differences we could propose a MOOD network in which the first choice is between imperatives and the other two (called indicative); and then within indicative, we have a choice between declarative and interrogative. These oppositions are presented as Figure 10.6. The network in effect classifies clauses according to ways in which interpersonal structures make differences in meaning in dialogue. The choices in the network represent clause classes (imperative, indicative, declarative and interrogative).

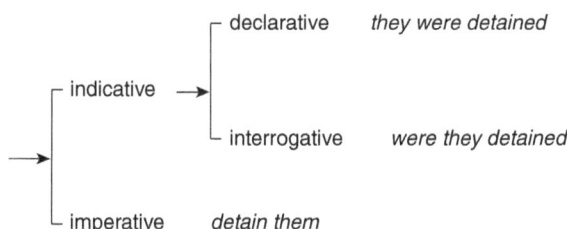

Figure 10.6 Two MOOD systems for English

Note that in systemic choice diagrams we move from left to right[19] – from more general classes to more specific ones. In chain diagrams on the other hand, referred to as tree diagrams above, we move from top to bottom – from larger units to smaller ones. The square brackets with the arrow pointing into them represent choice – logical 'or'. The terms in the diagram (indicative, imperative etc.) are called features and are the names of choices. Each choice is in fact a grammatical class (of clause, group / phrase, word or morpheme, depending on what kind of unit we are classifying). Some features (e.g. indicative above) act as entry conditions for other systems; in this respect system networks like that in Figure 10.6 organize paradigmatic choices as systems ordered in delicacy.

In another language, say Tagalog, comparable MOOD options are found even though the way in which they are realized is quite different (Martin, 1990). Like English, Tagalog uses a non-finite verb (with no ASPECT or MODALITY) to signal imperative (*maglaro* below); but unlike English it is usually explicit about the person responsible for carrying out the command (using the appropriate pronoun, e.g. *ka* for 'you' below). In indicatives, instead of moving around a noun and verb, Tagalog simply inserts an enclitic question particle after the verb (*ba* below). Note in the examples that unless there is a good textual reason not to, Tagalog begins with the verb, regardless of MOOD ('T' indexes the Topic marker, as above, which in SFG would be labelled Theme).

| naglaro | ang | bata | [declarative] |
| played | T | child | |

'The child played.'

| naglaro | ba | ang | bata | [interrogative] |
| played | ? | T | child | |

'Did the child play?'

| maglaro | ka | [imperative] |
| play | T-2nd person singular | |

'Play.'

From these examples we can see that there is no interpersonal reason to propose Subject and Finite functions for Tagalog; MOOD doesn't work that way. Tagalog and English are quite different languages in this regard. They are similar in that they both tend to establish the negotiability of the clause at its beginning (rather than at the end as with Japanese or Cantonese). And with respect to system, the two languages are so similar at this point in delicacy[20] that we can in fact use the MOOD systems suggested for English above for Tagalog as well. But the ways in which English and Tagalog structure the nub and terms of the argument are quite different. Fortunately, Halliday's complementary system and structure perspectives enable us to show how the languages are similar and different at the same time.

If we want to show explicitly how MOOD systems and structures are related in English, then we can provide formal specifications along the following lines (more formal statements are possible – cf. Halliday & Martin, 1981; Halliday & Matthiessen, 2009 for details):

[imperative]	⬎	(no Subject or Finite, Predicator only)
[indicative]	⬎	Subject & Finite present
[declarative]	⬎	Subject sequenced before Finite
[interrogative]	⬎	Finite sequenced before Subject

For TRANSITIVITY we can adopt the same network building strategy, focussing on VOICE relations:

Two Indian nationals were detained by authorities at Changi airport. [receptive]

Authorities detained two Indian nationals at Changi airport. [operative]

A bomb exploded at Changi airport. [middle]

Here we see the contrast between active and passive introduced above (re-labelled operative and receptive following Halliday & Matthiessen (2014) to help distinguish clause from verbal group 'voice' system[21]). In addition, as a third example, we have an 'intransitive' clause for which the choice of passive is not available. Halliday calls this clause type middle voice, since it involves just one inherent participant and so doesn't provide for alternative Subjects. The first two examples he refers to as effective clauses, for which an operative vs receptive choice is available.[22]

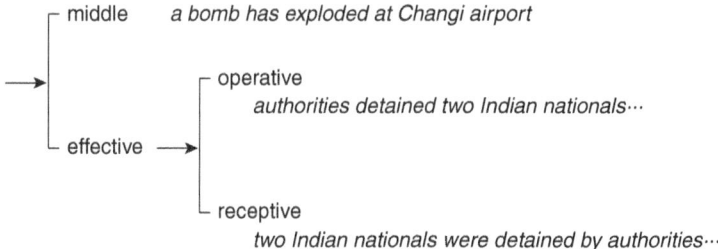

Figure 10.7 Two TRANSITIVITY systems for English

The structural implications of these choices are as follows (note that we need to refer to MOOD functions to make voice options explicit):

[middle]   Actor is Subject; verbal group realizing Process is active

[effective] Actor & Goal present

[operative] Actor is Subject; Goal is Complement; verbal group realizing Process is active

[receptive] Goal is Subject; Actor is 'by' phrase; verbal group realizing Process is passive

To account for the so-called agentless passive (*two Indian nationals were detained at Changi airport*), we'd have to add another system to the network (subclassifying receptives) and rework our rules relating system to structure so that Actors are not present when the agentless passive option is chosen.

6 System Networks

As the glimpses of English MOOD and TRANSITIVITY in Figures 10.6 and 10.7 have shown, systems formalizing paradigmatic relations can be related to one another as networks of systems (i.e. system networks). The networks proposed there each consisted of two systems, one dependent on the other – dependent in the sense that a feature in one system (indicative and effective) was the entry condition for another system (declarative/interrogative and operative/receptive respectively). Technically speaking the systems were related in delicacy, with the declarative/interrogative and operative/receptive systems subclassifying one selection from the indicative/imperative and middle/effective ones.

Another way in which systems can be related to one another is by cross-classification – where formally speaking two systems shared the same entry condition. The MOOD and TRANSITIVITY systems just discussed in fact cross-classify clauses in this way, as formalized by the right facing brace in Figure 10.8.

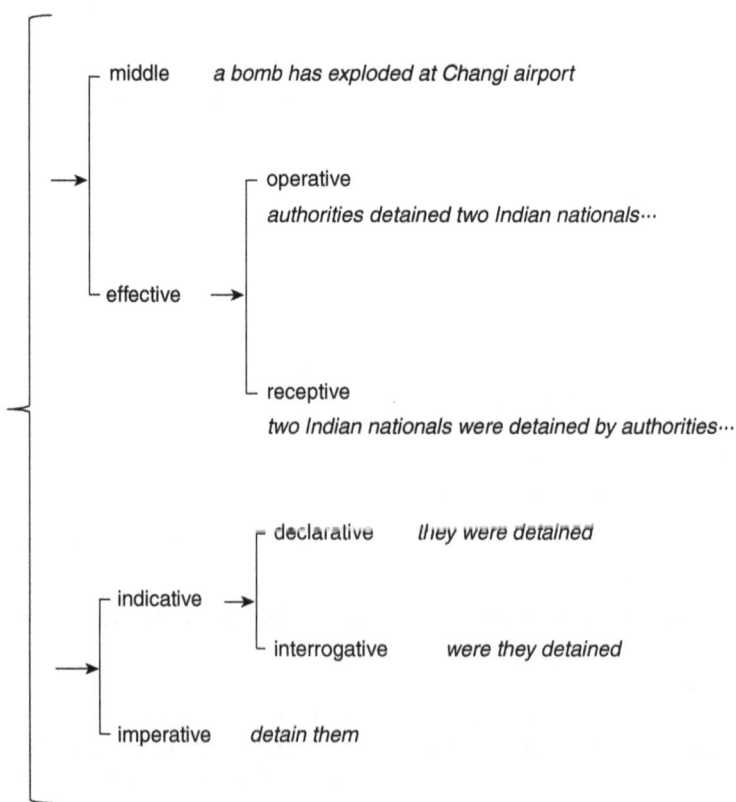

Figure 10.8 Cross-classifying systems for the entry condition clause

Cross-classification of this kind is a familiar pattern for linguists (and for many language learners), and where just two dimensions are at stake the relations involved can be displayed and exemplified as a paradigm (with rows for one system and columns for the other):

	middle	effective
indicative	*a bomb has exploded*	*they exploded a bomb*
imperative	*run*	*explode the bomb*

Where more than two systems are involved then presentation as a three (or more) dimensional table of this kind quickly becomes very difficult to view and formalization as a system network provides a clearer synoptic overview of the interrelations involved.

System network symbolism, to the point developed so far in this chapter, can be used to explore various interdependencies among systems, for example the relation of MOOD and MODALITY in English. As exemplified below, MODALITY is optional and only indicative clauses can be modalized (Halliday, [1970] 2005):

	unmodalized	modalized
indicative	*a bomb has exploded*	*they probably exploded a bomb*
imperative	*run*	**probably explode the bomb*

The dependency of the MODALITY system on the entry condition indicative is formalized in Figure 10.9.

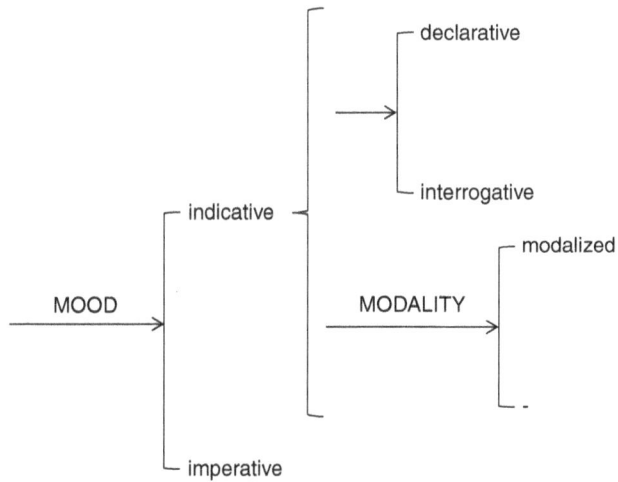

Figure 10.9 The dependency of MODALITY on indicative mood

Interdependency of this kind is the inspiration for Halliday's concept of metafunctions, which he uses to characterize the intrinsic functional organization of language. The relatively interdependent systems we are focusing on here cluster together as interpersonal meaning from a metafunctional perspective, complemented by additional clusters of experiential and textual systems. Critically, it is thus axis (i.e. system privileged over structure and formalized in system networks) that gave rise to and ultimately underpins this well-known dimension of SFL theory – the interpersonal, experiential and textual metafunctions (for discussion of experiential in relation to logical meaning, generalized as the ideational metafunction, see Section 7 below). Because the nature of relations among systems is so crucial to the theory, we'll explore what is meant by relative interdependency a little further, and problematize the discussion by focusing on POLARITY and the nature of its interaction with MODALITY and MOOD.

To begin let's make a further distinction in MOOD, this time between what we have been calling declarative clauses and exclamative ones:

	non-exclamative	exclamative
declarative	*they exploded a bomb*	*what a bomb they exploded*
interrogative	*did they explode a bomb*	**what a bomb did they explode*

As we can see, the exclamative option is not open to interrogatives, and shares with declaratives the Subject^Finite information giving structure sequence. Accordingly in Figure 10.10 a more delicate system is introduced, opposing declarative to exclamative to preserve the usual meaning of the feature declarative, and using the term informative to act as an entry condition for the new system (in opposition to interrogative).

At first blush, POLARITY looks to be relatively independent of these systems, cross-classifying as it does imperative, interrogative and declarative clauses, whether modalized or not, as positive or negative. But note that exclamative clauses must be positive:

	declarative	exclamative
positive	*they exploded a bomb*	*what a bomb they exploded*
negative	*they didn't explode a bomb*	**what a bomb they didn't explode*

We can formalize this interaction between MOOD and POLARITY by using an I/T (if/then) marking convention whereby the superscript ^{I} prescribes that exclamative clauses, marked with superscript ^{T}, are positive (as in Figure 10.11).

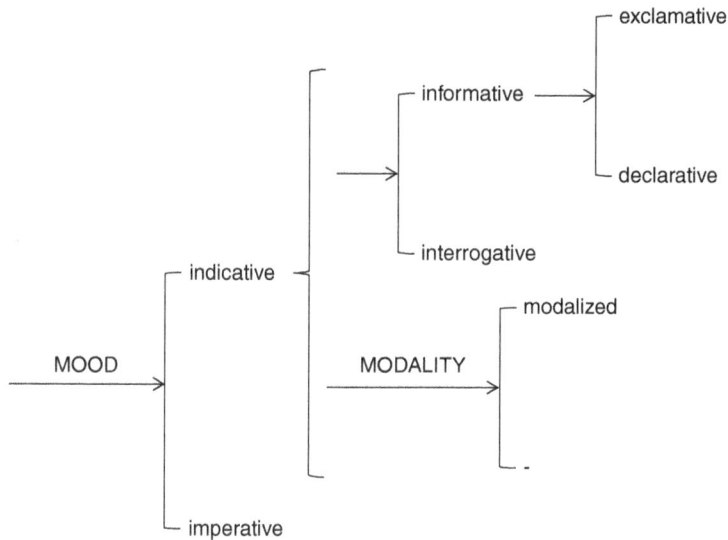

Figure 10.10 Expanding MOOD to allow for exclamative clauses

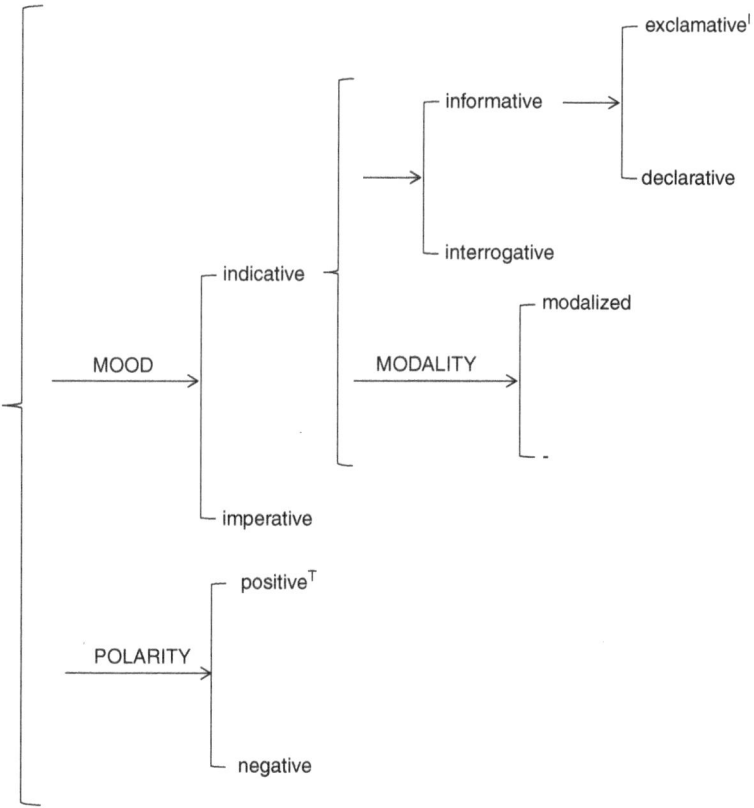

Figure 10.11 Interaction of MOOD and POLARITY (exclamatives)

Additional interdependency between POLARITY and MOOD can be seen in relation to tagging. In Canadian English for example only declarative and imperative clauses can be tagged. And the choice of reversed or constant polarity depends on selection of positive polarity (negative clauses, whether declarative or imperative, only allow reversed polarity).

	constant	reversed
declarative	*they exploded a bomb, did they*	*they exploded a bomb, didn't they*
	*they didn't explode a bomb, didn't they	*they didn't explode a bomb, did they*
imperative	*explode the bomb, will you*	*explode the bomb, won't you*
	*don't explode the bomb, won't you	*Don't explode the bomb, will you*

Part of this interdependency between POLARITY and MOOD is formalized in Figure 10.12, using a left-facing square bracket to show that either declaratives or imperatives can be tagged, and a left-facing brace to show that only positive clauses allow reversed or constant polarity.

Further interaction might be explored in relation to MODALITY, since as Halliday has shown ([1970] 2005) direct and transferred polarity operate differently with high and low modality as opposed to median – in the proportions *certainly won't : it's not possible :: possibly won't : it's not certain* but *probably won't : it's not probable*.

	direct negation	transferred negation
high	*they certainly won't explode the bomb*	*It's not possible they'll explode the bomb*
low	*they possibly won't explode the bomb*	*It's not certain they'll explode the bomb*
median	*they probably won't explode the bomb*	*It's not probable they'll explode the bomb*

We won't attempt to formalize this interdependency here – nor the need to arrange for the distinctive realization of negative imperatives (including Finite *do*: *don't explode the bomb*), nor the distinctive realization of negative polarity through certain Mood Adjuncts realizing modalities of usuality (*seldom, never, hardly*). Enough has been outlined to show what is meant by relative interdependency of systems, and thus to illustrate the empirical grounding of the concept of metafunction in axis (see Martin, [1984] 2010, 2013a for further discussion). It remains to show how two other further basic dimensions of SFL theory, rank and strata, are in fact grounded in axial relations in comparable ways.

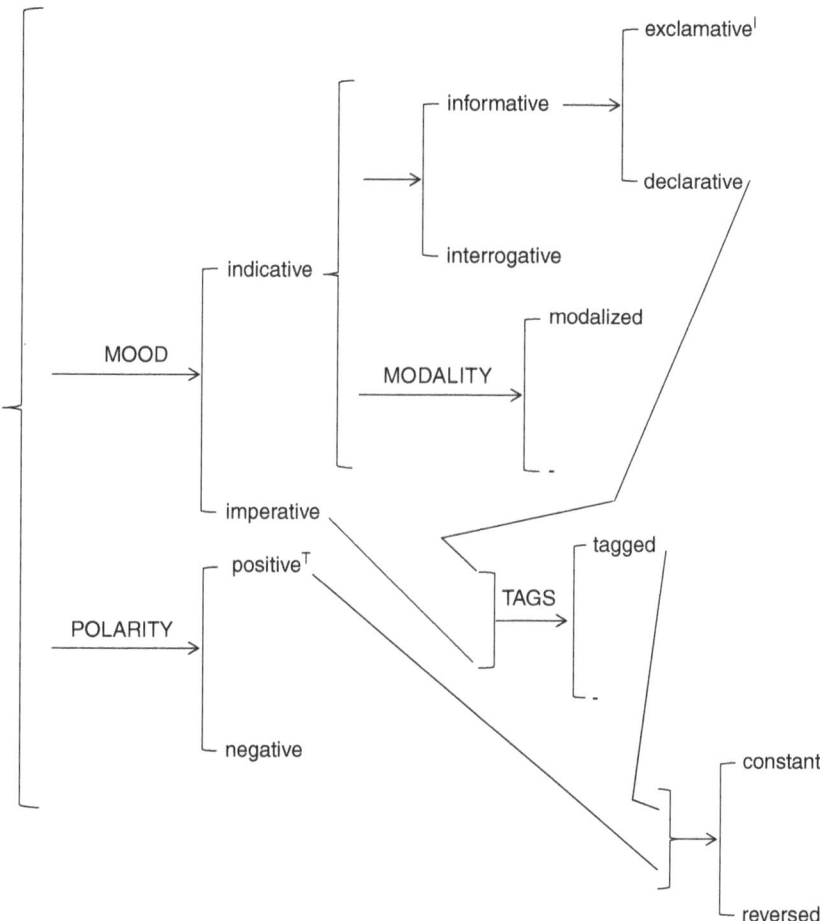

Figure 10.12 Interaction of POLARITY and MOOD (tagging)

First rank (cf. Huddleston, [1965] 1981; Hudson, [1967] 1982). As noted in Section 5 above, effective clauses involve two participants, referred to in material processes as Actor and Goal. Both participants are realized by nominal groups, with no categorical constraints[23] on the kind of nominal group selected (cf. mental processes where, as we have seen, one participant, the Senser, which must be conscious, is more constrained than the other, the Phenomenon, which can be any nominal group). The realization of clause participants by comparable nominal groups means that it would be very inefficient to introduce clause rank systems for each process type (e.g. material vs mental vs relational) or sub-type (e.g. middle vs effective material) specifying the kinds of nominal group at risk.

It is far more economical to recognize a distinctive bundle of systems formalizing the deep grammar of nominal groups and relate this bundle of features to clause bundles in terms of constituency – with clauses consisting of one or more nominal groups (alongside verbal and adverbial groups and prepositional phrases). Realization rules for clause functions can then be used to specify the realization of clause constituents by constitutes at group/phrase rank – Actor by nominal group, Senser by nominal group: conscious, Subject by a nominative nominal group if pronominal, Process by verbal group and so on. Once again we can see that like metafunction, the concept of rank is grounded in axis and the privileging of system over structure in the formalization of axial relations.

A schematic outline of the relation between bundles of features at different ranks in SFG is outlined in Figure 10.13. As mapped there, clause systems give rise to function structures; clause functions are specified by further realization rules as classes of unit at the rank below, thus forming syntagms (a sequence of classes); these classes are in fact features from lower rank networks, re-initiating the system/structure cycle. The cycles proceed until passes through the bundles of features at the different ranks of the grammar are exhausted.

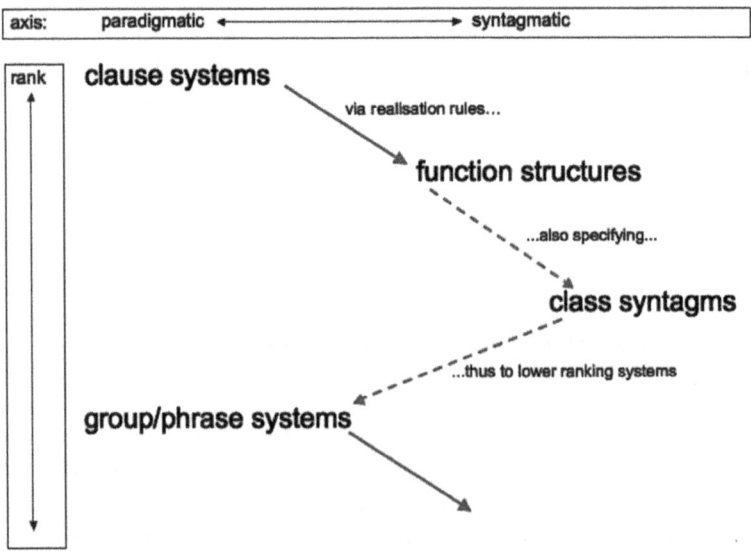

Figure 10.12 The relation of axis to rank in SFG

Next strata. As reflected in Figure 10.12, less delicate MOOD systems for example are motivated in fuller grammars of English by structural configurations of Subject, Finite, Wh/, Whex/ (cf. Halliday & Matthiessen, 2014, 2009; the function structures below use '^' to show sequence):

Needless to say the discourse semantic function of MOOD classes does not stand in a one-to-one relation to their distinctive function structures. There are various ways for example to ask for information (about someone's name for example):

MOOD	function structure	example
exclamative	Whex/C^Subject^Finite	**What a bomb they have** made!
declarative	Subject^Finite	**They have** made a bomb.
interrogative: polar	Finite^Subject	**Have they** made a bomb?
interrogative: wh	Wh/C^Finite^Subject	**What did they** make?
imperative/negative	Finite^Predicator	**Don't make** a bomb.

One of these, the wh-interrogative, can be treated as the congruent realization – since both the grammar and discourse semantics are playing the same role of seeking missing information. The others involve stratal tension, since the function structure is meaning one thing while at the same time symbolizing in one way or another a divergent discourse function – something we can confirm in relation to the compliant discourse semantic response *Sachin* in each example. Congruent and incongruent codings of this kind are the basis for SFG's concept of grammatical metaphor (Halliday & Matthiessen, 1999, 2014), which relies for its conception on structurally responsible axial argumentation in grammar. Axis thus underpins the development of discourse semantic systems accounting for exchange structure (as developed in Ventola, 1987; Martin, 1992) and enables the development of a stratified model of language with bundles of systems at successive levels of abstraction (phonology, lexicogrammar, discourse semantics), which bundles may themselves be grouped as further bundles by metafunction and rank and each stratum.

SPEECH FUNCTION	MOOD	function structure	example	compliant response
question	declarative	Subject^Finite	And your name is. . .?	- Sachin.
	interrogative: polar	Finite^Subject	Is your name Sachin or Ed?	- Sachin.
	interrogative: wh	Wh/C^Finite^Subject	What is your name?	- Sachin.
	imperative	Predicator	Tell me your name.	- Sachin

7 More on Systems

An overview of Halliday's perspective on axial relations would not be complete without a comment on kinds of system. In relation to metafunction, there is an important distinction between recursive and non-recursive systems. Recursive systems differ from those considered thus far in that they allow for re-entry once an option has been chosen. Halliday's description of English TENSE is one of the best-known examples of a recursive system, since past, present and future can be selected up to five times in English verbal groups (e.g. *will test, will have tested, will have been going to test, will have been going to have tested, will have been going to have been testing* – the last of these based on a recorded example of Halliday's, which also included passive *'ll 'v been going to 'v been being tested*; Halliday & Matthiessen, 2014: 339). Another well-known recursive system in English is AGENCY, which after an initial choice of middle or effective allows an indefinite number of 'initiators' to be added to a clause (involving the realization of a discontinuous verbal group complex in the process (*make . . . sing, let . . . make . . . sing, help . . . let . . . make . . . sing* below):

We sang.

They made us sing.

She let them make us sing

I helped her let them make us record the song.

etc.

A recursive AGENCY system, allowing for structures of this kind is presented as Figure 10.14. Halliday defines his logical metafunction as comprising all and only systems of this kind (e.g. Halliday & Matthiessen, 2009), and for English positions it alongside experiential systems as construing ideational meaning.

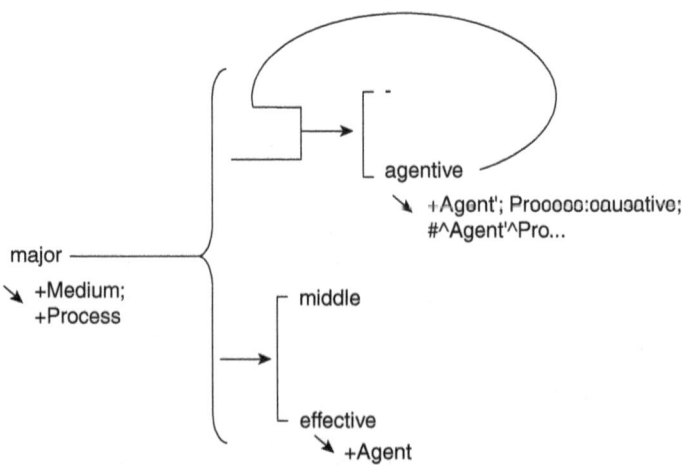

Figure 10.14 Recursive agency in English

Note that the meaning grammaticalized in recursive systems is a typological variable (cf. Tagalog where a comparable verbal system, ASPECT, is not recursive). Recursive systems are realized through serial rather than orbital[24] structures (univariate as opposed to multivariate ones), and apply to unit complexing at all ranks – clause complex (*we sang then they left*), group or phrase complex (*over the hills and through the woods*), word complex (*tea or coffee*) and morpheme complex (*pre- and post-inaugural celebrations*).

Recursive systems appear to have foregrounded for Halliday ([1991] 2005a: 46) the probabilistic nature of systems, since the choice of recursion tends to be made once out of every ten opportunities (so for every 4-term tense verbal groups in English, there would be 9 3-term, 90 2-term and 900 1-term ones for example). For non-recursive systems Halliday proposes that systems are equiprobable (e.g. singular/plural NUMBER, perfective/imperfective nonfinite ASPECT, specific/non-specific DEIXIS) or skewed on the ratio of 9 to 1 (positive/negative POLARITY, indicative/imperative MOOD, active/passive VOICE). Halliday (2005a) explores these patterns, including a survey of contextual variation studies by Plum, Nesbitt, Cowling, Hasan and others showing the way in which both users and uses of language push these inherent probabilities around – by way of realizing connotative semiotics in denotative ones (Hjelmslev, 1961).

As a closing comment we should acknowledge the possibility of treating systems as clines rather than as involving categorical oppositions (as exemplified by the PROCESS TYPE colour spectrum on the front cover of Halliday (1994), or his treatment of MODALITY on page 357 therein). The concept of clined systems opens the door for topological perspectives on agnation complementing typological ones (Martin & Matthiessen, [1991] 2010). In imagic terms, this involves setting up axes defining representing the poles of clined systems and positioning classes of item or instances of classes as more or less close to one pole or the other – with respect to as many axes as can be envisioned. With respect to Figure 10.15 for example, if the a/b axis represents vowel height

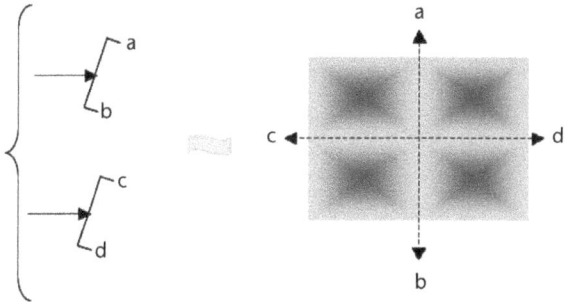

Figure 10.15 Clined systems in relation to a topology

and the c/d axis vowel frontedness, we could say that for the English phoneme /i/, its phonetic realization in New Zealand English is higher and further back than for Australian English (so that Kiwi *sick* sounds like Aussie *suck* to Australian ears).

8 Halliday the Grammarian

It is hard to do justice to Halliday as a grammarian, in no small part because of the brilliance of his descriptive work on English and Chinese. What I have tried to do here is focus on Halliday the grammatician, and consider the heart of the theory, axis, as it evolved to afford his searing insight. In doing so I have foregrounded his recontextualization of Firth's system/structure theory for grammar, and the concomitant privileging[25] paradigmatic relations from the 1960s as what is known as systemic functional grammar emerged. Central to this discussion is the nature of his axial argumentation, binding as it does system to structure – with system realized through structure and structure motivating system. By way of interpreting the nature of this argumentation Whorf's concept of cryptogrammar and Gleason's work on agnation provide essential meta-theoretical perspectives.

As shown, Halliday's particular formalization of paradigmatic relations in system networks, as deep grammar, gave rise to his theory-specific concepts of intrinsic functionality (metafunctions), constituency (organized by rank) and stratification (in particular his stratified content plane). These in turn laid the foundation for innovative work on language typology, context, multimodality and a wide range of applications in educational, forensic and clinical linguistics (as documented in this volume). The basic motif liberating this dialectic of theory and practice is Halliday's conception of system, and the relational thinking it affords – a toolkit materializing his dream of 'a socially accountable linguistics, and this in two distinct though related senses: that it put language in its social context, and at the same time it put linguistics in its social context, as a mode of intervention in critical social practices' (Halliday, 1993: 73) – an intellectual and political heritage we can deploy and develop, wherever linguistics and social semiotics take us in the generations to come.

Notes

1. This chapter has been adapted from Martin (2004b), a paper in which I attempt to introduce Halliday's approach to grammatical analysis to students of applied linguistics (further elaborated in Martin 2013a).

2. In the traditional school grammar the word class labels are referred to as the 'parts of speech', reflecting the 'sentences made up of words' perspective foregrounded in European writing systems.

3. An example of a 'notional' definition would be defining a noun as 'the name of a person place or thing'. Harris ([1946] 1957) (in Joos, 1957: 145) on the other hand concentrates on morphology and structural environment and so defines 'N' as 'morphemes which occur before plural -s or its alternants, or after *the* or adjectives'.

4. I've departed from strict binary branching here to simplify the presentation.

5 I've included the Aux as part of the MV in line with the IC analysis of this clause introduced above; in early generative grammar Aux would be treated as an immediate constituent of a higher node (VP or S) because of the way it 'moves' in various moods and bonds with the Subject (see the discussion of Subject, Finite and interpersonal meaning in functional grammar below). In addition, to simplify the figure I've treated *two Indian nationals* as involving three constituents rather than making an initial cut between *two* and *Indian. nationals.*

6. From this point on in the chapter we'll use the SFG term nominal group instead of the generative grammar term noun phrase, and the term verbal group to refer to the verb or group of verbs realizing the Process in a clause, excluding any Participants or Circumstances which follow; note that in formal grammars the VP (verb phrase) generally includes following NPs and PPs (as in Figures 10.1 and 10.2).

7. These three perspectives are exemplified in Halliday & Matthiessen, 2014; Nuyts et al., 1990 and van Valin, 1993 respectively.

8. The Topic is usually definite (an 'identity recoverable' participant) and in addition realizes a text's method of development (its angle on its content); see Martin, 1983, 2004b for discussion.

9. I have not attempted to use the English voice system to translate the shifts in thematic prominence here since to do so would give a misleading impression of the nature of information flow in Tagalog; I have however adjusted deixis to reflect the interaction of the systems of THEME and participant IDENTIFICATION (for discussion see Martin, 1983).

10. Had our commentator been a speaker of Indian English however this reactance would not have arisen, since mental processes in that dialect also deploy present in present tense for mental processing concurrent with the moment of speaking (e.g. *I am thinking that I am loving you very much.*).

11. Rose (2001a) develops Whorf's reasoning in his systemic functional grammar of Pitjantjatjara, an indigenous Australian language; see also Martin (1996) distinguishing process types in Tagalog.

12. The term agnation was introduced by Gleason (1965) to describe structures 'with the same major vocabulary items, but with different structures', and for which 'the relation in structure is regular and systematic, that is, (. . .) it can be stated in terms of general rules' (Gleason, 1965: 202); the concept afforded Gleason a non-mutational relational perspective on what at the time were described in formal grammar by structure changing processes called transformations. Davidse, 1998 demonstrates the significance of Gleason's work for SFL grammatics.

13. In SFG names of systems are formalized in graphology as small caps, a convention adopted from this point in the paper.

14. This clause is an agentive one, related to non-agentive *he was a Bosnian terrorist.*

15. Our discussion of informational prominence in English in particular needs to be extended to take into account the function of Theme to sustain a topic (the method of development of a text), and also Halliday's Given and New functions (Halliday & Matthiessen, 2014; Halliday & Greaves, 2008).

16. Figure 10.5 has been designed to partially reflect the different kinds of structure (particulate, periodic, prosodic) associated with different metafunctions (experiential, textual, interpersonal respectively); for discussion see Halliday, [1979] 2002; Martin, [1996] 2010).

17. Phenotype is Whorf's term for explicit categories marked by a segment, class sequence or morphology (Whorf, [1945] 1956).

18. Halliday recalls this as a matter of rotating Chomsky's tree diagrams 90 degrees counterclockwise and reinterpreting relations among terms as classification rather than composition.

19. Compare biology, where subclassification (taxonomy) is represented top-down, with more general classes on top of more specific ones.

20. Once we move to sub-types of interrogative and imperative however, the languages do look different systemically as well; see Martin, 1990 for discussion.

21. This is important since in English relational identifying clauses for example the verb *be* does not change voice to overtly mark the shift from operative to receptive (compare *Russell Crowe played the policeman/the policeman was played by Russell Crowe; Russell Crow was the policemen/the policeman was Russell Crowe*).

22. Australian English for example allows tagged interrogatives (if positive): *Is that for me, is it?*

23. Note that choice of case in pronouns depends on mood not transitivity, with a basic opposition between modally responsible Subject functions and non-Subject ones (*they detained them*).

24. See Halliday, [1979] 2002, 1981 and Martin, [1996] 2010 for the terminology used here.

25. For discussion of some limitations of this privileging, which I have not had space to consider here, see Bateman, 2008a.

11 Intonation

Bradley A. Smith and
William S. Greaves

Chapter Overview

---

1 Introduction: Intonation in Speech and Writing?

(Firth, [1957] 1962a: 121): Sweet himself bequeathed to the phoneticians coming after him the problems of synthesis which still continue to vex us.

We begin our account of Halliday's description of intonation ([1963] 2005a, [1963] 2005b, 1967, 1970; Halliday & Greaves, 2008) – the meaning-bearing organization of pitch – with a text, an excerpt from a play, George Bernard Shaw's *Pygmalion* (1916), and consideration of its interpretation in performance. The play is of course in two forms: the written script form; and the many performances (including readings) of that script. Here is the written script form of the text, a line from Act III, by the flower girl, Eliza:

What is wrong with that, young man? I bet I got it right.

A well-known performance of this play, the 1938 film production by Gabriel Pascal, co-written by George Bernard Shaw, is now in the public domain and is available online,[1] allowing us to hear the script 'brought to life' (as in the legend of Pygmalion from which Shaw derived his play) in speech (and, crucially, enabling *you*, the reader of this chapter, to become a *listener!*). In this performance we can hear pitch movements not represented in the written script, for example: the rising pitch contour beginning on the word 'that' and continuing through 'man'; and also a rising pitch contour on 'right'. We will discuss later the significance of these intonation choices.

The interpretation of written script into spoken performance is an excellent way of thinking and learning about intonation and its uses, especially when considered from the perspective of Halliday's account of such phenomena. In one of his most entertaining and accessible accounts of intonation, Halliday (1985b) explores significant differences between the two forms of language, making the point that (vii) '[w]riting and speaking are not just alternative ways of doing the same things; rather, they are ways of doing different things'. Writing and speech traditionally have tended to have different styles of discourse and social purposes, different patterning in terms of language choices within and corresponding to different social contexts: that is, they form different 'registers' of language use (Halliday, McIntosh & Strevens, 1964; Halliday & Hasan, 1985).

Importantly for our consideration of intonation, the two forms of language are different in terms of the capacity each has for making meaning: there are certain things one is able to do with speech that one cannot do (easily, at least) with writing (Halliday, 1985b: 30): '[t]here are various aspects of spoken language that have no counterpart in writing: rhythm, intonation, degrees of loudness, variation in voice quality ("tamber"), pausing, and phrasing'. Writing evolves for human cultures (1985b: vii) 'when language has to take on new functions in society', (1985b: 39) 'in response to needs that arise as a result of cultural changes . . . the complex of events whereby certain human groups changed over from a mobile way of life to permanent settlement'. These new social functions tend to be prestige ones (1985b: vii) 'those associated with learning, religion, government and trade': that is, writing has evolved for monologic authoritative statement (1985b: 32). 'The speaker's state of mind, the reservations and doubts he or she may be feeling, the hesitations, the weight given to different parts of an argument – these have no place in most uses of written language.' Writing, in its prototypical use, in general was (1985b: 32) 'not anchored in the here and now'; thus the meanings we find expressed with intonation weren't represented in the writing system.

Whereas intonation is absent in writing, it is obligatory in speech: speakers of English must and constantly do make choices from intonation systems. For example, in the *Pygmalion* excerpt above, Eliza speaks 'I bet I got it right' with a rising pitch contour, helping (with other language choices) to create what Halliday terms a 'protesting' or 'challenging' tone. This is in response to Freddy's comment on her 'small talk', 'how awfully funny!', which he speaks with a rising-falling tone, the natural choice for an exclamation such as this.

These (1985b: 32) 'on-the-spot features of language' play a crucial role in spontaneous, interactive dialogue, such as in dramatic dialogue between characters in a play. In addition to literary dialogue, other forms of written text designed to represent speech are, for example, transcripts of police interviews (read aloud in court), parliamentary proceedings and medical (e.g. doctor-patient) discourses. In each of these contexts (and many more in human society) misreadings of a written text can potentially have serious consequences in terms of the meanings thereby communicated. Punctuation notwithstanding (Halliday, 1985b: 32) 'the omission of prosodic features from written language is, in some respects and under certain circumstances, a genuine deficiency'.

In contemporary, digitally mediated communication (Halliday, [2002] 2005b: 160) 'the spoken / written distinction is increasingly blurred'. In emails, social media, text messages and blogs written language is brought into the service of often spontaneous, dialogic interaction. Such discourses, traditionally spoken, transient, and in which intonation traditionally plays such a crucial role, are now thus recorded, in writing. Meanwhile, registers of spoken discourse such as casual conversations or academic lectures are increasingly mediated and thus similarly 'on the record' (recorded and posted online). When discourse is mediated it becomes an object of study (see quotation from Halliday, 1985b: 36, below), available for much closer scrutiny, appraisal and critique. We are not yet accustomed to these sociocultural shifts and their consequences: a spontaneous remark made by a senior politician in the context of a relatively informal panel conversation (made available online) being subsequently taken up as part of a serious political debate[2]; an online lecture being critiqued by students or peers; or the common experience of 'tone' in an email or SMS being misinterpreted.

Because writing does not include intonation, a reader or actor wishing to interpret dialogue-as-writing into speech (including the reader of an email or SMS) must make decisions, whether conscious or otherwise, about choices of intonation. But upon what basis are such decisions made? Punctuation, Halliday (1985b) shows, has evolved to some extent as a response to this issue. However, commas, question marks, exclamation marks and the like only partially, inconsistently and often ambiguously fulfil the functions served in speech by intonation. Martin Davies, who has for over four decades made a study of this issue using Halliday's framework and description (e.g. 2014), shows how an intelligent reading of certain properties of a written text, in particular cohesion, can motivate and constrain the interpretation of certain aspects of intonation choice in 'reading aloud' that text. In general, an understanding of the use of intonation in spoken discourse registers is also a foundation for such decisions (Smith, 2008a); and knowledge of the functions of intonation in spoken registers is useful for crafting dialogic e-discourse (both written and spoken).

The interpretation of a written text into speech, particularly one purporting to represent spoken dialogue, is therefore problematic; but also of great interest and illustrative in terms of the study of intonation, especially within a meaning-based description such as Halliday's. Halliday's description of intonation is particularly well-adapted, or to use his term, 'appliable' (Halliday, 2005b) in this regard, being derived from a 'social semiotic', meaning-based theory of language (1978), termed 'systemic functional' theory. Halliday's theory relates language choice to social purpose, making the claim that the organization of language has evolved in adaptation to the social purposes which it serves and thus reflects, or rather, manifests: for example, in the different semiotic potentials of speech and writing, and shifts in the use of language, as in the changing roles of writing and speech, which thus serve as important data for studying changes in human culture and society. Halliday's social semiotic approach not only determines the nature of his description of intonation and other aspects of language, it is with reference to this theoretical framework that the description of intonation is properly to be understood and appreciated.

Halliday & Greaves (2008) present a discussion of the wide range of approaches to intonation study and description, each with their own points of view and areas of focus. For example (Halliday & Greaves, 2008: 9), for

> a social dialectologist the sounds of language . . . are the symptoms of linguistic change . . . [which] reveal aspects of the social structure of the speech community . . . For sociologists and psychologists interested in questions such as crisis management and conflict resolution . . . speech sounds . . . serve as indices of recognizable forms of human social behaviour, and typically correlate with other, non-linguistic behavioural traits.

While for many such scholars and practitioners (including actors) the purpose of the study of language and its expression in sound is (Halliday & Greaves, 2008: 10) 'in order to throw light on something else', linguists study (Halliday & Greaves, 2008: 10) 'language (and also other things) in order to throw light on language'. Yet linguists similarly specialize, as (Halliday & Greaves, 2008: 10) 'phoneticians, grammarians and lexicologists, and semanticists'. Halliday's approach from his earliest work has been to locate the description of intonation and other language phenomena within the framework of a general linguistic theory, known as systemic functional linguistics ('SFL'), and its derived language descriptions ([1961] 2002; Halliday & Matthiessen, 2004).

In the present chapter our aim is to provide a guide to Halliday's description of intonation in English with reference to his systemic functional theory of language, in the process showing what is distinctive about his approach. In the next section we present a brief guide to Halliday's description of intonation, and then in Section 3 we discuss Halliday's approach in general terms, in relation to other approaches to the study of intonation. In Section 4 we present a brief guide to Halliday's description of intonational systems as a part of the grammar of English; and conclude with some observations on the use of Halliday's description of intonation within linguistics.

2 Intonation: What It Is and What It Does

(Halliday & Greaves, 2008: 16) When we talk about the sound system of English, the significance of any category we refer to (whether a prosodic category, such as pitch movement, or an articulatory one, such as the shape and position of the tongue) will be its semogenic value – its function in the total meaning potential of the English language. This is a phonological consideration.

Intonation is the manipulation of pitch, in particular the use of distinctive falling and rising pitch contours and their combinations, to help make distinctions in meaning. Halliday gives an account of the crucial role pitch movement played in the early evolution of language in one infant he observed (1975), showing how this infant, at 19 months (1985b: 46) '. . . introduced an entirely new distinction into his speech, that between falling and rising tone. From this point on, all pragmatic utterances were spoken on a rising tone and all non-pragmatic (mathetic) ones on a falling tone'. The term 'pragmatic' here refers to the infant's use of language for doing, for interacting with others in his world, and 'mathetic' to the use of language for learning about his world. These two general uses of the infant 'proto-language' observed by Halliday were later to evolve into what Halliday terms the interpersonal and experiental 'metafunctions' of the adult language: language used to exchange meaning with others, and to construe experience, respectively.

Halliday shows in this book how the move from protolanguage to adult language crucially involves the move from a simple one-to-one relationship between expression and content (e.g. falling tone and mathetic function) to a more complex relation between sound and sense, a relation of crucial importance in understanding Halliday's description of intonation within the systemic functional theoretical model. In adult language there is no one-to-one correspondence between phonological distinctions – intonational ones such as tone (realized phonetically by rising/falling pitch movement); or phonemic distinctions such as, in English, between /t/ and /d/ (realized phonetically through the presence or absence of voicing) – and particular meanings. Instead, phonological choices 'realize' (express, manifest) choices in lexis and grammar – words and wordings – which in turn interact with each other to realize semantic choices. Importantly, the multiple levels of coding enable adults to (Halliday, [1974] 2003: 102) 'mean more than one thing at once': rather than having an inventory of simple signs as in the infant protolanguage, in adult language choices from different systems at different levels interact in complex ways to make nuanced meanings and provide a practically infinite variety of choice in terms of combinatory possibilities.

For example, in the Pygmalion excerpt, Eliza is in one sense making a statement in her second clause, 'I bet I got it right'; but the rising tone adds a sense of protest or challenge that demands an answer: that is, it is also in part a question, a polar (yes / no) question – 'don't you think?' is an implicit meaning of this utterance. Freddy's emphatic reply, 'killing', affirms this interpretation: it cannot be seen as a response to her wh-question, 'what is wrong with that young man', but to the implicit yes/no question as to whether or not she 'got it right'. Eliza's challenge is in fact an important point in the play: it is the first instance of Eliza asserting herself in her new social circle; setting up the later interpretation of her speech by her new social circle as, in Higgins' words a few lines later in this scene, 'the new small talk', which so enthralls Freddy.

The meaning of Eliza's line is the product of the interaction of choices: those represented in the written text – Subject-Finite[3] structure, *'I got* it right', rather than *'did I get* it right?'* – and those found only in the spoken performance – rising tone. Part of the meaning of this line is that it is a statement-and-question (rather than statement or question). Eliza could, furthermore, have instead chosen a command, (e.g. 'don't laugh at me'), another possibility from her repertoire of language. The result of the combination of these choices (and many more, even in this short excerpt) is a meaning more complex than a simple statement or yes / no question. Any literary or other consideration of this line (including by an actor) as an act of meaning, without due attention to this complex interaction of choices, is clearly impoverished and potentially misleading.

Halliday ([1963] 2005b, 1967, 1970; Halliday & Greaves, 2008) identifies five basic pitch contour shapes or 'tones' in the adult language, built upon the basic opposition between falling and rising pitch movement, which form a paradigm or 'system' from which speakers choose in English (cf. Halliday & Greaves, 2008: 50); as well as two compound tones composed of two pitch contours which have become 'fused' in English into a single tone (cf. Halliday & Greaves, 2008: 46). These are called the 'primary tones'.

This paradigm, termed by Halliday the 'TONE' system,[4] is 'exhaustive': speakers must select from one or other of these pitch contour shapes. The set of primary (simple and compound) tones are:

(1) falling pitch contour
(2) rising pitch contour
(3) level-rise pitch contour
(4) falling-rising pitch contour
(5) rising-falling pitch contour
(13) falling + level-rise pitch contour
(53) rising-falling + level-rise pitch contour

There is also a small set of secondary tone variations for each primary tone. For example, for tone 1, one can select the standard falling tone, a high falling tone, or a low falling tone; or a 'bouncing' pre-Tonic (the pattern of salient syllables before the Tonic).

Choices from the system of TONE are significant, or 'functional', in English. So too are choices in the location of such contours in an utterance, in the system of TONICITY; and the division thereby of the speech stream into tone groups – each of which is the domain of one tone choice – in the system of TONALITY. Furthermore, the organization of sound into accented and unaccented syllables – via distinct phonetic phenomena such as relative lengthening of a syllable, change in an established temporal patterning of syllables (rhythm) or change in pitch height (jump up or down) – is also significant. The division thereby of the speech stream into a succession of feet – a foot, analogous to a 'bar' in musical notation, being the domain of one accented syllable – is termed the system of RHYTHM; and the location of the accented syllable, called 'Ictus', is a choice in the system of SALIENCE.

One way to illustrate and think about what intonation is and what it does is to consider the different ways in which a written text may be interpreted in spoken performance, in terms of intonation choices, by comparing different performances of the same written text. For example, in the excerpt from *Pygmalion* quoted above, in 'What is wrong with that, young man?' the comma clearly indicates that this is to be spoken with some sort of break between 'that' and 'young man', but doesn't tell us the nature of that break: is it a choice in TONALITY, dividing the utterance into two tone groups? Or does it suggest only where the Tonic should fall, on 'that' as in the 1938 interpretation, rather than suggesting a division into two tone groups? The written script likewise doesn't tell us which words contain accented syllables, with a potentially humorous consequence, as we shall show below.

Nor does the script indicate which tone choice(s) should be made. A question mark is used in English writing for both yes / no – ('polar') and wh-interrogative ('content') questions – i.e., '?' doesn't differentiate the two types of question. Yet in speech these are, in the 'unmarked' (default) case – that is, in Halliday's words, unless there is 'good reason' for another choice – matched with different tones, a rising and a falling tone, respectively. Likewise, a full stop after a statement can be taken, in the 'default' case, to indicate a falling tone. However, in the 1938 performance of the line quoted earlier, these defaults are twice overridden: the wh-interrogative is spoken with a rising tone; while the 'statement' is also spoken with a rising tone.

We can make educated guesses about such choices in reading aloud from a script, based both upon our knowledge of English discourse and our literary interpretation of the play; and indeed, this is an essential part of the actor's craft. But each different interpretation results in a different meaning and a different text. All these phonological choices make meaning via their interactions with other choices in language.

One of the challenges of writing about intonation is that it *is* writing, rather than *speaking*: most academic discourse about intonation is done both through writing and with respect to written transcripts, so that the discussion (and analysis upon which discussion is based) is at a distance from the source text (in a way that it is not with written text as data), bringing issues of 'transcription as theory' to the fore (Ochs, 1979). One of the great strengths of systemic functional linguistics, its engagement with authentic, actual discourse as data, is thus severely hampered in the study of spoken discourse. There is no way of exemplifying by direct in-text reference to the source text: we are entirely dependent upon the reader's capacity to interpret intonation correctly transcription conventions, which rely on the reader making a correct link between a symbol, such as /, and its referent in actual speech, an 'accented syllable' – a term that is meaningless or ambiguous unless you can correctly hear its referent, either materially or mentally.

As a result of this, in order to study and discuss the phonological aspects of intonational systems we need to offer the reader both ready access to spoken text data (to listen to) and a transcription system which is able to capture those aspects of the speech signal of relevance to the discussion. The internet provides access to a vast databank of spoken language, including the performance of *Pygmalion* referenced earlier. Halliday's transcription system neatly captures those aspects of the sound signal of significance to the description of intonation, that is, which serve to make distinctions in meaning.

Below is a transcription of Eliza's line as performed in the 1938 film production of *Pygmalion*, using Halliday's system of transcription. Note, punctuation symbols, although included, are superfluous here: the meanings they attempt to express are more accurately captured by the intonation transcription.

//2 *what* is / *wrong* with / ***that***, young / ***man***? //2 ^ I / *bet* I / *got* it / ***right***. //

The numeral indicates the choice in TONE. Bold type indicates the Tonic syllable, which is the syllable upon which the locus (and beginning) of the tone choice occurs, and thus the choice in TONICITY. Double forward slashes // indicate the boundaries of a tone group and thus the choice in TONALITY. A single forward slash / (and also double forward slash) indicates the boundary of a foot and thus choices in the systems of RHYTHM and SALIENCE: the syllable following the forward slash is an accented syllable, termed 'Ictus', which is also in italics for ease of reading. A caret symbol ^ after a (single or double) forward slash indicates that the first syllable in the foot is not accented (termed a 'Remiss' syllable), as might occur when the foot begins an utterance or after a pause or break in an established rhythm.

Thus, in the 1938 performance of the line from *Pygmalion*, there are two tone groups, 'what is wrong with that young man' and 'I bet I got it right', which is an unmarked choice in TONALITY (one tone group per clause). In both tone groups the TONE choice is tone 2, the rising pitch contour. The two Tonics fall on the only syllable of each of the words, 'that' and 'right'; while the other accented syllables are 'what', 'wrong', 'man', 'bet' and 'got', making a total of seven feet, four in the first tone group and three in the second. Figures 11.1 and 11.2 show Praat pictures of these two tone groups.

Note that in the Praat picture of the first tone group, the pitch contour actually begins on 'that' but in fact the main part of the rise is on the final syllable 'man'. This is because TONE is prosodic: although 'that' is the locus of the tone choice – the point of focus which it picks out as the most important element in the utterance, and which begins the pitch contour shape – the entire contour is spread out over the remaining tone group. The rise certainly begins, albeit only slightly, at the Tonic syllable, 'that'; and the raised pitch level is maintained for 'young' following: a TONE choice has been 'instantiated' (made). But the final high rise tells us the important information that the choice of tone is in fact a tone 2 (high rise), rather than a tone 3 (level-rise); and also that these post-Tonic syllables are still part of this tone group, rather than the beginning of the next tone group. The fact that the pitch contour continues, unchanged, in the direction clearly set in the syllable 'that' and immediately after in 'young' indicates that 'that', rather than 'man', is in fact the Tonic syllable. A close listen

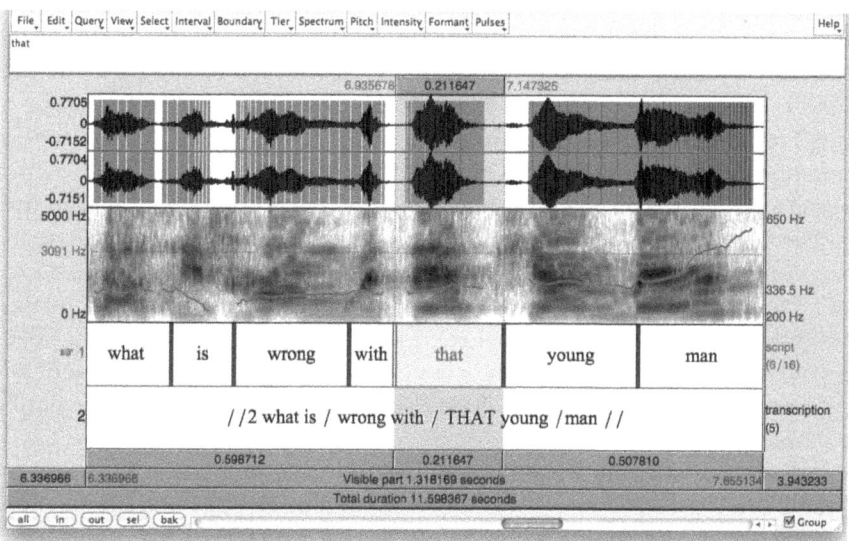

Figure 11.1 What is wrong with that young man

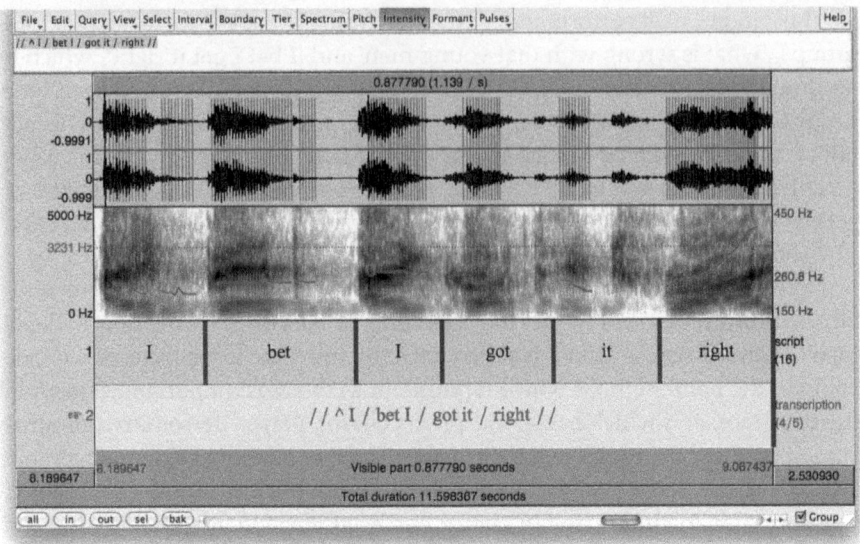

Figure 11.2 I bet I got it right

to the source text will confirm this (as will speaking the line yourself with 'that' as Tonic, i.e. beginning the rising pitch contour on this syllable: the choice in TONICITY will immediately appear distinct, especially if compared with the alternative of 'man' as Tonic).

But this is of course not the only (possible or actual) interpretation of this line. Another (amateur) production (one may find several by searching the internet) has the first sentence in this line spoken with a falling pitch contour, tone 1, creating a distinct sense from that of the rising tone with this type of question, the falling tone being the unmarked (default) choice with this type of question. This performance also has 'that' as Tonic. But a second Tonic, with a rising tone, follows on 'man': i.e., this utterance is divided into two tone groups, rather than the one tone group in the 1938 performance. This makes 'man', the head noun of 'young man' – the addressee of Eliza's line – a major point of focus also; which combines with the challenge in the rising tone to create a heightened sense of interpersonal energy. The second part of the line, 'I bet I got it right', also has a falling tone, changing the interpersonal meaning of this utterance: the challenging sense of the 1938 film performance is lost; it is simply a declarative statement.

We could also readily imagine other plausible interpretations of this line, for example, a compound tone 13 with the falling tone on 'that' and the level-rise on 'man'. The difference between the compound and simple tone is functional: a compound tone choice, being composed up of two pitch contours, is also thus a choice of double Tonic, but a major Tonic plus a minor Tonic; in this example, on 'that' and 'man', respectively. In this choice the addressee 'man' is not highlighted to the same extent as in the previous interpretation where it was major Tonic. This compound tone would in fact be the unmarked choice for this line, with its Nucleus + Adjunct structure, 'what is wrong with that + young man'. The minor Tonic tone, tone 3, is the choice that, as Halliday puts it, 'opts out' of the fundamental distinction between a falling or rising tone, the basis of the tone paradigm.

There are also a range of alternative interpretations of this line in terms of both SALIENCE and RHYTHM. An example is from an apocryphal anecdote (as told to one of the present authors) concerning a performance of this line at the end of a long-running season of the play. After performing the line, we assume, in some conventional way such as in the examples just discussed, on the last night (perhaps fatigued, bored, or simply annoyed beyond tolerance by the character Freddy's line to which Eliza's line is a response – cf. the video link provided in note 1), instead of the usual intonation, the line was spoken thus:

//1 ^ what / *is* / ***wrong*** with //1 *that* / *young* / ***man*** //

Here the intonation tells a very different story: the question is now, 'what is wrong with that young man' (a glance at the 1938 performance of Freddy's character might help to make this interpretation more plausible). The TONALITY – distribution of the flow of discourse into tone groups – is different; and 'that' is now Ictus (accented) rather than Tonic. In the 1938 version, 'young man' is a separate grammatical unit, a nominal group functioning as the Adjunct:addressee of the question, 'what is wrong with that'. But here the nominal group is 'that young man'; and is no longer directed at the addressee but to someone else.

This nominal group is distributed into three feet for the three syllables, a very unusual choice in RHYTHM adding extra prominence to this part of the utterance: English, as a stress-timed language, has an alternation of stressed / accented (Ictus) and unaccented (Remiss) syllables, with a tendency for more Remiss than Ictus syllables (Ictus tends to map together with lexical, Remiss with grammatical items). This non-default ('marked') division into feet is echoed in the higher-level division of this clause into two tone groups, again adding extra highlighting to the utterance. Furthermore, 'is' is Ictus, as is 'wrong' – again, a departure from the general pattern of alternating Ictus-Remiss syllables – adding emphasis to the utterance as a whole as well as highlighting the interpersonally charged Finite element 'is'. As a result of all of these choices, this line is given a dramatic 'boost' in relative emphasis and interactional energy, as befits this unconventional interpretation of the written script.

This humorous performance shows the powerful role intonation plays in making meaning in English speech, particularly in the interpretation of written text – or misinterpretation, wilful or otherwise. We have shown in this section what intonation is, how it works in spoken discourse and given some hints as to what it does, the consequences for meaning of changing the intonation of an utterance – something readily appreciated when considering the reading aloud of a play. In the next section we will discuss Halliday's approach, showing how it is distinctive and unique in its integration of intonational phenomena within the general linguistic description of English.

3 Intonation: Approaches to Its Study

(Pike, 1982: 3): The list and kind of things men will find will vary radically if they adopt different theories as tools with which to search for these units. The theory is part of the observer; a different theory makes a different observer; a different observer sees different things, or sees the same things as structured differently; and the structure of the observer must, in some sense or to some degree, be part of the data of an adequate theory of language.

The study of English intonation can be traced back at least as far as Hart's 1551 work (Danielsson, 1963), and studies by Steele ([1969] 1775) and Walker ([1970] 1787). Crystal (1969) provides an excellent review of early research on intonation, observing that (1969: 25) '[t]he main inadequacy with Steele's approach . . . was procedural, namely, that it is impossible to achieve any accurate and verifiable description of sounds . . . when they occur in actual speech'. He quotes Steele (in Crystal, 1969: 25) in this regard:

What ear can be so quick, nice, and discerning, as to keep pace with, discriminate, and ascertain the rapid and evanescent musical slides of the human voice . . . so as to enable the person to mark the limits of each syllable, with regard to gravity and acuteness, and to express them on paper?

Halliday's first large-scale study of spoken language was of dialects of the Pearl River Delta in Guandong, China, from 1949–50, under the training of the leading Chinese linguist Wang Li (Halliday, 2000). Halliday was chosen for this task for his ability to identify and analyse tones (a factor also in his earlier selection for foreign language training, during the Second World War, in Chinese). Halliday was trained in the transcription of responses using IPA (International Phonetic Alphabet) script, which he describes as (Halliday, 2002c: 7) 'excellent training for my later investigation of child language' – which was fortunate in that the wire recorder which (Halliday, 2002c: 7) 'Professor Wang was able to acquire . . . was not much use' as it kept breaking down.

But it was with the ready access to tape recording technology – which he cites as one of the most important advances for twentieth-century linguistics (cf. Halliday, 2002c: 7–8) – in the late 1950s that Halliday was able to begin the task of systematically accounting for the use of intonation in English. Recordings of (Halliday, 2002c: 7) 'natural conversations in the interactive situations of daily life' formed the basis for his description of intonation in English ([1963] 2005a, [1963] 2005b, 1967). His (1970) *A Course in Spoken English: Intonation* publication included tapes with examples of recorded speech from a variety of registers.

This tradition continues with the publication, together with William S. Greaves, of *Intonation in the Grammar of English*, which includes an accompanying CD with an e-copy of the book with embedded sound files: sound as source text becomes readily available, within the interactive digital media environment, as a part of the 'reading' (listening, speaking) and learning experience. With increasingly powerful technological resources, intonation-as-sound (rather than as transcription) has become substantially more accessible to study than a century ago.

To some extent because of the access to recordings of speech, for many scholars the approach to the study of intonation has been first to attempt a description of its form and only then to attempt a description of its function: i.e., a 'bottom-up' approach. This approach can be seen reflected in, for example, Schubiger's bold declaration ([1965] 1972: 175) that the 'investigation of English intonation has reached a point where its form has been explored almost to perfection . . . [but] the various attempts to assess its function have resulted in a mosaic of partly concordant, partly divergent opinions'. Another proponent of the bottom-up, formal approach is Crystal: (Crystal, 1969: 18):

All that emphasising a formal, as opposed to a 'semantic' or 'notional' approach to description implies is that, procedurally, considerations of meaning . . . do not enter in until a stable basis of formerly defined features has been determined. Then a more satisfactory classification of meanings can be carried out. Moreover, considerations of meaning enter in as criteria for discriminating between various kinds of formal contrast, as a method of indicating where linguistic significance may be said to lie.

Crystal's 'linguistic significance' has been a problematic concept for intonation study, bringing us to a central issue in the consideration of Halliday's intonation description: the nature of the theory that lies behind it, including conceptions of what 'linguistic significance' and indeed 'linguistics' are. Scholars in the twentieth century, from Saussure ([1916] 1974) onwards, sought to map out and delineate the appropriate domain and methods for linguistics as a nascent scientific discipline: what is to be considered part of language, and linguistics, or not. For Saussure (at least, according to the account we have of his lectures), 'langue' rather than 'parole' (the former ([1916] 1974: 9) 'not to be confused with human speech') was the proper and exclusive consideration of the linguistic scientist. Meaning was also excluded by leading linguists, such as the influential Bloomfield, who advocated a focus on the material plane as a proper basis for linguistics science ([1933] 2002: 38): '... it may be stated as a principle that in all sciences like linguistics, which observe some specific type of human activity, the worker must proceed exactly as if he held the materialistic view.'

Halliday ([1992] 2003a) observes:

> Those who study language have often been concerned with the status of linguistics as a science. They have wanted to ensure that their work was objective and scientifically valid. The natural way to achieve this aim has been to use other, earlier developed sciences as a model: theoretical physics, evolutionary biology, chemistry – some discipline that is currently valued as a leader in the field of intellectual activity.

Thus, we find critical references throughout twentieth-century work to what Crystal (1969: 2–3) terms the 'unscientific impressionism' in many intonation studies, resulting from 'the demands of English-language teaching in the early decades of this century'.

Data, in respect of the approach to intonation study, has also been crucial: theories of language are adapted to and reflect the data which are used to develop them, an important point in considering the history and development of intonation studies (Halliday, 1985b: 36):

> [w]hen language comes to be written down, people become aware of it; they start to speculate about it, and this is the origin of linguistics. Linguistics arose in all the great written cultures of the past ... and the centrepiece of linguistics is a theory of grammar.
>
> The grammar, of course, was a grammar of the written language. People were still unconscious of the nature of spontaneous conversation, and have remained so to this day; but they became aware of the structure of language through a study of what was written down.

Being developed in adaptation to the study of naturally occurring spoken discourse and in keeping with his teacher Firth's meaning-based approach to linguistics, Halliday's systemic functional linguistic theory is able to account for phenomena traditionally not considered part of language or grammar yet clearly meaningful (the same principle helping to establish the social semiotic approach to multimodal communication, e.g. van Leeuwen, 1999). Halliday is alone, in fact, (controversially) in assigning intonational meanings the status of being part of the grammar of English, precisely because his theory of 'grammar' is constructed so that it can accommodate the sort of meanings made by intonation in everyday spoken text. This stands in contrast to most working in the field, for example the prominent intonation expert Bolinger, who claimed that intonation is the ([1964] 1972: 29) 'half-tamed servant of language', and that (1958: 37) the 'encounters between intonation and grammar are casual, not causal . . . intonation is not grammatical'.

Halliday argues, in this respect, as follows (Halliday, 1970: 22) – using an example of the same type as that found in Eliza's question 'what is wrong with that, young man?' (note: Tonic, underlined in original, is here italicized):

The difference between

//1 where are you / *go*ing //   and

//2 where are you / *go*ing //

is a difference of the speaker's *attitude*: the first is a normal question, neither abrupt nor deferential, while the second is deferential: it is a question accompanied by a request for permission to ask, 'where are you going, may I ask?'. . . there is no clear line between these differences of attitude and differences in meaning such as found in a pair like

//2 would you like / *tea* //1 ^ or / *cof*fee //   and

//2 would you like / *tea* //2 ^ or / *cof*fee //

where the intonation expresses a clearcut logical distinction between the two kinds of 'or': the first means 'which would you like?', the second means 'would you like either?'.

Grammar is a central component of Halliday's linguistics, realizing semantic functions (such as statement and question) and being realized by phonological resources (such as phonemes and tones). For Halliday ([1963] 2005b: 238–9), in his well-known articulation,

[i]f we regard intonation as meaningful . . . then we should seek to state the place which such choices occupy relative to the total set of formal patterns in the language . . . The decision whether a given system that happens to be expounded by intonation is to figure in the grammar or not is a grammatical, not a phonological, decision.

Halliday differentiates between and relates phonetic, phonological, grammatical and semantic levels, or 'strata', in the description; hence, he distinguishes, in terminology, between 'intonation systems' in the phonological description, and 'intonational systems' in the grammatical description; and between the tone group and information unit, in phonology and grammar, respectively (the tone group realizes the information unit). This is to follow his teacher Firth's polysystemic, meaning-based approach to linguistics (Firth, [1957] 1962a: 192): '[t]he suggested procedure for dealing with meaning is its dispersion into modes, rather like the dispersion of light of mixed wave-lengths into a spectrum'. Stratification, outlined above, organizes the description into (phonetic, phonological, etc.) levels related by realization; metafunction differentiates systems of language which serve to represent experience, to interact with others and to weave coherent text (ideational, interpersonal and textual metafunctions, respectively); instantiation relates systemic potential to actual choice from that potential (with register configurations as intermediate between the two); rank accounts for the compositional organization of language (e.g. tone groups are composed of feet, which are composed of syllables); axis relates system and structure (e.g. Subject-Finite structure and the 'declarative' choice in the system of MOOD).

In the previous section we were looking at intonation from 'the bottom up' – from the perspective of (material) sound and its organization into intonation patterns, 'upwards' towards its functions in making (abstract) meaning. In this approach we were in a sense engaging in an artificial exercise at odds with Halliday's holistic approach to the description of intonation. One of Halliday's most significant contributions to the understanding and description of intonation is (Halliday, 1967: 7) 'to suggest how intonation patterns may be described in such a way as to integrate them within the description as a whole'. This in fact means beginning the description from an integrated perspective: as Halliday and Greaves (2008: 61), in discussing the systemic approach, put it, 'we do not first describe something and then ask how it can be related to everything else . . . describing something actually consists in relating it to all other possibilities.' This applies both to other possibilities within a system, for example the choice of tone 1 rather than tone 2, and in terms of relations to other systems – in the case of intonation, to particular systems of the grammar with which intonation choices interact most closely. Having viewed intonation 'from below' in Section 2, we will now present a discussion of Halliday's grammatical description of intonational systems in their interactions with other lexicogrammatical systems, as the realization of semantics in different metafunctions, at different ranks etc.; and conclude in Section 5 with a short discussion of the application of Halliday's description of intonation within linguistics, in the past and into the twenty-first century.

4 Intonational Systems of English Grammar

A pitch contour is a very distinct phonetic event for the human ear. The aural 'shapes' made by pitch contours take our attention; which perceptual phenomena are thus exploited for the purpose of making meaning in possibly all languages, although for different types of meaning. In Chinese and other 'tone' languages, pitch contours help distinguish what Halliday calls 'experiential' meanings, what are usually thought of as the content meanings of language: for example, in spoken Mandarin the difference between 'hai' 孩 with a rising tone, which means 'child', and 'hai' 害 with a falling tone, meaning 'harm'.

In spoken English these distinctive pitch contours function in the service of what Halliday terms 'interpersonal' and 'textual' meaning, as well as 'logical' meaning. Interpersonal meaning involves the exchange of information between dialogic interactants, e.g. making statements or asking questions, as in 'he went out yesterday / did he go out yesterday'; and the speaker's attitude towards a proposition, as in 'he should have gone out yesterday'. The major grammatical system serving to make interpersonal meaning is MOOD: declarative, interrogative and imperative options. While this system is concerned with the negotiation of propositions – e.g. 'it is' (declarative) as opposed to 'is it' (polar interrogative) – one of Halliday's most profound insights into intonation was to realize that the basic tonal distinction between falling and rising pitch makes comment upon the polarity of propositions: whether the polarity is known/not known (Halliday, 1970: 23):

> [b]asically, a falling contour means certainty and a rising contour means uncertainty . . . **with regard to yes or no** [bold font in original]. We go down when we know whether something is positive or negative, and we go up when we do not know.

This explains why the wh-interrogative is, in the unmarked case, spoken with a falling rather than rising tone: the polarity of the proposition is not at issue, as it is with a polar (yes / no) interrogative. The latter by default has a rising tone precisely because the polarity is what is at issue: a yes / no question seeks to know the polarity of a proposition. For the same reason a 'neutral' declarative key is realized by the falling tone. Tones 4 and 5 are combinations of this distinction: the falling-rising tone 4 is polarity 'known + unknown', a sense of reservation – 'yes, but'; while the rising-falling tone 5 is 'polarity unknown + polarity known', creating a sense of strong certainty – 'with respect to some issue regarding polarity, I am certain'. Tone 3 (Halliday, 1970: 24) 'is a sort of compromise between a fall and a rise', creating either a sense of confirmation or dependency between information units (the latter thus being a logical meaning – see below also on the logical function of tone 4).

However, as discussed in Section 2, in the adult language TONE does not make meanings on its own but as part of the grammar, in interaction with other grammatical systems, as the realization of complex acts of meaning (Halliday, 1967: 19–20):

> [i]f we therefore attempt a summary of the place of intonation in the English language, what we are summarizing is in fact the grammatical systems that are expounded by the phonological systems of intonation. What we can abstract as common to the grammatical meaning of a given choice in one of the (phonological) intonation systems may be extremely limited . . . it is only in the context of their occurrence in combination, both with each other and with grammatical systems not expounded by intonation, that we can fully account for the operation in English of tonality, tonicity and tone.

No doubt because of the intimate association of MOOD and POLARITY, KEY systems, realized by the system of TONE, serve as further (more 'delicate') options within the MOOD network: each option in the MOOD network has its own KEY system. Thus, for example, for the declarative mood, one may choose from the primary and secondary systems of TONE to realize: the 'neutral declarative' key (tone 1); the 'challenging declarative' key (rising tone); the confirmatory declarative key (tone 3); the 'reserved declarative' key (tone 4); the 'committed declarative' key (tone 5); as well as a range of other options realized by secondary tones, such as the 'strong declarative' (high falling tone 1+) or 'mild declarative' (low falling tone 1_) key options.

The same TONE choices mean differently in the environment of other mood choices, as Halliday and Greaves (2008: 51) explain:

> There is no proportionality such that
>
> // 1 she likes it //   is to   // 2 she likes it //
>
> as
>
> // 1 does she like it //   is to   // 2 does she like it //
>
> There is a different set of choices with interrogative mood, which we therefore represent as a different system.

As another aspect of the difference between the phonological and grammatical strata, the TONE system, in addition to being exploited in the interpersonal metafunction, is also taken up in the service of the logical metafunction, providing tactic relationships of coordination and subordination, through tones 3 and 4, respectively, between information units (cf. Halliday & Greaves, 2008: 130):

> //3 ^ it's / still / *rain*ing and I'm //1 *not* going / *out*//
>
> // 4 ^ un- / *less* it / *stops* / *rain*ing I'm //1 *not* going / *out* //

Logical relations between information unit choices may interact in a variety of ways (together with clause complex structures), for example in tone concord realizing elaboration (Halliday & Matthiessen, 2004: 483):

//2 *have* you / *seen* my / *green* / ***hat*** the //2 *one* with / *two* little / ***feath***ers //

Textual meaning is the organization of meanings into coherent text that is relevant to its context, for example in the relative importance and relevance of particular meanings within an utterance. The choice of Tonic location in TONICITY and incidence of occurrence in TONALITY realize two systems of grammar in Halliday's description of English. TONICITY realizes what is termed the focus of 'New' information, in the system of INFORMATION FOCUS. Making a lexicogrammatical item focus of New, via the perceptual salience of a pitch contour, picks it out as having special status in terms of its importance in the discourse.

Everything post-New in an information unit is 'Given' information: treated by the speaker as information that can be assumed in some way, from prior discourse or with reference to something in the context. Given-New structure is thus generated by 'the tension between what is already known or predictable and what is new and unpredictable' (Halliday & Matthiessen, 2004: 89) in the discourse and its context. The unmarked choice is for the final lexical item to be focus of New, with the information prior in the information unit as either Given or New. The extent of New may be anything from the Tonic item only, up to all the information prior to it in the information unit (see Halliday & Greaves, 2008 for indices of pre-Tonic Given-New structure).

Any other choice of focus of New/Tonic is marked, as in (the 1938) Eliza's // *what* is / *wrong* with / ***that*** young / *man* // ('that', rather than 'man' is given the prominence of marked New). In another example from the 1938 performance of Pygmalion, a little further on (from around 43 minutes in the first video cited in note 1) the following exchange occurs:

> MRS. EYNSFORD HILL. I'm sure I hope it wont turn cold. There's so much influenza about. It runs right through our whole family regularly every spring.
>
> LIZA [darkly] My aunt died of influenza: so they said.

The first mention of influenza is by Mrs Eynesford Hill; Eliza, picking up on the topic, thus speaks her line as

// *My* / *aunt* / ***died*** of influ- / *enza* //

'Influenza' is here treated as Given information, being post-Tonic lexis, because of its previous mention in the discourse. This makes 'died' marked New.

Speakers are at liberty to choose as they please in INFORMATION FOCUS, and it is often used strategically in discourse. For example, earlier in the same scene (39 minutes, 44 seconds), Mrs Higgins takes Colonel Pickering aside to ask,

// *what* is the e- / *xact* po- / *si*tion in / Wimpole / Street //

'Wimpole Street' – her son's residence, where Eliza has been staying while he and Pickering give her elocution lessons – hasn't, in the film, received prior mention (although it has in the original play); making it post-Tonic Given brings the topic of her son's living arrangements with respect to Eliza into the present context as though it has (as though it is 'in the air', to use Halliday's term). In another text, this time a casual conversation,[5] after a long discussion about one interactant's physiotherapy treatment a new topic is introduced, a recent extreme hailstorm event. Despite no prior mention, it is treated as Given information in the discourse:

// *while* you're / *speak*ing of being / *tor*tured // [Pause] // *what* happened to / all – / *you* had a */ **bit** of hailstorm / *dam*age // **did**n't you //

Treating 'hailstorm damage' as Given despite having no prior mention in this discourse enables the speaker to introduce this as a 'hot' topic that is 'in the air': as though it is so talked about in the general populace at that time that it can be treated as assumed knowledge in the context, as Given. This strategic aspect is part of the textual meaning of this marked choice of INFORMATION FOCUS; as well as being an effective way of creating dramatic interest in a new conversational topic.

Systems of the textual metafunction are 'enabling' systems (cf. Matthiessen, 1995c for a discussion): they 'map' onto other choices in language, enabling meanings of the other metafunctions to be woven together into 'text' that is coherent within itself and relevant to its context. Thus, tracking choices in INFORMATION FOCUS through a text in terms of the lexicogrammatical items they map onto provides an insight into the points of focus in that text: what gets made New reveals the 'point' of a text (Martin, 1992). Halliday and Matthiessen (2004: 581) track choices of THEME and NEW through a casual conversation, showing how these choices interact in meaningful ways with choices in COHESION systems (see also Bowcher, 2004; Smith, 2008a, for perspectives on choice in INFORMATION systems).

The rate of occurrence (or of 'instantiation') of New/Tonic is also a choice which is significant to the textual meaning of discourse, in the system of INFORMATION DISTRIBUTION. For example, in the 1938 performance of Eliza's line, 'what is wrong with that, young man', as discussed earlier, the choice between the division into one or two information units is significant, not only in terms of the mapping of New onto 'man' enabled by the latter choice, but also in adding textual 'focus' onto the utterance as a whole. Varying the rate of flow of information via INFORMATION DISTRIBUTION is a crucial means of highlighting particular areas of a discourse, irrespective of the decisions in INFORMATION FOCUS thereby enabled; although the two systems are closely related and usually work together. As suggested in Section 2, a similar significance may be found at the lower rank of the foot: the assignment of textual status through Ictus to particular lexicogrammatical items, and division into feet, are also significant to the textual meaning of a text (see Smith, 2008b for a grammatical perspective on the significance of systems of the foot).

Much work remains to be done, here, and elsewhere, in applying, exploring and developing Halliday's description of intonation: as Halliday suggested in his earliest work in this area ([1963] 2005a), 'no claim is made that the description is "complete", in the sense of being exhaustive in delicacy'. In the next section we make some concluding remarks on the use of Halliday's description of intonation in linguistics.

5 Halliday's Intonation Description: Its Use, Past and Future

Considering the value of Halliday's intonation description for accounting for meaning in actual text, perhaps the most remarkable aspect of Halliday's intonation description is its (lack of) application within linguistics. Although there is a rich vein of dedicated work on intonation within the SFL tradition (cf. Greaves, 2007 for a review), systemicists have tended to omit consideration of intonational systems in their various theoretical, descriptive and applied linguistics tasks. Outside of SFL work, although Halliday's is a well-recognized name within the field of intonation study, one mostly looks in vain for work applying or exploring Halliday's description, especially within mainstream phonological study.

One explanation is disciplinarity: the divide between phonetics-phonology studies on the one hand, and grammar-discourse studies on the other, seems firmly entrenched. Those in the former community tend still to shy away from considerations of meaning in their research; while those looking at the more abstract levels of language tend to avoid the study of intonation as being the preserve of those schooled in the phonetics and phonological (i.e. 'hard'[6]) sciences. Halliday observes, in this respect (2002c: 1), 'I have never really thriven in a discipline-based structure of knowledge', but (2002c: 7) 'by nature, and also by experience . . . was (and have always remained) a generalist'. This perhaps accounts for his holistic perspective on intonation, the integration of the description of the various aspects of intonational phenomena within his general linguistic description, within the framework of systemic functional theory. From the Hallidayan perspective, intonational systems should simply be a part of linguistic analysis, description and theory, not set apart as a dedicated study nor neglected when they may be relevant within particular linguistics projects: we need to integrate intonation within the practice of linguistics as it has been by Halliday within the description of language. It is the integrative aspect that makes Halliday's intonation description such a powerful, and thus vastly under-utilized resource for the study of spoken language, within and outside of systemics and the linguistics discipline in general.

One advantage of Halliday's approach is that any work on intonation, regardless of its theoretical origin, can be related to his description (as happens in Halliday & Greaves, 2008), providing a potentially fertile field for cross-disciplinary and theoretical collaboration (see Smith, 2011 for a discussion). In fact, in his early discussion of intonation Halliday makes the point that ([1963] 2005a: 265) 'although some features are, it is believed, being described for the first time, the attempt is rather to use a particular model to shed additional light on facts already known': much of the description was already in existence; it was primarily the sense Halliday made of existing descriptions, through the integration within his theoretical framework, which was novel. Henry Sweet (1877), for example, has a section on 'Tones and Pitch' (which also praises 'Mr Bell's Elocutionary Manual' on this subject), noting (1877: 94) 'three primary "forms" or "inflections" of tones', level, rising, falling, as well as 'compound tones', falling-rising and rising-falling – the basic paradigm in Halliday's description – with some brief observations on the use of these tones, for example (Sweet, 1877: 94):

> The level tone may be heard in 'well', as an expression of musing or meditation; the rising in questions or doubtful statements; the falling in answers, commands, or dogmatic assertions.

Halliday's genius has been to 'solve the problems of synthesis' referred to in the Firth quote at the beginning of this chapter, in reference to Sweet, a pioneer in the field of intonation study, and also a model, along with other phoneticists of his generation, for Shaw's character Henry Higgins (see the Preface to Shaw, 1916 for an interesting account of Sweet's character). Halliday saw how the work of Sweet and those before and after him could be given relevance and value within a general theory of language able to account for the meanings made with intonation, in concert with other language choices, in naturally occurring discourse. His attention both to detail and the big picture has provided a resource for dealing with the complexities and, for many, the seemingly intractable difficulties of natural, spontaneous spoken dialogue.

The present authors can attest that, although, as with any study, there is a learning curve to be undertaken in learning to analyse and interpret intonational phenomena, in essence their study is no different or more difficult than any other aspect of language. This is not to say there aren't serious difficulties: for example, as Halliday points out ([2002] 2005b: 158),

[i]t is ironical . . . that now that the technology of speech recording is so good that we can eavesdrop on almost any occasion and kind of spoken discourse, we have ethics committees and privacy agencies denying us access, or preventing us from making use of what we record.[7]

Nevertheless, as the social roles of speech and writing change in the twenty-first century, the study of intonation will become more central to our study of language and discourse in general, making it imperative to address obstacles both of access and technical competence. A vast wealth of recorded spoken discourse in a variety of registers is already available online – although of course, copyright remains an obstacle in many cases. Provided one understands the (nature and value of) the multidimensional theory of language behind it, the application of Halliday's intonation description offers a potential for an enriched insight into the nature and characteristics of English, and thus into our human capacity for making meaning in and through our social semiotic interactions.

Notes

1. <http://www.youtube.com/watch?v=tmdPj_XbF30> (the line spoken by Eliza can be found at 42 minutes, 29 seconds); also available at <http://archive.org/details/Pygmalion> (the line is at 42 minutes, 20 seconds); or simply search online for the 1938 production.
2. For example, the 'QANDA' programme in Australia – <http://www.abc.net.au/tv/qanda/>
3. Upper caps initial indicates a structural term in Halliday's description.
4. Halliday's convention is to write system names in upper caps.
5. Data from the Macquarie-UTS Corpus of Australian English.
6. 'Hard' meaning 'material' rather than 'difficult'!
7. See also Henry Higgins' surreptitious recording with his (Shaw, 1916) 'concealed microphone, for unsuspecting victims'.

12 Text Linguistics

Jonathan J. Webster

Chapter Overview

---

1 Introduction

'It is part of the task of linguistics to describe texts', states Halliday ([1964] 2002: 5). What is a text? Halliday describes a text as 'a semantic concept' ([1977] 2002: 45), 'a sociological event, a semiotic encounter' ([1977] 2002: 50); it is 'the means of exchange' ([1977] 2002: 51), 'the primary channel of the transmission of culture' ([1977] 2002: 53), 'the semantic process of social dynamics' ([1977] 2002: 53). No matter how long or short, whether prose or verse, spoken or written, literary or non-literary, traditional or spontaneous, any text is the outcome of choices from the total resources available, and thus accessible to linguistic analysis which is based on a descriptive account of those resources.

Halliday concludes his study of the final two paragraphs in Darwin's *The Origin of Species* ([1859] 1998) with the following statement which sums up well his approach to text linguistics:

> What is important is that we should be able to use the same theory and method of linguistic analysis – the same 'grammatics' – whatever kind of text (or subtext) we are trying to interpret, whether Tennyson or Darwin, Mother Goose or the *Scientific American*. Otherwise, if we simply approach each text with an *ad hoc* do-it-yourself kit of private commentary, we have no way of explaining their similarities and their differences – the aesthetic and functional values that differentiate one text from another, or one voice from another within the frontiers of the same text. (Halliday, [1990] 2002: 187)

2 Origin of a Theory of the Text

Perhaps because he is a language teacher turned linguist, M. A. K. Halliday has been able to maintain a perspective on language that is grounded in how we actually use language to construe reality and enact social relationships. What began as a 'laundry card grammar' – 'being written on the beautiful white cards that laundries inserted in one's shirts in the days before washing machines took over' – eventually developed into systemic-functional linguistics, which has become the *theory of choice* (in more ways than one) for those interested in achieving an 'appliable' description leading to an understanding of the enabling power of language.

For Halliday, the underlying quest has always been about description rather than theory. He maintains that it is 'not so much new theories but new descriptions' (2005b: xxx) that will enable us to engage more effectively with language. Theory becomes pertinent only insofar as it lays the foundation for grammatical description which embraces the complexity of language.

Halliday's first published work was the paper on 'Grammatical categories in Chinese', which appeared in the *Transactions of the Philological Society* in 1956, one year after he completed his Ph.D. at Cambridge, but three years before the subsequent publication of his Ph.D. dissertation 'The Language of the Chinese "Secret History of the Mongols"'. In this paper, he put forward a scheme of grammatical categories for the description of 'Modern Pekingese formal colloquial', or as he described it, 'the type of Chinese which a foreigner learns'. The textual basis for this description came from a small corpus of spoken material, which he recorded in Peking and elsewhere. Three types of grammatical categories served as the basis for description, including units, elements and classes, with the largest unit being the 'sentence', and the lower limit of grammatical description being the character, as the unit of word structure. As Halliday states,

'The Chinese language works, and the task of the descriptive linguist is to show how it works' ([1956] 2005a: 240).

When asked to compare his own approach with those of other linguists who helped shape not only his own thinking but also the discipline of linguistics as a whole, Halliday notes Firth's interest in varieties of a language, Hjelmslev's focus on language as a whole and Jakobson's search for universals across all languages. Halliday's early work with what he called 'New Chinese' or Modern Pekingese builds on and extends the general linguistic principles established by these scholars. As he indicates, however, it was a struggle to fit the frameworks which were then available with what he actually encountered in Chinese and later English. Such inadequacies in previous grammatical descriptions provided the motivation for Halliday to construct his 'own mapping, or projection, of the design and traffic flow of language' (2005b: xxvi). It was something he entered into, however, as he puts it, 'with many misgivings, because I never thought of myself as being a theorist' (2005b: xxvi).

3 Systemic Functional Theory[1]

Language, like other semiotic systems, is a systemic resource for making and exchanging meaning. Language is a particular kind of semiotic system which is based on grammar, characterized by both a stratal organization and functional diversity. Both this stratal organization and metafunctional diversity in language combine to form what M. A. K. Halliday refers to as a semiotic of higher-order consciousness, the basis for the human activity of meaning.

Linguistics is the study of language. The linguist's data comes from the observation of language events, language in use, i.e. the text, which may be spoken or written. The linguist's description of language at work must be grounded in a theory of how language works, i.e. general linguistic theory, providing both a theory of grammar and a theory of lexis. Grammar is what powers language, it is where the work is done. If linguistics is the study of language, then the study of grammar may be referred to as grammatics.

4 System in Language

Whereas *structure* involves the ordered arrangement of elements in a chain (place-ordered) relation, i.e. syntagmatic relations, the notion of *system* describes those features which are contrastive in a given functional environment (Halliday, [1966] 2002), i.e. paradigmatic relations.

Language is not only a semiotic system, it is also a semantic system, i.e. a system of meaning. What distinguishes language as a semantic system from other semiotic systems is the fact that it is founded on grammar. The semantic system is one of three levels, or strata, which together comprise the whole linguistic system. Below the semantic system is the lexicogrammar, and below the lexicogrammar is the phonological realization.

The semantic system incorporates a small number of discrete clusters of systems with 'very dense internal connections but relatively sparse connections with the rest of the grammar' (2005b: xx–xxi). These clusters correspond to the ideational (logical and experiential), interpersonal and textual components or 'metafunctions'. A clause is the complex realization of options from the three metafunctional components, or 'blocks' of options, each operating in parallel with the other two.

Each metafunctional component produces its own distinct dimension of structure. Experiential and logical meaning are included under ideational meaning. Logical meaning concerns the ability to make explicit certain fundamental logical relations such as 'and', 'or', 'if' and 'not'. Experiential meaning, i.e. the 'construing experience' function, is realized structurally by the configuration of process, participant(s), circumstance(s), i.e. transitivity structure; interpersonal meaning, i.e. the 'enacting social relationships' function, by mood and modality; and textual meaning, i.e. the 'creating discourse' function by theme and information structures.

The grammar of a language is thus represented in terms of features defined as terms in systems, with interrelated systems represented in the form of a system network, specifying the total systemic potential in terms of contrasting features and possible paths through the network. Each possible path through the network describes a class of linguistic items. In other words, 'class is a statement of potential: if you are a nominal group, you may function either as Subject or Complement within the clause, and you may select for NUMBER: singular/plural' (2005b: xvii). The specific role which each element of structure plays is its meaning, and may be stated in terms of a selection expression, or, in other words, 'the set of features that delineate its path through the network' (2005b: xix).

The point of origin into the system network is the clause. Halliday writes, 'It was clear to me already, when I taught my first Chinese class on 13 May 1945, that the clause was the centre of action in the grammar' (2005b: xv). It was 'the place, or the locus, where fundamental choices of meaning, were made' (2005b: xv). The clause as most basic lexicogrammatical unit creates and gives meaning to the text of which it is a constituent. But there is more to this relationship than constituency alone. Not only is the clause a constituent of the text, it is also the actualization of the text, inheriting properties from the text-as-model which is itself realized in relation to the context of situation.

The difference between a text and a clause is that a text is a semantic entity, i.e. a construct of meaning, whereas a clause is a lexicogrammatical entity, i.e.

a construct of wording. A text is an intersubjective event, in which speaker and listener exchange meaning in a context of situation. By means of my 'text', I participate in an act of interpersonal exchange, communicating my sense of my own identity, my world view, my interpretation of experience.

Language in use, i.e. text, is the instantiation of an indefinitely large meaning potential. Each text is an act of meaning which simultaneously construes experience and enacts social relationships. Acts of meaning are the linguistic instances of the linguistic system of meaning potential, which occur in context of situation. Context of situation is specified with respect to field, tenor and mode. The investigation of context of situation focuses on three main dimensions: (a) field – what is happening? (b) tenor – who is involved? (c) mode – how is it taking place? Likewise when analysing the text/utterance, we pose similar questions: what is happening? who is involved? how is it taking place? Corresponding to each question is a component of meaning or semantic metafunction: experiential, interpersonal and textual; and corresponding to each metafunctional component is a distinct dimension of structure.

In summary, the nature of the activity – *field* – is a determining factor in the selection of options from experiential systems, including choices related to transitivity structure, including process, participant, circumstance. Role relationships – *tenor* – have a hand in determining the selection of interpersonal options, such as those from the systems of mood and modality. The symbolic organization of the text – *mode* – is involved in the selection of options in *textual* systems, which relate to the overall texture of the text, including choices involving cohesion, and thematic and information structures.

5 Ideational Meaning

We talk about our experience of the world in terms of processes, plus the participants and circumstances that enter into them. Halliday uses the term *transitivity* to refer to all those features of the clause that contribute to the speaker's linguistic representation of process as an integrated phenomenon involving participants and circumstances.

Halliday uses the term 'process' for those words which are, grammatically speaking, typically verbs, and which describe 'happenings', i.e. events or actions (e.g. *Ted's flight **arrived** early; Tom **bought** the tickets at the reception desk*), states (mental or otherwise) or other abstract relations (e.g. *I **feel** fine; Mary **is** tall; Mary **is** the tallest girl at her school*), both in the world around us and within our own consciousness. Processes do not occur in isolation but also include (may even require) mention of participants (e.g. *Ted's flight, Tom, the tickets, Mary, the tallest girl in the class*) and circumstances (e.g. *early, at the reception desk, at her school*).

Corresponding to the different process types – material, mental, relational, verbal, etc. – are different role designations. While it is reasonable to talk about participating entities such as Actor and Goal in a material process (or Agent and Affected if analysed according to an ergative interpretation), it would not be sensible to use the same role labels for participants in a relational process, in which one is describing the attributes of some entity.

6 Interpersonal Meaning

Grammar is a resource not only for talking about our experience of the world around us and what is going on inside us, but also for communicating our attitudes towards and expectations of those with whom we are interacting. This 'interactive' dimension of language is referred to by Halliday as the interpersonal metafunction or component of language. The interpersonal metafunction deals with our use of language to relate to our listeners. When we communicate we deliver more than just content or information, we also communicate our role vis-à-vis our partners in the exchange.

In any exchange, there is give and take. When we ask a question – *Is it raining?* – we anticipate an answer. If our communication is successfully comprehended by our listener(s), then they will know what we expect of them, and, depending on their ability and willingness, provide us with the information we have requested. If we want someone to do something for us – *Please turn up the volume on the television* – then we need to use a suitable grammatical pattern for this purpose, and again hopefully elicit our desired response.

Language functions to facilitate exchange, both of information and goods-and-services. The interpersonal function of language addresses this issue of how we communicate our respective roles in this exchange. In English, the interpersonal function is realized in terms of choices involving declarative, interrogative and imperative clause types, or moods. The declarative typically expresses a statement – typically giving information; interrogative expresses a question – typically asking for information; imperative expresses a directive; exclamative an exclamation. Such choices are realized structurally by what Halliday refers to as mood-residue structure. *Mood* consists of the elements Subject and Finite. *Residue* consists of Predicator, and possibly Complement and Adjunct.

In English, it is the Mood element – consisting of the Subject and Finite – which indicates whether the clause is a statement or a question, whether the speaker is giving or asking for information. The sequence of Subject before Finite realizes a declarative; Finite before Subject realizes a yes/no interrogative. Indeed, the relationship between mood and illocutionary act is not one-to-one but instead many-to-many. While a declarative typically expresses a statement intended to give information, it may also function to make a request of the listener. For example, the statement, 'it sure is cold here' could in fact be a request to someone to turn off the air-conditioner. To understand the speaker's intended meaning, the situation context and the linguistic co-text are essential.

Modality is another aspect of interpersonal meaning related to the expression of the speaker's attitude about what he is saying. In English, modality is expressed by the use of modal adjuncts (possibly by certain adverbs like 'surely', 'possibly', or by various thematic structures such as 'it is possible that', 'there is a possibility that'), or through a small set of verbs known as modal auxiliaries, e.g. 'can', 'may', 'might', etc.

Intonation also plays a significant role in expressing what Halliday calls the 'key' or 'the particular tone of assertion, query, hesitation, doubt, reservation, forcefulness, wonderment, or whatever it is, with which the speaker tags the proposition' ([1979] 2002: 205). Intonation is described as 'a melodic line mapped on to the clause as a whole, running through from beginning to end' ([1979] 2002: 205).

7 Textual Meaning

Texture is what makes a text into a coherent piece of language, as opposed to simply being an unorganized string of sentences. One aspect of texture is cohesion, which deals with how successive sentences are integrated to form a whole, i.e. inter-sentence texture. The other aspect of texture has to do with fit to context, or those choices based on what the speaker wants to say (Theme), and those choices related to the flow of information (Given-New), i.e. intra-sentence texture.

Besides cohesion, texture is contributed by both information and thematic structures, both of which deal with the fit of the message to context. The organization of the message to fit the context comprises two aspects: one aspect, which Halliday refers to as the 'hearer angle', relates to the organization of the message so that it ties up with the preceding text, with that which the hearer has already heard about, i.e. the Given; the second aspect, the 'speaker angle', relates to how the message is organized around what the speaker wants to say, or what Halliday calls 'Theme'.

Each clause is a proposition which contributes new information to the text as a whole. Unlike Given information which is recoverable from the preceding text or the immediate context of situation, New information is not recoverable. Together, Given plus New information constitute information structure.

New information has a phonological realization in that it typically culminates in an element with tonic prominence called the *Focus*. Owing to this connection between tone group and information unit, analysis for information structure has been largely confined to investigations of spoken discourse, not written texts. However, as Halliday (1985: 315–16) explains, information structure is also relevant to the analysis of written texts: 'In writing, the principle is that (i) the information unit is a clause, unless some other unit is clearly designated by the punctuation; and (ii) the focus falls at the end of the unit, unless some positive signal to the contrary is given, either by lexical cohesion (no focus on repeated word) or by grammatical structure (predication: it is . . . that . . .).' One identifies the boundary between Given and New in written texts much the same way one does in spoken discourse – the Given refers to something recoverable or locatable in the text or the context of situation.

This distinction between Given and New information is but one consideration on the part of the speaker when it comes to deciding how best to convey the message in a particular linguistic and situational context. While what occurs at the end of the clause is typically the new and noteworthy information, the choice of what comes first is significant for reasons independent of this distinction between Given and New.

Theme is the speaker's choice for how to begin the clause. The speaker's choice for the point of departure may be related to textual, interpersonal or experiential meaning, or even a combination of meanings. As the writer/speaker launches into a new clause or message unit, he may include in his point of departure some grammatical device to link what he is about to say with what was previously said, i.e. textual meaning; and/or include something which communicates on an interpersonal level. But above all, the writer/speaker will provide an ideational/topical point of reference for the clause contents which follow.

8 Language as a Stratified, Multifunctional System

Language is a stratified system, which encompasses three strata: meaning (semantics), wording (lexicogrammar) and phonological realization (phonology). The three strata are interdependent. The interface between them is modelled as a system network of choice points, representing the meaning potential found in language. The product of multiple choices from this network is a text, an act of meaning.

The entry point to the semantic system is the text, which may be spoken or written, comprising just a single utterance (e.g. 'Help!') or many. A text is a semantic unit, consisting of clauses which begin with thematic prominence, and end in a peak of prominence – a tonic accent – related to information focus. Such periodicity is reinforced at clause boundaries by conjunctives which relate clauses cohesively to one another.

The entry point to the grammar is the clause, the most basic lexicogrammatical unit. The clause is the complex structural realization of ideational (experiential and logical), interpersonal and textual meanings. Corresponding to each kind of meaning – i.e. each metafunction – is a particular structural configuration. Experiential meaning may be accounted for by the configuration of process, participant and circumstance, or what Halliday calls 'transitivity structure'; interpersonal meaning by the configuration of mood-residue; textual meaning by theme-rheme.

The entry point to the phonological system is the tone group which extends across a continuous stretch of discourse, communicating the 'key' – 'the particular tone of assertion, query, hesitation, doubt, reservation, forcefulness, wonderment, or whatever it is, with which the speaker tags the proposition' ([1979] 2002: 205). Its realization – 'a melodic line mapped on to the clause as a whole, running through from beginning to end' ([1979] 2002: 205) – is 'prosodic'.

9 Halliday on Literary Texts

Much of Halliday's work in the area of text linguistics is included in the second volume of his collected works under the title: *Linguistic Studies of Text and Discourse.* The works included in *Linguistic Studies of Text and Discourse* illustrate text analysis of highly valued literary texts as well as everyday texts, including both spoken and written.

In his discussion of the linguistic study of literature, or 'linguistic stylistics', Halliday emphasizes that such 'is no different from any other textual description; it is not a new branch or a new level or a new kind of linguistics but the application of existing theories and methods' ([1964] 2002: 16). Halliday defines 'linguistics stylistics' as 'the description of literary texts, by methods derived from general linguistic theory, using the categories of the description of the language as a whole; and the comparison of each text with others, by the same and by different authors, in the same and in different genres' ([1964] 2002: 6).

On the role of linguistics in literary analysis, Halliday concludes,

> Linguistics is not and never will be the whole of literary analysis, and only the literary analyst – not the linguist – can determine the place of linguistics in literary studies. But if a text is to be described at all, then it should be described properly; and this means by the theories and methods developed in linguistics, the subject whose task is precisely to show how language works. The literary analyst is not content with amateur psychology, armchair philosophy, or fictitious social history; yet the linguistics that is applied in some accounts of literature, and the statements about language that are used as evidence, are no less amateur, armchair and fictitious. It is encouraging that literary scholars are coming more and more to reject such statements, and to demand a standard of objective linguistic scholarship that is no less rigorous than the standard of literary scholarship which they expect, and exact, from themselves. (Halliday, [1964] 2002: 19–20)

Among the 'highly valued texts' examined by Halliday are the works of the novelist, William Golding, whose prose offers 'a particular way of looking at experience' ([1971] 2002: 106); J. B. Priestley, the dramatist, who creates a world of meaning through dialogue ([1982] 2002); Alfred Lord Tennyson, whose poetry constructs 'a semiotic universe at the intersection of science and poetry' ([1987] 2002: 167); and Charles Darwin, the scientist, whose 450 pages of intense scientific argument has a unique place in the history of ideas ([1990] 2002).

What stands out in Golding's *The Inheritors* are selections in transitivity, 'the cornerstone of the semantic organization of experience' ([1971] 2002: 119) – see the discussion of transitivity in the section on 'Ideational meaning' above. In J. B. Priestley *An Inspector Calls*, the time theme is 'a motif that permeates the interaction of the participants, and is more or less covertly woven in to the dialogue' ([1982] 2002: 129). Once the dramatist stops 'defining the nature of the world' ([1982] 2002: 130) and starts 'implying his world rather than presenting it' ([1982] 2002: 131), the language is likely to become 'deautomatized'. Halliday prefers Mukařovský's term 'de-automatization' to 'foregrounding' 'since what is in question is not simply prominence but rather the partial freeing of the lower-level systems from the control of the semantics so that they become domains of choice in their own right' ([1982] 2002: 131). To 'deautomatize' means to 'try to interpret the grammar in terms that go beyond its direct realizational function' ([1982] 2002: 139); 'to focus out the background, and let the words and structures speak for themselves' ([1982] 2002: 139). In *An Inspector Calls* the complex interrelationship of themes related to obligation, personality and time are built from semantic systems of time, mood and polarity.

From his analysis of the final two paragraphs of Darwin's *The Origin of Species*, Halliday shows how 'the clauses are rather clearly organized, through their textual functions of Theme (in Theme-Rheme) and New (in Given-New), around a small number of distinct but interlocking motifs' ([1990] 2002: 184) culminating in a resounding lexicogrammatical cadence that 'brings the clause, the sentence, the paragraph, the chapter and the book to a crashing conclusion with a momentum to which I [Halliday] can think of no parallel elsewhere in literature – perhaps only Beethoven has produced comparable effects, and that in another medium altogether' ([1990] 2002: 185).

The grammar of Tennyson's *In Memoriam* is that of spoken rather than written language, as evidenced in the clause complexes and in the transitivity patterns. In particular, Halliday points to the dynamic, choreographic nature of the clause complexes: 'you cannot foresee the ending from the beginning, nor recover the beginning by looking at the end . . . So, for example, if we chart the passage from *So careful of the type she seems* to *and (I) faintly trust the larger hope,* we see how many and various are the steps that have been taken in between, each moving off from the point where the last one landed' ([1987] 2002: 160).

Another feature of the clause complexes is the occurrence of long paratactic chains launched by an initial hypotaxis. and as Halliday points out, 'in each case the hypotaxis undermines the whole effect, giving the entire sequence the status of a lost cause. "We trust that (all this will happen – but we know it won't)"; "Nature seems such that (I lose faith)"; "shall man (though he trusted) end up as dust and fossil?". . . .' ([1987] 2002: 160).

Examples from the text with their corresponding logical analysis are shown below. Here, I have converted Halliday's formulaic representation of logical structure into the more graphical format shown below. Hypotaxis is indicated by

<c 1a> OH yet we trust <c 1b> that somehow good
Will be the final goal of ill,
To pangs of nature, sins of will,
Defects of doubt, and taints of blood;

<c 1c> That nothing walks with aimless feet;
<c 1d> That not one life shall be destroy'd,
<c 1e> Or cast as rubbish to the void,
<c 1f> When God hath made the pile complete;

<c 1g> That not a worm is cloven in vain;
<c 1h> That not a moth with vain desire
Is shrivel'd in a fruitless fire,
<c 1i> Or but subserves another's gain.

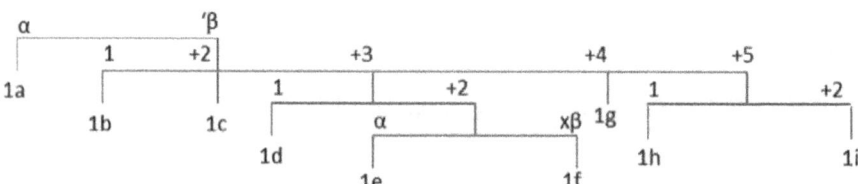

<c 6a> So careful of the type she seems,
<c 6b> So careless of the single life;

<c 6c> That I, <c 6d> considering everywhere
Her secret meaning in her deeds,
<c 6e> And finding <c 6f> that of fifty seeds
She often brings but one to bear;

<c 6c> I falter <c 6g> where I firmly trod,
<c 6h> And falling with my weight of cares
Upon the great world's altar-stairs
<c 6i>That slope thro' darkness up to God;

<c 6j> I stretch lame hands of faith, <c 6k> and grope,
<c 6l> And gather dust and chaff, <c 6m> and call

To what I feel is Lord of all,
<c 6n> And faintly trust the larger hope.

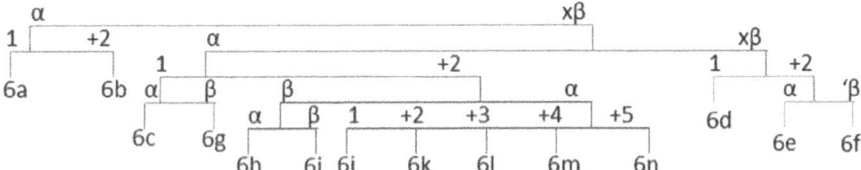

<c 12a> Man, her last work, <c 12b> who seem'd so fair,
<c 12c> Such splendid purpose in his eyes,
<c 12d> Who roll'd the psalm to wintry skies,
<c 12e> Who built him fanes of fruitless prayer,

<c 12f> Who trusted <c 12g> God was love indeed
<c 12h> And love Creation's final law –
<c 12i> Tho' Nature, <c 12j> red in tooth and claw
With ravine, <c 12i> shriek'd against his creed –

<c 12k> Who loved, <c 12l> who suffer'd countless ills,
<c 12m> Who battled for the True, the Just,
<c 12a> Be blown about the desert dust,
<c 12n> Or seal'd within the iron hills?

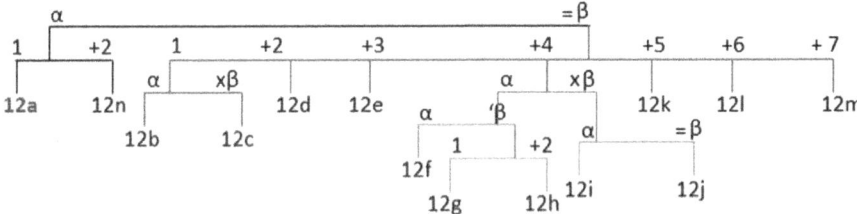

10 Everyday Texts

Halliday's paper 'Some lexicogrammatical features of the *Zero Population Growth* text' first appeared in 1991 in a collection of papers showing different analytical approaches applied by various authors to the same text, the ZPG text, which is an instance of a fund-raising letter. What Halliday refers to as only a 'partial interpretation' ([1992] 2002b: 197) covers theme; information structure; mood and modality; transitivity; clause complexes; lexical cohesion; nominalization and grammatical metaphor. Halliday notes how 'The thematic movement of the text clearly bears out Fries' interpretation of clause Theme in terms of the rhetorical concept of "method of development" (Fries, 1981)' ([1992] 2002b: 202). Based on the tonics of the text arrived at through reading the text aloud, Halliday attempts to establish the information structure emerging from the text. Looking next at mood and modality, including the writer's use of tense, and mood type – whether declarative or imperative, Halliday notes the single modalization occurring in the text, i.e. *may be*, and observes how this expression of probability 'has added a feature of tentativeness to the argument that your support now is critical (this may be our best opportunity, but it is important not to be too definite about that because we may want to ask for your support again later on)' ([1992] 2002b: 206). Halliday's strategy for exploring the ZPG letter writer's use of grammatical metaphor is particularly noteworthy. To arrive at a more congruent form of the text, he reworded the text along the lines of 'how would I say this to a 12-year-old?' describing it as 'an intuitive venture at making the text more accessible' ([1992] 2002b: 225). His rewording of the text helps to bring out the writer's use of clichés, ambiguities and grammatical metaphors.

A dissertation defense provides the context for the approximately 12.5 minutes of spoken text analysed in 'So you say "pass" . . . thank you three muchly' ([1994] 2002). This subtext begins with one of the speakers saying, 'So you say "pass"', and ends with the same speaker's closing, 'thank you three muchly'. Halliday presents 'a clause-by-clause analysis of the subtext in terms of the systems of theme, information, transitivity, mood, modality and key; and an analysis of each clause complex by interdependency and expansion/projection' ([1994] 2002: 232–3). He describes the dissertation defence as 'a lexicogrammatical event', one which exemplifies 'the power of discourse to change the environment that engendered it' ([1994] 2002: 254). Or as Halliday explains further: 'We might want to think of the entire text as a kind of expanded performative: "We dub thee Ph.D." But this would obscure a more fundamental point, which is that **every** text is performative in this sense. There can be no semiotic act that leaves the world exactly as it was before' ([1994] 2002: 254).

11 Conclusion

All texts are meaningful; each an instance formed from the total network of meaning potential; each accessible through the categories of the description of the language as a whole. Halliday's contribution, as a grammarian, has been to show how the grammar works to create meaning, providing the grounding for a linguistically sophisticated interpretation of the text under investigation.

Note

1. For further discussion on this topic, see Webster's entry on "Systemic Functional Theory", in Wiley-Blackwell's forthcoming International Encyclopedia of Language and Social Interaction (edited by Cornelia Ilie)

13 Halliday as an International Educator

Geoff Williams

To explore Halliday's contribution to language education, and taking account particularly of his wish to develop an *appliable linguistics*, I will take as a point-of-departure a specific, practical educational situation. Imagine the perspective of a teacher of young children, early in her career and working in an inner-urban school, in which English is the medium of instruction. Given the context of the school it is likely that the children come from a range of mother-tongue language backgrounds and a range of family social positioning. What key insights about education, specifically education in schools, might Halliday's work offer this teacher as she plans for the students' learning?

From the perspective of theoretical linguistics, this question seems oblique to Halliday's major interests because his intellectual focus has been the development of an expansive and descriptively detailed theoretical model of language. However, an interest in education has been sustained throughout most of his research career, from his early dialogues with Basil Bernstein about the role of language in social reproduction and transmission, through the Schools Council projects in the United Kingdom, the Australian Language Development Project (in which he became involved soon after taking up an appointment in that country) and through major engagement with educators on policy questions in Asia and Latin America. The influence of his work on education is so far most evident in countries in which English is the medium of instruction, but during the next two decades this influence will almost certainly expand in Putonghua- and Spanish-medium educational contexts, among others.

Here, rather than recounting his contribution to language education, I will focus on a sample of key educational concepts that he has introduced, ways in which these have substantially influenced practice, and their potential for further research and curriculum development. To develop the last point, I will focus specifically on a paper published in 1993, 'Towards a language-based theory of learning'. It is a paper that has often been cited as highly innovative but, so far, it has not been extensively utilized to produce research. So, as seems appropriate to the nature of Halliday's contribution, the purpose of the final movement of the paper is to open up prospects for new research by considering a small example based on one of his major interests and some of his specific suggestions.

With what concepts in Halliday's extensive body of work, then, should our example teacher begin? Because it informs literally everything Halliday has proposed about education, she should begin with the general concept on which his ideas about language, both as system and as instance, are based: that is the concept of language as social semiotic (Halliday, 1978), i.e. language is a *socially situated, meaning-making resource*. Such a suggestion for the starting point seems somewhat remote from the more immediate, urgent world of children wanting to know how to read, whether or not caregivers will be at school later to pick them up, and so on. But language as social semiotic has to be the orienting idea because it yields the further basic principle for what Halliday believes all education should be about: it should develop students' *meaning potential*. Expressed so, perhaps it appears to be not much more than a simple heuristic, analogous to something like 'developing students' full potential' or some such aphorism common in educational policy documents. What makes it qualitatively different is the next step: that 'meaning potential' is a technical concept embedded in a theory and description of language. These theoretical and descriptive resources have been designed specifically to assist teachers with the practical questions about learning that they face every day. So it is 'meaning potential', foregrounded against the background of 'language as social semiotic', that provides the basis for this overview. The theoretical complexity and descriptive range of Halliday's work has sometimes been seen as a reason for not asking teachers to engage with it. That has seemed to me to be an odd idea, not one that would be expected in other critically important fields of social practice that are basic to a civil society – primary healthcare, for example. Are the questions faced daily in the general practice of medicine really more complex than the questions faced daily by teachers in early childhood education?

In what senses, then, does Halliday use 'meaning potential' to inform work in educational contexts?[1] Foremost, he uses it to characterize language itself: language from this perspective is a

semantic potential. It is a range of possible meanings; together with the means whereby these meanings are realized, or expressed. (Halliday, 1975: 8)

Then, in a more specific sense, 'meaning potential' refers to what can be meant legitimately in some context of situation: 'legitimately' in the sense of capable of being understood as realizing meanings in that specific context. From this perspective a register is a 'meaning potential': the register is in operation so long as meanings habitually associated with the specific context within the institution are 'in play'. If meanings extraneous to the register are introduced then either the context will change or there will be some action to restore the context (often very subtle action, requiring minimal verbal intervention). Young children start-ing school have a lot of learning of this kind to do in order to become competent participants in the institution: from learning ways to interact linguistically in the playground with potential friends, to how to mean in school-appropriate ways when talking about written language (using such specialized terms as 'letter', 'sound', 'name of the letter') and so on. As they move through school they are introduced to a large number of new meaning potentials, new registers of school knowledge. These are, most typically, the privileged institutional meanings that are, in turn, privileging, to slightly paraphrase terms first introduced by Halliday's colleague, Basil Bernstein. (Bernstein's original terms were privileg-ing and privileged *'text'* (Bernstein, 1990: 172–8). Students are obviously not all equally well-placed to develop these registers, which is a very complex fact that will be obvious to our example teacher even before she has completed the first morning with her new class, and one that will preoccupy her, as a conscientious professional, for the rest of her career. I return to this key fact later in the chap-ter when discussing Halliday's linguistic dialogue with Bernstein's sociology. In overview, school learning can be usefully characterized as learning how to par-ticipate in institutionally required registers, both those that are primarily about 'content' and those that are primarily about 'relationships'.

Speaking in this way about meaning potential, however, is still to operate at a general conceptual level, sketching broad outlines in a map which looks more like the work of Eratosthenes (third century BCE) than that of a contem-porary digitally resourced cartographer. This is, in many ways, precisely the point of much of Halliday's contribution. It enables engagement with the detail of the registerial landscape. His theoretical and descriptive resources to char-acterize language from the perspective of meaning-making enable teachers to shift the scale of their thinking and planning from intelligent impressions about registers far down into the details of the meaning contours that are crucial to understanding how registers function in their contexts. It is the 'making visi-ble' of these contours to increase their accessibility to a larger range of students that has been central to Halliday's contribution, and subsequently to the work of many other SFL linguists (for example: Martin, 2012; Martin and Rose, 2003; Schleppegrell, 2004).

There is a closely associated third sense of 'meaning potential', dependent upon the two prior ones but equally educationally significant in its own right. This is the sense of 'what a particular person can mean': what the person can do semiotically in a range of contexts (using the technical, SFL sense of context). The personal sense of meaning potential is, of course, closely linked to the insti-tutional one but it is not equivalent and the difference is material to understand-ing Halliday's vision for education. This more personal sense is well-captured by the title of his major work on child language development: *Learning How to Mean* (Halliday, 1975). Learning is expanding a person's meaning potential: that is, achieving both the ability to mean in more expanded ways within familiar contexts and registers, and learning how to mean across an expanding range of contexts and registers.

The two processes of expansion are clearly visible in the language development of a child before about 18 months, which was the focus of the study reported in *Learning How to Mean*. Since Jane Torr discusses this work elsewhere in this volume, I cite it only briefly here to exemplify what Halliday means by expanding a person's meaning potential. (For detailed discussion of protolanguage, see Chapter 9.) Protolanguage comprises a small set of very general 'microfunctions', resources for making meanings in small regions of local experience in the family, for example, to satisfy immediate needs for food and cleansing; to interact with people; to find out about experience and so on. In principle, the meaning potential of each of these microfunctions could be expanded indefinitely by adding further features to the initial small systems the child has evolved. For example, at age 0:9–0:10.5 Nigel, the subject of Halliday's study, had developed just two features in his regulatory microfunction, his meaning resources for controlling the behaviour of other people. These were a [command: normal], glossed as 'do that again' and a [command: intensified], glossed as 'do that right now!' That is all he could do to regulate the behaviour of others at this age. However, after just 12 weeks, i.e. between 1;0 and 1;1.5 months, the regulatory microfunction had expanded considerably to include specific commands such as [go for a walk] and [play with cat], together with a new distinction between [initiation] and [response]. Additionally, between 1;0 and 1;1.5 months a whole new microfunction evolved, with major significance for the child's subsequent linguistic development. This was the imaginative microfunction, which comprised a small system of either pretending to go to sleep or pretending to sing a song. In turn, the imaginative microfunction expanded in a similar way over the next few months by evolving further differentiations and by adding new features to the existing ones. Halliday summarizes these processes in this way:

> First, children . . . can refine further the meanings they have already built up, introducing more delicate distinctions within the same topological region. Second, they can extend their meaning potential into new semantic domains, areas of experience or forms of interpersonal relationships that were not previously accessible. . . . The third strategy is really the intersection of these two, which is why it is a very powerful way of expanding a semiotic system; this is the strategy of dissociating associated variables, or deconstructing and recombining, like demanding iced coffee when the alternatives offered are hot coffee and iced tea. (1993: 101)

Sometimes all three processes can operate together, particularly when a child asks questions that bring together previously discrete elements of existing knowledge. For example, I recently heard a 5-year-old, who was reflecting on larva while eating his breakfast, ask the following questions in rapid succession: 'Is larva the hottest thing in the world?' to 'Is larva hotter than the Sun?' to 'So does the Sun heat the Earth and all the heat goes into the middle and makes the larva really hot?'. As can be imagined, the final question resulted in quite an extensive dissociation and recombining of previously associated variables!

While all three semogenic processes are observable in protolanguage, this phase is really the tip of the semogenic iceberg. It is when children begin to use their mother tongue, including crucially the new stratum of lexicogrammar, that the processes begin to make a much richer, more far-reaching contribution to development. Lexicogrammar is crucial to semogenic processes because it provides the means for *indefinite expansion of meaning potential*:

> The grammar opens the way to naming and reference, and hence can function as a theory of human experience. It allows for an ongoing exchange of roles between speaker and listener, and hence can function as the enactment of human relationships. It makes it possible to create discourse (text that is operational in its environment), and hence brings into being the commodity we call 'information.' It opens up a universe of meaning, a multidimensional semantic space that can be indefinitely expanded and projected. In other words, the grammar brings into being a semiotic that has unlimited potential for learning with. (Halliday, 1993: 97)

To foreshadow later discussion, Halliday's finding about the semogenetic significance of lexicogrammar raises an important educational question: what contribution, if any, might learners' *explicit* knowledge of 'grammar' make to these semogenic processes? That is, might metaknowledge of 'grammar' make a positive difference to semogenesis in schooling? While there are important differences between conditions for the initial development of lexicogrammar and those for explicit grammatical knowledge, from a semogenetic perspective there might also be some important commonalities. This is an issue to which I return in the last phase of the chapter.

Looking back over Halliday's contribution to educational thought, Gordon Wells suggests that it was his developmental studies of language and learning 'that ha[ve] probably had the greatest long-term educational impact through [their] influence on the thinking of teachers and teacher educators (1994: 43)'. (Wells made this comment about Vygotsky's work, too, while exploring relations between Halliday's and Vygotsky's theories.) His view is widely shared for at least three reasons.

First, the suggestion that *meaning* exchanged in social interaction is the basis for language development accords readily with the experience of educational professionals. They understand from daily practice that deep learning always has to be about meaning-making, so a theory of language development that situates meaning at the centre of the developmental process is a major professional resource. The proposal that language development itself could actually be led by meaning-making was simultaneously both intuitively familiar and institutionally radical in the educational contexts of the 1970s. Perhaps it appeared most radical in contexts for teaching of English as a second language. For an influential uptake of the ideas in the ESL field, see Mohan (1986).

Second, in Halliday's theory and research, meaning is understood in a richly nuanced way. It is modelled metafunctionally, which is to say that meaning-making is always considered from four simultaneous perspectives. 'Meaning' involves not only the familiar idea of language as representation of experience (the language of 'reflection' in Halliday's terms), but meaning from an interpersonal perspective, i.e. meanings that sustain interaction (the 'doing' meanings in Halliday's terms), together with textual meaning, i.e. resources for organizing information flow and making texts coherent, and logical meaning, i.e. meanings such as cause and effect, conditionality, adversitiveness and so on. These features are discussed in detail elsewhere in this volume so I merely note them here to emphasize the point that Halliday's work on language development was often taken up by teachers and teacher educators precisely because it focused on *meaning*, and because meaning was presented as multifaceted in a way that made sense in teachers' practical work contexts. His emphasis on the developmental significance of interpersonal meaning, consistent with his theoretical orientation to language as *social* semiotic, has been particularly important to educators. (For further comment on the significance of interpersonal exchange of information on the development of lexicogrammar, see Halliday, [2004] 2013, and for a sustained discussion of the 'interpersonal first' principle in language development, with implications for education, see Painter, 2004.)

Third, teachers know clearly that language is in some sense *the* basis on which learning is established, and that language affects all aspects of learning. Halliday extends this intuition to argue that, as well as language 'affecting' learning in various ways, in learning a mother tongue children simultaneously also learn the *process of learning* itself. That is, language is the resource through which children initially learn to learn. In the opening words of 'Towards a language-based theory of learning':

> When children learn language, they are not simply engaging in one kind of learning among many; rather, they are learning the foundation of learning itself. The distinctive characteristic of human learning is that it is a process of making meaning – a semiotic process; and the prototypical form of human semiotic is language. Hence the ontogenesis of language is at the same time the ontogenesis of learning. (1993: 5)

In overview, learning understood in terms of meaning development has proved a valuable and popular general perspective for educators. But learning understood as the development of *meaning potential*, with meaning potential in turn defined in terms of register and language as a meaning-making social system, is a much greater step, and one that has not been so widely taken in education. In the rest of this chapter I will discuss examples of work that has moved in this direction. Since Halliday's contribution to education has been so extensive and multi-faceted, resulting in work across many sub-fields, it has been necessary to select just a few of those examples. (Even volume 9 of Halliday's *Collected Works, Language and Education*, represents a fraction of his overall contribution.) In the following discussion I explore his work on language, education and social class; literacy development; spoken and written language, grammatical metaphor and education, and finally implications for research from his call for a 'language-based theory of learning' (1993).

These topics have been selected to exemplify work in the three regions of language education that Halliday first proposed in 1979: learning language, learning through language and learning about language. It is a sign of his influence on education that these distinctions have become so widely used in language education that their origin is rarely cited.[2] From the standpoint of the second decade of the twenty-first century, these regions might seem to a young teacher as distant from current discussion of multiliteracies and multimodality. And it is true that Halliday's attention to education has been exclusively focused on *language* development. In Halliday's thinking, consistently from his first research engagements with education at the beginning of the 1960s throughout his career, it is language that is foregrounded. But that choice is not merely a matter of personal or academic interest.

In his view, configurations of language features are the *primary* resources for meaning-making in social contexts and therefore for knowing. Recognizing these language configurations and understanding how they are formed is therefore critically important for learning. Of course, other semiotic modes contribute to education significantly (and usually more visibly) than language, and often other modes provide more accessible ways than technical language into complex fields. The potential for description of these semiotic modes is being interestingly explored by scholars using principles derived from Halliday's theory. (See, for example, the work of Unsworth, 2008a, 2008b; Painter, Martin and Unsworth, 2013 among many others.) However, for Halliday himself language is the focus of theoretical and research interest because it is the *primary* resource for learning. In a key paper on educational linguistics he comments:

'. . . it may be helpful to think of a single, multi-level construction process, in which the language – that is, the semantic system – **is** the representation of experience in the form of knowledge. In this perspective, language is not the means of knowing; it is the form taken by knowledge itself. Language is not **how we know** something else, it is **what we know**; knowledge is not something that is encoded in language – knowledge is made of language. (Halliday, [1988] 2007: 346–7, original emphasis)

He has sometimes been interpreted to mean that *all* knowledge is 'encoded' in language, and for this reason his work has sometimes been viewed as 'logocentric'. In my view, this is not an accurate representation, but the result of limited interpretation of his writing about language and education. For example, in a 1988 paper on language and socialization in which he discussed the concept of discourse, he commented:

Once we have language, of course, we tend to assume that there is nothing which is not – or at least nothing which could not be – represented in linguistic form, as meanings realized in wordings: if we can't say a thing then we don't know it. *I see no reason to assume that this is so.* ([1988] 2007: 96 emphasis added)

Nevertheless, he does certainly hold that, for education, language is primary. He goes on to say:

. . . in an age that is somewhat obsessed with the concept of discourse I think it is important to end on a contrary note. I strongly believe – otherwise I would not have spent my life working for it – that the concept of language education, of learning as primarily a linguistic process, will for as far ahead as we can see be the best way we have of understanding, and therefore of intervening in, the directions and practices of education. (Ibid.)

Looking at volume 9 of his *Collected Works*, one can see the interventions, the political engagements, expressed in a wide range of sub-fields, from the nature of literacy itself to language planning in multilingual societies, to critiques of the neglect of interpersonal meaning in second language development. Memorably, in addressing an international congress at the University of Sydney in 1987 as he retired from the Chair of Linguistics there, he spoke of the dilemma he had faced in the years immediately after the Second World War: whether he should continue working politically in rural areas of China, or to attempt to develop ways of thinking about, and working with, language that might in time be helpful to people engaged in key social practices such as education.

Halliday's political engagement in education is most visible in his work on language variation, and more specifically his work towards a sociological semantics, i.e. linguistic meaning-making understood through a dialogue with sociology. Commencing in the early 1960s, Halliday began conversations with

the sociologist Basil Bernstein about the roles language might play in reproducing the biasing effects of social structure on students' educational achievement (their 'official pedagogic success' in Bernstein's terms). Here, I will focus
specifically on the educational significance of this dialogue. Elsewhere in this
volume, Ruqaiya Hasan (Chapter 6) discusses the social background to the collaboration between Halliday, Bernstein and others.

The general idea that home language practices somehow affect student
achievement is, of course, very familiar and obvious to teachers. But how is a
teacher to understand this general impression and respond intelligently to the
differences? She most probably will have learned during professional preparation that some children enter school with learning deficits, and more specifically language deficits, resulting from their home backgrounds: that is the
dominant, commonsense professional response. It is also precisely the concept
of language deficit that Bernstein's theory *confronts*.

I have expressed his research focus in this way because, very frequently,
he has been positioned as a 'deficit theorist', whereas what he argued is, in
many respects, precisely the opposite. He proposed a radical theory of how
habitual and different ways of meaning characterize interaction in families as
a result of family positioning within the social division of labour. These variants are differentially selected by schooling, with the result that some children are structurally advantaged and others disadvantaged. What the teacher
will immediately see as difference between the students' abilities to learn in
school, Bernstein argued, is only partially a matter of variation in natural ability: it is also a matter of experience with different ways of meaning within local
contexts.

Bernstein identified two broad, general variants of habitual ways of meaning, which he called coding orientations: 'restricted' and 'elaborated' coding
orientations.[3] The origins of these lie in the relative proximity of the occupa-
tional categories of families to the material base of production. He writes:

> The simpler the social division of labour, and the more specific and local the
> relation between an agent and its material base, the more direct the relation
> between meanings and a specific material base and the greater the probability
> of a restricted coding orientation. The more complex the social division
> of labour, the less specific and local the relation between an agent and its
> material base, the more indirect the relation meanings and a specific material
> base, and the greater the probability of an elaborated coding orientation.
> (Bernstein, 1990: 20)

What Bernstein proposes, then, is not a theory of language deficit but a theory of variation in orientations to meaning-making and, consequently, a new
potential for thinking about differences between children entering school, and

new ways of thinking about relations between learning at home and learning at school.

Turning to a more specifically linguistic perspective, what Bernstein's theory evidently requires is a theoretical and descriptive semantics, a way of thinking about how meanings are (and can be) exchanged in various contexts together with a way of studying these exchanges in natural discourse. This he did not at first have. His initial attempts to specify relevant linguistic features associated with the contrasted coding orientations focused on isolated grammatical features (broadly speaking), which did not work. Bernstein withdrew them, having realized they were mistaken. In 1971, reflecting on a decade of work on coding orientation, he commented:

> One of the major difficulties of the research has always been the problem of inferring from micro counts of specific linguistic choices to macro characteristics of the speech as a whole. (1971a: 13)

This he was to find in Halliday's theory, though expressing it this way is somewhat misleading because crucial elements of SFL theory did not in fact pre-exist Bernstein's proposals. Rather, there was a sustained theoretical exchange, an example of the kind of transdisciplinary conversation that Hasan was later to call a 'meta-dialogue' between two 'exotropic theories' (Hasan, 1999b), each theory co-evolving with the benefit of theoretical input from the other, and each able to make contributions about the significant social and educational questions because of the other. The eventual outcome was a powerful sociological theory of cultural transmission, reproduction and change, and an equally powerful sociologically oriented semantics, including new methodologies for the analysis of discourse, initially proposed by Halliday and radically extended by Hasan, and the testing of hypotheses and methodologies by Hasan and her students.

Thinking now of the question of effects of social positioning on educational outcomes from a linguistic perspective, it is clear why Bernstein's questions were of such interest to Halliday. If, taking Halliday's theoretical starting point, language is a social semiotic, then social interaction is crucial to language development and if, by necessity, social interaction involves socially positioned interactants, and if the social positioning of interactants varies as a result of social structure, then we can expect variation in ways of meaning as a result of social structure. Variation in habitual ways of meaning is not a matter of linguistic deficit but of context-general orientations to ways of meaning resulting from features of social structure. For Bernstein, the primary structuring variable is social class, though it is by no means the only one involved. As Carmel Cloran's work has shown so clearly, differences in coding orientation are to be seen in the interaction between gender and social class positioning (Cloran, 1989).

Halliday's *political* engagement with these educational problems is clearly evident throughout this collaboration with Bernstein. It can be seen directly, for example, in his public defence of Bernstein's work in the Foreword contributed to *Class, Codes and Control*, volume 2, in which he directly addressed the 'linguistic deficit' accusation against Bernstein (Halliday, 1975). It must have been a complex political stance for a linguist to take at the time because Bernstein's ideas were so different (and remain very different) from dominant ways of thinking about relations between social class, educational opportunity and language. As Halliday commented, 'the left branded him as right wing and the right branded him as left wing' ([1988] 2007: 81). Halliday's political stance is also evident in his spirited defence of Bernstein's right to *evolve* his ideas through the metadialogue with linguistics, labelling as 'particularly moronic' the accusation that Bernstein was not consistent when he changed or elaborated his views about relationships between coding orientations and language (Halliday, [1988] 2007: 81). Halliday's position on language, social class and education has for many years restricted take-up of his work on education in North America, though that is now beginning to change.

Returning to the perspective of a teacher, then, what does this large body of research and theory offer her as she reflects, perhaps mainly for the longer term, about children's different and differentiating educational achievements? The most important outcome is that this work provides a systematically different way of understanding children's language development as they enter school, thus providing a resource for teachers to 'read' children very differently from commonsense observations and results on 'pre-tests' of knowledge. Two subsequent developments in theory and in pedagogy, both of whose origins lie in Bernstein's and Halliday's collaborative work are also noteworthy. The best-known of these is genre-based pedagogy, developed by J. R. Martin and his colleagues, which is an internationally significant initiative to which I will return shortly. Less well known, but of great long-term importance, is Hasan's work on language and education, which includes discussion of such important concepts as 'reflection literacy' and 'implicit versus explicit semiotic mediation' (Hasan, 2011c).

Halliday's own practical (and political) involvement with educational questions is also evident in more distributed activities, for example in the nature of the research projects he initiated in the Schools Council Project on Linguistics and English Teaching: the initial literacy project resulting in the *Breakthrough to Literacy* program (Mackay, Thompson and Schaub, 1970); the primary school project that produced the highly interesting but little known series, *Language and Communication* (Forsyth and Wood, 1977–9); and the secondary school language project which produced a resource that has been widely used internationally, *Language in Use* (Doughty, Pearce and Thornton, 1971). For economy *Breakthrough to Literacy* will have to serve as the example. (For an excellent discussion of the impact of the *Language in Use* materials in the United Kingdom, and that of similar work that followed, as for example in the publications of James Benson and Bill Greaves in Canada, see Keith (1990).)

Breakthrough to literacy is a set of practical materials for the initial teaching of literacy in school, together with a teacher's manual. The most significant point about it is that it increases *all* children's access to literacy through meaning-making in writing. The materials, properly used, enabled children to explore the new mode of writing by making meanings in writing with which they are already very familiar through speaking. It avoids the need for children to learn an artificial register, the language and meanings (or lack of meanings) of 'school readers' – *Janet and John* and the like. Writing and reading in this initial phase can thus be a 'natural' extension of spoken language, not an unpredictable disruption to established ways of meaning.

The practical materials through which this was achieved were very simple: a plastic slot into which children could insert pre-prepared words printed on cardboard. The words were selected as ones frequently used by children of five or so. The written words with which children became familiar were stored in a small folder as a kind of database for subsequent work, and new words were added as the child needed them. If children needed words that were not pre-prepared they could make them with a further resource of pre-prepared letters, the 'word-maker' resources. In practice the sentence maker was the most used resource because children often themselves wrote the new words they needed as their confidence with written language evolved.

The meanings made through writing in the sentence makers were not, of course, equivalent in complexity to the meanings they made in spoken language. (The development of meaning through writing, as Halliday has frequently asserted, typically lags about three years behind the development of meaning through speaking, and probably in the initial phase of literacy, even further than that.) For Halliday, the key point is that initial literacy development should be a modal, and then experiential, extension of existing meaning potential so that children could understand the purposes of reading and writing in functional terms. Initial literacy development is, again, *learning how to mean* in the written medium, necessarily using at first the resources of spoken medium. As Halliday comments:

> The principle is a familiar one: relate what the child is learning to his own previous experience. We repeat this slogan all the time, but we often forget that, in the case of learning to read and write, it means above all relating it to his previous **linguistic** experience. ([1979] 2007: 79 original emphasis)

This is an important contribution to the thinking of any young teacher, an appropriately theorized alternative position to what is still the majority practice, supported by massive corporate resources, which is the use of meaningless material, deriving from no register except the artificial one constructed for this pedagogical purpose. *Breakthrough's* materials might now be superceded by the affordances of digital technology but the concept of extending meaning potential modally has not.

So far I have foregrounded Halliday's view of the importance of continuity between spoken and written language in school learning. But his work also provides an important complementary perspective, also drawing attention to the educational significance of differences between spoken and written language. This is not merely a difference of channel, i.e. the material means through which language is encoded as talk or writing (Halliday and Hasan, 1985). If that were so, the difference would be fairly unimportant educationally. Rather, in his view spoken and written media involve *different ways of acting and reflecting*. Developmentally, students have to learn to move from initial reading and writing in spoken medium into the written medium, and thus these new ways of acting and reflecting. In brief,[4] Halliday draws attention to the relative independence of language from the material situation in which it is used, the specific consequences resulting from the writing system's omission of information signalled by intonation and rhythm (e.g. important use of the passive voice so that new information is positioned at the end of clauses, where it can be given tonic prominence in the typical English pattern), and difference in the rate of information flow in clauses, more technically, their lexical density. Written medium typically 'packs' information densely into clauses, averaged across a text, while spoken medium 'distributes' information over a larger number of clauses in a text. The denser the information per clause, the greater the level of difficulty a reader/listener is likely to experience in construing meaning from the lexicogrammar (Halliday, [1979] 2007; Halliday and Hasan, 1985). Conversely, the denser the information per clause the more economically information can be conveyed. It might seem from everyday views about writing that written language is more complex than spoken, but in Halliday's view this is not so.

> Contrary to what many people think, spoken language is on the whole more complex than written language in its grammar, and informal spontaneous conversation, especially sustained and rather rapid conversation, is the most grammatically complex of all. The more unselfconscious the language, the more complex it is liable to become. (Halliday, [1979] 2007: 74)

For work in language and education, there are several important consequences from this work. The first is a general one: his analysis of the educational importance of spoken language *on linguistic grounds*. In the 1970s, when he first began to produce this work, there were many voices promoting the importance of talk in education. (It was, for example, officially promoted in the Bullock Report,

A language for life (Department of Education and Science, G.B., 1975), and in a wide range of publications from scholars, particularly some at the Institute of Education, University of London.) What Halliday adds to this view is explicit information about the linguistic features that are crucially implicated in how the two media function. This information is itself a significant pedagogical resource. More specifically, his work clarifies why systematic teaching about written medium is so important. Students do not develop writing just by writing, as was widely asserted in education during the 1980s: control of written medium is not a natural development. Students typically need a lot of explicit information about the contextual features that writing has to address, such as its use out of immediate contexts, and about the expected patterns of registers, including especially interpersonal features. Even more importantly, through developing knowledge of written medium they have to learn new ways of construing experience, and this is perhaps the toughest task of all.

Spoken language tends to represent the world as dynamic, creating a sense of a rapid flow of experience. In contrast, written language represents the world as static, creating a sense of how entities relate rather than of what actants do. Educationally, then, students need opportunities to reflect on experience initially in spoken medium and then to be assisted into the more abstract, generalized 'uncommonsense' knowledge construed through the written medium. (The precept might therefore be reworded as 'talk is the basis for *knowing*'. For a discussion of teacher-student interaction exemplifying this trajectory, see Butt (2004).)

One other descriptive concept that has proved to be critically important for work on written medium is grammatical metaphor. Again, it is Halliday's analytic and theoretical extension of a familiar concept that is significant. He has shown that the familiar concept of nominalization (nominals such as 'the transportation of food' and 'intraoperative electron radiation therapy') is just one aspect of a much broader linguistic phenomenon in which congruent ways of encoding experience (typical, for example, of ways children represent experience) are reformulated into more abstract, and typically more condensed, forms. Crucially for education, he argues that grammatical metaphor is distributed metafunctionally rather than constrained just to the experiential representation, as in nominalization. Interpersonal grammatical metaphor has been of particular interest in tertiary educational contexts, where students have to learn, for example, to recode and project personal opinion 'objectively': not 'I think' but 'it would seem probable that'. Grammatical metaphor has also proved to be a powerful resource for students to use to make 'deconstructive' readings of text. (In tertiary contexts it can be particularly entertaining for students to deconstruct philosophical texts about deconstruction.) I point here only to the importance of Halliday's description of grammatical metaphor for the development of secondary school and tertiary academic reading and writing, thus complementing the more detailed discussion in Chapter 2 of this volume. For extended discussion relevant to education see Simon-Vandenbergen et al., (2003).

In the final movement of the chapter I turn to what may arguably be the most important long-term legacy from all of Halliday's contributions to education: his proposals towards a language-based theory of learning. At many points in his writing about language education over the last five decades he shows how it would be productive to rethink educational practices in linguistic terms. One example discussed earlier concerned children's experience of talk as the basis for their new *linguistic* experience of reading and writing. However, in 1993, he systematically set out 21 features of language development that he proposed might form the basis of a new approach to theorizing learning. He derived the features both from his own research and that of colleagues working in the systemic functional linguistic framework such as Hasan (2005), Painter (1984), Oldenburg [Torr] (1987) and Phillips (1985).

The article was enthusiastically received when it appeared. Gordon Wells, for example, commented that 'there can hardly be a topic of greater interest to readers of this journal than the one announced in the title of Halliday's recent article: towards a language-based theory of learning' (Wells, 1994: 41), and it has been cited frequently. However, research use of these features for thinking about language and educational problems and research into them has been infrequent, so here I explore one possible use, returning to a question raised earlier in this chapter, the question of the semogenic potential of explicit grammatical knowledge. I am thus also returning to the third aspect of language knowledge that Halliday proposed: learning *about* language.

To address this question it is important to note a distinction Halliday introduced between knowledge of 'grammar' and knowledge of 'grammatics'. In everyday ways of saying 'grammar' is used to refer to two distinct phenomena: knowledge of lexicogrammatical structure that every speaker of a language possesses; and the explicit description of lexicogrammatical structure such as one would expect to study in linguistics courses. From an ontogenetic perspective, the first develops naturally in the vast majority of children, without recourse to metadescription. (We learn to talk without needing to know about gerunds.) The second, grammatics, does not: it always results from explicit teaching, and it is dependent on teachers using a metadescription. Halliday's proposal is to use the term 'grammatics' for the second type of knowledge and restrict 'grammar' to the first. He comments about the problems of using the term 'grammar':

> *grammar*, the name of the phenomenon (as in *the grammar of English*) slides over to become the name of the study of the phenomenon (as in *the grammar of English*). This was already confusion enough: it was made worse by the popular use of the term to mean rules of linguistic etiquette (for example *bad grammar*)

So:

> ... as a way of getting round part of the problem I started using the term *grammatics* ... this was based on the simple proportion grammatics : grammar :: linguistics : language. (Halliday, [1996] 2002: 384–6)

With this distinction in mind, we can then consider work in the SFL framework on developing students' knowledge about language. To do so, it is useful to distinguish between work specifically on grammatics and work on other aspects of metaknowledge.

By far the best-known SFL work on the development of knowledge about language is genre-based pedagogy, initiated by Jim Martin and developed by many others (e.g. Frances Christie, Joan Rothery, Len Unsworth, Beverly Derewianka, David Rose, John Polias and Brian Dare). For a recent useful overview see Rose and Martin (2012). Genre-based pedagogy has made a major contribution to the reform of literacy education internationally. While it has often included discussion of grammatical features, usually to assist learners to recognize differences between generic types and stages, thus supplementing schematic structural descriptions,[5] it is helpful to distinguish it from educational work specifically on grammatics itself. There is no inherent pedagogical incompatibility, but the longer-term goals of work on grammatics and work on genres are not necessarily equivalent so it is useful to discuss the two sets of work separately.

Additional to genre-based pedagogy, there has been a long experience of working with SFL on developing knowledge about language in the British education system. This work is well-represented in several of the papers in Carter's influential book, *Knowledge about Language and the Curriculum* (1990). A paper in that volume by Keith includes a helpful discussion of problems with teaching and examining traditional school grammatics in the senior secondary school, together with a report on imaginative alternatives to that kind of teaching. However, there is little about systematically developing students' knowledge of grammatics.

Halliday has himself frequently advocated grammatics as an important element in education, as for example in a major paper on literacy education in which he discusses the importance of deconstructing written language:

> The value of having some explicit knowledge of the grammar of written language is that you can use this knowledge not only to analyse the texts, but as a critical resource for asking questions about them: why is the grammar organized as it is? Why has written language evolved in this way? What is its place in the construction of knowledge, the maintenance of bureaucratic and technological power structures, the design and practice of education?

You can exploit disjunctions and exploit their potential for creating new combinations of meanings. ([1996] 2007: 107)[6]

He does, however, acknowledge that not everyone finds studying grammatics an easy task.

Some people find it threatening to have to bring language to the level of consciousness; and many others, though they may not feel threatened by it, find it extraordinarily difficult. And I think until you have taken that critical step the study of language may seem rather arid. (Halliday, [1981] 2007: 333)

Some SFL research focused specifically on grammatics in primary schools has been conducted over the last two decades, for example in work by Williams, French and Rothery in the mid-1990s. This work demonstrated both the *accessibility* and the *efficacy* of SFL grammatical knowledge in school literacy in a range of projects with children aged 6 and 11 years (Williams, 1999, 2000, 2004, 2005a). The grammatics proved to be accessible to children as young as 6. Even in formal written tests of grammatical knowledge 11-year-old students were able to demonstrate their understanding of SFL concepts, and marked positive effects on writing development were observed. Subsequently, French conducted her own significant study (French, 2013), and currently there is a small range of systematic research on grammatics under weigh in various centres in Australia, North America and Hong Kong (e.g. work by Schleppegrell, Palinscar and their colleagues at the University of Michigan in a curriculum development project 'The iterative development of modules to support teachers' engagement in *Exploring Language and Meaning in Text* with English language learners').

This work notwithstanding, quite literally nothing is currently known from an SFL perspective about how grammatics might first commence in school, when that might be done, and what terms (functional or class) might be used to begin it. In other words, there is no meaning potential for taking the very first steps in a systemic functionally based grammatics in school. Returning, then to Halliday's proposals in 'Towards a language-based theory of learning', my question is this: could any of the 21 features in Halliday's list assist with conceptualizing the initial steps in young children's study of grammatics?

Two developmental features he proposes are of particular interest, 'the magic gateway' and 'semogenic strategies', both of which were discussed above. 'The magic gateway'[7] refers to the phenomenon in language development in which a child 'finds a way in to a new activity or a new understanding' (Halliday, 1993: 116). Halliday discusses two senses, that of a 'generalized interpersonal' gateway and a more specific instance of a 'gateway' through which Nigel, the child in his own case study, entered grammar for the first time. The first of these senses has already been mentioned: it concerns the fact that expansion in meaning potential frequently originates in the exchange of interpersonal meanings, rather than the more commonly assumed experiential ones. Halliday cites initial learning of abstract meanings as one example, which is particularly clear:

> It seems likely that abstract meanings are first understood when children come to terms with strongly interpersonally oriented expressions such as 'you're a nuisance', 'that's not fair'. (Halliday, 1993: 104)

As additional evidence he cites examples from Cloran's (1989) account of the social construction of gender.

The second example, of entry to lexicogrammar itself, is more systemic in nature and therefore of particular interest to questions about the ontogenesis of grammatics. To illustrate this sense of the 'magic gateway' Halliday recounts a specific moment in Nigel's development:

> Where is the magic gateway into the grammar? This is again from my own data, when Nigel was 1;3. He was beginning to incorporate names (Mummy, Daddy, Anna) into his protolanguage, but they were not yet referential; they were still microfunctional signs meaning 'play with me', 'I'm giving this to you', and so on. Then, within three consecutive days he constructed the system shown in Table 13.1 (cf. Halliday, 1975, pp. 67, 154–155). By separating articulatory from prosodic features in the expression, Nigel had deconstructed the sign; in doing so, he had succeeded in varying one dimension of meaning (one system, in the technical sense) while keeping the other one constant, and in the process marked out one of the two meaning systems as referential. Thus, the combination of 'proper name' (Mummy/Daddy/Anna) with mood, or protomood (seeking/finding), provided the magic gateway into this new stratum of lexicogrammar; it enabled him to mean two things at once, so that one of the two meanings became a name. (Halliday, 1993: 98)

In this case development into grammar was of course a spontaneous, unplanned one, and that is precisely *not* the kind of development on which teachers ought to rely in classrooms. The 'magic gateway' must be explicitly constructable for the group if the general principle is to prove useful. Could that be achievable?

Semogenic strategies, also discussed above, are succinctly summarized by Halliday as: expanding the meaning potential (refining distinctions, moving into new domains, deconstructing linked variables) (Halliday, 1993: 116). The introduction of grammatics obviously involves a movement into new domains

Table 13.1 Dimension of meaning in a protolanguage system

Expressed by prosody	'Where are you?' (mid level + high level)	'There you are!' (high falling + low level)
Expressed by artivulation		
'Mummy' [ama]	[ā m ā]	[à m ā]
'Daddy' [dada]	[d ā s ā]	[d à d ā]
'Anna' [an:a]	[ā n: ā]	[à n: ā]

of knowledge. Might it also usefully be thought about in terms of deconstructing linked variables and refining existing distinctions?

My colleague Emily Moreton and I have recently begun to explore these questions in a school curriculum development project with a class of Kindergarten children in an inner-city school. The children had been in school for three terms. In a context in which national curricula are beginning to give more prominence to grammatics we asked ourselves whether there might be ways to begin the study of grammatics productively as early in schooling as Kindergarten. The approach and outcomes were reported to a recent international SFL congress and will be further reported in a forthcoming paper (Williams and Moreton, 2013). Here I can report that we have found the concept of a 'magic gateway', both in the generalized interpersonal and the systemic sense, to be both applicable and very productive.

Entry to grammatics for these children was oriented from register, and thus meaning-making. We asked the children to begin noticing and recording examples of language as it was being used in a range of institutional contexts, contexts such as the school playground, parks, shops and at home. The children gathered examples of both spoken and written language and recorded them, through photographs and in writing, in community walks, conversations with their caregivers and peers, and then in classroom discussion. One finding that emerged for these young learners was that language was used frequently to regulate actions in public contexts, from STOP signs on the street, to 'No Dogs Allowed' in parks, to their teacher saying 'If you have finished go to the reading corner'. These observations in turn led to discussion of various ways in which commands could be worded, and that different wordings that made commands more or less effective in their contexts. (Making very dysfunctional STOP signs was a source of great enjoyment ('YOU MIGHT LIKE TO STOP HERE'), as were small dramatizations of the longest way the children could think of to tell a classmate to do something very simple such as to close the door.) That is, the making of interpersonal meanings was brought to the fore playfully, and provided a base for the children to begin to think systematically about relations between contexts,

345

meanings and wordings. From a more systemic perspective, we then used commands as a basis from which to try a 'magic gateway' into grammatics. This 'gateway', was the concept Event, as defined in systemic functional grammar (Halliday and Matthiessen, 2004: pp. 335–7). For example, in the clauses 'she **smiled** happily because she had been **awarded** three medals', the Events are 'smiled' and 'awarded').

Did Events prove to be a magic gateway into grammatics? Such a complex research experience requires a longer account, but I can report that after work over just two school terms almost all of these Kindergarten children could identify Events in commands, even in clauses with Marked Themes (which meant that the Event was not in first position). They could also compose their own examples of clauses and identify Events in them, including in several clause complexes.

From this small experiment, then, it does seem that 'magic gateways' and semogenic strategies are useful resources with which to begin to think about a language-based approach to learning. Semogenic strategies are more obviously relevant, but searching for a constructed 'magic gateway' also proved relevant in our experience.

Generalizing, it does seem that the 21 features proposed by Halliday as moves towards a language-based theory of learning could prove to be a very important legacy for educational linguistics, and one that can be used to conceptualize educational research into the large range of educational problems of a globalized, information-oriented world. It could, for example, enable ways to support existing positive practices, rethinking them from a language-based perspective and thus providing stronger theorization and creating possibilities for empirical research. This possibility is exemplified by the Schools Council work on initial literacy, the *Breakthrough to literacy* programme. Additionally, it could create possibilities for research on educational questions about which we currently know almost nothing, as with the ontogenesis of grammatics just discussed.

Concluding, Halliday's contribution to language education has been both an enduring and an extraordinary one. Few educators, and I suggest no other linguist, could reasonably claim to have given education such a broad and genuinely appliable body of theoretical and descriptive resources for practicing and researching meaning-making in education. A comment Halliday himself made about Bernstein's work seems equally apposite to his own: 'His ideas are, of course, not simple, because the things that he was trying to explain are not simple, and he didn't distort them by pretending that they were' (Halliday, [1988] 2007: 82). The task of productively and adequately recontextualizing his work for the kind of teacher whose perspective has oriented this chapter remains a major task for teacher education.

Notes

1. Halliday's paper 'The notion of "context" in language education' (Halliday, [1991] 2007) includes a frequently cited, helpful diagram of relations between contexts, language and text (p. 275).
2. The extent of influence of his ideas can actually be arranged in that order. By far the greatest influence has been on learning language, then on learning through language (as, for example, in 'language across the curriculum' initiatives). There has been important, but much more limited, influence in work concerning learning about language.
3. Bernstein (1990, chapter 3) presents an overview of misrepresentations of coding orientation theory, together with rebuttals. Further exposition and linguistic testing of his theory from an educational perspective is available in Williams (1995b, 2005).
4. Details of the lexicogrammatical and semantic differences between the two media are discussed in Chapter 11 of this volume.
5. However, in some education systems it has also been the case, regrettably, that curricula based on genres (or 'text types') have included traditional descriptions of grammatics – primarily just 'parts of speech' –, in parallel but without reference to the genres.
6. Informally, when he was teaching systemic functional grammar to graduate students Halliday would often suggest that they might think about problems in terms of entities in grammatical relations. He would typically remark: 'And now I'm going to teach you to think grammatically. If you have a problem, grammaticalise it.'
7. I find this term difficult and wonder if 'toehold', evoking a sense of children climbing on existing structures to gain a new perspective, might be a useful alternative. However, for obvious reasons I have retained Halliday's own term here.

14 A Linguistics of Style: Halliday on Literature

Annabelle Lukin

Chapter Overview

---

1 Introduction

We owe to literature Halliday's discovery of linguistics as a scholarly activity. In his entry in the book *Linguistics in Britain: Personal Histories*, Halliday wrote:

> I had always been fascinated by language. My father was an English teacher, with equal love for grammar and for Elizabethan drama, and also a dialectologist and dialect poet. At school I enjoyed the study of English literature; but I thought that what my teachers said about its language made no sense, and so I searched in the library, where I discovered a subject called 'linguistics' and a book about language by an American professor called Bloomfield. (Halliday, in Brown & Law, 2002: 117)

Looking back on his more than 60 years of study of language, we are in a position to consider where this combined fascination for language and love of literature took him as he has 'wander[ed] the highways and byways of language' (Halliday, 2002c: 14). Halliday has published five[1] papers on the linguistic analysis of literature, which span the period of 1964 to 1987. Four of these papers signal their preoccupation with literary text in their titles: 'The linguistic study of literary texts' (1964), 'Linguistic function and literary style: an inquiry into the language of William Golding's *The Inheritors*' (1971), 'The deautomatization of grammar: from Priestley's *An Inspector Calls*' (1982) and 'Poetry as scientific discourse: the nuclear sections of Tennyson's *In Memoriam*' (1987). The fifth is 'Text as semantic choice in social contexts' (1977), an important theoretical paper in systemic functional linguistics. This paper was published in an edited volume titled *Grammars and Descriptions* (van Dijk & Petöfi, 1977), in which the text for analysis for contributors (Thurber's essay 'The Lover and His Lass') was pre-selected by the book's editors. All five papers are republished in volume 2 of Halliday's *Collected Works*, called *Linguistic Studies of Text and Discourse*. Two of the five articles ('The linguistic study of literary texts' and 'Text as semantic choice in social context') form Part I of this book, under the heading 'Linguistic analysis of textual meaning'. The other three are in part 2, collected together under the title 'Highly valued texts'. This suggests Halliday sees the 1964 and 1977 papers as distinct from the three on Golding, Priestley and Tennyson. And it is in these latter papers that Halliday sets out his argument about how grammar can be recruited to aesthetic projects. The terms 'prominence' and 'deautomatization', deriving largely from Mukařovský, are key to Halliday's views on language in literature.

In this chapter, I explore Halliday's approach to language in literature. To begin, it is important to see the influences on Halliday's explorations of literature, so I consider which linguists and linguistic ideas have been most influential in his work on literary text. Then, I consider why Halliday argues that, in some sense, all texts are like literature, and what his grounds are for seeing the analysis of literary text as requiring the same method as the study of any other text. Thirdly, and given the centrality of the notion of 'context' to systemic functional linguistics, I will explore what Halliday has said about the conception of context with respect to literary texts. Then, his views on how it is that grammar can be an aesthetic resource will be considered. This will require an examination of his use of the terms 'prominence' and 'deautomatization'. Finally, the specific analysis conducted in Halliday's studies of *The Inheritors, An Inspector Calls,* and *In Memoriam,* will be examined, in order to show what it means to make an argument about the meaning of these texts from the perspective of SFL. In this final section I will be evaluating Halliday's arguments against his own claims about the task for 'a linguistics of style', which is 'to demonstrate that the meaning of a text . . . is a great deal more than the manifest propositional content' ([1987] 2002: 149).

2 Influences on Halliday's Ideas

All of the influences on Halliday as linguist have influenced his account of the language of literature, by virtue of the fact that he draws on his general linguistic theory as the point of departure for the study and analysis of literary text. Malinowski and Hjelmslev, Firth and Whorf, who are so consistently present in his accounts of his general linguistic theory, are also part of the picture when we explore Halliday's contribution to stylistics. Below I discuss the relation of context of situation and context of culture to Halliday's stylistics; these are terms from Malinowski (1923), elaborated by Firth (e.g. 1957a). Firth in particular is an important influence on Halliday's general linguistic theory (e.g. Butt, 2001 – and see the references to Firth in Halliday's early papers on grammar, in Halliday, 2002a). In his analysis of literary texts, Halliday makes particular reference to Firth's [1951] 1957 paper, 'Modes of meaning'; here Firth argues that 'the main concern of descriptive linguistics is to make statements of meaning', and that 'the suggested procedure for dealing with meaning is its dispersion into modes, rather like the dispersion of light of mixed wave-lengths into a spectrum' (Firth, [1951] 1957: 190–2). Halliday uses this notion of Firth's in his discussion of Golding (e.g. 'the syntax is effective as a "mode of meaning"' (Halliday, [1971] 2002: 120)); of Priestley (e.g. 'It is a general assumption of structuralism that the meanings of a work of literature are dispersed throughout the text not just at different places in the syntagm but also, and more significantly, at different levels within the code. This dispersal into what Firth called "modes of meaning" . . . is typically an unconscious feature of the writing process' [1982] 2002: 129–30); and of Tennyson ([1987] 2002: 150). The idea that all strata are meaning-making is relevant also to the discussion of the idea of 'deautomatization' of grammar that is central to Halliday's account of the language of literary text. The idea that analysis incorporates processes of contextualization is also a Firthian legacy in Halliday's stylistics (e.g. [1987] 2002: 150).

From Hjelmslev comes the critical perspective that the text and the system must be kept in view at the same time. The significance of this concept for Halliday's stylistics is that:

> The stylistic interpretation of the text is not . . . a 'close reading' or 'explication de texte', because these undertakings, admirable though they are, fail to relate the text to the linguistic system. Without this perspective, in which the system and the text are in focus at the same time (as they are with Hjelmslev, almost alone among theoretical linguists), interpretation may become either another 'new criticism', under the guise of pragmatics, or a new formalism on a more macroscopic scale. (Halliday, [1982] 2002: 128; see also Halliday, [1987] 2002: 150)

Halliday notes that while the point of the analysis of a literary text is its unique-ness, it is in its relationship to a systemic potential that it can function at all. The text 'would not be a text if it was not a product – an "instantiation" – of the linguistic system' (Halliday, [1982] 2002: 128).

The Whorfian[2] basis of Halliday's grammar is also central to Halliday's theory and description of the language of literature. Halliday has argued that Whorf's notion of the 'crypotype', and his conception of 'how grammar models reality' will 'turn out to be among the major contributions of twentieth century linguistics' ([1985] 2003: 188). When elaborating his claim about the deautoma-tization of grammar, Halliday draws in particular on the idea of 'crypotype' both in his theoretical claims and his discussion of method. In his 1971 paper on Golding, for instance, Halliday draws on Whorf in his elaboration of the ideational function: 'in serving this function, language lends structure to his [i.e. man's – sic] experience and helps to determine his way of looking at things' (Halliday, [1971] 2002: 91). Halliday notes here that Whorf's views have been mis-represented on these matters, as if he argued the relation of language to reality was deterministic and in one direction – that language determines how its speakers see the world. Whorf, he notes, was never so extreme. The speaker 'can see through and around the settings of his semantic system; but he is aware that, in doing so, he is seeing reality in a new light' (Halliday, [1971] 2002: 91). The notion of grammar as crypotype is set out in Whorf as follows:

A covert linguistic class may not deal with any grand dichotomy of objects, it may have a very subtle meaning, and it may have no overt mark other than certain distinctive 'reactances' with certain overt marked forms. It is then what I call a crypotype. It is a submerged, subtle, and elusive meaning, corresponding to no actual word, yet showing by linguistic analysis to be functionally important in the grammar. (Whorf, 1956: 70)

The idea that meanings can be 'submerged, subtle and elusive' is the founda-tion for Halliday's particular interpretation of Mukařovský's notion of 'deau-tomatization'. Halliday argues that Mukařovský 'offered a rich multifunctional view of language' ([1987] 2002: 149). Halliday follows Mukařovský's claim that what made a text highly valued was not the use of special literary language. Rather 'poetic language is permanently characterized only by its function: how-ever, function is not a property but a *mode of utilizing* the properties of a given phenomenon' (Mukařovský, 1977: 3–4). Halliday, as we will see below, is also influenced by Mukařovský's (and Jakobson's) ideas about the orientation of poetic language being towards the essence of the sign itself. As Mukařovský wrote 'poetic language . . . concentrates attention on the linguistic sign itself . . . poetic language is more suited than other functional languages for con-stantly reviving man's attitude toward language and the relation of language to reality, for constantly revealing in new ways the internal organization of the linguistic sign, and for showing new possibilities of its use' (Mukařovský, 1977: 4, 6). Halliday's analyses of Golding, Priestley and Tennyson are all exemplars of these propositions; I would suggest that even for many linguists, Halliday's analysis is remarkable for what it brings out about the grammar's potential as a construer of deep and profound cultural concerns.

For Mukařovský, aesthetic deautomatization can occur in relation to any linguistic (even paralinguistic) unit. Of grammar, he argues that 'a grammatical category can acquire aesthetic effect by the accumulation of words belonging to it and especially by their accumulation in prominent places in the text' (Mukařovský, 1977: 35). Even morphology, Mukařovský argues, can be recruited to aesthetic ends. In a discussion which is echoed in Halliday's conception of the aesthetic potential of grammar, Mukařovský argues:

> The deautomatization of desinence . . . calls attention above all to the meaning which the ending introduces into the form. It does not matter that this meaning is only 'abstract'; on the contrary, the poetic word can often penetrate right to the roots of the poet's epistemology precisely by means of this semantic abstractness of a desinence. (Mukařovský, 1977: 36)

Halliday combines Mukařovský's view with his (i.e. Halliday's) more elaborated conception and description of lexicogrammar. Thus, the grammar can be freed from the control of semantics to express itself directly, with the kind of semantic 'abstractness' Mukařovský is writing of here; and this is the means by which one gets to the heart of the expression of the writer's 'epistemology'.

From within the systemic stylistic tradition, Halliday's work is very closely related to the account of language in verbal art by Hasan. Her work during the period of Halliday's stylistics studies – Hasan, 1964, 1967, 1971, 1975, 1985a[3] – are referenced in Halliday's work. In his discussions of Golding and Tennyson, he refers to Hasan's claims about layers of semiosis in verbal art; in his discussion of Priestley, he makes reference to her claim about 'symbolic articulation'. Both Halliday and Hasan take Mukařovský's work on poetic language as a central resource, although they use his notion of 'foregrounding' (in Czech *ackualizace*[4]) in different ways. For Hasan, foregrounding has two dimensions: stability of 'semantic direction', and stability of 'textual location' (1985a: 95). In his Golding paper, Halliday draws on a notion of 'foregrounding' that would be something like Hasan's 'stability of semantic direction'. In his 1982 and 1987 papers, he comes to use the term 'deautomatization' which he argues is more apt than the concept of 'foregrounding'. This point is explored below.

Halliday's stylistics work has inspired many scholars to pursue systemic studies of the language of selected literary texts. Butler (2003: 445–6) has a summary of some of this work; see also Lukin and Webster (2005), and Butt and Lukin

(2009). Butler notes that Halliday's work has influenced a number of monographs on stylistics, including Leech and Short (1981) and Toolan (1988, 1990).

3 Literature as Text, Text as Literature

In sorting his papers into his *Collected Works*, Halliday put his papers on literary text in a volume containing papers on decidedly non-literary texts. For instance, his analysis of a fundraising text, and of a section of a thesis defence appear in the same book as his studies of Yeats, Golding, Priestley and Tennyson. This choice is one manifestation of his view that the literary text is a text like any other, deserving of the same kind of comprehensive analysis as any other text. It was a view articulated in his first paper on literature, where he argued against 'the ad hoc, personal and arbitrarily selective statements offered, frequently in support of a preformulated literary thesis, as "textual" or "linguistic" statements about literature' (Halliday, [1964] 2002: 5). Linguistic stylistics, he argued, should be founded on 'general linguistic theory and descriptive linguistics' (Halliday, [1964] 2002: 5). 'Close reading' or 'explication de texte' he argued, fail to 'relate the text to the linguistic system' ([1982] 2002: 128). The text 'would not be a text if it was not a product – an "instantiation" – of the linguistic system' ([1964] 2002: 5). All of these claims relate to text per se, and as such hold for a literary text. It follows that claims about a literary text can only be evaluated when put 'in relation to the total "pure" description of the language concerned' ([1964] 2002: 6).

Text analysis of any kind is, for Halliday, a question of putting the instance against the system, since 'text is meaningful not only in virtue of what it is but also in virtue of what it might have been' (Halliday, [1964] 2002: 6). Thus 'a work of literature, like any other piece of language activity, is meaningful only in the perspective of the whole range of uses of the language' (Halliday, [1964] 2002: 19). Stylistics is a contrastive activity, in which each text is compared 'with others by the same and by different authors, in the same and in different genres' (Halliday, [1964] 2002: 6). But this method is only viable if we are able to use 'the same theory and method of linguistic analysis – the same "grammatics"' with any text. Otherwise, Halliday argues:

> if we simply approach each text with an ad hoc do-it-yourself kit of private commentary, we have no way of explaining their similarities and their differences – the aesthetic and functional values that differentiate one text from another, or one voice from another within the frontiers of the same text. (Halliday, [1990] 2003: 187)

This claim that the literary text ought to be treated like any other text is the basis for linguistics having a central place in the analysis of literary text. The language of a literary work can only be understood 'as the selection by the individual writer from the total resources at his disposal' ([1964] 2002: 17). But Halliday also makes clear his view that linguistics 'is not and will never be the whole of literary analysis' and he argues that 'knowing what a text means is achieved in the first place not by coming to it as a linguist, but rather by bringing to bear on it the whole of one's antecedent experience' ([1982] 2002: 127). But he insists that 'if the text is to be described at all, then it should be described properly', by 'the subject whose task it is to show how language works' ([1964] 2002: 19). This means 'the only valid unit for textual analysis is the whole text', and that it can take 'many hours of talking to describe exhaustively even the language of one sonnet' ([1964] 2002: 9).

What is the significance of the inclusion of Halliday's paper on the closing section of Darwin's *The Origin of Species* ('The construction of knowledge and value in the grammar of scientific discourse: with reference to Charles Darwin's *The Origin of Species*') with three papers on literary texts? Beyond the idea of the selected texts being instances of 'highly valued texts' there is a more general theoretical principle, that 'we can treat any text as a unique semiotic object / event' (Halliday, [1990] 2003: 177). This is to treat a scientific text as if it were literature. Halliday in fact suggests that it follows from a social-semiotic perspective on text that in some sense all text is literature, in that, like the literary text, texts of all kinds 'involve many orders of cultural values, both the value systems themselves and the many specific sub-systems that exist as metaphors for them' (Halliday, [1977] 2002: 60).

But Halliday suggests that over and beyond the fact that we can treat any text is if it is unique, *The Origin of Species* is 'a product of the impact between an intellectual giant and a moment in the space-time continuum of our culture' (Halliday, [1990] 2003: 186). In other words, it is not simply that we can treat any text as if it is unique; but that *The Origin of Species* is unique. Some texts, he argues 'by their own birthright lie at the intersection of science and verbal art . . . [they] are not merely reconstituted in this dual mode by us as readers, but are themselves constituted out of the impact between scientific and poetic forces of meaning' (Halliday, [1990] 2003: 177). A later paper (Halliday, n.d.) gives a more explicit account of the relations between a text of the significance of Darwin's *The Origin of Species*, and literature. In the paper, Halliday suggests that scientific text might be considered 'verbal science', by analogy with the conception of 'verbal art' (e.g. Hasan, 1985a). Halliday is arguing that scientific text resembles literature in that it is associated with a process of 'double articulation' (Hasan, 1985a). But what is construed is not 'theme' but 'theory'. He argues:

> Verbal science and verbal art are both concerned with the more abstract construal of human experience; but they arrive at it by different routes – and it is not such a very long time since the two diverged. (Halliday, n.d.)

The idea that the literary text can be treated like any other kind of text holds only up to a point. Halliday argues for instance that 'the discreteness of a literary text is untypical of texts as a whole' ([1977] 2002: 48), which is itself a significant statement on the notion of 'text'. As we will see below, he suggests also that the construct of context has a particular complexity in the context of literary texts. And while Halliday insists on the same methods and categories as for non-linguistic descriptions, he argues that 'such studies may require new alignments of groupings or descriptive categories, through which the special properties of a text may be recognized' ([1964] 2002: 6). Later, he would formulate these ideas through Gregory's conception of 'interpretative stylistics', summarized with these questions: 'Why does the text mean what it does? Why is the text valued as it is?' Halliday argues that these two questions are the central concern of stylistics (Gregory, 1978, cited in Halliday, [1982] 2002: 127).

4 'Situation', 'Culture' and the Construal of a 'Higher-order Semiotic'

Since the notion of context of situation and context of culture are central to Halliday's account of how language works, then it is important to consider what work these terms do in Halliday's account of language in literature. Halliday argues the notion of situation is complex in relation to the written text, and 'that of a fictional narrative is about as complex as it is possible for it to be' (Halliday, [1977] 2002: 58). Central to Halliday's account of context has been the contextual parameters of field, tenor and mode, defined in Halliday ([1977] 2002, 1985). How do they apply in the context of a literary work? Halliday addresses this issue most extensively in his 1977 paper,[5] where he argues that two 'levels' of field and tenor are construed by a literary text. In relation to field, he describes these two levels as 'the social act of narration, and the social acts that form the content of the narration' ([1977] 2002: 58). He describes the two levels of tenor as 'one between the narrator and his readership, which is embodied in the narrative, and one among the participants in the narrative, which is embodied in the dialogue' ([1977] 2002: 58). Two orders of field and tenor do not construe two distinct texts, however. Although 'as a purely abstract model this could be made to stand . . .', Halliday argues it would be 'misleading' both because the text is an integrated unity, and also because the meaning of 'two levels' is distinct for these two context variables. He argues that with respect to tenor 'the text does fall into two distinct segments, the narrative, and the dialogue' each characterized by its own tenor values. In relation to field, on the other hand, he proposes that there is 'no division in the text corresponding to the two levels of social action' (Halliday, [1977] 2002: 59).

It is a reminder of the special status of the vector of 'mode' that Halliday does not suggest two orders of mode. Instead, he argues that 'the oneness of the text also appears in the characterization of the mode, the symbolic structure of the situation and the specific role assigned to the text within it' (Halliday, [1977] 2002: 59). Note also that Halliday treats the literary conception of 'genre' as a dimension of mode (Halliday, [1977] 2002: 57). He describes these categories of literary genre, like discourse genres of other kinds, as 'specific semiotic functions of text that have social value in the culture' (Halliday, [1977] 2002: 57). But Halliday relates literary genres to the other components of meaning, arguing that 'there are often associations between a particular genre and particular semantic features of an ideational or interpersonal kind' (Halliday, [1977] 2002: 57). This claim would seem to follow from Firth's conception of the context of situation as 'a patterned process conceived as a complex activity with internal relations between its various factors' (Firth, 1937: 110).

Literary texts, like texts of all kinds, are both the realization of, and the 'realizers' of, a context of situation; as we will see below, for Halliday the lexicogrammatical patterning – especially the 'crypto-grammar' – in a literary text can function in one of two ways, with the grammar functioning as realizer of semantic patterns in its usual way (in an 'automatized' fashion, where grammar is activated by the semantic stratum at the same time that it is the construer of meanings) or in the 'deautomatized' mode, whereby the lexicogrammar is 'creating meanings of its own' (Halliday, [1987] 2002: 152). At the same time, and along this realizational dimension, the process of analysis takes one into the 'context of situation, the contextual configuration in terms of field, tenor and mode; and this in turn leads in to the context of culture, the socio-historical and ideological environment engendering, and engendered by, the text' (Halliday, [1987] 2002: 152). Halliday has argued that the relation between the situational and cultural context is one of instantiation. This is, like realization, a two-way process: 'each instance disturbs the probabilities of the system and hence destroys and recreates it – almost identically, but not quite'. Halliday notes the particular property of highly valued texts along this dimension of language:

> One property of a highly valued text is its capacity to disturb the system beyond its simple quantitative function: the writer – or speaker – that we call innovative is one whose text causes perturbations greater than those associated with a single instance. (Halliday, [1987] 2002: 152)

These theoretical relations of realization and instantiation are relevant to the method for the analysis of literary texts. One step is to consider the metafunctional grammatical patterns, separately at first, but then in interaction, since 'it is the intersection of these patterns in a unique combination that gives a text its characteristic flavor' (Halliday, [1987] 2002: 151). These patterns must also be related to patterns at other levels in the linguistic system. Because language is a realizer of context of situation, one should also at some point enter into consideration of the context of situation. Since '"the context of situation" is seen as the essential link between the social system (the "context of culture", to use another of Malinowski's terms) and the text, then it is more than an abstract representation of the relevant material environment; it is a constellation of social meanings, and in the case of a literary text these are likely to involve many orders of cultural values, both the value systems themselves and the many specific subsystems that exist as metaphors for them' (Halliday, [1977] 2002: 60). The context of culture is 'the socio-historical and ideological environment engendering and engendered by, the text' ([1987] 2002: 152).

This method is not linear however, since what the theoretical relations reflect is the 'interdependence of all parts' (Halliday, [1987] 2002: 151). He notes also that making the text a close object of study in no way backgrounds the social and historical context of the text. The reader's own personal history is not irrelevant either: Halliday notes in his study of Priestley the significance of the fact that both share the same home town (Bradford). Thus, 'this community of origins means that I understand him more roundedly than I could expect to understand an author from Manchester, London, Scotland or the United States' (Halliday, [1982] 2002: 127).

5 Grammar as Aesthetic Resource

With respect to the work the text can be said to be doing, the prime mover for Halliday is the lexicogrammar, a view built on the rich conception of grammar that is central to Halliday's linguistic theory. Halliday has a strong conception of what lexicogrammar does: he has called it the 'powerhouse' of language. Since grammar is 'internal to language (not located at either material interface)' grammar can 'to a certain extent "take off" on its own'; but 'since it is the powerhouse for construing experience there can never be a total disjunction between the symbolic forms and the material conditions of their environment' (Halliday, [1990] 2003: 146–7). For Halliday, language is as it is because of what it has evolved to do. What it does is no less than '"semioticizing" our complex eco-social environment in a way that is favourable to our survival' (Halliday, 2003c: 29). In this process, the grammar's 'theorizing of the human condition is nothing more than a massive reconciliation of conflicting principles of order' (Halliday, 2003c: 29). Halliday, in his particular expression of the functional and semiotic traditions in linguistics, gives a maximal degree of agency to lexicogrammar in the lives of humans.

5.1 Prominence and Foregrounding

In his paper on Golding, Halliday considers the problem of distinguishing the linguistic regularity which is significant for a poem or prose work. The question requires an examination of 'the place of semantics in the study of style', which itself demands a consideration of functional theories of language ([1971] 2002: 89). It is noteworthy that it is in this stylistics paper that Halliday first sets out his 'function/rank' matrix ([1971] 2002: 94); one function in particular turns out to take on particular prominence in the grammar of *The Inheritors*. Halliday uses the term 'prominence' to name the phenomenon of 'linguistic highlighting, whereby some feature of the language of a text stands out in some way' ([1971] 2002: 99). Halliday selects the term at least partly because one's attention can be brought to a feature not merely because that feature constitutes a departure from a norm. Quoting Wellek, he rejects a tendency in linguistic stylistics to 'focus on deviations from, and distortions of, the linguistic norm' (Wellek, in Sebeok, 1960, cited in Halliday, [1971] 2002: 99). Halliday's analysis of *The Inheritors* shows that 'syntax need not be deviant in order to serve a vision of things; a foregrounded selection of everyday syntactic options may be just as visionary, and perhaps more effective' (Halliday, [1971] 2002: 104–5; cf. his quote from McIntosh, p. 100).

A further theoretical point is made by Halliday here; that is, that there is no universal linguistic norm against which one can judge an instance of linguistic frequencies. For the purposes of an investigation, a comparative benchmark has to be established on the basis of reasoned argument. A text may be compared with 'the author's complete works, or the tradition to which it belongs'; what might be globally a departure could be locally a norm; the relevant comparison could be 'language as a whole', in a diatypic variety or register characteristic of some situation type (Halliday, [1971] 2002: 100). Halliday argues that we always have a choice between saying 'either "this departs from a pattern" or "this forms a pattern"' (Halliday, [1971] 2002: 100). Linguistic stylistics is 'essentially a comparative study' (Halliday, [1964] 2002: 6). Whether one views a pattern as positive prominence (confirming an existing tendency) or negative (departing from a norm) depends on the 'standpoint of the observer' (Halliday, [1971] 2002: 100). He adds that linguistic prominence in itself provides 'no criterion of literary value' (Halliday, [1971] 2002: 103). While Halliday argues for the value of quantitative statements in the study of linguistic patterns in literature, he also argues that:

> What cannot be expressed statistically is foregrounding: figures do not tell us whether a particular pattern has or has not 'value in the game' . . . The figures, obviously, do not alone constitute an analysis, interpretation, or evaluation of the style. (Halliday, [1971] 2002: 103)

In Golding's writing, a particular set of grammatical patterns have significance because they '"belong" in some way as part of the whole'; they are relevant by virtue of having 'congruence with our interpretation of what the work is about'. Hence, 'the criteria of belonging are semantic ones' (Halliday, [1971] 2002: 120). The criterion for 'eliminating what is trivial and for distinguishing true fore-grounding from mere prominence of a statistical or an absolute kind' is to con-sider whether and how a linguistic pattern relates to 'the underlying functions of language' (Halliday, [1971] 2002: 98). Halliday argues, beautifully, that what is foregrounded in *The Inheritors* are selections in transitivity. And, while he does not use the term 'deautomatization' in his account of Golding – this term comes into his work in his 1982 paper on Priestley – the ideas encapsulated in the term are present in his 1971 work. But his interpretation of foregrounding in *The Inheritors* depends on his metafunctional conception of lexicogrammar:

> since the role of syntax in language is to weave into a single fabric the different threads of meaning that derive from the variety of linguistic functions, one and the same syntactic feature is very likely to have at once both a deeper and a more immediate significance. (Halliday, [1971] 2002: 105)

In the patterns which are key to the expression of 'subject matter', namely choices in the transitivity system, Halliday draws attention to the 'vision' in Golding's work; 'subject matter' and 'vision', he argues, are 'merely different levels of meaning' in a literary work (cf. Hasan's model which distinguishes the level of 'verbalization' from the level of 'theme', Hasan, 1985a). In *The Inheritors*, the vision and the subject matter are 'closely interwoven' (Halliday, [1971] 2002: 105), a position that follows when one assumes that 'there are no regions of lan-guage in which style does not reside' (Halliday, [1971] 2002: 97). Here he draws on Hasan, who claims:

> Each utterance has a thesis: what it is talking about uniquely and instantially; and in addition to this, each utterance has a function in the internal organization of the text: in combination with other utterances of the text it realizes the theme, structure and other aspects. . . . (Hasan, 1967, cited in Halliday, [1971] 2002: 105)

Halliday brings out what Golding's work shows about the aesthetic power of language:

> The immediate thesis and the underlying theme come together in the syntax; the choice of subject-matter is motivated by the deeper meaning, and the transitivity patterns realize both. This is the explanation of their powerful impact. (Halliday, [1971] 2002: 106)

5.2 Deautomatization

The term 'deautomatization' does not come into Halliday's account of the language of literature until his 1982 paper on Priestley, although the discussion above of the two orders of meaning carried in transitivity selections in Golding are very much in harmony with Halliday's discussions of grammar in his 1982 and 1987 papers. He argues that the term 'deautomatization' is, however, more apt than 'foregrounding' because:

> what is in question is not simply prominence but rather the partial freeing of the lower-level systems from the control of the semantics so that they become domains of choice in their own right. In terms of systemic theory the de-automatization of the grammar means that grammatical choices are not simply determined from above: there is selection as well as pre-selection. Hence the wording becomes a quasi independent semiotic mode through which the meanings of the work can be projected. (Halliday, [1982] 2002: 131)

'Deautomatized' implies that grammar can also be 'automatized'. Halliday describes this state as 'words and structures . . . in their automatic function as the "output" of semantic choices'; as realizing 'the semantic selections in an unmarked way – getting on with expressing the meanings, without parading themselves in patterns of their own' (Halliday, [1982] 2002: 141, 130). A literary text like any other requires this automatic function of grammar to 'carry forward the movement of the text'; but the 'words and structures' can also become deautomatized, and 'take on a life of their own as engenderers of meaning' ([1982] 2002: 141). This is this basis for Halliday arguing for the term 'deautomatization' over 'prominence'. Deautomatization, he argues, is 'more than prominence'; while prominence is 'achieved through an untypical distribution of symbols in their typical function in the text . . . here we are referring to their appearance in a transcendent function, whereby a grammatical system as a whole directly encodes some higher-level semiotic, bypassing the semantic organization of the text' ([1982] 2002: 141). Halliday uses the notion of deautomatization both as a descriptor of phenomena in the context of literature, and as a feature of the interpretative process, arguing that once a metafunctional analysis has been conducted, the analyst's role is to 'deautomatize', to 'interpret the grammar in terms that go beyond its direct realizational function'. This is a process in which the analyst must 'distance the text, and respond to the language: to focus out the background, and let the words and structures speak for themselves' ([1982] 2002: 139).

The idea some particular arrangement of grammatical features can produce something which can be called 'a semiotic helix' is one which requires Halliday's particular understanding, and development, of the work of scholars like Whorf

and Firth. As far as Google is aware, only one searchable text has the collocation 'semiotic' with 'helix' – a book called *Space in Musical Semiosis* (Ojala, 2009).
Halliday's work is remarkable for its vision of the agency of grammar in the
construction of meanings, and for what he is able to bring out about the work
that grammar does in making sense of the deep human cultural preoccupations
and experiences, despite the limits that he claims for our metalanguage – our
'grammatics' to use the term he coined – for the description of grammar. In
a simile he borrowed from Whorf, Halliday has argued that 'the grammatics
(grammar as metalanguage) is to the grammar (the language) as a bludgeon is
to a rapier' (Halliday, [1987] 2002: 129). By contrast to grammar – the abstract
mode of organization wholly internal to language – our grammatics is 'feeble
and crude'. Yet with his 'feeble and crude' grammatics, Halliday shows that the
'incisive penetration and positive indeterminacy' achieved by the human mind
are properties of human language, which is 'the very system by which they are
developed, stored and powered' (Halliday, [1987] 2002: 129).

6 What Do Halliday's Analyses Show?

6.1 Yeats and the Scale of 'Verbness'

Halliday's case for the role of linguistics in stylistics includes the argument that
the meaning of a text is 'accessible . . . but that it encompasses a great deal more
than the manifest propositional content' (Halliday, [1987] 2002: 149). But the
proof of the pudding is in the eating: how do Halliday's own analyses stack up
as exemplars of his theoretical claims and contributions? Since his published
writings on literary text span nearly a quarter of a decade (the period 1964 to
1987) it is not surprising that his work has evolved over this time. His first
paper, a discussion of general methodological matters in a linguistic stylistics,
includes some analysis of a set of short texts, such as W. B. Yeats' *Leda and the
Swan*. His discussion of the poem draws attention to certain grammatical features, and uses a contrastive method to explore them (comparing aspects of the
language with selections of prose, and later with another poem by Yeats and
one of Tennyson's). The discussion lacks the directedness of his other papers, in
particular the papers on Golding, Priestley and Tennyson; he does not, at any
point, present an interpretation of the significance of the grammatical patterns
in *Leda and the Swan*.

But his analysis shows already a deep understanding about how much work
grammar does, and how close attention to its patterns will bring out a renewed
appreciation for the distinctions that can made through grammatical choices.
He proposes, for instances, the idea of 'a sort of scale of "verbness" in the use
of verbal items – the "cline of verbality" to give it a jargonistic label' (Halliday,

[1964] 2002: 12). His 'sort of scale' consisted in six points. At one end he locates the most 'verbish' selection of all, a finite verbal group in a free clause. As one moves towards the other end of the cline, 'the more the status of the verb is attenuated, until finally it is subordinated altogether to the nominal element without even the formality of a rankshift'. In *Leda*, he argues, 'the verbal items are considerably deverbalized' (Halliday, [1964] 2002: 12), and that it is in particular the lexical items construing violence where the 'deverbalizing' is prominent; they get lexically 'more powerful' as they get grammatically 'less "verbal"'. Thus, *hold, push, put on, feel* are finite verbal groups in free clauses; while *stagger, loosen* and *caress* do not even function within the verbal group (Halliday, [1964] 2002: 13). Halliday does not reach a conclusion about the significance of this pattern in this poem; but it is a demonstration of how one applies paradigmatic descriptions of grammar to the process of text analysis.

6.2 Prominence in Golding's *The Inheritors*

With respect to Golding, Halliday's focus is the grammar of transitivity, 'the linguistic resources as they are used first to characterize the people's world and then to effect the shift of world-view' (Halliday, [1971] 2002: 108). Halliday's method is to select from three points in the logogenesis of the novel: first, from the early part of the book, where Golding presents a 'narrative of the people'; this section provides a strong contrast with the end of the novel, where the world view has shifted over to that of the 'inheritors', the hominid species that invades the world of the Neanderthals. A third passage is selected at the point in the novel where the transition between these cosmologies is taking place. It should be noted first of all that Halliday's analysis is 'lexicogrammatical', in that his findings are a function of the combination of patterns in closed systems, such as process type and voice, with tendencies in open systems, such as more delicate lexical choices of items within a grammatical function (delicacy with respect to Actor / Subject selection, delicacy in lexical choices of process type). Thus, in building the world view of the Neanderthals, it is important to notice Golding's choice of material processes, of simple movement in intransitive structures, of things that lack description or classification of any kind. Thus 'the picture is one in which people act, but they do not act on things; they move, but they move only themselves not other objects'. The genius of such writing is the realization of a 'semantic drift' (Butt, 1983) by a wide range of linguistic selections. As Halliday notes, 'even such normally transitive verbs as *grab* occur intransitively: *he grabbed at the branches*'. The 'syntactic tension expresses this combination of activity and helplessness', a world view in which 'there is no cause and effect', where 'people do not bring about events in which anything other than themselves, or parts of their bodies, are implicated', where 'people do not act on the things around them; they act within the limitations imposed by the things' (Halliday, [1971] 2002: 109, 113, 114). In the world of the 'inheritors', the 'horizons have broadened'; 'Where the people were bounded by tree and river and rock, the tribe are bounded by sky and sea and mountain' (Halliday, [1971] 2002: 118). This transformation is, as Halliday shows, encoded lexico-grammatically; in the final section of the novel, transitive structures predomi-nate, agency belongs to humans not inanimate things, humans intentionally act on external objects, their actions are more varied, and they produce results, and things in the world are increasingly taxonimized.

6.3 Deautomatization in Priestley's *The Inspector Calls*

In his analysis of Priestley's play, *The Inspector Calls*, Halliday suggests that 'to create a partially differing reality by conversational means within the space-time of a dramatic performance is almost bound to demand some de-automati-zation of the language' (Halliday, [1982] 2002: 131). Halliday notes the negative appraisals of Priestley's language – 'flat naturalistic prose'; language that 'he cannot persuade to leave the ground' (Lloyd Evans, 1964; Hughes, 1958; cited in Halliday, [1982] 2002). But Halliday shows otherwise. Priestley's play dra-matizes the relations between a middle-class, mill-owning, family (the Birlings) and a young working-class woman who has taken her own life. *The Inspector* uncovers the many facets of the family's relations to this woman, including the father who denies her decent wages, and his daughter's fiancé, who takes her as his mistress, but leaves her when she becomes pregnant. In a complex social drama such as this, what meanings might be apparent when 'the words and structures speak for themselves' (Halliday, [1982] 2002: 139)? Halliday selects for his study an exchange more or less at the middle point of play, in which a tense interaction between the Inspector and members of the Birling family unfolds around a photo of the young woman, Eva. Halliday draws attention to selections from the grammatical systems of modality, selections both about probabilities and obligations. These meanings are expressed in different ways, and, Halliday argues, with different meaning effects. Where a modal selection is expressed by a modal verb, the modality is assigned by the speaker implicitly; an option such as the use of a first person mental process ('I think') makes this subjective assignation explicit. Other options provide the speaker with a mode for 'objectifying' modality. In *it's possible she has changed* or *you are required to do so*, the speaker 'is claiming that the probabilities are inherent in the situation, or that the source of the obligations is elsewhere' (Halliday, [1982] 2002: 135). Halliday sets out the meanings of Priestley's selections in their 'automatized' function. As the scene unfolds, the characters engage in a verbal parry around the photograph. Halliday describes the scene as a challenge from the Inspector, from which a conflict between himself and Mrs Birling arises, leading to a confrontation between the Inspector and Mr Birling. Mr Birling's daughter, Sheila, then takes over and gives an explanation of what has transpired, and evaluates the meanings of these events.

The passage 'encapsulates the theme of social responsibility not just as a topic but as an issue: as something that has to be accepted, but that also is associated with opinions, interpretations and conflicts' (Halliday, [1982] 2002: 140). In a claim which resounds with both Jakobson (see citation in Halliday, [1964] 2002: 8) and Mukařovský (1977), Halliday argues that the lexicogrammatical selections not only construe these themes, but draw attention to their own construing power. The thrust of this combination in this work of verbal art is, Halliday argues, to bring into the foreground the semiotic basis of the social order, and therefore, its status as something negotiated, via language, between people. Social obligations, however much they may be expressed as objectively required, are established and maintained through 'the subjective reality of this world' (Berger & Luckmann, 1966, cited in Halliday, [1982] 2002: 130). Halliday also argues Priestley is drawing our attention to 'then and now', bringing together the two themes of 'time and social obligation' in this play, themes which 'are so often associated in Priestley's plays' (Halliday, [1982] 2002: 146). Halliday shows these themes 'turn out to be closely associated also in the linguistic system' (Halliday, [1982] 2002: 146). Priestley's play, through its grammatical patterning, draws attention to the temporally contingent nature of social obligation:

> The individual's social responsibilities are the actualization of the timeless fabric of existence which guarantees us and gives us the 'I-now' such contingent reality as it has. (Halliday, [1982] 2002: 148)

6.4 Deautomatization in Tennyson's *In Memoriam*

The focus of Halliday's exploration of *In Memoriam* is the central passage of the poem. He selects three sections from the middle of the poem (constituting 17 stanzas in all). While his study of *The Inheritors* and *The Inspector Calls* focus on the meanings of choices in one metafunction, his analysis of Tennyson involves the examination of logical, interpersonal and experiential meanings, and their co-selections in this passage. Halliday shows how selections from these functions create semantic waves in parallel; the mood, for instance 'oscillates' between various selections creating 'a pattern of assertion and challenge, terminating in an apostrophic coda where the clauses are exclamatory in function' (Halliday, [1987] 2002: 155). The experiential selections run in phase with the logical selections, creating 'a second dimension of structure having an ideationally based phasal organization' which is 'slightly, but not randomly, out of phase with the pattern set up by the interpersonal structure' (Halliday, [1987] 2002: 157). The experiential patterns of this extract are material (first destructive, then dispositive), a combination of mental and verbal, and relational of the attributive type. Halliday's interpretation of these co-selecting features creates a dynamic exploration of the social implications of emerging scientific interpretations of nature (that humans are descended from other life forms), combined with the motif of the grief of personal loss.

Halliday's exploration of Tennyson is titled 'Poetry as scientific discourse'. Halliday regards the poem to be one with 'an important place in English semo-history, in the struggle to come to terms with the scientific ideology of the century following Newton' (Halliday, [1987] 2002: 152). 'These stanzas' he argues 'fall within the tradition of the scientific imagination: the works of the great poet-scientists from Lucretius onwards whose poetic text displays in a unique form the grammatical construction of reality' (Halliday, [1987] 2002: 152, 162). The grammar of these stanzas 'has created an intricate semiotic helix', which moves from the view that the idea of evolution 'rehumanizes science', that this idea restores 'man's place in nature', that nature destroys both species and individuals, and that his beloved friend has died. Halliday's summary is a 'crude' paraphrase; *In Memoriam* 'construct[s] a semiotic universe at the intersection of science and poetry' through 'the poeticization of science' (Halliday, [1987] 2002: 166–7).

7 Concluding Remarks

For some scholars in stylistics, Halliday's work is central to modern stylistics (e.g. Nørgaard et al., 2010; Simpson, 2004). It is somewhat frustrating, with Halliday in the latter part of his career, that he was not able to give more attention to this domain of his linguistic study. Moreover, his three central papers (on Golding, Priestley and Tennyson), could each have been their own monograph; but more time spent on his stylistic explorations would have taken time from other areas of his investigations. Halliday's papers on literature are few in number, but are full of insights about grammar as a mode of meaning, and the kinds of patterning that can be observed when one looks closely, theoretically and descriptively, at texts created by great writers (literary and scientific), whose work rewards such close attention.

Notes

1. Technically 6, since 'The linguistic study of literary texts' was original published as two papers. See Halliday, [1964] 2002.
2. Lee argues that Whorf's notion of 'cryptotype' is more narrowly conceived than Halliday's use of the concept (Lee, 1996: 181–2).

3. Hasan's work on verbal art goes beyond 1985a; but Halliday's concludes in 1987.
4. 'Foregrounding' is Garvin's (1964) translation of the Czech word *ackualizace* (Fulton 1999: 180; O'Toole & Shukman, 1977: 16). Fulton writes that 'deautomatization' is another translation of this term (Fulton, 1999: 181). Fludernik (Fludernik, 2005: 329) writes that Mukařovský replaced the term *ostranenie* (translated as 'marking strange', a key term in the Russian Formalist tradition – see O'Toole & Shukman, 1977) with *ackualizace*.
5. See also Hasan, 1996, for a more extensive discussion of field, tenor and mode in verbal art.

Part IV

Directions of Development
from Halliday

15 Halliday's Three Functions and Their Interaction in the Interpretation of Painting and Music

Michael O'Toole

1 Functions

In this part of the chapter, I want to compare and relate two concepts of 'function' in a comparison of two paintings. One is the Hallidayan concept of 'semantic metafunction', which, for language, distinguishes between the Ideational, the Experiential and the Textual functions in the construction of spoken and written texts. Since the material of a visual art like painting is radically different from verbal language and works through quite distinct systems of choice,

I have adopted the labels 'Representational function', 'Modal function' and 'Compositional function' for my sketch for a systemic functional semiotics of painting, sculpture and architecture (O'Toole, [1994] 2011).

The other concept of 'function' was applied by the Russian Formalist theorists of the 1920s. Their main focus was on the structure of literary texts, but they also applied many of their key concepts to the theory and analysis of the visual – indeed multimodal – art of film. Yurii Tynyanov wrote in 1927:

> The work of art is a system of correlated factors. Correlation of each factor with the others is its *function* in relation to the whole system. It is quite clear that every literary system is formed not by the peaceful interaction of all the factors, but by the supremacy, the foregrounding of one factor (or group) that functionally subjugates and colours the rest. This factor bears the name that has already become established in Russian scholarly works of *the dominant*. (Tynyanov, 1927; translation O'Toole & Shukman (eds) RPT, 1977)

A key difference between these concepts of 'function' is that the Hallidayan one applies to every genre of spoken and written language – and by extension to multimodal genres – while the Russian one is specific for works of literature and other arts: it is what unifies the elements, foregrounding some and subjugating others in such a way as to point to preferred, or dominant, readings of the text as an integrated whole. I have chosen the term 'hot spots' to designate those areas of systemic choice where the artist seems to have concentrated his or her selections from the ones available in different functions and ranks of unit.

2 The Interplay of Compositional and Modal Functions in Hinder's *Abstract Painting*

My chart (Table 15.1) for the Functions and Systems in Painting (O'Toole, 2011: 24 – Table 1.5) seems to confirm that an abstract painting such as the one (Figure 15.1) by the Australian painter Frank Hinder 'Abstract Painting' (1947) exploits systems in the Compositional function at every rank:

- at the rank of Work the 'depicted' elements relate to the outer Frame in geometric terms of Horizontals, Verticals and Diagonals, and to each other in terms of Line, Rhythm and Colour;
- their relative position and alignment within and between visual Episodes involves both Parallelism and Opposition, as well as a degree of Subframing; Figure elements relate to each other in Shape, Line, Intersection, Colour, Light, Transparency and Texture.

Table 15.1 Functions and systems in painting

Function \ Unit	REPRESENTATIONAL	MODAL	COMPOSITIONAL
WORK	Narrative themes Scenes Portrayals Interplay of episodes	Rhythm Modality Gaze Frame Light Perspective	*Gestalt:* Proportion Framing Geometry Horizontals Line Verticals Rhythm Diagonals Colour
EPISODE	Actions, events Agents—patients—goals Focal/side sequence Interplay of actions	Relative Prominence Scale Centrality Interplay of Modalities	Relative position in work Alignment Interplay } of forms Coherence

FIGURE	Character Object
	Act/Stance/Gesture
	Closing Components
		Gaze Contrast: Scale
		Stance Line
		Characterization Light
		           Colour
			Relative position in
			    episode
			Parallelism/Opposition
			Subframing

MEMBER	Part of body/object Natural form	Stylization	Cohesion: Reference (Parallel/Contrast/Rhythm)

Figure 15.1 Frank Hinder: *Abstract Painting* (1947), Collection,
Art Gallery of Western Australia.

The rectangular Frame of Hinder's painting is broadly divided horizontally into the top two-thirds (dominated by blue tones and the upper parts of the larger cones) and the bottom third (dominated by pinkish-beige tones, the pointed ends of the cones, and the intersections between the small and large cones).

Vertically, the space is apportioned between the left five-twelfths (with the straight-edged large cone almost touching the left edge of the frame and with three smaller straight-edged cones, two arranged vertically and one horizontally) and the seven-twelfths on the right dominated by a large curved-edge cone (a full twelfth from the right edge) and the small horizontal cone intersecting with it near their points.

Three parallel bands appear significant:

(1) the one running horizontally across the painting, which is interrupted by the right edge of the intruding (and largest) oblique cone, but resumes in shades of blue, slightly narrower at its left edge, interrupted again by the small blue vertical cone;

(2) the parallel band separating the large left-hand cone from the large oblique cone; its upper section is dominated by the darkest blue in the painting;

(3) the narrow parallel band separating the left edge of the small blue cone and the large cone that contains it. (Note that both 2 and 3 are intersected, but not masked, by the small horizontal orange cone, bottom left.)

Although, as we have seen, many lines and curves intersect and interrupt one another, most of the lines are smooth and geometrically precise. Some slight deviations from this (the exceptions that prove the rule) are the wavy line separating light blue and dark blue between the tops of the main vertical cones; the sudden break in the width of the horizontal oblique cone; the complex 'knot' of small triangles around the point of the large right-hand cone (bottom right), which highlights the onset of the reddish parallel strip along most of the bottom of the painting. This also appears to cut into the cream non-geometric shape, bottom left.

I take Hinder's painting to be very much about intersections (like life!). The only shape that almost does not intersect with anything is the small blue vertical cone within the large left-hand cone on the left. Only its sharpest point pierces the straight side of the horizontal orange-red cone below it. This latter cuts right across the point of the large left cone (but does not mask it) and the oblique parallel band (2), masking it, and pierces the left side of the large oblique cone.

Meanwhile, the small bright orange-red vertical cone intersects with (but does not mask) the top curved edge of the large left cone and the wavy blue line above, but does not quite touch the small blue vertical cone below it, with which it is parallel.

The large oblique cone has its point cut off by the bottom frame but inter-sects three times with the large right cone and the hemisphere, which also cuts into it from the left (but without masking either shape). Apart from this rela-tion between the right cone and the oblique cone, the right cone twice inter-sects with the parallel horizontal band (1) and twice with the small orange-red horizontal cone, bottom right. It is semi-transparent and does not mask any of these shapes. It does, however, mask the bright cream shape, bottom right, with which it intersects four times.

It is clear from the foregoing that we cannot describe any of the other abstractions without mentioning Colour and Transparency – perhaps because these offer us ready labels for more abstract relations. As far as Colour itself is concerned, the top left quadrant is dominated by a rich blue, shading off to a lighter blue at the top edge; the top right is a kind of sage-green interrupted by the orange-beige of the right-hand curve of the large right cone. The bot-tom third of the painting is predominantly cream, though this shades off to brown (bottom right), orange (bottom left) and sage (bottom mid-left). Of the four smaller cones, three are mainly in a range of tones from red to brown or orange (depending on their intersections), while the largest of them, contained within the large left cone, is blue shading into pink.

You could describe the whole of this abstract painting as a play with the abstractions of Transparency and Intersection, as the shapes all involve differ-ent degrees of transparency or masking and they intersect with each other to varying degrees, and we read these detail-by-detail as we scan the work.

The Textures in the painting relate closely to the colour, not least because the pastel hues are a product of the *tempera* paint Hinder often uses (pigment mixed with water and egg yolk: see his *Flight into Egypt*, which is analysed in detail in O'Toole, 1995). The tempera wash produces areas of relatively solid colour, like the central blue area between the large cones or the brownish-red of the three small cones (two horizontal and one vertical) and the geometrical com-plex of cones, triangles and trapeziums, bottom left and bottom right. However, it also thins out to a lighter and more speckled wash (left background and the rounded part of the large right-hand cone, where it almost seems to be reflect-ing light). It is at its thinnest in the cream-coloured areas, which actually appear to be illuminated from outside the image – and *that is a Modality*, one aspect of the Address of the painting to the viewer.

I want to argue that for all the foregrounding of abstract Compositional shapes and relationships, a series of 'hot spots' on our Functions chart (Table 15.1) is where these interact with systemic choices in the Modal function in terms of

- Scale, Line, Light and Colour at the rank of FIGURE;
- Scale, Centrality and Relative Prominence at the rank of EPISODE; and
- Rhythm, Framing and Light at the rank of the whole WORK.

I am aware that this formal analysis seems very abstract, but I think it helps the viewer to focus on an *Abstract Painting*. It obliges the viewer to stand in front of the painting for more than the 10 seconds we usually allow ourselves and to learn to 'think with our own eyes', as I have said elsewhere (O'Toole, [1994] 2011). The complex interaction of abstract relations is probably more akin to the interrelation of Key, Notes, Melody, Tempo and Orchestral Colour in a piece of music – all of which can only be described abstractly, unless we are looking for a story-line.

It is intriguing to consider why abstract relations are so much better defined, and learned, and *valued* in musical theory, analysis and interpretation than in the visual arts. Is it because music is already composed and transposed from sounds (or their imaginings) to the abstract notation of notes, tempi, key signatures and indications of volume and style of performance – all of which get interpreted and reproduced by instrumental soloists, sections of orchestras, whole orchestras and conductors? Is it because all music teaching starts with this notation, or because the practice of notation – with variations – has been used and taken for granted and passed on for centuries? It is a collective cultural tradition, whereas painting involves an individual artist expressing their meanings on some surface for individual viewers to interpret.

3 The Representational Function in an Abstract Painting

If I am right in thinking that the 'hot spots' in Hinder's 'Abstract Painting' are produced by the interaction of the Compositional and Modal functions, is there any place for an analysis of the Representational function? A website devoted to Frank Hinder (All Images © Estate of Frank Hinder) entitles this painting 'Floating' (a reproduction with the colours washed out – almost bleached – compared to the original in the Art Gallery of Western Australia). We do not know whether this was Hinder's own title, but it seems to tie down the meaning of the cone shapes to balloons. This seems to me to impoverish the shapes and the relationships between them. We can all recognize a cone, and the universal relationships of contrast (in size, colour and positioning), and the processes of containment and of intersection are all represented in this painting. Of the two large vertical cones, the one on the left relates variously to three small ones:

- it contains one, the blue vertical cone;
- nearly contains one, the orange-red vertical cone; and
- cuts across the middle of the brown horizontal cone below it.

The large cone on the right is less of a pure cone (its rounded top extends down to what should be straight sides) and it cuts across the tip of the horizontal small cone below it. It is more dominated by circular forms as it is 'invaded' by hemispheres from the large oblique cone and the large blue-to-indigo form crossing horizontally from top left.

This play with represented shapes and their relationships is a good example of what Hinder called 'Dynamic Symmetry' ('Dynamic = movement; Symmetry = relationship: Dynamic Symmetry is concerned with the actual living movement you get in growth.') (Hinder website, www.frankhinder.com.au: 'A Visual Language for the 20th Century')

If you have read my analysis of Hinder's neo-Cubist painting *Flight into Egypt* (O'Toole, 1995), or more particularly of the Russian Suprematist poster *Arrange a 'Red Gift Week' Everywhere and All Over* (1920–1) in chapter 6 of my book (O'Toole, 2011: 140–4), you will not be surprised to find a more anthropomorphic reading of the forms represented in 'Abstract Painting'. The two main vertical cones could be human heads: the straight-edged one on the left being male, the more rounded one on the right leaning towards 'him' being female. If they are a couple, the man seems to have three mini-cones, or children, on his side (a blue 'boy' and two pinkish 'girls', whereas the woman has a close intersecting relationship with just one 'girl'-cone. And what might the oblique cone emerging from the bottom edge of the painting (i.e. outside their world) and leaning towards the 'female'-cone? Is that the stranger threatening their marriage? I don't know, but you can fill out the rest of the novel, including the relations between the little cones, if that is your bent.

Many paintings – and not just landscapes – have a 'horizon line' about a third, or two-thirds, of the way down. In the case of Hinder's painting, this is either a scale establishing the proportions of the other abstractions or a table across which the 'couple' face each other. The horizontal cones below their heads could then be their shoulders and arms (articulating joints) rather than children. In any case, Hinder seems to be aiming at 'Dynamic Symmetry'.

4 The Representational Function in Lowry

If we avoid doing what we usually do in our tours of art galleries, i.e. looking first at the title, and leave aside for the moment the modality of its enigmatic title, Lowry's painting represents a street scene in urban Manchester or Salford during the Depression or the Second World War. The left-hand Episode involves a small crowd of passers-by listening to a male speaker; the right-hand Episode has a slightly less dense crowd listening to a woman speaker. The foreground Episode has men observing the speakers, a mother with her daughter pushing a pram with the baby, two children fighting (left), four children playing (right) and two dogs 'going on with their doggy life' (as W. H. Auden would say).

The background behind the crowds constitutes its own Episode: an urban skyscape behind the speakers and their crowds. Note two features here:

(1) An Episode in painting does not have to be in a sequential relation to other episodes as in narrative. It is simply a distinct visual segment and part of our 'reading' of the painting involves focusing on each of these segments of the visual array in no particular order.
(2) The background Episode seems to divide horizontally between the factory roofs and chimneys and some kind of domed civic building behind the male speaker, while the female speaker is silhouetted against terraces of houses and a church tower with a clock.

5 Lowry's Modalities in '*The Rival Candidate*'

This brings us back to the enigma of the painting's title, which addresses us, the viewers, and is therefore Modal (verbally Interpersonal): what are the candidates (for what?) making speeches about, and who is whose rival? My guess is that

Figure 15.2 Laurence Stephen Lowry: *The Rival Candidate* (1942), Collection, Art Gallery of Western Australia. © Laurence Stephen Lowry/DACS. Licensed by Viscopy, 2014.

the speakers are candidates for different parties in a parliamentary or local council election and that in this male-dominated world of industry in the 1930s the
'rival' is the woman speaker. (She may be a suffragette.) Even Compositionally,
the audience is denser and more focused around the male speaker – although
an elderly man, a thin old lady and a youth in a brown sweater are facing out
towards us with their backs to the male speaker. At Figure rank these three may
be read as Intermediaries between us viewers and the speakers' world – like the
dwarf maid of honour and the dog in Velazquez' 'Las Meninas'.

Here we seem to have a 'hot spot' in this painting, with figures fulfilling a
Representational Function on the edge of a crowd, a Modal function 'gazing'
us into the painting, and a Compositional function bunching together the audience for the male speaker while themselves standing apart from it.

At the rank of Figure the men and women, children and dogs are heavily
stylized, caught in typical poses and actions but simplified to basic outlines
of heavy dark clothing heavy shoes and spiky legs, walking sticks and pipes.
As the British 'Top of the Pops' song for Christmas 1978 by Manchester sing-
ers Brian and Michael termed them: 'Matchstalk Men and Matchstalk Cats and
Dogs'. And yet at the ranks of Work and Episode there is a sense of 'frozen'
action drained of colour, as in early sepia photographs of townscapes anywhere
in the world.

6 Lowry's Composition

As in all of Lowry's urban scenes, the Composition is very strongly geometric (as
we can observe better by slightly screwing up our eyes and observing the canvas
as bands of light and dark rather than as containing recognizable figures):

- the central 'thematic' band across the middle of the painting has the rival
  candidates and their audiences in heavy dark clothes;
- the far more palely sketched background has the city buildings offering a
  kind of virtual reality beyond the candidates and their claims;
- meanwhile the passers-by silhouetted against the pavement in the foreground episode are sparser, more varied and less involved with either
  each other or the discourse of politics.

The painting as a whole is **X**-shaped, with the pair of fighting children (representing the rival parties?) at its centre. Our eye is drawn to them along the light-
paths of the foreground: the girl and boy fighting, bottom left, the dog looking
at the boy in brown and that boy himself forms the left side of an inverted **V**,
while the children playing in the gutter, bottom right, lead our eye through the
mother walking on the pavement and the baby's head pointing straight up the
widest light path to form the right side of the **V**.

Our Representational hunch about the woman speaker as the authentic 'rival candidate' on the grounds of social status and gender politics seems to be supported Compositionally by the visual complexity of her episode:

- her head and gesticulating arm are at the centre of the top-right quarter of the painting, framed by the edge of the building behind her and its neighbouring telegraph pole, and 'squared off' by the lamp-post, two telegraph poles and the chimney belching smoke at the rear of her audience;
- her arm is silhouetted against a light patch of railings, house roofs and the church tower, while the male candidate's gesture hardly emerges from the crowd of bowler-hatted listeners around him.

Once again, the interplay of the three functions (in Halliday's sense) at the different ranks of Figure, Episode and the whole Work points to *light* and *density* as the dominant functions in Tynyanov's sense, both in a classic of abstraction (Hinder) and a classic of social realism (Lowry). I do not believe that this involves any semiotic contradiction – although the systems work differently in each case. It tests the power and flexibility of a detailed analysis of visual art forms along Hallidayan lines, which I like to think will help art lovers to 'think with their own eyes'.

7 Some Notes towards a Systemic Functional Semiotics of Music

Our analysis of Hinder's 'Abstract Painting' focused on a dominant repeated figure of the cone, with three large vertical (or near-vertical) cones and four small cones (two vertical and two horizontal) either contained by or intersecting with the larger ones (Representational function). All four small cones have a dominant and fairly solid colour, while the larger ones share tones of a thinner colour-wash with each other and with the remaining areas of the painting (Modal function). A large horizontal shape – not conical, but with a rounded end – intrudes into the conical discourse from the left, while two horizontal and one oblique parallel bands hold the composition together (Compositional function).

I want to claim that musical themes involving repetition, variation and intersection, comprising melody, are Representational/Experiential in function, like the cones in 'Abstract Painting'. We focus on – and remember, and whistle or hum – whole melodies as if they were isolated entities in the flow of the music. However, melodies vary in Tone, Rhythm, Mood and relative Prominence. These combine with the composer's instructions and the performers' interpretations to perform a Modal function. Meanwhile, each phrase, figure, theme, phase, section and movement – and even the pause – has its place in the Composition as a whole.

Before I attempt to analyse how these functions are realized in two contrasting musical compositions, I should stress how inadequate my qualifications are for this task and how tentative my conclusions. My mother was a Royal Academy-trained music teacher and I grew up with a love of classical music, folk music and blues, but no formal training. Largely self-taught on the guitar, I can pick out tunes but cannot read music fluently. I accompany simple songs and learned some basic studies from the classical guitar repertoire. My acquaintance with musical theory is via *The Language of Music* by Deryck Cooke (1959), *The Unanswered Question* by Leonard Bernstein (1976) and the two chapters on music in *Psychology of the Arts* by Hans and Shulamith Kreitler (1972).

Lacking both the knowledge and the courage to construct my own Systemic Functional chart for music, analogous to the ones for painting, sculpture and architecture in my book *The Language of Displayed Art* ([1994] 2011), I have borrowed the chart devised by my friend and postgraduate student Kristene Thompson, a piano teacher and musical theorist, for her paper 'Music: a systemic functional approach' (2002, unpublished).

8 'Tarrega's '*Recuerdos de la Alhambra*'

'Memories of the Alhambra' (1896) by Francisco Tarrega (1854–1909) is a classic of the guitar repertoire. The title suggests a narrative involving memories of the famous Moorish palace outside Granada, but apart from the cultural influence of classical Moorish architecture and non-representational mural decoration, its metaphors are 'intrinsic' to the music, not 'extrinsic' and imported from the world outside (see Leonard Bernstein's comments when we discuss Tchaikovsky's '1812', further).

Tarrega's piece starts from the motifs of repetition and variation which I have claimed are the essence of melody. Each bar (in 3/4 time) consists of six sets of notes played 'tremolo style' (ring finger–middle finger–index finger rapidly playing a single treble note), accompanied by a single-note bass line played on the lower strings by the thumb. This repetition at the ranks of note and bar varies as the pitch and relation between the melody and bass (i.e. harmonies) change. The piece divides into two sections, each with a repeat. The first is in the key of A minor, while the second moves into A major, so the harmonies and mood differ greatly, but the tremolo pattern is sustained until a short coda at the end. Thus an underlying rhythmic and melodic pattern of repetitions is varied as each section progresses. Like many pieces of classical music, each section has the structure of a five-line stanza, reminding us of the origins of symphonic music in song forms ('airs' and 'arias'), and the last three lines of the stanza include a skipping grace note, which both produces a mini-climax to the melody and ties the two sections together. The coda is preceded by bars with an

Table 15.2 Functions and systems in Music Place chart

Unit/Function	REPRESENTATIONAL	MODAL	TEXTUAL
WORK (MOVEMENT)	Synthesis Self-actualizing Descriptive -extramusical -musicological Interplays of sections	Prominence Tone Rhythm Mood /Character Overall Complexity Certainty Ambiguity	Relation to Work (Mov't) Title Phasing of sections Coherence
SECTION	Broader patterns of Themework Melodic) new/ Harmonic) old/ Rhythmic) modified Transition: Sequencing/ Interplay of Articulations	Relative Prominence Relative Centrality Parallels/Contrasts: Melody/Tonality Rhythm/Tempo Harmonic Rhythm Dynamics Character Cadence	Relative position in work/ Movement Cohesion: Key relations Rhythmic relations Cadence Transitions Coherence Cohesion/Relation of Phrases
PHRASE	Phases Antecedent/Consequent Imitation/Mimicry Character Stance Span/Process: Melodic Harmonic Rhythmic Sequencing / Interplay of Articulations	Complexity Independent/ Melodic Subordinate Harmonic Rhythmic Fortifying/ Disruptive Modifiers Intensifiers Climactic(tense)/ Cadence Anticlimactic (lax) Major/minor key	Relative position in section Cohesion: Musical texture Key Tempo Metre) Connectors:) (upbeat, pauses,) 'Phoric' pivots, sequences,) cadence)) Cohesion/Relation of Articulations
ARTICULATION (sound groups)	Sound groups Timbre: Intonation) Duration Register) Range) Direction	Stylization Loudness Fluid Accentuation Broken Ornamentation Solid Similarity Difference Instrumentation (voices)	Intervallic Cohesion/ Reference: Melodic Harmonic Rhythmic Marks of Articulation Instrumentation (voicing) Instruments

insistent E flat, then D pedal in the bass line, which anticipates the rallentando, or slowing down, of the closing three bars, where the tremolo figure is replaced by an ascending arpeggio and two held chords in A major.

If I am right in claiming that melody constitutes the essence of the Experiential function in a piece of non-programmatic music (the bits we can hum or whistle when we are not in the recital hall), it is clear from the above analysis that the Experiential and Textual functions are inseparable – perhaps why Walter Pater claimed that 'all the arts aspire to the condition of music', i.e. the relations of key, tempo, melodic, harmonic and rhythmic cohesion all realize melody.

If shifts of key, harmonic progressions and intervals, rhythm and tempo all realize a Modal function, what is the role of the composer in affecting his/her listeners' mood? Even in this fairly straightforward solo work, Tarrega has indicated 'Andante' below the title and a 'forte-piano-forte' marking between the first two pairs of bars, which presumably sets the pattern for the whole piece until the strongly marked *pp* of the arpeggio and held chords of the last three resolving bars of the coda.

These shorthand ways of instructing the performer about the preferred mood(s) of the work are clearly signs of the Modal function at work. But in an art form that depends ultimately on the interpretation of a performer (or a conductor and a stage full of performers on every kind of musical instrument), how are we to describe the Modal contribution of the instrumentalist?

Two of the best public performances of Recuerdos de la Alhambra can be googled online and the interpretations of two of the world's best guitarists compared to show the distinctive style and interpretation of each.

- John Williams (1941–), the Australian guitarist, made a recording of Tarrega's work within the Alhambra Palace, which incorporates an unbelievably smooth tremolo and deep respect for the dynamics of the work itself and the building in which he is performing.
- Narciso Yepes (1927–97), the Spanish guitar virtuoso, can be seen and heard performing in a concert hall in Tokyo. His performance uses a greater dynamic range than Williams in both volume, tempo and timbre (i.e. the contrast between the 'sharp' sound of guitar strings plucked near the bridge of the instrument and the mellow sound from nearer the sound hole).

These direct ways in which the composer, with his score marking, and the performer, with his/her fingering and bowing, influence our feelings about the musical piece could be seen as *extrinsic* modalities in the Interpersonal function. But modalities of key and harmony are *intrinsic* to the music itself. Deryck Cooke (1959) and Leonard Bernstein (1976) devote much detailed attention to rising and falling melodies where the very sequence of tones evokes an emotional response in the listener. Here are two strongly contrasting sequences as analysed by Cooke:

> We have postulated that to rise in pitch is to express an outgoing emotion; we know that, purely technically, the tonic is the point of repose, from which one sets out, and to which one returns; that the dominant is the note of intermediacy, towards which one sets out, and from which one returns; and we have established that the major third is the note which 'looks on the bright side of things', the note of pleasure, of joy. All of which would suggest that to rise from the tonic to the dominant through the major third – or in other words to deploy the major triad as a melodic ascent 1–3–5 – is to express an outgoing, active, assertive emotion of joy. Composers have in fact persistently used the phrase for this very purpose. (Cooke, 1959: 115)

> Substituting the minor for the major third in the descending 5–3–1 progression, we have a phrase which has been much used to express an 'incoming' painful emotion, in a context of finality: acceptance of, or yielding to grief; discouragement and depression; passive suffering; and the despair connected with death. (Cooke, 1959: 133)

> [and the author gives many examples from composers over four centuries – including songs and operatic arias where the mood of the words parallels that of the melodies, M.O'T].

The composer–conductor Leonard Bernstein, in a series of lectures at Harvard University in 1973, had recently fallen under the spell of his linguist neighbour at MIT, Noam Chomsky, so tends to discuss musical syntax and semantics in terms of transformations. He regards all metaphors, whether literary or musical, as 'forms of poetic transformations':

> First, those intrinsic musical metaphors I have already mentioned, which are of a purely musical order, and operate rather like those puns-and-anagram games we were speaking of. All these metaphors derive from transformations of musical material – those very *Chomskian* transformations [repetition, inversion, modulation, etc., M.O'T] we investigated last week. By transforming any given musical material from one state to another, . . . we automatically arrive at the test equation of any metaphor: this-is-that; Juliet is the sun. Secondly, we must define *extrinsic* metaphors, by which musical meanings relate to nonmusical meanings. In other words, certain semantic meanings belong to the so-called 'real world', the 'world out there' – the *non*musical world – are assigned to musical art in terms of literal semantic values, namely extramusical ones. This form of this-equals-that is typified in Beethoven's *Pastorale* Symphony, in which certain notes are meant to be associated in the listener's mind with certain images, such as merry

peasants, brooks, and birds; *these are those*. It is a variation of the old formula. (Bernstein, 1976: 131–3)

From a systemic functional perspective, we would, I think, consider Bernstein's *intrinsic* musical metaphors as primarily Textual in function, while his *extrinsic* ones are Experiential. In other words, his insistence on transformations as the motivation for all variation in music blurs an important distinction. Cooke's semantics of tone sequences, on the other hand, clearly argues for an Interpersonal function in the very choice and sequencing of keys and the notes that comprise them.

9 Tchaikovsky's *1812 Overture*: Classical Meets Pop

The notes accompanying the DVD recording of Vladimir Ashkenazy conducting the St Petersburg Philharmonic Orchestra, 'using authentic cannons and bells from St Petersburg', tell us:

> Today the *Ouverture solennelle '1812'*, to give it its original title, is without question his most popular piece, and very likely the most popular piece in the entire classical repertoire. The reason it has achieved such status is surely precisely because Tchaikovsky tossed it off in such a hurry. It is a piece that draws on raw musical instinct, free from the intellectual and emotional constraints of profound self-exploration or questioning. (Decca Record Company, 1998, DVD No. 455, 971–2)

It is what Bernstein would call the *extrinsic* musical metaphors that make this piece so popular and so memorable – 'mere programme music' – as many critics would say, and have said.

Telling the story of the defeat of Napoleon's army by the Russians' smaller and less well-equipped army in defence of Moscow at Borodino in 1812, the musical narrative moves

- from a Russian Orthodox choir chanting in a pious but monotone plainsong 'Lord Preserve Thy People';
- through a jaunty Russian regimental march played by a military band;
- the approaching and increasingly aggressive strains of 'La Marseillaise';
- a long sweeping lyrical melody representing the beauty and simplicity of the Russian countryside and its threatened people;
- a children's choir singing a simple folk song 'At the Gateway';
- the hectic skittering of strings + 'La Marseillaise' in the brass section + a section with the whole orchestra, including cymbals and several types of drum (in counterpoint, but *rallentando*);

- the Russian lyrical melody + anxious skittering + 'At the Gateway', gradually hushing to a *pp*;
- 'La Marseillaise' for the French army in heavy *staccato* + the sweeping Russian theme, rising in pitch and tempo to a loud cannon shot;
- a descending four-note figure (G-F#-E-D) repeated ten times, slowing and softening as the French troops retreat into the impenetrable snow of the Russian winter;
- the Cathedral choir chanting and bells tolling victory, merging into the tsarist anthem 'God Save the Tsar' (A. L'vov);
- brass fanfares of repeated chords + tolling bells;
- the now victorious Russian regimental march in counterpoint with 'God Save the Tsar', the booming cannon and massed choirs;
- a final trumpet fanfare of the Russian military march and final chords.

The extrinsic metaphors here retell a historic narrative deeply embedded in the Russian psyche (and Tolstoy's *War and Peace*) and they all have their origins in a variety of musical genres, sacred and royal, military and civilian, adult and childish. All represent the Experiential function which seems to dominate the work. But as the italics for musical indications of pitch, tempo, and the like, and the adjectives *monotone, jaunty, aggressive, sweeping, lyrical, simple, hectic, anxious, heavy, skittering, softening, booming*, and the like, reveal, the Experiential is constantly Modalized, so that the story is simultaneously factual and emotional.

It is also highly dialogic: hostile armies clash; sopranos and basses harmonize in the plainsong; the orchestra merges with the choir; cellos and basses are in dialogue with the woodwind; in the long lyrical section before the battle the orchestration moves through different sections of the strings, woodwind, brass and timpani; at the climax of the battle itself the strings struggle against the brass; the musical instruments and voices merge with the precisely timed cannon shots.

Moreover, all the resources of the Textual function in music are exploited: the whole work constitutes a single narrative with complication, crisis and denouement; each episode of the battle, its preparations and the victory are dramatized into a continuous text by moments of quiet solemnity, brooding anxiety or riotous celebration before the next phase. And, as with lexical and thematic cohesion in a verbal text, the musical motifs and instrumentation recur as the story progresses.

Tchaikovsky, of course, is one of the great 'classical' composers of symphonies, concertos, ballets and operas and many shorter serenades and sonatas, so how did he come to get caught up in composing such a programmatic piece of 'pop' music as the *1812*? He wrote it in six weeks between 12 October and 19 November 1880 in response to Nikolai Rubinstein's commission for the opening of the Moscow Arts and Industry Exhibition in 1882, the seventieth anniversary of Napoleon's defeat at Borodino and a year after the twenty-fifth anniversary of the coronation of Tsar Alexander II. The Cathedral of Christ the Saviour commissioned by the Tsar was nearing completion, so the social semiotic around 1882 was in a fever for commemorative gestures. The impetus was deflated by the assassination of the Tsar in March 1881, but for the church, civic, commercial and cultural authorities 'the show had to go on'. As the DVD notes tell us,

> The *1812* received its premiere a year late, on 20 August 1882, to the same kind of rapturous reception with which it has been received ever since.
>
> Tchaikovsky undertook the task unwillingly, finally persuaded only by Rubinstein's appeal to write it as a personal favour. But even in accepting the commission he made it abundantly clear that he disliked having to compose music for such public occasions. It was without much agonising that he duly provided something very festive and noisy, complete with cannon shots and bells. . . . It is exactly what Rubinstein had hoped it would be: a work of thrilling celebration that holds the attention of even the most hardened critical ears from the first [barely audible] notes of the opening solemn hymn, through the busy but carefully controlled build up of excitement (helped by the incorporation into the texture of the *Marseillaise*) to the final outrageously clamorous climax.

No chronological or geographic anomalies are too outrageous for this piece of classical 'pop'. 'La Marseillaise' had been the French national anthem since 1795, but was banned by Napoleon in 1805, so it could not have been heard at Borodino in 1812. However, by the time the overture was commissioned it had been reinstated as the French anthem. Meanwhile, back home in Russia, there was no official national anthem in 1812. From 1815 to 1833 an anthem called 'Prayer of the Russians' (sung to the tune of the British 'God Save the King'). 'God Save the Tsar' had become the national anthem, sung to Alexander L'vov's music by the time Tchaikovsky was writing *1812* in 1880.

I have quoted from one of the many fine recordings of Tchaikovsky's overture. That most refined of Russian pianist-conductors, Vladimir Ashkenazy, conducted this historic piece of music about Moscow in her rival city of St Petersburg with the St Petersburg Philharmonic Orchestra, the St Petersburg Chamber Choir, the bells and cannon of the Peter-and-Paul fortress in St Petersburg and the Leningrad Military Band and the shots were fired by an artillery battery of the Leningrad Military District. This was in 1990, a year after the collapse of Communism in Russia, when Leningrad was given back its original name of St Petersburg after 67 years: a further historic excuse for popular celebration.

16 Multimodal Semiosis and Semiotics

Kay L. O'Halloran, Marissa K. L. E and Sabine Tan

Chapter Overview

---

1 Introduction

Michael Halliday's social semiotic theory (Halliday, 1978; van Leeuwen, 2005) provides the basis for the study of language and other semiotic resources in the research field known as 'multimodality' and 'multimodal analysis'. This area of research, pioneered by Kress and van Leeuwen (2006) and O'Toole (2011) in their respective studies of visual design and displayed art, is derived from Halliday's SF theory, developed as systemic functional linguistics (SFL) (Halliday & Matthiessen, 2004; Martin, 1992; Martin & Rose, 2007). Today, multimodal research has expanded to include the study of other semiotic resources (e.g. photographs, music, mathematical symbolism, three-dimensional space) and the integration of semiotic choices in different media texts (e.g. documents, film, hypertext) (see overview in Djonov & Zhao, 2014; Iedema, 2003; Jewitt, 2014; O'Halloran, 2011). While multimodal analysis includes other theoretical perspectives, for example, interactional analysis (Norris, 2004; Norris & Jones, 2005; Scollon, 2001) and cognitive approaches (Forceville & Urios-Aparisi, 2009), Halliday's SF theory provides the underlying basis for the bulk of multimodal research undertaken today, including the present study which, given the centrality of Halliday's social semiotic theory, is referred to as *multimodal semiotics*[1] (see Unsworth, 2008a).

In what follows, we describe how key SF theory concepts can be used to theorize and analyse semiotic resources and their interactions in video texts (see also Bateman, 2014; Bateman & Schmidt, 2014) and images. This includes capturing and modelling combinations of multimodal choices over time using interactive digital technology and information visualization techniques (see further approaches in Bateman, 2014; O'Halloran, E & Tan, 2014). Following Halliday and Hasan's (1985) conception of culture as sets of interrelated semiotic systems, we adopt the view that the meanings of individual semiotic choices are derived in relation to semiotic configurations in discourse, society and culture which themselves are multimodal in nature (O'Halloran, Tan & E, 2014).

We demonstrate the multimodal semiotic approach by investigating two contrasting building projects featured in the British television series 'Grand Designs', hosted by the British designer, writer and television producer Kevin McCloud and produced by Talkback Thames and broadcast on Channel 4.[2] In this study, we use O'Toole's (2011) systemic functional framework for architecture to contextualize the two building projects. Following this, we analyse the 3D computer-generated imagery (CGI) animations from the 'Grand Designs' DVD and television program to explore how different semiotic resources, namely architecture, camera choices and language, work together to create different views of the two housing designs. Lastly, we analyse images of the actual houses to explore what meanings are made in the built structures, and how these compare with the 3D CGI animations and the accompanying voice-over narration.

The overall aim of the study is to present analytical techniques and tools which provide empirical data to support claims about the nature of multimodal semiosis (Bateman, 2008, 2014; Bateman & Schmidt, 2012; O'Halloran et al., 2014), in this case, with respect to the functions of architecture, camera choices and language and their associated intersemiotic interactions over time. In this way, we demonstrate how the multimodal semiotic approach provides theoretical and analytical tools to understand discourse, social practices and culture in ways which to-date have been theorized, but not yet fully operationalized. In this regard, this study is a modest step towards situating multimodal concepts and frameworks in relation to empirical data.

In what follows, we introduce some basic SF theory concepts, O'Toole's (2011) framework for architecture, and systems for camera movement, distance and angle based on Bordwell and Thompson (2010). We use these theoretical frameworks to contextualize the two building designs in the 'Grand Design' series before analysing the 3D CGI 'walk-throughs' of these designs using *Multimodal Analysis Video*[3] software. That is, we use facilities in the software to create time-stamped annotations of systemic choices in the CGI animations and we visualize the resulting multimodal data. Following this, we use facilities in *Multimodal Analysis Image*[4] software to analyse images of the two buildings using O'Toole's (2011) systems for architecture. We discuss the results of the multimodal analyses, and conclude with suggestions for future research directions in multimodal semiotics.

2 Multimodal Semiotic Theory

Halliday (2008: ii–iii) explains how language can be conceptualized as both *system* and *text* which forms the central tenet of SF theory; namely that the system and text are parts of the same conceptual construct:

> 'language as system' and 'language as text' . . . highlights the fact that 'system' and 'text' are two aspects of one single phenomenon. The system is the potential – an open ended network of possibilities; the text is a process and product of selecting from within this overall potential. This complementarity between text and system is realized in the constant shifting between the instantial activity of the moment, and the long-term patterns, which have been built up through textual experience, and thus come to serve as the basis for processing this activity.

Halliday's fundamental insights about language can be extrapolated to other semiotic resources – namely that semiotic resources have underlying *systems of meaning*, where the meaning of an individual semiotic choice is derived from the intersemiotic relations which are established when semiotic choices combine, that is, when multimodal semiosis takes place. As the concept of 'system' in SF theory is explained in detail elsewhere (e.g. Halliday, 2009; Halliday & Matthiessen, 2004), only a brief description of the term and its relation to the functionality of semiotic resources are provided here (see also O'Halloran & Lim, 2014).

Semiotic resources are conceptualized as systems of meaning with options which together capture the meaning potential of that resource. The systems are described as system networks and in some cases, paradigmatic systems with graduated scales of meaning, for example, for descriptions of different dimensions of voice quality (van Leeuwen, 2009) and colour (van Leeuwen, 2011). In some cases, the systems for semiotic resources are organized according to ranks (O'Halloran, 2005, 2008; O'Toole, [1994] 2011), following Halliday's approach to language (Halliday & Matthiessen, 2004). However, regardless of the approach taken in the systemic descriptions of semiotic resources, the meanings of system choices are seen to be context-based (Halliday & Hasan, 1985) – that is, meaning arises in the context of semiotic interactions, giving rise to the multimodal formulations of discourse, context and culture (O'Halloran et al., 2014).

In accordance with SF theory, semiotic resources are seen to be functional, and following Halliday, these functions are called *metafunctions*: namely, *textual* (or compositional) to organize the multimodal text; *interpersonal* (or modal) to negotiate social relations; *experiential and logical* (or representational) to construe the world and logical relations in that world. While there is debate regarding the 'metafunctional configurations' of semiotic resources (van Leeuwen, 1999: 190), semiotic resources are generally seen to serve different functions which accord with Halliday's metafunctional hypothesis. In this study, we focus on the functions of architecture, film framing, language and images and demonstrate how 'resemiotization' of the two housing designs (Iedema, 2001, 2003) across different media, in this case, the 3D CGI video animations and photographs of the actual buildings in the 'Grand Design' series, involve shifts of metafunctional-based meaning. In this manner, we demonstrate the usefulness of SF theory for multimodal semiotics, in this case for providing detailed semantic descriptions of built spaces, video texts and images.

2.1 O'Toole's Systemic Framework for Architecture

O'Toole (2011: 65) proposes a metafunctionally organized and ranked framework for the study of architecture, arguing that buildings have largely a practical function which is clearly signified by semiotic choices at the rank of element, room, floor and building. Simultaneously, built spaces also '"address" the viewer' (O'Toole, [1994] 2011: 64) at these different ranks to create an interpersonal orientation to the experiential elements, which, as O'Toole explains, is a major factor in architectural design choices. As Stenglin (2009: 42) explains, built spaces 'are also designed to make us *feel* – some spaces make us feel comfortable, protected and secure while other spaces evoke a range of negative feelings'. Moreover, built spaces have a close textual relationship to their environment and a specific internal organization making them to some extent (more or less) coherent as a whole. O'Toole's (2011) systemic framework for experiential, interpersonal and textual metafunctions, displayed in Table 16.1, provides the theoretical basis for the analysis of the two 'Grand Designs'.

Table 16.1 Systemic functional framework for architecture (O'Toole, 2011: 65)

Units	Functions		
	EXPERIENTIAL	*INTERPERSONAL*	*TEXTUAL*
BUILDING	Practical function: Public/Private; Industrial/Commercial/Agricultural/ Governmental/Lducational/Medical/ Cultural/Religious/Residential Domestic/Utility Orientation to light Orientation to wind Orientation to earth Orientation to service (water/sewage/ power)	Size Orientation to neighbours Verticality Orientation to road Chthonicity Orientation to entrant Facade Intertextuality: Cladding reference Colour mimicry Modernity contrast Exoticism Opacity Reflectivity	Relation to city Relation co road Relation to adjacent buildings Proportions Rhythms: contrasting shapes, angles Textures: rough/ smooth Roof/wall relation Opacity Reflectivity
FLOOR	Sub-functions: Access Working Selling Administration Storing Waking Sleeping Parking	Height Sites of power Spaciousness Separation of groups Accessibility Openness of vista View Hard/soft texture Colour	Relation to other floors Relation to outer world Relation to connectors; stairs/lift escalator (external cohesion) Relation of landing/ corridor/foyer/room (internal cohesion) Degree of partition Permanence of partition
ROOM	Specific functions: Access Study Foyer Entry Toilet Restaurant Living room Laundry Kitchen Family room Gamesroom Bar Kitchen Retreat Bed room Bathroom En suite Bedroom Servery	Comfort Lighting Modernity Sound Opulence Welcome Style: rustic, pioneer, colonial, suburban 'Dallas', working class, tenement, slum Foregrounding of function	Scale Lighting Sound Relation to outside Relation to other rooms Connectors: doors/ windows/hatches/ intercom Focus (e.g. hearth, dais, altar, desk)
ELEMENT	Light: window, lamp, curtains, blinds Air: window, fan, conditioner Heating: central, fire, stove Sound: carpet, rugs, partitions acoustic, treatment Seating (function/comfort) Table (dining/coffee/occasional/desk/ computer/drawing board)	Relevance Functionality: convention/ surprise Texture: rough/smooth Newness Decorativeness 'Stance' Stylistic coherence Projection (e.g. TV)	Texture Positioning: to light/ heat/other elements Finish

2.2 Framing

As Bordwell and Thompson (2010: 186) explain: '[i]n any image, the frame is not simply a neutral border; it imposes a *certain vantage point* onto the material within the image. In cinema, the frame is important because it actively *defines* the image for us.' In this regard, film framing realizes experiential, interpersonal and textual meanings through the size and shape of the frame (in this case, the standard 4:3 ratio), the formulation of off-screen and on-screen space and the definition of the vantage point via mobile framing, camera distance and camera angle (Bordwell & Thompson, 2010). In this study, we investigate the on-screen space and the vantage point of the viewer in the 3D CGI animations of two housing designs in 'Grand Designs'. The basic systems of analysis for framing are described as follows.

2.2.1 Mobile Framing
Mobile framing involves camera movement where the viewer approaches, moves away and circles what is depicted in the on-screen space. Mobile framing is an important resource in the CGI animations in 'Grand Designs' as the viewer is taken on a 'walk-through' the designs, which basically involves moving through 3D space (see the description of 'Grand Designs 3D' software[5]). In this way, camera movements in the CGI animations are not confined to the physical limitations of a camera. On the contrary, the mobile framing in the CGI animations permit the viewer to 'fly' around the 3D space without constraint. As a consequence, the systems for film in Bordwell and Thompson (2010: 199–203) are expanded to include the following choices.

> *Mobile Framing*: Arc Up; Arc Down; Forward; Backward; Circular, Diagonal, Side to Side, Pan Left to Right, Pan Right to Left, Pedestal Up, Tilt Up, Tilt Down, Stationary, Zoom In and Zoom Out.

2.2.2 Camera Distance and Camera Angle
The position from which the building designs are viewed in the 3D CGI walk-through animations are in part determined by the distance of the shot and the camera angle, which are not predetermined measures, but matters of degree. Following Bordwell and Thompson (2010: 194–6), we use the following choices which are generally accepted and understood in film theory.

> *Camera Distance*: Extreme Close; Close; Medium; Long Shot; Extreme Long
> *Camera Angle*: High Angle; Eye-Level; Low Angle

2.2.3 The Functions of Camera Choices

Significantly, as Bordwell and Thompson (2010) claim, there are no absolute meanings attached to technical choices such as mobile framing, camera distances and camera angles. That is, viewing an object or a person from a low angle does not automatically imbue that object or person with power, and vice versa, looking down on a person or object does not diminish the status of that person or object because these choices derive their meaning in collaboration with other choices in the film. Bordwell and Thompson (2010: 196) emphasize this point: 'The fact is that framings have no absolute or general meanings' and '[t]o rely on formulas is to forget that meaning and effect always stem from the film, from its operation as *a system*' [emphasis added]. With this in mind, we introduce the two building designs and explore how viewers engage with these designs in the 3D CGI video and actual photographs of the houses. As we shall see, the metafunctional basis of multimodal semiotics provides valuable insights into how we interpret what we see and hear.

3 Multimodal Semiotic Analysis: 'Loch House' and 'Space Pod'

The case studies examined here are two buildings featured on 'Grand Designs' which chronicles the building and conceptualization process of innovative building projects from start to finish. The 'Grand Design' series aims to present 'unusual and often elaborate architectural homebuilding projects'[6] to the public. Each episode contains commentary and interviews from all parties involved in the building project as it progresses. The CGI walk-through of each building is featured in each episode of the program, together with voice-over commentary provided by Kevin McCloud. The CGI walk-throughs are featured on the DVDs as separate video files, and for this reason, we analyse these video animations in detail.

In this study, we examine two contrasting projects featured in two separate episodes of 'Grand Designs' – 'Killearn: Loch House' (Series 6, Episode 1, 5 April 2006) and 'Peckham: Urban Space Pod' (Series 5, Episode 2, 13 April 2005), henceforth respectively referred to as the 'Loch House' and the 'Space Pod'. The first residence, the Loch House, is a luxurious, spacious property located at a private loch in rural Scotland. The second residence, the Space Pod, is an innovative urban residence located between two Georgian villas and confined within an extremely limited land space in suburban London. The owners of the Loch House are a successful businessman and his wife who are funding the building project through the sale of their current property and a substantial inheritance. The owners of the Space Pod are a couple working as a freelance film producer and dance instructor. Their financial situation is much more constrained than the first couple, as evidenced by their reliance on themselves and their friends as a team of 'Do-It-Yourself' designers and labourers in the construction of the Space Pod, and the loans they had to take in order for the building project to take place.

The two housing designs involve architectural innovation in relation to the constraints of finance. To illustrate, the Loch House has been put on the market for sale with offers over £1,250,000, together with a downloadable brochure which is available from Savills estate agents.[7] The property has been given the name 'Stilwater', which emphasizes its main feature – the large private loch that the Loch House has been built on. On the other hand, the Space Pod, now named 'Peckham House', is not available for sale, although a website offers merchandise for sale, including a DVD for £14.95, and building plans of the house for £2.25, together with an advertisement for dancing lessons.[8] Thus, the owners of the Space Pod seem to be leveraging on the ideals of self-reliance that made their property a reality by offering paid information and advice about 'how to build a dream design' using one's own capabilities and resources, rather than embarking on a building project via the conventional method of hiring design and construction professionals.

The aim of this study is to use multimodal semiotic frameworks to analyse the two building designs, with a view to examining and comparing how the designs are presented to the public in the 3D CGI walk-throughs and images of the actual houses themselves. We begin with a contextual description of both residences, before examining framing techniques and the voice-over narration in the CGI animations to explore how the two designs are presented to viewers. Following this, we examine select images taken from the online brochure of 'Stilwater' and the 'Peckham House' website, looking specifically at the exterior and certain interior rooms of each building to show how different meanings are communicated for each property. We interpret the results in relation to the features of each house, the individual concepts and ideas which motivated each step of the design and building process and the situational context of the photographs which we relate to social and cultural values of consumer society.

3.1 Design and Architecture

The Loch House and the Space Pod are very different in terms of design and architecture. Using O'Toole's (2011: 65) framework for architecture, at the rank of 'Building' (see Table 16.1), the Loch House is situated in a private site, where the building is interpersonally and experientially orientated to its natural sur-roundings, especially water from the loch and light from wide acres of fields and meadows. In contrast, the Space Pod is confined within a restricted urban space that is textually defined by the buildings adjoining the block and the road,

Figure 16.1(a) The Loch House

Figure 16.1(b) The Space Pod

as displayed in the screenshots from *Multimodal Analysis Image* in Figures 16.1a and 16.1b. This difference in orientation (i.e. experiential and interpersonal versus textual) is the result of each building's external environment, where space functions as a semiotic resource that can either be a source of potential to be exploited (by the designers of the Loch House) or a source of constraint that has to be accommodated (by the designers of the Space Pod). In fact, the only constraint on the external appearance of the Loch House was that its design had to conform to local designs which blend with the natural environment. However, for the Space Pod, there was a single storey height restriction, which meant that the builders could not build vertically to create space. In addition, windows could not be built on either side of the house due to the pre-existing walls of two adjoining properties. A further restriction was that the house had to be hidden from view from the street, which meant even less potential for an interpersonal orientation to the road, neighbours and visitors to the building. In contrast, the Loch House is in full view to visitors in a beautiful open natural environment.

On the inside, at the ranks of 'Floor' and 'Room' (see Table 16.1) there are further differences. That is, textually, the interiors of both houses have characteristics of an open-plan concept, but in the case of the Loch House, this concept is applied to all parts of the building, whereas in the Space Pod the open-plan concept applies to the main living area only, which consists of a kitchen, living-room, family space and dining-room all combined into one open space. In contrast, the Loch House has self-contained spaces which are clearly demarcated with minimal use of partitions, yet do not interfere with the free-flowing characteristic of its open-plan concept. Moreover, the full expanse of the two-storey layout of the Loch House is exploited using a double-height living-room that reaches from floor to ceiling, thus allowing for an unobstructed view of the second-floor staircase landing. Consequently, the second storey is not separated from the first in the Loch House, maximizing the use of space to achieve the effect of openness and freedom across spaces which are experientially marked as communal spaces (e.g. sitting room, kitchen/breakfast room, dining area and lounge).

In terms of height and spaciousness, the Loch House, with its two-storey structure, exhibits an extravagance that flaunts the luxury of height and space. In addition, the use of reflective surfaces such as glass brings the outside loch and mountain landscape into the house and creates a free-flowing environment that is light and spacious. The careful selection of certain fixtures, such as the cantilevered glass staircase with steps that appear to be floating in the air, and an unusually large, specially designed aquarium which connects the kitchen and sitting room, also enhance the impression of unimpeded movement and lightness throughout the house, highlighting how the textual, experiential and interpersonal meanings can be woven together to create a unique experience. However, such extravagance comes at a price because the Loch House appears to be a 'designer home' which aims to impress, unlike the personalized space of the Space Pod, as we shall soon see.

3.2 Viewer Vantage Points in the CGI Animation

In what follows, we explore how the respective designs are presented to viewers through camera movement, camera distance and camera angle in the 3D CGI animation walk-throughs. Using *Multimodal Analysis Video* software, we annotated the semiotic choices from these systems over time and calculated the relative percentage of video time assigned to individual choices and combinations of choices. For example, screenshots of the system choices for 'Mobile Framing' for the Loch House and the Space Pod from *Multimodal Analysis Video* are displayed in Figures 16.2a and 16.2b and the accompanying percentages are displayed in Table 16.2.

As Table 16.2 shows, there are similarities and differences in camera movement in the CGI videos for the Loch House and the Space Pod. For example, the

Table 16.2 Camera movement – The Loch House and Space Pod

Camera movement	Percentage in terms of total video time	
	Loch House (%)	Space Pod (%)
Stationary	23.42	22.47
Backward	9.01	15.73
Backward, diagonal	3.60	3.37
Backward, circular	4.50	–
Circular	19.82	12.36
Forward	13.51	11.24
Forward, circular	1.80	10.11
Forward, tilt down	–	2.25
Forward pedestal up	2.70	–
Pan left to right	6.31	4.49
Pan right to left	8.11	–
Arc up	3.60	4.49
Arc down	–	4.49
Tilt up	–	2.25
Tilt down	–	1.12
Tilt down, circular	–	4.49
Diagonal	2.70	–

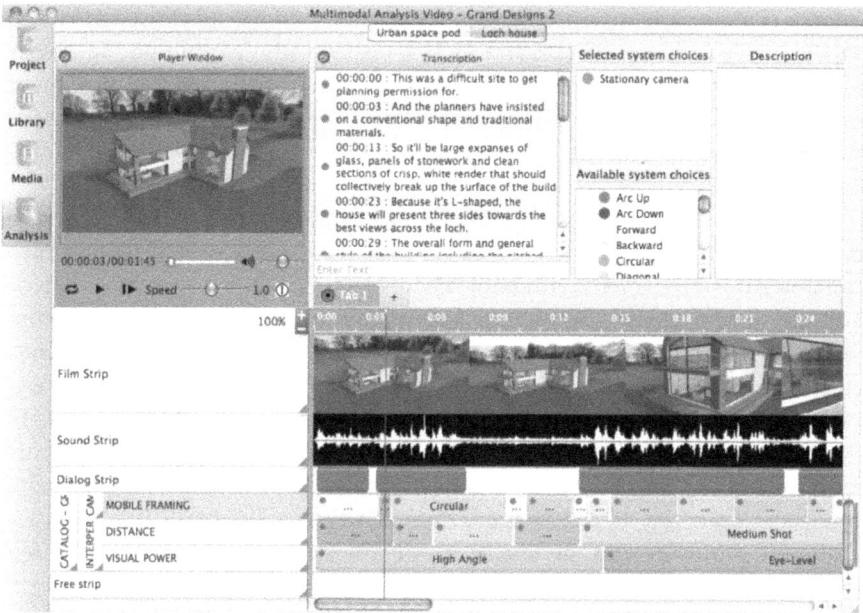

Figure 16.2(a) Camera movement: Loch House

Figure 16.2(b) Camera movement: Space Pod

camera is stationary for approximately the same relative time in Loch House and Space Pod videos (23.42% and 22.47% respectively) permitting the viewer to engage with the on-screen space without being distracted by movement around and through the buildings. However, there are differences in the ways the viewer approaches the two house designs via camera movement, as discussed further.

The use of backward camera movement in the Space Pod (15.73%) with diagonal movements (3.37%) may be contrasted to Loch House (9.01%), which combines this movement with both diagonal and circular movements (3.60% and 4.50% respectively). A possible explanation for this difference is the confined linearity of the Space Pod's layout which reduces the possibility of wide, circular movements, and makes backward linear camera and diagonal movements more common in order to navigate the narrow, elongated structure. In this regard, the circular camera movements for the Space Pod (12.36%) are used mainly to show the exterior of the house, perhaps to avoid the walls confining the premises. In comparison, the Loch House has the luxury of space both on the outside and the inside, thus allowing for combinations of different camera movements which include wide, sweeping, circular camera movements (19.82%) which afford a 360 degree view, emphasizing the vastness of unbounded space in which the building is situated.

The use of forward camera movement in the CGI videos for both house designs is similar (13.51% for Loch House and 11.24% for Space Pod). However, their metafunctional purpose appears to be different. In the Space Pod, the forward camera movement appears to be associated with the textual arrangement of the elongated living space, while forward camera movement in the Loch House performs an interpersonal function for showcasing the high-class, expensive, stylish and exclusive amenities and furnishings contained in the house, for example, the jacuzzi bathroom, the aquarium, black-gloss kitchen and cantilevered glass staircase.

Lastly, the combination of tilt down and tilt down circular camera movements in the Space Pod animation (1.12% and 4.49% respectively) focuses on the sliding-glass roof which provides light and ventilation. Thus, in order to foreground this retractable glass roof as a main feature of the Space Pod, it is necessary for the camera to approach this confined space tilting downwards, in a circular movement that allows the viewer to see as many angles of the room as possible. The Loch House, on the other hand, has many points of entry because of its floor to ceiling glass windows on nearly every vertical face of the residence. As a result, there is little need for the camera to be tilted in the CGI animation for the Loch House.

As displayed in Table 16.3, the camera distances for the Loch House are largely medium shots with some close shots (77.87% and 3.70% respectively) to showcase the various features of the house, followed by some long and extreme

Table 16.3 Camera distance – The Loch House and Space Pod

Camera distance	Percentage in terms of total video time	
	Loch House (%)	Space Pod (%)
Extreme close shot	–	–
Close shot	3.70	13.95
Medium shot	77.78	33.72
Long shot	13.89	51.16
Extreme long shot	3.70	–

Table 16.4 Camera angle – The Loch House and Space Pod

Camera angle	Percentage in terms of total video time	
	Loch House (%)	Space Pod (%)
High angle	21.50	76.74
Eye-level	72.90	19.77
Low angle	4.67	2.33

long shots of the building and surrounding scenery (13.89% and 3.70% respectively). On the other hand, the majority of shots for the Space Pod are long shots of the exterior of the house (51.15%), followed by close and medium shots of the house and its interior (13.95% and 33.95% respectively). These marked differences in camera distance extend to the camera angle (see Table 16.4) where the viewer mainly engages with the Loch House at eye-level (72.90%) while looking down at the Space Pod from a high angle (76.74%).

The combinations of system choices for camera movement, camera distance and camera angle for the Loch House and the Space Pod are displayed as state-transition diagrams in Figures 16.3a and 16.3b. These visualizations are automatically generated from the database of time-stamped annotations for the CGI animations in *Multimodal Analysis Video*. As seen from Figures 16.3a and 16.3b, the interactive visualizations display the different combinations of system choices (bottom right panel) and the relative time spent in each state which is indicated by the size of the circles and accompanying percentages, together with transitions between those states (left panel). These combinations of systemic choices are synchronized with the CGI animations (top right panel) so we can see where these semiotic selections occur in the videos.

The four most common combinations of the camera choices in the Loch House and Space Pod walk-through videos in terms of time (accounting for 43.20% and 40.78% of total time respectively) are displayed in Table 16.5 where

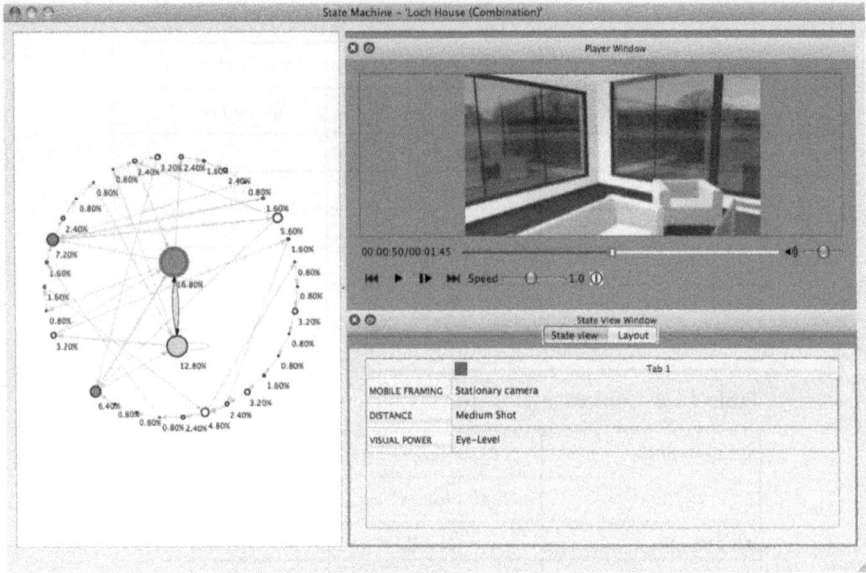

Figure 16.3(a) Vantage points: Loch House

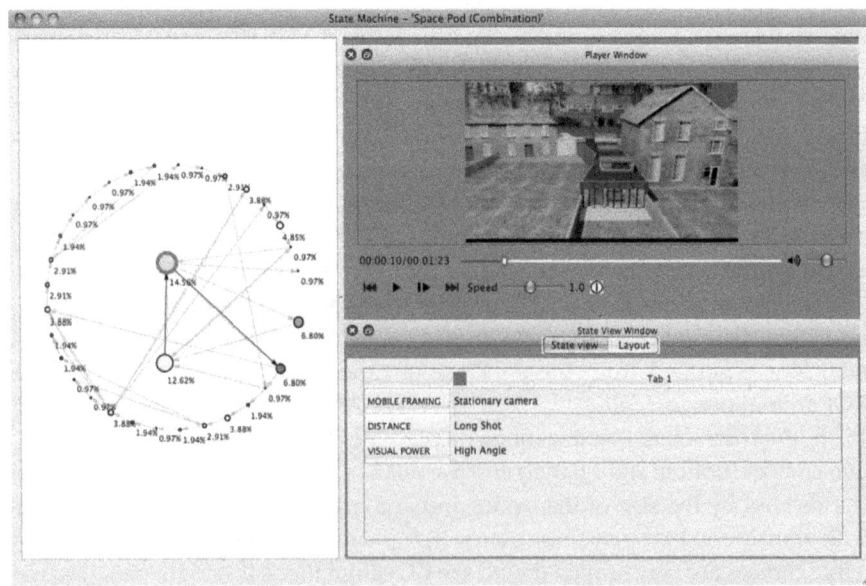

Figure 16.3(b) Vantage points: Space Pod

Table 16.5 Vantage points: The Loch House and Space Pod

House design	Multimodal combinations: Mobile framing Camera distance Camera angle			
	1	*2*	*3*	*4*
Loch House	Stationary Medium Eye-Level	Circular Medium Eye-Level	Forward Medium Eye-Level	Pan Right-to-Left Medium Eye-Level
(43.20%)	16.80%	12.80%	7.20%	6.40%
Space Pod	Stationary Long High angle	Backward Long High angle	Forward Long High angle	Forward-Circular Long High angle
(40.78%)	14.56%	12.62%	6.80%	6.80%

we see distinct differences in the vantage point offered to the viewer in the two CGI animations. That is, variations in mobile framing for the Loch House (i.e. stationary, circular, forward and pan left to right) which occur in combination with medium shots at eye-level, offer a vantage point which positions the viewer as a 'real' participant in the walk-through. In other words, the viewer interpersonally engages and experiences the design features of the Loch House and its relationship to the outside as a cohesive whole through the camera movements which reflect the actual experience of walking through a house, spending 52.83 per cent of video time in the interior. However, the vantage points offered to the viewer in the Space Pod walk-through are quite different. The mobile framing (stationary, backward, forward and forward-circular) does not always accord with the real experience of a walk-through (i.e. one does not approach a house moving backwards) and the long shots and high angle function to position the viewer as a more distant observer. In contrast to Loch House, the viewer spends only 24.42 per cent of video time inside the Space Pod. While many of the camera choices are the product of the actual design, namely the spaciousness of the Loch House versus the bound elongated space of the Space Pod, the different vantage points offered to viewers means that the viewer's experience of each house and its design are quite different.

3.3 Voice-Over Narration in CGI Videos

The vantage points offered to the viewer in the CGI animations are related to the different concepts and ideas forming the overarching theme for each house, as reflected in Kevin McCloud's voice-over narration in the CGI walk-through.

401

For example, our analysis of tag-cloud visualizations generated from the transcripts of the voice-over narration[9] in Figures 16.4a and 16.4b reveal some of the concepts and features that Kevin McCloud wishes to highlight in each house. That is, the lexical choices in the tag-cloud for the Loch House are 'house (5)', 'around (2)', 'bathroom (2)', 'bespoke (2)', 'building (2)', 'designed (2)', 'glass (2)', 'materials (2)', 'planners (2)', 'reflect (2)', 'traditions (2)', 'views (2)' and 'water (2)', while the lexical choices for the Space Pod are 'house (4)', 'space/ space-saving (4)', 'build (2)', 'light (2)', 'mezzanine-pods (2)', 'sliding-glass roof (2)', 'solution (2)' and 'window (2)'. In this respect, Kevin McCloud appears to be more concerned with architectural features of the Loch House and the technical innovations in the Space Pod, as discussed further.

In the Loch House's CGI walk-through, for example, Kevin McCloud highlights the concepts relating to the exclusivity of the owners' taste ('bespoke') and the private loch as a major feature of the property ('water') which represent significant components in the design of the house. In contrast, in the Space Pod CGI walk-through, there is an emphasis on 'solution' and 'space/space-saving' because of the physical constraints of the location that required innovative solutions to overcome the lack of space. Other lexical choices such as 'mezzanine-pods' and 'sliding-glass roof' focus attention on the main architectural and engineering features that allow light and air to come into the house. Thus, it is no coincidence that the lexical item 'light' is repeated. In the Space Pod, light is of particular importance because of the lack of suitable wall-space to construct windows. This reduces the avenues by which light enters the house, and makes innovative means, such as the 'mezzanine pods' and the 'sliding-glass roof' particularly important features in Kevin McCloud's assessment of the success of the design.

In this way, visual framing techniques and linguistic choices in the CGI animations work together to create a different focus on the two building designs. That is, the viewer engages interpersonally with the 'designer' features of the Loch House, while observing the technical innovations of the Space Pod. The interpersonal and experiential orientations to the two building designs are further explored and developed in relation to images of the actual houses.

4 The Actual Houses

We have shown how the vantage point provided to the viewer in the CGI animations reflect particular views of the architecture, approach and design concepts of the Loch House and the Space Pod. In the first case, the viewer is drawn into the Loch House and experiences the architectural features as a coherent whole with regards to the interior and exterior of the building and its relationship with the environment. In a sense, the CGI animation reinforces the desires of the

although (1) aquarium (1) area (1) **around** (2) axis (1)

bathroom (2) bedrooms (1) **bespoke** (2) best (1) break (1)

budget (1) **building** (2) built (1) clean (1) collectively (1) conservative (1)

continuous (1) conventional (1) cost (1) course (1) crisp (1) **designed** (2)

dialogue (1) dictated (1) difficult (1) dining (1) double-height (1) downstairs (1) en-suite (1)

expanses (1) exterior (1) financed (1) fire (1) form (1) general (1) **glass** (2) gloss-

black (1) half (1) happy (1) **house** (5) including (1) inheritance (1)

insisted (1) jacuzzi (1) **jim** (2) kitchen (1) l-shaped (1) living-room (1) local (1) loch (1)

luxurious (1) master-bedroom (1) match (1) **materials** (2) million (1) open-

plan (1) open (1) outside (1) overall (1) panels (1) permission (1) pitched (1)

planners (2) planning (1) pounds (1) present (1) recently (1)

reflect (2) render (1) roof (1) room (1) sale (1) sauna (1) sections (1) shame (1)

shape (1) sides (1) **simone** (3) sit (1) site (1) staircase (1) stonework (1)

style (1) surface (1) think (1) throughout (1) towards (1) **traditions** (2)

transparent (1) tv (1) upstairs (1) via (1) **views** (2) **water** (2) white (1)

Figure 16.4(a) Tag-cloud: Loch House

---

accessed (1) additional (1) architectural (1) bedroom (1) **build** (2) catch (1)

claire (1) comes (1) courtyard (1) creates (1) critical (1) crucially (1) dictated (1) dual (1)

engineering (1) experimental (1) features (1) form (1) front (1) half-attic (1) hall (1) heart (1)

height (1) help (1) hidden (1) high-tech (1) **house** (4) huge (1)

hundred (1) ingenious (1) introduces (1) **light** (2) living (1) low-cost (1) main (1)

making (1) master-bedroom (1) **mezzanine-pods** (2)

monty (3) open-air (1) open-plan (1) panels (1) pigeon-step (1)

planners (1) planted (1) pounds (1) protrude (1) provide (1) restriction (1) roman (1)

roof (2) row (1) screened (1) single (1) **sliding-glass** (2)

solution (2) **space-saving** (2)

space (2) squeeze (1) stacks (1) staircase (1) story (1) street (1) summer (1)

ten (1) third (1) thousand (1) unusual (1) upstairs (1) wall (1) willow (1)

window (2)

Figure 16.4(b) Tag-cloud: Space Pod

actual house designers themselves, given that the façade of the Loch House is meant as an impressive display of both structural and design features to reflect a harmonious yet eclectic mix of the traditional and the contemporary that is in line with those local planning requirements which dictate minimal conflict with the natural landscape. This meant that the exterior of the Loch House had to blend with the natural environment, as displayed in Figure 16.5a.

On the other hand, the viewer is cast as observer of the technical innovations of the Space Pod and the ingenuity behind such a remarkable design. In this regard, the Space Pod was constructed as a result of negotiating the various limitations and constraints placed upon it. The exterior of the Space Pod is somewhat exotic because of how its modern, unconventional, industrial-type exterior contrasts with the neighbouring Georgian villas. The simplicity of its modern, efficient design culminates in an exterior façade that is less feature-rich and less outwardly impressive, both structurally and design-wise, as displayed in Figure 16.5b. With reference to the awkwardness of the external appearance, with its lack of height and grey roof membrane, Kevin McCloud points to the necessity of viewing the house from the inside in order to fully appreciate the degree of ingenuity, innovation and inventiveness that made this D-I-Y project an engineering success.

While the concepts from the exterior of each building are repeated inside the house, the photographs posted on the sales brochure for the Loch House and the Space Pod website (for example, see Figures 16.6a and 16.6b) realize new configurations of experiential and interpersonal meanings compared to the CGI videos, in part due to the situational context of the images – that is, the owners of the Loch House aim to sell the property, while the owners of the Space Pod clearly live in the house.

For example, in the master bedroom of the Loch House, a large bed, furnished with luxurious black bed sheets and a fur throw-over, faces the floor to ceiling windows that surround the bed and provides views onto the private loch, orientating the room to the natural elements outside, as displayed in Figure 16.6a. According to the property sales brochure, expensive polished imported American walnut flooring is used throughout the house, reflecting the modern tastes and flexible budget of the owners.

In contrast, the master bedroom in the Space Pod has rough, concrete flooring with only a single wall panel of windows that slide towards the side to allow access to the outside wooden deck, as displayed in Figure 16.6b. Even with sliding-glass panels, there is nothing much to see in terms of scenery, since the glass panels open out towards a wooden deck in the backyard that is bordered by walls on each side. The position of the bed in the Space Pod is also different from that in the Loch House in that it does not allow a full view of the outside via the glass panels. The occupants in the room are therefore not oriented towards the outside, unlike in the Loch House. In terms of style, the

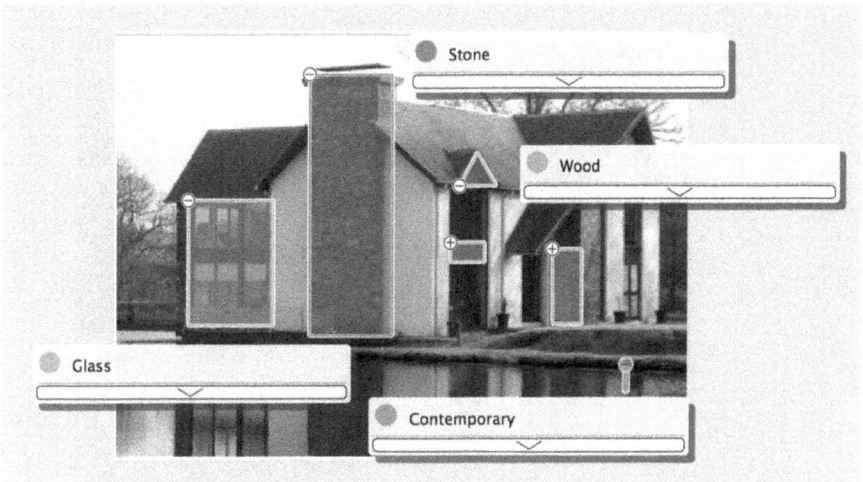

Figure 16.5(a) Exterior design feature: Loch House

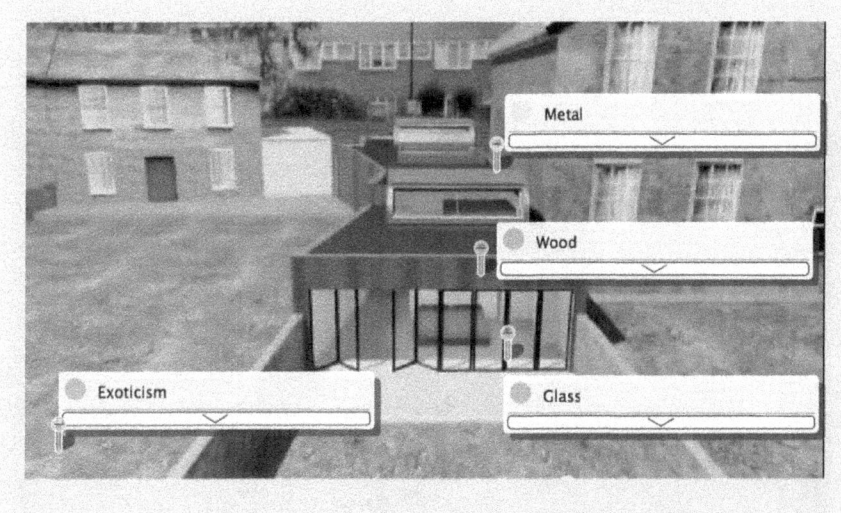

Figure 16.5(b) Exterior design features: Space Pod

modern, stylish opulence of the Loch House is absent; what is present is an 'IKEA'-type functional design that foregrounds basic utility, ease of use and convenience. However, the inward-orientation of the Space Pod creates a focus on elements in the room which enhance utility and exhibit surprise and creativity. An example of this is a built-in space-saving spa-bath located under the

405

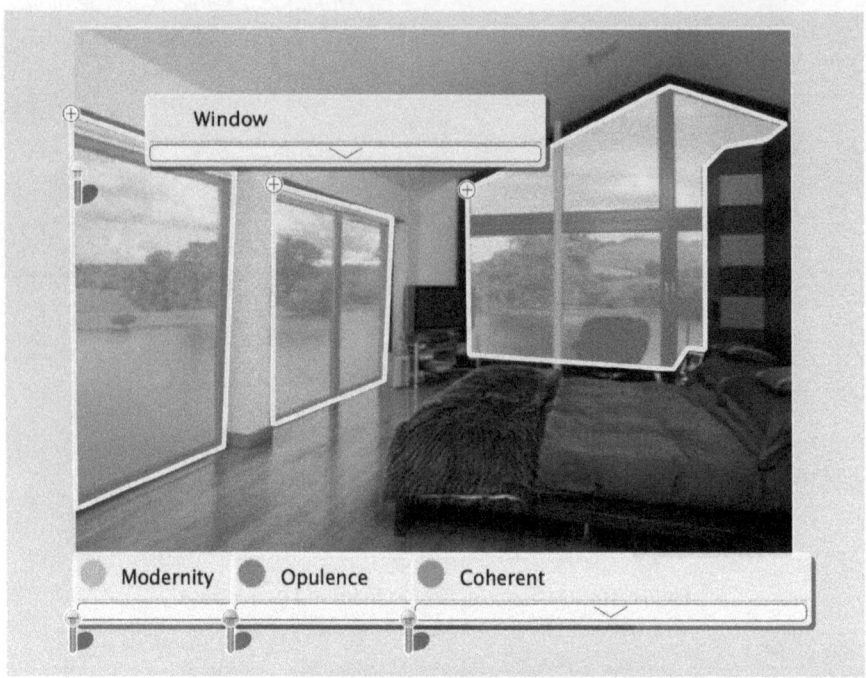

Figure 16.6(a) Master bedroom: Loch House

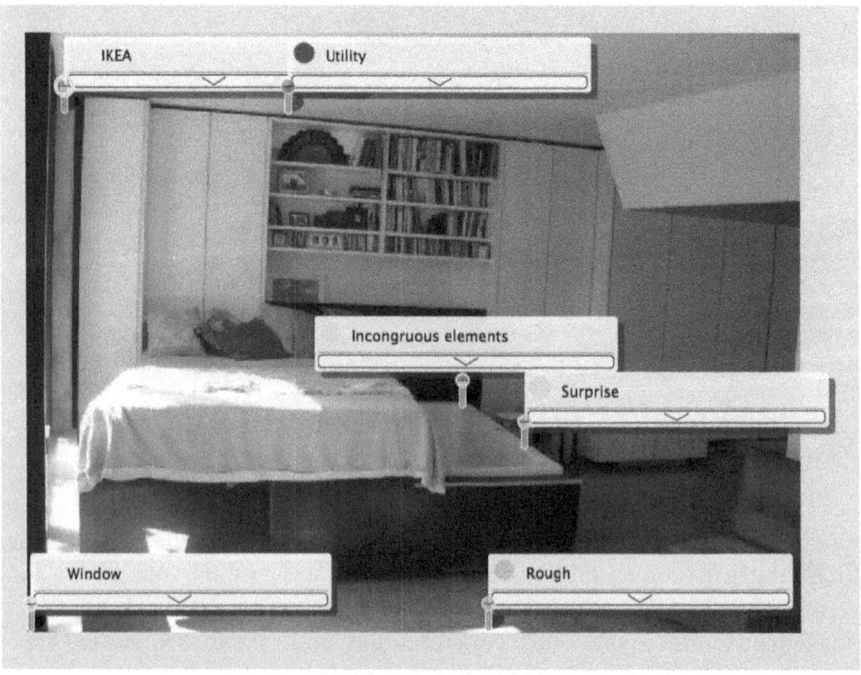

Figure 16.6(b) Master bedroom: Space Pod

bed in the master bedroom in the Space Pod. It is a highly 'marked' choice as the functionalities of a bed and a spa-bath are different and incongruous (see Figure 16.6b). Moreover, the personal belongings in the bedroom (and other rooms) create a sense of intimacy and close family relationships in the photos of the interior of the house.

As evident in the 'Grand Designs' television program, the Space Pod is a house which is lived in, unlike the Loch House, which aims to impress but at the same time, lacks the intimacy of the Space Pod. In this sense, in comparison with the CGI walk-through, the Loch House becomes a building to be observed and desired, while the Space Pod becomes a building to engage with at close range, and in doing so, the viewer experiences the nature of family life in the house. In this way, the various semiotizations of the two housing designs realize different configurations of interpersonal and experiential meanings for the two residences. The reconfiguration of metafunctional meanings across different media is further discussed in relation to the specific context of the CGI videos and the images analysed in the study.

5 Discussion

Our analysis has shown that for both projects there seems to be a central theme that motivates how each project has been conceptualized, designed and built, and ultimately showcased in the CGI walk-throughs, the sales brochure and the website. For the Loch House, the overarching motifs are high quality and perfection, and the house is advertised as 'A Grand Design' in the sales brochure – no doubt an intertextual reference to the television program it has been featured in. The images in the sales brochure focus on the finished product highlighting its impressive modern and contemporary fixtures, furnishings and facilities. These are evidence of a project that reflects the owners' drive for glamour and perfection, unencumbered by physical and financial limitations, a valued attribute in contemporary society and culture.

For the Space Pod, the central theme revolves around the notion of overcoming physical and financial limitations by using ingenuity and creativity in building and design, taking risks by using low-cost, unconventional materials with an emphasis on keeping costs low, and relying on non-professional help from friends and family to complete the project. Hence, the focal points for the Space Pod are its inventive architectural and engineering features in the CGI animations, rather than its interior design and furnishings. Unlike the images on the Loch House website which features the finished house, people are portrayed as active participants in the process of building the whole project from start to finish on the Space Pod website.

The images on the websites and sales brochure, and indeed in the 'Grand Design' television program, reveal the key metafunctional distinctions between the Loch House and the Space Pod that extend beyond the obvious differences in the practical functionalities afforded by the different spaces in each house. That is, despite the viewer being cast as a participant and observer in the CGI walk-throughs for the Loch House and Space Pod respectively, the latter foregrounds intimacy, close personal relationships and family life in images on the website and the 'Grand Designs' television program, unlike the distant glamour of the Loch House in the sales brochure. For example, the personal belongings scattered throughout the Space Pod and the highly 'marked' fixtures and amenities, like a light that has the dual-purpose function of a shower, and the spa-bath beneath the bed in the master bedroom, function to engage the viewer with images of family life. Indeed, the television program, photographs and the website foreground practicality and personal relations. As Kevin McCloud states in the television program, 'the romance of this house [the Space Pod] is all inside'.

In contrast, the Loch House is a professional designer home with high quality materials, fittings and furniture that function coherently as a whole. That is, architects and interior designers are 'trained to look at a home "from a distance"' (Ventola, 2011: 237), and in doing so, make specific interpersonal, experiential and textual choices to position the building as something to be observed, admired and desired by others in accordance with current consumer values, as evidenced in the Loch House sales brochure which keeps evidence of the owner's presence to a minimum precisely for this reason. In this way, the architectural features of the Loch House are displayed to attract potential house buyers, rather than depicting actual life inside the house. The house is 'empty' in a personal sense, with a view to new ownership.

In this way, the various semiotizations of the two building designs resonate with the aims of the producers of the different media: 'Grand Designs' CGI video aims to engage viewers and provide them with an understanding and appreciation of the design features of each house; the owners of the Loch House and Savills estate agency aim to sell the property, and the owners of the Space Pod aim to promote the process of building a 'dream design' while living in their house. Each involves a series of semiotic selections which function together to achieve these objectives.

In this regard, multimodal semiosis can be viewed in terms of a 'metafunctional mixing board', similar to consoles with channels, sliders, controls and meters which sound engineers use to combine, route and change the level, timbre and dynamics of audio signals for voices and instruments which are summed in the combined output signal. In our case, however, the metafunctional mixing board is used to calibrate the meanings of system choices from different semiotic resources in the combined signal (i.e. different media and events) with an output which identifies the functionalities of the different semiotic resources and the interactional patterns of the semiotic choices which achieve particular objectives, as illustrated in this study. The problem is complex, however, because meanings of the semiotic choices are derived in relation to the multimodal 'system', that is, the combined signal and the immediate context, which are situated in relation to established semiotic conventions for different social practices and cultural activities. Regardless of difficulty, the nature of multimodal semiosis points to the necessity of using empirical data in order to further develop multimodal semiotic theory and analysis.

6 Conclusion

We have attempted to demonstrate how the concepts and tools provided by multimodal semiotics may be operationalized to investigate the interaction of semiotic choices in our abstract multimodal semiotic world where meanings are negotiated and reconfigured for different purposes, as demonstrated in the analysis of the CGI animations and photographs of the two house building projects. Multimodal semiosis provides the key for understanding discourse, society and culture, yet we still have much to learn with regard to mapping socio-cultural patterns and trends using the theoretical concepts at our disposal. Indeed, the complexity of intersemiotic and resemiotization processes necessitates the use of computational tools which permit multimodal data to be compiled, modelled and visualized in order to understand and interpret semiotic patterns as they unfold. In this regard, the future of multimodal semiotics will in part depend on our ability to develop theory in accordance with insights gained from analysing multimodal data using computer-based approaches and, in turn, understanding the usefulness and limitations of this research approach.

Acknowledgements

This inspiration for this chapter arose from *The Design of Grand Designs: Testing the SF Model for Architecture Symposium*, organized by Professor Michael O'Toole (Chair and Presenter: Murdoch University, Western Australia) in collaboration with Eija Ventola (Presenter: Aalto University,

Finland) and Kay O'Halloran (Presenter: National University of Singapore) at the Thirty-Ninth International Systemic Functional Linguistics Congress at the University of Technology Sydney, Australia on 16–20 July 2012. Also, we thank Michael O'Toole for his insightful comments on the draft version of this chapter.

Notes

1 http://semioticon.com/semiotix/2010/03/multimodal-semiosis-multimodal-semiotics-digital-technologies-and-techniques-for-studying-multimodal-communication
2 www.channel4.com/programmes/grand-designs
3 http://multimodal-analysis.com/products/multimodal-analysis-video
4 http://multimodal-analysis.com/products/multimodal-analysis-image
5 www.3dhomesoftware.co.uk
6 http://en.wikipedia.org/wiki/Grand_Designs
7 http://search.savills.com/property-detail/gbglrsgls090027
8 www.peckhamhouse.com
9 Kevin McCloud's Voice-Over Narration for CGI Videos

    (a) Loch House
       This was a difficult site to get planning permission for, and the planners have insisted on a conventional shape and traditional materials. So it'll be large expanses of glass, panels of stonework and clean sections of crisp, white render that should collectively break up the surface of the building. Because it's L-shaped, the house will present three sides towards the best views across the loch. The overall form and general style of the building including the pitched roof has been designed to reflect the local traditions. Although Jim and Simone are happy, I think it's a shame that the planners have dictated a conservative exterior. Downstairs will be open-plan and designed around the views. And throughout the house will be a continuous use of transparent and reflective materials in dialogue with the water outside. So, a bespoke aquarium will sit between the TV room and a gloss-black kitchen. On the other axis of the house will be a dining area and a double-height living-room with a large open fire. Upstairs, via the bespoke glass staircase will be four bedrooms, three with their own en-suite bathrooms. The master bedroom will also have its own sauna and a Jacuzzi bathroom. And of course, it will look right out over the water. This will be a large luxurious house built on a budget to match. It'll cost around half a million pounds, financed by the sale of Jim and Simone's old house and an inheritance that Simone recently came into.
    (b) Space Pod
       So, two ingenious solutions that are both big architectural and big engineering features of this low-cost, high-tech house. The first is a huge sliding-glass roof above the main, open-plan living space. Crucially, it introduces light into the heart of the building, and in summer creates Monty's open-air Roman courtyard. The second solution comes in the form of two space-saving mezzanine-pods, which protrude from the roof to catch yet more light. They each just squeeze an upstairs bedroom under the single storey height restriction. They're accessed by a space-saving pigeon-step staircase. These mezzanine-pods, half-attic, half dual window, should help provide critical additional space. At the back of the

house will be a third master-bedroom, with the only wall where Monty and Claire can have windows. So, they are making the most of it with sliding-glass panels. The planners have also dictated that the house has to be hidden from the street, that the front will be screened by a row of planted willow stacks. To build this unusual experimental house, Monty's got just a hundred and ten thousand pounds.

17 Halliday's Contributions to a Theory of Translation

Erich Steiner

Chapter Overview

---

1 Introduction[1]

When I was an undergraduate a story went round among students in my college that a fellow called Harris had refused to teach translation classes on the grounds that he did not know what 'translation' was. He'd challenged the faculty board to tell him what it was that he was being asked to teach. Everyone knows what it is! They said. Translation has been taught here for centuries. But knowing how to perpetuate an academic tradition is not the same thing as knowing what you're doing. Harris could not possibly teach a subject his seniors were unable to define (Bellos, 2011: 1). . . . Finding out what translation has done in the past and does today, finding out what people have said about it and why, finding out whether it is one thing or many – these inquiries take us far and wide, to Sumer, Brussels and Beijing, to comic books and literary classics, and into the fringes of disciplines as varied as anthropology, linguistics and computer science. What translation *does* raises so many answerable questions that we can leave the business of what it *is* to the side for quite some time. (Bellos, 2011: 3)

In this quote, Bellos poses a few highly relevant questions which may open our eyes for the discussion to follow. Among those questions are whether you can teach something of which you do not have explicit knowledge, whether the question of what translation *is*, and what it *does* refer to the same, or closely related knowledge, and the question of whether a phenomenon which extends over a long period of time, a great diversity of locations, and into disciplines as diverse as empirical humanities, arts, and computer science can be seen as a unified phenomenon at all. Michael Halliday, the scholar in focus here, would certainly be the last person to claim that he has given all the answers to what translation does, and even less so to what translation is, in the last resort. However, and as we shall see, it is quite striking to see how he started early on with questions centering around what translators do, and what translation is. And many of those working within his model of language would claim that the model developed by him – while not answering the questions raised by Bellos in an easy and immediate sense – opens a controlled space for addressing them. And maybe this is not a bad way to start on the quest for an answer.

The view expressed by Bellos comes from a context of comparative literature, and literary translation in particular, that is to say the kind of translation in which ultimately the translation unit is the entire text in its context of culture, and nothing less (cf. already Halliday et al., 1964: 130). It is thus anchored in the literary and methodologically hermeneutic end of the very broad spectrum of translation (studies). A view of translation studies from a somewhat more linguistics-influenced angle, assessing the impact of Halliday's work on modelling translation, can be found in Jeremy Munday's (2012) *Evaluation in Translation. Critical Points of Translator Decision Making*:

> As well as providing a vital link between language, social practice and value orientation, the usefulness of SFL ['Systemic Functional Linguistics' as developed by Michael Halliday, ES] in translation has to do with the significance allotted to choice. The reader (and translator or interpreter) approaches the ST in the belief that the writer's choice is meaningful, asking questions such as: Why this wording rather than another? What choices did the writer have at each point? What is the function of the writer's choice? And what form of communication is produced by this choice? The translator needs to uncover the ST writer choice and to re-encode that choice as appropriate in the target language. Thus, the translator's choices are also meaningful and represent conscious or unconscious decisions at the lexical level that, together, represent the translator's interpretation of the ST. (Munday, 2012: 16)

This is a strong and fairly far-reaching statement from the field of translation studies in general, rather than literary translation only, linking up in significant ways with Halliday's views about 'good translations' explained at the very end of this chapter.

As we said earlier, translation extends from the literary and hermeneutic end of linguistic activity to its very technical and formal end, which is machine translation and related areas. Below follows a citation from one of the most influential figures of computational linguistics, and machine translation in particular:

> In practice, I take it that the factors that govern the production of sentences typically come from a great variety of different sources, logical, textual, interpersonal, and so forth. In general, each of these, taken by itself, underdetermines what comes out. When they jointly overdetermine it, there must be priorities enabling a choice to be made among the demands of the different sources. When they jointly underdetermine the outcome, the theory must provide defaults and unmarked cases. The point is that we must be prepared to take seriously the claim that language in general, and individual utterances in particular, fill many different functions and that these all affect the theory, even at the syntactic level. (Kay, 1985: 252–3)

Kay's remarks here are clearly reminiscent of Halliday's thinking about language, and, indeed, Kay's views expressed here come from a period during which he and Michael Halliday had had a period of personal contact. And it is very clearly the influence of the latter's multifunctional view on language which informs Kay's remarks about *parsing in functional unification grammar* and machine translation here. And as we shall see further, the interaction between computational linguistics and Halliday's model of language was never a dominant one in either field, but something of a constant dialogue between a creative context of application and a model attempting to develop responses to some of that context's questions (cf. Chapter 19 – John Bateman's contribution in this volume).

Michael Halliday's views on language in general, and on translation in particular, have had a wide-ranging influence on translation studies, even though it usually was the general model of language as such which was influential, rather than the few and scattered remarks about translation in particular, which were perceived and taken up in translation studies – which does not constitute a problem, in my view, as fields of relevant application and theoretical development are intimately related to each other in Halliday's thinking.

Let us trace some main lines of historical development before going into Halliday's view on translation as such and then into some of its implications, as I see them, for future developments.

2 Formative Influences

Halliday's thinking on language, and on translation in particular, owes much to earlier work by Malinowski and Firth (cf. Chapter 4 by Braj B. Kachru in this volume). The important role which the anthropologist Malinowski played in the development of Halliday's functional approach to language has often been outlined, especially the issue of why and how translation as a phenomenon proved focal for Malinowski's understanding of language. Translating, as he saw it, was a decisive way of bringing home the difference of some other culture's meanings to the investigator and his/her (English-speaking) readership. In other words, translation for him was less an instrument in the service of assimilation of some foreign culture to our own than a way of becoming aware of differences between cultures. In terms of modelling the phenomenon, translation for him was a process of iterative contextualization of linguistic structures, e.g. words in phrases in clauses in sentences in situational and then ultimately cultural contexts. The elucidation of 'meaning' was thus to proceed through a sequence of linguistic and ultimately cultural levels until the full meaning of the linguistic activity under study became understandable to its readership. It was the acknowledgement of difference and the motivation to understand it which made translation for the anthropologist a different matter than it usually was for the missionary – an early foreshadowing of Venuti's advocacy of 'foreignizing translation' (1995: 148–86).

Translation for Malinowski ([1935] 1965) was not a decontextualized substitution of words (or larger structures) from different languages for each other, but rather an iterative contextualization, both intra-linguistically and extra-linguistically, of hitherto unknown meanings so as to make them understandable. In addition to a method for acknowledging and recognizing difference between cultures, translation as a process became a prototypical linguistic activity, a source of methodology. Now, even if the methodological task identified here was not accomplished by Malinowski, at least not with hindsight and in the full sense of the term 'linguistic methodology', what he did derive from translation was a fundamental methodological orientation which he bequeathed on functional and Firthian linguistics. And, although translation as such did not figure prominently in Firth's writing (but cf. Firth, 1956b), what he did inherit from Malinowski was a general programme of linguistic analysis as a process of iterative contextualizations intra- and extra-linguistically – a programme which took methodological shape only in Firth's later work (e.g. Firth, 1957c). And the fulfilment of this programme became the focus of Halliday's work, known as 'scale-and-category grammar' in its early influential version.

3 Evolving Functional Thinking about Translation in Halliday

Halliday's interest in a model of translation can, at least partly, be inferred from his earlier published remarks on translation ([1956] 2005b, 1962; Halliday et al., 1964: 111–134). In his early paper, he already formulated something like the general problem of machine translation, which, however, is lurking in the background of human translation as well, if we want to model it (Halliday, [1956] 2005b: 6–7):

> A fundamental problem of mechanical translation, arising at the levels of both grammar and lexis, is that of the carry-over of elements ranged as terms in particular systems; i.e. systems established non-comparatively, as valid for the synchronic and syn-topic description of what is regarded for the purpose as 'one' language. The translation process presupposes an analysis, generally unformulated in the case of human translation, of the source and target language; and it is a commonplace that a one-to-one translation equivalence of categories – including not only terms within systems but even the systems themselves – does not by itself result in anything which on contextual criteria could be called a translation.

From the perspective of a theory of translation, Halliday's overall work on modelling language can thus be seen as necessary groundwork for developing sufficiently rich descriptions of languages, systematically related through relationships of 'translation', iteratively from 'bottom' to 'top' of the descriptive hierarchy, where units on the next higher level always provide the context for relationships to be established at the current level. Halliday's later paper shows this in an instructive illustration of a 'rank by rank' English translation of Chinese and Russian sentences (Halliday, 1962: 33–6). But alongside this illustration of his translation-by-rank method, he makes statements towards a more general model of translation (1962: 29):

> It appears clearly that, while equivalence can be stated, in terms of probabilities, for all ranks, translation in the accepted sense does not occur below the rank of the clause, and a good translation needs to be based on the sentence as its unit. So-called 'literal' translation is, roughly, translation at group rank, or at a mixture of group and word.

This privileging of one rank – the sentence – clearly is a step beyond the formal possibility of mapping translation relationships at all ranks of description. It points towards a contextually and possibly even psychologically plausible model of human translation – although Halliday always makes it clear that a 'model' here is not to be equated with a 'description of the process' (cf. Halliday et al., 1964: 126). Another important clarification entailed in Halliday's words here is that 'equivalence' and 'translation' are not the same thing – an equivocation which translation studies often criticized as typical of structural linguistics, but one which was less frequently asserted by linguists than was usually thought in translation studies, certainly not by those of a more 'functional' and text-oriented methodological linguistic stance.

The chapter on 'Comparison and translation' (in Halliday et al., 1964: 111–34) takes this thinking some steps further and this time contextualizes it more in language teaching methodologies, rather than in machine translation. In particular, we find a clear picture of the relationship between language comparison and translation as *relationships* on the one hand, and the *activities* of language teaching and translating on the other. Very early on, Halliday avoids the fallacy of equating systemic correspondence (a highly problematic notion in itself), with translation (1964: 123–4):

> [T]he occurrence of an item or pattern in language A, and of another item or pattern in language B, in actual use and under conditions that allow us to refer to these items as 'equivalent', is a piece of evidence of a kind that is crucial to useful comparative studies. The nature of this equivalence is not formal but contextual. It is not formal correspondence that we accept as translation: if we are assessing whether an English text is an acceptable translation of a French one we do not judge it by whether each grammatical category has been replaced by its nearest formal equivalent. . . . We regard translation as the relation between two or more texts playing an identical part in an identical situation. . . . What we can ask about two texts is therefore strictly speaking not 'are these in translation or not' but 'how far are these in translation?' In practice in normal life we postulate a kind of threshold of acceptability for translations, at some point along the scale of 'more or less equivalent'. The point tends to shift with different registers.

In all of Halliday (1956, 1962) and Halliday et al. (1964), we see one of the important pervasive principles of Halliday's thinking about language: different areas of application – in these cases machine translation and foreign language teaching – provide contexts for the development of the theory. Application and theory are thus not divided, but strongly related to each other as developing system – the theory – and its contexts of development – the applications. Theory needs guiding applications to stimulate further development, with the corollary that theory is interested in applications as stimulants and guidance, not in application for applications sake. This is a thoroughly 'dialectical view' of the relationship between theory and practice, and one which has strong implications for the philosophy of science.

Probably the most influential attempt at modelling translation against the background of the early version of Halliday's linguistics is Catford's *A Linguistic Theory of Translation* (1965). He clearly demonstrated how the scale-and-category-type architecture of linguistics, and especially grammar, can be exploited for an understanding of the complex phenomenon of translation, or more precisely for an understanding of the relationship of translation that may obtain between texts. This was a significant, and at its time rare, step away from models of translation based on some version of the 'container metaphor', within which translation was seen as the transfer of some equivalent content from the 'container' of one language to that of another. Instead, he showed how translation could be seen as a relationship between units in structures arranged in a hierarchy of ranks and levels. Apart from these relationships, no separate level of 'mental representation' or 'sense' would have been needed. Functional and also early systemic linguistics were strongly anti-mentalist in that they did not foresee the necessity of a separate level of 'mental representations' in addition to whatever 'meanings' the contextualizations of units in their structures and systems made available. Catford in his 'Linguistic Theory of Translation' was very much a representative of this orientation, as was Ellis (1966) for contrastive linguistics.

After these early attempts, some time elapsed before other attempts were made at an understanding of translation in Halliday's footsteps. Within the translation studies community, it has nevertheless often been acknowledged that his linguistics was of particular usefulness for translation pedagogy and didactics (cf. e.g. Newmark, 1991: 65 and elsewhere, Munday, 1997/2001: 89; Munday, 2012: 16). And, indeed, a number of systemicists and translation studies scholars have used the ongoing development of his linguistic framework as a guideline for modelling aspects of translation, both as a relationship between texts and as an activity.

After developing some cornerstones of a model of translation as indicated earlier, Halliday's published views on language developed further by foregrounding the system as opposed to structure, by strengthening a rhetorical and semantic, rather than only structural view on grammar, and by developing the notion of 'function' from a programme to a specialized tool in linguistic analysis. This 'systemic functional thinking', as it came to be known, gave increasing space to the system rather than the structure, to a semanticized grammar rather than the more formal one of the scale-and-category version, and to context in addition to text. Because of this methodological refinement, a significant extension of the range of phenomena covered under the term of 'translation' became possible. At the same time, systemic functional approaches maintained a firm linguistic and text-oriented base for the whole enterprise, at a time when some strands in translation studies disclaimed any grounding in linguistics under the global methodological orientation of the 'cultural turn' in the social sciences and humanities. Translation began to be modelled on different levels and, possibly more uniquely due to Halliday's thinking, on different scales of abstraction.

One strand of work exploited the level of 'local' clause-based semantics, or semanticized networks, for explorations of a suitable level of transfer in transfer-based architectures for (machine) translation, sometimes and characteristically related to work in multilingual text generation (cf. Steiner et al., 1988, who used a Fawcett-type version of SFL (cf. Fawcett, 1980), but also Matthiessen & Bateman, 1991 and work mentioned therein). It is in this strand of work that Halliday's elaboration of a clause semantics throughout the late 1960s and 1970s showed a very clear and enlightening influence, and one in which his early interest in 'machine translation' reoccurred as a context generating new facets of a model of translation. And Halliday continued to have a fairly direct influence on the people mentioned here, less through published work of his own at this stage, but through intense personal and working contacts.

Another strand of work more clearly oriented towards human translation considered translation at the level of 'register' (Baker, 1992; Hatim & Mason, 1990, 1997; House, 1977/1997; Steiner in various publications throughout the 1990s collected in Steiner, 2004; Yallop, 2001). House provides an important attempt at using notions from register and genre in a framework for translation quality assessment, intersecting systemic ideas with ideas from pragmatics and comparative culture studies in a wider sense. Some of my own attempts can be seen as similar, though they probably focus more on microlevel considerations than those of House or Taylor (1998), for example, in their extensive exploitation of the notion of 'grammatical metaphor' and its implication for translation (cf. Steiner, 2002). Part of Halliday's appeal to people working in translation (studies) certainly is that he uses terms such as 'register', and some of his colleagues also 'genre', which link up easily with the more general usage of these terms within traditional textual and literary studies. Yet, more than this superficial point of contact, he interfaces them with and embeds them within an overall model of language, within which 'register' in particular becomes a key organizing concept linking context and lexico-grammar – something which to my knowledge is not found anywhere else in modern linguistics. Halliday's linguistics is strongly embedded within a broadly rhetorical tradition in the history of linguistics, and this proves attractive in a natural way to people working on texts, either as practising translators, or else as theoreticians of translation.

The development of a systemically based modelling of translation after the initial scale-and-category based phase can be seen as a development away from a more lexico-grammatically based modelling, and one mainly in terms of structure, towards a modelling which privileged the strata of semantics and context. This represents a movement of theorizing mainly along the stratification dimension. Another important move of theorizing happened along the instantiation dimension, and included, apart from work on exploiting the notion of register already referred to earlier, some work exploiting corpus-based methodologies in investigations of translations and parallel texts as instances (Hansen, 2003; Hansen-Schirra et al., 2012; Neumann, 2003; Steiner, 2002; Teich, 2003). The more comprehensive development of theorizing of translation and related phenomena against Halliday's model of language is perhaps best represented in papers by Matthiessen (2001: 41–126) and Teich (2001: 191–228).

Matthiessen outlines a model of the environments for theorizing translation in what I would at the moment regard as the most comprehensive statement of an SFL-based view and, indeed, programme for theorizing translation (2001). He locates translation within a typology of systems, characterizing it as a semiotic process. This includes, significantly, an acknowledgement of non-linguistic semiotic systems, and the possibility of translation between those and language. It then focuses on translation between languages and, also significantly, within languages between varieties. The latter possibility has been quite extensively discussed in work on registerial variation (e.g. Ghadessy (ed.), 1999), especially between expert and non-expert registers (e.g. Halliday & Martin, 1993). Matthiessen then proceeds to exploit the environments for thinking about translation within an overall SFL-architecture (2001: 73–87) making full use of scales of abstraction in several dimensions. He also gives due weight to the possibility of 'metafunctional shifts' in translation (pp. 101–4), which may arise from different metafunctional orientations of language systems and/or from constraints of the intended register and genre of the target text. He furthermore locates important concepts of translation studies, such as 'equivalence, shift, free vs. literal' in this model (pp. 104–14). His instantiation–stratification matrix (p. 92) defines a significant space for types of systemic investigations of translation for the future. Teich (2001) builds on the same methodological base as Matthiessen, adding to it some more in-depth considerations to do with contrastive-linguistic resources in thinking about language comparison and translation, with an emphasis on English and German. Concepts investigated and placed inside an overall SFL-architecture include 'translation strategy, type, and procedure, as well as equivalence', inside the stratification–instantiation matrix.

Within the development traced here, we find a significant extension of the range of options for the translator during his/her activity, as well as a broadened range of phenomena to consider and to model for the researcher. The translator is freed to shift between ranks, levels and metafunctions when searching for translational equivalents. At the same time, the meaning of the term 'translation' is extended to translating between diachronic and synchronic variants on the one hand, and to translations between different semiotic systems on the other. We do not claim that other models, or indeed active translators, have never seen these possibilities, but it does appear that the explicit modelling of these highly complex relationships within one overall architecture makes Halliday's views on language fairly unique as a theory within which to work on translation. This theory has a clear semiotic 'flavour', indeed explicitly acknowledged in many places, and thus belongs into that wider family of approaches to cultural phenomena.

As we have traced the development here, most of the more recent published work on translation arising from Halliday's model of language is not published by him, but by other people, many of whom have had fairly frequent and long-lasting working contacts with him. And it is probably fair to say that the over-all model of language, within which all of the partial models referred to are located, is very much Michael Halliday's. This becomes clear from reading even early publications by him, some of which we have quoted. The rich semioti-cally inspired model of language nowadays referred to as 'systemic functional linguistics' was present from early on in Halliday's thinking and – just as impor-tantly – teaching. There is little in the contemporary extravagant architecture of Halliday's linguistics which is not genuinely his own original work – and it is this ability to construct and consistently master such complex architectures of thought which characterize the outstanding scholar that Michael Halliday is. Such personalities stand out even from the communities of excellent experts, while at the same time maintaining the mutually rewarding dialogue all the time.

4 Contextualization and Appreciation

One clear attraction of Halliday's views on language and translation is their potential to strengthen connections to higher-level and transdisciplinary questions in investigations of the semiotics of culture and language: texts are networks of relations among configurations of meanings within and across sit-uations and cultures. The central units of meaning in cultural environments are not microlevel configurations such as individual words, or units of clause struc-ture, but rather more macrolevel units, such as those realizing register, genre and ideology in a culture – units and relationships of discourse. And some key concepts referred to in Halliday's work on translation, such as the concepts of 'register, situation, culture', are clearly essential here. Important concepts such as 'foreignizing vs. domesticating' translation (Venuti, 1995: 148–86) and 'static vs. dynamic' (Hatim & Mason, 1997: 27–35) require operationalization in terms of textual detail in order to become as convincing as they deserve to be, and theoretically motivated studies of translation are one possible way of achieving such operationalizations. If a systemically based discourse semantics, as pre-sented in Martin and Rose (2003), and as thoroughly explored in Munday (2012) for a model of evaluation (in the sense of 'judgement' and 'subjective stance') in translation, can be exploited in studies of translation, and if its connections to the more 'microlevel' strata of the model can be upheld and strengthened, we should be able to arrive at highly valuable concepts and operationalizations for linking macro-, mezzo- and microlevels of semiotic analyses of translations and other kinds of texts in situations of contact between different cultures.

However, there are other, though related, questions that we hope systemically based studies of translation will be able to address.

Among such key questions are those of 'language contact', 'multilinguality' and 'language change' (cf. Oesterreicher, 2001; Thomason & Kaufmann, 1988). What a specifically SFL-oriented perspective on these phenomena would imply in terms of methodology and of domain is only very gradually becoming visible on the horizon of systemic theorizing. Such a perspective would give due consideration to systems alongside structures, to the instance alongside the system, and to more abstract (and at the same time, more empirical) types of contrast than have often been in the centre of theorizing (Hansen-Schirra et al., 2012: 8–14; 255–80). Language contact along the channels of system, instance and contrast may be shown to be the process through which ultimately socio-cultural motivations drive language change. The way languages influence each other is often through relative frequencies of use, changes in 'markedness', directness and explicitness, rather than through directly changing lexico-grammatical categories. We would hope that theoretically motivated studies of translations and other forms of multilingual text production prove to be a significant step of Systemic Linguistics towards addressing questions of this nature – important in the last resort not only for an understanding of language, but also for an understanding of specifically human existence. And it is quite striking to read those early papers by Michael Halliday which we have quoted (Halliday, [1956] 2005b, 1962; Halliday et al., 1964): Although they are located within very specific contexts of application, many fundamental issues to do with language contrast, contact and translation are already on the horizon there.

There is yet another sense in which Halliday's theorizing may lead us beyond the limits of linguistics as defined traditionally. Halliday writes, in his *Towards a Theory of Good Translation* (2001) about how translation studies and linguistics could move beyond their traditional boundaries: what he tentatively outlines there would be a movement towards investigating the nature of the value systems themselves which underlie translation criticism, the systems which constrain what types of equivalence we privilege in our evaluation of a given (translated) text:

> [T]here are two groups of professionals who theorize about translation in its entirety: the translators themselves, and the linguists. Both these groups are concerned with a general theory of translation; but they interpret this in rather different ways. For a linguist, translation theory is the study of how things are: what is the nature of the translation process and the relation

between texts in translation. For a translator, translation theory is the study of how things ought to be: what constitutes good or effective translation and what can help to achieve a better or more effective product (cf. Bell, 1991: chapter 1). (Halliday, 2001: 13)

At this point, Halliday appears to reconfirm the conventional divide between the merely descriptively oriented scientist on the one hand, and the evaluating, decision-making practitioner. He then refers to the concept of 'equivalence', and to the fact that there are different types of equivalence on different ranks and levels, and that they must be differentially weighted depending on the specific context of some given translation. The fact that 'equivalence' must be conceptually subdivided into different types, which are differently ordered or ranked depending on the task at hand, and depending on the language types and text types involved, has been stated by several translation studies scholars and linguists (cf. Koller, [1979] 1997: 214–71 or Schreiber, 1993: 29 on types of 'invariance' and 'equivalence'). What Halliday's linguistics is offering beyond yet another programmatic statement is an architecture of a theory and a model to provide a 'scaffolding' for this ranking and these subdivisions:

To summarize the discussion of 'equivalence value': in any particular instance of translation, value may be attached to equivalence at different ranks, different strata, different metafunctions. In rank, it is usually at the higher lexicogrammatical units that equivalence is most highly valued; lower units are then exempted (e.g. words can vary provided the clauses are kept constant). In strata, likewise, equivalence is typically most valued at the highest stratum within language itself, that of semantics (where again the lower strata may be allowed to vary); value may also attach explicitly to the level of context, especially when equivalence at lower strata is problematic. In metafunction, high value may be accorded to equivalence in the interpersonal or textual realms – but usually only when the ideational equivalence can be taken for granted (it is interesting to speculate on why this should be so). (Halliday, 2001: 17)

A 'good' translation in a given context is one which achieves equivalence with respect to those linguistic features which are most valued in that context. Halliday here takes us to the point at which the linguist transcends his or her own role, as conventionally conceived: As long as we stay inside language in our notion of 'evaluation', we can still conceive of the entire process as an essentially descriptive exercise within which the active role of the human analyser only intrudes as an agent relating types of information which are already given. If we know that in statements of 'equivalence value' (cf. Yallop, 2001) among the ranks, it is the higher ones which are privileged against the lower ones, that among the strata, likewise the higher ones constitute the evaluative context for the lower ones, and that among the metafunctions, equivalence of the ideational one needs to be satisfied necessarily before equivalence on the interpersonal and/or textual one, then 'evaluation' can – at least in principle – be conceived of as an 'objective', almost 'mechanistic' exercise, encoded through the 'appraisal' in our discourse realizing the evaluation. The deontic 'ought to', as in 'this translation under such and such circumstances ought to read like this and this . . .' does have deontic force, but the source of the obligation is in intralinguistic constraints.

However, if we admit, or even require, judgements about how and why a highly valued text is highly valued *in terms of its cultural context*, we are taking our process of iterative contextualization of the semiotic act at hand – the text to be evaluated – significantly further. We are now embedding the text not only inside its context of situation, which is still directly indexed in the text, but also, through this context, in the wider context of culture. And we are using the judgements 'good' or 'bad', or even 'effective', no longer only in terms of whatever 'higher' or 'adjacent' levels of representation may specify in terms of constraints, but in terms of what constraints a given culture, often our own, may encompass.

Traditionally, for the 'modernist' understanding of science, our goals as scientists would have been twofold: Descriptive goals, in the pursuit of which we are analysing 'how' a piece of discourse works, and explanatory goals, in the face of which we would have explained 'how' and 'why' this state of affairs was brought about. Very often this was not really a dichotomy, as can be seen in many so-called historical explanations, which, if looked at closely, are nothing but a 'thick description'. Halliday's 'why is the text evaluated as it is?', though, seems to point to something beyond: A highly valued text in some context of culture is partly valued because of its qualities as a text, including qualities such as 'creativity' on the formal levels. These qualities, though, very often form only a (necessary?) condition for this culturally conditioned evaluation. Highly valued, canonical texts are usually so valued because they conform or develop, initially sometimes contradict, a given set of cultural beliefs – which is why during the period of their establishment in a culture, highly valued texts are often at the centre of controversy. They also privilege ideational, interpersonal and textual meanings to different extents. But can, and should, a linguistic theory, or a theory of 'good' translation, describe, or even explain to us why these texts are canonical in their cultures? And if translated, should they become highly valued in their target cultures at the price of possibly no longer conforming to their original set of values?

Where does Halliday's work stand as a theory of language and textuality relevant to translation? Let me quote here from an influential and representative assessment of what a translation theory is, or ought to be. Venuti, after convincing arguments to the effect that 'the history of translation theory can be imagined as a set of changing relationships between the relative autonomy of the translated text, or the translator's actions, and two other concepts: equivalence and *function* [emphasis by Venuti]' concludes (cf. Venuti (ed.) 1999: 5):

> The changing importance of a particular theoretical concept, whether autonomy, equivalence or function, may be determined by various factors, linguistic and literary, cultural and social. Yet the most decisive determination is a particular theory of language or textuality.

Observe that there is no claim implied that there be only *one* such theory, but that *some* theory of language and textuality is necessary as an evaluation matrix for assessing the relative importance of key notions such as *autonomy*, *equivalence* or *function*. The first privileges the autonomy of the translated text and of the translator's textual actions, the second the source text and the third gives priority to the function in the target contexts of situation and culture. Depending on the type of translation, any of these priorities may be warranted, yet not following from some arbitrary decisions by an evaluator, but arising out of the context of an overall model which gives conceptual space to such considerations. And Halliday's views on language and textuality offer one such model – not the only one, yet one of only few currently in existence.

May I add a few remarks by Gideon Toury (1995: 264–5), one of the significant voices in translation theory over the past decades, on the probabilistic nature of translational laws, which tie in well with another core notion of Halliday's view on language:

> Obviously, descriptive-explanatory investigations can be rewarding not only in the attempt to draw the applied extensions of Translation Studies closer to real-life behaviour. . . . They also form a vital link in the elaboration of translation theory itself . . .: from the most elementary kind of theoretical framework, equipped only to deal with what translation *can*, in principle, *involve*, through that which translation *does involve*, under varying circumstances, to the statement of what it is *likely to involve*, under one set of conditions or another. The latter represents a more elaborate form of a theory, and one which is bound to become more and more intricate with each subsequent study. . . . The desired theory . . . would thus acquire a **probabilistic** form, which would put it in line with recent developments in other sciences of man. (See especially Halliday, [1991] 2005a)

Where I see Halliday's gesture towards a 'theory of good translation' as a significant way forward is in the sense that for any progress in fields where evaluations are called for – as in translation quality assessment, or as in literary stylistics, or in the assessment of textual quality in general – we need to carry our contextualizations beyond and outside the linguistic levels of description, through the interlevel of context of situation and into the cultural context. And many of the regularities which we then need to fall back on may well be of a probabilistic, rather than categorical, nature. Once we have made some progress there, we shall have placed the linguistic sciences in the centre of textual studies – and maybe have begun to productively dissolve them in their proper situational and cultural context. The academic discipline 'linguistics' would be dissolved into the general meaning-making activity itself – the end of disciplinary specialization, and reintegration of its essence into where it came from: generalized semiotic human activity itself.

Note

1. Parts of the ground covered in this volume, especially in Chapters 2 and 4, can be found in an earlier version in Steiner, 2005.

18 Halliday in Relation to Language Comparison and Typology*

Kazuhiro Teruya and
Christian M. I. M. Matthiessen

1 Introduction

The contributions in the part of the Halliday Companion, Part IV, are concerned with 'Directions of development from Halliday'. There are many such directions, and six of them are covered here. Two of them, Steiner's chapter on translation and the present chapter, complement one another in the coverage of what we have called **multilingual studies** (e.g. Matthiessen, Teruya & Wu, 2008). The concerns in these two chapters can be distinguished along different dimensions; but let us focus on two of them – the cline of instantiation and the number of languages in focus: see Figure 18.1.

Translation is, of course, translation of texts in their contexts of situation – the recreation of instances of meaning identified in one language in another languages (or possibly a small number of other languages). It is thus located at the **instance** pole of the cline of instantiation, although texts may of course

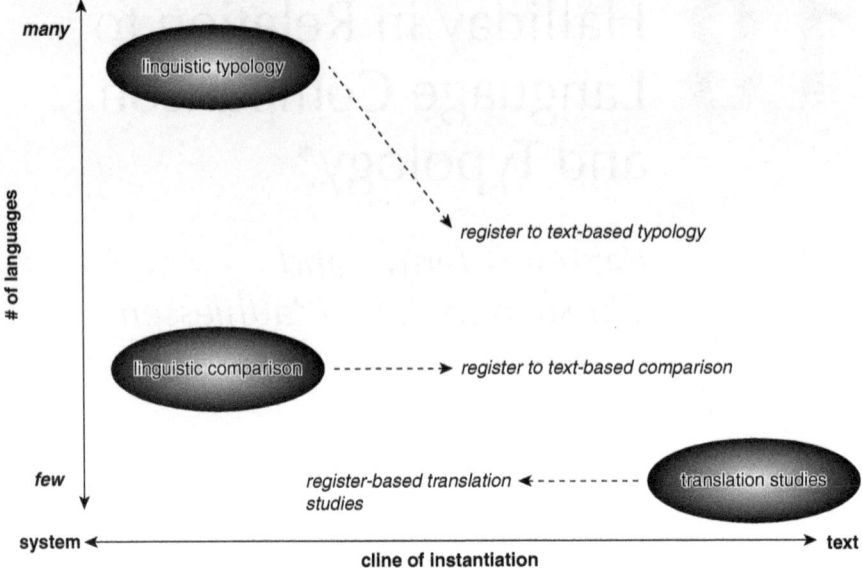

Figure 18.1 The territory of multilingual studies differentiated in terms of the cline of instantiation and the number of languages in focus

be referred to text types or registers higher up the cline of instantiation (cf. e.g. Snell-Hornby, 1995). Consequently, this is also the primary focus of **translation studies**.

Prototypically, translation studies are concerned with texts at the instance pole of the cline of instantiation covering a fairly small number of languages (small even in the context of translation within the European Union, involving all the languages of the members). In contrast, **linguistic typology** has prototypically been concerned with parts of linguistic systems in many languages, thus with a focus on the **potential** pole on the cline of instantiation. The sample size has ranged from a little over 30 in Greenberg's (1966) pioneering study to well over one thousand for certain features in WALS (Haspelmath et al., 2005); but it tends to be much larger than the number of languages considered together in translation studies.

In between translation studies and linguistic typology, we find **linguistic comparison**. Here researchers have tended to focus on a small number of languages – usually a larger number than in translation studies but always a much smaller number than in linguistic typology.[1] As a method in historical linguistics, linguistic comparison was focused on the system end of the cline of instantiation – on items, or on phonological systems such as vowel systems and lexico-grammatical systems such as pronominal systems. Here the goal was usually to assist in the reconstruction of earlier varieties of languages. However, linguistic comparison is now also conducted to shed light on synchronic similarities and differences among systems in different languages based on the analysis of texts – with many contributions in the journal *Languages in Contrast*, often within one or a small set of registers. This is an active area of research in SFL – an early influential one being Teich (1999b), which we will return to now.

This form of linguistic comparison can also serve as a new way of doing **contrastive analysis**. When contrastive analysis was first developed as a method designed to support second/foreign language teaching by Lado (1957) and other scholars in the 1950s and 1960s, it was based essentially on American structuralist linguistics. It fell out of fashion – it was displaced by error analysis (e.g. Corder, 1967) and by other methods and conceptions (like interlanguage). But there would be a considerable benefit in returning to contrastive analysis in the form of systemic functional contrastive analysis based on a conception of language as a meaning potential and grounded in the analysis of texts from different registers.

All types of multilingual research presuppose the existence of **descriptions of particular languages**, and in systemic functional multilingual research, this means systemic functional descriptions of particular languages – and thus descriptions that have been based on the analysis of texts and are oriented towards meaning. We will start with a review of the development of systemic functional descriptions of different languages before we move on to comparison and typology. However, let us first provide an overview of Halliday's early contributions that have influenced later developments in description and multilingual studies.

In 1956, Halliday published two papers that are directly relevant – one the **description of Chinese** (Halliday, [1956] 2005a) and one on **translation** (Halliday, [1956] 2005b), more specifically a demonstration of the potential value of using a thesaurus (rather than just a dictionary[2]) in (what later came to be called) machine translation (cf. also Halliday, 1962).

Halliday's ([1956] 2005a) description of Modern Chinese was grounded in text, which was both theoretically and methodologically important; and this contribution to the description of contemporary Chinese was followed by Halliday ([1959] 2005), his description of fourteenth-century Medieval Chinese based on a corpus consisting of one long text, *The Secret History of the Mongols*.

During this period, Halliday also worked on, and wrote about, comparison and typology. In Halliday ([1957] 2002), he explores the conditions for comparing linguistic systems; and he offers one example (to put it in terms that would be used today) the possibility of recognizing 'classifiers' as an areal feature of languages spoken in South East Asia ([1957] 2002: 34). Halliday further explores issues relating to comparison and typology, **interlinguistic classification**. He cautions against the late nineteenth-century tendency to classify **languages**; instead of classifying languages, we should focus on **systems** within languages:

> The first problem in linguistic typology is to decide what is being classified. Traditionally, the answer has been: languages. But this raises a difficulty. This is not primarily the difficulty of defining 'a language', since within limits any definition would suffice provided it was adhered to rigorously. Rather the difficulty is that if we want to say that two languages are alike, that Lx resembles Ly, then we must presuppose that Lx resembles itself. (Halliday, 1959–60/1966: 166)

> Linguistic typology can thus perhaps be regarded as the typology of language features, rather than as the typology of languages. (177)

Thus by the early 1960s, language description, language comparison and typology and translation were all part of the agenda of Halliday's general linguistics. Let us now trace the development of descriptions of different languages, first by Halliday and then by other systemic functional linguists building on his work.

2 The Development of Descriptions of Different Languages in SFL

The first descriptions of different languages in (proto)systemic functional terms were produced by Halliday himself – first on Chinese (Halliday, [1956] 2005a, [1959] 2005; Halliday & Ellis, [1951] 2005; his articles on Chinese are collected in Halliday, 2006) and then on English (e.g. Halliday, [1966–8] 2005; his articles on English are collected in Halliday, 2005b); and the 1960s, he supervised Ph.D. theses concerned with the description of other languages – the account of Mbembe by Barnwell (1969) and the account of Nzema by Mock (1969), both during Halliday's time in London. The engagement with different languages was a natural continuation of the tradition that Firth had established. Students had to study the systems of different languages, and quite a range of languages were described in terms of prosodic analysis and system-structure theory.

Relative to the multilingual work in the 1950s and the 1960s, research in the 1970s was less multilingually oriented, and there were few descriptions of languages other than English – but this was because scholars were busy expanding the theory and the areas of application: this was a period when scholars developed the systemic functional approach to text, including the work on cohesion in English (Halliday & Hasan, 1976) and Hasan's (e.g. 1978) early work on the modelling of text, worked on semantic system networks (see Hasan et al., 2007), Halliday proposed the correlation between context and language based on the contextual parameters of field, tenor and mode and the metafunctional organization of language (Halliday, 1978) and developed his pioneering account of how young children learn how to mean (Halliday, 1975). There were some accounts of languages other than English, including Hasan's (1972) work on Urdu and Hudson's (1973) systemic description of the morphology of Beja, an Afro-Asiatic language.

By the early 1980s, the situation was changing again: at the University of Sydney, Halliday supervised a number of MA thesis on various systems in the grammar of Mandarin Chinese, including CLAUSE COMPLEXING, TRANSITIVITY, MODALITY, THEME and COHESION. The Chinese scholars who produced these descriptions all went on to play important roles in the development of SFL in China (cf. Hu, Zhu & Zhang, 1989), producing further descriptions of Chinese and supervising research into Chinese by Ph.D. students at various universities in China.

However, it was really in the 1990s that systemic functional work on a range of different language began to take off, as can be seen from Table 18.1. A number of the accounts that originated as Ph.D. theses in the 1990s are reflected in publications recorded in the table in the column for the 2000s. In the first decade of the twenty-first century, there was an 'explosion' of new accounts of languages that had not been described in systemic functional terms before. Publications included Caffarel, Martin & Matthiessen (2004) and a new series of systemic functional grammars launched by Continuum in 2006 (Caffarel, 2006a; Lavid, Arús & Zamorano-Mansilla, 2009; Li, 2007; Teruya, 2007).

Once a new description of a language previously not described in systemic functional terms has been produced, it becomes a resource for systemic text analysis. For example, based on her description of the lexico-grammar of French in Caffarel (2006a) – a long-term effort of around a decade and a half, Caffarel has been able to undertake illuminating projects of text analysis like her investigation of the construal of alienation in Camus' *L'Etranger* based on her description of the system of TRANSITIVITY in French (e.g. Caffarel, 2004b). At the same time, new descriptions have also paved the way for applications in second/foreign language education: see Caffarel (2006b) and Teruya (2006, 2009) for examples of how their comprehensive descriptions of French and Japanese, respectively, can be deployed in educational contexts.

And new descriptions lay the foundation for comparative and typological research – areas to which we will now turn.

Table 18.1 Seminal and comprehensive descriptions of different languages in (proto) systemic functional terms

	1950s	1960s	1970s	1980s	1990s	2000s
Chinese [Mandarin]	Halliday (1956a, 1959)			A series of MA thesis supervised by MAKH at Sydney University	Halliday (1992, 1993)	Halliday & McDonald (2004); Halliday (2006); Li (2007)
Chinese [Cantonese]						Tam (2004)
Vietnamese					Hoang (1997); Thai (1998)	Thai (2004)
Thai						Patpong (2005)
Japanese					Teruya (1998)	Teruya (2004, 2007)
Tagalog						Martin (2004)
Telugu						Prakasam (2004)
Bajjika						Kumar (in press)
Western Desert						Rose (2001a)
Gooniyandi					McGregor (1990)	
Arabic (Modern Standard)						Bardi (2008)
Beja			Hudson (1973)			
Mbembe		Barnwell (1969)				
Nzema		Mock (1969)				
Akan				Matthiessen (1987a,b)		
Oko						Akerejola (2005)
English		Halliday [see Halliday, 2005]	Halliday [see Halliday, 2005]; Halliday & Hasan (1976)	Halliday (1985)	Martin (1992); Matthiessen (1995)	
French		Huddleston & Uren (1969)				Caffarel (2004a, 2006a)
Spanish						Lavid, Arús & Zamorano-Mansilla (2009)
German						Steiner & Teich (2004)
Danish						
Swedish						
Finnish					Shore (1992)	

3 Comparison

3.1 Comparative Linguistics

The interest in comparative linguistics was a natural development within the 'Firthian' and 'Neo-Firthian' tradition; we have already referred to Halliday's early contributions (Halliday, [1957] 2002, 1959–60/1966).[3] The first extended treatment of comparative linguistics in this tradition was provided by Ellis (1966) – based on the first phase of Halliday's SFL, the phase that came to be known as 'scale-and-category theory' after the publication of Halliday ([1961] 2002).

Ellis (1966: 15) distinguishes between different kinds of comparative linguistics, the primary distinction being between 'all-purpose comparative linguistics' and 'specialized comparative linguistics':

> All-purpose comparative linguistics and comparative linguistics with specific purposes differ in that the first abstracts from purposes and ways of comparison, the second abstracts from purposes, the third comprises kinds defined by purpose (study of translation and bilingualism, of genetic relation, etc.) and only secondarily by kind of tongue comparison [. . .].

Under the heading of 'all-purpose comparative linguistics', he includes descriptive (synchronic) and historical (diachronic) comparison; and under the heading of 'specialized comparative linguistics', he includes research into translation, genetic relations, languages in contact (including 'areal convergence') and dialectology.

Ellis (1966) thus provided a very broad framework for exploring comparative linguistics, and he followed it up in subsequent research (in particular, Ellis, 1987). Within this very broad vision for comparative linguistics, only certain themes have been followed up in systemic functional work; but they represent developments that became possible after the 1960s. We will discuss them under the headings of 'multilingual system networks' and 'text- and register-based studies'.

3.2 Multilingual System Networks

When linguists develop comparative descriptions, the nature of the comparison naturally depends on the general theory of language, the descriptions are cast in terms of syntagmatic patterns. Thus the kind of contrastive analysis that was proposed by Lado (1957) and others in the late 1950s and early 1960s was largely focused on syntagmatic patterns.[4] In contrast, comparison in SFL has always foregrounding the comparison of systems; systems provide the environment for comparing structures.

One central tool that can be used in systemic comparison was developed starting in the early 1990s in research on multilingual text generation. This tool is **multilingual system networks**; they were first described by Bateman et al. (1991), and then elaborated by Bateman, Matthiessen and Zeng (1999: 615), who specify the following two goals for such networks:[5]

- Integration of the different languages so that commonality is separated from particularity and reused: resources should maximize the factoring out of generalizations across the languages of the system and the particulars of individual languages in the linguistic resources;
- Integrity of each individual language so that it can be used separately: integrated resources should support consistent access from both the point of view of their multilinguality and the point of view of the individual languages.

If we start with system networks of separate languages, we obtain a multilingual system network by **merging** or **integrating** them, while keeping the parts that are not shared across the languages distinct. The language-specific parts are represented as **partitions** within the general system network. Such partitions may be **tagged** as being specific to one or more languages, but they are not general across all the languages represented by the multilingual system network. Partitions may include whole systems, or parts of systems – one or more systemic terms, and also realization statements.

Let us illustrate a multilingual system network of the system of mood for English and Chinese (for a version representing several more languages, see Teruya et al., 2007): see Figure 18.2. Partitions are tagged according to the language or languages they are valid for. For example, the realization statement attached to 'declarative' is specific to English, whereas the realization statement attached to 'jussive' is specific to Chinese.

The mood network for English and Chinese in Figure 18.2 illustrates two general **principles regarding degree of congruence** between languages that emerge (cf. Figure 18.3) when we compare languages systemically using system networks:

(1) **Hierarchy of axis**: Languages tend to be more congruent with one another – i.e. have a higher degree of sharing – in terms of system than in terms of structure; we can call this the axial principle of congruence across languages. Systemic contrasts such as 'indicative'/'imperative', 'declarative'/'interrogative' in the mood network illustrated here are the same for English and Chinese, but these systemic contrasts are realized in different ways in the two languages.

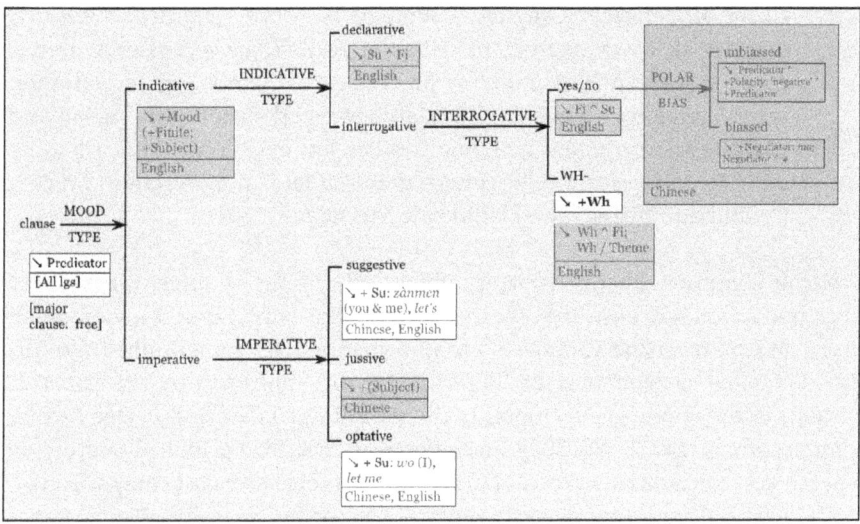

Figure 18.2 Example of multilingual system network with largely shared potential – mood in Chinese and in English

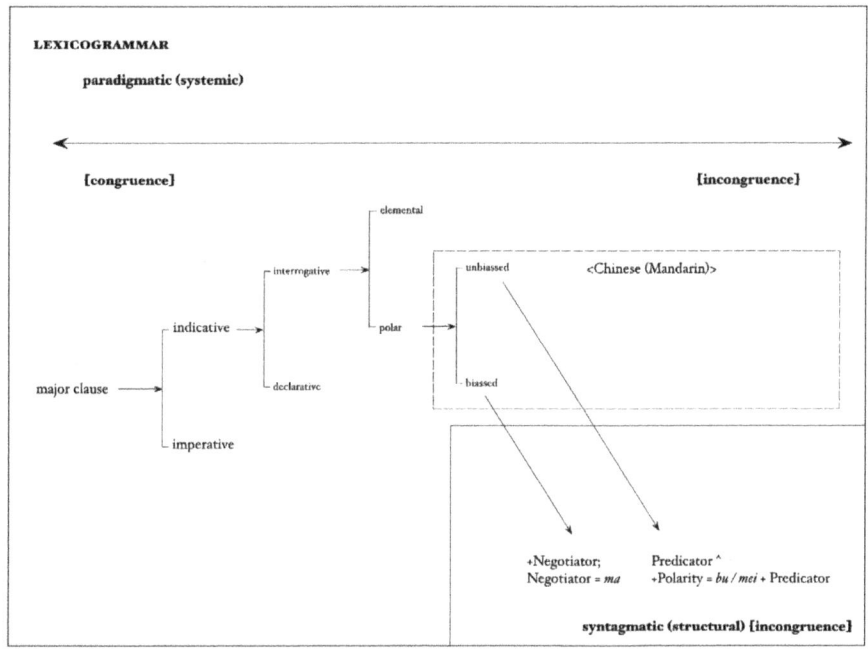

Figure 18.3 Degree of congruence across languages in terms of axes

(2) **Cline of delicacy**: Languages tend to be more congruent with one another at lower degrees of delicacy; as delicacy increases within a given system such as mood or process type, there is greater variation across languages. Thus the low-delicacy mood systems in English and Chinese are congruent with one another, but in Chinese there is a more delicate option for 'yes/no' interrogatives that is not present in English ('unbiased'/'biased': see Halliday & McDonald, 2004).

Systemic congruence across lexico-grammatical systems of different languages does not mean, however, that the systems are the same when we view them 'from above', from the vantage point of semantics. As we will illustrate further, the same systems may be 'deployed' in different ways by the semantic systems of the languages included in the multilingual description (see further Matthiessen, Teruya & Wu, 2008, and references therein, e.g. to the literature on 'speech act realizations' across languages and on register-based comparison).

By means of multilingual system networks, we can thus reveal congruence across languages, while at the same time identifying points of incongruence. One kind of common difference is that one language will organize a lexico-grammatical space in terms of two systemic vectors where another one only uses one.

We can illustrate this situation by representing the English and Indonesian pronominal systems in a multilingual system network (Figure 18.4). Here there are some differences at higher degrees of delicacy; Indonesian offers options for 'speaker +' and 'addressee' person that are not part of English. However, the major difference is really that Indonesian intersects the PERSON systems with another systemic dimension, STATUS. Any trace of such a system has disappeared in Modern English although it was part of its Germanic inheritance: more local status contrasts are found in, e.g. German, and also in Romance languages. We can relate this to the question of what kinds of tenor parameters are grammaticalized in the pronominal system of a language, as Brown and Gilman (1960) did in their classic study of the pronouns of power and solidarity.

We have not included the realization statements in the multilingual system network in Figure 18.4; but they can easily be spelt out. We have tabulated them in Table 18.2.

When we compare two or more languages in this way, it may turn out that for some system or set of systems the languages are basically incongruent – that is, they provide different models for doing some kind of semiotic work. As an illustration of this situation, a multilingual system network incorporating the Chinese and English systems for construing the unfolding of a process through time, see Figure 18.5. In Chinese, the model for construing process time is that of ASPECT (for systemic functional accounts, see Halliday & Matthiessen, 1999: chapter 7; Halliday & McDonald, 2004): the unfolding of the process is

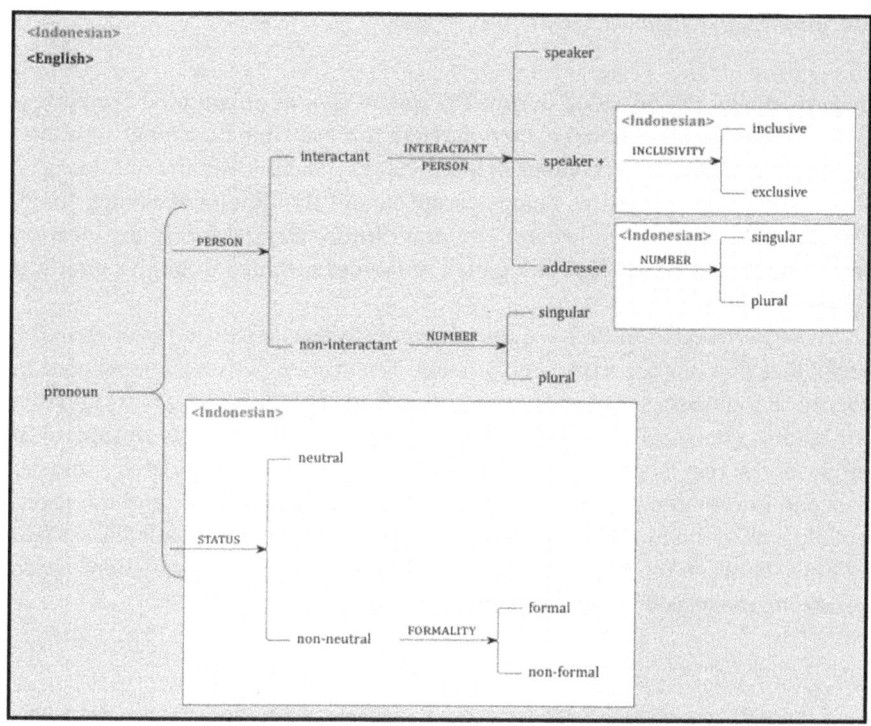

Figure 18.4 Example of multilingual system network with partially shared potential – pronominal system in Indonesian and in English

Table 18.2 Pronouns in English and Indonesian

			English	Indonesian		
				non–formal	neutral	formal
interactant	speaker		*I*	*aku*	*saya*	
	speaker+	inclusive	*we*	*kita*		
		exclusive		*kami*		
	addressee	singular	*you*	*kamu; engkau*	*anda*	*saudara; anda*
		plural		*kalian*		
non-interacant	singular		*he, she, it*	*dia*		*beliau*
	plural		*they*	*meréka*		

construed either as bounded in time ('perfective') or as unbounded ('imperfective'). In English, the model is that of TENSE (for systemic functional accounts, see Halliday, 1976, 1985: chapter 6; Matthiessen, 1983b, 1996): the unfolding of the process is construed as being located before the time of speaking, 'now' ('past'), at the same time ('present') or after ('future'); and this primary location in relation to the 'now' of speaking may be further specified through secondary tense selections.

These two models of time are **complementary**, but they do not overlap in the sense that they do not share any systems. The system network represented in Figure 18.5 consists simply of two partitions, one for Chinese (ASPECT) and one for English (TENSE). This reflects the difficulties faced by learners starting with either of the two languages and embarking on the other, and also by translators and interpreters. To overcome these difficulties, translators and interpreters must master a multilingual temporal semantic system that will allow them to move between the two languages, reconstruing temporal distinctions made in one language as they translate into the other.

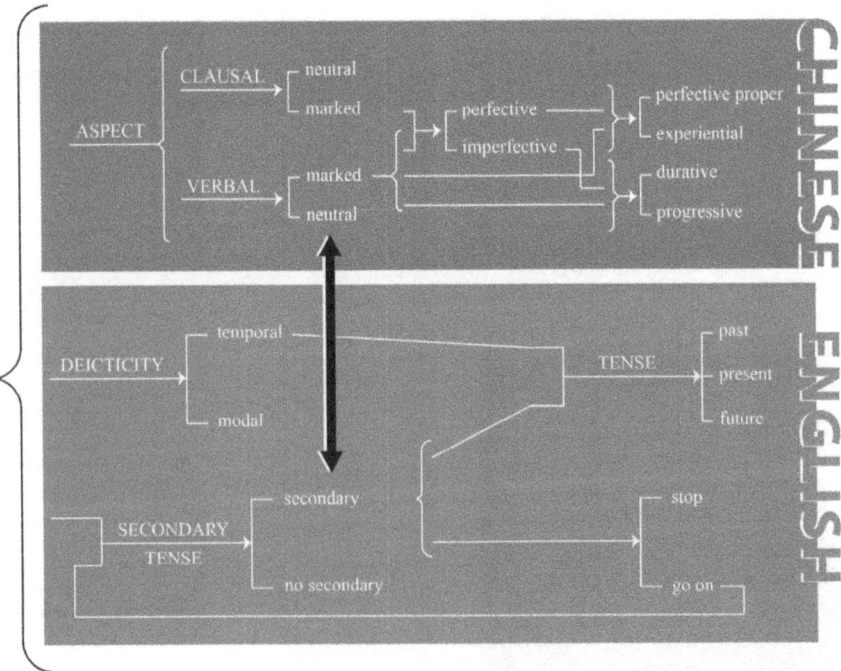

Figure 18.5 Example of multilingual system network with no shared potential – aspect in Chinese and tense in English

3.3 Text- and Register-Based Studies

The example of the multilingual system network incorporating Chinese ASPECT and English TENSE illustrates a general principle in systemic functional comparison: comparison within the content plane of languages cannot be limited to lexico-grammar (content form); it must be extended to include semantics (content substance) – in fact, to semantics embedded within context. This principle was brought out very clearly 30 years ago by Martin (1983). He showed that to be able to compare REFERENCE – the tracking of participants in text, 'participant identification' – in English, Tagalog and Kâte, we must move up to the level of semantics, and examine how these languages achieve this task as texts unfold as units of meaning. Summarizing his findings, he writes:

> In this paper, discourse function, rather than a grammatical category of process, has been taken as the point of departure for contrastive analysis. Participant identification has been considered in three languages, English, Tagalog and Kâte. Two important observations can be drawn from contrastive analysis along these lines. The first is that the systems which identify participants appear at different ranks in different languages. While all the languages considered make us of pronouns, demonstratives and proper names to refer to participants recoverable from the context, only English depends solely on nominal group systems to accomplish this task. In Tagalog the clause rank systems of focus and theme are also involved. And in Kâte the clause complex rank systems of Subject switching and conjunction are also relevant. [. . .] The second important observation has to do with the interaction of participant identification with other discourse functions. In English the task of identifying participants is independent of other discourse tasks because the system coding participant identification, reference, is systematically independent of other grammatical systems. In Tagalog and Kâte, on the other hand, this independence is not found. (Martin, 1983: 70)

In terms of Halliday's **trinocular vision** (e.g. Halliday, 1978, [1996] 2002; Halliday & Matthiessen, 2004), we should thus **shunt** when we conduct comparative or contrastive analysis, and the view 'from above', from the vantage point of semantics – in context, is essential if we are to understand how different languages achieve similar meaning-making tasks such as 'participant identification' by deploying different lexico-grammatical resources.

By the late 1990s, systemic functional linguists began to produce text-based comparative studies of languages within particular registers: Teich (1999b) [English, German and French], Lavid (2000) [English, German and Italian] and Murcia-Bielsa (1999, 2000) [English and Spanish] investigated selections in interpersonal systems, viz. SPEECH FUNCTION and MOOD, in texts from a few different registers (for a summary and discussion of these studies, see Matthiessen, Teruya & Wu, 2008: section 6.3.3.6., 182–90). These studies show how very similar lexico-grammatical resources – the options within the system of MOOD – are deployed in interestingly different ways in comparable registers across languages.

For example, Teich (1999b) shows that, in instructional texts, while straight instructions are realized by 'imperative' clauses in English, French and German, recommendations (another subtype of commands) are realizationally a bit more varied. In English and in French, they are realized by 'addressee-oriented' imperative clauses, the only difference being that French has a more delicate 'polite' option (cf. the discussion earlier of the difference between the English and Indonesian pronominal systems: see Figure 18.4). In contrast, in German, recommendations are realized grammatically be 'modulated' declarative clauses, as illustrated by the following examples from Teich (1999b):

English:

Set the switch to OFF when carrying the radio to prevent turning the power on accidentally.

French:

Réglez-la sure OFF quand vous transportez la radio pour éviter de la mettre sou tension accidentellement.

German:

Beim Transportieren sollte der Schalter auf OFF gestellt werden, damit das Gerät nicht versehentlich eingeschaltet wird.

The similarities and differences among these three languages in the realization of recommending commands in instructional texts are represented schematically in Figure 18.6.

Other systemic functional studies have followed the same or comparable lines of investigation. For example, in unpublished work, we have examined various aspects of topographic procedures in guidebooks in different languages. Contextually, such procedures tend to cycle through a number of phases or elements: movement, where the (potential) tourist is instructed in how to walk or drive around the place s/he is visiting, followed by an introduction of a Place of Interest, which may then optionally be described (Description and historical Background): see Figure 18.7. As the figure shows, there are different register-specific semantic strategies for introducing a place of interest. If we compare English and German, it turns out that they tend towards different strategies, partly because of differences between 'existential' clauses in the two

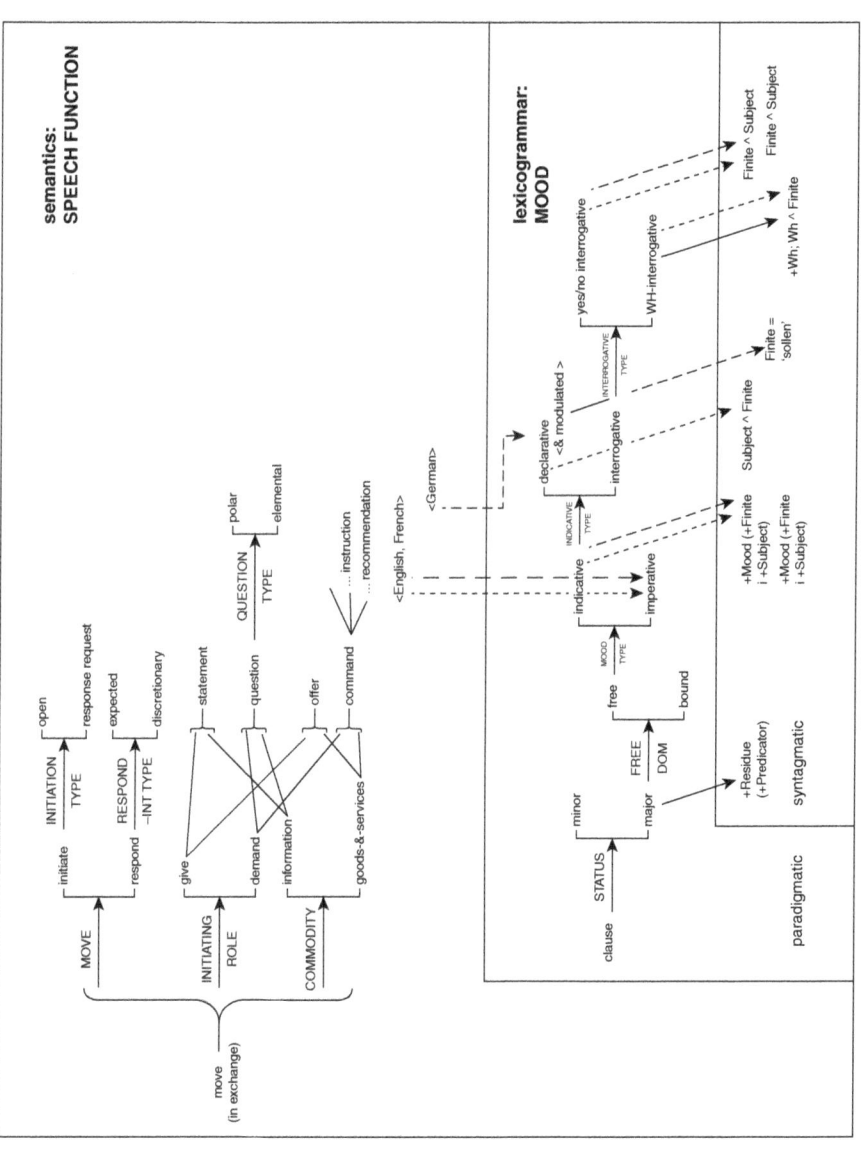

Figure 18.6 Variation across languages in the semantic deployment of the 'same' lexicogrammatical resources – speech function and mood in English, French and German: the realization of recommendations in procedural texts (based on Teich, 1999b)

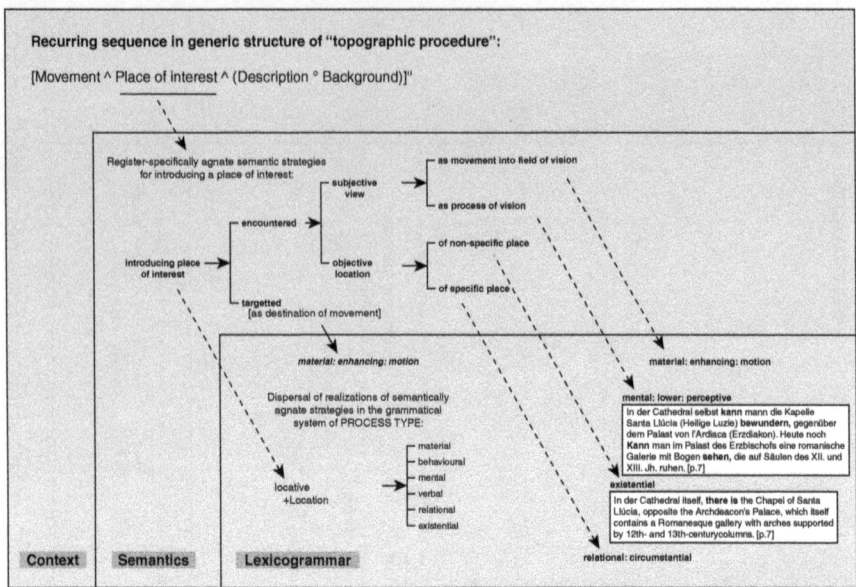

Figure 18.7 English and German strategies for introducing places of interest in topographic procedures

languages (cf. Matthiessen, 2001, and references therein). Thus German tends to introduce places of interest 'subjectively', using 'mental' clauses of the 'perceptive' subtype, whereas English tends to introduce them 'objectively', using 'existential' clauses (although the subjective option is also available): again, see Figure 18.7.

Other systemic functional studies also illustrate the value of register-based comparative research.[6] For example, Martinec (2003) compares instructional texts in English and Japanese in terms of both language and image showing that there are different tendencies in both these semiotic systems, Japanese having more of an interpersonal orientation. Rose (2005) examines features in narratives in languages around the world – but his scope is actualized more on the order of typology or generalized comparison (see Section 4.1). We can also mention Thomson & White's (2008) volume with contributions dealing with news media in different languages. In our own work, we have examined the construal of motion in different languages using texts from registers where the construal of motion plays a particularly important role (e.g. topographic procedures and both recounts and narratives of journeys) and also the deployment of projection in different languages in registers where projection plays a particularly central role.

4 Towards Systemic Typology

4.1 From Comparison to Typology; Sample Size

The studies that we have just discussed in the previous section have been concerned with a small handful of languages – and in this sense they are in the field of linguistic comparison rather than in the field of linguistics typology, or generalized comparison (see Halliday, [1957] 2002; cf. also Ellis, 1966: 19). The difference between comparison and typology is of course a cline or a continuum; but, in typology, linguists strive towards empirical generalizations that in principle apply to all languages around the world.

In empirical typological linguistics,[7] there has been considerable discussion since the 1960s of the size and nature of samples of languages used as a basis for typological generalizations.

Since Greenberg's (1966) pioneering typological study based on a sample of just over 30 languages, typological linguists have worked hard to increase the number of languages that are sampled as a basis for typological generalizations. In the World Atlas of Language Structures (Haspelmath et al., 2005), some linguistic variables ('features') are based on samples of just over 1,500 languages; this has become possible in particular in the investigation of 'word order' variables. However, just over 100 languages are covered by a large number of variables (e.g. Comrie & Cysouw, n.d.).

To estimate what would constitute a reasonable sample size, we need to know the approximate number of languages spoken today but we also need to know how they are distributed genetically into language families or stocks and how they are distributed geographically (to take language contact and areal features within a given Sprachbund into consideration).

The estimate given of the number of languages spoken around the world today vary considerably. These languages vary from megalanguages such as Mandarin, English and Spanish to microlanguages that are about to disappear forever unless we make a concerted effort to preserve **semo-diversity** alongside **bio-diversity** and to support members of the human family who live on the fringes of modern nation-states (e.g. Evans, 2010; Grenoble & Whaley, 2006; Hagège, 2000; Harrison, 2007; Nettle & Romaine, 2000). The 83 biggest languages, around 1.3% of the world's languages, account for nearly 80% of the world's population, or around 4.5 billion speakers; so there are not many speakers left over for the remaining 98% of the world's languages. How many are there? The Ethnologue, which is often quoted as the most reliable authority, puts the number at just over 6,900. However, Dixon (2010: xiii) thinks that the number is much lower, estimating that a more accurate figure would be 'no more than 4,000, quite likely a fair number fewer'.

Clearly, the number of languages spoken today will help determine how many languages we should sample to support typological considerations. But it is not just the number of languages that is important; it is also how they are distributed genetically and geographically: Nichols (1992) discusses different ways of sampling languages based on these considerations. And there are of course additional issues. For example, if we decide that in our typological sample of languages, we should include one from the Germanic branch of Indo-European, what criteria could we use to decide between, e.g. English and Danish? Should we exclude English because of its motley nature – probably creolized, with strands not only of Germanic but also of Celtic and Romance through Norman French (not to mention Germanic overlays, and Latin and Greek)?

In practice another kind of consideration often comes to dominate the picture: the descriptive coverage of the languages spoken (or signed, or written) around the world is very uneven. Only a relatively small number of languages have been described in terms that we might call 'comprehensive' (documented in 'reference grammars' based on sizeable corpora of authentic text), whereas the majority of the world's languages are at best documented through field notes and brief linguistic sketches. This situation is visualized very schematically in Figure 18.8.

These are thus some central aspects of the working conditions of researchers in empirical linguistic typology – with a level of funding that is obviously vanishingly small compared to the levels of funding in sciences concerned with material systems (biological and physical systems): compared to the levels of funding needed for the human genome project and for quantum physics dependent on particle accelerators. What we need is substantial funding for a

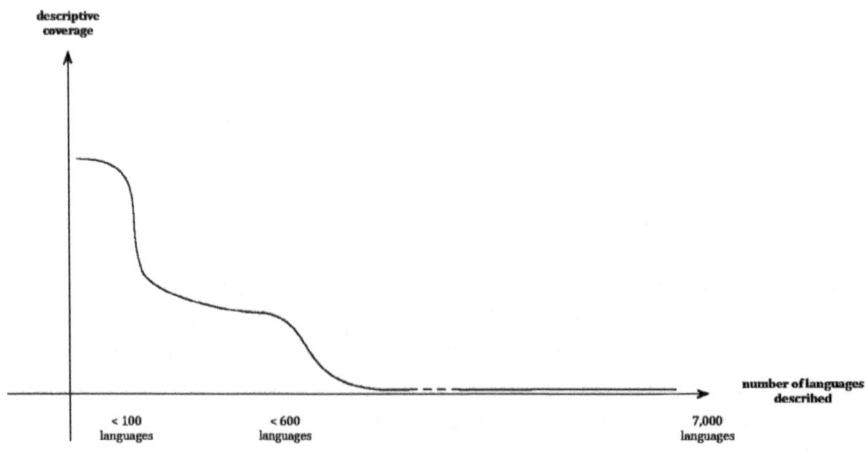

Figure 18.8 Descriptive coverage in linguistics in relation to the number of languages described

human sememe project, with a serious commitment to the understanding and preservation of semo-diversity.

Against this background and given these serious constraints on linguistic typology, what kind of contribution can systemic functional typology possibly make? We believe systemic functional contributions can be very central, in terms of both description and theory. Exploratory contributions along these lines include Caffarel, Martin and Matthiessen (2004), Matthiessen, Teruya & Wu (2008), Rose (2001b, 2005) and Teruya et al. (2007).

In terms of description, systemic functional linguists have produced a unique body of text-based and meaning-oriented accounts of the lexico-grammatical systems of a range of languages – a growing range of languages, as is clear from Table 18.1. Since these descriptions are all based on the same framework, they are as it were designed to form the basis of comparison and typology; they rest on shared standards – a property that has turned out to be of critical importance in many collective efforts in the area of computational technology, including open-source projects such as Apache and Linux. One early example of what can be achieved is presented in Teruya et al. (2007), a step towards a typology of mood systems in languages.

In terms of theory, SFL can also make a very considerable contribution. This contribution certainly includes the 'metatheoretical' insight articulated by Halliday (1959–60/1966) that comparison and typology should be conducted in terms of **linguistic systems** (such as mood, tense, aspect, pronominal systems) rather than **whole languages**, and the metatheoretical decision to continue to develop the Firthian tradition in terms of the division of labour between the general **theory** of language and **descriptions** of particular languages (cf. Matthiessen & Nesbitt, 1996), avoiding the danger of building descriptive categories such as subject and topic into the general theory.

But the contribution also includes the nature of systemic functional theory itself. Unlike theories that have formed the basis of mainstream empirical work in linguistic typology, systemic functional theory foregrounds the conception of language as a resource for making meaning – a meaning potential that is represented by means of system networks with realization statements. As we have already shown in our discussion of comparison based on system networks, they open up new possibilities in comparative research, and also in typological research.

Drawing on descriptive and theoretical contributions by SFL, we can adopt a two-pronged approach where we relate these contributions to empirical typological studies involving large samples of languages – in particular, the typological database now made available through WALS (http://wals.info). In this way, we can achieve a complementarity between generalizations based on a relatively small number of languages described in comprehensive terms based on authentic text and generalizations based on relatively large numbers of languages whose descriptions range from fairly comprehensive ones to linguistic sketches.

4.2 Typology Based on Systems

Casting typological generalizations in terms of systems, and systems forming system networks, makes it possible to bring out principles and patterns in the languages of the world that would remain more implicit if we only take structure as our point of departure. Many typological generalizations have, of course, normally been stated in paradigmatic terms: obvious examples include generalizations about phonological systems such as vowel systems (as in Jakobson, 1941; and more recently in, e.g. Maddieson, 2005) and about morphological systems such as pronominal or person systems (e.g. Siewierska, 2004).

However, the further we move away from phonology and low-ranking lexico-grammar (morphological paradigms), the more likely we are to find typological generalizations stated in terms of structures – so-called word order typology being an obvious example.[8] Importantly, such typologies can be restated in systemic terms since systemic order underpins structural order. To take just one example: so-called accessibility hierarchies have tended to be stated in terms of implicational hierarchies referring to elements of structure. For example, if the Complement ('Object') of a relative clause can be conflated with the relative element, Wh, so can the Subject; and if Adjuncts ('obliques') are candidates in terms of relativization, so are Complements and Subjects. But this implicational hierarchy is really a statement about the elaboration of the system of relativization: see Figure 18.9.

This 'hierarchy' is now an ordering of systems – an ordering of increasingly elaborated systems. From left to right: languages with relative clauses may have only one candidate for relativization, the Subject (i.e. Subject/Wh); if they have another option – another candidate, this will be the Complement

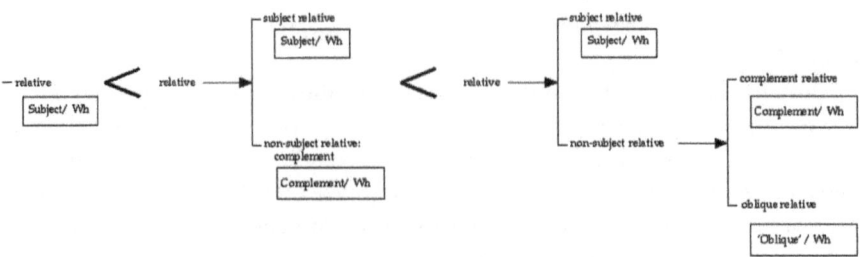

Figure 18.9 Accessibility hierarchy interpreted in systemically

(Complement/Wh); and if there is yet another option, this will be an Adjunct (an 'Oblique' element).

Once we begin to explore typological generalizations stated systemically in this way, new ways of conceiving of typological generalizations open up. These include the following:

- typology of **probabilistic systems**: it becomes possible to relate categoricity to high or low probability (cf. Matthiessen, this volume, on Halliday's conception of language as a probabilistic system); for example, in one language 'passive' clauses may be 'non-agentive' with a probability of 0.9 but in another they may be 'non-agentive' with a probability of 1 – typological generalizations are inherently probabilistic (cf. a point made a long time ago by Givón, 1979, about the likelihood that Subject is constrained to be 'definite' in a language).
- typology in terms of the **cline of delicacy (1): location along the cline**: it becomes possible to conceptualize grammar and lexis as part of a lexicogrammatical continuum extending from the very general grammatical end to the very delicate lexical end with intermediate patterns of the kind studied under the heading of constructions (cf. Matthiessen, this volume: section 4.5). When we compare and typologize systems within languages, we can investigate where a given field of meaning tends to be lexicogrammaticalized – more towards the grammatical end (grammaticalization, in one sense of the term: i.e. constructing meaning grammatically) or more towards the lexical end (lexicalization).
- typology in terms of the **cline of delicacy (2): movement along the cline – grammaticalization**: as just noted, it becomes possible to locate grammaticalization along the continuum of lexico-grammar as part of the lexico-grammaticalization of meaning, and, by another step, to grammaticalization in the sense of turning lexical items into grammatical ones as a move along this continuum from lexis to grammar.
- typology in terms of the **community of meaners** (speech fellowship): it becomes possible to theorize a language as inherently variable, and as an aggregate of varieties (dialectal, registerial and codal), so variation can be taken into account in typological generalization; and, by another step, the size and nature of the community of meaners of a given language and their contact with other speakers and degree of multilinguality.

In addition to comparing and typologizing systems across languages in terms of the probability attached to terms in these systems, we can of course also investigate the probability of the presence of particular systems (contrasts between systemic terms), the occurrence of systemic terms or combinations of systemic terms in a sample of languages – adding quantitative information to generalizations about systemic elaboration of the kind illustrated in Figure 18.9. For example, based on the frequency of the presence of the system of vowel nasalization in a sample of 244 languages[9] (Hajek, 2011), we can assume that the likelihood of a language having this system is about 0.25: see Figure 18.10.

The illustration in Figure 18.10 suggests that there is a relationship between the degree of systemic elaboration of a system – the extension in delicacy – and the number of languages: the greater the systemic elaboration, the fewer languages we will find in a sample. This seems plausible in very general terms, and can be illustrated for the systemic elaboration of 'addressee' person in pronominal systems, based on the data from Helmbrecht (2011): see Figure 18.11. In his sample of 207 languages,[10] the majority have no distinction in 'politeness' for 'addressee' pronouns, a good number have a binary distinction between 'intimate' and 'respectful' and a fairly small number have a further distinction

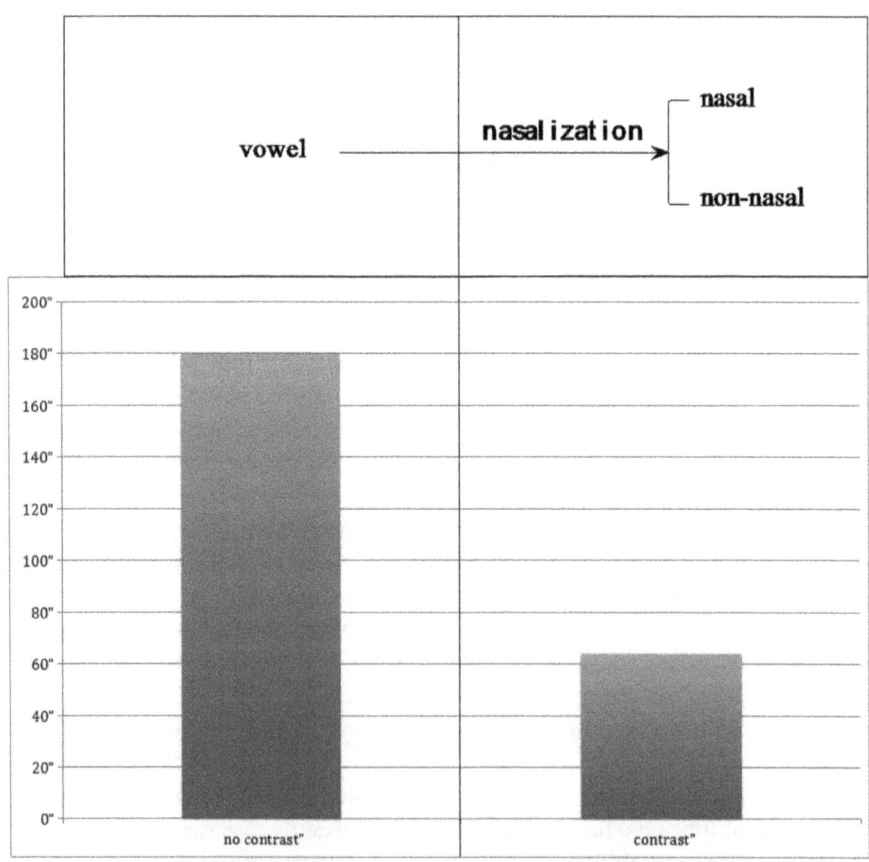

Figure 18.10 Presence of system of vowel nasalization in a sample of 244 languages (based on data from Hajek, 2011)

within 'respectful' having to do with the status of the person being addressed (with two ore more terms). Of course, it is perfectly possible that the system of politeness is simultaneous with the system of person, as in our earlier example of Indonesian: see Figure 18.4. In this case, the system network fragment in Figure 18.11 can be thought of as a 'displayed' system network in Fawcett's (1988) sense. There are many obvious examples of systems to be explored along similar lines, e.g. case, number, tense, aspect, mood type, process type.

The examples given involve systems ordered in delicacy – as in Figures 18.10 and 18.11. However, it is equally important to investigate patterns involving potentially simultaneous systems. When we consider two or more different variables that may be systemicized in languages, we can ask to what extent

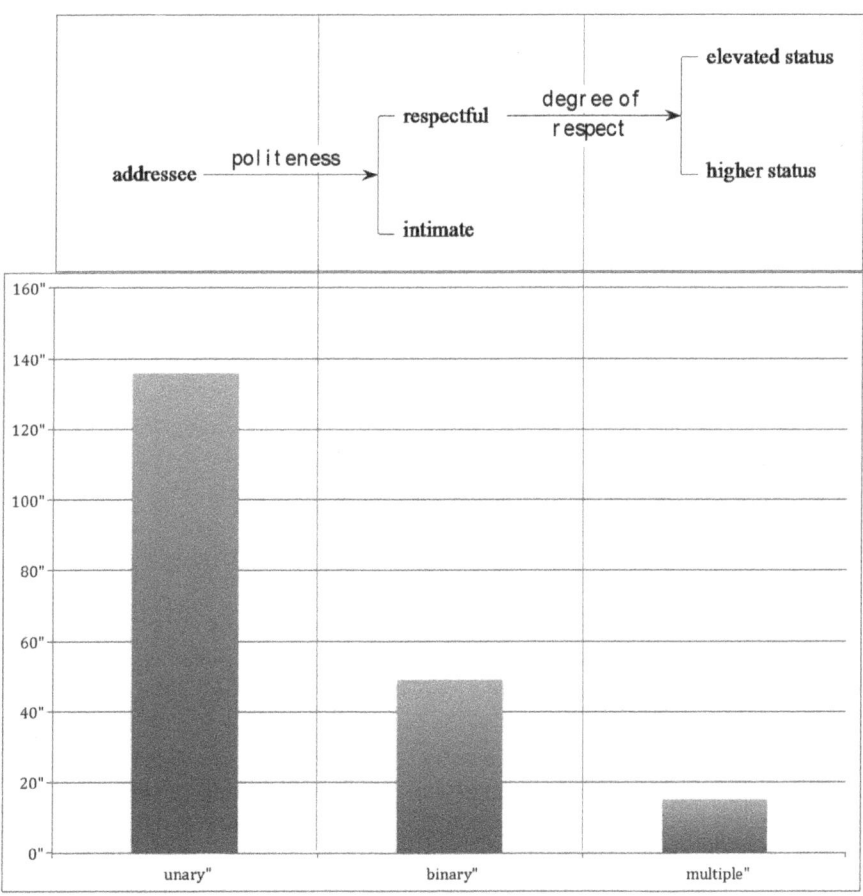

Figure 18.11 Addressee person in pronominal systems and degree of systemic elaboration in politeness in a sample of 207 languages (based on data from Helmbrecht, 2011)

they tend to be systemicized as simultaneous systems or as delicacy-ordered systems. For example, for front vowels, lip rounding and nasalization are phonetic variables that may be systemicized in the phonological system of a language. Lip rounding is not very common as a systemic contrast for front vowels (see Maddieson, 2011), and as we have already seen neither is nasalization (see Figure 18.10, based on Hajek, 2011). But do they occur as simultaneous systems? When we intersect the two, we find that there are only three languages in the intersection of Hajek's (2011) and Maddieson's (2011) samples where they are simultaneous: mid- and high front vowels can be 'round'/'spread' and 'nasal'/'non-nasal' in French and two other languages.

Typology based on systems is certainly worth pursuing; it involves **systems thinking**, also with respect to how systems evolve. System-based typology includes the syntagmatic patterns that realize terms in systems, and it is such patterns that are really best represented in the WALS database (e.g. generalizations about the sequence of elements in a given unit, 'word order') – not surprisingly since it is easier to find information about such patterns in most descriptions.

5 Conclusion

In this chapter, we have provided an overview of work on language comparison and typology that draws on Halliday's development of SFL, and also of the kinds of descriptions that form the basis of systemic comparison and typology – comprehensive systemic descriptions based on the analysis of registerially varied samples of authentic text.

We have discussed past contributions, going back to Halliday's own work in the 1950s and 1960s – his descriptions of Chinese and English in terms that can support comparison and his exploration of system-based comparison and typology.

We traced the development of systemic functional descriptions of languages from different parts of the world belonging to different families, noting that there's been a marked increase in the number of new descriptions, particularly in the 2000s – including both languages that have been described before in terms of other frameworks and languages that have essentially never been described before, at least not systematically with extensive evidence from authentic text.

This was also the period when a number of linguists in Europe developed a new approach to linguistic comparison – coinciding more or less with the launch of the journal *Languages in Contrast*, where systemic functional contributions have been published alongside other text-based studies. We referred in particular to studies exploring differences in languages based on texts from comparable registers.

As noted by Halliday (1959–60/1966: 173), linguistic typology can be understood as generalized comparison. Since comparison has now come to include evidence from text analysis, this method should also be added to typology: one central approach to typology should be based on text samples from comparable registers, and outside systemic functional work, this has indeed been developed within functional typology. The challenge here is the sample size: as soon as we begin to link typology to text-based evidence, we have to reduce the size of the sample of languages quite dramatically (possibly down to the sample size used in linguistic comparison) in order to keep the investigation manageable.[11] However, we can adopt the kind of two-pronged approach suggested earlier – a combination of studies based on a relatively small sample of languages and based on text and studies drawing on large typological databases such as WALS.

Systemic functional typology has great potential, for theoretical and descriptive reasons discussed. The actualization of this potential can emerge from recent studies in the future if enough researchers are attracted to the new insights that can be derived from systemic functional typology. This would be a very important and exciting 'direction of development from Halliday'.

Notes

* This research was sponsored in part by Faculty of Humanities Dean's Reserve 1-ZV6R. The Hong Kong Polytechnic University; the opinions in this chapter are solely those of the authors.

1 This research was sponsored in part by Faculty of Humanities Dean's Reserve 1-ZV6R. The Hong Kong Polytechnic University; the opinions in this chapter are solely those of the authors.

   To bring out the connection between typology and comparison, systemic functional linguists have sometimes characterized typology as 'generalized comparison'. Halliday (1959–60/1966: 173) writes: 'Typology is, so to speak, generalized comparative descriptive linguistics; or generalized "contrastive" linguistics, to use a term that has come into use, particularly with reference to language teaching, for the comparative description of languages.'

2. The organization of Roget's thesaurus is systemic in orientation whereas the organization of dictionaries is based on items.

3. In his introduction to *Studies in Linguistic Analysis*, Firth ([1957] 1962b: vi) writes: 'Dr. Halliday, whose work is primarily in Chinese linguistics, points out that we in Britain have a long tradition of the description of the languages of Asia, Africa, and the Pacific, and gives it as his experience that the general linguistic principles and theories expounded and put into practice in London and elsewhere by my colleagues and myself are of particular value because most of the work has been done on non-Indo-European languages.'

4. Lado (1957) called his chapter on comparison of phonological systems 'how to compare two sound systems' (his chapter 2), but his chapter on the comparison of grammatical systems 'how to compare two grammatical structures' (his chapter 3). In phonology chapter, he shows how 'a phoneme is a complex unit in the system of a language' (pp. 10), bringing out the different phonological variables. The chapter on grammar is more syntagmatically oriented, but Lado (1957: 57) does talk about system, emphasizing that 'each pattern, each structure, contrasts not just with one other pattern but with many others. It is a complex net of these contrasts which constitutes a system for each language.' It is not difficult to see how one could develop this insight with the help of multilingual system networks.

5. Cf. also Ellis (1987) on dia-categories.

6. Such comparative studies are of course complemented by translation studies such as Hasselgård (1998, 2004) and Kim (2007).

7. By empirical typological linguistics, we mean the tradition that was pioneered in the Prague School (e.g. Sgall, 1995) – noting in particular Trubetzkoy's work on phonology, and later in the tradition developed by Greenberg and his colleagues, leading to linguistic typological databases such as WALS (Haspelmath et al., 2005) and its online version (Dryer & Haspelmath, 2011). Here typology is empirical in the sense that it is based on large samples of descriptions of languages – samples constructed according to considerations of the kind we mention in this subsection.

8. There are certainly exceptions. The most natural interpretation of Hopper and Thompson's (1980) transitivity hypothesis is probably systemic: their transitivity parameters are systemic variables, and their generalizations about correlations among these parameters between low and high values are precisely generalizations across systems.

9. This excludes nasalization as a feature of syllables.

10. Helmbrecht (2011) includes in his sample languages that avoid pronouns as a politeness strategy, but there are only seven such languages in his sample.

11. Typological linguists have started using parallel corpora as an important source of typological data. This is of course only possible where one text has been translated into a very large number of languages; see, for example, Stolz (2007) on the use by him and his team of parallel corpora based on *Le petit prince* and *Harry Potter.*

19 Computational Linguistics: The Halliday Connection

John Bateman and Mick O'Donnell

Chapter Overview

1 Introduction

Computational linguistics has become increasingly central to our lives, albeit mostly in ways remaining invisible to the casual computer user. Each search that is carried out on the internet using a web browser and search engine is already making use of basic computational linguistic techniques, such as stemming words so that documents involving all forms of given words can be found and not just 'exact' matches. Spell checking and grammar/style correction are now common techniques offered without comment by word processors, web forms and email programs. And more explicitly linguistic investigators have long since grown used to being able to search in corpora for linguistic patterns, initially with words but nowadays also often extending to grammatical and semantically tagged information. Behind each of these capabilities lie results that have their origins in computational linguistics, the field of study concerned with exploring descriptions of language and language use by employing computational techniques and algorithms. This field began with work on dictionaries and automatic translation in the 1950s and has passed through several phases dominated by quite different approaches to linguistics and language.

Over this entire period, it is remarkable that there have been significant and reoccurring interactions between the newest developments of the time and Michael Halliday. As the hardware capabilities of computers increased so that they became ever more able to deal with the prodigious quantities of linguistic information necessary for effective language processing, new opportunities for addressing linguistic phenomena were created and, within each of these cycles, input from Michael Halliday had a lasting effect on the approaches adopted and the mechanisms explored. One of the reasons for this lies in the flexibility and scope of the systemic functional model itself: its concerns were always more practical and inclusive than many other theories that arose in this period of history and, as the ambitions and capabilities of those employing computational means to explore language grew, systemic-functional linguistics (SFL) was always ready to meet the new challenges and offer theoretically motivated but practically grounded advice. This could not, however, occur without an investment of effort, and here Halliday's readiness to engage with the new technologies played a crucial role.

In this chapter, we will briefly set out the main points of interaction between Halliday and the developing field of computational linguistics, emphasizing the places where there was a considerable and lasting effect on subsequent research. As we shall see, Halliday's lifelong exploration of the functional basis of language has often impacted on the developing strands of computational linguistics. We will then conclude with the current state of affairs, in which computational studies of language are dramatically different to those in the late 1950s while nevertheless, in some ways, having become more compatible with some basic tenets of systemic functional theorizing than ever.

2 The Emergence of Machine Translation

One of the earliest motivations for employing computational techniques for the processing of natural human language was the desire to achieve automatic translation. This can be seen as a natural outgrowth of the early application of computers for military code breaking and was originally funded for many of the same reasons. Within this context, language was considered very much like a 'code' requiring only the appropriate codebook to be converted into various forms. Naturally, this kind of view of language did not succeed and, particularly in the United States, led to a widespread disillusionment with computational techniques for translation lasting almost a decade. However, as with many goals which were overambitious for their time, the research questions that were raised did create an environment for intellectual inquiry that brought together highly gifted research teams addressing phenomena in new and exciting ways.

It was in exactly such an environment that Halliday first became involved in computational linguistics, very soon after completing his Ph.D. in Chinese language at Cambridge. At that time, a research group called the Cambridge Language Research Unit (CLRU) was established with a particular focus on machine translation (MT). The CLRU

> was not part of the University at all and housed an extraordinary collection of eccentrics. It survived, in a way that would now seem almost miraculous, on the instincts and energy of Margaret Masterman its Director (MMB), and the grants she extracted from the UK and US governments and later the EEC Commission. (Wilks, 1995)

Halliday was part of the team from the first meeting, along with Margaret Masterman, Arthur Frederick Parker-Rhodes and Richard Richens. The work produced by the unit had lasting influence, mainly on MT, but also on other areas of language processing. Several prominent computational linguists got their start working in the unit, including Yorick Wilks, Karen Sparck-Jones and Martin Kay – all of whom have played a major role in shaping computational linguistics as a field.

Halliday became interested in the work of the unit because of the hope he believed MT offered for facilitating education in languages where a lack of native-language text books had previously pushed education towards the languages of dominant cultures. The linguistic notions of Firth and colleagues were also influential on the project (Léon, 2000: 3; Masterman, 1965: iv–18) and Firth himself attended the first project meeting at King's College London, presenting a paper on 'Linguistic analysis and translation' (Firth, 1956b). This influence manifested itself most strongly in the group's awareness that, for texts to be properly translated, one needed to take into account the context of situation, and also that meaning was a valuable component in language description. Other approaches developing at that time were largely dictionary-based (i.e. word-for-word translation, with possible reordering applied afterwards), or attempted to map syntactic structures from the source language onto those in the target language.

The unit's ideas on MT and the role of semantics were presented at a meeting in the United States. where it attracted the attention of the US National Science Foundation (NSF). The NSF agreed to fund their approach and exploration of meaning-based translation, where the set of concepts expressed in a source sentence were first to be derived and then generated in the target language as a

455

corresponding sentence which best expressed those concepts, given the context of use. This ambitious goal led to the development of two principal approaches: one involving a language-neutral interlingua and the other, promoted particularly by Masterman, Parker-Rhodes and Halliday, a thesaurus to organize a language's different word senses in a manner analogous to that of Roget's thesaurus. In the use of a thesaurus we already see in embryo form many of the ideas that came later to form central themes of Halliday's SFL. Organizing language as a resource involving alternative options growing ever finer is intrinsic to a thesaurus style of approach and thus established very early an awareness of the potential role of paradigmatic organization in language description. The idea of employing a thesaurus for translation was then to determine which thesaurus sense was intended by each source word so as to choose among the words/phrases corresponding to that sense in the target language. This basic style of approach has reappeared over the years in many forms and is still one of the basic ways in which MT is performed.

A further fundamental problem for translation directly considered by the CLRU group was that of involving context appropriately. Masterman had been trained formerly in Wittgenstein's philosophy of language and so was convinced that a word's use in context had to be a, if not the, major determinant of its meaning. This contributed to her openness to the Firthian and, increasingly Hallidayan, views of language developing at that time. Masterman (1957) describes this task in terms of a word-sense disambiguation task: deciding which of the source-language senses of a word was intended, and then finding the target-language word or phrase which best expresses this sense. Word-sense disambiguation still forms today one of the basic challenges of computational linguistics and the most common method is to rely on co-text in order to derive statistically most likely readings in context. This is precisely the approach taken by Masterman, Halliday and Parker-Rhodes: when translating a word, e.g. 'plant', from English to another language, one would look up the term in the thesaurus, producing several senses, each associated in Roget's with a numerical code. The words around the term in the source text would then be explored to find terms with intersecting senses. For instance, if the preceding term was 'flowering', then its associated senses intersect with those of 'plant' in only one code. The proposed thesaurus contained a translation of each sense, and thus the word or phrase to translate 'plant' with this sense would be provided. This was one of the earliest uses of automatic word-sense disambiguation, and perhaps the earliest using a thesaurus. Similar techniques are still in use today, forming one of the fundamental operations within automatic text processing (e.g. Carpuat & Wu, 2007).

The use of a thesaurus style of organization for computational representations of language resources is also strongly echoed in knowledge representation and modern work on ontologies, particularly as employed for the Semantic

Web. This connection is rarely drawn out but is certainly an interesting branch in the family tree of modern generally accepted computational approaches. As Masterman (1965: iv–18) states: Halliday 'put us on the original thesaurus idea, on which all our more recent semantics work has directly or indirectly been founded'.

Halliday's work in the translation project also concerned the translation of syntax as opposed to lexical meaning. Halliday took issue with a trend at the time of syntactic-level translation: the assumption of translation equivalence of syntactic structures across languages, e.g. that occurrences of passive in one language should be translated as the equivalent of passive in the other language. He took seriously the Hjelmslevian principle that the meaning of a category is relative to the other categories that it is in opposition to. Thus, the categories of two languages, even if given the same names, do not have the same meanings. For instance, the feature 'nominative' in a system with four features does not then have the same sense as a feature 'nominative' in a system with 2 or 14 features (Léon, 2000). This has as automatic consequence that one cannot assume translation equivalence of syntactic features. Halliday's idea was then to extend the project's language descriptions to combine semantic information and the information coded in the syntactic structure of each particular language. To achieve this he proposed identifying the contextual conditions under which particular syntactic items are appropriate. He argued that if one could identify all of the determining factors that led the writer of the source text to produce the text they did, then the original text would not be needed in the translation process, one could just produce a text in the target language appropriate to those determining factors (Halliday, [1956] 2005b: 82); this is perhaps the earliest statement of the basic principle underlying what later became multilingual natural language generation (cf. Hartley & Paris, 1997). Halliday was, however, also well aware of the practical limitations of this approach: one cannot derive all the determining factors needed to produce the target text from the source text (some factors relevant to the target language may not be relevant in the source language), and even those that can be derived, could not be derived without a full description of the language, which even today we lack. Nevertheless, for the factors that could be identified this offered a principled approach to form selection going far beyond lexical or syntactic transfer.

Halliday's approach required a more sophisticated representation of the languages to be translated. This, however, was not without cost. Masterman (1957: 40) says that while using a more straightforward 'inter-lingua'-style approach, only 20 bits would be needed to store one entry, Halliday's approach required 120 bits. She concluded 'it should be borne in mind by those linguists who are seriously interested in developing MT as a concrete reminder that, for every increase in linguistic analytic complexity, a heavy electronic price has to be paid' (Masterman (1957: 41). This then marked the end of a first cycle of inter-action: linguistic theory and descriptive practice had developed to the point where there were clear hypotheses concerning how the translation task, as well as monolingual linguistic description, could be beneficially addressed, but the limited capabilities of the computational tools available began to place seri-ous hurdles in the path of pursuing those hypotheses in actual instantiations of language descriptions and computational systems. For more on Halliday's contribution to the early phase of MT, see Halliday ([1956] 2005b, [1957] 2002, 1962) and Masterman (1957), some of which can be found within the *Collected Works* volume appearing as Halliday (2005a).

As well as offering specific directions in which to look for solutions to the problems of processing languages and achieving usable linguistic descriptions, Halliday's involvement in computational linguistics at that time, as often since, had a direct impact on the work of his colleagues on the project. Masterman, director of the project, said that Halliday (along with W. S. Allen) shaped her conception of linguistics (Masterman, 1965), and that Halliday's thesaurus approach was central to the project even after Halliday left. The cooperation between Halliday and Parker-Rhodes also continued after Halliday had left the project: in the early 1960s, Parker-Rhodes developed a method for syntactic parsing based on Halliday's grammatical theories at that time. Around 1962–3, the task of programming this method was given to Yorick Wilks, who subse-quently became a highly influential figure in MT, knowledge representation and computational linguistics in general and is still active in shaping the field today.

One of Halliday's principal regrets within the project was that he did not get his colleagues to think paradigmatically.[1] This style of approaching the orga-nization of linguistic information was at that time rather far from the kinds of representations adopted computationally. This changed substantially in the 1990s when organizing resources into so-called type lattices of linguistic information became the dominant descriptive framework employed in com-putational approaches to language; this approach was primarily popular-ized in the more formal computational work of Pollard and Sag (1994). The involvement of SFL in MT subsequently remained largely indirect, however. In the late 1980s, Erich Steiner constructed a model of clause types and par-ticipant roles for the German component of the large-scale European transla-tion project Eurotra (Steiner et al., 1988). Steiner also subsequently interacted with the Natural Language group at the Information Sciences Institute (ISI) in Los Angeles (home of the Penman project: see section 4) in their first moves towards considering MT (Bateman et al., 1990). In the early 1990s, Graham Wilcock investigated the possible advantages of using Systemic Functional Grammar (SFG) in MT, although only part of an MT system was produced (Wilcock, 1993).

3 Early Computational Versions of Systemic Functional Grammar: Natural Language Parsing

By the 1970s, computational capabilities had developed substantially and Artificial Intelligence (AI) had become a thriving field of research. The general goal within AI is to produce computational systems that carry out tasks that would normally be said to require 'intelligence' and to use those systems as instantiated theoretical models for improving our understanding of how such intelligence operates. Naturally, one of the primary examples of intelligent behaviour investigated within AI has always been the human ability to use language and a range of computational systems had been explored that appeared to employ natural language in sophisticated ways. The earliest influential system of this kind to be developed was SHRDLU, written by Terry Winograd as part of his Ph.D. This pioneer system represented a breakthrough in the state of the art and was the first fully functional system to engage in a convincing (written) dialogue with a human user. The program presented a number of coloured blocks lying around in a simulated environment on a computer screen and a human operator could type in sentences, for instance, giving instructions ('Move the green block onto the red block'), or asking questions ('Which block is under the green block?'). The computer program would then respond, either performing the instructed action, or answering the question (see Winograd, 1972).

Winograd's undergraduate degree was in Mathematics in Colorado and, following this, he decided to learn more about natural human language. Taking advantage of a Fullbright scholarship, he travelled to London for a year's study during 1966–7 in Halliday's department, attending lectures under Halliday, Dick Hudson and Bob Dixon. Halliday's approach to language influenced Winograd to the extent that, on his return to the United States to pursue his doctoral research at the Artificial Intelligence Lab at MIT, he made direct use of Halliday's linguistic theory. As he later described:

> My direct source of inspiration came from the year in London where I studied with Halliday. If you look at what Halliday was doing in the context of the larger picture of generative grammar, he was trying to adapt his theories, which came more from a social perspective, to a generative form. (Quoted in Thanning Vendelø, 2002: 10–11)

The computational linguistic component of Winograd's system employed a direct computational instantiation of Halliday's early SFG, complete with system networks for clause, group and word. This grammar provided the linguistic information necessary for the syntactic analyser of SHRDLU to provide semantic interpretations for users' input sentences. The system had a very high

459

impact at the time. The focus in the early 1970s was on the parsing of problem sentences, or on making syntactic parsers more efficient. Winograd, following a more functional line, dealt with the core sentences of the language, and focused on making the system work, not proving that it should work in theory. Thus, where the current work was mostly focusing on syntax, Winograd made a system which analysed input text, interpreted it semantically, decided on the appropriate response to the input, and then acted upon it. The system required work in knowledge representation (modelling the 'blocks world') and on problem solving. Many considered the system to have demonstrated that natural language interaction with AI was possible, if not solved. The success of this work was then responsible for a much broader spread of awareness for functional approaches to language, SFG and Halliday across the natural language processing community.

Halliday's linguistics also influenced another computational linguist, Michael McCord. McCord, inspired by Winograd's work, found Dick Hudson's book, *English Complex Sentences* (1971), and started up a correspondence with him. He spent the fall of 1977 with Hudson on a sabbatical. McCord developed a modified version of SFG (1975), that he used for parsing (1977).

There have been several subsequent research efforts exploring the use of SFG for sentence analysis, both in its Hallidayan variants (Kasper, 1988b; O'Donnell, 1993) and that of Robin Fawcett's variant (Day, 2007; O'Donoghue, 1991; Weerasinghe, 1993). In all of these systems however, Halliday's influence has been fairly indirect: although his description of English grammar was used as resources, and the systemic formalism could be said to drive the abstract design of the corresponding systems (e.g. the choice of a paradigmatic approach to language analysis, multiple layers of syntactic functions conflated together), the actual mechanisms involved often needed to draw on further sources of input in order to operate. Some of the theoretical reasons for this are discussed in more detail in Bateman (2008b).

4 Text Generation

The next major interaction between Halliday and computational linguistics was in the area of computational linguistics called *text generation* or, more generally, *natural language generation* (NLG). This is often talked of as the 'opposite' of analysis or parsing, although there are many asymmetries between the two, both in terms of approaches and methods and in terms of research communities. Simply stated, NLG is the computational process of automatically producing sentences in some human language on the basis of a specification of communicative intention. A program that performs this task is called a *sentence generator*. Such programs require more or less extensive linguistic descriptions of the lexico-grammatical resources of the languages they are to cover and there are examples of such systems for most linguistic theories. It is in NLG, however, that some of the most close and productive exchanges between SFL and computational linguistics have occurred – generally because the generation task is one that has always been characterized computationally most naturally in terms of *choice*. When generating a sentence to express some communicative intent, the question is always one of choice between grammatical and lexical alternatives so as to best express the intended semantics. Linguistic descriptions that make considerations of choice more accessible have a natural advantage for this task.

Halliday's early characterization of language as a systemic potential that is organized paradigmatically offers precisely such a perspective. In many respects, a Hallidayan systemic network as found within a lexico-grammar *is* a statement of how to construct a sentence or other grammatical unit. Following the network through, from left to right, invoking realization statements as they are encountered, is a recipe for constructing corresponding grammatical units. Thus, despite the fact non-computational users of systemic theory tend to think first of analysis, within the computational context it is generation that the systemic functional framework has shown itself most suited to. This feature, which has actually only become clear because of the attempts to apply SFL for both analysis and generation, has some fairly deep consequences for theory and for how systemic potential can be best captured (cf. Bateman, 2008b).

There were several early attempts to provide direct computational instantiations of systemic specifications; Henrici ([1965] 1981), for example, took the notions of systemic network (paradigmatic organization) and realization statements constraining structure (syntagmatic organization), and specified them sufficiently explicitly for a computer program to carry them out. This demonstrated that it was possible at least in theory to construct a computational implementation of a paradigmatically organized grammar, although at that time the computational capabilities available again limited the scope of what could be demonstrated. In the 1970s, a paradigmatically organized computational grammar was developed as part of the PROTEUS system, another system written as part of a doctoral dissertation – that of Anthony Davey in Edinburgh in 1974 (published as Davey, 1978). This system was particularly significant both for computational linguistics and for the interaction between SFG and computation because it addressed for the first time not the generation of isolated sentences but of running texts. Although very simple, basic textual phenomenon still had to be considered, including issues of pronominalization and clause connectives. This then placed a clear emphasis on accepting textual organization and capabilities into the specification of the necessary linguistic resources, a move that Halliday had been promoting all along and including explicitly in his metafunctionally organized systemic networks. Davey's system was a

461

convincing demonstration that it was feasible to produce extended texts auto-matically on the basis of machine-internal non-linguistic information and most recent NLG systems generally follow in this tradition, producing information from database contents, from knowledge bases of expert systems and from user-provided abstract input.

These moves paved the way for the next cycle of close interaction and col-laboration between Halliday and computational linguistics which took place in the context of the original development of the Penman text generation system in the 1980s, a system designed and conceived by William Mann of the Information Sciences Institute in Los Angeles. Mann has been planning a large-scale NLG project, but found in an extensive study of the technology of the time that the tools available showed little linguistic sophistication. On the basis of previous computational experiences, Mann had been convinced that making a computer 'function as an author' (Mann & Moore, 1980) would require detailed and linguistically valid models of lexis, grammar, semantics and discourse in order to succeed. The existence of proof-of-concept specifi-cations of Hallidayan paradigmatically organized grammars produced ear-lier in work such as that of Henrici and Davey suggested a way to proceed. Mann decided that what his project required was a large-scale computational instantiation of Halliday's SFG as the 'front-end' of a larger, general-purpose NLG system. This system, called Penman, was intended to be a register-non-specific, broad-coverage generation system, capable of producing texts in nat-ural English for as broad a range of domains as required. To achieve this aim, he directly involved Halliday, and a fresh graduate student at UCLA work-ing on a systemic interpretation of tense in English, Christian Matthiessen. Together they started on the computational specification and implementation of the extant fragments of English grammar within the systemic functional framework that Halliday had been working on over the previous 15 years. The result of these efforts was the Nigel grammar of English, a fully explicit computational SFG for sentence generation that, by the late 1980s, had become the most extensive such computational grammar in any framework (Mann & Matthiessen, 1985; Matthiessen, 1985). Even today, there are few grammars with comparable coverage and the Nigel grammar continues to be used and developed; many researchers have contributed to the grammatical descrip-tions it contains. A detailed overview of all aspects of the Penman system is given by Matthiessen and Bateman (1991).

The existence of the Nigel grammar as a functioning resource for large-scale natural language generation did much to motivate the take-up of systemic func-tional approaches in other computational projects, the largest example of which is Robin's Fawcett's COMMUNAL project and its Cardiff grammar (Tucker, 1996, 1998). The Penman system was also extended to work with multilin-gual linguistic resources by incorporating the results of discussions originally involving Halliday, Matthiessen, Bateman, Licheng Zeng and Keizo Nanri on functional typology (cf. Bateman et al., 1991). This then formed the basis of the KPML (Komet-Penman Multi-Lingual) system that is still actively used and developed for linguistic resources in a variety of languages and applications today (Bateman, 1997).

5 Linguistic Formalisms

Computational linguistics is also very much concerned with providing representational forms which are appropriate for capturing linguistic information. Appropriate representational forms should possess the expressive capabilities to capture linguistic generalizations without adopting an 'anything goes' policy that would undermine the intended semantics of the representation. Here also there has been an interesting interaction between Halliday and computational approaches. The problem of specifying linguistic information in a 'computationally responsible' fashion had been placed on the linguistic agenda very clearly with the mathematical proof from Peters and Ritchie (1973) that transformational generative grammars of the form proposed by Chomsky at that time were in fact equivalent to general computer programs. This meant that they were very unlikely candidates for convincing descriptions of natural human languages since there would be, on this reading, no real reason why there are not languages in which passives are formed by reversing the order of the words. It is clear that there are a considerable number of further constraints to be considered that would distinguish appropriate linguistic accounts from general computer programs. This then is the goal when considering computational linguistic representations: to capture linguistically appropriate means of representing information.

One of the most influential developments in computational linguistics in this regard was made by Martin Kay in the late 1970s and early 1980s. Kay also started working on language at the CLRU, although several years after Halliday had left. Subsequently, however, Kay visited Halliday several times in London in the 1960s and, in the 1970s, while Kay was working at Rand Corp (Los Angeles), Halliday visited him there also. Kay (1979) started to work on SFG and this task led him to develop the formalism that was then termed Functional Unification Grammar (FUG). As Kay says:

> FUG was in large measure an attempt to provide a formalization of Systemics that would be amenable to computation. In particular, Halliday spoke of 'realization rules' that would effectively translate the choices made in his networks into strings, but there was virtually nothing said about what these would be like, and I was eager to fill that gap. (Personal Communication)

FUG exhibited many clear correspondences with SFG and offered the first well-defined computational representation that was particularly suited to capturing some of the basic features of systemic grammars, such as the description of grammatical units in terms of recursive functionally labelled constituents and the co-description of grammatical units by multiple labels. Co-description was achieved by a computational operation termed *unification*: the merging together of distinct but compatible functional descriptions. Unification has always been implicit in SFG, via the use of simultaneous systems which need to be considered together to construct structure and, to a certain extent, via some aspects of conflation and the cumulative nature of realizations of successive features related by delicacy. Kay made this notion computationally explicit, bringing out its central role for linguistic description. Kay himself was not happy with the parsing results that his formalism produced and so abandoned it (Personal Communication). The formalism caught on however and unification and unification-based grammars are now the standard representation of choice in all branches of computational linguistics.

An important difference between the original FUG formalism and SFG was, however, a lack of paradigmatic organization: an FUG-style grammar included no system networks. This lack was largely overcome in subsequent work on typed unification, which relies essentially on organizing functional descriptions, such as are produced by traditional FUG, into inheritance hierarchies. These hierarchies are defined in terms of linguistic *types* and correspond closely to the features of an SFG. The most developed perspective on this close correspondence between typed unification formalisms and SFGs is given in Henschel (1994) and subsequent work. Almost all modern computational linguistic formalisms employ some version of typed unification, although very few of these can be described as Hallidayan in any sense in terms of their content. One exception to this is the NLG system developed by Michael Elhadad called FUF (Functional Unification Formalism) (Elhadad & Robin, 1996). Michael Elhadad's FUF is an extension of Kay's FUG specially tailored for generation and whose main linguistic resource is a very large grammar of English called SURGE ('Systemic Unification Realization Grammar of English'), a direct typed unification variant of an SFG combining elements of both the Hallidayan and Fawcett variants.

6 Corpus Linguistics and Language as a Probabilistic Phenomenon

An early orientation of Hallidayan linguistic work was the commitment to studying occurrences of language in use. It was always assumed that real instances of language were the final word concerning the data to be considered when constructing theories. This was established at a time when access to such data was still difficult: large-scale bodies of linguistic data were beyond the storage capabilities of computers of the time and there were few developed tools for interacting with such data even when available. In this sense, the Hallidayan perspective on language as instance was considerably ahead of its time. Now, with substantial bodies of linguistic data available and growing exponentially with each document added into the World-Wide Web, the application of corpus methods and statistical approaches to language appears to many to be the obvious, for some even the only, road to follow.

Due to the considerable time lag between theory and practice, the influence and interaction of Halliday on current approaches to corpus linguistics and to statistical approaches to linguistic phenomena has mostly been quite indirect. Halliday and Hasan's model of cohesion has influenced the field of reference resolution and there are several tools available now for tracking reference chains and lexical cohesion. The general idea of collocation (Halliday, 1966, [1966] 2002b) has also influenced the field of modern statistical computing in several areas, and collocation is often used to resolve parsing decisions. One of the few direct interactions with modern corpus linguistics is reported in Halliday and James ([1993] 2005), which presents a quantitative study of the co-occurrence of polarity and primary tense.

It is particularly interesting, however, how the consideration of language as a probabilistic phenomenon is now coming into its own in computational linguistics at large. This has only become possible with the availability of really substantial bodies of data since otherwise statistical patterns cannot be reliably uncovered. The original version of the Penman system required that its generation grammars include specifications of probabilities in each of the choices defined within its system networks: this followed directly from Halliday's commitment to the role of probabilities and distributions in linguistic description and language use. These probabilities were however never used in generation: there were at that time few linguistically relevant ways of employing the statistics to control the generation process and even fewer ways of obtaining appropriate values for the probabilities from real data. Now there are a host of available methods that work directly with probabilistic descriptions of linguistic data; these do not generally work with the resources defined previously from a Hallidayan perspective, however.

7 Conclusions

As we have now seen, the long interaction and contribution of Michael Halliday to computational linguistics has been of considerable significance – both directly, in terms of cooperative work and personal interaction, and indirectly, in terms of influences on entire approaches towards the treatment of linguistic phenomena. Some of these interactions have contributed to methods whose general application has gone far beyond their original intentions and where the precise sources of contributions become difficult to disentangle. There is little doubt, however, that the view of language as a multidimensional, multifunctional, paradigmatic, socially anchored probabilistic phenomenon has repeatedly provided important impetuses that have beneficially pushed the development of computational treatments of language further at several points over its brief history. That interaction has now been rather quiet for some time: it remains to be seen whether the current explosion of interest in statistical approaches to linguistic phenomena will lead to a further round of exchange as machine-learning techniques sweep the field in all areas from language learning, through corpus annotation to mechanisms for dialogic interaction. The success of these methods given sufficiently strong statistical techniques goes a long way to supporting once again the essential core of Halliday's views on the nature of language.

Note

1. Unpublished interview, recorded July 2003, Leeds, UK, by M. O'Donnell.

Bibliography

Abercrombie, D. (1948) 'Forgotten phoneticians', *Problems and Principles*. London: Longmans.
— (1957) *Problems and Principles*. London: Longmans.
— (1967) *Elements of General Phonetics*. Edinburgh: Edinburgh University Press.
Akerejola, E. (2005) *A Systemic Functional Grammar of Òkó*. Macquarie University: Ph.D. thesis.
Albright, D. (1997) *Quantum Poetics: Yeats, Pound, Eliot, and the Science of Modernism*. Cambridge: Cambridge University Press.
Alford, D. M. (2002) 'The great Whorf hypothesis hoax: Sin, suffering and redemption in academe', <http://www.hilgart.org/enformy/dma-Chap7.htm>.
Allan, K. (2010) *The Western Classical Tradition in Linguistics*. Second edition. London: Equinox.
Allen, W. S. (1953) 'Relationship in comparative linguistics', *Transactions of the Philological Society*.
Amsler, R. A. (1981) 'A taxonomy for English nouns and verbs', Proceedings of the 19th Annual Meeting of the Association for Computational Linguistics. Stanford, CA, pp. 133–8.
Anderson, John M. (1968) 'Ergative and nominative in English', *JL* 4, pp. 1–32.
Antilla, R. (2003) 'Analogy: The warp and woof of cognition', B. D. Joseph and R. D. Janda (eds), *The Handbook of Historical Linguistics*. Carlton, VIC: Blackwell Publishing, pp. 425–40.
Arbib, M. (2012) *How the Brain Got Language: The Mirror System Hypothesis*. Oxford and New York: Oxford University Press.
Australian Government Department of Education, Employment and Workplace Relations (2009) *Belonging, Being and Becoming: The Early Years Learning Framework for Australia*. Canberra: Commonwealth of Australia.
Baker, M. (1992) *In Other Words: A Course Book on Translation*. London: Routledge.
Ball, P. (2004) *Critical Mass: How One Thing Leads to Another*. London: Heinemann.
Bardi, M. A. (2008) *A Systemic Functional Description of the Grammar of Arabic*. Macquarie University: Ph.D. thesis.
Barnwell, K. G. L. (1969) A *Grammatical Description of Mbembe (Adun Dialect): A Cross River Language*. University of London: Ph.D. thesis.
Bateman, J. (1997) 'Enabling technology for multilingual natural language generation: The KPML development environment', *Journal of Natural Language Engineering* 3: 1, pp. 15–55.
— (2008a) 'Systemic functional linguistics and the notion of linguistic structure: Unanswered questions, new possibilities', Jonathan J. Webster (ed.), *Meaning in Context: Implementing Intelligent Applications of Language Studies*. London and New York: Bloomsbury Academic, pp. 24–58.
— (2008b) *Multimodality and Genre: A Foundation for the Systematic Analysis of Multimodal Documents*. Hampshire: Palgrave Macmillan.
— (2014) 'Looking for what counts in film analysis: A programme of empirical research', Machin (ed.), *Visual Communication*. Berlin: Mouton de Gruyter, pp. 301–30.
Bateman, J. and Schmidt, K. H. (2012) *Multimodal Film Analysis: How Films Mean*. London and New York: Routledge.

Bateman, J., Emele, M. and Momma, S. (1992) 'The nondirectional representation of systemic functional grammars and semantics as typed feature structures', Proceedings of COLING 92. Nantes: COLING, pp. 916–20.

Bateman, J., Matthiessen, C. M. I. M. and Zeng, L. C. (1999) 'Multilingual language generation for multilingual software: A functional linguistic approach', *Applied Artificial Intelligence: An International Journal* 13: 6, pp. 607–39.

Bateman, J., Hois, J., Ross, R. and Tenbrink, T. (2010) 'A linguistic ontology of space for natural language processing', *Artificial Intelligence* 174, pp. 1027–71.

Bateman, John A., Kasper, R., Schütz, J. and Steiner, E. (1989) 'A new view on the translation process'. Proceedings of the European Chapter of the Association for Computational Linguistics. Manchester, England. April, 1989. Association for Computational Linguistics.

Bateman, J., Kasper, R., Moore, J. and Whitney, R. (1990) *A General Organization of Knowledge for Natural Language Processing: The Penman Upper Model*. Information Sciences Institute, University of Southern California.

Bateman, J., Matthiessen, C., Nanri, K. and Zeng, L. C. (1991) 'The rapid prototyping of natural language generation components: An application of functional typology', Proceedings of the 12th International Conference on Artificial Intelligence, Sydney, 24–30 August 1991, Sydney. San Mateo, CA: Morgan Kaufman, pp. 966–71.

Bates, E. (1979) *The Emergence of Symbols: Cognition and Communication in Infancy*. New York: Academic Press.

Baudouin de Courtenay, J. (1972) *A Baudouin de Courtenay Anthology: The Beginnings of Structural Linguistics*, translated by Stankiewicz (ed.), Bloomington and London: Indiana University Press.

Beaugrande, R. (1991) *Linguistic Theory: The Discourse of Fundamental Works*. London: Longman.

Beckman, M. E., Hirschberg, J. and Shattuck-Hufnagel, S. (2005) 'The original ToBI system and the evolution of the ToBI framework', Sun (ed.), *Prosodic Typology – The Phonology of Intonation and Phrasing*. Oxford: Oxford University Press, chapter 2, pp. 9–54.

Beckner, C., Blythe, R., Christiansen, M. H., Croft, W., Ellis, N. C., Holland, J., Ke, J., Freeman, D. L. and Shoenemann, T. (2009) 'Language is a complex adaptive system: Position paper', Ellis and Freeman (eds), *Language Learning* 59: Supplement 1, Language as a Complex Adaptive System, pp. 1–26.

Beer, G. (2000) *Darwin's Plots: Evolutionary Narrative in Darwin, George Eliot and Nineteenth-Century Fiction*. Second edition. Cambridge: Cambridge University Press.

Bell, R. T. (1976) *Sociolinguistics: Goals, Approaches and Problems*. London: Batsford.

— (1991) *Translation and Translating*. London: Longman.

Bellos, D. (2011) *Is That a Fish in Your Ear? Translation and the Meaning of Everything*. London: Particular Books/Penguin.

Bernstein, B. (1958) 'Some sociological determinants of perception: An inquiry in subcultural differences', *British Journal of Sociology* 9, p. 174.

— (1959) 'A public language: Some sociological implications of a linguistic form', *British Journal of Sociology* 10, pp. 311–26.

— (1970) 'Education cannot compensate for society', *New Society* 15: 387, pp. 344–7.

— (ed.) (1971a) *Class, Codes and Control*. Volume 1. *Theoretical Studies Towards the Sociology of Language*. London: Routledge & Kegan Paul.

— (1971b), 'Social class, language and socialization', *Current Trends in Linguistics*. A. S. Abramson et al. (eds). The Hague: Mouton.

— (1973) *Class, Codes and Control*. Volume 3. *Towards a Theory of Educational Transmission*. Second edition. London: Routledge & Kegan Paul.

— (ed.) (1975) *Class, Codes and Control*. Volume 2. *Applied Studies Towards a Sociology of Language*. London: Routledge & Kegan Paul.

— (1990) *Class, Codes and Control*. Volume 4. *The Structuring of Educational Discourse*. London: Routledge.

— (2000) *Pedagogy, Symbolic Control and Identity: Theory, Research, Critique*. Revised version. Oxford: Rowman and Littlefield Publishers.

Bernstein, L. (1976) *The Unanswered Question: Six Talks at Harvard*. Cambridge, MA and London: Harvard University Press.

Berwick, R. C. (1997) 'Syntax facit saltum: Computation and the genotype and phenotype of language', *Journal of Neurolinguistics* 10: 2, pp. 231–49.

Biber, D. (1986) 'Spoken and written textual dimensions in English: Resolving the contradictory findings', *Language* 62: 2, pp. 384–414.

— (1988) *Variation across Speech and Writing*. Cambridge: Cambridge University Press.

— (2006) *University Language: A Corpus Based Study of Spoken and Written Registers*. Amsterdam and Philadelphia: John Benjamins.

Biber, D., Conrad, S. and Reppen, R. (1998) *Corpus Linguistics: Investigating Language Structure and Use*. Cambridge: Cambridge University Press.

Birch, C. (1990) *On Purpose*. Kensington: University of New South Wales Press.

Birch, D. (1988) 'Expanding semantic options for reading early modern English', D. Birch and M. O'Toole (eds), *Functions of Style*. London and New York: Pinter Publishers, pp. 157–68.

Birch, D. and O'Toole, L. M. (eds), *Functions of Style*. London and New York: Pinter.

Blake, J. and de Boysson-Bardies, B. (1992) 'Patterns in babbling: A cross-linguistic study', *Journal of Child Language* 19, pp. 51–74.

Bloch, B. ([1946] 1957) 'Studies in colloquial Japanese II: syntax', *Language* 22, pp. 20–48. [Reprinted in Joos (1957), pp. 154–85.]

Bloom, L. (1993) *The Transition from Infancy to Language*. New York: Cambridge University Press.

Bloomfield, L. ([1933] 2002) *Language*. New York: Holt. [Reprinted by Foreign Language Teaching and Research Press (Beijing) (2002).]

Bod, R., Hay, J. and Jannedy, S. (eds) (2003a) *Probabilistic Linguistics*. Cambridge, MA: MIT Press.

— (2003b) 'Introduction', Body, Hay and Jannedy (2003a), pp. 1–10.

Bohm, D. (1980) *Wholeness and the Implicate Order*. London: Routledge & Kegan Paul.

Bohr, N. (1961) *Atomic Physics and Human Knowledge*. New York: Science Editions.

Bolinger, D. L. (1958) 'Intonation and grammar', *Language Learning* 8, pp. 31–7.

— ([1964] 1972) 'Around the edge of language: Intonation', *Harvard Educational Review* 34: 2, pp. 282–93. [Reprinted in Bolinger, D. L. (ed.), *Intonation: Selected Readings*. Harmondsworth: Penguin, pp. 19–29.]

Bordwell, D. and Thompson, K. (2010) *Film Art: An Introduction*. Ninth edition. New York: McGraw-Hill.

Bowcher, W. L. (2004) 'Theme and new in play-by-play radio sports commentating', Banks (ed.), *Text and Texture: Systemic Functional Viewpoints on the Nature and Structure of Text*. Paris: L'Harmattan, pp. 455–93.

Brachman, R. J. (1978) A Structural Paradigm for Representing Knowledge, BBN Report No. 3605. Cambridge, MA: Bolt Beranek and Newman, Inc.

— ([1979] 1985) 'On the epistemological status of semantic networks', Findler (ed.), *Associative Networks: Representation and Use of Knowledge by Computers*. New York: Academic Press, pp. 3–50. [Reprinted in Brachman, R. J. and Levesque, H. J. (eds) (1985) *Readings in Knowledge Representation*. Los Altos, CA: Morgan Kaufman.]

Bréal, M. ([1897] 1900). *Essai de Sémantique*, translated by Nina Cust as *Semantics: Studies in the Science of Meaning* (1900). New York: Henry Hold & Co.

Bresnan, J. (1982) 'The passive in lexical theory', Bresnan (ed.), *The Mental Representation of Grammatical Relations*. Cambridge, MA: MIT Press, pp. 3–86.

— (2000) 'Linguistic theory at the turn of the twentieth century', AILA '99 Organizing Committee (eds), Selected Papers from AILA'99 Tokyo, Plenary Addresses, Keynote Addresses, Special Lectures, Special Symposia, Twelfth World Congress of Applied Linguistics, Waseda University Press, Tokyo, pp. 98–115.

Brooks, M. (2011) *The Secret Anarchy of Science*. London: Profile Books.

Brown, E. K. and Law, V. (eds) (2002) *Linguistics in Britain: Personal Histories*. Oxford: Blackwell.

Brown, R. and Gilman, A. (1960) 'The pronouns of power and solidarity', Sebeok (ed.), *Style in Language*. Cambridge, MA: MIT Press, pp. 253–76.

Bullowa, M. (ed.) (1979) *Before Speech: The Beginning of Interpersonal Communication*. Cambridge: Cambridge University Press.

Bursill-Hall, G. L. (1961) 'Levels analysis: J. R. Firth's theories of linguistic analysis', *Journal of the Canadian Linguistic Association* 6, pp. 124–5, 164–91.

Butler, C. (2003) *Structure and Function: From Clause to Discourse and Beyond*. Amsterdam: John Benjamins.

Butt, D. (1983) 'Semantic drift in verbal art', *Australian Review of Applied Linguistics* 6, pp. 34–48.

Butt, D. G. (1988) 'Randomness, order and the latent patterning of text', D. Birch and L. M. O'Toole (eds), *Functions of Style*. London: Pinter.

— (1991) 'Some basic tools in a linguistic approach to personality: A Firthian concept of social process', F. Christie (ed.), Literacy in Social Processes: Papers from the Inaugural Australian Systemic Functional Linguistics Conference, Deakin University, January 1990. Darwin: Centre for Studies of Language in Education, Northern Territory University, pp. 23–44.

— (2000) 'The meaning of a network XXXX', Matthiessen and Butt XXXX Xian

— (2001) 'Firth, Halliday and the development of systemic functional theory', S. Auroux, E. F. K. Koerner, H. Niederehe and K. Versteegh (eds), *History of the Language Sciences*. New York: Walter de Gruyter.

— (2004) 'How our meanings change: School contexts and semantic evolution', G. Williams and A. Lukin (eds), *The Development of Language: Functional Perspectives on Species and Individuals*. London: Continuum.

Butt, D. G. (2008a) 'Whiteheadian and functional linguistics', M. Weber and W. Desmond (eds), *Handbook of Whiteheadian Process Thought*. Frankfurt: Ontos Verlag.

— (2008b). 'The robustness of realizational systems', J. J. Webster (ed.), *Meaning in Context: Implementing Intelligent Applications of Language Studies*. London and New York: Continuum, pp. 59–83.

— (2010) '…"mysterious butterflies of the soul"? One linguistic perspective on the efficacy of meaning in the "mind-brain" system', C. Wu, C. M. I. M. Matthiessen and M. Herke (eds), *Proceedings of ISFC 35: Voices Around the World*. Volume 2. Sydney: Macquarie Lighthouse Press, pp. 1–23.

— (2014) 'The history of ideas and Halliday's natural science of meaning', Jonathan J. Webster (ed.), *Bloomsbury Companion of M.A.K. Halliday*. London: Bloomsbury Academic (Chapter 2, this volume).

Butt, D. G. and Lukin, A. (2009) 'Stylistic analysis: Construing aesthetic organization', Halliday and Webster (eds), *Continuum Companion to Systemic Functional Linguistics*. London: Continuum.

Butt, D. G. and O'Toole, M. (2003) 'Transactions between matter and meaning: A functional theory for the science of text', M. Amano (Nagoya, Nagoya University) (ed.), Proceedings of the Second International Conference Studies for the Integrated Text Science, 21st Century Centre of Excellence Program International Conference Series No. 2, pp. 1–23.

Byrnes, H. (ed.) (2006) *Advanced Instructed Language Learning: The Complementary Contribution of Halliday and Vygotsky*. London and New York: Bloomsbury Academic.

Caffarel, A. (2004a) 'Metafunctional profile of the grammar of French', Caffarel, Martin and Matthiessen (eds), *Language Typology: A Functional Perspective*. Amsterdam: John Benjamins, pp. 77–137.

— (2004b) 'The construal of a second-order semiosis in Camus' L'Etranger', Banks (ed.), *Text and Texture: Systemic Functional Viewpoints on the Nature and Structure of Text*. Paris: L'Harmattan, pp. 204–24.

— (2006a) *A Systemic Functional Grammar of French: From Grammar to Discourse*. London and New York: Continuum.

— (2006b) 'Learning advanced French through SFL: Learning SFL in French', Byrnes (ed.), *Advanced Instructed Language Learning: The Complementary Contribution of Halliday and Vygotsky*. London and New York: Continuum, pp. 204–24.

Caffarel, A., Martin, J. R. and Matthiessen, C. M. I. M. (2004) *Language Typology: A Functional Perspective*. Amsterdam and Philadelphia: John Benjamins.

Campbell, L. (2003) 'How to show languages are related: Methods for distant genetic relationship', B. D. Joseph and R. D. Janda (eds), *The Handbook of Historical Linguistics*. Malden, MA: Blackwell Publishing, pp. 262–82.

— (2006) 'Why Sir William Jones got it all wrong, or Jones' role in how to establish language families', *Anuario del Seminario de Filología Vasca Julio de Urquijo: International Journal of Basque Linguistics and Philology*, pp. 245–64.

Capra, F. (1996) *The Web of Life: A New Synthesis of Mind and Matter*. London: HarperCollins.

Carter, R. (1987) *Vocabulary: Applied Linguistic Perspectives*. London: Unwin Hyman.

— (ed.) (1990) *Knowledge about Language and the Curriculum*. Sevenoaks: Hodder and Stoughton.

Cassidy, David (1992) *Uncertainty: The Life and Science of Werner Heisenberg*. New York: W.H. Freeman & Co.

Catford, J. C. (1965) *A Linguistic Theory of Translation*. Oxford: Oxford University Press.

— (1969) 'J. R. Firth and British linguistics', Hill (ed.), *Linguistics Today*. New York and London: Basic Books, Inc., pp. 218–28.

— (1977) *Fundamental Problems in Phonetics*. Indiana: Indiana University Press.

— (1985) '"Rest" and "open transition" in a systemic phonology of English', Benson and Greaves (eds), *Systemic Perspectives on Discourse*. Norwood, NJ: Ablex, pp. 333–48.

Čermák, F. (1997) 'Synchrony and diachrony revisited: Was R. Jakobson and the Prague Circle right in their criticism of de Saussure?' *Folia Linguisica Historica* XVII: 1–2, pp. 29–40.

Chalmers, A. (2013) *What Is This Thing Called Science?* Fourth edition. Brisbane: University of Queensland Press.

Chao, Y. (趙元任) (1968) *A Grammar of Spoken Chinese* (中國話的文法). Berkeley, Los Angeles and London: University of California Press.

Chargaff, E. (1978) *Heraclitean Fire*. New York: Warner/Murray Curtin.

Charter, N., Tenenbaum, Joshua B. and Yuille, A. (2006) 'Probabilistic models of cognition: Conceptual foundations', Editorial in Probabilistic models of cognition, a special issue of *TRENDS in Cognitive Sciences* 10:7, pp. 287–91.

Chater, N. and Oaksford, M. (eds) (2008) *The Probabilistic Mind: Prospects for Bayesian Cognitive Science*. Oxford: Oxford University Press.

Chater, N., Tenenbaum, J. B. and Yuille, A. (2006) 'Probabilistic models of cognition: Conceptual foundations', *TRENDS in Cognitive Sciences* 10: 7, pp. 287–91.

Chomsky, N. (1957) *Syntactic Structures*. The Hague: Mouton.

— (1965) *Aspects of the Theory of Syntax*. Cambridge, MA: MIT Press.

— (1970) 'Remarks on nominalization', Jacobs and Rosenbaum (eds), *Readings in English Transformational Grammar*. Waltham, MA: Ginn-Blaisdell, pp. 184–221.

— (1975) *Reflections on Language*. New York: Pantheon.

— (1979) *Language and Responsibility*. New York: Pantheon.

— (1993) *Language and Thought*. Wakefield, Rhode Island and London: Moyer Bell.

— (2000) *New Horizons in the Study of Language and Mind*. Cambridge: Cambridge University Press.

— (2012) *The Science of Language: Interviews with James McGilvray*. Cambridge: Cambridge University Press.

Chomsky, N. and Halle, M. (1968) *The Sound Patterns of English*. New York: Harper & Row.

Chow, I. and Webster, Jonathan J. (2008) 'Supervised clustering of the WordNet verb hierarchy for systemic functional process type identification', Proceedings of the 1st International Conference on Global Interoperability for Language Resources (ICGL). Hong Kong, PRC, 9–11 January 2008, pp. 51–8.

Christie, F. (ed.) (1999) *Pedagogy and the Shaping of Consciousness: Linguistic and Social Processes*. London: Cassell.

— (2002) *Classroom Discourse Analysis: A Functional Perspective*. London: Continuum.

Christie, F. and Derewianka, B. (2008) *School Discourse: Learning to Write across the Years of Schooling*. London and New York: Bloomsbury Academic.

Christie, F. and Unsworth, L. (2005) 'Developing dimensions of an educational linguistics', Hasan, Matthiessen and Webster (eds), *Continuing Discourse on Language: A Functional Perspective*. Volume 1. London: Equinox, pp. 217–50.

Cicourel, Aaron V. (1969) 'Generative semantics and the structure of social interaction', *International Days of Sociolinguistics*. Rome.

— (1973) *Cognitive Sociology, Language and Meaning in Social Interaction*. Harmondsworth: Penguin.

Cloran, C. (1989) 'Learning through language: The social construction of gender', *Language Development: Learning Language, Learning Culture*. Volume 1. *Meaning and Choice in Language*. Norwood, NJ: Ablex.

Cobb, J. B. (1993) *Alfred North Whitehead: Founders of Constructive Post Modern Philosophy*. Albany: State University of New York Press.

Cohen, J. and Stewart, I. (1995) *The Collapse of Chaos: Discovering Simplicity in a Complex World*. London: Penguin.

Cohen, M. (2005) *Wittgenstein's Beetle and Other Classic Thought Experiments*. Oxford: Blackwell Publishing.

Cole, P. (1978) *Syntax and Semantics: Pragmatics*. Volume 9. New York: Academic Press.

Comrie, B. and Cysouw, M. (n.d.) 'New Guinea through the eyes of WALS', <http://web.mac.com/cysouw/publications/index_files/cysouwNEWGUINEAtext.pdf>.

Cooke, D. (1959) *The Language of Music*. Oxford and New York: Oxford University Press.

Copestake, A. and Flickinger, D. (2000) 'An open-source grammar development environment and broad-coverage English grammar using HPSG', Proceedings of the Second Conference on Language Resources and Evaluation (LREC-2000). Athens, Greece.34

Corder, S. P. (1967) 'The significance of learners' errors', *International Review of Applied Linguistics* 5, pp. 160–70.

Crosby, A. W. (1997) *The Measure of Reality: Quantification and Western Society 1250–1600*. Cambridge: Cambridge University Press.

Cross, M. (1992) 'Choice in lexis: Computer generation of lexis as most delicate grammar', *Language Sciences* 14: 4, pp. 579–607.

Crystal, D. (1969) *Prosodic Systems and Intonation in English*. Cambridge: Cambridge University Press.

Cummings, M. (2010) *An Introduction to the Grammar of Old English: A Systemic Functional Approach*. London: Equinox.

Curtis, D. and Carter, M. (2008) *Learning Together with Young Children: A Curriculum Framework for Reflective Teachers*. St Paul, MN: Redleaf Press.

Damasio, A. (2012) *Self Comes to Mind: Constructing the Conscious Brain*. London: Vintage.

Danes, F. (1974) 'Functional sentence perspective and the organisation of the text', Danes (ed.), *Papers on Functional Sentence Perspective*. The Hague: Mouton, pp. 106–28.

Danielsson, B. (1963) *John Hart's Works on English Orthography and Pronunciation 1551, 1569, 1570*: Part II: Phonology. Stockholm, Goteborg and Uppsala: Almqvist and Wiksell.

Darwin, C. ([1859]1998) *The Origin of Species*. New York: The Modern Library.

Davey, A. (1978) *Discourse Production: A Computer Model of Some Aspects of a Speaker*. Edinburgh: Edinburgh University Press.

Davidse, K. (1986) 'M. A. K. Halliday's functional grammar and the prague school', Dirven and Fried (eds), *Functionalism in Linguistics*. Amsterdam: John Benjamins, pp. 39–79.

— (1998) 'Agnates, verb classes and the meaning of construals. The case of ditransitivity in English', *Leuvense Bijdragen* 87: 3–4, pp. 281–313.

Davies, M. (2014, in press) 'The black hole in graphology', Bowcher and Smith (eds), *Systemic Phonology: Recent Studies in English*. London: Equinox.

Davies, Paul and Gregersen, N. H. (eds) (2010) *Information and the Nature of Reality*. Cambridge: Cambridge University Press.

Davis, Phillips W. (1973) *Modern Theories of Language*. Englewood Cliffs, NJ: Prentice Hall.

Dawkins, R. (1995) *River Out of Eden: A Darwinian View of Life*. New York: Basic Books.

— (2004) *The Ancestor's Tale*. Boston: Houghton Mifflin.

Dawkins, R. and McKean, D. (2011) *The Magic of Reality: How We Know What's Really True*. London: Bantam Books.

Day, M. D. (2007) *A Corpus-consulting Probabilistic Approach to Parsing: The CCPX Parser and its Complementary Components*. Cardiff University: Ph.D. thesis.

Deacon, T. (1992) 'Brain-language Coevolution', Hawkins and Gell-Mann (eds), *The Evolution of Human Languages*. Redwood City, CA: Addison-Wesley (Proceedings volume XI, Santa Fe Institute Studies in the Sciences of Complexity), pp. 49–85.

— (1997) *The Symbolic Species: The Co-evolution of Language and the Human Brain*. Harmondsworth: Penguin Books.

— (2010) 'What is missing from theories of information?', P. Davies and N. H. Gregersen (eds), *Information and the Nature of Reality: From Physics to Metaphysics*. Cambridge: Cambridge University Press, pp. 146–69.

— (2012) *Incomplete Nature: How Mind Emerged from Matter*. London and New York: W.W. Norton & Co.

Department of Education and Science, Great Britain (1975) *A Language for Life: Report of the Committee of Inquiry appointed by the Secretary of State for Education and Science under the Chairmanship of Sir Alan Bullock*. London: HMSO.

Derewianka, B. (1998) *A Grammar Companion for Primary Teachers*. Sydney: Primary English Teachers Association.

De Saussure, F. ([1916] 1983) *Course in General Linguistics*, translated by R. Harris. London: Gerald Duckworth and Co.

Deutsch, D. and Ekert, A. (2012) 'Beyond the quantum horizon', *Scientific American* 307: 3, pp. 70–5.

DeWitt, R. (2004) *Worldviews: An Introduction to the History and Philosophy of Science*. Oxford: Blackwell Publishing.

Diamond, J. (2005) *Collapse: How Societies Choose to Fail or Survive*. Camberwell, VIC: Penguin/Allen Lane.

Dineen, F. P. (1967) *An Introduction to General Linguistics*. New York: Holt, Rinehart & Winston.

Dixon, R. W. (1965) *What Is Language? A New Approach to Linguistic Description*. London: Longmans.

Dixon, R. M. W. (2010) *Basic Linguistic Theory: Methodology*. Volume 1. Oxford: Oxford University Press.

Djonov, E. and Zhao, S. (2013) 'From multimodal to critical multimodal studies through popular discourse', Djonov and Zhao (eds), *Critical Multimodal Studies of Popular Discourse*. London and New York: Routledge.

D'Odrico, L. and Franco, F. (1991) 'Selective production of vocalization types in different communication contexts', *Journal of Child Language* 18, pp. 475–99.

Donaldson, M. (1978) *Children's Minds*. Glasgow: Fontana.

Doughty, Peter, Pearce, J. and Thornton, G. (1971) *Language in Use*. London: Arnold (for Schools Council Programme in Linguistics and English Teaching).

Douglas, M. (1966) *Purity and Danger: An Analysis of Concepts of Pollution and Taboo*. London: Routledge & Kegan Paul.

— (1975) *Implicit Meanings: Essays in Anthropology*. London: Routledge & Kegan Paul.

— (1979) 'Taboo', Cavendish (ed.), *Man, Myth and Magic*. Volume 20. London: Phoebus Publishing, pp. 2761–71.

Dryer, M. S. and Haspelmath, M. (eds) (2011) *The World Atlas of Language Structures Online*. Munich: Max Planck Digital Library. [Available online at http://wals.info/]

Dunn, M., Greenhill, S. J., Levinson, S. C. and Gray, R. D. (2011) 'Evolved structure of language shows lineage-specific trends in word-order universals', *Nature*. Published online 13 April 2011.

Edelman, G. M. (1988) *Topobiology: An Introduction to Molecular Biology*. USA: Basic Books.

— (1992) *Bright Air, Brilliant Fire: On the Matter of the Mind*. New York: Basic Books.

— (2006) *Second Nature: Brain Science and Human Knowledge*. New Haven: Yale University Press.

Edelman, G. and Tononi, G. (2000) *A Universe of Consciousness: How Matter Becomes Imagination*. New York: Basic Books.

Eggins, S. and Slade, D. (1997) *Analysing Casual Conversation*. London: Cassell.

Elhadad, M. (1990) 'Types in functional unification grammars', Proceedings of the 28th Annual Meeting of the Association for Computational Linguistics, pp. 157–64.

Elhadad, M. and Robin, J. (1996) 'A reusable comprehensive syntactic realization component', Demonstrations and Posters of the 1996 International Workshop on Natural Language Generation (INLG '96). Herstmonceux, England, pp. 1–4.

Ellegård, A. (1971) *Transformationell Svensk-engelsk Satslära*. Lund: Gleerup.

Ellis, J. (1966) *Towards a General Comparative Linguistics*. The Hague: Mouton.

— (1987) 'Some "dia-categories"', Steele and Threadgold (eds), *Language Topics: Essays in Honour of Michael Halliday*. Volume 2. Amsterdam: John Benjamins, pp. 81–94.

Ellis, J. and Davies, R. (1951) 'The Soviet linguistics controversy', *Soviet Studies*. Glasgow: University of Glasgow.

Ellis, J. and Ure, J. (1974) 'Register in descriptive linguistics and linguistic sociology', *International Journal of Sociolinguistics*.

Ellis, J. (1993) *Language, Thought, and Logic*. Evanston, IL: Northwestern University Press.

Elmenoufy, A. (1969) *A Study of the Role of Intonation in the Grammar of English*. University of London: Ph.D. thesis.

— (1988) 'Intonation and meaning in spontaneous discourse', Benson, Cummings and Greaves (eds), *Linguistics in a Systemic Perspective*. Amsterdam: John Benjamins, pp. 1–27.

Evans, N. (2010) *Dying Words: Endangered Languages and What They Have to Tell Us*. Oxford: Wiley-Blackwell.

Evans, N. and Levinson, S. C. (2009) 'The myth of language universals: Language diversity and its importance for cognitive science', *Behavioural and Brain Sciences* 32, pp. 429–92.

Favareau, D. (ed.) (2010) *Essential Readings in Biosemiotics: Anthology and Commentary.* Dordrecht: Springer.

Fawcett, R. P. (1980) *Cognitive Linguistics and Social Interaction.* Exeter and Heidelberg: University of Exeter & Julius Groos.

— (1988) 'What makes a "good" system network good?', Benson and Greaves (eds), *Systemic Functional Approaches to Discourse.* Norwood, NJ: Ablex, pp. 1–28.

— (2010) *A Theory of Syntax for Systemic Functional Linguistics.* Amsterdam and Philadelphia: John Benjamins.

Fawcett, R. P. and Weerasinghe, A. R. (1993) 'Probabilistic incremental parsing in systemic functional grammar', Bunt and Tomita (eds), Proceedings of the Third Workshop on Parsing Technologies. Tilburg: Institute for Language Technology and Artificial Intelligence, pp. 349–67.

Feyerabend, P. K. (1975) *Against Method.* London: New Left Books.

Fillmore, C. J. (1968) 'The case for case', Emmon Bach and R. T. Harms (eds), *Universals in Language.* New York: Holt, Rinehart & Winston.

Fillmore, C. J., Kay, P. and O'Connor, M. C. (1988) 'Regularity and idiomaticity in grammatical constructions: The case of Let Alone', *Language* 64, pp. 501–38.

Firth, J. R. (1936) 'Phonological features of some Indian languages', Proceedings of the Second International Congress of Phonetic Sciences (held at) London 1935. Cambridge, pp. 197–182.

— (1937) *The Tongues of Men.* London. [Reprinted in Oxford Series Language and Language Learning No. 2. London: Oxford University Press (1964).]

— (1956a) 'Philology in the philological society', *Transactions of the Philological Society*, pp. 1–5.

— (1956b) 'Linguistic analysis and translation', Palmer (ed.) (1968) *Selected Papers of J. R. Firth 1952–1959.* London: Longman.

Firth, J. R. ([1935] 1957) 'The technique of semantics', *Papers in Linguistics 1934–1951.* London: Oxford University Press, pp. 7–33.

— ([1946] 1957) 'The English school of phonetics', *Transactions of the Philological Society*, pp. 92–132.

— ([1948] 1957) 'The semantics of linguistic science', *Papers in Linguistics 1934–1951.* London: Oxford University Press, pp. 139–47.

— ([1950] 1957) 'Personality and language in society', *Papers in Linguistics 1934–1951.* London: Oxford University Press, pp. 177–89.

— ([1951] 1957) 'Modes of meaning', *Essays and Studies of the English Association* N.S.4, pp. 118–114.

Firth, J. R. (1957a) *Papers in Linguistics 1934–1951.* London: Oxford University Press.

— (1957b) 'Ethnographic analysis and with reference to Malinowski's views', R. Firth (ed.), *Man and Culture: An Evaluation of the Work of Bronislav Malinowski.* London: Routledge & Kegan Paul.

— (1957c) 'A synopsis of linguistic theory 1930–1955', Palmer (ed.) (1968) *Selected Papers of J. R. Firth 1952–1959.* London: Longman.

— ([1957] 1962a) 'A synopsis of linguistic theory 1930–1955', *Studies in Linguistic Analysis.* Oxford: Philological Society, pp. 1–32.

— ([1957] 1962b) 'Introduction', *Studies in Linguistic Analysis.* Oxford: Philological Society, pp. v–vii.

— ([1957] 1968a) 'A synopsis of linguistic theory 1930–55', *Philological Society: Studies in Linguistic Analysis* (special volume). Oxford, pp. 1–31.

Firth, J. R. (1968b) *Selected Papers of J. R. Firth 1952–1959.* F. R. Palmer (ed.), London: Longmans.

Fischer-Jørgensen, E. (1975) *Trends in Phonological Theory: A Historical Introduction.* Copenhagen: Akademisk Forlag.

Fishman, J. A. (1965) 'Who speaks what language to whom and when?', *La Linguistique* 2, pp. 67–88.

— (1971) *Sociolinguistics: A Brief Introduction.* Rowley, MA: Newbury House.

Fludernik, M. (2005) *The Fictions of Language and the Languages of Fiction.* London: Routledge.

Flynn, J. R. (2007) *What Is Intelligence? Beyond the Flynn Effect.* Cambridge: Cambridge University Press.

Fontaine, L., T., Bartlett, G. O'Grady (2013) *Systemic Functional Linguistics. Exploring Choice.* Cambridge: Cambridge University Press.

Forceville, C. J. and Urios-Aparisi, E. (eds) (2009) *Multimodal Metaphor.* Berlin and New York: Mouton de Gruyter.

Forsyth, Ian J. and Wood, K. (1977) *Language and Communication.* Volume 1. London: Longman.

— (1978) *Language and Communication.* Volume 2. London: Longman.

— (1979) *Language and Communication.* Volume 3. London: Longman.

Frake, C. O. (1961) 'The diagnosis of disease among the Subanum of Mindanao', *American Anthropologist* 63, pp. 13–132. [Reprinted in Hymes, D. (ed.) (1966) *Language in Culture and Society.* New York: Harper & Row, pp. 192–206.]

French, R. (2013) *Teaching and Learning Functional Grammar in Junior Primary Classrooms.* University of New England: Ph.D. thesis.

Fulton. G. (1999) *Styles of Meaning and Meanings of Style in Richardson's Clarissa.* Quebec: McGill-Queen's University Press.

Fung, Y. (1948) *A Short History of Chinese Philosophy,* translated by D. Bodde (ed.). New York: Free Press.

Gao, M. (高名凱) (1948) *On Chinese Grammar* (漢語語法語). Shanghai: Kaiming Press.

— (高名凱) (1960) *The Theory of Grammar* (語法理語). Beijing: Commercial Press.

Garvin, P. L. (ed.) (trans.) (1964) *A Prague School Reader on Esthetics, Literary Structure and Style.* Washington, DC: Georgetown University Press.

Ghadessy, M. (ed.) (1999) *Text and Context in Functional Linguistics.* Amsterdam: John Benjamins.

Gilder, L. (2008) *The Age of Entanglement: When Quantum Physics Was Reborn.* New York: Vintage.

Givón, T. (1979) *On Understanding Grammar.* New York: Academic Press.

Gleason, H. A. (1961) *An Introduction to Descriptive Linguistics.* New York: Holt, Rinehart & Winston.

— (1965) *Linguistics and English Grammar.* New York: Holt, Rinehart & Winston.

Gleick, J. (2011) *The Information: A History, a Theory, a Flood.* London: Fourth Estate.

Goldberg, A. (1995) *Constructions: A Construction Grammar Approach to Argument Structure.* Chicago: University of Chicago Press.

Goldsmith, J. (1990) *Autosegmental and Metrical Phonology.* Oxford: Blackwell.

— (2001) 'On information theory, entropy, and phonology in the 20th century', *Folia Linguistica* XXXIV: 1–2, pp. 85–100.

Grant, E. (1997) *The Foundations of Modern Science in the Middle Ages: Their Religious, Institutional, and Intellectual Contexts.* Cambridge: Cambridge University Press.

Greaves, W. S. (2007) 'Intonation in systemic functional linguistics', Hasan, Matthiessen and Webster (eds), *Continuing Discourse on Language.* Volume 2. London and Oakville, ON: Equinox.

Greenberg, J. H. (1966) 'Some universal of grammar with particular reference to the order of meaningful elements', Greenberg (ed.), *Universal of Language.* Second edition. Cambridge, MA: MIT Press, pp. 73–113.

Greenblatt, S. (2011) *The Swerve: How the Renaissance Began*. London: The Bodley Head.
Greenfield, S. (1997) *The Human Brain: A Guided Tour*. London: Weidenfeld and Nicholson.
— (2008) *ID: The Quest for Identity in the 21st Century*. London: Sceptre.
Gregory, R. (1981) *Mind in Science: A History of Explanations in Psychology and Physics*. Harmondsworth: Penguin.
Grenoble, L. A. and Whaley, L. J. (2006) *Saving Languages: An Introduction to Language Revitalization*. Cambridge: Cambridge University Press.
Gross, M. (1972) *Mathematical Models of Language*. Englewood Cliffs, NJ: Prentice Hall.
— (1979) 'On the failure of generative grammar', *Language* 55: 4, pp. 859–85.
Gumperz, J. J. (1964) 'Linguistic and social interaction in two communities', J. J. Gumperz and D. Hymes (eds), *American Anthropologist* 66: 6 *The Ethnography of Communication* (special publication Part 2).
— (1967) 'The social setting of linguistic behavior', D. L. Slobin (ed.), *A Field Manual for Cross-Cultural Study of the Acquisition of Communicative Competence*. Berkeley: University of California Press.
Gumperz, J. J. and Hymes, D. (eds) (1964) *American Anthropologist* 66: 6 *The Ethnography of Communication* (special publication Part 2).
— (eds) (1972) *Directions in Sociolinguistics: The Ethnography of Communication*. New York: Holt, Rinehart & Winston.
Haas, W. (1966) 'Linguistic relevance', C. E. Bazell, J. C. Catford, M. A. K. Halliday and R. H. Robins (eds), *In Memory of J. R. Firth*. London: Longmans.
Hagège, C. (2000) *Halte à la mort des langues*. Paris: Odile Jacob.
Hajek, J. (2011) 'Vowel nasalization', Dryer and M. Haspelmath (eds), *The World Atlas of Language Structures Online*. Munich: Max Planck Digital Library, chapter 10, <http://wals.info/chapter/10> [accessed 2 March 2013].
Halliday, M. A. K. (1959–1960/1966) 'Typology and the exotic', Combination of two lectures, one delivered at the Linguistics Association Conference, Hull, in May 1959, the other to the St. Andrews Linguistic Society, in May 1960, Halliday, M. A. K. and McIntosh, A. (1966) *Patterns of Language: Papers in General, Descriptive and Applied Linguistics*. London: Longman, chapter 10, pp. 165–82.
— (1962) 'Linguistics and machine translation', *Zeitschrift für Phonetik, Sprachwissenschaft und Kommunikationsforschung* 15: i/ii, pp. 145–58 (reprinted in Webster. Jonathan Ed. (2005). *The Collected Works of M.A.K. Halliday*. Volume 6. Computational and Quantitative Studies. London: Continuum, pp. 20–36).
— (1966) 'Patterns in words', *The Listener* LXXV: 1920, pp. 53–5.
— (1967) *Intonation and Grammar in British English*. The Hague: Mouton (Janua Linguarum Series Practica 48).
— (1970) *A Course in Spoken English: Intonation*. Oxford: Oxford University Press.
— (1971) 'Review of selected papers of J. R. Firth 1952–59', F. R. Palmer (ed.), *Bulletin of the School of Oriental and African Studies* 34, pp. 664–7.
— (1973a) *Explorations in the Functions of Language*. London: Arnold.
— (1973b) 'Foreword', Basil Bernstein (ed.), *Class, Codes and Control*. Volume 2. *Applied Studies Towards a Sociology of Language*. London: Routledge & Kegan Paul.
— (1974a) 'Language and social man', *Schools Council Programme in Linguistics and English Teaching: Papers Series II*. Volume 3. London: Longman (for the School's Council).
— (1974b) 'The place of "Functional Sentence Perspective" in the system of linguistic description', Daneš (ed.), *Papers on Functional Sentence Perspective*. Prague: Academia, pp. 43–53.
— (1975) *Learning How to Mean: Explorations in Language Development*. London: Arnold.
— (1976) *Halliday: System and Function in Language*. Kress (ed.), London: Oxford University Press.

— (1978) *Language as Social Semiotic: The Social Interpretation of Language and Meaning.* London: Edward Arnold.
— (1980) 'Foreword', de Joia and Stenton (eds), *Terms in Systemic Linguistics: A Guide to Halliday.* London: Batsford, pp. vii–xii.
— (1981) 'Types of structure', Halliday and Martin (eds), *Reading in Systemic Linguistics.* London: Batsford, pp. 29–41.
— (1984) 'Linguistics in the university: The question of social accountability', Copeland (ed.), *New Directions in Linguistics and Semiotics.* Houston, TX: Rice University Studies, pp. 51–67.
— (1985a) *An Introduction to Functional Grammar.* London: Arnold.
— (1985b) *Spoken and Written Language.* Waurn Ponds, VIC: Deakin University Press.
— (1988) 'On the language of physical science', Ghadessy (ed.), *Registers of Written English: Situational Factors and Linguistic Features.* London and New York: Pinter Publishers, pp. 162–78.
— (1993) 'Towards a language-based theory of learning', *Linguistics and Education* 5, pp. 93–116.
— (1994) *An Introduction to Functional Grammar.* Second edition. London: Edward Arnold.
— (2000) 'Phonology past and present: A personal retrospect', *Folia Linguistica* 34: 1/2, pp. 101–11.
— (2001) 'Towards a theory of good translation', Steiner and Yallop (eds) (2001), pp. 13–18.
— ([1957] 2002) 'Some aspects of systematic description and comparison in grammatical analysis', Jonathan J. Webster (ed.), *The Collected Works of M.A.K. Halliday.* Volume 1. *On Grammar.* London and New York: Bloomsbury Academic, pp. 21–36.
— ([1961] 2002) 'Categories of the theory of grammar', Jonathan J. Webster (ed.), *The Collected Works of M.A.K. Halliday.* Volume 1. *On Grammar.* London and New York: Bloomsbury Academic, pp. 37–94.
— ([1963] 2002) 'Class in relation to the axes of chain and choice in language', Jonathan J. Webster (ed.), *The Collected Works of M.A.K. Halliday.* Volume 1. *On Grammar.* London and New York: Bloomsbury Academic, pp. 95–105.
— ([1964] 2002) 'The linguistic study of literary texts', Jonathan J. Webster (ed.), *The Collected Works of M.A.K. Halliday.* Volume 2. *Text and Discourse.* London and New York: Bloomsbury Academic, pp. 5–22.
— ([1966] 2002a) 'Some notes on "deep" grammar', Jonathan J. Webster (ed.), *The Collected Works of M.A.K. Halliday.* Volume 1. *On Grammar.* London and New York: Bloomsbury Academic, pp. 106–17.
— ([1966] 2002b) 'Lexis as a linguistic level', Jonathan J. Webster (ed.), *The Collected Works of M.A.K. Halliday.* Volume 1. *On Grammar.* London and New York: Bloomsbury Academic, pp. 158–72.
— ([1970] 2002) 'Language structure and language function', Jonathan J. Webster (ed.), *The Collected Works of M.A.K. Halliday.* Volume 1. *On Grammar.* London and New York: Bloomsbury Academic, pp. 173–95.
— ([1971] 2002) 'Linguistic function and literary style: An enquiry into the language of William Golding's "The Inheritors"', Jonathan J. Webster (ed.), *The Collected Works of M.A.K. Halliday.* Volume 2. *Text and Discourse.* London and New York: Bloomsbury Academic, pp. 88–125.
— ([1977] 2002) 'Text as semantic choice in social contexts', Jonathan J. Webster (ed.), *The Collected Works of M.A.K. Halliday.* Volume 2. *Text and Discourse.* London and New York: Bloomsbury Academic, pp. 23–81.
— ([1979] 2002) 'Modes of meaning and modes of expression: Types of grammatical structure and their determination by different semantic function', Jonathan J. Webster

(ed.), *The Collected Works of M.A.K. Halliday*. Volume 1. *On Grammar*. London and New York: Bloomsbury Academic, pp. 196–218.

— ([1982] 2002) 'The de-automatization of grammar: From Priestley's "An Inspector Calls"', Jonathan J. Webster (ed.), *The Collected Works of M.A.K. Halliday*. Volume 2. *Text and Discourse*. London and New York: Bloomsbury Academic, pp. 126–48.

— ([1984] 2002) 'On the ineffability of grammatical categories', Jonathan J. Webster (ed.), *The Collected Works of M.A.K. Halliday*. Volume 1. *On Grammar*. London and New York: Bloomsbury Academic, pp. 291–322.

— ([1987] 2002) 'Poetry as scientific discourse: The nuclear sections of Tennyson's In Memoriam', Jonathan J. Webster (ed.), *The Collected Works of M.A.K. Halliday*. Volume 2. *Text and Discourse*. London and New York: Bloomsbury Academic, pp. 149–67.

— ([1990] 2002) 'The construction of knowledge and value in the grammar of scientific discourse: With reference to Charles Darwin's *The Origin of Species*', Jonathan J. Webster (ed.), *The Collected Works of M.A.K. Halliday*. Volume 2. *Text and Discourse*. London and New York: Bloomsbury Academic, pp. 228–54.

— ([1992] 2002a) 'How do you mean?', Jonathan J. Webster (ed.), *The Collected Works of M.A.K. Halliday*. Volume 1. *On Grammar*. London and New York: Bloomsbury Academic, pp. 352–68.

— ([1992] 2002b) 'Some lexicogrammatical features of the Zero Population Growth text', Jonathan J. Webster (ed.), *The Collected Works of M.A.K. Halliday*. Volume 2. *Text and Discourse*. London and New York: Bloomsbury Academic, pp. 197–227.

— ([1994] 2002) 'So you say "pass". Thank you three muchly', Jonathan J. Webster (ed.), *The Collected Works of M.A.K. Halliday*. Volume 2. *Text and Discourse*. London and New York: Bloomsbury Academic, pp. 228–86.

— ([1996] 2002) 'On grammar and grammatics', Jonathan J. Webster (ed.), *The Collected Works of M.A.K. Halliday*. Volume 1. *On Grammar*. London and New York: Bloomsbury Academic, pp. 384–417.

— (2002a) *The Collected Works of M.A.K. Halliday*. Volume 1. *On Grammar*. Jonathan J. Webster (ed.), London: Bloomsbury Academic.

— (2002b) *The Collected Works of M.A.K. Halliday*. Volume 2. *Linguistic Studies of Text and Discourse*. Jonathan J. Webster (ed.), London: Bloomsbury Academic.

— (2002c) 'Introduction: A personal perspective', Jonathan J. Webster (ed.), *The Collected Works of M.A.K. Halliday*. Volume 1. *On Grammar*. London and New York: Bloomsbury Academic, pp. 1–14.

— ([1964] 2003) 'Syntax and the consumer', Jonathan J. Webster (ed.), *The Collected Works of M.A.K. Halliday*. Volume 3. *On Language and Linguistics*. London and New York: Bloomsbury Academic, pp. 36–49.

— ([1972] 2003) 'Towards a sociological semantics', Jonathan J. Webster (ed.), *The Collected Works of M.A.K. Halliday*. Volume 3. *On Language and Linguistics*. London and New York: Bloomsbury Academic, pp. 323–54.

— ([1974] 2003) 'A socio-semiotic perspective on language development', Jonathan J. Webster (ed.), *The Collected Works of M.A.K. Halliday*. Volume 4. *The Language of Early Childhood*. London and New York: Bloomsbury Academic, pp. 90–112.

— ([1975] 2003) 'The context of linguistics', J. Webster (ed.), *The Collected Works of M.A.K. Halliday*. Volume 3. *On Language and Linguistics*. London and New York: Bloomsbury Academic, pp. 74–91.

— ([1975] 2003) 'Learning how to mean: The language of early childhood', Jonathan J. Webster (ed.), *The Collected Works of M.A.K. Halliday*. Volume 4. *The Language of Early Childhood*. London and New York: Bloomsbury Academic, pp. 28–59.

— ([1977] 2003) 'Ideas about language', Jonathan J. Webster (ed.), *The Collected Works of M.A.K. Halliday*. Volume 3. *On Language and Linguistics*. London and New York: Bloomsbury Academic, pp. 92–115.

— ([1980] 2003) 'Three aspects of children's language development: Learning language, learning through language, learning about language', Jonathan J. Webster (ed.), *The Collected Works of M.A.K. Halliday*. Volume 4. *The Language of Early Childhood*. London and New York: Bloomsbury Academic, pp. 308–26.

— ([1984] 2003) 'Language as code and language as behaviour: A systemic-functional interpretation of the nature and ontogenesis of dialogue', Jonathan J. Webster (ed.), *The Collected Works of M.A.K. Halliday*. Volume 3. *On Language and Linguistics*. London and New York: Bloomsbury Academic, pp. 226–50.

— ([1985] 2003) 'Systemic background', Jonathan J. Webster (ed.), *The Collected Works of M.A.K. Halliday*. Volume 3. *On Language and Linguistics*. London and New York: Bloomsbury Academic, pp. 185–98.

— ([1987] 2003) 'Language and the order of nature', Jonathan J. Webster (ed.), *The Collected Works of M.A.K. Halliday*. Volume 3. *On Language and Linguistics*. London and New York: Bloomsbury Academic, pp. 116–38.

— ([1990] 2003) 'New ways of meaning: A challenge to applied linguistics', Jonathan J. Webster (ed.), *The Collected Works of M.A.K. Halliday*. Volume 3. *On Language and Linguistics*. London and New York: Bloomsbury Academic, pp. 139–74.

— ([1992] 2003a) 'Systemic Grammar and the concept of a "science of language"', Jonathan J. Webster (ed.), *The Collected Works of M.A.K. Halliday*. Volume 3. *On Language and Linguistics*. London and New York: Bloomsbury Academic, pp. 199–212.

— ([1992] 2003b) 'The history of a sentence', Jonathan J. Webster (ed.), *The Collected Works of M.A.K. Halliday*. Volume 3. *On Language and Linguistics*. London and New York: Bloomsbury Academic, pp. 355–74.

— ([1992] 2003c) 'The act of meaning', Jonathan J. Webster (ed.), *The Collected Works of M.A.K. Halliday*. Volume 3. *On Language and Linguistics*. London and New York: Bloomsbury Academic, pp. 375–89.

— ([1993] 2003) 'Language in a changing world', Jonathan J. Webster (ed.), *The Collected Works of M.A.K. Halliday*. Volume 3. *On Language and Linguistics*. London and New York: Bloomsbury Academic, pp. 62–81.

— ([1994] 2003) 'Appendix: Systemic theory', Jonathan J. Webster (ed.), *The Collected Works of M.A.K. Halliday*. Volume 3. *On Language and Linguistics*. London and New York: Bloomsbury Academic, pp. 433–41.

— ([1995] 2003a) 'A recent view of "missteps" in linguistic theory', Jonathan J. Webster (ed.), *The Collected Works of M.A.K. Halliday*. Volume 3. *On Language and Linguistics*. London and New York: Bloomsbury Academic, pp. 232–47.

— ([1995] 2003b) 'On language in relation to the evolution of human consciousness', Jonathan J. Webster (ed.), *The Collected Works of M.A.K. Halliday*. Volume 3. *On Language and Linguistics*. London and New York: Bloomsbury Academic, pp. 390–432.

— ([1997] 2003) 'Linguistics as metaphor', Jonathan J. Webster (ed.), *The Collected Works of M.A.K. Halliday*. Volume 3. *On Language and Linguistics*. London and New York: Bloomsbury Academic, pp. 248–70.

— ([1998] 2003) 'Representing the child as a semiotic being (one who means)', Jonathan J. Webster (ed.), *The Collected Works of M.A.K. Halliday*. Volume 4. London and New York: Bloomsbury Academic, pp. 6–27.

— (2003a) *The Collected Works of M.A.K. Halliday*. Volume 3. *On Language and Linguistics*. Jonathan J. Webster (ed.), London: Bloomsbury Academic.

— (2003b) *The Collected Works of M.A.K. Halliday*. Volume 4. *The Language of Early Childhood*. Jonathan J. Webster (ed.), London: Bloomsbury Academic.

— (2003c) 'Introduction: On the architecture of human language', *The Collected Works of M.A.K. Halliday*. Volume 3. *On Language and Linguistics*. Jonathan J. Webster (ed.), London and New York: Bloomsbury Academic.

— ([1988] 2004) 'On the language of physical science', Jonathan J. Webster (ed.), *The Collected Works of M.A.K. Halliday*. Volume 5. *The Language of Science*. London and New York: Bloomsbury Academic.

— ([1998] 2004) 'Things and relations: Regrammaticizing experience as technical knowledge', Jonathan J. Webster (ed.), *The Collected Works of M.A.K. Halliday*. Volume 5. *The Language of Science*. London and New York: Bloomsbury Academic.

— (2004) *The Collected Works of M.A.K. Halliday*. Volume 5. *The Language of Science*. Jonathan J. Webster (ed.), London and New York: Bloomsbury Academic.

Halliday, M. A. K. and Greaves, W. S. (2008) *Intonation in the Grammar of English*. London: Equinox.

Halliday, M. A. K. and Matthiessen, C. M. I. M. (1999) *Construing Experience Through Meaning: A Language-Based Approach to Cognition*. London: Cassell. [Republished by Contiuum (2006).]

— (2009) *H Systemic Functional Grammar: A First Step into Theory*. London: Arnold.

— (2014) *Halliday's Introduction to Functional Grammar*. Fourth edition. London: Arnold.

— (2004) *An Introduction to Functional Grammar*. Third edition. London: Arnold.

— ([2004] 2014) *An Introduction to Functional Grammar*. Second revised edition. London: Edward Arnold.

— ([1956] 2005a) 'Grammatical categories in modern Chinese', Jonathan J. Webster (ed.), *The Collected Works of M.A.K. Halliday*. Volume 8. *Studies in Chinese Language*. London and New York: Bloomsbury Academic, pp. 209–48.

— ([1956] 2005b) 'The linguistic basis of a mechanical thesaurus, and its application to English preposition classification', Jonathan J. Webster (ed.), *The Collected Works of M.A.K. Halliday*. Volume 6. *Computational and Quantitative Studies*. London and New York: Bloomsbury Academic, pp. 209–48.

— ([1959] 2005) 'The language of the Chinese "Secret History of the Mongols元朝秘史"', Jonathan J. Webster (ed.), *The Collected Works of M.A.K. Halliday*. Volume 8. *Studies in Chinese Language*. London and New York: Bloomsbury Academic, pp. 5–171.

— ([1963] 2005a) 'Intonation in English grammar', Jonathan J. Webster (ed.), *The Collected Works of M.A.K. Halliday*. Volume 7. *Studies in English Language*. London and New York: Bloomsbury Academic, pp. 264–86.

— ([1963] 2005b) 'The tones of English', Jonathan J. Webster (ed.), *The Collected Works of M.A.K. Halliday*. Volume 7. *Studies in English Language*. London and New York: Bloomsbury Academic, pp. 237–63.

— ([1966–1968] 2005) 'Notes on transitivity and theme in English part 1–3', Jonathan J. Webster (ed.), *The Collected Works of M.A.K. Halliday*. Volume 7. *Studies in English Language*. London and New York: Bloomsbury Academic, pp. 5–153.

— ([1969] 2005) 'Options and functions in the English clause', Jonathan J. Webster (ed.), *The Collected Works of M.A.K. Halliday*. Volume 7. *Studies in English Language*. London and New York: Bloomsbury Academic, pp. 154–63.

— ([1970] 2005) 'Functional diversity in language as seen from a consideration of modality and mood in English', Jonathan J. Webster (ed.), *The Collected Works of M.A.K. Halliday*. Volume 7. *Studies in English Language*. London and New York: Bloomsbury Academic, pp. 164–204.

— ([1981] 2005) 'The origin and early development of Chinese phonological theory', Jonathan J. Webster (ed.), *The Collected Works of M.A.K. Halliday*. Volume 8. *Studies in Chinese Language*. London and New York: Bloomsbury Academic, pp. 275–93.

— ([1984] 2005) 'Grammatical metaphor in English and Chinese', Jonathan J. Webster (ed.), *The Collected Works of M.A.K. Halliday*. Volume 8. *Studies in Chinese Language*. London and New York: Bloomsbury Academic, pp. 325–33.

— ([1991] 2005a) 'Towards probabilistic interpretations', Jonathan J. Webster (ed.), *The Collected Works of M.A.K. Halliday*. Volume 6. *Computational and Quantitative Studies*. London and New York: Bloomsbury Academic, pp. 42–62.

— ([1991] 2005b) 'Corpus studies and probabilistic grammar', Jonathan J. Webster (ed.), *The Collected Works of M.A.K. Halliday*. Volume 6. *Computational and Quantitative Studies*. London and New York: Bloomsbury Academic, pp. 63–75.

— ([1992] 2005a) 'Language as system and language as instance: The corpus as a theoretical construct', Jonathan J. Webster (ed.), *The Collected Works of M.A.K. Halliday*. Volume 6. *Computational and Quantitative Studies*. London and New York: Bloomsbury Academic, pp. 76–92.

— ([1992] 2005b) 'A systemic interpretation of Peking syllables studies in Chinese language', Jonathan J. Webster (ed.), *The Collected Works of M.A.K. Halliday*. Volume 8. *Studies in Chinese Langauge*. London and New York: Bloomsbury Academic, pp. 294–320.

— ([1993] 2005a) 'Analysis of scientific texts in English and Chinese', Jonathan J. Webster (ed.), *The Collected Works of M.A.K. Halliday*. Volume 8. *Studies in Chinese Langauge*. London and New York: Bloomsbury Academic, pp. 334–45.

— ([1993] 2005b) 'Quantitative studies and probabilities in grammar', Jonathan J. Webster (ed.), *The Collected Works of M.A.K. Halliday*. Volume 6. *Computational and Quantitative Studies*. London and New York: Bloomsbury Academic, pp. 130–56.

— ([2001] 2005) 'On the grammatical foundations of discourse', Jonathan J. Webster (ed.), *The Collected Works of M.A.K. Halliday*. Volume 8. *Studies in Chinese Langauge*. London and New York: Bloomsbury Academic, pp. 47–58.

— ([2002] 2005a) 'Computing meanings: Some reflections on past experience and present prospects', Jonathan J. Webster (ed.), *The Collected Works of M.A.K. Halliday*. Volume 6. *Computational and Quantitative Studies*. London and New York: Bloomsbury Academic, pp. 239–67.

— ([2002] 2005b) 'The spoken language corpus: A foundation for grammatical theory', Jonathan J. Webster (ed.), *The Collected Works of M.A.K. Halliday*. Volume 6. *Computational and Quantitative Studies*. London and New York: Bloomsbury Academic, pp. 157–89.

— (2005a) *The Collected Works of M.A.K. Halliday*. Volume 6. *Computational and Quantitative Studies*. Jonathan J. Webster (ed.), London: Bloomsbury Academic.

— (2005b) *The Collected Works of M.A.K. Halliday*. Volume 7. *Studies in English Language*. Jonathan J. Webster (ed.), London: Bloomsbury Academic.

— (2005c) 'Introduction: Towards an applicable description of the grammar of English', *The Collected Works of M.A.K. Halliday*. Volume 7. *Studies in English Language*. Jonathan J. Webster (ed.), London and New York: Bloomsbury Academic, pp. xii–xxx.

— (2006) *The Collected Works of M.A.K. Halliday*. Volume 8. *Studies in Chinese Language*. Jonathan J. Webster (ed.), London: Bloomsbury Academic.

— ([1978] 2007) 'Is learning a second language like learning a first language all over again?', Jonathan J. Webster (ed.), *The Collected Works of M.A.K. Halliday*. Volume 9. *Language and Education*. London and New York: Bloomsbury Academic, pp. 174–93.

— ([1979] 2007) 'Differences between spoken and written language', Jonathan J. Webster (ed.), *The Collected Works of M.A.K. Halliday*. Volume 9. *Language and Education*. London and New York: Bloomsbury Academic, pp. 63–80.

— ([1981] 2007) 'A response to some questions on the language issue', Jonathan J. Webster (ed.), *The Collected Works of M.A.K. Halliday*. Volume 9. *Language and Education*. London and New York: Bloomsbury Academic, pp. 331–40.

— ([1988] 2007) 'Language and socialization: Home and school', Jonathan J. Webster (ed.), *The Collected Works of M.A.K. Halliday*. Volume 9. *Language and Education*. London and New York: Bloomsbury Academic, pp. 81–96.

— ([1988] 2007) 'Some basic concepts of educational linguistics', Jonathan J. Webster (ed.), *The Collected Works of M.A.K. Halliday*. Volume 9. *Language and Education*. London and New York: Bloomsbury Academic, pp. 341–53.

— ([1991] 2007) 'The notion of "context" in language education', Jonathan J. Webster (ed.), *The Collected Works of M.A.K. Halliday*. Volume 9. *Language and Education*. London and New York: Bloomsbury Academic, pp. 269–90.

— ([1994] 2007) 'Language and the theory of codes', Jonathan J. Webster (ed.), *The Collected Works of M.A.K. Halliday*. Volume 10. *Language and Society*. London and New York: Bloomsbury Academic, pp. 231–46.

— ([1996] 2007) 'The Literacy and linguistics: A functional perspective', Jonathan J. Webster (ed.), *The Collected Works of M.A.K. Halliday*. Volume 9. *Language and Education*. London and New York: Bloomsbury Academic, pp. 97–129.

— ([1998] 2007) 'Where languages meet: The significance of the Hong Kong experience', Jonathan J. Webster (ed.), *The Collected Works of M.A.K. Halliday*. Volume 9. *Language and Education*. London and New York: Bloomsbury Academic, pp. 254–63.

— ([2002] 2007) 'Applied linguistics as an evolving theme', Jonathan J. Webster (ed.), *The Collected Works of M.A.K. Halliday*. Volume 9. *Language and Education*. London and New York: Bloomsbury Academic, pp. 1–19.

— (2007) *The Collected Works of M.A.K. Halliday*. Volume 9. *Language and Education*. Jonathan J. Webster (ed.), London and New York: Bloomsbury Academic, pp. 1–19.

— (2008) *Complementarities in Language*. Beijing: Commercial Press.

— (2008a) 'Working with meaning: Towards an appliable linguistics', Jonathan J. Webster (ed.), *Meaning in Context*. London and New York: Bloomsbury Academic.

— (2009) *The Essential Halliday*. New York: Bloomsbury Academic.

— ([2004] 2013) 'On grammar as the driving force from primary to higher-order consciousness', Jonathan J. Webster (ed.), *The Collected Works of M.A.K. Halliday*. Volume 11. *Halliday in the 21st Century*. London and New York: Bloomsbury Academic, pp. 159–90.

— ([2005] 2013) 'On matter and meaning: The two realms of human experience', Jonathan J. Webster (ed.), *The Collected Works of M.A.K. Halliday*. Volume 11. *Halliday in the 21st Century*. London and New York: Bloomsbury Academic, pp. 191–214.

— ([2010] 2013) 'Language evolving: Some systemic functional reflections on the history of meaning', Jonathan J. Webster (ed.), *The Collected Works of M.A.K. Halliday*. Volume 11. *Halliday in the 21st Century*. London and New York: Bloomsbury Academic, pp. 237–54.

— ([2011] 2013a) 'Why do we need to understand about language?', Jonathan J. Webster (ed.), *The Collected Works of M.A.K. Halliday*. Volume 11. *Halliday in the 21st Century*. London and New York: Bloomsbury Academic, pp. 71–82.

— ([2011] 2013b) 'On text and discourse, information and meaning', Jonathan J. Webster (ed.), *The Collected Works of M.A.K. Halliday*. Volume 11. *Halliday in the 21st Century*. London and New York: Bloomsbury Academic, pp. 55–70.

— (2013) 'That 'certain-cut': Towards a characterology of Mandarin Chinese', Plenary paper delivered to ISFC 40, Sun Yat-Sen University, Guangzhou.

— (2014) 'Marxist orientations', Jonathan J. Webster (ed.), *Bloomsbury Companion of M.A.K. Halliday*. London: Bloomsbury Academic (Chapter 5, this volume).

— (in press [a]) 'A fragment of autobiography', *Selected Papers by M.A.K. Halliday on Applied Linguistics*. Beijing: Foreign Languages Teaching and Research Press (2015).

— (in press [b]) 'Meaning as choice', Fontaine, Bartlett and Grady (eds), *Systemic Functional Linguistics: Exploring Choice*. Cambridge: Cambridge University Press.

— (n.d.) *Text, Discourse and Information: A Systemic-Functional Overview*.

Halliday, M. A. K. and Ellis, J. O. ([1951] 2005) 'Temporal categories in modern Chinese verb', Jonathan J. Webster (ed.), *The Collected Works of M.A.K. Halliday*. Volume 8. *Studies in Chinese Language*. London and New York: Bloomsbury Academic, pp. 177–208.

Halliday, M. A. K. and Hasan, R. (1976) *Cohesion in English*. London: Longman.

— (1985) *Language, Context and Text: Aspects of Language in a Social-Semiotic Perspective*. Geelong, VIC: Deakin University Press. [Revised version of *Text and Context: Aspects of Language in a Social-Semiotic Perspective: Sophia Linguistica VI*. Tokyo: Sophia University Press. 1980.] [Reprinted by World Publishers of Beijing, 2012.]

Halliday, M. A. K. and James, Z. L. ([1993] 2005) 'A quantitative study of polarity and primary tense in the English finite clause', Jonathan J. Webster (ed.), *The Collected Works of M.A.K. Halliday*. Volume 6. *Computational and Quantitative Studies*. London and New York: Bloomsbury Academic, pp. 93–129.

Halliday, M. A. K. and Martin, J. R. (eds) (1981) *Reading in Systemic Linguistics*. London: Batsford.

— (1993) *Writing Science: Literacy and Discursive Power*. London and Washington, DC: Falmer Press.

Halliday, M. A. K. and McDonald, E. (2004) 'Metafunctional profile of the grammar of Chinese', Caffarel, Martin and Matthiessen (eds), *Language Typology: A Functional Perspective*. Amsterdam: John Benjamins, pp. 305–86.

Halliday, M. A. K. and Webster, Jonathan J. (eds) (2009) *Bloomsbury Companion to Systemic Functional Linguistics*. London: Bloomsbury Academic.

Halliday, M. A. K., McIntosh, A. and Strevens, P. (1964) *The Linguistic Sciences and Language Teaching*. London: Longmans.

Hansen, S. (2003) The Nature of Translated Text: An Interdisciplinary Methodology for the Investigation of the Specific Properties of Translations. Saarbrücken: Saarbrücken Dissertations in Computational Linguistics and Language Technology. Volume 13. German Research Center for Artificial Intelligence and Saarland University.

Hansen-Schirra, S., Neumann, S. and Steiner, E. (2012) *Cross-linguistic Corpora for the Study of Translations. Insights from the Language Pair English – German*. Series Text, Translation, Computational Processing. Berlin, New York: Mouton de Gruyter.

Harris, Z. ([1946] 1957) 'From morpheme to utterance', *Language* 22, pp. 161–83. [Reprinted in Joos (1957), pp. 142–53.]

Harrison, K. D. (2007) *When Languages Die: The Extinction of the World's Languages and the Erosion of Human Knowledge*. Oxford: Oxford University Press.

Hart, B. and Risley, R. 'The early catastrophe: The 30 million word gap by age 3', American Educator, <http:archive.aft.org/pubsreports/American_Educator/spring2003 /catastrophe.html> [accessed Spring, 2003].

Hartley, A. and Paris, C. (1997) 'Multilingual document production: From support for translating to support for authoring', *Machine Translation* 12: 1–2, pp. 109–29.

Hasan, Ruqaiya (1964) *A Linguistic Study of Contrasting Features in the Style of Two Contemporary English Prose Writers*. University of Edinburgh, Edinburgh: Unpublished Ph.D. thesis.

— (1967) 'Linguistics and the study of literary texts', *Études de Linguistique Appliqué* 5. Paris: Didier.

— (1968) 'Grammatical cohesion in written and spoken English', *Programme in Linguistics and English Teaching* 7.

— (1971) 'Rime and reason in literature', Chatman (ed.), *Literary Style: A Symposium*. New York: Oxford University Press.

— (1972) 'The verb "be" in Urdu', Verhaar (ed.), *The Verb 'Be' and Its Synonyms*. Part 5. *Foundations of Language*.

— (1973) 'Code, register and social dialect', Basil Bernstein (ed.), *Class, Codes and Control*. Volume 2. *Applied Studies Towards the Sociology of Language*. London: Routledge & Kegan Paul.

— (1975) 'The place of stylistics in verbal art', Ringbom (ed.), *Style and Text: Studies Presented to Nils Erik Enkvist*. Stockholm: Skriptor.

— (1978) 'Text in the systemic-functional model', W. U. Dressler (ed.), *Current Trends in Text-linguistics*. Berlin: Mouton de Gruyter.

— (1984) 'What kind of resource is language?', *Australian Review of Applied Linguistics* 7: 1, pp. 57–85.

— (1985a) *Linguistics, Language and Verbal Art*. Geelong, VIC: Deakin University Press.

— (1985b) 'Meaning, context and text – fifty years after Malinowski', J. D. Benson and W. S. Greaves (eds), *Systemic Perspectives on Discourse*. Volume 1. Norwood, NJ: Ablex.

— (1986) 'The ontogenesis of ideology: An interpretation of mother child talk', Threadgold, Grosz and Kress (eds), *Semiotics, Ideology, Language: Sydney Studies in Society and Culture 3*. Sydney: University of Sydney.

— (1987) 'The grammarian's dream: Lexis as most delicate grammar', M. A. K. Halliday and R. P. Fawcett (eds), *New Developments in Systemic Linguistics: Theory and Description*. London: Pinter.

— (1989) 'Semantic variation and sociolinguistics', *Australian Journal of Linguistics* 9: 2.

— (1991) 'Questions as a mode of learning in everyday talk', Thao Lê and Mike McCausland (eds), *Language Education: Interaction and Development*. Launceston, Tasmania: University of Tasmania.

— (1992a) 'Rationality in everyday talk: From process to system', Jan Svartvik (ed.), *Directions in Corpus Linguistics*. Berlin and New York: Mouton de Gruyter.

— (1992b) 'Meaning in sociolinguistic theory', K. Bolton and H. Kwok (eds), *Sociolinguistics Today: International Perspectives*. London and New York: Routledge.

— (1992c) 'Speech genre, semiotic mediation and the development of higher mental functions', *Language Sciences* 14: 4, pp. 489–528.

— ([1984] 1996) 'Ways of saying; ways of meaning', C. Cloran, D. Butt and G. Williams (eds), *Ways of Saying; Ways of Meaning: Selected Papers of Ruqaiya Hasan*. London: Cassell, pp. 191–242.

— (1996) 'Semantic networks: A tool for the analysis of meaning', C. Cloran, D. Butt and G. Williams (eds), *Ways of Saying; Ways of Meaning: Selected Papers of Ruqaiya Hasan*. London: Cassell, pp. 104–32.

— (1999a) 'Speaking with reference to context', M. Ghadessy (ed.), *Text and Context in Functional Linguistics: Systemic Perspectives*. Amsterdam and Philadelphia: John Benjamins, pp. 219–328.

— (1999b) 'Society, language and the mind: The meta-dialogism of Basil Bernstein's theory', Christie (ed.), *Pedagogy and the Shaping of Consciousness: Linguistic and Social Processes*. London: Cassell.

— (2005) *The Collected Works of Ruqaiya Hasan*. Volume 1. *Language, Society and Consciousness*. Jonathan J. Webster (ed.), London: Equinox.

— (2006) 'Retrospective on language and literacy', (Part 2 with M. A. K. Halliday) Rachel Whittaker, Mick O'Donnell and Anne McCabe (eds), *Language and Literacy: Functional Approaches*. London: Equinox.

— (2009) *The Collected Works of Ruqaiya Hasan*. Volume 2. *Semantic Variation: Meaning in Society and in Sociolinguistics*. Jonathan J. Webster (ed.), London: Equinox.

— (2011a) 'English process, English tense: Foreign learner, foreign teacher', *The Collected Works of Ruqaiya Hasan*. Volume 3. *Language and Education: Learning and Teaching in Society*. Jonathan J. Webster (ed.), London: Equinox.

— (2011b) 'A timeless journey: On the past and future of present knowledge', *Introductory Chapter of Selected Works of Ruqaiya Hasan on Applied Linguistics*. Beijing: Foreign Languages Teaching and Research Press.

— (2011c) *The Collected Works of Ruqaiya Hasan*. Volume 3. *Language and Education: Learning and Teaching in Society*. Jonathan J. Webster (ed.), London: Equinox.

— (2013) 'Choice, system, realization: Describing language as meaning potential', L. Fontaine, T. Bartlett and G. O. Grady (eds), *Systemic Functional Linguistics: Exploring Choice*. Cambridge: Cambridge University Press.

— (2014) 'Linguistic sign and the science of linguistics: The foundations of applicability', Y. Fang and Jonathan J. Webster (eds), *Developing Systemic Functional Linguistics: Theory and Application*. London: Equinox.

— ([2001] in press) 'Wherefore context?: The place of context in the system and process of language', to appear in Jonathan J. Webster (ed.), *The Collected Works of Ruqaiya Hasan*. Volume 4. *Context in the System and Process of Language*. London: Equinox. Original in S. Ren, W. Gutherie and I. W. R. Fong (eds), *Grammar and Discourse: Proceedings of the International Conference on Discourse Analysis*. Macau: University of Macau.

— (in press) 'Towards a paradigmatic description of context: Systems, metafunctions and semantics', *Functional Linguistics* (2014) 1: 2.

Hasan, R. and Cloran, C. (1990) 'A sociolinguistic interpretation of everyday talk between mothers and children', M. A. K. Halliday, J. Gibbons and H. Nicholas (eds), *Learning, Keeping and Using Language: Selected papers from the 8th World Congress of Applied Linguistics, Sydney, 16–21 August 1987*. Amsterdam: John Benjamins, pp. 67–99.

Hasan, R., Matthiessen, C. M. I. M. and Webster, Jonathan J. (2005) *Continuing Discourse on Language: A Functional Perspective*. Volume 1. London: Equinox.

— (2007) *Continuing Discourse on Language: A Functional Perspective*. Volume 2. London: Equinox.

Hasan, R., Cloran, C., Williams, G. and Lukin, A. (2007) 'Semantic networks: The description of linguistic meaning in SFL', Hasan, Matthiessen and Webster (eds), *Continuing Discourse on Language*. Volume 2. London: Equinox, pp. 697–738.

Haspelmath, M., Dryer, M. S., Gil, D. and Comrie, B. (eds) (2005) *The World Atlas of Language Structures*. Oxford: Oxford University Press.

Hasselgård, H. (1998) 'Thematic structure in translation between English and Norwegian', Stig and Oksefjell (eds), *Corpora and Cross-linguistic Research: Theory, Method, and Case Studies*. Amsterdam: Rodopi, pp. 145–67.

— (2004) 'Thematic choice in English and Norwegian', *Functions of Language* 11: 2, pp. 187–212.

Hatim, B. and Mason, I. (1990) *Discourse and the Translator, Language in Social Life Series*. London: Longman.

Hatim, B. and Mason, I. (1997) *The Translator as Communicator*. London: Routledge.

Haugen, E. (1958) 'Review of J. R. Firth's Papers in Linguistics 1934–1951', *Language* 34, pp. 498–502.

Hauser, M. D., Chomsky, N. and Fitch, W. T. (2002) 'The faculty of language: What is it, who has it, and how did it evolve?', *Science* 298, pp. 1569–78.

Heisenberg, W. (1958) *Physics and Philosophy: The Revolution in Modern Science*. New York: Harper & Row.

Heller, L. G. and Macris, J. (1967) *Parametric Linguistics*. The Hague: Mouton.

Helmbrecht, J. (2011) 'Politeness distinctions in pronouns', Dryer and Haspelmath (eds), *The World Atlas of Language Structures Online*. Munich: Max Planck Digital Library, chapter 45, <http://wals.info/chapter/45> [accessed 2 March 2013].

Helmer, John (1969) 'The sociology of language', *International Days of Sociolinguistics*. Rome.

Henderson, E. J. A. (1987) 'J. R. Firth in retrospect: A view from the eighties', Steele and Threadgold (eds), *Language Topics: Essays in Honour of Michael Halliday*. Volume I. Amsterdam: John Benjamins, pp. 57–69.

Henrici, A. ([1965] 1981) 'Some notes on the systemic generation of a paradigm of the English clause', Halliday and Martin (1981), pp. 74–98.

Henschel, R. (1994) 'Declarative representation and processing of systemic grammars', Martin-Vide (ed.), *Current Issues in Mathematical Linguistics*. Amsterdam: Elsevier Science Publisher B.V., pp. 363–71.

Hill, A. A. (1961) 'Suprasegmentals, prosodies, prosodemes', *Language* 31, pp. 457–68.

Hinder, F. (1947) *Abstract Painting* (Art Gallery of Western Australia).

Hjelmslev, L. (1943) *Omkring sprogteoriens grundlæggelse. København: Akademisk Forlag* [English version. (1961) *Prolegomena to a Theory of Language*. Madison: University of Wisconsin Press].

— (1953) *Prolegomena to a Theory of Language*, translated by F. J. Whitfield. Bloomington: Indiana University Publications in Anthropology and Linguistics.

— (1961) *Prolegomena to a Theory of Language*. Madison: University of Wisconsin Press.

Hoang, V. V. (1997) *An Experiential Grammar of the Vietnamese Clause: A Functional Description*. Macquarie University: Ph.D. thesis.

Hobsbawm, E. (2011) *How to Change the World: Tales of Marx and Marxism*. London: Yale University Press.

Hockett, C. (1955) *A Manual of Phonology, Indiana University Publications in Anthropology and Linguistics, Memoir 11* (IJAL).

Hoekstra, T., van der Hulst, H. and Moortgat, M. (eds) (1980) *Lexical Grammar*. Dordrecht: Foris.

Hoey, M. (2006) 'Language as choice: What is chosen?', Hunston and Thompson (eds.), *System and Corpus: Exploring Connections*. London: Equinox, pp. 37–54.

Hoff, E. (2003) 'Causes and consequences of SES-related differences in parent-to-child speech', Bornstein and Bradley (eds), *Socioeconomic Status, Parenting, and Child Development*. Mahwah, NJ: Erlbaum, pp. 147–60.

Hoffmeyer, J. (2010) 'Semiotic freedom: An emerging force', P. Davies and N. H. Gregersen (eds), *Information and the Nature of Reality: From Physics to Metaphysics*. Cambridge: Cambridge University Press.

Holldobler, B. and Wilson, E. O. (2009) *The Superorganism: The Beauty, Elegance, and Strangeness of Insect Societies*. New York and London: W.W. Norton & Co.

Hopper, P. J. and Thompson, S. A. (1980) 'Transitivity in grammar and discourse', *Language* 56, pp. 251–99.

House, J. (1977/1997) *A Model for Translation Quality Assessment*. Tübingen. Gunter Narr Verlag.

Hu, Z. (1991) 'Wang Li and Halliday', *Journal of Peking University* 1, pp. 49–57.

Hu, Z. L., Zhu, Y. S. and Zhang D. (1989) *A Survey of Systemic Functional Grammar* [in Chinese]. Changsha: Hunan Educational Publishing House.

Huang, C. R., Calzolari, N., Gangemi, A., Lenci, A., Oltramari, A. and Prévot, L. (eds) (2010) *Ontology and the Lexicon: A Natural Language Processing Perspective*. Cambridge: Cambridge University Press.

Huddleston, R. (1965) 'Rank and depth', *Langauge* 41, pp. 574–86. [Reprinted in Halliday and Martin (eds) (1981), pp. 42–53.]

— (1981) 'Systemic features and their realization', Halliday and Martin (eds) (1981), pp. 59–73.

— (1984) *Introduction to the Grammar of English*. Cambridge: Cambridge University Press.

Huddleston, R. and Uren, O. (1969) 'Declarative, interrogative, and imperative in French', *Lingua* 22, pp. 1–26.

Huddleston, R., Hudson, R. A., Winter, E. O. and Henrici, A. (1968) *Sentence and Clause in Scientific English: A Report of the Research Project on the Linguistic Properties of Scientific English*. Mimeo.

Hudson, R. A. (1967) 'Constituency in a systemic description of the English clause', *Lingua* 18, pp. 225–50. [Reprinted in Halliday and Martin (eds) (1981), pp. 103–21.]

— (1971) *English Complex Sentences: An Introduction to Systemic Grammar*. Amsterdam, North-Holland Publishing Company.

— (1973) 'An item-and-paradigm approach to Beja syntax and morphology', *Foundations of Language* 9, pp. 504–48.

Hunston, S. and Francis, G. (2000) *Pattern Grammar: A Corpus-Driven Approach to the Lexical Grammar of English*. Amsterdam: John Benjamins.

Hymes, D. (1962) 'The ethnography of speaking', T. Gladwin and W. Sturtevant (eds), *Anthropology and Human Behavior*. Washington, DC: Anthropological Society of Washington, pp. 13–53.

— (1964) 'Introduction: Toward ethnographies of communication', J. J. Gumperz and D. Hymes (eds), *American Anthropologist* 66: 6, *The Ethnography of Communication* (special publication Part 2), pp. 1–34.

— (1969) 'Linguistic theory and the functions of speech', *International Days of Sociolinguistics*. Rome.

— (1971a) 'Sociolinguistics and ethnography of speaking', E. Ardener (ed.), *Social Anthropology and Language*. London: Tavistock.

— (1971b) *On Communicative Competence*. Philadelphia: University of Pennsylvania Press.

— (1974) *Foundations in Sociolinguistics*. Philadelphia: University of Pennsylvania Press.

— (1966) 'Indian English: A study in contextualization', C. E. Bazell, J. C. Catford, M. A. K. Halliday and R. H. Robins (eds), *In Memory of J. R. Firth*. London: Longmans.

Iedema, R. (2001) 'Resemiotization', *Semiotica* 137: 1/4, pp. 23–39.

— (2003) 'Multimodality, resemiotization: Extending the analysis of discourse as a multisemiotic practice', *Visual Communication* 2: 1, pp. 29–57.

Jakobson, R. (1941) *Kindersprache, Aphasie und allgemeine Lautgesetze*. Uppsala: Uppsala Universitets Årsskrift. [Translated (1968) Child Language, Aphasia and Phonological Universals. The Hague: Mouton.]

— ([1942] 1990) 'Langue and parole: Code and message', L. R. Waugh and M. Monville-Burston (eds), *On Language by Roman Jakobson*. Cambridge, MA: Harvard University Press (1990), pp. 80–109.

— ([1949] 1962) 'On the identification of phonemic entities', *Recherches Structurales, Travaux du Cercle Linguistique de Prague* V, pp. 205–13. [Reprinted in Jakobson, R. (1962) *Selected Writings I: Phonological Studies*. The Hague: Mouton, pp. 418–25.]

— ([1961] 1971) 'Linguistics and communication theory', Presented in the Symposium on Structure of Language and its Mathematical Aspects, New York, 15 April 1960, Published in Proceedings of Symposia in Applied Mathematics XII. [Reprinted in Jakobson, R. (1971) Selected Writings II. The Hague: Mouton, pp. 570–79.]

— (1973) *Main Trends in the Science of Language*. London: George, Allen and Unwin.

— ([1977] 1985) 'The grammatical buildup of child language', *Vorträge* G281, translated by Brent Vine. Geisteswissenschaften: Academy. [Reprinted in Rudy, S. (ed.) (1985) *Roman Jakobson's Selected Writings* VII *Contributions to Comparative Mythology; Studies in Linguistics and Philology 1972–1982*. Berlin, New York and Amsterdam: Mouton, pp. 141–47.]

— (ed.) (1987) *Language in Literature*. Cambridge, MA: Belknap Press of Harvard University Press.

Jakobson, R. and Waugh, L. R. ([1979] 1987) 'Dynamic synchrony', *The Sound Shape of Language*. Second edition. The Hague: Mouton, pp. 168–76.

Jakobson, R., Fant, G. and Halle, M. (1952) 'Preliminaries to speech analysis: The distinctive features and their correlates', Acoustics Laboratory, Massachusetts Inst. of Technology, Technical Report No. 13. MIT Press. Seventh edition, 1967.

Janet, P. (1924) *Principles of Psychotherapy*. London: George, Allen and Unwin.

Jespersen, O. (1924) *The Philosophy of Grammar*. London: George, Allen and Unwin.

— (1949) *A Modern English Grammar*. Volume 3. Copenhagen: Ejnar Munksgaard.

Jewitt, C. (2013) *Handbook of Multmodal Analysis*. Second edition. London and New York: Routledge.

Johnson, W. R. (2000) *Lucretius and the Modern World*. London: Duckworth.

Jones, A. A. (1998) *Towards a Lexicogrammar of Mekeo (An Austronesian Language of Western Central Papua)*. Canberra: Pacific Linguistics.

Jones, S. (2000) *Almost Like a Whale. The Origin of Species Updated*. London: Anchor books.

Joos, M. (ed.) (1957) *Readings in Linguistics I: The Development of Descriptive Linguistics in America 1925–1956*. Chicago: University of Chicago Press.

Joseph, Brian D. and Janda, Richard D. (2003) 'On language, change, and language change – or, of history, linguistics, and historical linguistics', B. D. Joseph and R. D. Janda (eds), *The Handbook of Historical Linguistics*. Malden, MA: Blackwell Publishing, pp. 3–180.

Jurafsky, D. (2003) 'Probabilistic modeling in psycholinguistics: Linguistic comprehension and production', Body, Hay and Jannedy (2003a), pp. 39–95.

Kachru, B. B. (1965) 'The Indianness in Indian English', *Word* 21, pp. 391–410.

— (1983) *The Indianization of English: The English Language in India*. New Delhi: Oxford University Press.

— ([1981] in press) '"Socially realistic linguistics": The Firthian tradition', Jonathan J. Webster (ed.), *Bloomsbury Companion of M.A.K. Halliday*. London: Bloomsbury Academic.

Kandel, E. R. (2005) *Psychiatry, Psychoanalysis, and the New Biology of Mind*. Washington, DC and London: American Psychiatric Publishing Inc.

— (2012) *The Age of Insight: The Quest to Understand the Unconscious in Art, Mind, and Brain from Vienna 1900 to the Present*. New York: Random House.

Kasper, R. (1988a) 'Systemic grammar and functional unification grammar', Benson and Greaves (eds), *Systemic Functional Approaches to Discourse*. Norwood, NJ: Ablex, pp. 176–99.

— (1988b) 'An experimental parser for systemic grammars', Proceedings of the 12th Int. Conf. on Computational Linguistics. Budapest: Association for Computational Linguistics.

Kay, M. (1979) 'Functional grammar', Proceedings of the Fifth Annual Meeting of the Berkeley Linguistic Society, pp. 142–58.

— (1985) 'Parsing in functional unification grammar', Dowty, Karttunen and Zwicky (eds), *Natural Language Parsing*. Cambridge: Cambridge University Press, pp. 251–77.

— (1994) 'A life of language', *Computational Linguistics* 16: 1, pp. 1–13.

Kay, P. and Fillmore, C. J. (1999) 'Grammatical construction and linguistic generalizations: What's X doing Y? construction', *Language* 73: 1, pp. 1–33.

Keith, G. (1990) 'Language study at Key Stage 3', R. Carter (ed.), *Knowledge About Language and the Curriculum*. Sevenoaks: Hodder and Stoughton.

Kiełtyka, R. (2010) 'A panchronic account of equine verbal zoosemy', *Skase Journal of Theoretical Linguistics* 7: 3, pp. 53–63.

Kim, M. (2007) *A Discourse Based Study on THEME in Korean and Textual Meaning in Translation*. Macquarie University: Ph.D. thesis.

Kline, M. (1953) *Mathematics in Western Culture*. London: George, Allen and Unwin.

— (1980) *Mathematics: The Loss of Certainty Oxford*. New York: Oxford University Press.

Kobayashi, I., Sugeno, M., Sugimoto, T., Iwashita, S., Ito, N., Iwazume, M. and Takahashi, Y. (2006) 'Everyday-language computing project overview', *Journal of Advanced Intelligence and Intelligent Informatics* 10: 6, pp. 773–81.

Koller, W. ([1979] 1997) *Einführung in die Übersetzungswissenschaft*. Wiesbaden: Quelle und Meyer.

Kreitler, H. and Kreitler, S. (1972) *Psychology of the Arts*. Durham, NC: Duke University Press.

Kress, G. (ed.) (1976) *Halliday: System and Function in Language*. London: Oxford University Press.

Kress, G. and van Leeuwen, T. (1996) *Reading Images: The Grammar of Visual Design*. London: Routledge.

Kumar, A. (2009) *A Systemic Functional Description of the Grammar of Bajjika*. Macquarie University: Ph.D. thesis.

— (in press) *A Functional Grammar of Bajjika: A Systemic Functional Perspective*. Leiden: Brill.

Labov, W. (1963) 'The social motivation of a sound change', *Word* 19, pp. 273–309.

— (1966) *The Social Stratification of English in New York City*. Washington, DC: Center for Applied Linguistics.

— (1970) 'The study of language in its social context', *Stadium Generate* 23: 1, pp. 30–87.

— (1972) *Sociolinguistic Patterns*. Philadelphia: University of Pennsylvania Press.

— (1978) 'Sociolinguistics', W. O. Dingwall (ed.), *A Survey of Linguistic Science*. Stamford, CT: Graylock, pp. 33–75.

Ladefoged, P. (1979) 'Review of Catford (1977) fundamental problems in phonetics', *Language* 55: 4, pp. 904–7.

Ladd, D. R. (1996) *Intonational Phonology*. Cambridge: Cambridge University Press.

Lado, R. (1957) *Linguistics across Cultures: Applied Linguistics for Language Teachers*. Ann Arbor: University of Michigan Press.

Lakatos, I. and Musgrave, A. (eds) (1970) *Criticism and the Growth of Knowledge*. Cambridge: Cambridge University Press.

Lakoff, R. (1972) 'Language in context', *Language* 48: 4, pp. 907–38.

— (1973) 'The language of politeness', Papers from the Ninth Regional Meeting of the Chicago Linguistic Society. Chicago: Department of Linguistics, University of Chicago.

— (1975) 'Linguistic theory and the real world', *Language Learning* 25: 2, pp. 309–38.

Lamb, S. (1962) *Outline of Stratificational Grammar*. Berkeley: ASUC.

— (1964) 'On alternation, transformation, realization and stratification' C. I. J. M. Stuart (ed.), *Report of the 15th Annual Round Table Meeting on Linguistics and Language Study*. Monograph Series on Language and Linguistics No. 17. Washington, DC: Georgetown University Press.

— (1965) *Outline of Stratificational Grammar*. Washington, DC: Georgetown University Press.

— (1966) 'Epilegomena to a theory of language', *Romance Philology* 19, pp. 531–73.

— (1973) 'Linguistic and cognitive networks' A. Makkai and D. Lockwood (eds), *Readings in Stratificational Linguistics*. Alabama: University of Alabama Press, pp. 60–83.

— (1984) 'Semiotics of language and culture: A relational approach', R. P. Fawcett, M. A. K. Halliday, S. M. Lamb and A. Makkai (eds), *The Semiotics of Culture and Language*. Volume 2. *Language and Other Semiotic Systems of Culture*. London: Frances Pinter.

— (1999) *Pathways of the Brain: The Neurocognitive Basis of Language*. Amsterdam and Philadelphia: John Benjamins.

Langendoen, T. (1968) *The London School of Linguistics: A Study of the Linguistic Contributions of B. Malinowski and J.R. Firth*. Cambridge, MA: MIT Press.

Lao, Tzu (1934) *Resources for the Study of the Dao De Jing*, translated by Tao Te Ching and A. Waley, <http://www.faculty.umb.edu/gary_zabel/Courses/Phil%20100--08/Taoism/Dao%25252520de%25252520Jing%25252520--%25252520Multiple%25252520Versions. html>.

Larsen-Freeman, D. (2011) 'Saying what we mean: Making a case for "language acquisition" to become "language development"', Plenary at AILA 2011. Beijing.

Lass, R. (1997) *Historical Linguistics and Language Change*. Cambridge: Cambridge University Press.

Lavid, J. (2000) 'Cross-cultural variation in multilingual Instructions: A study of speech act realisation patterns', Ventola (ed.), *Discourse and Community: Doing Functional Linguistics*. Tübingen: Günter Narr Verlag, pp. 71–85.

Lavid, J., Arús, J. and Zamorano-Mansilla, J. R. (2009) *Systemic Functional Grammar of Spanish: A Contrastive Study with English*. London and New York: Continuum.

Lee, P. (1996) *The Whorf Theory Complex: A Critical Reconstruction*. Amsterdam: John Benjamins.

Leech, G. (1970) *Towards a Semantic Description of English*. Bloomington: Indiana University Press.

— (1974) *Semantics*. Harmondsworth: Penguin. [Second revised edition (1981).]

Leech, G. and Short, M. (1981) *Style in Fiction*. London: Longman.

Leff, M. C. (1996) 'Agency, performance and interpretation in Thucydides: Account of the Mytilene debate', C. L. Johnstone (ed.), *Theory Text Context: Issues in Greek Rhetoric and Oratory*. New York: State University of New York Press.

Leggett, A. J. (2008) 'Realism and the physical world', *Reports on Progress in Physics* 71.

Lemke, J. L. (1984) *Semiotics and Education*. Toronto, ON: Victoria University. (Toronto Semiotic Circle Monographs, Working Papers and Pre-publications, no. 2.)

— (1995) *Textual Politics: Discourse and Social Dynamics*. London: Taylor and Francis.

Léon, J. (2000) 'Traduction Automatique et Formalisation du Langage. Les Tentatives du Cambridge Language Research Unit (1955–1960)', Desmet, Jooken, Schmitter, Swiggers (eds), *The History of Linguistics and Grammatical Praxis*. Louvain and Paris: Peeters, pp. 369–94.

— (2007) 'From universal languages to intermediary languages in machine translation: The work of the Cambridge language research unit (1955–1970)', Guimaraes and Pessoa de Barros (eds), *History of Linguistics 2002*. Amsterdam and Philadelphia: John Benjamins, pp. 123–32.

Lewontin, R. (1993) *Biology as Ideology: The Doctrine of DNA*. London: Penguin.

— (2000a) *The Triple Helix: Gene, Organism and Environment*. Cambridge, MA: Harvard University Press.

— (2000b) *It Ain't Necessarily So: The Dream of the Human Genome and Other Illusions*. London: Granta Books.

Li, C. N. and Thompson, S. A. (1976) 'Subject and topic: A new typology of language', Li (ed.), *Subject and Topic*. New York: Academic Press, pp. 457–90.

Li, E. (2007) *Systemic Functional Grammar of Chinese: A Text-Based Analysis*. London and New York: Continuum.

Lieberman, P. (2000) Human Language and Our Reptilian Brain: The Subcortical Bases of Speech, Syntax and Thought. Cambridge, MA: Harvard University Press.

Lloyd, G. E. R. (1970) *Early Greek Science: Thales to Aristotle*. New York and London: W.W. Norton & Co.

— (2002) *The Ambitions of Curiosity: Understanding the World in Ancient Greece and China*. Cambridge: Cambridge University Press.

Locke, J. (1996) 'Why do infants begin to talk? Language as an unintended consequence', *Journal of Child Language* 23, pp. 251–68.

Lounsbury, F. G. (1956) 'Semantic analysis of the Pawnee Kinship usage', *Language* 32, pp. 159–94.

Lowry, L. S. (1942) *The Rival Candidate* (Art Gallery of Western Australia).

Lucretius (1992) *De Rerum Natura*. Loeb Classical Library, translated By W. H. D. Rouse, revised M. F. Smith, Cambridge, MA and London: Harvard University Press.

Lukin, A. and Webster, J. (2005) 'SFL and the study of literature', Hasan, Matthiessen and Webster (eds), *Continuing Discourse on Language*. Volume 1. London: Equinox.

Luo, C. (羅常培) (1949) *Introduction to Chinese Phonology* (漢語音韻學導語). Peiping: Peking University Press.

Luria, A. R. (1979) *The Making of Mind: A Personal Account of Soviet Psychology*. Harvard: Harvard University Press.

Lv, S. (呂叔湘) (1947) *Outline of Chinese Grammar*, 3 Volumes (中國文法要略). Shanghai: The Commercial Press.

— (呂叔湘) ([1959] 1984) 'Survey of the problem of "word" in Chinese (漢語裏「詞」的問題概述)', *Russian Linguistics* 5. [Reprinted in *the Collection of Studies on Chinese Grammar* (漢語語法語文集). Revised edition. Beijing: Commercial Press, pp. 359–69.]

Lyons, J. (1962) 'Phonemic and non-phonemic phonology: Some typological reflection', *IJAL* 28, pp. 127–34.

— (1966) 'Firth's theory of 'meaning', C. E. Bazell, J. C. Catford, M. A. K. Halliday and R. H. Robins (eds), *In Memory of J. R. Firth*. London: Longmans.

— (1968) *Theoretical Linguistics*. Cambridge: Cambridge University Press.

— (1969) 'Structural semantics: An analysis of part of the vocabulary of Plato', *Philological Society* XX. Oxford: Blackwell.

— (ed.) (1970) *New Horizons in Linguistics*. Harmondsworth: Penguin Books.

— (1977) *Semantics*. 2 volumes. Cambridge: Cambridge University Press.

— (1978) 'Foreword', *Sociolinguistic Patterns*. William Labov (ed.), British edition. Oxford: Blackwell, pp. x–xxiii.

Mackay, D., Thompson, B. and Schaub, P. (1970) *Breakthrough to Literacy*. [For the pupil; (i) My Sentence Maker, with insert word cards and stand; (ii) My Word Maker, with insert letter cards; (iii) Breakthrough Books (24); (iv) Big Breakthrough Books (2); (v) Sally Go Round the Sun (LP Record). For the teacher: (i) Teacher's Sentence Maker, with insert word cards and stand; (ii) Magnet board, magnet and figurin Maddieson, I. (2005) 'Vowel quality inventories', Haspelmath et al., pp. 14–17.

Maddieson, I. (2011) 'Front rounded vowels', Dryer and Haspelmath (eds), The World Atlas of Language Structures Online. Munich: Max Planck Digital Library, Chapter 11, <http://wals.info/chapter/11> [accessed 18 April 2013].es; (iii) Teacher's Manual]. London: Longman.

Mainzer, K. (2004) *Thinking in Complexity: The Computational Dynamics of Matter, Mind, and Mankind*. Third edition. Berlin: Springer.

Mair, C., and Leech, G. (2006) 'Current changes in English syntax', B. Aarts and A. McMahon (eds), *The Handbook of English Linguistics (Blackwell Handbooks in Linguistics)*. First edition. London: Wiley-Blackwell, pp. 318–42.

Malinowski, B. (1923) 'The problems of meaning in primitive languages', C. K. Ogden and I. A. Richards (eds), *The Meaning of Meaning*. New York: Harcourt Brace and World, pp. 296–336.

— ([1935] 1965) *Coral Gardens and Their Magic*. Volume 2. New York: American Book Company.

— (1970) *Nya vägar inom språkforskningen: En orientering i modern lingvistik. Fjärde upplagan*. Stockholm: Kungliga Boktryckeriet P.A. Nordstedt & Söner.

Mann, W. C. and Matthiessen, C. (1985) 'Demonstration of the Nigel text generation computer program', Benson and Greaves (eds), *Systemic Functional Approaches to Discourse*. Norwood, NJ: Ablex, pp. 50–83.

Mann, W. C. and Moore, J. A. (1980) Computer as Author – Results and Prospects, Technical report, Information Science Institute, USC/Information Sciences Institute. Marina del Rey, CA.

Manning, C. D. (2003) 'Probabilistic syntax', Bod, Hay and Jannedy (2003a), pp. 289–341.

Manning, C. D. and Schütze, H. (1999) *Foundations of Statistical Natural Language Processing*. Cambridge, MA: MIT Press.

Margulis, L. (1998) *Symbiotic Planet: A New Look at Evolution*. New York: Basic Books.
— (2006) 'The conscious cell', *Annals of the New York Academy of Sciences* 929: 1, pp. 55–70.
Marine, C. and Wu, D. (2007) 'Improving statistical machine translation using word sense disambiguation', Proceedings of the 2007 Joint Conference on Empirical Methods in Natural Language Processing and Computational Natural Language Learning (EMNLP-CoNLL 2007). Prague, June 2007, pp. 61–72.
Martin, J. R. (1983) 'Participant identification in English, tagalog and Kâte', *Australian Journal of Linguistics* 3: 1, pp. 45–74.
— (1985) 'Process and text: Two aspects of human semiosis', J. D. Benson and W. S. Greaves (eds), *Systemic Perspectives on Discourse*. Volume 1. Norwood, NJ: Ablex
— (1990) 'Interpersonal grammatization: Mood and modality in tagalog', *Philippine Journal of Linguistics* 21: 1 (Special Issue on the Silver Anniversary of the Language Study Centre of Philippine Normal College 1964–1989 – Part 2), pp. 2–51.
— (1991) 'Intrinsic functionality: Implications for contextual theory', *Social Semiotics* 1: 1, pp. 99–162.
— (1992) *English Text: System and Structure*. Amsterdam: John Benjamins.
— (1996a) 'Transitivity in tagalog: A functional interpretation of case', Berry, Butler, Fawcett and Huang (eds), *Meaning and Form: Systemic Functional Interpretations*. Norwood, NJ: Ablex (Meaning and Choice in Language: Studies for Michael Halliday), pp. 229–96.
— (2000) 'Beyond exchange: APPRAISAL systems in English', Hunston and Thompson (eds), *Evaluation in Text*. Oxford: Oxford University Press, pp. 142–75.
— (2004a) 'Metafunctional profile: Tagalog', Caffarel, Matthiessen and Martin (eds), *Systemic Functional Typology*. Amsterdam: John Benjamins, pp. 255–304.
— (2004b) 'Grammatical structure: What do we mean?', Coffin, Hewings and O'Halloran (eds), *Applying English Grammar: Functional and Corpus Approaches*. London: Arnold, pp. 57–76.
— (2004c) 'Metafunctional profile of the grammar of Tagalog', Caffarel, Martin and Matthiessen (eds), *Language Typology: A Functional Perspective*. Amsterdam: John Benjamins, pp. 255–304.
— ([1984] 2010) 'Functional components in a grammar: A review of deployable recognition criteria', *Nottingham Linguistic Circular* 13, pp. 35–70. [Reprinted in Martin (2010), pp. 9–43.]
— ([1996] 2010) 'Types of structure: Deconstructing notions of constituency in clause and text', Hovy and Scott (ed.), *Computational and Conversational Discourse: Burning Issues – an Interdisciplinary Account*. Heidelberg: Springer (NATO Advanced Science Institute Series F – Computer and Systems Sciences. Volume 151), pp. 39–66. [Reprinted in Martin, (2010), pp. 343–85.]
— (2012) *The Collected Works of J.R. Martin*. Volume 3. *Genre Studies*. Shanghai: Shanghai Jiao Tong University Press.
Martin, J. R. (2013a) *Systemic Functional Grammar: A Next Step into the Theory – Axial Relations* (Chinese translation and extensions by Wang Pin and Zhu Yongsheng). Beijing: Higher Education Press.
— (ed.) (2013b) *Interviews with M.A.K. Halliday: Language Turned Back on Himself* (with R. Hasan, G. Kress and J. R. Martin (1986)). London: Bloomsbury Academic. [Reprinted from *Social Semiotic* 2: 1, pp. 176–95 and 2: 2, pp. 58–69. Taylor & Francis Ltd], <http://www.tandfoline.com>.
— (2014) 'Halliday, the grammarian: Axial functions', Jonathan J. Webster (ed.), *Bloomsbury Companion to M.A.K. Halliday*. London: Bloomsbury Academic (Chapter 10, this volume).
Martin, J. R. and Doran, Y. (eds) (in press) *Grammatics*. London: Routledge (Critical Concepts in Linguistics: Systemic Functional Linguistics, Vol. 1).

Martin, J. R. and Matthiessen, C. M. I. M. ([1991] 2010) 'Systemic typology and topology', Christie (ed.), Literacy in Social Processes: Papers from the Inaugural Australian Systemic Functional Linguistics Conference, Deakin University, January 1990. Darwin: Centre for Studies of Language in Education, Northern Territory University. pp. 345–83. [Reprinted in Martin, J. R. and Wang, Z. (ed.) (2010) *The Collected Works of J.R. Martin*. Volume 1. *SFL Theory*. Shanghai: Shanghai Jiao Tong University Press, pp. 167–215.]

Martin, J. R. and Rose, D. (2003) *Working with Discourse: Meaning beyond the Clause*. London: Continuum.

— (2007) *Working with Discourse: Meaning beyond the Clause*. Second edition. London: Continuum.

Martin, J. R. and Wang, Z. (ed.) (2010) *The Collected Works of J.R. Martin*. Volume 1. *SFL Theory*. Shanghai: Shanghai Jiaotong University Press.

Martin, J. R. and White, P. R. R. (2005) *The Language of Evaluation: Appraisal in English*. London and New York: Palgrave Macmillan.

Martinec, R. (2003) 'The social semiotics of text and image in Japanese and English software manuals and other procedures', *Social Semiotics* 13: 1, pp. 43–69.

Mashburn, A., Pianta, O., Hamre, B., Downer, J., Barbarin, O., Bryant, D., Burchinal, N., Early, D. and Howes, C. (2008) 'Measures of classroom quality in prekindergarten and children's development of academic, language and social skills', *Child Development* 79: 3, pp. 732–49.

Masterman, M. (1957) 'The thesaurus in syntax and semantics', *Mechanical Translation*. Volume 4, Nos 1 and 2, November 1957, pp. 35–43.

— (1965) 'Semantic algorithms', Proceedings of the Conference on Computer-Related Semantic Analysis, Wayne State University. Las Vegas, Nevada 3–5 December 1965, Section IV, pp. 1–97.

— (2005) *Language, Cohesion and Form*. Cambridge: Cambridge University Press.

Matthiessen, C. M. I. M. (1983) 'Systemic grammar in computation: The Nigel case', Proceedings of the First Annual Conference of the European Chapter of the Association for Computational Linguistics, Pisa, pp. 155–64.

— (1983b) 'Choosing primary tense in English', *Studies in Language* 7: 3, pp. 369–430.

— (1985) 'The systemic framework in text generation: Nigel', Benson and Greaves (eds), *Systemic Perspectives on Discourse*. Volume 1. Norwood, NJ: Ablex, pp. 96–118.

— (1987a) *Notes on Akan Phonology: A Systemic Interpretation*. Mimeo.

— (1987b) *Notes on Akan Lexicogrammar: A Systemic Interpretation*. Mimeo.

— (1988) 'Representational issues in systemic functional Grammar', Benson and Greaves (eds), *Systemic Functional Perspectives on Discourse*. Norwood, NJ: Ablex, pp. 136–75.

— (1990) 'Two Approaches to semantic interfaces in text generation', COLING-90, Helsinki, August 1990, Helsinki, August 1990, pp. 322–9.

— (1991) 'Lexico(grammatical) choice in text-generation', Paris, Swartout and Mann (eds), *Natural Language Generation in Artificial Intelligence and Computational Linguistics*. Boston: Kluwer, pp. 249–92.

— (1993) 'Register in the round: Diversity in a unified theory of register analysis', Ghadessy (ed.), *Register Analysis: Theory and Practice*. London: Pinter, pp. 221–92.

— (1994) 'Paradigmatic organization: 30 years of system networks', Written version of paper presented at ISFC 21, Ghent, Belgium, July 1994, Manuscript.

— (1995a) *Lexicogrammatical Cartography: English Systems*. Tokyo: International Language Sciences Publisher.

— (1995b) 'Fuzziness construed in language: A linguistic perspective', Proceedings of FUZZ/IEEE, Yokohama, March 1995. Yokohama, pp. 1871–8.

— (1995c) 'THEME as an enabling resource in ideational "knowledge" construction', Ghadessy (ed.), *Thematic Development in English Texts*. London and New York: Pinter.

— (1996) 'Tense in English seen through systemic-functional theory', Butler, Berry, Fawcett and Huang (eds), *Meaning and Form: Systemic Functional Interpretations*. Norwood, NJ: Ablex, pp. 431–98.
— (1998) 'Construing processes of consciousness: From the commonsense model to the uncommonsense model of cognitive science', Martin and Veel (eds), *Reading Science: Critical and Functional Perspectives on Discourses of Science*. London: Routledge, pp. 327–57.
— (1999) 'The system of TRANSITIVITY: An exploratory study of text-based profiles', *Functions of Language* 6: 1, pp. 1–51.
— (2001) 'The environments of translation', Steiner and Yallop (eds) (2001), pp. 41–126.
— (2002a) 'Lexicogrammar in discourse development: Logogenetic patterns of wording', Huang and Wang (eds), *Discourse and Language Functions*. Shanghai: Foreign Language Teaching and Research Press, pp. 91–127.
— (2002b) 'Combining clauses into clause complexes: A multi-faceted view', Bybee and Noonan (eds), *Complex Sentences in Grammar and Discourse: Essays in Honor of Sandra A. Thompson*. Amsterdam: John Benjamins, pp. 237–322.
— (2004a) 'Descriptive motifs and generalizations', Caffarel, Martin and Matthiessen (eds), *Language Typology: A Functional Perspective*. Amsterdam: John Benjamins, pp. 537–673.
— (2004b) 'The evolution of language: A systemic functional exploration of phylogenetic phases', Williams and Lukin (eds), *Language Development: Functional Perspectives on Evolution and Ontogenesis*. London: Bloomsbury Academic, pp. 45–90.
— (2005) 'Remembering Bill Mann', *Journal of Computational Linguistics* 31: 2, pp. 161–71.
— (2006) 'Frequency profiles of some basic grammatical systems: An interim report', G. Thompson and S. Hunston (eds), *System and Corpus: Exploring Connections*. London: Equinox, pp. 103–42.
— (2007a) 'The lexicogrammar of emotion and attitude in English', Published in electronic proceedings based on contributions to the Third International Congress on English Grammar (ICEG 3) Sona College, Salem, Tamil Nadu, India, 23–27 January 2006.
— (2007b) 'The "architecture" of language according to systemic functional theory: Developments since the 1970's', Ruqaiya Hasan, C. M. I. M. Matthiessen and Jonathan J. Webster (eds), *Continuing Discourse on Language: A Functional Perspective*. Volume 2. London: Equinox.
— (2009a) 'Meaning in the making: Meaning potential emerging from acts of meaning', *Anniversary Issue of Language Learning* 59 (Supplement 1), pp. 211–35.
— (2009b) 'Léxico-gramática y colocación léxica: Un estudio sistémico funcional' [Translation of 'Lexicogrammar and collocation: A systemic functional exploration'], *Revista Signos* 42: 71, pp. 333–83.
— (2009c) 'Ideas and new directions', M. A. K. Halliday and Jonathan J. Webster (eds), *Bloomsbury Companion to Systemic Functional Linguistics*. London: Bloomsbury Academic.
— (2012a) 'Extending the description of process type in delicacy: Verb classes', Manuscript submitted to Functions of Language.
— (2012b) 'Systemic functional linguistics as appliable linguistics: Social accountability and critical approaches', *D.E.L.T.A. (Revista de Documentação de Estudos em Lingüística Teórica e Aplicada)* 28: 437–71.
Matthiessen, Christian M. I. M. (2014) 'Extending the description of process type in delicacy: verb classes', *Functions of Language* 21: 2, pp. 139–75.
— (2014) 'Halliday on language', Jonathan J. Webster (ed.), *Bloomsbury Companion to M.A.K. Halliday*. London: Bloomsbury Academic (Chapter 7, this volume).

— (2014) 'Language as a probabilistic system', Jonathan J. Webster (ed.), *Bloomsbury Companion to M.A.K. Halliday*. London: Bloomsbury Academic (Chapter 8, this volume).

Matthiessen, Christian M. I. M. (in press) 'Appliable discourse analysis', Fang Yan and Jonathan J. Webster (eds), *Developing Systemic Functional Linguistics: Theory and Application*. London: Equinox, pp. 135–205.

Matthiessen, C. M. I. M. and Bateman, J. A. (1991) *Systemic Linguistics and Text Generation: Experiences from Japanese and English*. London: Frances Pinter.

Matthiessen, C. M. I. M. and Nesbitt, C. (1996) 'On the idea of theory neutral descriptions', Hasan, Cloran and Butt (eds), *Functional Descriptions: Theory in Practice*. Amsterdam: John Benjamins, pp. 39–85.

Matthiessen, C. M. I. M., Kobayashi, I. and Zeng, L. (1995) 'Generating multimodal presentations: Resources and processes'. Mimeo.

Matthiessen, C. M. I. M., Teruya, K. and Wu, C. Z. (2008) 'Multilingual studies as a multidimensional space of interconnected language studies', Webster (ed.), *Meaning in Context*. London and New York: Continuum, pp. 146–221.

McCartney, K. (2002) 'Language environments and language outcomes: Results from the NICHD study of early child care and youth development', Girolametto and Weitzman (eds), *Enhancing Caregiver Language Facilitation in Child Care Settings*. Toronto, ON: Hanen Centre.

McCord, M. (1975) 'On the form of a systemic grammar', *Journal of Linguistics* 11, pp. 195–212.

— (1977) 'Procedural systemic grammars', *International Journal of Man-Machine Studies* 9, pp. 255–86.

McEnery, T. and Hardie, A. (2011) *Corpus Linguistics: Method, Theory and Practice*. Cambridge: Cambridge University Press.

McGregor, W. (1990) *A Functional Grammar of Gooniyandi*. Amsterdam and Philadelphia: John Benjamins.

McMullin, E. (2010) 'From matter to materialism and (almost) back', P. Davies and N. H. Gregersen (eds), Cambridge: Cambridge University Press, pp. 13–37.

Meares, R. (2005) *The Metaphor of Play: Origin and Breakdown of Personal Being*. Third edition. London and New York: Routledge.

— (2012) *A Dissociation Model of Borderline Personality Disorder*. New York: W.W. Norton & Co.

Meares, R., Bendit, N., Haliburn, J., Korner, A., Mears, D. and Butt, D. (2012) *Borderline Personality Disorder and the Conversational Model: A Clinician's Manual*. New York: W.W. Norton & Co.

Medawar, P. (1984) *Pluto's Republic*. Oxford: Oxford University Press.

Mel'chuk, I. (1982) 'Lexical functions in lexicographic description', Proceedings of the EighthAnnual Meeting of the Berkeley Linguistic Society, pp. 427–44.

Mellish, C. S. (1988) 'Implementing systemic classification by unification', *Journal of Computational Linguistics* 14: 1, pp. 40–52.

Meščanionv, Glagol [The verb] or Myšlenie i Yazik [Thought and Language] HALLIDAY

Milroy, L. (1987) *Language and Social Networks*. Second edition. Oxford: Basil Blackwell.

Mitchell, T. F. (1957) 'The language of buying and selling in Cyrenaica: A situational statement', *Hesperis Tamuda* [Reprinted in Mitchell (1975) 44, pp. 31–71.]

— (1975) *Principles of Firthian Linguistics*. London: Longmans.

— (1978) 'Meaning is what you do – and how he and I interpret it: A Firthian view of pragmatics', *Die Neueren Sprachen* 3: 4. Frankfurt am Main: Verlag Moritz Diesterweg.

Miyagawa, S., Berwick, R. C. and Okanoya, K. (2013) 'The emergence of hierarchical structure in human language', *Frontiers of Psychology*. Language Series.

Mock, C. C. (1969) *The Grammatical Units of the Nzema Language: A Systemic Analysis.* University of London: Unpublished Ph.D. thesis.

Mohan, B. A. (1986) *Language and Content.* Reading, MA: Addison-Wesley.

Mohrmann, C., Norman, F. and Summerfelt, A. (eds) (1963) *General Linguistics in Great Britain 1930–1960 Trends in Modern Linguistics.* Antwerp: Spectrum.

Monaghan, James (1979) *The Neo-Firthian Tradition and Its Contribution to General Linguistics.* Tübingen: Niemeyer.

Morgan, J. L. (1977) 'Linguistics: The relation of pragmatics to semantics and syntax', *Annual Review of Anthropology.* Palo Alto, CA: Annual Reviews Inc, pp. 57–67.

Mukařovský, J. (1964) 'Standard language and poetic language', P. L. Garvin (ed.), *A Prague School Reader on Esthetics*, Literary Structure and Style. Washington, DC: Georgetown University Press.

Mukařovský, J. (1977) *The Word and Verbal Art.* New Haven: Yale University Press.

Munday, J. (1997) Systems in Translation: A Computer-assisted Systemic Analysis of the Translation of Garcia Marquez, Ph.D. dissertation. Bradford: University of Bradford.

— (2001) *Introducing Translation Studies: Theories and Applications.* London and New York: Routledge.

— (2012) *Evaluation in Translation. Critical Points of Translator Decision Making.* London: Routledge.

Munro, R. (2004) 'A probabilistic representation of systemic functional grammar', The 31st International Systemic Functional Congress (ISFC31). Kyoto, Doshisha University, <http://www.robertmunro.com/research/munro04probabilistic.pdf>.

Murcia-Bielsa, S. (1999) *Instructional Texts in English and Spanish: A Contrastive Study.* Universidad de Córdoba: Ph.D. thesis.

— (2000) 'The choice of directives expressions in English and Spanish instructions: A semantic network', Ventola (ed.), *Discourse and Community: Doing Functional Linguistics.* Tübingen: Günter Narr Verlag, pp. 117–46.

Nanri, K. (1993) *An Attempt to Synthesize Two Systemic Contextual Theories through the Investigation of the Process of the Evolution of the Discourse Semantic Structure of the Newspaper Reporting Article.* University of Sydney: Ph.D. thesis.

Neale, A. (2002) *More Delicate TRANSITIVITY: Extending the PROCESS TYPE System Networks for English to Include Full Semantic Classifications.* Cardiff University: School of English, Communication and Philosophy: Ph.D. thesis.

Needham, J. (1985) *The Shorter Science and Civilisation in China.* Cambridge: Cambridge University Press.

Neef, M. and Vater, H. (2006) 'Concepts of the lexicon in theoretical linguistics', Wunderlich (ed.), *Advances in the Theory of the Lexicon.* Berlin: Mouton de Gruyter, pp. 27–55.

Nesbitt, C. N. and Plum, G. (1988) 'Probabilities in a systemic grammar: The clause complex in English', Fawcett and Young (eds), *New Developments in Systemic Linguistics: Theory and Application.* Volume 2. London: Frances Pinter, pp. 6–39.

Nettle, D. and Suzann, R. (2000) *Vanishing Voices: The Extinction of the World's Languages.* Oxford: Oxford University Press.

Neumann, S. M. (2003) *Die Beschreibung von Textsorten und ihre Nutzung beim Übersetzen. Eine Systemisch-funktionale Korpusanalyse Englischer und Deutscher Reiseführer.* Frankfurt/M. et al: Peter Lang Verlag.

Newmark, P. (1991) *About Translation.* Clevedon, Philadelphia, Adelaide: Multilingual Matters Ltd.

New Zealand Ministry of Education (1996) *Te Whàriki: Early Childhood Curriculum.* Wellington: Ministry of Education.

Nichols, J. (1992) *Linguistic Diversity in Space and Time.* Chicago: Chicago University Press.

Nooteboom, S. (1997) 'The prosody of speech: Melody and rhythm', Hardcastle and Laver (eds), *The Handbook of Phonetic Sciences*. Oxford: Blackwell, pp. 640–73.

Nørgaard, N., Busse, B. and Montoro R. (2010) *Key Terms in Stylistics*. London and New York: Continuum.

Norris, S. (2004) *Analyzing Multimodal Interaction: A Methodological Framework*. London: Routledge.

Norris, S. and Jones, R. H. (eds) (2005) Discourse in Action: Introducing Mediated Discourse *Analysis*. London: Routledge.

Nuyts, J., Bolkestein, A. M. and Vet, C. (eds) (1990) *Layers and Levels of Representation in Language Theory: A Functional View*. Amsterdam: John Benjamins (Pragmatics and Beyond), pp. 101–22.

Ochs, E. (1979) 'Transcription as theory', Ochs and Schieffelin (eds), *Developmental Pragmatics*. New York: Academic Press, pp. 43–72.

Ochs, E. and Keenan, E. (1979) 'Becoming a competent speaker of Malagasy', Tim Shopen (ed.), *Languages and Their Speakers*. USA: University of Pennsylvania Press.

O'Donnell, M. (1993) 'Reducing complexity in a systemic parser', Proceedings of the Third International Workshop on Parsing Technologies. Tilburg, The Netherlands, August 10–13, 1993.

O'Donnell, M. and Bateman, J. A. (2005) 'SFL in computational contexts', Hasan, Matthiessen and Webster (eds), *Continuing Discourse on Language a Functional Perspective*. Volume 1. London: Equinox Publishing, pp. 343–82.

O'Donoghue, T. F. (1991) 'The vertical strip parser: A lazy approach to parsing', Research Report 91.15, School of Computer Studies, University of Leeds, Leeds, UK.

Oesterreicher, W. (2001) 'Historizität – Sprachvariation, Sprachverschiedenheit, Sprachwandel', Haspelmath, König, Oesterreicher and Raible (eds) (2001) Language Typology and Language Universals Volume 2 [Handbücher zur Sprach- und Kommunikationswissenschaft 20.1. und 20.2.]. Berlin and New York: Mouton de Gruyter, pp. 1554–96.

O'Halloran, K. L. (2005) *Mathematical Discourse: Language, Symbolism and Visual Images*. London and New York: Continuum.

— (2008) 'Inter-Semiotic expansion of experiential meaning: Hierarchical scales and metaphor in mathematics discourse', Jones and Ventola (eds), N*ew Developments in the Study of Ideational Meaning: From Language to Multimodality*. London: Equinox.

— (2011) 'Multimodal discourse analysis', Hyland and Paltridge (eds), *Companion to Discourse Analysis*. London: Continuum, pp. 120–37.

O'Halloran, K. L. and Lim, F. V. (2014). Systemic functional multimodal discourse analysis', S. Norris and C. Maier (eds), *Texts, Images and Interactions: A Reader in Multimodality*. Berlin: Mouton de Gruyter, pp. 137–54.

O'Halloran, K. L. and Smith, B. A. (2011) 'Multimodal studies', O'Halloran and Smith (eds), *Multimodal Studies: Exploring Issues and Domains*. New York and London: Routledge.

O'Halloran, K. L., Tan, S. and E, M. K. L. (2014) A multimodal approach to discourse, context and culture', J. Flowerdew (ed.), *Discourse in Context: Contemporary Applied Linguistics Volume 3*. London: Bloomsbury, pp. 247–72.

— (2014) 'Multimodal analytics: Software and visualization techniques for analyzing and interpreting multimodal data', C. Jewitt (ed.), *The Routledge Handbook of Multimodal Analysis*. Second edition. London: Routledge, pp. 386–96.

O'Halloran, K. L. and Lim, F. V. (2014) 'Systemic functional multimodal discourse analysis', S. Norris and C. Maier (eds), *Texts, Images and Interactions: A Reader in Multimodality*. Berlin: Mouton de Gruyter, pp. 137–54.

Oldenburg, J. (1987) *From Child Tongue to Mother Tongue: A Case Study of Language Development in the First Two and a Half Years*. University of Sydney, Sydney: Ph.D. thesis.

Organisation for Economic Co-operation and Development (2006) *Starting Strong II: Early Childhood Education and Care*. Paris: OECD Publishing.

O'Toole, M. ([1994] 2011) *The Language of Displayed Art*. Second edition. London and New York: Routledge.

— (1995) 'A systemic-functional semiotics of art', Fries and Gregory (eds), *Discourse in Society: Systemic Functional Perspectives*. Norwood, NJ: Ablex, pp. 159–82.

O'Toole, M. and Shukman, A. (eds) (1977) *Russian Poetics in Translation: Formalist Theory*. Volume 4. Oxford: Holdan Books Ltd.

Oyelaran, O. O. (1967) 'Aspects of linguistic theory in Firthian linguists', *Word* 23, pp. 428–52.

Painter, C. (1984) *Into the Mother Tongue*. London: Frances Pinter.

— (1999) *Learning through Language in Early Childhood*. London: Cassell.

— (2004) 'The "interpersonal first" principle in child language development', G. Williams and A. Lukin (eds), *The Development of Language: Functional Perspectives on Species and Individuals*. London: Continuum.

Painter, C., Derewianka, B. and Torr, J. (2007) 'From microfunctions to metaphor: Learning language and learning through language', Hasan, Matthiessen and Webster (eds) (2007), *Continuing Discourse on Language: A Functional Perspective*. Volume 2. London: Equinox, pp. 563–88.

Painter, C., Martin, J. and Unsworth, L. (2013) *Reading Visual Narratives: Image Analysis of Children's Picture Books*. Sheffield: Equinox Publishing.

Palmer, F. (ed.) (1968) *Selected Papers of J.R. Firth 1952–1959*. London: Longman.

— (1970) *Prosodic Analysis*. London: Oxford University Press.

— (1974) *The English Verb*. London: Longman.

Parker-Rhodes, A. F. (1978) *Inferential Semantics*. Hassocks: Harvester Press.

Pascal, G. (Producer and Director). (1938) *Pygmalion* [Film]. United Kingdom: General Film Distributors; United States: Metro-Goldwin-Mayer.

Patpong, P. (2005) *A Systemic Functional Interpretation of Thai Grammar: An Exploration of Thai Narrative Discourse*. Macquarie University: Ph.D. thesis.

Patten, T. (1988) *Systemic Text Generation as Problem Solving*. Cambridge: Cambridge University Press.

Patten, T. and Ritchie, G. (1987) 'A formal model of systemic grammar', Kempen (ed.), *Natural Language Generation*. Dordrecht: Martinus Nijhof, pp. 279–99.

Peng, Alex X. (2014) 'Halliday in China', Jonathan J. Webster (ed.), *Bloomsbury Companion to M.A.K. Halliday*. London: Bloomsbury Academic (Chapter 3, this volume).

Peters, P. S. and Ritchie, R. W. (1973) 'On the generative power of transformational grammars', *Information Sciences* 6, pp. 49–83.

Phillips, J. (1985) 'The development of modality and hypothetical meaning: Nigel 1;7½ – 2; 7½', *Working Papers in Linguistics* 3. Sydney: Department of Linguistics, University of Sydney, pp. 3–20.

Pike, K. L. (1945) *The Intonation of American English*. University of Michigan Publications, Linguistics, Ann Arbor: University of Michigan Press.

— (1948) *Tone Languages: A Technique for Determining the Number and Type of Pitch Contrasts in a Language, with Studies in Tonemic Substitution and Fusion*. Ann Arbor: University of Michigan Press.

— ([1959] 1967) *Language in Relation to a Unified Theory of the Structure of Human Communication*. The Hague: Mouton.

— (1982) *Linguistic Concepts: An Introduction to Tagmemics*. Lincoln, London: University of Nebraska Press.

Pittman, R. S. ([1948] 1957) 'Nuclear structures in linguistics', *Language* 24, pp. 287–92. [Reprinted in Joos (1957), pp. 275–8.]

Plum, G. A. and Cowling, A. (1987) 'Social constraints on grammatical variables: Tense choice in English', Steele and Threadgold (eds) *Language Topics, Essays in Honour of Michael Halliday*. Amsterdam: John Benjamins, pp. 281–305.

Pollard, C. and Sag, I. A. (1994) *Head-Driven Phrase Structure Grammar*. University of Chicago Press and CSLI Publications.

Pollock, E. (2006) *Stalin and the Soviet Science Wars*. Princeton University Press.

Popper, F. (1979) *Objective Knowledge*. Oxford: Oxford University Press.

Popper, K. (1972) *Objective Knowledge: An Evolutionary Approach*. Oxford: Clarendon Press.

Popper, K. and Eccles, J. C. ([1977] 1983) *The Self and Its Brain: An Argument for Interactionism*. Germany: Springer International.

Postal, P. M. (1964*) Constituent Structure: A Study of Contemporary Models of Syntactic Descriptions*. Bloomington, IN: Indiana University Publications in Anthropology, Folklore and Linguistics, Publication 30.

Prakasam, V. (2004) 'Metafunctional profile of Telugu', Caffarel, Martin and Matthiessen (eds), *Language Typology: A Functional Perspective*. Amsterdam: John Benjamins, pp. 433–78.

Qiu, S. (1985) 'Transition period in Chinese language development', *Australian Review of Applied Linguistics* 8: 1, pp. 31–49.

Ramos, T. (1974) *The Case System of Tagalog Verbs*. Canberra: The Linguistic Circle of Canberra. (Pacific Linguistics Series B 27).

Ridley, M. (2000) *A Darwin Selection: Understanding Darwin*. London: Orion Audio Books.

Rissanen, M. (1991) 'Spoken language and the history of do-periphrasis', Kastovsky (ed.), *Historical English Syntax*. Berlin and New York: Mouton de Gruyter, pp. 321–42.

Robins, R. H. (1957) 'Malinowski, Firth, and the "context of situation"', E. Ardener (ed.), *Social Anthropology and Language*. London: Tavistock.

— (1961) 'John Rupert Firth', *Language* 37: 2, pp. 199–200. [Reprinted in Sebeok (ed.) (1967), pp. 543–44.]

— (1971) *General Linguistics*. London: Longmans.

Roochnik, D. (1996) *Of Art and Wisdom: Plato's Understanding of Techne*. Pennsylvania: Pennsylvania State University Press.

Rose, D. (2001a) *The Western Desert Code: An Australian Cryptogrammar*. Canberra: Pacific Linguistics.

— (2001b) 'Some variations in theme across languages', *Functions of Language* 8: 1, pp. 109–45.

— (2005) 'Narrative and the origins of discourse: Construing experience in stories around the world', *Australian Review of Applied Linguistics* 19, pp. 151–73.

Rose, D. and Martin, J. R. (2012) *Learning to Write, Reading to Learn: Genre, Knowledge and Pedagogy in the Sydney School*. Bristol: Equinox.

Rose, D., Gray, B. and Cowey, W. (1999) 'Scaffolding reading and writing for indigenous children in school', Wignell (ed.), *Double Power: English Literacy and Indigenous Education*. Canberra: National Language and Literacy Institute of Australia.

Rose, S., Lewontin, R. and Kamin, L. J. (1984) *Not in Our Genes: Biology, Ideology and Human Nature*. New York: Pantheon.

Rosenblueth R., Wiener, N. and Bigelow, J. (1943) 'Behaviour, purpose and teleology', *Philosophy of Science* X.

Rothery, J. (1984) 'The development of genres: Primary to junior secondary school', Christie (ed.), *Children Writing. Geelong*. Vic: Deakin University Press, pp. 67–114.

Ruppenhofer, J., Ellsworth, M., Petruk, M. R. L., Johnson, C. R. and Scheffczyk, J. (2006) FrameNet II: Extended Theory and Practice.35

Sag, I. A. (2010) 'Sign-based construction grammar: An informal synopsis', Boas and Sag (eds), Sign-based Construction Grammar, Center for the Study of Language and Information.

Sag, I. A., Kaplan, R., Karttunen, L., Kay, M., Pollard, C., Shieber, S. and Zaenen, A. (1986) 'Unification and grammatical theory', Proceedings of the Fifth Annual Meeting of the West Coast Conference on Formal Linguistics. Stanford: SLA, CSLI Publications, pp. 238–54.

Sapir, E. (1921) *Language: An Introduction to the Study of Speech*. New York and London: Harcourt Brace Jovanovich.

— (1985) *Selected Writings in Language, Culture, and Personality*. David G. Mandelbaum (ed.), USA: California University Press.

— (1928/1999) 'The unconscious patterning of behaviour in society', R. Darnell and J. Irvine (eds), *The Collected Works of Edward Sapir*. The Hague: Mouton de Gruyter.

Saussure, F. ([1916] 1974) *Course in General Linguistics*. Revised edition. Bungay, Suffolk: Fontana/Collins.

— (1959) *Course in General Linguistics*, translated by W. Baskin. London: Peter Owen Ltd.

— (2008) *Writings in General Linguistics*, translated by C. Sanders and M. Pires, S. Bouquet and R. Engler (eds). Oxford: Oxford University Press.

Schachter, P. (1976) 'The subject in Philippine languages: Topic, actor, actor-topic, or none of the above', Li (ed.), *Subject and Topic*. New York: Academic Press, pp. 491–518.

— (1977) 'Reference-related and role-related properties of subjects', Cole and Saddock (eds), *Grammatical Relations* (Syntax and Semantics 8). New York: Academic Press, pp. 279–306.

Schachter, P. and Otanes, F. (1972) *Tagalog Reference Grammar*. Berkeley: University of California Press.

Schenkein, J. (ed.) (1978) *Studies in the Organization of Conversational Interaction*. New York: Academic Press.

Schleppegrell, M. J. (2004) *The Language of Schooling: A Functional Linguistics Perspective*. Mahwah, NJ: Erlbaum.

Schreiber, M. (1993) *Übersetzung und Bearbeitung. Zur Differenzierung und Abgrenzung des Übersetzungsbegriffs*. Tübingen: Gunter Narr Verlag.

Schubiger, M. ([1965] 1972) 'English intonation and German modal particles – a comparative study', *Phonetica* 12: pp. 65–84. Reprinted in D. Bolinger (ed.), *Intonation*. Middlesex; Baltimore; Ringwood: Penguin Books, pp. 175–93.

Scollon, R. (2001) *Mediated Discourse: The Nexus of Practice*. London and New York: Routledge.

Searle, J. (1969) *Speech Acts: An Essay in the Philosophy of Language*. Cambridge: Cambridge University Press.

Sebeok, T. A. (1967) *Portraits of Linguists: A Biographical Source Book for the History of Western Linguistics 1746–1963*. Bloomington: Indiana University Press.

Seuren, P. A. M. (1998) *Western Linguistics: An Historical Introduction*. Oxford: Blackwell.

Sgall, P. (1995) 'Prague school typology', Shibatani and Bynon (eds), *Approaches to Language Typology*. Oxford: Oxford University Press, pp. 49–84.

Shannon, C. E. (1948) 'A mathematical theory of communication', *The Bell System Technical Journal* 27.

Shannon, C. E. and Weaver, W. (1949) *The Mathematical Theory of Communication*. Urbana: University of Illinois Press.

Shapiro, J. A. (2011) *Evolution: A View from the 21st Century*. New Jersey: FT Press Science.

Shaw, B. (1916) *Pygmalion*. New York: Brentano.

Sheldrake, R. (1988) *The Presence of the Past*. Fontana/Collins.

Shieber, S. (1986) *An Introduction to Unification-based Approaches to Grammar*. Stanford: Center for the Study of Language and Information: CSLI Publications, pp. 39–156.

Shonkoff, J. and Philips, D. (eds) (2000) *From Neurons to Neighbourhoods: The Science of Early Childhood Development*. Washington, DC: National Academy Press.

Shore, S. (1992) *Aspects of a Systemic Functional Grammar of Finnish*. Macquarie University: Ph.D. thesis.

Siewierska, A. (2004) *Person*. Cambridge: Cambridge University Press.

Simon-Vandenbergen, A.-M., Taverniers, M. and Ravelli, L. (eds) (2003) *Grammatical Metaphor: Views from Systemic Functional Linguistics*. Amsterdam: John Benjamins.

Simpson, P. (2004) *Stylistics: A Resource Book for Students*. London: Routledge.

Smith, B. (2008a) 'Intonational systems and register: A multidimensional exploration', Sydney: Macquarie University: PhD thesis, <http://www.isfla.org/Systemics/Print/Theses.html> [accessed 16 December 2012].

— (2008b) 'The language of the heart and breath: Bridging strata, bridging discourses of INFORMATION systems', Conference Proceedings for the 2007 ASFLA Congress: Bridging Discourses, <http://www.asfla.org.au/2008/07/31/the-language-of-the-heart-and-breath-bridging-strata-bridging-discourses-of-information-systems/> [accessed 16 December 2012] [held at Wollongong University, 29 June–1 July 2007. Australian Systemic Functional Association].

— (2011) 'Intonation within ,ultimodal studies', O'Halloran, Kay and Smith (eds), *Multimodal Studies: Exploring Issues and Domains*. New York and London: Routledge.

Smith, B. and Greaves, W. S. (2014) 'Intonation', Jonathan J. Webster (ed.), *Bloomsbury Companion of M.A.K. Halliday*. London: Bloomsbury Academic (Chapter 11, this volume).

Smith, N. and Wilson, D. (1979) *Modern Linguistics: The Results of Chomsky's Revolution*. London: Penguin.

Snell-Hornby, M. (1995) *Translation Studies: An Integrated Approach*. Second edition. Amsterdam: John Benjamins.

Snow, C., Pan, B., Imbens-Bailey, A. and Herman, J. (1996) 'Learning how to say what one means: A longitudinal study of children's speech act use', *Social Development* 5: 1, pp. 56–84.

Solm, M. (February/March 2006) *Freud Returns. Scientific American Mind*.

Souter, C. and Atwell, E. (1992) 'A richly annotated corpus for probabilistic parsing', AAAI Technical Report WS-92-01.

Stark, R., Bernstein, L. and Demorest, M. (1993) 'Vocal communication in the first 18 months of life', *Journal of Speech and Hearing Research* 36, pp. 548–58.

Steele, J. ([1775] 1969) *An Essay Towards Establishing the Melody and Measure of Speech*. Menston, UK: The Scolar Press Limited.

Steels, L. (1998) 'Synthesizing the origins of language and meaning using coevolution, self-organization and level formation', Knight, Studdert-Kennedy and Hurford (eds), *Approaches to the Evolution of Language: Social and Cognitive Bases*. Cambridge: Cambridge University Press, pp. 384–404.

— (ed.) (2012) *Design Patterns in Fluid Construction Grammar*. Amsterdam and New York: John Benjamins.

Steiner, E. (1988) 'Semantic relations in EUROTRA-D and LFG – a comparison', Schmidt, Zelinsky-Wibbelt and Steiner (eds), From Syntax to Semantics – Insights from Machine Translation. London: Pinter.

— (2002) 'Grammatical metaphor in translation – some methods for corpus-based investigations', Hasselgard, Behrens and Fabricius-Hansen (eds) (2002) *Information Structure in a Cross-Linguistic Perspective*. Amsterdam: Rodopi, pp. 213–28.

— (2004) *Translated Texts: Properties, Variants, Evaluations*. Frankfurt/M.: Peter Lang Verlag.

— (2005) 'Halliday and translation theory – enhancing the options, broadening the range, and keeping the ground', Hasan, Matthiessen and Webster (eds) (2005) *Continuing Discourse on Language. Festschrift for Michael Halliday*. London: Equinox.

Steiner, E. and Teich, E. (2004) 'Metafunctional profile of the grammar of German', Caffarel, Martin and Matthiessen (eds), *Language Typology: A Functional Perspective*. Amsterdam: John Benjamins, pp. 139–84.

Steiner, E. and Yallop, C. (eds) (2001) *Exploring Translation and Multilingual Text Production: Beyond Content*. Berlin and New York: Mouton de Gruyter.

Steiner, E., Eckert, U., Weck, U. B. and Winter, J. (1988) 'The development of the EUROTRA-D system of semantic relations', Steiner, Schmidt and Zelinsky-Wibbelt (eds), *From Syntax to Semantics – Insights from Machine Translation*. London: Frances Pinter, pp. 40–103.

Steiner, P. (1984) *Russian Formalism: A Metapoetics*. Ithaca, London: Cornell University Press.

Štekauer, P., Franko, Š., Slančová, D., Liptáková, L. and Sutherland-Smith, J. (2001) 'A comparative research into the transfer of animal names to human beings', *View[z]: Vienna English Working Papers* 10:2, pp. 69–75.

Stenglin, M. (2009) 'Space odyssey: Towards a social semiotic model of 3D space', *Visual Communication* 8: 1, pp. 35–64.

Stephens, M. (1995) *A'aisa's Gifts: A Study of Magic and the Self*. Berkeley: University Of California Press.

Stevens, W. (1957) *Opus Posthumous: Poems, Plays; Prose*. New York: Vintage.

Stillings, N. A., Feinstein, M. H., Garfield, J. L., Rissland, E. L., Rosenbaum, D. A., Weisler, S. E. and Baker-Ward, L. (1987) *Cognitive Science: An Introduction*. Cambridge, MA: MIT Press.

Stockwell, R. P. (1959) 'Review of studies in linguistic analysis', *IJAL* 29, pp. 254–59.

Stockwell, R. P., Schachter, P. and Partee, B. H. (1973) *The Major Syntactic Structures of English*. New York: Holt, Rinehart & Winston.

Stoel-Gammon, C. (1998) 'Role of babbling and phonology in early linguistic development', Wetherby, Warren and Reichle (eds), *Transitions in Prelinguistic Communication*. Baltimore: Brookes Publishing Co., pp. 87–111.

Stolz, T. (2007) 'Harry Potter meets Le petit prince: On the usefulness of parallel corpora in crosslinguistic investigations', *Sprachtypologie und Universalienforschung* 60: 2, pp. 100–17.

Straumann, Heinrich (1935) *Newspaper Headlines: A Study in Linguistic Method*. London: George, Allen and Unwin.

Strevens, P. (1964) 'Editor's preface', J. R. Firth (ed.), *The Tongues of Men*. London: Oxford University Press.

Striedter, J. (1989) *Literary Structure, Evolution, and Value: Russian Formalism and Czech Structuralism Reconsidered*. Cambridge MA: Harvard University Press.

Svartvik, J. (1966) *On Voice in the English Verb*. The Hague: Mouton.

Sweet, H. (1877) *A Handbook of Phonetics, Including a Popular Exposition of the Principles of Spelling Reform*. Oxford: Clarendon Press.

Tam, H. S. R. (2004) *A Systemic-functional Interpretation of Cantonese Clause Grammar*. University of Sydney: Ph.D. thesis.

Taylor, C. (1998) *Language to Language*. Cambridge: Cambridge University Press.

Tchaikovsky, P. (1880) 1812 Overture, op. 49. (DVD of Vladimir Ashkenazy conducting the St, Petersburg Philharmonic Orchestra, using authentic cannons and bells from St Petersburg, Decca, No. 455, 971–972, 1990.)

Teich, E. (1999a) *Systemic Functional Grammar in Natural Language Generation: Linguistic Description and Computational Representation*. London: Cassell.

— (1999b) 'System-oriented and text-oriented comparative linguistic research: Cross-linguistic variation in translation', *Languages in Contrast* 2: 2, pp. 187–210.

— (2001) 'Towards a model for the description of cross-linguistic divergence and commonality in translation', Steiner and Yallop (eds) (2001), pp. 229–48.

— (2003) *Cross-linguistic Variation in System and Text – a Methodology for the Investigation of Translations and Comparable Texts*. Berlin and New York: Mouton de Gruyter.

— (2009) 'Computational linguistics', Halliday and Webster (eds), *A Companion to Systemic Functional Linguistics*. London and New York: Bloomsbury Academic, pp. 113–27.

Teich, E., Watson, C. I. and Pereira, C. (2000) 'Matching a tone-based and tune-based approach to English intonation for concept-to-speech generation', Proceedings of the 18th Conference on Computational Linguistics. Volume 2. Morristown, NJ: Association for Computational Linguistics, pp. 829–35.

Tench, Paul (ed.) (1992) *Studies in Systemic Phonology*. London and New York: Pinter.

Teruya, K. (1998) *An Exploration into the World of Experience: A Systemic Functional Interpretation of the Grammar of Japanese*. Macquarie University: Ph.D. thesis.

— (2004) 'Metafunctional profile of the grammar of Japanese', Caffarel, Martin and Matthiessen (eds), *Language Typology: A Functional Perspective*. Amsterdam: John Benjamins, pp. 185–254.

— (2006) 'Grammar as resource for the construction of language logic for advanced language learning in Japanese', Byrnes (ed.), *Advanced Instructed Language Learning: The Complementary Contribution of Halliday and Vygotsky*. London and New York: Continuum, pp. 109–33.

— (2007) *A Systemic Functional Grammar of Japanese*. 2 volumes. London and New York: Bloomsbury Academic.

— (2009) 'Grammar as a gateway into discourse: A systemic functional approach to SUBJECT, THEME, and Logic', *Linguistics and Education* 20: 1, pp. 67–79. [Special issue edited by Heidi Byrnes, Instructed foreign language acquisition as meaning-making: a systemic-functional approach.]

Teruya, K., Akerejola, E., Andersen, T. H., Caffarel, A., Lavid, J., Matthiessen, C., Petersen, U. H., Patpong, P. and Smedegaard, F. (2007) 'Typology of MOOD: A text-based and system-based functional view', Hasan, Matthiessen and Webster (eds) (2007) *Continuing Discourse on Language: A Functional Perspective*. Volume 2. London: Equinox, pp. 859–920.

Thai, M. D. (1998) *A Systemic Functional Interpretation of Vietnamese Grammar*. Macquarie University: Ph.D. thesis.

— (2004) 'Metafunctional profile: Vietnamese', Caffarel, Martin and Matthiessen (eds), *Language Typology: A Functional Perspective*. Amsterdam: John Benjamins, pp. 397–431.

Thanning, V. M. (2002) 'An interview with Terry A. Winograd', <http://openarchive.cbs.dk/bitstream/handle/10398/6460/2002-7.pdf> (accessed 21 August 2014).

Thibault, P. J. (2005) 'Brains, bodies, contextualising activity and language: Do humans (and bonobos) have a language faculty, and can they do without one?', *Linguistics and the Human Sciences* 1: 1, pp. 99–125.

Thomas, M. (2011) *Fifty Key Thinkers on Language and Linguistics*. London and New York: Routledge.

Thomason, S. G. and Kaufman, T. (1988) *Language Contact, Creolization, and Genetic Linguistics*. Berkeley: University of California Press.

Thompson, K. (2002) *Music: A Systemic-functional Approach*. [Murdoch University, unpublished Honours paper, analysing a movement from a Haydn quartet.]

Thomson, E. and White, P. R. R. (eds) (2008) *Communicating Conflict: Multilingual Case Studies of the News Media*. London: Continuum.

Toolan, M. (1988) *Narrative: A Critical Linguistic Introduction*. London: Routledge.
— (1990) *The Stylistics of Fiction: A Literary-linguistic Approach*. London: Routledge.
Torr, J. (1997) 'From child tongue to mother tongue: A case study of language development in the first two and a half years', *Monographs in Systemic Linguistics*. Volume 9. Nottingham: University of Nottingham.
Toulmin, S. (1961) *Foresight and Understanding: An Enquiry into the Aims of Science*. New York: Harper Torchbooks.
— (1972) *Human Understanding*. Princeton: Princeton University Press.
Toury, Gideon (1995) *Descriptive Translation Studies and Beyond*. Amsterdam: John Benjamins.
Trevarthen, C. (1974) 'Conversations with a two-month old', *New Scientist* 2.
— (1987) 'Sharing makes sense: Intersubjectivity and the making of an infant's meaning', R. Steele and T. Threadgold (eds), *Language Topics: Essays in Honour of M.A.K. Halliday*. Amsterdam: John Benjamins, pp. 177–200.
Trevarthen, C. and Hubley, P. (1978) 'Secondary intersubjectivity: Confidence, confiding and acts of meaning in the first year', A. Lock (ed.), *Action Gesture and Symbol*. London: Academic Press, pp. 183–229.
Tucker, G. (1996) 'So grammarians haven't the faintest idea: Reconciling lexis-oriented and grammar-oriented approaches to language', Hasan, Cloran and Butt (eds), *Functional Descriptions – Theory in Practice*. Amsterdam: John Benjamins, pp. 145–79.
— (1998) *The Lexicogrammar of Adjectives: A Systemic Functional Approach to Lexisi*. London: Cassell.
Turner, G. J. (1987) 'Sociosemantic networks and discourse structure', Halliday and Fawcett (eds), *New Developments in Systemic Linguistics*. London: Frances Pinter, pp. 64–93.
Tynjanov, J. (1978) 'On literary evolution', L. Matejka and K. Pomorska (eds), *Readings in Russian Poetics: Formalist and Structuralist Views*. MIT Press.
Tynjanov, J. and Jakobson, R. (1978) 'Problems in the study of literature and language', L. Matejka and K. Pomorska (eds), *Readings in Russian Poetics: Formalist and Structuralist Views*. MIT Press.
Uglow, J. (2002) *The Lunar Men: The Friends Who Made the Future*. London: Faber and Faber.
Ullmann, S. (1957) *The Principles of Semantics*. Glasgow and Oxford: Basil Blackwell.
Unsworth, L. (2002) *Teaching Multiliteracies Across the Curriculum: Changing Contexts of Text and Image in Classroom Practice*. Buckingham and Philadelphia: Open University Press.
— (ed.) (2008a) *Multimodal Semiotics: Functional Analysis in Contexts of Education*. London: Continuum.
— (ed.) (2008b) *New Literacies and the English Curriculum*. London: Continuum.
Vachek, J. (1959) 'The London group of linguists', *Sbornik Praci Filosoficke Faculty Brenske University Rocnik* 8 (Rada Jazykovidn'a A 7), pp. 106–13.
Vaihinger, H. (1924) *The Philosophy of 'As if': A System of the Theoretical, Practical and Religious Fictions of Mankind*, translated by C. K. Ogden. New York: Harcourt, Brace & Co.
Van de Walle, J. (2009) 'Roman Jakobson, cybernetics and information theory: A critical assessment', *Folia Linguistica Historica* 29: 1, pp. 87–123.
van Dijk, T. A. and Petöfi, J. S. (eds) (1977) *Grammars and Descriptions*. Berlin: Mouton de Gruyter.
van Leeuwen, T. (1999) *Speech, Music, Sound*. Hampshire and London: MacMillan Press; New York: St. Martin's Press.
— (2005) *Introducing Social Semiotics*. London: Routledge.
— (2009) 'Parametric systems: The case of voice quality', Jewitt (ed.), *The Routledge Handbook of Multimodal Analysis*. London and New York: Routlege, pp. 68–77.

— (2011) *The Language of Colour: An Introduction*. London and New York: Routledge.

van Trijp, R., Steels, L., Beuls, K. and Wellens, P. (2012) 'Fluid construction grammar: The new kid on the block', Proceedings of the 13th Conference of the European Chapter of the Association for Computational Linguistics, pp. 63–8.

van Valin, R. D. (1993) 'A synopsis of role and reference grammar', van Valin (ed.), *Advances in Role and Reference Grammar*. Amsterdam: John Benjamins (Current Issues in Linguistics Theory, 82), pp. 1–164.

Veneziano, E. and Sinclair, H. (1995) 'Functional changes in early child language: The appearance of references to the past and of explanations', *Journal of Child Language* 22, pp. 557–81.

Ventola, E. (1987) *The Structure of Social Interaction: A Systemic Approach to the Semiotics of Service Encounters*. London: Pinter.

— (2011) 'Semiotisation processes of space: From drawing our homes to styling them', O'Halloran and Smith (eds), *Multimodal Studies: Exploring Issues and Domains*. London and New York: Routledge, pp. 220–38.

Venuti, L. (1995) *The Translator's Invisibility: A History of Translation*. London: Routledge.

— (ed.) (1999) *The Translation Studies Reader*. London and New York: Routledge.

Vygotsky, L. S. (1962) *Language and Thought*, translated by Hanfmann and Vakar (eds), Cambridge, MA: MIT Press.

— (1978) *Mind in Society: The Development of Higher Psychological Processes*. Harvard: Harvard University Press.

— (1986) *Thought and Language*, translated by A. Kozulin (ed.). Cambridge, MA: MIT Press.

Waddington, C. H. (1977) *Tools for Thought*. Frogmore: St Albans, Paladin.

Walker, J. ([1787] 1970) *The Melody of Speaking*. London. G. G. J. and J. Robinson and T. Cadell. Reproduced as *The Melody of Speaking*, Menston: Scolar Press.

Wan, Y. N. (2011) *Call Centre Communication: An Analysis of Interpersonal Meaning*. Hong Kong Polytechnic University: Ph.D. thesis.

Wang, Li (王力) (1936) *Chinese Phonology* (漢語音韻學). Shanghai: The Commercial Press.

— (王力) ([1947] 1971) *Theory of Chinese Grammar*. 2 volumes (中國語法理語). Shanghai: Commercial Press.

Warner, A. (2005) 'Why do dove: Evidence for register variation in early modern English negatives', *Language Variation and Change* 17, pp. 257–80.

Wasow, T. (1977) 'Transformations and the lexicon', Culicover, Akmajian and Wasow (eds), *Formal Syntax*. New York: Academic Press, pp. 327–60.

Webster, Jonathan J. (2005) 'M.A.K. Halliday: The early years 1925–1970', J. Webster, C. Matthiessen and R. Hasan (eds), *Continuing Discourse on Language*. Volume 1. London: Equinox.

Weerasinghe, A. R. (1994) *Probabilistic Parsing in Systemic Functional Gramma*. Department of Computing Mathematics, University of Wales College of Cardiff: Ph.D. thesis.

Weerasinghe, A. R. and Fawcett, R. (1993) 'Probabilistic incremental parsing in systemic functional grammar', Proceedings of the Third International Workshop on Parsing Technologies. Tilburg, the Netherlands, 10–13 August 1993.

Wegener, Ph. (1885) *Untersuchungen über die Grundfragen des Sprachlebens*. Halle: M. Niemeyer.

Weinreich, H. (1972) 'Die Textpartitur als heuristische Methode', *Der Deutschunterricht* 24: 4, pp. 43–60.

Weinreich, U. (1980) *On Semantics*. Labov and Weinreich (ed.), Philadelphia: University of Pennsylvania Press.

Weinreich, U., Labov, William and Herzog, Marvin I. (1968) 'Empirical foundations for a theory of language change', *Directions for Historical Linguistics: A Symposium*. Austin: University of Texas Press.

Wells, G. (1994) 'The complementary contributions of Halliday and Vygotsky to a "language-based theory of learning"', *Linguistics and Learning* 6, pp. 41–90.

Wells, R. (1947[1957]) 'Immediate constituents', *Language* 3: 2, pp. 81–117. [Reprinted in Joos, pp. 186–207.]

Whitaker, A. (2006) *Einstein, Bohr and the Quantum Dilemma: From Quantum Theory to Quantum Information*. Cambridge: Cambridge University Press.

Whorf, B. L. ([1945] 1956) 'Grammatical categories', *Language* 21, pp. 1–11 [Reprinted in Carroll, J. B. (ed.) (1956) *Language, Thought and Reality: Selected Papers of Benjamin Lee Whorf*. Cambridge, MA: MIT Press, pp. 87–110.]

— (1956) *Language, Thought and Reality: Selected Writings of Benjamin Lee Whorf*, J. B. Carroll (ed.), Cambridge, MA: MIT Press.

Wignell, P., Martin, J. R. and Eggins, S. (1993) 'The discourse of geography: Ordering and explaining the experiential world', Halliday and Martin, *Writing Science: Literacy and Discursive Power*. London: Falmer, pp. 136–65.

Wilcock, G. (1993) *Interactive Japanese-European Text Generation – an Approach to Multilingual Export Translation Based on Systemic Functional Grammar*. University of Manchester: MSc thesis.

Wilks, Y. (1995) 'Arthur Frederick Parker-Rhodes: A memoir', Paper given as a Parker-Rhodes Memorial Lecture at the annual meeting of the Alternative Natural Philosophy Association in Cambridge, September 1995, <http://www.dcs.shef.ac.uk/~yorick/papers/cs-95-22.ps>. (accessed 21 August 2014).

Williams, G. (1995a) 'A package of information', Brockman (ed.), *The Third Culture*. New York: Touchstone Books, pp. 38–50.

— (1995b) *Joint Book-reading and Literacy Pedagogy: A Socio-semantic Examination*. Macquarie University, North Ryde: Ph.D. thesis.

— (1998) 'Children entering literate worlds: Perspectives from the study of textual practices', F. Christie and R. Misson (eds), *Literacy and Schooling*. London: Routledge.

— (1999) 'Grammar as a metasemiotic tool in child literacy development', C. Ward and W. Renandya (eds), *Language Teaching: New Insights for the Language Teacher*, Series 40. Singapore: Regional Language Centre, SEAMO.

— (2000) 'Children's literature, children and uses of language description', L. Unsworth (ed.), *Researching Language in Schools and Communities*. London: Cassell.

— (2004) 'Ontogenesis and grammatics: Functions of metalanguage in pedagogical discourse', G. Williams and A. Lukin (eds), *The Development of Language: Functional Perspectives on Species and Individuals*. London: Continuum.

— (2005a) 'Grammatics in schools', J. Webster, C. Matthiessen and R. Hasan (eds), *Continuing Discourse on Language*. Volume 1. London: Equinox.

— (2005b) 'Semantic variation', J. Webster, C. Matthiessen and R. Hasan (eds), *Continuing Discourse on Language*. Volume 1. London: Equinox.

Williams, G. and Moreton, E. (2013 and forthcoming) 'Learning grammatics in the first year of school', Paper presented to the 40th International Systemic Functional Congress, Sun Yat-Sen University, Guangzhou, 15–19 July.

Winograd, T. (1972) *Understanding Natural Language*. Academic Press.

— (1983) *Language as a Cognitive Process 1: Syntax*. USA: Addison-Wesley.

Wittgenstein, Ludwig (1953) *Philosophical Investigations*, translated by G. E. Enscombe. G. E. Enscombe, R. Rhees and G. H. von Wright (eds), London: Blackwell.

Woods, W. ([1975] 1985) 'What's in a link: Foundations for semantic networks', Bobrow and Collins (eds), *Representation and Understanding: Studies in Cognitive Science*. New York: Academic Press, pp. 35–82. [Reprinted in Brachman, R. J. and Levesque, H. J.

(eds) (1985) *Readings in Knowledge Representation*. Los Altos, CA: Morgan Kaufman, pp. 217–41.]

Wu, C. (2009) 'Corpus-based research', Halliday and Webster (eds), *Bloomsbury Companion to Systemic Functional Linguistics*. London and New York: Bloomsbury Academic, pp. 128–42.

Yallop, C. (2001) 'The construction of equivalence', Steiner and Yallop (eds) (2001), pp. 229–48.

Zipf, G. K. (1935) *The Psychobiology of Language*. Boston: Houghton Mifflin.

Index